THE BRITISH
CARRIER
STRIKE FLEET
After 1945

THE BRITISH
CARRIER
STRIKE FLEET
After 1945

David Hobbs

NAVAL INSTITUTE PRESS
Annapolis, Maryland

Copyright © David Hobbs 2015

First published in Great Britain in 2015 by
Seaforth Publishing,
Pen & Sword Books Ltd,
47 Church Street,
Barnsley S70 2AS

www.seaforthpublishing.com

Published and distributed in the United States of America and Canada
by the Naval Institute Press, 291 Wood Road, Annapolis, Maryland 21402-5043

www.nip.org

Library Of Congress Control Number: 2015948087

ISBN 978 1 59114 601 8

Typeset and designed by M.A.T.S., Leigh-on-Sea, Essex
Printed and bound in Great Britain by CPI Group (UK) Ltd, Croydon, CR0 4YY

Contents

Foreword

[Sailors have always] learned, in the grimmest schools, precision and resolution. The sea endures no makeshifts. If a thing is not exactly right it will be vastly wrong. Discipline, courage and contempt for all that is pretentious and insincere are the teaching of the ocean and the elements and they have been qualities, in all ages, of the British sailor.

John Buchan

I do not usually begin my books with a quotation but these words by John Buchan seemed so apt for the opening page of a book about the Royal Navy's carrier strike fleet after 1945 that I decided to begin it with them. Unlike any other form of warfare that I have been involved with, operating fixed-wing aircraft from a carrier in the open ocean really does 'endure no makeshifts' and has to be 'exactly right', especially at night or in bad weather. Naval aviation also delivers a whole range of capabilities that have proved to be invaluable in the defence of the United Kingdom and its interests around the world, often when nothing else was available.

In my earlier book about the British Pacific Fleet I explained the great effect that Fleet was to have on the post-war Royal Navy. In this book I take that story forward and give examples of the many operations in which British aircraft carriers have played a critical role and describe the ships and aircraft that achieved so much. In the seventy years since the end of the Second World War the RN and its integral Fleet Air Arm have undergone huge changes and, despite their conspicuous success, aircraft carriers have had to undergo greater scrutiny than any other British weapons system. The Fleet Air Arm has had to fight not only against the nation's enemies but also against politicians who have often failed to understand what an enormous asset these ships and their aircraft are. The independent Air Force has been principally concerned about preserving its own identity and has often been less helpful than it should have been, despite the Government's attempts to promote joint activity. In order to show how this see-saw balance developed I have alternated examples of carrier operations with descriptions of a succession of defence reviews with comment on their impact. I have described how technology evolved from the simple Seafire FR 47 operating from the ubiquitous light fleet carriers in 1946 to the technologically complex Lightning II Joint Strike Fighter in 2015 and the *Queen Elizabeth* class carriers that are to operate them. Carrier strike operations were inevitably compared with the British nuclear deterrent and I have included a chapter on how the deterrent force evolved for comparison.

It is, in part, my story for I served as a fixed and rotary-wing pilot for over thirty years, during which I served in seven aircraft carriers, a number of naval air squadrons and two appointments in the Ministry of Defence. Lest readers should feel that I lack knowledge of the RAF and how it operates when commenting on it, I might also add that I did my advanced flying training in the RAF's Number 4 Flying Training School, flying Gnats, and completed two exchange appointments, in one of which I flew Hunter FGA 9s and in the other Canberra B 2s and T 17s. I am one of the few pilots to include qualifications on Gannets, RN and RAF Hunter variants, Canberras and Wessex helicopters in their log books and take enormous pride in having carried out over 800 deck landings. After leaving the RN, I served in the Naval Historical Branch for a period and then became the Curator and Deputy Director of the Fleet Air Arm Museum at RNAS Yeovilton. In both those appointments I was able to carry out a prodigious amount of detailed research into naval aviation which I have put to good use in this book. I have included the activities of a number of people to create a balance between what happened, why it happened and an informative level of human interest. I am, of course, conscious that for every name mentioned there are literally dozens of others that I have omitted but, at the very least, I hope to have kept the spirit of the Fleet Air Arm in these exciting years alive and brought its magnificent achievements to a wider audience. The Fleet Air Arm has always been a relatively small organisation but mobility gives it the ability to 'punch above its weight' and be there when it is needed. I am proud to have been part of its story.

David Hobbs MBE
Commander Royal Navy (Retired)
Crail
February 2015

Acknowledgements

As always I have been helped and supported by my wife Jandy and my son Andrew together with his wife Lucyelle. During a career that lasted more than three decades in the Royal Navy I met a number of clever and inspirational people who broadened my knowledge of RN strike carrier tactics, techniques and operations. It would take too long to name them all and invidious to name only some of them but I thank them all wholeheartedly and those still alive will know who they are. As my focus shifted from current operations and projects to a study of naval history, many people have provided direct or indirect help, some of them in the margins of symposia and conferences around the world. Among them are the late David Brown together with Christopher Page and Stephen Prince, sequentially heads of the Naval Historical Branch, and their colleagues Jennie Wraight the Admiralty librarian, Jock Gardner and Malcolm Llewellyn-Jones. Mike MacAloon has always had the invaluable capacity not only to decide immediately which document would exactly answer a particular question but, more importantly, the knowledge of exactly where to find it within the Branch. The late D K Brown was a valued source of information on design issues that related to carrier performance. Andrew Choong and Jeremy Michel of the Historic Photograph and Ship Plans Department of the National Maritime Museum at the Brass Foundry in Woolwich have also been a considerable source of information and encouragement; I have greatly enjoyed my all-too-brief time with them poring over ships' plans and drawings. I am also grateful to Graham Edmonds for keeping me up-to-date with what is in newspapers and other publications.

Both in Australia at King-Hall Naval History Conferences and during his visits to the UK, I have received valuable insight about both the RAN and the RN from my friend David Stevens, formerly the Director of Strategic and Historical Studies at the Sea Power Centre – Australia, and much other useful information from Joe Straczek. John Perryman, Senior Historian at the Sea Power Centre, was kind enough to locate several RAN images and to obtain permission for me to use them. Rear Admiral James Goldrick, whose father was a pilot in the RAN, has also contributed through discussions over many years, to my knowledge of the part played by the RAN's Fleet Air Arm.

From the United States I have learnt a great deal from my friend Norman Friedman, the pre-eminent naval analyst of our generation, and from others with whom I have come into contact including A D Baker III, Edward J Marolda, Thomas Wildenberg and, not least, Tom Momiyama of the Naval Air Systems Command with whom I carried out the AV-8 Harrier trial on the USS *Tarawa* during 1981. The USNI digital News Daily Update provided important and relevant information.

Michael Whitby, Chief of the Canadian Naval History Team, contributed to my knowledge of the RCN Fleet Air Arm, as did J Allan Snowie from whom I learnt a great deal about aircraft operations from HMCS *Magnificent* and *Bonaventure*.

As before, I have found it possible to illustrate the book largely from the photographic collection that I have built up over many years but I am grateful to several people who were kind enough to help fill the gaps. Among these were Steve Bush of Maritime Books who allowed me to use images from the T Ferrers-Walker Collection, and the Crail Museum.

Discussions with Conrad Waters over my contributions to the *Seaforth World Naval Review* every year have also stimulated my thought processes and been of considerable value, I am grateful for his interest and support.

This publication contains Public Sector information licensed under the Open Government Licence v 1.0 in the UK.

I am grateful to Rob Gardiner and Seaforth Publishing for their encouragement and support with this book, as with its predecessors. Our successful partnership has lasted for nearly a decade now and I have already started work on our next book together.

David Hobbs

Glossary

A/A	Anti-Aircraft
A&AEE	Aeroplane & Armament Experimental Establishment (Boscombe Down)
AAC	Army Air Corps
AAG	Advanced Arrester Gear
AAM	Air-to-Air Missile
ACA	Aircraft Carrier Alliance
ACNB	Australian Commonwealth Navy Board
ACNS	Assistant Chief of the Naval Staff
ACR	Aircraft Control Room (in a carrier)
ACS	Aircraft Carrier Squadron
ADA	Action Data Automation
ADAWS	Action Data Automated Weapons System
ADR	Aircraft Direction Room
AED	Air Engineering Department (in a carrier)
AESA	Airborne Electronically-Scanned Array
AEW	Airborne Early Warning
AF	Admiral of the Fleet
AFC	Air Force Cross
AFO	Admiralty Fleet Order
AFWR	Atlantic Fleet Weapons Range (USN)
AHU	Aircraft Holding Unit
AI	Air Intercept (radar)
AIM	Air Intercept Missile
ALIS	Autonomous Logistic Information System
AMRAAM	Advanced Medium-Range Air-to-Air Missile
AN/APS	Army-Navy/Airborne Pulse Search (radar) (USN designation)
A/S	Anti-Submarine
ASaC	Airborne Surveillance and Control
ASM	Air-to-Surface Missile

ASOC	Air Support Operations centre
ASR	Air-Sea Rescue
ASV	Air-to-Surface Vessel (radar)
ASW	Anti-Submarine Warfare
avcat	Aviation Catoline Spirit
avgas	Aviation Gasoline
avtur	Aviation Turbine Spirit
BBC	British Broadcasting Corporation
BOAC	British Overseas Airways Corporation
BPF	British Pacific Fleet
BR	Book of Reference
BuAir	Bureau of Aircraft USN
CAF	Canadian Armed Forces
CAFO	Confidential Admiralty Fleet Order
CAG	Carrier Air Group
CAH	NATO designation for a helicopter-carrying light cruiser
CALE	Catapult/Aircraft Line-Up Equipment
CAP	Combat Air Patrol
CB	Confidential Book
CCA	Carrier Controlled Approach
CCH	Helicopter-operating Cruiser (USN/NATO designation)
CDS	Comprehensive Display System/Chief of the Defence Staff
CEC	Co-operative Engagement Capability
CENTO	Central Treaty Organisation
CGRM	Commandant General Royal Marines
C-in-C	Commander-in-Chief
CIWS	Close-In Weapons System
CNO	Chief of Naval Operations USN
COD	Carrier On-board Delivery (aircraft)
COMFEF	Commander Far East Fleet
COMNAVFE	Commander Naval Forces Far East (USN)
COMUKTG	Commander UK Task Group
CRBFD	Close-Range Blind Fire Director
CS	Cruiser Squadron
CV	Aircraft Carrier (USN/NATO designation)
CVA	Attack Aircraft Carrier (USN/NATO designation)
CVE	Escort Aircraft Carrier (USN/NATO designation)

CVL	Light Aircraft Carrier (USN designation)
CVN	Nuclear-Powered Aircraft Carrier (USN/NATO designation)
CVS	Support Aircraft Carrier (USN/NATO designation)
CW	Continuous Wave
DAPS	Deck Landing Approach Sight
DC	Direct Current
DCNS	Deputy Chief of Naval Staff
DGA(N)	Director General Aircraft (Naval)
DG Ships	Director General Ships
DLCO	Deck Landing Control Officer
DLMS	Deck Landing Mirror Sight
DLPS	Deck Landing Projector Sight
DLT	Deck Landing Training
DNAW	Directorate of Naval Air Warfare
DNC	Director of Naval Construction
DNO	Director of Naval Ordnance
DRPC	Defence Research Policy Committee
DSC	Distinguished Service Cross
DSO	Distinguished Service Order
ECCM	Electronic Counter-Countermeasures
ECM	Electronic Countermeasures
EMALS	Electro-Magnetic Aircraft Launch System
ESM	Electronic Support Measures
F/A	Fighter/Attack (aircraft)
FADEC	Full Authority Digital Engine Control
FAMG	Fleet Aircraft Maintenance Group
FAW	All-Weather Fighter (aircraft)
FB	Fighter Bomber (aircraft)
FCBA	Future Carrier-Borne Aircraft
FCS	Flight Control System
FEBA	Forward Edge of the Battle Area (on land)
FEF	Far East Fleet
FES	Far East Station
FFO	Furnace Fuel Oil
FFWP	Future-Fleet Working Party
FGA	Fighter Ground Attack (aircraft)

FLASH	Folding Lightweight Acoustic System for Helicopters
Flyco	Flying Control Position
FM	Frequency Modulated
FO	Flag Officer
FOAC	Flag Officer Aircraft Carriers
FOB	Forward Operating Base
FOCAS	Flag Officer Carriers and Amphibious Ships
FOF	Flag Officer Flotillas
FOGT	Flag Officer Ground Training
FO2	Flag Officer Second-in-Command
FO2FEF	Flag Officer Second-in-Command Far East Fleet
FOME	Flag Officer Middle East
FONFT	Flag Officer Naval Flying Training
FOTEX	Fleet Operational Training Exercise
FPDA	Five Power Defence Agreement (UK, Australia, New Zealand, Singapore, Malaysia)
FRC	Fleet Requirements Committee
FRS	Fighter, Reconnaissance & Strike (aircraft)
GPMG	General-Purpose Machine Gun
GWS	Guided Weapons System
HAAU	Helicopter Acoustic Analysis Unit
HAR	Helicopter Air Rescue
HAS	Helicopter Anti-Submarine
HDS	Helicopter Delivery Service
HF	Home Fleet/High Frequency
HM	Her/His Majesty
HMS	Her/His Majesty's Ship
HMAS	Her/His Majesty's Australian Ship
HMCS	Her/His Majesty's Canadian Ship
HMNZS	Her/His Majesty's New Zealand Ship
hp	horsepower
HRH	Her/His Royal Highness
HTP	High-Test Hydrogen Peroxide
IFF	Identification Friend or Foe
IFTU	Intensive Flying Trials Unit
INS	Indian Naval Ship

IR	Infrared
IRBM	Intermediate-Range Ballistic Missile
JASS	Joint Anti-Submarine School
JCA	Joint Combat Aircraft
JFH	Joint Force Harrier
JFSC	Joint Fire Support Committee
JHDU	Joint Helicopter Development Unit
JHF	Joint Helicopter Force
JMC	Joint Maritime Course
JSF	Joint Strike Fighter
KCB	Knight Commander of the Order of the Bath
knot	measurement of speed, 1 knot equals 1 nautical mile per hour
LABS	Low Altitude Bombing System
LAPADS	Lightweight Acoustic Processing and Display System
LAST	Low Altitude Surveillance Task
lb	pound (weight)
LCA	Landing Craft Assault
LCT	Landing Craft Tank
LCVP	Landing Craft Vehicles and Personnel
LHA	Landing Ship Helicopter Assault
LHD	Landing Ship Helicopter/Dock
LPD	Landing Platform Dock
LPH	Landing Platform Helicopter
LSO	Landing Signal Officer
LTC	Long Term Costing
MAD	Magnetic Anomaly Detector
MAP	Ministry of Aircraft Production
MATCH	Medium Anti-submarine Torpedo Carrying Helicopter
MASC	Maritime Airborne Surveillance and Control (Project)
MC	Military Cross
MDAP	Mutual Defence Assistance Programme
MF	Mediterranean Fleet
MFAS	Multi-Function Active Sensor
MG	machine gun
mm	millimetre

MOD	Ministry of Defence
MONAB	Mobile Operational Naval Air Base
MOS	Ministry of Supply
MRBM	Medium-Range Ballistic Missile
MRH	Multi-Role Helicopter
MRR	Maritime Radar Reconnaissance
MVO	Member of the Royal Victorian Order
MW	megawatt
NAS	Naval Air Squadron/Naval Air Station (USN)
NATO	North Atlantic Treaty Organisation
NATSU	Naval Aircraft Transport and Salvage Unit
NBMR	NATO Basic Military Requirement
NCRE	Naval Construction Research Establishment
NKPA	North Korean People's Army
ORI	Operational Readiness Inspection
pdr	pounder (as in 12pdr gun)
PGM	Precision-Guided Munition
PLA	People's Liberation Army (China)
PLA/N/AF	People's Liberation Army/Navy/Air Force
psi	pounds per square inch
RA	Rear Admiral
RAAF	Royal Australian Air Force
RAE	Royal Aircraft Establishment
RAF	Royal Air Force
RAN	Royal Australian Navy
RANAS	Royal Australian Naval Air Station
RANR	Royal Australian Naval Reserve
RANVR	Royal Australian Naval Volunteer Reserve
RARA	Rear Admiral Reserve Aircraft
RAS	Replenishment At Sea
RATOG	Rocket-Assisted Take-Off Gear
RCAF	Royal Canadian Air Force
RCN	Royal Canadian Navy
RCNAS	Royal Canadian Naval Air Station
RCNR	Royal Canadian Naval Reserve

RCNVR	Royal Canadian Naval Volunteer Reserve
RCNC	Royal Corps of Naval Constructors
RDU	Receipt and Dispatch Unit
RFA	Royal Fleet Auxiliary
RIMPAC	'Rim of the Pacific' Allied naval exercise
RIO	Radar Intercept Officer (USN)
RM	Royal Marines
RN	Royal Navy
RNAS	Royal Naval Air Station
RNAY	Royal Naval Air Yard
RNR	Royal Naval Reserve
RNVR	Royal Naval Volunteer Reserve
RNZAF	Royal New Zealand Air Force
RNZN	Royal New Zealand Navy
RNZNVR	Royal New Zealand Naval Volunteer Reserve
ROP	Report of Proceedings
RP	Rocket Projectile
RRE	Royal Radar Establishment
SAC	Strategic Air Command (USAF)
SAGW	Surface-to-Air Guided Weapon
SAM	Surface-to-Air Missile
SAR	Search And Rescue
SDR	Strategic Defence Review
SDSR	Strategic Defence and Security Review
SEATO	South East Asia Treaty Organisation
SHP	Shaft Horsepower
SSBN	Nuclear-powered Ballistic missile Submarine
SSM	Surface-to-Surface Missile
SSN	Nuclear-powered Attack Submarine
STOBAR	Short Take-Off But Arrested Recovery
STOVL	Short Take-Off Vertical Landing
TACAN	Tactical Air Navigation System
TAG	Telegraphist Air Gunner/Tailored Air Group
TASMO	Tactical Air Support of Maritime Operations
TE	Task Element
TEZ	Total Exclusion Zone
TF	Task Force

| TG | Task Group |
| TU | Task Unit |

UAV	Unmanned (uninhabited) Air vehicle
UCAS-D	Unmanned (uninhabited) Combat Air System – Demonstrator
UCAV	Unmanned (uninhabited) Combat Air Vehicle
UCLASS	Unmanned (uninhabited) Carrier-Launched Airborne Strike, Surveillance System (USN)
UDI	Unilateral Declaration of Independence (Rhodesia/Zimbabwe)
UHF	Ultra High Frequency
UK	United Kingdom
UN	United Nations
US	United States
USAF	United States Air Force
USMC	United States Marine Corps
USN	United States Navy
USS	United States Ship
UN	United Nations

VA	Vice Admiral
VC	Victoria Cross
VHF	Very High Frequency
V/STOL	Vertical/Short Take-Off and Vertical Landing
VTO	Vertical Take-Off
VTOL	Vertical Take-Off and Landing

WF	Western Fleet
WOD	Wind Over the Deck
WRE	Weapons Research Establishment
WRNS	Women's Royal Naval Service
W/T	Wireless Telegraphy

1 Manpower, Fleets and Changes

The effective strike operations carried out by the British Pacific Fleet (BPF) in 1945 against Japanese strategic, industrial, military and naval targets drew the Royal Navy into a new era of warfare. It had been the only British strike force capable of attacking mainland Japan and had done so with an economy of manpower and equipment that should have demonstrated to post-war British governments how a maritime strategy could be deployed affordably in the nation's best interests across the world when required in the uncertain years after 1945. The BPF had also harnessed the potential of the Commonwealth to act together in support of a common aim, besides fighting seamlessly alongside the armed forces of the United States. At the dawn of an era when the United Nations was expected to be the guardian of the world's peace these were factors as important as the fleet's effectiveness in combat. The BPF's embarked aircraft had been the core of the fleet's power and those who understood its achievements predicted a bright future for naval aviation in the post-war era. After the end of hostilities, the BPF had shown further flexibility by transforming a number of ships, especially aircraft carriers, to repatriate former prisoners of war and internees and to provide humanitarian relief to places such as Hong Kong left destitute by Japanese occupation forces. In the power vacuum after the collapse of Japan the BPF had moved seamlessly into a constabulary role to put down piracy and insurrection across the Far East so that peacetime trade could be restored. The fleet demonstrated its ability to deploy the right amount of force or humanitarian aid in the right place at the right time, often using the same resources for both tasks.

For much of late 1945 and 1946, BPF warships and their ships' companies proved to be not only the most suitable entity for a wide variety of sensitive and difficult new tasks but, in many cases, they represented the only organisation available in the short term to implement UK government policies that had not been anticipated or prepared for. The former French and Dutch colonial empires in Indo-China and the East Indies had to be held against nationalist insurgents until suitable colonial forces could be shipped to them from Europe where the colonial powers were, themselves, trying to recover from German occupation. The

The BPF led the Royal Navy into a new era of warfare in which carrier air groups would be used with powerful effect against enemies at sea, in the air and on land, if necessary at considerable distances from the UK. A running range of Corsairs and Avengers is seen here on *Victorious*, about to take off to strike targets in Japan. RN carrier-borne aircraft like these were the only British aircraft to attack the Japanese mainland during the Second World War. (Author's collection)

restoration of French and Dutch rule in the region, whilst distasteful to some, was supported by the United Nations in the short term to restore stability and was accepted as British government policy. It was an important aspect of the restoration of global trade and, therefore, vital to the recovery of the United Kingdom's economy after six years of war. The BPF contributed to the restoration of stability and British trade in a number of ways including the protection of shipping against piracy and the illegal use of force by non-state forces. More subtly it 'showed the flag' in many ports to emphasise that Britain was a victorious power with global reach, able to act for good as a permanent member of the United Nations Security Council.

Many urgent operational tasks remained after VJ-Day, among them the clearance of wartime minefields. On the initiative of the Admiralty, an international organisation was created, based in London, to supervise the work of clearance[1] and 1900 minesweepers from many nations were employed on the task. Despite this effort, 130 merchant ships and fishing vessels of all nationalities were sunk or damaged in late 1945 and early 1946, most of them vessels that strayed outside specified channels despite published advice, but no minesweepers were lost. At the beginning of 1946 the Royal Navy operated 513 minesweepers across the world on active duty, all of which had to be manned by skilled personnel available for long enough to avoid constant disruptions to their ships' companies. By the beginning of 1947 the number had reduced to sixty-five[2] and over 4600 mines had been swept by British and Commonwealth vessels during 1946[3] in areas as far apart as the Atlantic, North Sea, Mediterranean, Singapore, Malaya, Hong Kong, Indo-China and Borneo.

Powerful strike carrier operations had continued in the BPF until the last hours of the war but the Home Fleet had already run down considerably before the Japanese surrender and the Mediterranean Fleet had effectively become a training force, providing operational sea training facilities in good weather for newly commissioned ships. The end of hostilities and the urgent need for the UK Government to recover an economy that was on the verge of bankruptcy after re-armament and six years of global war meant that the Admiralty had to carry out a programme of demobilisation and force reduction on a massive scale. In 1945 there was already a manpower crisis, with new ships including sixteen of the new light fleet carriers coming into service and older ships including the carriers *Furious* and *Argus* and several battleships having to be reduced to reserve to find the experienced men needed to man them. The Admiralty had expected the war in the Pacific to last into 1946 but, under pressure from the Government to make manpower available for the restoration of British industry, had already begun to release men in certain categories back into civilian life. The Japanese surrender in August 1945 meant that large numbers of men would have to be demobilised while maintaining operational capability where it was still needed urgently. The RN in general, and its Fleet Air Arm in particular faced a number of problems once the imperative to mount major combat operations at long range ceased and the Service had to revert to a peacetime size and structure.

Manpower and Training

In mid-1945 approximately 866,000 men and women were serving in the Royal Navy, Royal Marines and Women's Royal Naval Service (WRNS) but over 75 per cent of the officers were mobilised members of the Royal Naval Reserve (RNR) and Royal Naval Volunteer Reserve (RNVR) and a large percentage of ratings enlisted since 1939 had joined under 'hostilities only' rules, although these had allowed for some of them to be retained until 'normal' conditions were restored and men on peacetime engagements trained to replace them. This number was far in excess of the Royal Navy's approved war strength of 450,000 in 1918 and demobilisation had to be carried out, therefore, on a scale and at a pace that was unprecedented. Some organisations could be demobilised quickly as the requirements for them had ended with the enemy's surrender. These included Western Approaches Command in Liverpool; the wartime Home Fleet base at Scapa Flow; airfields, air yards and stores depots in Ceylon, Australia, the Admiralty Islands and many more. By 1946 the manpower total was reduced to 492,800 and by 1947 it was 192,665.

Demobilisation was not just a question of numbers, although reductions of 300,000 men per year in two consecutive years were difficult enough to manage. The majority of the pre-war regulars still serving had become senior rates or officers and virtually every branch had shortages of junior rates, felt most keenly in the newer branches such as radar, fighter control, electronic warfare and particularly naval aviation. The RN had only regained full control of its embarked aircraft together with their procurement, shore training and support in May 1939, although recruiting for aircrew and maintenance personnel had begun shortly after the decision by Sir Thomas Inskip, the Minister for Defence Co-ordination, in July 1937 that both the administration and operation of naval aviation should be under Admiralty and not joint control. By 1945 one man in four of those serving in the RN and its reserves was directly concerned with naval aviation. The Fleet Air Arm was not, therefore, in a position to allow as many early releases as the larger, longer-established branches such as seamen and stokers. The result was that the release of some rating categories had to be held back behind the average level[4] and by 1947 the disparity between the most advanced release group and the most retarded was eleven. Equality was not achieved before 1948 when the last of the 'hostilities only' ratings were released. The manpower crisis between 1945 and 1948 was one of the reasons why the WRNS was retained as a permanent element within the Naval Service.

A number of regular RN officers had qualified as pilots prior to 1939 and others were recruited as short-service RN pilots and observers after 1937. Many of these subsequently gained permanent commissions and several rose to high rank but after September 1939 the great majority of pilots and observers were commissioned into the RNR and especially the RNVR. While some of these were interested in transferring to the regular Navy, many were not. Faced with a serious shortage of aircrew in 1946, the Admiralty decided to cease the training of observers and train officers as pilot/observers to fill the gap.[5] Officers undergoing observer training at the time, or ear-marked for it, were to be re-trained as pilot/observers. Surprisingly, it was decided not to repeat the pre-war practice of entering officers on short-service commissions as pilots. At the same time it was decided that two-thirds of all naval pilots should, in future be ratings,[6] the majority to be recruited direct from civil life into a re-constituted rating pilots' branch but some to be taken from RN branches particularly, it was hoped, aircraft artificers although it was not made clear how this would help the existing shortage of artificers. The first rating pilot intake took place in November 1946 and comprised volunteers from the residue of deferred wartime 'Y' Scheme candidates together with a few transfers from other branches. Another new rating branch was created to replace the wartime telegraphist air gunners (TAGs); known as aircrewmen, the new rear-seat crews were to specialise as 'maintainer-users' of airborne electronic equipment and were to be recruited, it was hoped, mainly from the electrical branch. Aircrewmen in the higher rating grades were to be trained to navigate aircraft and suitable TAGs were to be offered conversion courses to allow them to join the branch which was expected to fill about 80 per cent of the rear seats in future squadrons.

Changes were also made in the maintenance and servicing branches and those connected with other duties concerning aircraft. The naval airman branch was re-constituted and ratings employed in both aircraft handling and safety equipment duties were transferred into it from the seaman branch. The branch also included photographers, meteorological ratings and mechanics used for aircraft servicing and general duties connected with air ordnance. More highly-qualified mechanics, now known as skilled air mechanics (SAMs), were to be introduced to replace the air fitter branch for employment on aircraft maintenance that required a lower degree of skill than that of artificers.[7] Artificers themselves were the most highly-skilled rating maintenance personnel and they were qualified in either airframe/engine or electrical/ordnance categories. In accordance with the recommendations of the Naval Aircraft Maintenance Committee, centralised maintenance was introduced for both front-line and training units within which personnel and aircraft were to be formed into cohesive air groups.

Within a year it had to be accepted the changes introduced for aircrew categories and their training had been a failure that had, arguably, made the situation worse rather than better. Few volunteers for the rating pilot scheme had come forward and the Admiralty had to accept that only officers would have the full range of qualities and access to briefing material and intelligence that it required its pilots to have.[8] This accorded with wartime experience, making the decision to rely heavily on rating pilots difficult to understand. Also, the RAF, which was responsible for all UK military pilot training, had decided that its own pilots should all, in future, be officers and training ratings for the RN alone would have been difficult. The termination of the rating pilot scheme was announced in December 1948[9] and it was announced at the same time that in future pilot entry was to comprise approximately one-third from volunteer executive officers on the permanent list and two-thirds direct entry officers on short-service commissions. A small number of Royal Marines and engineer specialist officers were also to be recruited to provide a broad base of knowledge in front-line units.

The first conversion course to train pilot/observers started in July 1948 but it immediately became apparent that the concept of appointing dual-trained officers as either pilots or observers was impractical and very uneconomical since the training was excessively long and the maintenance of currency in both skills difficult to achieve. The few dual-trained officers were designated as (F) for 'flying' rather than the more usual (p) for a pilot or (o) for an observer in the Navy List. The last pure observer courses in 1946 were composed of RCN and Dutch officers but by 1948 it was accepted that a new scheme for the direct entry of short-service officers for training as observers must be restored. The aircrewman branch took a long time to get started but eventually attracted a number of TAGs; all TAGs rated petty officer or above were offered the choice of conversion to the aircrewman branch or of re-training as naval airmen or air electrical specialists. About 150 opted to continue flying and completed their training in November 1949. The original concept that the branch should draw its recruits from the air electrical branch was abandoned after it proved impractical and a direct-entry scheme was approved. This, likewise, never materialised and by 1949 the branch was composed entirely of former TAGs. A new entry of some form of rating aircrew was anticipated, however, for the three-seat anti-submarine aircraft project that materialised as the Fairey Gannet. Broadly, the changes in the structure of the maintenance branches proved more workable and these stayed in place. One other change was introduced in 1949; since May 1939 officers involved with aviation duties had formed what was known as the Air Branch, although the term Fleet Air Arm used since 1924 had remained in common use. Short-service officers and those mobilised from the RNR and RNVR into the Air Branch, who had not qualified as executive officers able to keep watches or command HM ships had the fact denoted by a letter 'A' inside the executive curl of the their rank lace. In 1949 the Branch was disestablished and officers were transferred into the executive or engineering Branches[10] as appropriate and the use of the 'A' in rank lace lapsed.

The last course of pilots cross-trained as observers completed its training in September 1949 and there were no plans to train more although, in the normal course of events, it remained possible for some suitable observers to re-train as pilots. At the same time specialisation as observers was re-opened to officers in the executive branch and direct-entry into observer training continued. By 1949 the training of aircrew had, therefore, stabilised although numbers were still significantly below those required. Two very practical schemes were introduced to expand the number of aircrew available at short notice in emergencies, however. The first of these was the establishment of four RNVR naval air squadrons, three fighter and one anti-submarine, in July 1947. These were based at RN air stations and had a core of regular pilots and maintainers. Initially sixty-five pilots and six observers, all officers, were enrolled,[11] thus ensuring that their extensive wartime experience continued to be available. The Admiralty also sought to recruit experienced RNVR air engineer officers, supply officers and air traffic control specialists together with an initial ninety ratings with aircraft servicing and maintenance experience to make the RNVR air squadrons fully capable of embarkation at need. They had to commit to carrying out fourteen days' continuous training per year in addition to 100 hours non-continuous training spread over at least twelve weekends per year. In practice it was found that commitment was needed to two or three weekends per month for the pilots to maintain reasonable currency on their aircraft. RNVR aircrew with a wartime background were obviously a wasting asset as they grew older, however, and the second scheme involved the training of new reserve aircrew. In 1949 it was decided to introduce pilot training, and in due course observer training, for National Servicemen deemed to be suitable for a commission.[12] They were entered as Midshipmen RNVR and followed the normal RN flying training syllabus to 'wings' standard during their National Service time. They were then to be fed into the RNVR air squadrons for conversion onto operational types and continuation flying, meeting the normal requirements for training. Both reserve schemes provided a valuable means by which the front-line naval air squadrons could be reinforced in an emergency and both were to be tested sooner than had been envisaged.

As a means of making the most use of the manpower that was available, another 1949 decision led to the civilianisation of several tasks previously undertaken within the Home Air Command training establishment. The main object of this was to enable the release of large numbers of maintenance personnel and a proportion of aircrew for duties more closely connected to front-line operations.[13] These included the twin-engined aircraft conversion unit and the provision of targets for the aircraft direction school taken over by Airwork Services at RNAS Brawdy, flying in support of the naval air signal school by Air Service Training at Hamble and the provision of an instrument flying school and practice flying facilities for pilots in Admiralty appointments by Short Brothers & Harland at Rochester. Introduced for an initial trial period until 1950, civilianisation worked well and other tasks were considered.

Ships

In 1945 all six operational fleet carriers had served in the 1st Aircraft Carrier Squadron (ACS) as part of the BPF. By 1947 all of them had returned to the UK, some having been used for trooping duties to the Far East before being reduced to reserve status. *Illustrious* was modernised and re-commissioned but with accommodation that was far below acceptable peacetime standards she was used with a reduced ship's company as a trials and training carrier. Even then it proved impossible to keep her running during the manpower crises during demobilisation and she spent periods in reserve. It had to be accepted between 1945 and 1948 that these big ships were manpower-intensive and expensive to operate. *Implacable* and *Indomitable* underwent refits to allow them to return to operational service but their low hangar heights and small lifts limited the type of aircraft they could operate. *Indefatigable* and *Victorious* were brought out of reserve for service with reduced ships' companies to act as training ships in the Home Fleet Training Squadron based at Portland, replacing battleships that were placed in reserve or scrapped. *Formidable* was found to be in such a poor material state after her wartime damage and the years laid up without maintenance that she was never returned to service.

Although they were relatively young, these six ships suffered from the fact that they had been designed before the 1942 Joint Technical Committee decision that aircraft must be embarked in greater numbers with larger dimensions than had previously been allowed and maximum launch weights up to 30,000lbs. None of the existing fleet carriers were capable of operating such aircraft without major reconstruction and their accommodation, designed in the late 1930s was totally inadequate for the increased number of sailors required for their enlarged air groups, radar and other technical advances including the big increases in the size of their close-range armament. In mid-1945 the Admiralty had authority from the Government to build seven new fleet carriers, three of the *Audacious* class and four of the later and bigger *Malta* class. The latter could never have been completed during the war and were designed with the post-war fleet in mind but with the nation on the verge of bankruptcy, the Admiralty was unable to persuade the new Labour Government that it needed at least two *Malta* class and they were all cancelled by December before construction had begun. One of the *Audacious* class was scrapped on the slipway when 27 per cent complete. The two others were eventually completed as *Eagle* and *Ark Royal*, both modified to operate new generations of aircraft and both had a major role to play in the RN strike fleet for two decades.

The light fleet carriers proved to be valuable ships in the immediate post-war years. Four of them, *Colossus*, *Venerable*, *Vengeance* and *Glory*, had joined the BPF in 1945 just too late for active operations against the Japanese but in time to play an important role in the stabilisation of the Far East when limited force had to be applied in several local conflicts that followed the removal of Japanese occupation forces. By the end of 1946 only two light fleet carriers remained with the BPF and they returned to the UK to be reduced to reserve in 1947 as the manpower crisis reached its height. Other ships of this class were completed after 1945 and were brought into service when manpower and worked-up squadrons were available. None of the improved *Majestic* class were completed for the RN but *Magnificent* was completed for loan to the RCN and *Terrible* was sold to the RAN as HMAS *Sydney* III. Both navies adopted RN squadron numbers and procedures for their embryonic Fleet Air Arms and the provision of manpower to fill gaps in their establishments and training their air groups absorbed a significant amount of RN effort. 1948 found nearly all RN carriers immobilised in UK ports because of manpower shortages,[14] but by the end of the year the position had improved and it proved possible to re-commission one fleet and four light fleet carriers for operational service with full air groups with one fleet and one light fleet carrier engaged in trials and training duties.

During the Second World War the RN had operated thirty-eight escort carriers built in the USA and made available under Lend-Lease arrangements; a further six were converted from merchant ships in the UK together with nineteen small Merchant Navy-manned escort carriers known as MAC-Ships. By 1947 the surviving American ships had all been returned, the MAC-Ships returned to mercantile use and all but one of the British conversions returned to their former owners. The exception was *Campania* which was to be converted into an aircraft ferry but that plan failed to materialise and she was converted into an exhibition ship to support the Festival of Britain in 1951. Her naval career subsequently resumed and in 1952 she was refitted to become the flagship of the task force that carried out the first British atomic bomb test at Monte Bello Island off north-west Australia. She operated helicopters and seaplanes on a variety of administrative tasks. Three maintenance carriers, a type unique to the RN, were reduced to reserve by 1946 but *Unicorn* was subsequently to give valuable service during the Korean War and *Perseus* as a trials ship and prototype helicopter carrier.

Beyond the short term, once manpower stability had been achieved, the Admiralty still faced major problems. To keep the RN effective, a new generation of aircraft would have to be introduced but the existing large carriers were clearly handicapped by their low hangar height, small lifts and cramped workshops and accommodation. They would need radical reconstruction to make them effective and that would be expensive; just how expensive was not appreciated until work started on the first ship, *Victorious* in 1950. Reconstruction on this scale had never been attempted in a Royal Dockyard before but in 1949 Admiralty approval in principle, with Treasury acceptance, was given to modernise three of the existing fleet carriers.[15] The flight deck and hangars were to be strengthened to operate aircraft at maximum weights up to 30,000lbs. The hangars were to retain their armoured protection but their height was to be increased to 17ft 6in and a complete gallery deck was to be built in over the hangars, beneath their flight decks. The ships were to be fitted with new, larger lifts including a side-lift, together with steam catapults, improved arrester gear and barriers. Even in 1949, however, it was admitted that 'owing to the small size of these ships, the full possibilities which should result from fitting all the latest aircraft operating equipment will not be attainable'.[16] There was no immediate intention of modernising any light fleet carriers despite their current usefulness.

Aircraft

In many ways the Royal Navy's problems with aircraft mirrored those with its ships; it had a lot of them in 1945, some of which remained in production but new technological developments and the requirement for long-range strike warfare meant that most of these were already obsolescent. A considerable number, roughly half the total, had been provided by the United States under Lend-Lease arrangements and after the end of hostilities these had to be paid for in dollars, returned to the USA or destroyed. Unsurprisingly the last option was the cheapest and thousands of aircraft were dumped into the sea off Australia, India, Ceylon, South Africa and in the waters around the United Kingdom. To add to the problem, the British aircraft industry was going through its own post-war convulsions with the shutting-down of the shadow factory scheme and the financial difficulties that followed the cancellation of large numbers of aircraft under contract.

Two aircraft types were under development for the RN in 1945 which were intended specifically for use in the *Malta*, *Audacious* and *Hermes* class carriers. Both were too big and heavy to operate from the existing fleet or light fleet carriers and with the cancellation of the *Malta*s and likely long delays before the ships that became *Eagle* and *Ark Royal* and the four remaining *Hermes* class ships would be completed there seemed little point in continuing with aircraft which were expected to be obsolete before they could go to sea and both were cancelled. The first was the Fairey Spearfish, intended as a Barracuda replacement in the strike and reconnaissance roles, ordered to meet Specification O.5/43.[17] Unlike its predecessor, dive-bombing was considered the primary attack method with torpedo attack relegated to secondary status. The first prototype, RA 356, flew in 1946 and it was followed by two other prototypes which were used for development work until 1952 but production orders for 208 Spearfish were cancelled and the airframes broken up on Fairey's Stockport production line.[18] It had a wingspan of 60ft 3in and a maximum launch weight of 22,083lbs, making it considerably larger and heavier than its predecessor, and had a large internal weapons bay capable of carrying a single Mark 15 or 17 torpedo or up to four 1000lb bombs. Defensive armament comprised a single 0.5in Browning machine in a turret aft of the cockpit that was controlled remotely by the observer. Another advanced feature was the torpedo and sight which included an early example of an analogue computer. It would have had a radius of action of about 400 miles. The prototypes and the first 100 production aircraft were powered by a single 2320hp Bristol Centaurus 58 radial engine; subsequent production aircraft were to have been fitted with the projected Rolls-Royce Pennine engine which was to be more powerful.[19] The Spearfish was one of the largest single-engined aircraft ever flown.

The other cancelled project was the Short Sturgeon which was designed to meet Specification S.11/43 for a long-range reconnaissance and light strike aircraft. Like the Spearfish, it was specified after the Joint Technical Committee's decision to increase the size and weight of aircraft and intended for the new generation of carriers. The only twin propeller-driven aircraft to be designed for the Royal Navy from the outset rather than evolved from a design intended for the RAF, it was too big and too heavy for operation from the existing carriers. Powered by two Rolls-Royce Merlin 140 engines, each developing 2080hp, it had a wingspan of 59ft 11in and a maximum all-up weight of 23,000lbs.[20] A small internal bomb-bay was capable of carrying a single 1000lb bomb or four depth charges; it was also

The Sturgeon T 2 was an unusual target facilities aircraft in that it was fully equipped for deck landing. This aircraft of 728 NAS at RNAS Hal Far is about to be given the 'cut' by the batsman as it lands on a light fleet carrier of the Mediterranean Fleet.

intended to have two 0.5in Browning 'front-guns' fitted in the wings and hardpoints under the wings for sixteen 3in rockets with 60lb warheads. These gave it a useful attack capability but its principal role equipment would have been two F-52 cameras with 36in or 20in lenses which would have given the aircraft a strategic reconnaissance capability. It would also have carried ASH radar in the nose and was capable of both radar and visual surface search and shadowing an enemy force at sea. The radius of action on internal fuel would have been an impressive 700 miles in still air and maximum speed was 325 knots. Like all twin-engined propeller-driven naval aircraft, the Sturgeon suffered from an asymmetric problem if a single engine failed on the approach to a carrier. Shorts tackled this by fitting the two engines with contra-rotating propellers which solved the problem of yaw on take-off but successful deck landing with asymmetric thrust after a single engine failure would still have been marginal because of the 'good' engine being necessarily offset from the aircraft's centreline to give space for the propeller's rotation. A single prototype of this variant, RK 787, flew in 1946.

In August 1945 a contract had been placed for thirty Sturgeon S1 aircraft and, rather than cancel them, the Admiralty tasked Shorts to modify them into high-speed target-towing aircraft to meet specification Q.1/46 and two further prototypes were built, VR 363 and VR 371. These retained the ability to operate from a carrier with tail hooks and power-folding wings but had a lengthened nose with extensive glazing to house cameras. It is a measure of the importance placed on realistic weapons training required after 1945 that twenty-three aircraft from the original production order were completed as target-tugs to this modified TT 2 standard for service with RN fleet requirements units in the UK and Malta. Of these, nineteen aircraft were further modified in the mid-1950s to TT 3 standard with the deck landing and photographic equipment removed together with a reversion to the original nose design. They remained in service until replaced by Meteor TT 20 jets in 1958.

Another aircraft that saw limited production in the years immediately after the Second World War was the Blackburn Firebrand, originally conceived to meet specification N.11/40 for a fleet air-defence fighter. Large, robust and never to prove popular with its pilots, the Firebrand's first prototype, DD 804, first flew in February 1942 by which time the Seafire appeared to fill the role adequately and it was decided to modify the Firebrand into a long-range torpedo-carrying strike fighter. Further development spanned the remaining war years and the first production version, the TF 4, only entered service with 813 NAS in September 1945. It took part in the victory flypast over London in June 1946. A total of 220 aircraft were produced, mostly to TF 4 standard but a small batch was built to the definitive TF 5 standard. A number of TF 4s were upgraded to TF 5 standard.

A Firebrand of 813 NAS armed with a Mark 17 torpedo taking off from *Indomitable*. The aircraft parked aft are Sea Furies and Firebrands. (Author's collection)

The Firebrand[21] had a maximum all-up weight of 17,500lbs and a wingspan of just over 51ft which meant that it could only be operated from *Implacable*, *Indefatigable*, *Eagle* and the modernised *Indomitable*. By 1946 it lacked the essential performance needed from a fighter but with no strike aircraft other than the obsolescent Barracuda capable of carrying a torpedo it had a limited usefulness and equipped two front-line units, 813 and 827 NAS. It was expected that both would re-equip with the new turbo-prop Westland Wyvern in 1948 but development difficulties delayed their replacement until 1953. The Firebrand TF 5 had a 2520hp Bristol Centaurus 9 engine giving a maximum speed of 380 knots. It had four 20mm cannon, each with 200 rounds per gun, in the wings and a single 1850lb Mark 15 or 17 torpedo on a hardpoint on the fuselage centreline which could be fitted with alternative loads of a single 2000lb, 1000lb, 500lb bomb, Mark 6, 7 or 9 mine or 100-gallon fuel tank. Hardpoints under each wing could be fitted with 500lb or 250lb bombs or depth charges, 50-gallon tanks or eight 3in rockets with 60lb heads. Radius of action with internal fuel was about 250nm; this could be extended with external tanks but the aircraft's handling qualities would have been marginal with a heavy load. In any event it was a cumbersome aircraft to fly to the deck and was considered obsolete by 1950.

A specialised variant of the Mosquito fighter/bomber, known as the Sea Mosquito, had been developed after Lieutenant Commander E M 'Winkle' Brown landed a modified Mosquito on *Indefatigable* on 25 March 1944; the world's first carrier landing by a twin-engined aircraft.[22] Designed to meet specification N.15/44, the RN variant was designated the Sea Mosquito TR 33 and a contract for three prototype examples was followed by another for 100 production aircraft, the first of which was delivered in late 1945. 811 NAS re-formed with former RAF Mosquito FB 6 aircraft to convert aircrew onto the new type at the end of 1945 and re-equipped with Sea Mosquitoes in April 1946. By then, there was literally no deck from which the type could operate at its maximum all-up weight of 22,500lbs with a torpedo and full fuel although its wingspan of 54ft was acceptable. It could have operated at reduced weight from *Indefatigable* or *Implacable* but there were concerns about its marginal single-engine deck landing performance and, while these might have been acceptable in wartime, they were not in peacetime. 811 NAS operated ashore at RN Air Stations Ford, Brawdy and Eglinton before disbanding in July 1947.[23] The production Sea Mosquitoes were subsequently used by second-line squadrons until the mid-1950s, together with a small batch of improved TR 37 versions.

A Sea Hornet NF 21 seconds before catching number 2 wire on its parent carrier. The batsman has his bats lowered in the 'cut' position and is continuing to watch the aircraft's arrival from his position aft of his wind-break. (Author's collection)

The Mosquito's designers, de Havilland, had also produced a later twin-engined design from 1943 which was wisely produced in both land and carrier-based versions as a single-seat strike fighter. Both had two Merlin engines of 2030hp with propellers that rotated in opposite directions so that there was no yaw on take-off but the problem of asymmetric recovery after a single engine failure remained.[24] The naval version was modified to meet specification N.5/44 from the basic design by Heston Aircraft and the first prototype, PX 212, flew for the first time in April 1945 with deck-landing trials on the new light fleet carrier *Ocean* following in August. The naval variant was given the name Sea Hornet and the RN eventually procured three versions; the F 20 long-range strike-fighter, the NF 21 night fighter and the PR 22 reconnaissance aircraft. The NF 21 was the heaviest version, equipped with ASH radar and a second crew member to operate it. It had a maximum all-up weight of 19,530lbs and, like all versions, a wingspan of 45ft which meant that it could be operated from *Indefatigable*, *Implacable*, the modernised *Indomitable*, *Eagle* and even, in limited numbers, from a modernised light fleet carrier. With a maximum speed of 406 knots the Sea Hornet F 20 was the fastest piston-engined fighter ever to serve with the RN and it had a radius of action of 600nm with internal fuel which could be extended to 800nm with drop tanks fitted under the wings. The F 20 and NF 21 had four 20mm cannon in the nose with 180 rounds per gun[25] and both versions had wing hardpoints, each capable of carrying a single drop tank, 1000lb bomb or mine. Alternatively, rails for up to eight 3in rockets with 60lb warheads could be fitted under the wings. Surprisingly, the addition of radar and the extra crew member in the NF 21 only reduced its maximum speed by 4 knots. The PR 22 was a strategic reconnaissance version which lacked the guns but could still be fitted with underwing drop tanks. It was fitted with two F52 vertically-mounted cameras for day reconnaissance or a single K19B for night work.[26] Later F 20s were fitted to take oblique photographs from cameras fitted in the rear fuselage and designated FR 20s. Only one front-line unit embarked with Sea Hornet F 20s and PR 22s, 801 NAS, which re-commissioned with the types on 1 June 1947 although 806 NAS was partially equipped with Sea Hornets together with Sea Vampire jets and Sea Furies for a demonstration tour of the USA in 1948. Although it had a greater radius of action than any other fighter, the F 20 was withdrawn from front-line service in 1951 so that the fighter force could be standardised on a single type, the Sea Fury. The PR 22 was withdrawn at the same time although both variants continued to serve with second-line units until 1957. The NF 21 equipped 809 NAS on 20 January 1949 and continued in service until 1954 when it was replaced by Sea Venom jets. A total of 178 Sea Hornets was built, comprising seventy-seven F 20s, seventy-eight NF 21s and twenty-three PR 22s.[27]

The other new type was the Hawker Sea Fury which flew for the first time in February 1945 and carried out deck landing trials on *Victorious* during 1946. Development then proceeded at a slow pace because of the run-down of Hawker's production facilities after 1946 and the RN's large stock of legacy Seafire fighters which did not need immediate replacement. The first version was the F 10,[28] intended for use as an interceptor fighter for fleet air-defence duties, and it equipped 807 NAS at RNAS Eglinton in August 1947.[29] Development work continued, however, towards what would become the outstanding piston-engined fighter of its generation, the Sea Fury FB 11. This had a 2480hp Bristol Centaurus engine driving a five-bladed propeller. The four 20mm cannon fitted in the wings had 580 rounds per gun, making the Sea Fury a persistent ground-attack aircraft as well as an effective fighter for the period and hardpoints under each wing were capable of carrying a single 1000lb or 500lb bomb, or 90- or 45-gallon drop tanks in addition to a maximum of twelve 3in rockets with 60lb warheads on underwing rails.[30] With a maximum all-up weight of 14,555lbs and a wingspan of only 38ft 4in spread, the Sea Fury could operate from any British carrier and its usefulness as a strike fighter operating from the light fleet carriers that formed the backbone of the RN and Commonwealth carrier strike forces by 1950 was obvious. It had a radius of action of 300nm on internal fuel which could be doubled if 90-gallon tanks were fitted, although they limited its manoeuvrability as a fighter. The first FB 11-equipped unit, 802 NAS, re-commissioned at RNAS Eglinton in May 1948 and the type eventually replaced the Seafire and equipped eight front-line fighter squadrons in the RN plus another eight RNVR fighter squadrons and twelve second-line units. Logically the Commonwealth navies that bought light fleet carriers bought Sea Furies to operate from them and squadrons were formed by the RAN and RCN. The Dutch Navy also operated the type from its light fleet carrier and land-based versions were exported to Burma, Cuba and Germany. Eventually 665 Sea Furies were built for the RN with the last batch of thirty ordered in October 1951. The early jet fighters were only marginally faster than the Sea Fury and were unable to out-turn it, so it remained a viable fighter into the mid-1950s and was not finally withdrawn until 1957.

Although the majority of American types were destroyed soon after VJ-Day, several squadrons retained them for a short period. The four light fleet carriers serving with the BPF in 1945 retained their Corsair squadrons because there was no viable replacement until stocks of the Seafire F 15 arrived in the Far East. The last Corsair unit, 1851 NAS, was not disbanded until August 1946. Sufficient Hellcat NF 2 night fighters, the equivalent of the USN F6F-5N, were retained to re-commission 892 NAS as a night fighter unit in April 1945 for service in the night carrier *Ocean* which was originally intended to join the BPF. Another night fighter unit, 1792 NAS equipped with Firefly NF 1s, joined *Ocean* in late 1945 and in the

A Sea Fury photographed from above seconds before landing on *Illustrious*. (Author's collection)

first half of 1946 the ship and her squadrons carried out a trial of night operations in the Mediterranean, based in the Malta area and using RNAS Hal Far as a diversion airfield. The trial was also intended to evaluate the difference in capability between the single-seat Hellcat and the two-seat Firefly and the importance placed on its outcome can be judged from the fact that the Admiralty had to pay, in US dollars, for the retention of the Hellcats and their AN/APS-6 radar mounted in a pod on the wing. The Fireflies were fitted with a pod under the fuselage which contained an American-supplied AN/APS-4 radar which also had to be paid for as there was no British equivalent. It was found that the APS-6 was the better air-intercept radar but that the APS-4 had a useful secondary surface-search capability and both the pod and 'black boxes' could be fitted into any Firefly as role equipment to convert it into a night fighter. It was also felt that having an observer to concentrate on the radar while the pilot concentrated on flying the aircraft was a safer option in bad weather at night. The trial ended in April 1946, having concluded that the Firefly was the better night fighter since it was available in large numbers and could also be used in other roles with a minimum of modification by squadron engineers. The contemporary decision to cease observer training is interesting but it was assumed that the new aircrewmen branch would be able to provide a suitable number of radar operators for the radar intercept role. The Hellcats were returned to the USN. During the trial *Ocean* logged 1100 day and 250 night deck landings without accident.

The Firefly was one of several legacy types that the RN retained in service after 1945. Eventually 1702 were built with the last examples being used as pilotless target aircraft by 728 NAS at RNAS Hal Far in Malta. The last production Firefly was delivered to this unit in March 1956, nearly fifteen years after the prototype first flew in December 1941. Wartime Fireflies had a single Rolls-Royce Griffon XII engine of 1990hp.[31] Post-war development led to the improved FR 4 and FR 5 versions with the more powerful Rolls-Royce Griffon 74 engine developing 2250hp.[32] With a maximum all-up weight of 13,480lbs and a wingspan of 41ft 2in the Firefly could operate from any contemporary British aircraft carrier and made an ideal companion to the Sea Fury in the strike-fighter wings embarked in the light fleet carriers. It had four 20mm cannon in the wings with 160 rounds per gun and could carry single 1000lb or 500lb bombs or depth charges on hardpoints under each wing. Up to four 3in rockets with 60lb heads could be mounted on rails under each wing. Fireflies equipped sixteen front-line RN squadrons at various times after 1945, seven RNVR air squadrons and no less than twenty-one second-line squadrons. It operated in the fighter, fighter-reconnaissance, night fighter and anti-submarine roles with different equipment fits and was also operated by the RAN, RCN and Dutch Navy besides being exported to operate ashore in Thailand, Sweden, Ethiopia and Denmark.[33] A further mark, the AS 7, intended for use purely as a three-seater anti-submarine aircraft, was not a success and only operated ashore with training squadrons.

Seafire FR 47s equipped front-line squadrons but a number of earlier versions, such as this Seafire F 17 of 771 NAS at RNAS Lee-on-Solent, continued in use until the early 1950s. (Author's collection)

The other legacy types were the Seafire and the Barracuda. The latter had been built in large numbers for the RN during the war as a torpedo/dive-bomber /reconnaissance aircraft. With the reduced torpedo attack role being assumed by the Firebrand, a number of Barracudas were scrapped or ditched at sea but a single unit, 815 NAS, was retained with the radar-equipped AS 3 variant for the development of airborne anti-submarine tactics based ashore at RNAS Eglinton after 1945. The type's 1642hp Merlin 32 engine had only given it a marginal performance and Lend-Lease Grumman Avengers had replaced it in the BPF. Of interest, delays in producing a replacement led to the transfer by the USN of 100 Avengers to the RN under the Mutual Defence Assistance Plan (MDAP). Some of these re-equipped 815 NAS in 1953 giving the Barracuda the unique distinction of having been replaced in service by the same type on two occasions nine years apart.

The Seafire was also built in large numbers and both production and development continued after 1945 as the Griffon-engined F 15 replaced the Mark III.[34] They were the only fighters available to replace the Lend-Lease Corsairs and Hellcats and gradually equipped all the operational fighter squadrons as the situation stabilised after 1946. The RN procured 791 Griffon-engined Seafires after 1945, the final variant being the FR 47 with a 2375hp Rolls-Royce Griffon engine. It had an improved undercarriage which made it less susceptible to deck landing accidents and an armament of four 20mm cannon.[35] Hardpoints under the fuselage and wings could each carry a single 500lb bomb or 90-gallon drop tanks and rails for four 3in rockets with 60lb warheads could be fitted under each wing. Oblique cameras could be installed aft of the cockpit to give a reconnaissance capability, hence the FR designation. The type's weakest feature was its radius of action of only 150nm on internal fuel, although drop tanks could increase this to 250nm with a small bomb load. The Seafire FR 47 was the last variant of the Spitfire/Seafire line and differed radically from the early versions produced a decade earlier but it was never able to overcome its diminutive size and the weakness stemming from its lightweight airframe and undercarriage. A developed airframe with a new 'laminar-flow' wing named the Seafang was flown in prototype form but had unpleasant handling qualities, offered little advantage over the FR 47 and was cancelled.

The British aircraft industry ran down quickly after 1945 with the end of the 'shadow' factory scheme and every firm sought to rationalise its production capacity to meet the new peacetime reality. Aircraft such as the Seafire and Firefly had been ordered in large batches but many of these were cancelled and, henceforward, types were generally ordered in small numbers which increased the individual price of an aircraft but decreased the sums required in the annual naval estimates, a process that became familiar over the next seventy years. The methods used to develop new types by the British aircraft industry were outdated and in need of radical modernisation as aircraft became more complex and this contributed to the slow progress with which the new generation of jet and turbo-prop aircraft were introduced during this period. However, the massive reduction in orders after 1945 gave little inducement for change. The Royal Aircraft Establishment (RAE) at Farnborough was tasked by the Government with developing the technology of flight and would suggest new developments to both the Admiralty and industry. 'Undercarriage-less' landing on a flexible deck, 'swing-wings', swept wings and 'zero-length' launches are examples of the Establishment's advanced ideas, some of them derived from captured German technology. The Admiralty took up ideas that appeared useful for the next generation of naval aircraft and issued requirements to the Ministry of Supply which took over the responsibility for military aircraft procurement from the Ministry of Aircraft Production after 1945. The Ministry would give advice on the practicality of producing aircraft to meet the specification and, if general agreement was reached, issue a specification and request for proposals to firms it deemed 'suitable'. Of interest, Saunders Roe had to meet all the costs of its own submission to the specification that evolved into the SR 177 Joint Strike Fighter because, with background of flying boat manufacture, the Ministry of Supply did not consider it to be 'suitable'.

A number of firms would often offer sketch designs and it was usual to give a contract to two of these for the construction of one or two prototypes which were evaluated against each other. It would have been impossible for the firms to cost a project accurately at this stage because they would not know the size of the production quantity. The prototypes that were selected would then undergo proof testing by the manufacturer followed by acceptance tests of the airframe, systems and armament by the RAE and, finally, service trials including deck landing so that the type could eventually be released for naval use. This tortuous process was made even longer by the separate development of systems such as radar at the Royal Radar Establishment (RRE), which designed sets speculatively without a defined aircraft project in mind, and engine manufacturers who designed new power units which often had no specific application at first. Radios, armament and other systems were usually Admiralty or Air Ministry-supplied items and modifications to new aircraft designs might be needed to fit them. No matter how good the initial specification had been, protracted development led to changes being specified to meet the latest front-line requirement and these added to the time needed to achieve front-line capability. As if these potential causes of delay were not enough, the majority of British aircraft manufacturers built prototypes by hand in special departments that were often remote in both location and thought processes from the production sites. If they were selected for production, the prototype would have to be 'reverse-engineered' to make the design suitable for large-scale production. Prototypes were ordered in small numbers, as they had been with the simple biplanes of the 1930s, but now had to fulfil a number of different tests to evaluate airframes, engines, armament, radar avionics and carrier compatibility which had to be carried out sequentially and added to the delay. The loss of a prototype could set a new type's entry into service back by years. The lesson was eventually learnt and in the mid-1950s the Admiralty ordered twenty Blackburn NA39 Buccaneer prototypes so that testing could be carried out concurrently

This was the situation in the late 1940s, made even worse by limited funding, but the Admiralty had to maintain a latent capability through the manpower crisis and replace obsolescent aircraft types at a time when politicians saw no immediate threat to the UK. Existing stocks of legacy aircraft had to equip the front line for longer than had been intended and it was against this background that the requirements for the new generation of jet and turbo-prop naval aircraft were drawn up. Jet fighters had entered service with the RAF in 1944; they were at the start of their development process whereas piston-engined aircraft were probably close to their limits. A prototype RN Sea Vampire, LZ 551/G, was the world's first jet aircraft to land on a carrier when Lieutenant Commander E M Brown landed on *Ocean* in December 1945. It had a good view of the deck but had to use a new technique in which the aircraft was flown into the deck at constant speed without closing the throttles. This, together with a slow engine response, gave concerns

Vengeance taking part in Operation 'Rusty' during 1949. This was a six-week deployment into the Arctic to evaluate the effect of extremely cold weather on men, ships and aircraft. Her air group included Sea Vampire jets and Dragonfly helicopters as well as more usual front-line types. (Author's collection)

about climbing away after a baulked approach. The Sea Vampire had a high top speed but its endurance was even more limited than the Seafire and although the RN formed second-line jet fighter units to give pilots experience of the new technology and tactics, none were embarked on a regular basis as a component part of a carrier air group. To add to the Admiralty's concern, aviation turbine fuel, known as avtur, was not yet refined in the UK and had to be bought from the USA in dollars, making jet aviation expensive. On the other hand, it had a higher flashpoint than avgas and could be stored in carriers' double bottoms like furnace fuel oil, greatly increasing the amount a single ship could carry and significantly reducing the risk of fire or explosion.

The first jet fighter to enter service was the Supermarine Attacker which had the same 'laminar-flow' wing as the cancelled Seafang and was expected to be an interim type while better fighters were developed. It had a single Rolls-Royce Nene

3 centrifugal-flow turbojet engine of 5000lbs thrust and a maximum all-up weight of 12,210lbs,[36] but the design was marred by having a tail-wheel undercarriage, the only jet fighter to date ever to have this feature. Attackers equipped three front-line units, 800, 803 and 890 NAS, They only operated from *Eagle* and were replaced by Sea Hawks in 1954 although a number continued to serve in five RNVR fighter squadrons until 1957 together with a number of second-line units.

A number of other advanced projects began at this time. The first among these began with specification GR 17/45 which evolved into the Fairey Gannet which I flew in the 1970s. Initially described[37] as being specially designed for anti-submarine work, including operation from escort carriers; it was originally to be a two-seat aircraft with a tricycle undercarriage and powered by two gas turbine engines driving contra-rotating, co-axial propellers. This would give twin-engine performance without the asymmetric problem after a single engine failure. Two prototypes each were ordered from Blackburn, whose version was to have two Napier Naiad engines and Fairey Aviation whose version was to have two Armstrong Siddeley Mamba engines. The production aircraft were to have ASV 15 radar, initially with a 22in scanner but later with an improved one of 36in, eight sono-buoys and a sono-buoy receiver and a 2000lb homing torpedo. Alternative armament loads were to include bombs, rocket projectiles or mines. GR 17/45 was to have no fixed armament but the capability to be fitted with two detachable 20mm gun installations. The estimated top speed was to be 290 knots and the aircraft was to fly comfortably at 150 knots on patrol. Optimistically, the Admiralty expected the type to come into service during 1949.

The Westland Wyvern was a single-seat strike fighter and an initial production batch of fifteen had been built with Rolls-Royce Eagle piston-engines. In 1947 it was hoped that trials with these would lead to a speedier release to service for a Mark 2 version fitted with a Rolls-Royce Clyde turbo-prop engine. The estimated top speed was to be 416 knots with a radius of action of 650nm[38] or an endurance of five hours with a torpedo or up to 2000lb of bombs. It was designed to take the 1000lb anti-surface ship rocket known at the time under the project name of 'Uncle Tom' or up to sixteen 3in rockets and 100-gallon drop tanks to extend the combat radius still further. It was expected to enter service in 1949 but development problems and the need to fit a new engine, the Armstrong Siddeley Python, delayed its entry into service until 1953 by which time it was already obsolescent and the last squadron was disbanded only five years later, in 1958.

Last of the new types was the Hawker N.7/46 which evolved into the Hawker Sea Hawk jet fighter. It was to have the same Nene engine as the Attacker but its more refined design was expected to give a top speed of 537 knots[39] with a combat radius of 386nm on internal fuel which could be extended by the use of two

65-gallon drop tanks, one under each wing. It was hoped that the type would enter service in late 1949 or early 1950 but, again, delays in development meant that the first unit, 806 NAS, did not form until March 1953 at RNAS Brawdy.

Air Weapons

Air weapons were rationalised after 1945, beginning with guns. The 0.5in machine gun was removed from service after the last American Lend-Lease aircraft were withdrawn in 1946 but the 0.303in machine gun was retained for use in the Seafire F 17. Otherwise all strike and fighter types carried 20mm cannon as their standard front guns. Stocks of bombs were reduced and standardised on 2000lb armour-piercing, 1000lb and 500lb medium-capacity, 500lb semi armour-piercing and 250lb general-purpose weapons, the latter only retained for the early marks of Seafire while they remained in operational service. The wartime 'B' bomb, a buoyant weapon intended to be dropped close to a ship in order to float up under the hull to detonate under the keel, had proved a disappointment in service and was discarded despite the existence of large stockpiles. A new standard bomb-carrier was introduced capable of carrying all types of bomb on all types of aircraft.[40]

The 3in rocket projectile remained standard and could be fitted with either a 25lb solid armour-piercing head or a 60lb high-explosive head for use against different targets. The solid head was intended for use against submarines to penetrate the pressure hull and against armoured vehicles on land. A new 10in rocket remained in development; it was known as 'Uncle Tom' and was expected to subsume the torpedo as the primary ship-killing weapon used by strike aircraft. In the event, development difficulties, lack of funds and lack of RAF interest in such a weapon in the late 1940s led to its eventual cancellation.

Training for torpedo attack pilots ceased in 1946, a year in which 813 NAS with its Firebrands was the only operational unit capable of dropping them. It carried out a few experimental drops before disbanding in September 1946 and the Admiralty stated that torpedo-attack training would resume when the necessary aircraft and manpower became available but, in the event, it never returned to the earlier level of importance. A homing torpedo intended for use against submarines continued in development under the codename 'Dealer' and was eventually to emerge as the Mark 30. It had a weight of only 670lbs, a running range of 5000 yards at 15 knots and its acoustic sensor could acquire a target at 300 yards in shallow water; it had, therefore, to be dropped at less than this distance ahead of its intended target. During 1946 all mobile torpedo maintenance units were reduced to care and maintenance as there was no work for them but considerable stocks of Mark 15 and 17 torpedoes were retained at RN Armament Depots to fill the need for a powerful anti-shipping weapon if it became necessary. Similarly a stock of airborne mines was retained after 1947 although there were few opportunities to practice dropping them. After 1948 facilities were created for the laying of practice minefields and some training resumed so that the experience gained during the war would not be lost.

Although not weapons, cameras formed an important element of strike fighters' equipment and these too were rationalised. Fittings for vertical and oblique F.24 cameras were retained in the Seafire FR 47, Sea Hornet F 20 and Sea Fury FB 11 aircraft. They could be controlled from the cockpit and used for tactical reconnaissance. In 1947 an RN strategic reconnaissance unit was formed to work in close liaison with the Central Photographic Unit at RAF Benson. It was equipped, initially, with Sea Mosquito TR 33 aircraft equipped with two F.52 cameras which could be fitted with either 36in or 20in lenses for strategic reconnaissance. They were replaced by Sea Hornet PR 22s.

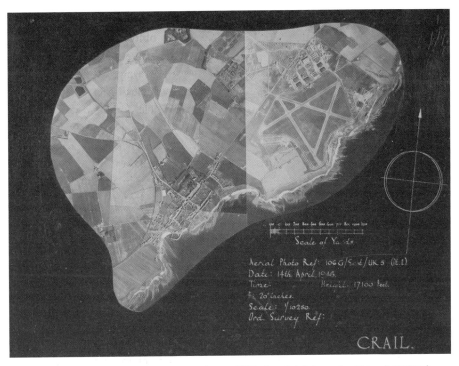

RNAS Crail was part of the post-war run-down of RN air establishments. This photograph was taken in 1946, shortly before it was reduced to care and maintenance status. Note the fields to the north of the hangars and east of the runways which are full of surplus Barracudas waiting for the scrap dealers to remove them. (Crail Museum Trust)

RN Air Stations

During the Second World War the RN commissioned eighty-three naval air stations and ten air establishments throughout the world. Of these, twenty-nine were overseas and the remainder in the UK. By 1 December 1947 there were nineteen air stations and six air establishments commissioned in the UK with a further fifteen retained in reserve that could be commissioned at short notice in an emergency. Overseas there were a further four air stations in commission, one each in Ceylon and Singapore, two in Malta and four others in reserve. The wartime Mobile Naval Air Bases (MONABs), had all been disbanded although a nucleus of men and equipment was retained at RNAS Lossiemouth for use in an emergency and to keep the art alive.[41]

The UK air stations carried out a number of functions that were vital to the support of front-line units embarked in carriers. These included the receipt, despatch and storage of new aircraft and those held in long-term reserve. Others provided facilities including ranges for squadrons to maintain their operational proficiency when disembarked from their parent carriers. Some provided training facilities for aircrew and maintenance personnel in specialised roles such as fighters, anti-submarine operations and strike warfare while others contained specialised units to function as aircraft repair yards. Until 1947, the Admiralty had tended to build a large number of relatively small task-specific airfields. With the completion of RNAS Culdrose, Cornwall, in 1947,[42] however, this changed and a move began towards a smaller number of 'super-stations' to reduce the requirement for manpower by basing more tasks on a single airfield. From then onwards surviving airfields were expanded to absorb tasks from smaller air stations which were closed. The overseas airfields provided direct support for the ships on their deployed stations including facilities for squadrons disembarked from carriers, second-line squadrons for fleet requirements duties and small holdings of reserve aircraft to replace those lost or damaged.

By December 1949 the number of air stations in the UK had reduced to sixteen with five air establishments with sixteen air stations held in reserve. Overseas, only the two air stations in Malta remained in commission with Ceylon reduced to reserve at eighteen months' notice to re-commission and Sembawang in Singapore lent to the RAF. However, with the Communist advances in China and a deteriorating situation in the Far East it was intended to re-commission Sembawang as HMS *Simbang* in January 1950.[43] The timing of this measure could hardly have been better conceived.

Operations

In March 1947 the First Lord of the Admiralty, George Hall,[44] stated that the fundamental role of the Royal Navy was to maintain operational fleets that were strong enough to ensure that the UK's vital lines of supply could be kept open and to provide such support for the United Nations as might be required.[45] At the same time, the Navy was to make the minimum demand on the nation's manpower and material resources. Several commitments that followed the end of the Second World War remained incomplete and continued to absorb effort. These included the support of occupation forces in former enemy territory and the maintenance of law and order in other disturbed regions. Whilst the winding-up of wartime organisations and infrastructure was not yet complete, considerable emphasis had to be placed on the study and application of the wartime lessons learned by the Allies and those which were coming to light from a study of German and Japanese records. As if all this was not enough, the Admiralty was committed to improving conditions of service for peacetime personnel.

The number of aircraft carriers in full commission had reduced quickly after 1946 as the manpower and financial crises took effect. By early 1948, only *Ocean* and *Triumph* were in full commission with air groups embarked although *Victorious* was running as a training ship with a reduced ship's company.[46] After her night-fighter trial, *Ocean* formed part of the Mediterranean Fleet and demonstrated the various operational roles that aircraft carriers were capable of fulfilling. In October 1946 she gave medical assistance to support the wounded from the destroyers *Saumarez* and *Volage* when they were damaged by Albanian mines in the Corfu Channel. In May 1948 with 805 (Seafire F 17) and 816 (Firefly FR 1) NAS embarked she formed part of the RN task force that covered the withdrawal of British forces from Palestine. Her squadrons provided the only air cover available once the RAF airfields ashore were evacuated. In June 1948 she returned to the UK and the squadrons disembarked to re-form as part of the RAN's first air group.

East of Suez, the last aircraft carrier to serve with the BPF was *Theseus* with 804 (Seafire FR 47) and 812 (Firefly FR 4/5) NAS embarked between February and December 1947. After she returned to the UK, the BPF was re-designated as the Far East Fleet (FEF) and its air element was run down, with the RN air station in Singapore lent to the RAF and all stocks of aircraft and spare parts on the Far East Station returned to the UK or otherwise disposed of. The civil war between the Communists and Nationalists in China, however, posed a threat to the considerable British interests in the region, including the colony of Hong Kong and the trading city of Shanghai where more than 4000 UK nationals were based. In February 1949 the Nationalist cruiser *Chungking*, the former RN *Arethusa* class *Aurora*, went over to the Communists and was renamed *Tchoung King*. She was bombed and sunk by Nationalist forces in Taku harbour in March 1949[47] but was raised and returned to service, albeit in poor condition, in 1951. The maritime threat to the region's trade was becoming serious but worse was to follow in April

1949 when the frigate *Amethyst* was on passage up the Yangtze River to relieve the destroyer *Consort* in providing support for the British Embassy in Nanking, the Nationalist capital. She was fired on and driven ashore on mud banks near Rose Island[48] and attempts by *Consort* to tow her off proved unsuccessful, with both ships suffering damage and a number of dead and injured. The heavy cruiser *London* attempted to reach her with the frigate *Black Swan* but after an exchange of fire with Chinese Communist shore batteries she suffered a number of men killed and wounded and had to withdraw. *Amethyst* managed to break out under cover of darkness in July.

Against this deteriorating background, the decision to reinforce the FEF with an aircraft carrier was a logical step and measures were taken to provide support for the deployed carrier air group. The first of these was the re-commissioning of the naval air station at Sembawang in Singapore. The maintenance carrier *Unicorn* was re-commissioned from reserve in Devonport and loaded with a considerable outfit of air stores which were intended to re-stock Sembawang. She also carried

Search and rescue before the helicopter; a Sea Otter ASR 2 seen being lowered into the water by crane from *Theseus'* flight deck. Note that the engine is running and the aircrewman is on the upper wing ready to release the hook. The ladder, down which he must climb to the cockpit, is just visible below the aircraft's engine. The aircraft is being held steady by a rope run through the tail wheel strut and held taut by sailors. (Author's collection)

a number of Seafire FR 47s and Firefly FR 1s in a state of preservation to support the operational carrier air group and replace losses. Having unloaded her stores and aircraft to form an aircraft holding unit (AHU) ashore, *Unicorn* was in Singapore Naval Base preparing for her passage back to the UK in June 1950. The light fleet carrier *Triumph*, which had emerged from a refit in Sheerness Dockyard to re-commission on 21 April 1949, was selected as the operational carrier for the FEF. She worked up with 13 Carrier Air Group (CAG), which comprised 800 (Seafire FR 47) and 827 (Firefly FR 1) NAS embarked together with a single Sea Otter amphibian for SAR duties. She sailed in July and on 23 October 1949 took part in Operation 'LEO', air strikes against Communist guerrillas in the Malayan jungle areas south of Gemas and Baru Anam in co-operation with ground forces and RAF aircraft.[49] On 8 June 1950 she visited Ominato in Japan with other ships of the FEF and six days later began a series of exercises in Japanese waters with ships from the RN and USN. Their extent and timing soon proved to be of critical importance.

A Firefly landing on *Glory*, seen from the 'plane-guard' destroyer. The batsman is just visible below the aircraft, his arms and conspicuous bats are slightly below level indicating that he considers the aircraft to be below the ideal glide-slope. Both barriers are raised and the aircraft that have already landed are parked forward in Fly 1. (Author's collection)

2 The Korean War

At 04.00 local time on 25 June 1950 the Communist North Korean People's Army (NKPA) launched an unprovoked attack on South Korea across the 38th Parallel with eight combat divisions, one of which was armoured. It came as a complete surprise, unpredicted by any Western agency and must rank as one of the greatest intelligence failures of the modern era[1] although it was not to be the worst in that eventful year. The South Korean Army lacked tanks, artillery and air support and was forced to retreat to the south along roads choked by large numbers of civilian refugees. News of this aggression reached Mr Trygve Lie, the Secretary-General of

Triumph and *Cossack* off the coast of Japan in May 1950 during exercises with the USN. The aircraft in Fly 1 with their wings folded are Seafire FR 47s. (Author's collection)

the United Nations, in New York at 03.00 local time, some fourteen hours after the attack. He called an emergency meeting of the UN Security Council immediately and, by unanimous agreement of the nine member nations who were present and who voted,[2] the Council placed the blame for the conflict squarely on the North Korean Government. The Secretary-General called on the aggressor to end hostilities immediately and withdraw its forces north of the 38th Parallel but the North Koreans took no notice.

The Origins of the War

Korea had gained independence from China in 1895 after the Sino-Japanese War but was annexed by Japan in 1910 and subsequently exploited ruthlessly.[3] The Allied leaders' wartime conference at Cairo in December 1943 had discussed Korea and the UK, USA and China had minuted that 'in due course Korea shall become free and independent'. This policy was re-affirmed by the Potsdam Conference in July 1945 but this straightforward intention was complicated when the Soviet Union declared war on Japan a month later in August. In September Korea was occupied by Soviet forces in the north and United States' forces in the south and an *ad hoc* agreement between the two powers fixed the 38th Parallel as the line of demarcation between them. In December 1945 an agreement was reached in Moscow for the re-establishment of Korea as an independent state with a democratically-elected government under the initial 'trusteeship' of the four signatory powers who had guaranteed the nation's independence, the UK, USA, USSR and Nationalist China. The Chinese Communist regime subsequently accepted the agreement and stated its intention to adhere to it in principle. Significantly no agreement emerged on the method of implementing this aim and the UK and USA took the matter to the United Nations. In 1947 two UN Resolutions were passed calling for democratic elections to be overseen by a UN Commission. The Soviet authorities flouted them, however, and all the Commission could do was monitor elections south of the 38th Parallel where a National Assembly was established and the Republic of Korea established in 1948. Shortly afterwards, the area of Korea under Soviet occupation north of the 38th Parallel proclaimed itself to be the Democratic People's Republic of Korea but, since the UN Commission had not been allowed to monitor the elections that were claimed to have taken place, it recommended against recognition of the People's Republic and identified South Korea as the only legal Korean government. The UN General Assembly subsequently endorsed this view.

The UN Commission continued to strive for unification under the terms of the Moscow Agreement but in a report dated 8 September 1949[4] its Chairman stated that it was hopeless to attempt to gain access to, or even to communicate with

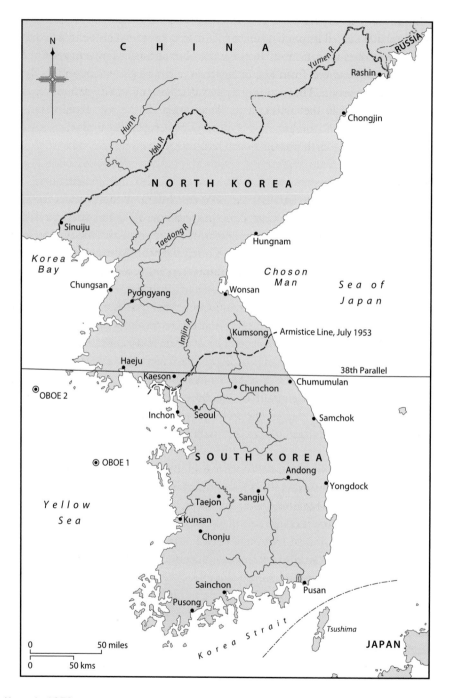

Korea in 1950.

North Korea. The report described the North as 'the creature of a military occupation' that denied its population any chance to express their opinion upon its claim to rule. Communication between the two Koreas broke down completely but US troops were removed from South Korea in June 1948, leaving only a small military advisory group. There could be no verification of when Soviet forces left the North but by 1949 they had equipped and trained a North Korean People's Army, of over 130,000 combat troops equipped with 500 Soviet tanks and 132 aircraft. Neither the North nor the South had a significant navy.

Reactions

The US President, Harry S Truman, waited until 26 June, giving the UN Security Council time to discuss the matter, before stating his position swiftly and unambiguously. He ordered US sea and air forces to support South Korean military forces and immediately sought international support from other heads of government for armed intervention to counter North Korean aggression. There were credible fears that this was but the first step in a major offensive in the Far East now that the Communists had emerged victorious from the Chinese civil war and the President ordered the Seventh Fleet to prepare to meet any potential attack on the Nationalist-held island of Formosa. C-in-C Pacific was ordered to form new carrier battle groups as quickly as possible for deployment to the western Pacific. On 30 June President Truman ordered a naval blockade of the whole Korean peninsula and authorised General Douglas MacArthur to send combat troops to Korea and to carry out air strikes against targets in Korea both north and south of the 38th Parallel. MacArthur had, in fact, ordered the first attack on the North a day earlier on his own initiative.

The US Army still maintained an occupation force in Japan under MacArthur who had his headquarters in Tokyo. He was immediately placed in supreme command of all United States' forces in the region. These comprised four US Army divisions that were being used for constabulary duties as an occupying power and were not equipped or trained for combat on the scale now required of them. The USAF units placed under his command included about 400 aircraft which were intended for the air defence of Japan, Okinawa, the Philippines and Guam and there were a small number of warships forming US Naval Forces Far East under its Commander, Vice Admiral C Turner Joy USN (COMNAVFE). These comprised a light cruiser, four destroyers and six minesweepers. Further away but immediately available was a Seventh Fleet strike carrier task force which included the USS *Valley Forge*, a heavy cruiser and eight destroyers under Vice Admiral Arthur Struble USN. There was also a British Commonwealth Occupation Force in Japan under Lieutenant General Sir Horace Robertson of the Australian Army but by June 1950 this had been reduced to a single Australian infantry battalion, a single RAAF fighter squadron and a small naval contingent based ashore in Kure Dockyard under a Commander RAN. The BPF had, initially, maintained a sizeable naval force in Japanese waters and in 1946 this had comprised two British or Australian cruisers, several British and Australian destroyers or frigates and an Indian frigate. Such numbers could not be maintained through the manpower crisis, however, and from mid-1947 ships were not replaced as they left Japan, the last to leave being the British frigate *Hart* on 18 December 1947. A number of ships from the Far East Station and Australia continued to visit Japanese ports whenever possible, however, both to provide a Commonwealth presence and to practice operations with the USN. Having failed to anticipate or prevent the conflict, the UN had at least condemned North Korean aggression and, within a week, taken steps to defend the south. On 7 July 1950 MacArthur was named as the supreme commander of all Allied forces allocated to the UN in the Far East in addition to those of the US. His line of responsibility, however, remained directly to the US Joint Chiefs of Staff rather than to the UN General Assembly for this wider role.

The British Prime Minister, Clement Attlee, announced British support for the UN in the House of Commons on 27 June 1950. On 28 June he announced that warships of the FEF were to be placed at the disposal of the US authorities to operate on behalf of the UN. The Canadian Government offered naval support on the same day, followed by the Governments of Australia and New Zealand, who were some nine hours ahead of GMT, a day later on 29 June. The Commander-in-Chief of the Far East Station, Admiral Sir Patrick Brind, who flew his flag at a shore headquarters in Singapore, had elected to deploy substantial units of his fleet to Japanese waters in the late spring and early summer under the tactical command of Rear Admiral William Andrewes, Flag Officer Second-in-Command Far East Station (FO2FES), who flew his flag in the cruiser *Belfast*.[5] Whilst there, the British task force formed part of the occupation forces and came under the command of Vice Admiral Turner Joy USN. It had maintained close contact with its American counterparts and had carried out joint exercises using USN signal procedures. The British task force included the light fleet carrier *Triumph* with 800 (Seafire FR 47) and 827 (Firefly FR 1) NAS embarked, the cruisers *Belfast* and *Jamaica*, two destroyers, three frigates and a number of auxiliaries including tankers and a hospital ship.

When fighting began on 25 June 1950, *Belfast* was visiting Hakodate in northern Japan. FO2 heard of the invasion that evening, ordered the ship to raise steam immediately and sailed at 01.30 on 26 June on his own initiative to position himself further south where he would be available to meet any eventuality. The C-in-C ordered another cruiser, *Kenya*, together with further destroyers, frigates and auxiliaries to raise steam in Singapore and Hong Kong and prepare for operations off Korea. In his subsequent report of proceedings (ROP) FO2 said that he wished to concentrate his ships without delay since it seemed probable that any action would be off South Korea and that, should the Soviet Union intervene, the best place for his task force would be further to the south.[6] Later on 26 June Admiral Brind signalled COMNAVFE offering the use of British warships for any humanitarian mission he might require. Later still he warned FO2 by signal that his ships might be required to engage North Korean armed forces in order to implement the UN Security Council's Resolutions.

Allied Preparations

After a rough but fast passage, *Belfast* arrived at Yokosuka Naval Base at noon on 27 June and Admiral Andrewes drove immediately to meet COMNAVFE in Tokyo where he found that the latter had just come from a meeting with General MacArthur. Both were deeply concerned about the deteriorating situation in South Korea but Admiral Joy advised that since all British and Commonwealth citizens had already been evacuated, there was no requirement for a humanitarian operation. However, since the Soviet reaction to the mobilisation of UN forces was uncertain, he thought it best for the British task force to concentrate south of Japan having taken on fuel and, as far as possible, provisions. On 28 June Admiral Brind received a signal from the Admiralty authorising him to 'place the Royal Navy at present in Japanese waters at the disposal of the United States' Naval Commander for Korean Operations (Vice Admiral C T Joy) in support of the UN Security Council Resolutions'.[7] The early meeting between COMNAVFE and FO2 meant that the two admirals understood each other's views and they now had the authority to move quickly. On 29 June COMNAVFE ordered Admiral Andrewes to deploy his ships immediately to join USN task groups. *Jamaica* with the frigates *Black Swan* and *Alacrity* joined Admiral Higgins USN in the cruiser *Juneau* off the east coast of South Korea. FO2 himself, now back in *Belfast*, in company with *Triumph* and the destroyers *Consort* and *Cossack* and the newly-joined HMAS *Bataan* joined Task Force 77, which included *Valley Forge*, off Okinawa. From this position the carriers could be used to defend Formosa or Okinawa if necessary or to strike at targets in Korea. All Commonwealth ships adopted USN signal procedures and the joint task forces were able to work well together from the outset. Admiral Andrewes wrote in his report 'it all seemed so familiar as it was just what we had done so often before during the exercises in March with very similar forces'. It was also only five years since the US and British Pacific Fleets had worked together so successfully in the final phase of the war against Japan.

The First Carrier Strikes

Valley Forge and *Triumph* formed Task Group 77.3 which was commanded by Rear Admiral Hoskins USN, Commander Carrier Division 3 (COMCARDIV3). Planning for strikes against targets in North Korea began as the force moved north-west into the Yellow Sea and the first strikes by aircraft from the two carriers were flown off between 05.45 and 06.15 on 3 July 1950. *Valley Forge* launched eight Corsairs, twelve Skyraiders and twelve Panther jet fighters to strike at the North Korean capital Pyongyang which was beyond the radius of action of the USAF B-29 bombers based in Guam. B-29 units were ordered to deploy to airfields in Okinawa but it took considerable time to move their support, weapons, main-tenance and spares infrastructure into place, without which the aircraft were useless. Of course, these were all things the aircraft carriers carried with them as they moved, enabling them to choose their ideal launch positions for strike operations. *Triumph* launched nine Fireflies and twelve Seafires to attack the airfield at Haeju and adjacent railway bridges. Seafire FR 47s were notoriously difficult to maintain and 800 NAS did well to get all the squadron's aircraft serviceable for the strike. The Seafires were armed with 3in rockets and the Fireflies with 500lb bombs. The two carriers had been allocated separate target areas to take into account the shorter radius of action of the British aircraft but also to spread the impact of their strikes for which the enemy was totally unprepared. The geographical separation of strike targets for aircraft of differing performance or command structure was to become a major feature of strike warfare over Korea in the years ahead. The North Korean Air Force was felt to pose a negligible threat but TF 77 was only 100 miles from Communist Chinese airfields in the Shantung peninsula and 220 miles from Soviet airfields at Port Arthur. The Panthers' task was to defend the area against both North Korean fighters and any others that might intervene. They shot down two airborne North Korean Yak fighters and destroyed a further nine by strafing them on the ground. Both strikes proved to be successful and all their aircraft returned safely although several had been hit by small-arms fire. Later in the day both carriers 'aircraft struck at railways in their respective target areas.[8] Because the full extent of Communist aggression was not yet clear, these strikes had been planned as a one-day operation but in view of the deteriorating situation in South Korea, TG 77.3 was ordered to remain in action to continue the strikes as long as practical, again showing the flexibility of carrier-based aviation. The greatest priority for strike operations was given to attacks on railway facilities that were being used in support of the NKPA's drive to the south.

The first British aircraft was lost on 28 July 1950 when Commissioned Pilot White RN of 800 NAS, on combat air patrol (CAP) over the task group in his Seafire, was ordered to intercept a radar contact that was not showing the correct

IFF[9] response. The contact tuned out to be a USAF B-29 bomber and as White flew up alongside it, one of the gunners opened fire and shot him down 'for no very apparent reason'.[10] He managed to parachute into the sea, suffering from burns, and was rescued from his dinghy by the USN destroyer *Eversole* which returned him to *Triumph* later in the day. When informed of the incident COMNAVFE said that 'the calculated risk of damage to friendly forces must be accepted'; Mr White's comments were not recorded. It is significant to note that although the RN and USN were familiar with each other's equipment, the USAF had clearly not been adequately briefed about its Allies' equipment. After the initial strike operations, FO2 detached from TF 77 with *Belfast* and his two destroyers and returned to Sasebo Dockyard which Commonwealth warships were to share with their USN counterparts as a forward base throughout the conflict.

Blockade

On his arrival FO2 was able to have further discussions with COMNAVFE who confessed that both he and General MacArthur had been surprised by the UN decision to defend South Korea but were convinced of the correctness of the decision. Rear Admiral Higgins USN joined their discussions and COMNAVFE instructed the two rear admirals to set up a blockade of northern Korea as TF 96. TG 96.5 under Higgins, comprising largely USN ships, was to cover the east coast and TG 96.8, comprising largely British and Commonwealth ships under Andrewes, was to cover the west coast although ships of both task groups could move to the other coast when necessary. This command structure worked well and lasted until the end of the conflict in 1953. COMNAVFE gave clear instructions for the conduct of the blockade which included notes on international law and directions for the treatment of ships that attempted to evade interception. In October 1951 the west coast task group was re-designated as TG 95 with separate elements including the British carrier and its destroyer escort, blockading units, minesweepers and other activities.

There were immediate concerns about the possibility of Soviet submarines from Vladivostok being used to support the NKPA offensive and, after a signalled discussion between Admiral Brind and Admiral Forrest Sherman, the US Chief of Naval Operations, authorisation was given to attack unidentified, submerged submarines inside the designated war zone. The first open-water naval engagement occurred on 2 July 1950 when *Jamaica* was operating off the east coast with Admiral Higgins' task group. Four fast patrol boats attacked the group and were engaged by gunfire. Three were sunk and the fourth made off to seaward, zigzagging at high speed. The first action off the west coast occurred on 12 July when the *Cossack* was engaged by NKPA field guns while she passed inside the

Techong islands. She returned their fire at an initial range of 5000 yards, subsequently opening to 8000 yards and destroyed two enemy guns for the expenditure of 140 rounds of 4.5in ammunition, suffering no damage herself. FO2 issued his own instructions for the implementation of the west coast blockade on 8 July. His object was to dominate the coastline occupied by the NKPA; prevent any infiltration by sea into coastal areas held by the South Koreans and to provide naval gunfire support against any enemy target at sea or on land. His initial dispositions centred on three task units, each comprising a cruiser and several destroyers or frigates, the latter having the advantage that they could operate close inshore to engage targets inland. During the conflict a number of warships were used for shore bombardment including, once, the maintenance carrier *Unicorn*.

The objects of the British and US patrol areas were obviously similar but their methods differed because of the dissimilar geography of the east and west Korean coasts. The east comprised steep cliffs with a narrow coastal strip along which both road and rail communications ran. The terrain was so mountainous that in 1140 miles of railway track there were 956 bridges and 231 tunnels, making the route particularly vulnerable to interdiction by gunfire and commando raids as well as air strikes. There were few islands off the east coast. On the other hand, the west coast had shallow seas and a number of islands surrounded by extensive mud flats and heavily silted river estuaries. The enemy frequently attempted to move supplies in small junks close inshore where larger warships were unable to operate. In August when *Triumph* left TF 77, she joined the west coast blockading force where her aircraft made a big difference by locating and destroying these junks in large numbers.

Inchon – A Triumph of Amphibious Warfare

As soon as operations to support the South Koreans were authorised, General MacArthur decided to mount an amphibious assault against Inchon, Seoul's seaport on the west coast, in order to outflank the NKPA and exploit the UN's naval superiority. For this daring operation the UN assembled a remarkable total of 230 ships from the USA, UK, Australia, Canada, New Zealand, France, South Korea and Japan and prepared the run-down 1st US Marine Division for combat operations in only a few weeks. The US Army initially opposed the plan and the USN was hesitant because of the poor hydrographical conditions at Inchon, among them a tidal range of 33ft and other factors that limited a landing to one of only three days in the autumn of 1950. MacArthur over-rode the opposition and selected 15 September 1950, declaring that an amphibious assault was the most powerful tool available to the UN and the only one that could strike hard and deep into enemy territory at such short notice. The landings, supported by carrier-borne aircraft and naval gunfire, proved to be a first-class example of both amphibious warfare and Allied co-operation and, once commenced, the result was never in doubt. The NKPA had not believed it possible that the UN could mount such an assault so soon, nor that the US would risk landing its marines on the treacherous beaches of Inchon. Once the decision to land was taken, the USMC and Navy led the way and MacArthur said of them that 'their star never shone brighter'. The NKPA was forced to retreat to prevent the forces that were encircling the southern port of Pusan from being isolated and captured.

British and Australian Aircraft Carriers in Action

HMS Triumph – *July 1950 to September 1950*
After joining TF 77, *Triumph*'s Fireflies flew constant anti-submarine patrols and two Seafires were held at readiness on deck alert to intercept unidentified aircraft if necessary. Aircraft from both carriers flew low round the task force to allow gunners to recognise unfamiliar shapes but, as we have seen, one of 800 NAS

A Firefly FR 1 being 'waved-off' from *Triumph* with three other aircraft closing the ship to 'slot' into the visual circuit. After Commissioned Pilot White was shot down in his Seafire by a USAF B-29, RN aircraft were painted with the conspicuous black and white identification stripes seen here and a large Union flag has been painted on the flight deck. (Author's collection)

Seafires was shot down in error by a USAF B-29.[11] To prevent any further misidentification, all RN and RAN aircraft were painted with black and white 'invasion stripes' on their fuselage and wings as an aid to identification and a Union flag was painted prominently on *Triumph*'s flight deck when the ship entered Sasebo for a replenishment period. On 15 July 1950 *Triumph* re-joined *Valley Forge* for a series of strikes from an operating area off the east coast. To free the longer-ranged USN aircraft for strikes 827 NAS flew anti-submarine patrols and 800 NAS concentrated on flying CAP sorties over the task force. On 19 July 1950 *Triumph*'s Sea Otter search and rescue (SAR) aircraft landed in the sea to rescue a USN Corsair pilot; the last recorded occasion on which a British amphibian carried out an operational rescue using this technique. After this *Triumph* suffered a leaking stern gland and had to return to Sasebo Dockyard for repairs which took two days. She was back with TF 77 on 24 July, however, and resumed her defensive flying task. By the end of the month more USN carriers arrived in TF 77 and *Triumph* was re-allocated to FO2's west coast task group and her aircraft immediately improved the group's ability to locate and engage small junks operating close inshore.

There were no combat casualties at this stage but deck landing on a straight-deck carrier always had the potential to be hazardous. On 29 August a Firefly missed all the arrester wires on landing and went into the barrier. The propeller blades broke up as the engine was shock-loaded to a standstill and a large piece of one of them flew up, bounced off the bottom of the flying control position (Flyco), smashed through the operations room scuttle and struck the commanding officer of 800 NAS, Lieutenant Commander I M MacLachlan RN who was there to discuss his squadron's flying programme. His injuries, unfortunately, proved to be fatal despite all the medical team could do and he was buried at sea that evening off the coast of South Korea. Lieutenant T D Handley RN, the squadron's Senior Pilot, took over command. On 5 September *Triumph* moved to the east coast and replaced the American carriers while they carried out underway replenishment of fuel and ammunition. Later in the month she moved back to the west coast to act in support of the 1st Marine Division's landing at Inchon. By then, the ship's two months of intensive operations had depleted the number of serviceable aircraft within the air group and the surviving aircraft were proving difficult to maintain. There were no replacement Seafire FR 47s or Firefly FR 1s left in the FEF reserve stock, her stern gland was still giving trouble and so, after Inchon, FO2 decided reluctantly that she had reached the end of her operational usefulness and ordered her withdrawal. She had only eleven serviceable aircraft left and *Theseus* was already on her way from the UK to replace her. On 25 September, after she had returned to Sasebo for further temporary repairs in dry dock, COMNAVFE

Fireflies from *Triumph* photographed over Inchon. One aircraft is visible above the causeway leading to the small island. (Author's collection)

British warships in Sasebo in either late September or early October 1950. Furthest away, *Triumph* is secured to a jetty with *Belfast* to starboard of her. The ships at moorings are, from left to right, the hospital ship *Maine*, *Theseus,* which had just arrived, and *Unicorn*. The ship in the right foreground surrounded by lighters is the armament stores issuing ship RFA *Fort Rosalie*. (Author's collection)

signalled 'On the departure of HMS *Triumph* from the Command of the Naval Forces Far East, I take pleasure in saying to the Captain, the Officers, the Flying personnel and the Crew of this splendid fighting ship "Well done". Your enthusiastic and effective efforts have contributed immeasurably to the United Nations' cause in Korea.'[12]

HMS Theseus – *October 1950 to April 1951*
Theseus was serving with the Home Fleet in 1950 with 17 CAG comprising 807 (Sea Fury FB 11s) and 810 (Firefly FR 5s) NAS embarked and in August the decision was taken to bring her ship's company and squadrons up to war complement and deploy her to the FEF as a replacement for *Triumph*. She also embarked a Sea Otter amphibian for SAR duties and sailed from the UK on 18 August 1950 for a brief work-up in the Mediterranean after which she arrived in the war zone in early October. Her first period of operations began on 8 October in the Yellow Sea off the west coast of Korea[13] flying searches and tactical missions in support of the advancing UN forces' left flank. However, on 27 October the wire reeving in her single catapult's pulley system was found to be badly frayed and, therefore, not safe to use. Consequently, during her second operational period, aircraft had to be flown without bombs, rockets or drop tanks, relying on a free take-off from the deck which limited the number of aircraft that could be ranged for take-off. It also meant that six Fireflies had to be disembarked to Iwakuni to reduce the size of her deck park. By the end of October the defeated NKPA had been driven back into northern Korea close to the Yalu River and with less urgency for continued operations, *Theseus* returned first to Sasebo and then sailed for repairs in Hong Kong Dockyard. While she was on passage, the ship's engineering department managed to re-reeve the catapult, a major and unprecedented achievement at sea. Deadweight launches were carried out off Hong Kong, followed by live launches to prove its restored efficiency.

When *Theseus* left Korean waters it had been thought that the war was nearly over and other warships had been withdrawn at the same time but the massive and totally unexpected Chinese offensive across the Yalu River in December 1950 began a new phase of the conflict which forced UN forces to retreat to the south. The lack of any warning that such an offensive was being prepared was the second significant failure by Allied intelligence agencies. *Theseus*, therefore, returned to the war zone to begin a new period of operations with her squadrons brought back up to their full numbers in the bitter winter of 1950. Despite atrocious weather conditions she maintained 95 per cent aircraft serviceability and flew 338 sorties in seven days. Notwithstanding the widely-held view earlier in 1950 that her piston-engined fighters were obsolescent, they proved to be the ideal aircraft for the task

A Firefly FR 5 photographed from another aircraft over North Korea. It has just dropped bombs on a target and smoke from them can be seen at the top of the picture. (Author's collection)

confronting the RN and the emerging generation of jet fighters could not have done as well in the circumstances. Their targets included railway bridges and rolling stock, trucks and enemy troops on the march. During the critical month of December 1950 *Theseus* spent twenty-three days at sea and flew 630 sorties during which her aircraft expended 38,000 rounds of 20mm ammunition and fired 1412 rocket projectiles. These figures were way beyond the ship's normal outfit and the RN armament supply organisation did a superb job replenishing her stocks at sea from RFA armament stores issuing ships at the end of a very long supply chain.

Theseus entering Sasebo for the last time on 20 April 1951 with sailors spelling out her name on the flight deck. (Author's collection)

During January 1951 she flew sixty sorties in a single day, a record at the time for a light fleet carrier, targeting railways, trucks and junks. On 18 January 1951 the Admiralty announced that 17 CAG had been awarded the Boyd Trophy for its operations off Korea.[14] At the end of January the Sea Otter was disembarked and replaced on board by a USN S-51 helicopter for SAR duties. On 2 February a run of 1463 accident-free deck landings ended when a Sea Fury landed heavily and broke its undercarriage but a day later a new record of sixty-six sorties in a single day was achieved. *Theseus'* tenth and last war patrol off Korea began on 8 April 1951; this was off the east coast in company with the USS *Bataan*,[15] one of the USN light carriers that replaced the British carriers on task when they went into harbour for a period of rest and replenishment. The two carriers were intended to deter a possible Chinese attack on Formosa but *Theseus* managed to maintain reconnaissance sorties off the west coast by flying aircraft across the peninsula. Her targets in the east included railway marshalling yards in Wonsan. On 17 April she moved back to her more familiar area off the west coast and on 20 April 1951 she entered Sasebo for the last time with members of her ship's company spelling out her name on the flight deck. On 25 April she sailed for the UK and arrived on 29 May 1951. Admiral of the Fleet Lord Fraser of North Cape, the First Sea Lord, came on board at once to present the Boyd Trophy.

Glory in Korean waters with Sea Furies and Fireflies ranged aft. (Author's collection)

Replenishing liquids at sea. *Glory* and HMAS *Bataan* taking on fuel from RFA *Wave Premier* using the method perfected by the BPF in 1945. (Author's collection)

HMS Glory – *April 1951 to September 1951*

Glory had been serving in the Mediterranean Fleet during 1950 but late in the year she was ordered to make preparations to relieve *Theseus* in the Far East. Her 14 CAG, comprising 804 (Sea Fury FB 11s) and 812 (Firefly FR 5s) NAS, was disembarked to RNAS Hal Far in Malta where its aircraft and personnel were brought up to war strength and worked up to a high state of operational efficiency. Meanwhile the ship returned to Devonport and paid off on 16 December. She re-commissioned with a full war complement on 29 December 1950 and returned to the Mediterranean, arriving in Malta on 2 February 1951. A work-up with squadrons embarked lasted until March, after which she sailed for the Far East Station, arriving in Sasebo on 23 April where she took on board personnel, aircraft, stores and ammunition from *Theseus* and *Unicorn*. The USN S-51 helicopter detachment was embarked for SAR duty. *Glory* sailed for her first period of

A Sea Fury FB 11 bombing a bridge in North Korea. One of its bombs can be seen falling on the left-hand side of the picture, slightly above the small, circular crater with water in it. The photograph was taken by his wing-man who had things other than photography on his mind and is, unfortunately, of poor quality but it is just possible to see the steam from a train which has just crossed the bridge at its right-hand extremity. The bombs might, therefore, hit the bridge while rolling stock is still on it. (Author's collection)

An exhausted crane landed on *Glory* during a war patrol off Korea and is seen here standing on the cockpit of a Sea Fury FB 11, which is armed with 500lb bombs outboard of the drop tanks. Kind-hearted sailors fed it on milk and kippers for several days and it eventually flew off revived and happy! (Author's collection)

operations on 26 April 1951 off the west coast, her aircraft attacking railway lines bridges, enemy logistics and junks. In addition to these offensive sorties, Sea Furies maintained a CAP over the task group and Fireflies flew anti-submarine patrols.

The SAR helicopter saw its first use on 14 May 1951 when Stoker McPherson fell overboard and was subsequently winched to safety, the first time such a rescue had been carried out from an RN ship. During her first operational tour of duty off Korea, *Glory* carried out nine war patrols, during one of which her aircraft achieved a new light fleet carrier record of eighty-nine sorties in a single day's flying. Between April and the end of September 1951 *Glory*'s aircraft had flown 2875 hours in 107 days at sea with only nine accidents. The tally of targets destroyed included 679 junks, 794 ox-carts[16] and 236 railway wagons for the expenditure of 1450 500lb bombs, 9242 rocket projectiles and 538,000 rounds of 20mm cannon ammunition. On 22 September 804 NAS completed its 1000th accident-free deck landing and for much of this period it had maintained 100 per cent serviceability. By September the ship was badly in need of a refit and it was decided to carry this out in Her Majesty's Australian Dockyard at Garden Island in Sydney, Australia and she berthed in Kure on 27 September to hand over to HMAS *Sydney*.

HMAS Sydney 3 – *September 1951 to January 1952*

The RAN had formed its own Fleet Air Arm in 1948 with considerable help from the RN and Australia's first aircraft carrier, HMAS *Sydney*, had only arrived at her new home port in 1949. The need to withdraw *Glory* for a refit in Australia posed a problem for the Admiralty since *Ocean*, the next light fleet carrier intended for service in the war zone, would not be ready to deploy until May 1952. To fill the gap the First Sea Lord, Admiral of the Fleet Lord Fraser, asked the First Naval Member of the Australian Commonwealth Naval Board, Vice Admiral Sir John Collins, if it would be possible for '*Sydney* to relieve *Glory* for two or three months operational flying if the Korean business is still going'.[17] Collins supported the idea and put it to the Australian Government which approved the deployment in May 1951. This was a substantial increase in the nation's commitment to the war and a significant development in Australian history since only three nations, the UK, USA and Japan, had previously deployed aircraft carriers in combat operations. For the deployment *Sydney* embarked elements of 20 and 21 CAGs and sailed for the war zone after a work up with 805 and 808 (Sea Fury FB 11) and 817 (Firefly FR 5) NAS embarked. She secured alongside *Glory* in Kure Dockyard, Japan on 27 September 1951 to transfer aircraft, stores and the USN S-51 helicopter detachment for SAR duties. *Sydney* sailed for her first war patrol on 3 October 1951 and sent her aircraft into action from a position off the east coast two days later. On only her fifth day of operations she equalled the record number of eighty-

A Firefly FR 5 on HMAS *Sydney*'s catapult with its engine running but not quite ready to launch. The ship's USN S-51 'plane-guard' helicopter has just launched and taken up its position off the port bow. (RAN)

A replacement Firefly FR 5 being lowered onto HMAS Sydney's flight deck in Sasebo. (RAN)

nine sorties flown in a single day set by *Glory*. Judged by the standards of her peers with their recent extensive wartime carrier-operating experience, *Sydney* had started well and continued to do so.

On 14 October she had to stand out to sea to avoid Typhoon RUTH and although she managed to avoid the epicentre, high winds and seas destroyed six aircraft in her deck park. Replacement aircraft were provided from the RN Aircraft Holding Unit (AHU), at Iwakuni and *Sydney* began her second war patrol on 18 October. During this period she flew 474 sorties which included the provision of close air support for the Commonwealth Division which formed part of the UN land forces in Korea. Rear Admiral Scott-Moncreiff had succeeded Rear Admiral Andrewes as FO2FES on the latter's promotion and he flew his flag in *Sydney* during her third war patrol which began on 4 November so that he could gain first-hand experience of carrier operations. Her aircraft carried out a number of strikes on rail targets that were synchronised with other Allied air arms. After a brief respite, *Sydney* took part in Operation 'Athenaeum' from 18 November, a series of co-ordinated attacks by aircraft and naval gunfire against Hungnam, a transport

Aircraft storm-lashed on HMAS *Sydney*'s flight deck while she rides out Typhoon RUTH.

hub on Korea's east coast. She resumed operations off the west coast during early December and then spent Christmas 1951 in Kure Dockyard.

Individual accounts of every sortie would make this a very long narrative but I will include several within the accounts of individual carrier operations that are illustrative of overall Commonwealth carrier operations. For example, on 26 October 1951 Firefly WB 393 of 817 NAS was hit by anti-aircraft fire while attacking a railway tunnel near Chaeryong, north of Haeju. The pilot, Sub Lieutenant N D MacMillan RAN, managed a successful forced landing in enemy territory and both he and his observer, Chief Petty Officer J Hancox RAN, got out of the wrecked aircraft and took cover in a ditch, keeping NKPA soldiers that had encircled them at bay with their Owen submachine-guns. *Sydney* had a section of Sea Furies in the area and these were instructed to provide top cover, strafing enemy troops to prevent them from capturing the downed aircrew. *Sydney* herself was 75 miles away and her captain, Captain D H Harries CBE RAN, had doubts about the wisdom of sending her USN helicopter to rescue them because of fears that it might not locate the crash-site and clear enemy territory before nightfall. The crew insisted that they be given the chance to try, however, and Harries approved the sortie. Meanwhile Meteor jet fighters of 77 Squadron RAAF joined the Sea Furies in giving top cover. By 17.15 the jets had to go but the Sea Fury pilots, Lieutenants Cavanagh and Salthouse RAN, elected to remain, despite their low fuel state, another advantage of the piston-engined Sea Fury over the early generation of jet fighters. At 17.25 the SAR helicopter arrived, having flown at a speed considerably above the maximum quoted in the S-51's aircrew manual. As it landed the observer, Chief Petty Officer Gooding USN, jumped out and shot dead two NKPA soldiers who had crawled to within fifteen yards of the wrecked Firefly. An hour later the helicopter with the two rescued aircrew on board, and still escorted by the Sea Furies, landed at the Allied airfield at Kimpo just as darkness fell.

Sydney sailed on 28 December for her sixth war patrol during which emphasis was placed on the defence of small islands off the west coast held by South Korean forces. Her seventh and last patrol began on 16 January 1952 and when she entered Sasebo for the last time on 26 January, FO2 described her work in the Korean war zone as being 'quite excellent'. She had flown a total of 2366 sorties in forty-three operational flying days, an average of 55.2 per day, and her expenditure of ammunition amounted to 154 500lb and 1000lb bombs, 1197 rocket projectiles and 73,440 rounds of 20mm ammunition. All replacement aircraft, ammunition and stores came from RN stocks. She lost fifteen aircraft in action and three pilots killed.

HMS Glory – *February 1952 to May 1952*

On 1 February 1952 *Glory* arrived in Hong Kong after her Australian refit to take over aircraft, stores and equipment from *Sydney*. She had the same squadrons embarked as in her previous deployment and arrived in Sasebo on 5 February, beginning a war patrol off the west coast a day later. Her tasks included reconnaissance in support of the UN blockade, close air support for the army ashore, especially the Commonwealth Division, and the defence of small Allied-held islands including Chodo and Paengyong-do. On 9 February Fireflies operating in the strike role armed with 1000lb bombs blocked a railway tunnel north of Haejin and Sea Furies spotted for a bombardment by the cruiser *Ceylon*. When she returned to Sasebo for a break, she was relieved off the west coast by the USS *Bairoko*, one of a number of USN escort carriers now operating in the war zone. *Glory* was able to resume her combat routine quickly and her operations were recognised by the UN command as making a significant and very visible contribution to the Allied war effort.

On 1 March 1952 Lieutenant Fraser's Sea Fury suffered an engine failure as he 'slotted' to starboard of *Glory* to join her visual circuit. The USN helicopter was already airborne as a planeguard and was able to winch him out of the water in seconds. He actually stepped onto the carrier's deck two minutes later, in less time than it would have taken him to complete the circuit and land in his own aircraft! After a replenishment period in Kure, *Glory* sailed with FO2 embarked on 12 March to take part in a number of Allied deep-penetration raids against targets in the Anak area which were intended to destroy enemy logistical targets on the ground. On 17 March 1952 she flew the maximum number of sorties possible in

Tugs 'cold-moving' *Glory* towards the Captain Cook Dry Dock during her 1951 refit in HMA Dockyard Garden Island in Sydney. (RAN)

order to defend Allied troops against a Communist attack on Sok-to. 804 NAS flew sixty-five sorties and 812 NAS a further forty, a combined total of 105, setting a new record for a light fleet carrier. Both squadrons maintained their aircraft at 100 per cent serviceability. From 1 April both Sea Furies and Fireflies regularly carried 500lb bombs on armed reconnaissance sorties and successful attacks were carried out on enemy warehouses at Kyomipo and Simpo. On 4 April *Glory*'s aircraft flew a number of close air support missions north of the Imjin River in support of the Commonwealth Division and two days later they bombed and destroyed an important rail bridge north of Chinnampo. On 9 April her aircraft gave close air support to the 1st US Marine Division.

After a brief spell in Kure to take on replacement aircraft and stores from *Unicorn*, *Glory* sailed for the fifth war patrol of her second period of operations on 17 April 1952. On 22 April Fireflies destroyed an enemy ammunition dump in the centre of the village of Singsongdong and Sea Furies destroyed a factory near Pyongyang.[18] On 27 April Sea Furies accurately bombed and dropped one span of the important railway bridge near Sariwon, an appropriate end to this period of operations. On 1 May 1952 *Glory* left the Korean war zone for Hong Kong where she transferred pilots, aircraft and stores to *Ocean*. During her two tours off Korea, *Glory* had flown 4835 sorties for the loss of twenty-seven aircraft and nine aircrew. Her running total of ammunition expenditure now amounted to 886,300 rounds of

A Sea Fury FB 11 being ranged on *Glory*'s after lift. The squadron duty officer, in battle-dress, is monitoring the move. (Author's collection)

20mm ammunition, 126 1000lb bombs, 3114 500lb bombs and 13,098 rocket projectiles. By then targets destroyed totalled 796 junks, 1001 ox carts and 308 railway trucks.

HMS Ocean – *May 1952 to October 1952*

Ocean had been serving in the Mediterranean Fleet until January 1952 when she was relieved by *Theseus*, showing how tight the programming of operational aircraft carriers remained in the RN during this period. She arrived in Hong Kong in May with 802 (Sea Fury FB 11s) and 825 (Firefly FR 5s) NAS, which had transferred from *Theseus* in April, embarked.[19] *Ocean* was commanded by Captain C L G Evans DSO DSC RN, one of the top-scoring RN fighter pilots of the Second World War, a man determined that his ship and its squadrons would set an outstanding example of carrier capability. She sailed for her first war patrol on 10 May 1952 and operated off the west coast. Only a week later, on 17 May 802 NAS flew seventy-six sorties and 825 NAS flew forty-seven, creating a new light fleet carrier record of 123 sorties in a single day during which 90 tons of bombs were

A deck-load strike of Sea Furies and Fireflies ranged on *Ocean*. (Author's collection)

dropped. A second war patrol began on 29 May and on 8 June she arrived in Kure to take on replacement aircraft from the AHU at Iwakuni. During her third period of operations she anchored off Inchon on 15 June to be visited by Field Marshal Lord Alexander of Tunis, the Minister of Defence, who had come to study RN carrier operations and to visit the Commonwealth Division ashore.

On 24 June 1952 *Ocean* joined the USN carriers of TF 77 to carry out combined strikes against North Korean power stations and electrical installations. She often sailed with *Unicorn* in company during this period so that the maintenance carrier could act as a spare deck for aircraft that had to recover with an emergency, allowing her own finely-balanced tempo of strike operations to continue without interruption. *Unicorn* also embarked detachments from 802 NAS to provide CAP over the task force, further freeing *Ocean* to concentrate on strike operations. From 11 July 1952 *Ocean* and her aircraft played an important part in Operation 'Pressure Pump', a combined offensive against the North Korean capital Pyongyang by RN, USN, USMC, USAF and RAAF aircraft co-ordinated by the

US 5th Air Force. *Ocean* contributed thirty-nine sorties to a grand total of 1254; her target was a large railway marshalling yard thought to contain crated MiG-15 fighters in railway wagons which were successfully hit and destroyed. Later in July she continued to attack interdiction targets including railway bridges as well as all the usual carrier tasks.

On 1 August *Ocean* arrived in Kure to take on replacement aircraft and aircrew. The latter included the first five RNVR pilots to arrive in the Korean war zone, a vindication of the system of aircrew reserve training established in the late 1940s which was now providing a flow of competent replacement pilots. By then communist MiG-15 jet fighters were being deployed into North Korea and on 9 August 1952 a flight of four Sea Furies from 802 NAS was attacked by one from a section of MiGs. This MiG-15 was shot down by the flight's leader, Lieutenant P Carmichael RN, the first occasion on which a jet fighter was shot down by any British armed forces and, again, the incident emphasises the versatility of the Sea Fury as a practical strike fighter aircraft. Flying operations were curtailed on 16 August by Hurricane KAREN and after it had passed *Ocean* returned to Kure for a replenishment period. Her impressive list of achievements continued in the next war patrol; five bridges were destroyed by bombing on 28 August and three more a day later. The squadron ROPs show that they had reached a peak of operational efficiency during this period and one of *Ocean*'s innovations was the extensive use of pre-dawn launches for interdiction missions. None of the British carriers carried out night missions during the Korean War, principally because the light fleet carriers lacked the manpower to sustain operations by both day and night. The nights also gave the squadron maintenance personnel a chance to work on their aircraft to repair damage and carry out routine maintenance. However, the enemy used the hours of darkness to move men and supplies towards the front line in trucks with dimmed headlights. By carrying out night launches, *Ocean*'s aircraft could position themselves to interdict vehicles that were still on the move in the open in the twilight before dawn. They could then recover to carry out a conventional day landing. At first this technique proved very successful but by the time *Glory* relieved *Ocean* in November 1952 the enemy would devise methods to counter it.

A further, typical, war patrol began on 13 September and during it *Ocean*'s aircraft flew 749 sorties in nine days, an average of eighty-three sorties a day, maintaining 100 per cent serviceability. The last of the railway bridges between Pyongyang and Chinnampo were destroyed on 16 September while attacks on trucks and other transport continued. After her ninth war patrol she was visited by the First Sea Lord, Admiral Sir Roderick McGrigor, who congratulated the ship's company on their achievements. She sailed for the last war patrol of this

A Sea Fury FB 11 from *Ocean* over North Korea. (Author's collection)

deployment on 23 October 1952 and on 28 October Sea Furies accurately bombed and destroyed sluice gates at Yonan with 1000lb bombs and destroyed more rail bridges. On 30 October a short service was held on the flight deck for the eight aircrew who had died during Korean operations and wreaths were dropped into the sea in their memory. 802 and 825 NAS were subsequently awarded the 1952 Boyd Trophy for their operations.

Throughout the Korean War the light fleet carriers had to be prepared, at short notice, to concentrate with the bulk of the FEF in order to defend Hong Kong against a Communist attack and frequent exercises were carried out to test the Colony's defences. One of these was Exercise 'Tai-Pan' on 4 November 1952 when *Ocean* and *Glory* combined to simulate attacks against Hong Kong's air defences. At the time the Colony was defended against air attack by RAF de Havilland Vampire fighters based at Kai Tak, all of which had been transported to their new base by *Unicorn* and light fleet carriers operating in the ferry role. On completion of the exercise, *Ocean* was relieved by *Glory* which was to carry out its third and last war deployment.

HMS Glory – *November 1952 to May 1953*
In May 1952 *Glory* had returned to the Mediterranean Fleet and, on her arrival in Malta on 26 May she disembarked her squadrons which subsequently returned to

the UK in *Theseus* to be disbanded. She embarked 807 and 898 (Sea Fury FB 11s) NAS, which had been embarked in *Theseus* for the Fleet's summer cruise and showed her versatility by taking part in a major Mediterranean Fleet visit to Istanbul in July 1952 in company with the Canadian light fleet carrier HMCS *Magnificent*, the cruiser *Cleopatra* and the destroyers *Chevron* and *Chivalrous*.[20] On 22 July Egyptian Army officers led by Colonel Gamal Abdel Nasser launched a coup which toppled the government of King Farouk who abdicated on 26 July and left the country in his yacht for Naples. *Glory* formed part of a concentration of the Mediterranean Fleet off Tobruk from where it could act to defend the Suez Canal and other British interests if necessary. The diplomatic crisis eased during August and after a spell anchored off Cyprus, she returned to Malta on 15 August and flew off her temporary air group.

On 1 September 1952 she embarked a new air group comprising 801 (Sea Fury FB 11s) and 821 (Firefly FR 5s) NAS and began an extensive work-up prior to re-joining the FEF. She returned to Hong Kong on 23 October and on 4 November took part in Exercise 'Tai Pan' with *Ocean* to test the Colony's air defence organisation. Two days later, having taken on aircraft and stores from *Ocean*, she sailed for Sasebo and on 10 November 1952 she sailed to begin the first patrol of her third period of operations in the Korean war zone. By then peace talks had been making slow progress for more than a year and both the type and number of targets in enemy-held territory that could be attacked were strictly limited although anti-aircraft fire remained intense. At first *Glory*'s aircraft continued to use the pre-dawn interdiction tactic introduced by *Ocean* but they found that the enemy had reacted to it with a simple but effective air-raid warning system. This comprised warning fires lit rapidly on the ground under the aircraft as they flew inland; looking behind them, *Glory*'s pilots could see a long line of fires, about a mile apart, that led Communist fighters to the strike's position. Like the Soviet Air Force, the North Koreans used night fighters in tight radar-controlled 'boxes' and this technique lent itself particularly well to indicating the position of strikes to defensive fighters. To make the enemy's warning system more difficult, strikes flew at low level but the season of winter fog made this tactic impractical on most days.

After taking on replacement aircraft from *Unicorn* in Sasebo, *Glory* relieved the USS *Badoeng Strait* off western Korea on 28 November 1952. Much of the tasked flying was now intended to support Allied forces on the islands of Chodo and Sok-to as the NKPA tried to gain territorial advantage before a potential ceasefire but bad weather hampered operations *Glory* sailed for her last period of operations in 1952 on 15 December. Unfortunately her SAR helicopter was lost, together with its crew, a day later. It was an RN Dragonfly flown by Lieutenant A P Daniels RN and Aircrewman E R Ripley and was caught by a strong crosswind while taking off and crashed over the starboard side into the sea. Strike sorties concentrated on blocking railway tunnels and on 20 December a Firefly carried out the 10,000th deck landing since *Glory* had left the UK in May 1951. She left the operational area on 26 December to take on replacement aircraft from the AHU at Iwakuni which were ferried out to her by lighter.

A further war patrol began on 4 January 1953 with the emphasis placed on bombing attacks on villages where intelligence sources believed enemy troops to be billeted. Numerous cuts were also made in the railway network. A further patrol began on 19 January with similar tasking and on 6 February she began her sixth war patrol. Intelligence had warned of a possible pre-armistice submarine offensive against Allied warships and there were heightened anti-submarine precautions including visual searches by Fireflies and an enlarged screen of destroyers. Rivers and the ground froze so hard in January 1953 that trucks could drive round any damage inflicted on roads. It was well known that railway bridges could be repaired quickly and so attacks were directed at railway lines in the most inaccessible parts of their routes. Thirty-three such cuts were made in the month and, at first, repair rates were encouragingly slow but as NKPA engineers became aware of the tactic, repairs were made more quickly. On 5 January a Sea Fury, piloted by Lieutenant D G 'Pug' Mather RN, was hit by enemy fire after an attack on a railway line north of Chaeryon.[21] His aircraft caught fire and he bailed out but the remainder of his section was unable to see where he landed and for 90 minutes aircraft searched for him without success. A USAF helicopter, escorted by two Sea Furies, was sent to the scene but, unfortunately, it was forced to turn back by bad weather and Mather was taken prisoner by the NKPA. He was tortured but eventually released after the armistice. One of the escorting Sea Furies, flown by Sub Lieutenant B E Rayner RN, lost radio contact and disappeared without trace and later in the day a Sea Fury flown by Sub Lieutenant B J Simonds RNVR spun from 3000ft and exploded on hitting the ground. Lieutenant Foster RN made a wheels-up landing in his Sea Fury at Pengyong-do with a rough-running engine and electrical failure. A day later a Firefly flown by Lieutenant W R Heaton RN was hit by ground fire and ditched north of Kirin-do. He was rescued from his dinghy by a USAF helicopter from Pengyong-do. On 10 February a section of Sea Furies was attacked by MiG-15s but the communist fighters failed to gain an advantage in their first firing pass and, unable to get into a firing position in a turning fight, they broke off the action and withdrew at high speed. After further replenishment in Kure, *Glory* sailed on 25 February for a further period of operations in some of the worst weather encountered during the entire war. Targets included troop concentrations and lorry convoys. As part of a pre-armistice 'hearts and minds' campaign, leaflet raids were carried out over the larger villages and towns in the north.

Pre-dawn strikes against lorry convoys resumed in March and war patrols with high-intensity rates of flying followed in March and April. On 5 April 1953 *Glory* equalled the record set by *Ocean* of 123 sorties flown in a single day. It could have been exceeded but the sensible decision was taken to equal it rather than risk lives by chasing statistics. As it was, the achievement required every pilot to fly four combat sorties in the day and Commander 'Air', the Flight Deck Officer and the Landing Signals Officer to fly two each. Weapons expended included 104 500lb bombs and 384 rocket projectiles fitted with the new shaped-charge warheads for use against hardened targets. Targets destroyed included seven road and railway bridges, twenty-eight buildings and five 'exploding' ox-carts with four further bridges and three gun positions damaged.

On 19 April *Glory* sailed for her tenth war patrol during this period of operations. By now sick and wounded prisoners of war were being exchanged at Panmunjon and target restrictions were particularly tight but close air support for the Commonwealth Division was given when requested. Her last war patrol began on 5 May; this was the eleventh of this tour of operations and her twenty-fifth overall. The Commander Seventh Fleet had signalled all carriers in theatre that the war was drawing to a close and no unnecessary risks were to be taken by aircraft attacking heavily-defended targets. Her last day of operational flying was 14 May 1953 after which she returned to Sasebo to pass personnel, aircraft and stores to *Ocean* which had arrived to relieve her. Since leaving the UK in May 1951 she had made an unrivalled contribution to the Korean War. This involved steaming 157,000nm and flying 13,700 sorties, 9500 of which were operational over Korea, using a million gallons of avgas. The ship had used 25,000 tons of furnace fuel oil. Her aircraft had destroyed seventy bridges, 392 vehicles and forty-nine railway trucks for the loss of twenty aircrew. The expenditure of ammunition amounted to 278 1000lb bombs, 7080 500lb bombs, 24,238 rocket projectiles and 1,441,000 rounds of 20mm ammunition. Once she had handed over operational duties, *Glory* returned to the UK, arriving in Portsmouth on 8 July 1953 to be de-commissioned for a major refit.

HMS Ocean – *May 1953 to July 1953*

Ocean returned to the Korean War zone in May 1953 after a spell in the Mediterranean. She had a new air group embarked which comprised 807 (Sea Fury FB 11s) and 810 (Firefly FR 5s) NAS. After a few days in Sasebo she sailed for a war patrol on 19 May and provided close air support for the Commonwealth Division as well as interdicting enemy troop movements. She returned to Sasebo on 31 May but had been unable to disembark her Sea Furies to Iwakuni as planned because of fog and low cloud. This was unfortunate as they were intended to carry out a fly-past over Allied ships in harbour to mark the forthcoming Coronation of HM

Queen Elizabeth II. Not to be put off, fourteen Sea Furies were launched from *Ocean* while she lay at anchor in Sasebo using Rocket-Assisted Take-off Gear (RATOG), so that they could carry out a fly-past from Iwakuni. This had never been done before and provided as great a spectacle for the ships in harbour as the subsequent fly-past a day later. On Coronation Day, 2 June 1953, Commonwealth ships dressed overall, there was a parade in *Ocean*'s hangar and the fly-past took place as planned.

Ocean sailed again on 8 June with tasking limited to close air support for the Commonwealth Division as the front line stabilised prior to the armistice. A replenishment period in Kure was followed by a further patrol but fog limited the number of close air support sorties that could be flown. A further operational period was carried out in early July and three Fireflies were disembarked to K6 airfield at Pyongtaek as night fighters to counter interdiction raids by North Korean aircraft that were too slow for jets to intercept. They proved to be a successful deterrent although no enemy aircraft were shot down. On 27 July 1953 the armistice was finally signed at Panmunjon but *Ocean* carried out a further four patrols off the west coast of Korea to monitor ceasefire arrangements and ensure that there were no infringements of the armistice terms. She left the area for Hong Kong flying her paying-off pennant on 31 October and was relieved as the FEF carrier by HMAS *Sydney*. On arrival back in Devonport in December she paid off for a refit.

HMS Unicorn – *June 1950 to July 1953*
Unicorn had been re-commissioned in 1949 to ferry aircraft, stores and equipment to the FEF so that a light fleet carrier could be fully supported on station.[22] She was in Singapore Dockyard undergoing a refit to prepare for her passage back to the UK when the Korean War broke out and, with the BPF a recent memory and no British base nearer to the war zone than Hong Kong, it was clear that earlier lessons applied directly to the new conflict. *Unicorn* was ordered to remain in the FEF to form the nucleus of an air train to support the fleet's operational carriers but the best method of employing her had to be given careful consideration. She could operate at a forward base as she had done at Leyte Gulf and Manus in 1945 or she could land her aircraft repair department to RNAS Sembawang in Singapore and operate as a replenishment carrier. The latter alternative was decided to be the more flexible and efficient and was the one adopted, although she retained a light repair and maintenance capability. She sailed from Singapore on 11 July, arriving in Sasebo on 20 July to transfer seven Seafires and five Fireflies to *Triumph*.

The range of capabilities *Unicorn* offered were quickly realised and the light fleet carrier *Warrior* was re-commissioned in the UK to provide further support by

Unicorn receiving a rousing welcome from US armed forces, including a military band, as she arrives in Pusan with men of the Middlesex Regiment and their vehicles, the first British troops to arrive in Korea. (Author's collection)

ferrying aircraft, stores and personnel to Singapore. In August 1950 *Unicorn* was in Hong Kong Dockyard being loaded with stores as diverse as aircraft engines, rum, flour and ammunition when the British Government took the decision to commit ground troops to the conflict. She proved to be capable of embarking the headquarters of 27 Infantry Brigade, the 1st Battalion of the Middlesex Regiment and loading their vehicles tightly into her lower hangar. The cruiser *Ceylon* embarked the 1st Battalion of the Argyle & Sutherland Highlanders. The two ships entered Pusan, the last port in UN hands, on 29 August to unload their military force. After that *Unicorn* returned to Singapore Dockyard to complete the refit that had been interrupted by the outbreak of war before returning to the war zone in December with a further 400 troops and their kit in addition to replacement aircraft for *Theseus* which had replaced *Triumph*. As in the BPF she provided a spare deck for new pilots to practice their deck landing technique, leaving the operational carrier free to concentrate on its primary role.

In early 1951 she ferried Meteor jet fighters for 77 Squadron RAAF from Hong Kong to Iwakuni, an airfield across the bay from Hiroshima, and later in the year she continued to ferry RAAF Meteors into the war zone in addition to large numbers of replacement Sea Furies and Fireflies for the RN. She also ferried RAF Vampire fighters for Hong Kong which bolstered its defences against potential communist aggression. For a while *Unicorn* acted as an accommodation ship for Commonwealth naval personnel in Sasebo and she had the distinction of being 'adopted' by the Middlesex Regiment after her continuous close association with the Regiment ferrying in replacements for the battalion fighting in Korea. She sailed north of the 38th Parallel to bombard North Korean coast-watchers with her 4in guns and retains, at the time of writing, the distinction of being the only aircraft carrier of any nation to have carried out a bombardment of enemy targets on shore under wartime conditions. She often used the Shimonoseki Strait to pass between Honshu and Kyushu and, despite careful checks on the state of the tide, she struck power cables stretched between the islands on 2 October 1951 because they were covered in ice and snow in the unseasonable cold weather prevailing at the time which caused them to sag much lower than normal. Replacing them took weeks and *Unicorn* invariably sailed south of Kyushu after that. Later in October she had to sail in order to ride out Typhoon RUTH, encountering 100-knot winds and waves 50ft high.

Unicorn was too important to be spared from the FEF but she had been away from the UK for over two years on 24 November 1951 when she was re-commissioned in Singapore Naval Base with a new ship's company that had steamed *Warrior* from the UK. *Unicorn*'s former ship's company steamed *Warrior* home. Changing ship's companies on station in the Far East was to become commonplace a decade later but it was a novel concept in 1951. After a short refit she resumed her varied duties and continued to support the operational carriers. In March 1952 she played the part of a light fleet carrier with a small embarked air group to test the air defences of Hong Kong in Exercise 'Vortex'. In April the Middlesex Regiment presented her with the Regimental March and a special Regimental Order of the Day, both of which were mounted on the quarterdeck next to the ship's battle honours board. The only other British warship to have been similarly honoured by an Army unit in the modern era was the battleship *Vanguard* which had a close relationship with the Royal Artillery.

Unicorn sailed on several war patrols with *Ocean* during 1952, acting as a spare deck to recover unserviceable aircraft and to maintain CAP with 'borrowed' Sea Furies. After a further refit she was in Singapore dressed overall to mark the

Unicorn at Kure in Japan delivering Meteor fighters for 77 Squadron RAAF. (Author's collection)

Coronation of HM Queen Elizabeth II. On 17 July she sailed with replacement aircraft for Sasebo and, while on passage, she picked up a 'Mayday' signal from the ss *Inchkilda* saying that she was being attacked by a pirate gunboat. *Unicorn* went to her aid immediately and closed the scene with all armament manned and circled the pirate vessel at 3000 yards with all her medium and close-range weapons trained on it. This was too much for the pirates who re-boarded their vessel and fled at high speed. *Inchkilda* was returned to her master to go about her lawful business and *Unicorn* proceeded to Sasebo. A day later the armistice that ended the conflict was signed and *Unicorn* eventually sailed for the UK in October 1953 after four years away and two separate commissions in the Far East. During the Korean War, *Unicorn* spent 500 days at sea, steamed 130,000 miles and handled some 600 replacement aircraft. She also ferried 6000 troops and passengers into the war zone. She arrived back in Devonport on 17 November and reduced to reserve.

Lessons Learned by the Carrier Air Groups

The static nature of the war by 1952 led *Glory* and *Ocean* to plan flying operations on a programmed, rather than a reactive, basis.[23] This was easier for the running of the ships and it was found that sixty sorties per day could be flown without undue strain for protracted periods. Every evening at about 17.00, a programme was worked out for the next day's flying which consisted of a number of fly-offs known as Events. Event 'A' would fly off and approximately two hours later Event 'B' would launch, allowing Event 'A' to land on, and this carried on throughout the day. During the day the ship operated in an area bounded by a circle of 15 miles diameter with its centre at Point 'Oboe'. The ship's area of responsibility was sub-divided into smaller operational areas with the aim of covering each at least once every other day. Each area had a primary target and this was duly attacked unless a more promising opportunity target appeared. Blockade enforcement was undertaken by armed coastal reconnaissance sorties and the threat to friendly islands was countered by attacking adjacent mainland targets. Railways were kept out of use by continuous interdiction and aircraft were always included in the Events for close air support tasking by outside agencies. Close air support could take several distinct and different forms.

Before every sortie, pilots and observers were briefed on the amount and types of anti-aircraft fire, known at the time as 'flak', that the enemy was known to have in the areas in question, their location, tactics and camouflage. The NKPA had guns ranging from 88mm to 12.7mm but made no use of tracer and only limited use of radar control at first. NKPA radars were believed to be pirated versions of British wartime sets designed for anti-aircraft fire control. Predicted fire was encountered around Pyongyang and the airfield at Yongdang Dong where Soviet forces were believed to be based. NKPA and Chinese People's Liberation Army flak made extensive use of terrain and camouflage and was tightly disciplined. Troops in the open would remain absolutely still when attacked and then engage aircraft as they pulled away with massed, concentrated small-arms fire which was often very effective. Units on the move would post anti-aircraft sentries on hills which would fire warning shots when Allied aircraft were seen. Heavy anti-aircraft guns were deployed in batteries of four or eight dug into diamond-shaped positions. To attract UN pilots and make them waste ammunition, dummy targets 'reasonably well camouflaged' were set up, many of which formed the basis of flak traps and cables were often slung across valleys to catch low-flying pilots. Several measures were adopted to counter these tricks; phony camouflage was looked at carefully, reported and only attacked after careful photographic reconnaissance and analysis. It was normal to fly at 3000ft in transit, above the danger of small-arms fire and never attack targets more than once. Line astern formation was never used in attacks as the enemy could easily shift accurate fire onto the second and subsequent aircraft after the first had made its pass. Instead, converging attacks from different angles were made to disperse anti-aircraft fire and flak suppression was carried out by specialised sections of Sea Furies. These countermeasures resulted in fewer aircraft being hit and more damage inflicted on targets.

Captain Evans of *Ocean* warned his pilots not to regard MiG-15 jet fighters, when they were first encountered over Korea, as 'something legendary as we had done with Rommel in the desert' after claims on Radio Tokyo that they were shooting down Allied aircraft.[24] Lieutenant Carmichael's flight encountered a group of MiGs at 06.00 on 9 August 1952. His number 2, Lieutenant Haines called 'MiGs at five o'clock' but Carmichael did not see them himself at first. His number 4, Sub Lieutenant Ellis, called a break and the Sea Furies all turned towards the enemy aircraft and good hits were obtained by Carmichael and others on two MiGs, one of which went down trailing smoke and flame and the other broke away, clearly damaged. The remaining enemy aircraft broke off the engagement to escort the damaged aircraft away after the first MiG crashed. Carmichael considered the main reason for his flight's success was the ruggedness and dependability of the Sea Fury. His men had kept a good lookout and used their aircraft to better advantage than the enemy, taking their opportunity to knock down a superior aircraft. Despite their piston-engined fighters' supposed limitations, they had not been intimidated by the enemy and the skill and experience of the Sea Fury pilots was, clearly, also a significant factor.

All bombardment spotting by RN aircraft used American procedures regardless of the ship carrying out the shoot. Some were pre-briefed, some impromptu and some briefed whilst the aircraft were in flight to the target area. A special card was printed for pilots' guidance with the correct procedure sequence, definitions and terms. It was found to be extremely useful. Cruisers with their 6in guns and fire control systems were the most accurate and pilots preferred to spot for them; destroyers' 4.5in guns were less accurate and frigates with their small 4in guns were the least accurate of all. Their usual inaccuracy led to them being used to engage area targets although they were sometimes used against enemy guns. The most frustrating discovery was that, in general, American ships did not know the American procedures and nor did their pilots. There were a number of cases of Sea Fury pilots having to give lectures on bombardment procedure to a USN ship whilst actually flying over the target! 1:50,000 scale maps were used for spotting and found to be satisfactory; gridded photographs were not used.

Pilots flying armed reconnaissance sorties were usually given an area or line along which to search and tasked to answer specific questions. For close air support sorties pilots were briefed on the position of Allied forward troops which they plotted on 1:50,000 scale maps. Targets in this static phase of the war were most likely to be dug-outs, bunkers or underground shelters and, therefore, 500lb bombs with 30-second delay fuzes were the preferred weapons. Once close to the forward edge of the battle area (FEBA), pilots reported to a forward air control pilot or 'Mosquito' in a North American Harvard aircraft who talked him onto the target with a six-figure map reference and/or accurately dropped smoke markers. Under Plan 'Victor', all friendly artillery ceased fire while the attack went in but after experience and discussions with Army officers ashore, RN pilots became confident that they could keep out of the way of shells if warned of the line of fire and 'Victor' was used less often. Close air support sorties were generally popular because pilots felt they were directly helping their colleagues in action on the ground. Through necessity the enemy became adept at camouflage and it took time for pilots to get used to their methods. On a number of occasions even experienced pilots had returned with reports that nothing was going on in the area they had covered but analysis of their photographs revealed good targets which had been well concealed. Successive carriers found that enemy movement stopped in their areas of interest by day and that enemy guns would not open fire against ships when aircraft were overhead.

Aircraft Maintenance

It proved difficult to apply consistent lessons to the carriers deployed off Korea because seasonal variations had a significant impact. Fewer hours of daylight and worse weather in winter meant fewer sorties per day but far higher averages could be maintained in summer. There was, thus, no such thing as a standard figure for logistic requirements, aircraft wastage or the consumption of air stores. To achieve an average of seventy-five sorties per day, a number often exceeded by both *Glory* and *Ocean*, maintenance personnel had to carry out very quick turnarounds with unserviceable aircraft. If an aircraft could be made serviceable for the next Event, work had to start on it as soon as its engine had shut down and it had been lashed to the deck. This included refuelling, re-arming and re-spotting into the launch range aft within a very tight time frame. It was vital that pilots reported problems immediately so that 'Snag Parties' could have the right tools and ground equipment ready together with serviceable spares. There was no time to fetch things from deep storage. Striking down aircraft that needed more extensive repairs in the hangar also needed careful planning. If a series of engine runs would be required to prove an aircraft serviceable, care had to be taken not to lock it into the back of the hangar. It was also important to avoid continually moving aircraft that were actually being worked on by mechanics to enable serviceable aircraft to be ranged on deck. In fact such movements could be rendered impossible if aircraft under repair were on jacks or had a wing spread.

When pilots made their post-flight reports in the aircraft control room (ACR), there was often a lot of congestion as aircraft, electrical and radio snag parties, flight deck marshallers and arming parties with notebooks poised attempted to get the information they needed quickly. Flying started before dawn and ended shortly after sunset, after which the range for the next day's first two Events had to be moved into position, accurately spotted, fuelled armed and lashed to the deck. Since the ship was darkened it was not possible to carry out routine inspections while these aircraft were ranged on deck. Daily inspections were, therefore, carried out between Events during the day's flying and this required careful supervision to ensure that aircraft were not lost to the flying programme for this reason alone. Other routine inspections were easier to plan. Daily starred inspections were carried out every six days instead of once per week since this fitted in better with the programming of a war patrol. By doing them on a replenishment day in the middle of a patrol, on return to harbour and just prior to leaving harbour, none fell due on a flying day. Minor inspections were either anticipated or extended and engine changes anticipated to coincide with a period in harbour since every aircraft in any way immobilised in the hangar at sea was one more obstacle to overcome. In harbour there was the luxury of space and the ability to use 'Jumbo', the mobile crane, to help speed the work.

After each patrol there was always a heavy programme of ammunitioning and the embarkation of new aircraft, air, naval, armament and victualling stores to be completed and aircraft maintenance ratings were naturally called on to do their part. This was most satisfactorily solved by virtually abandoning all attempts at doing any maintenance on the first day alongside while up to 150 maintenance ratings helped to take in ammunition. From then on no further call was made on the Air Engineering Department (AED), or squadrons for the remainder of the period in harbour. To conserve spares while the ship was on a patrol or even to make them available at all sometimes, it was necessary to rob aircraft with major damage fairly extensively; aircraft thus stripped were known as 'Christmas Trees'. In nearly all cases the item removed was replaced by the original unserviceable one with the result that aircraft returned to *Unicorn* were usually deeply unserviceable. The most common items in this respect were arrester hooks, oleos, hydraulic piping, G4F magnetic compasses, oil pressure gauges and artificial horizons. Quite often it was possible to use a mainplane off a damaged Sea Fury to service another aircraft rather than use a new spare. One of the more inexplicable aspects of Korean operations was the constant recurrence of a certain type of defect during a particular patrol, it neither having appeared previously nor subsequently. To the air maintenance sailors, patrols frequently became known by their common defects rather than by any other particular incident. For example there were 'over-speeding', 'spark-plug', 'bomb-carrier' and 'magneto' patrols during 1952 but none of them prevented the number of tasked flying sorties from being met.

The Aircraft Holding Unit at Iwakuni

One of *Unicorn's* first tasks was to establish an aircraft holding unit (AHU), at an airfield at Iwakuni which was situated on the other side of Hiroshima Bay from the dockyard at Kure. The airfield was administered by the RAAF and apart from acting as an operational base for 77 Squadron with its Meteor fighters, it hosted a squadron of USAF B-25 bombers, USN Neptune maritime patrol aircraft and a small detachment of RAF Sunderland flying boats. It also acted a staging post for Allied transport aircraft and turned round large numbers of flights organised by the US Military Air Transport Service, RAF Transport Command and QANTAS which was contracted to support the Australian armed forces. Like the wartime MONABs, the sailors that set up the AHU had to make do at first with primitive facilities and their first move was to make an office out of engine crates and a workshop in the back of a 3-ton lorry. The 'team' comprised a single officer, initially Lieutenant Foster RN, one chief petty officer aircraft artificer, four petty officers and twenty sailors. Its primary task was to hold twenty-four replacement aircraft of which two, one Sea Fury and one Firefly, had to be at 24 hours' notice for issue to an operational carrier.[25] Their workload varied from intense when *Unicorn* unloaded aircraft or the operational carrier arrived to take them on board and unload 'duds' for repair or scrap to dull when neither were present. During the quiet periods the sailors turned to with a will to improve their facilities and help other lodger units at the base. They were, in turn, helped by them whenever necessary. The AHU proved to be a fine example of inter-Allied co-operation throughout the conflict.

SAR Helicopter Coverage

The value of helicopters as combat SAR platforms was demonstrated both on land and at sea during the Korean War. As a 'planeguard' during day carrier operations it offered unrivalled efficiency but a destroyer with its sea-boat ready was still needed close to the carrier at night. At different times RN aircrew were rescued by helicopters operating from the quarterdecks of bombarding cruisers at Wonsan and Inchon, from tank landing ships acting as small flight decks close inshore and from USAF airfields as well as from their own carriers. Their morale value was important but the limitations of the Sikorsky S-51 and its licence-built British derivative the Westland Dragonfly had to be appreciated and understood. These included a relatively small radius of action, made even smaller by the strong headwinds often encountered and a reliance on dead-reckoning navigation with its potentially large errors. The ability to fly on instruments was minimal, limiting their usefulness in adverse weather and their VHF radios were limited to 'line-of-sight' ranges. For all these reasons, the ubiquity of their basing was a critical factor and some of the aircrew that were rescued would not have been recovered if only the carrier-borne helicopters had been available. The dedication and skill of the USN and USAF helicopter crews to their combat rescue task was worthy of the highest praise.

Destroyers and frigates also formed part of the SAR organisation and were frequently placed in 'rescue stations' close inshore where they could move to recue aircrew from Allied aircraft that managed to cross the coast and ditch after being damaged. On 7 April 1951, for instance, the destroyer *Cockade* was acting as Allied air search and rescue ship in the Yalu Gulf when she was ordered to search for the crew of a crashed US bomber. This involved moving close inshore among shoals in foggy weather and searching in co-operation with a USAF amphibious aircraft which was able to land on the water to pick up the one survivor that was located;[26] the rest of the crew were never found. Fortuitously, however, *Cockade* was able to rescue another US airman who had been shot down in January, concealed by friendly Koreans and brought out to the destroyer in a junk when she was seen to be close inshore.

RAF and British Army Involvement

The Royal Navy provided the only British contribution to tactical air operations throughout the Korean War but the other Services made contributions to the overall UN air effort. The RAF maintained a detachment of four Sunderland flying boats at Iwakuni drawn from 205, 88 and 209 Squadrons which constituted the Far East Air Force Flying Boat Wing based at RAF Seletar in Singapore. They flew daily sorties under naval operational control in support of the Commonwealth warships that implemented the blockade to the west and south-west of Korea.[27] Air observation was important for troops on the ground and two units were formed to provide it in 1951. These were 1903 Air Observation Post (AOP) Flight which formed part of the 1st Commonwealth Division. It was a joint unit equipped with Auster AOP 6 aircraft flown by pilots drawn from the Royal Artillery with maintenance personnel provided by the RAF. 1913 Light Liaison Flight was also formed in 1951 with Auster AOP 6 aircraft which were flown by officers and NCOs of the Glider Pilot Regiment[28] and RAF maintenance personnel. Both units were disbanded after the armistice.

Screening the Carrier Battle Groups

There was a latent threat, throughout the war, that the Soviet Union would seek to escalate the conflict with attacks on UN warships by aircraft and submarines. It was necessary, therefore, to ensure that a proportion of aircraft sorties maintained defensive anti-submarine patrols and CAP and that a screen of destroyers remained with the operational carrier. The screen was not always made up entirely of RN warships but often included a mix of British, Australian, American, Canadian and Dutch destroyers. Anti-submarine capability had to be maintained at high proficiency but this was not always easy to achieve, given the emphasis on other tasks and the lack of training opportunities. The rotation of destroyers between the war zone and other areas of the FEF helped by allowing ships to take part in exercises and in 1951 *Cossack*, *Consort*, *Charity* and *Cockade* took part in USN 'hunter-killer' anti-submarine exercises off Okinawa that helped to keep standards at a high level. The opportunity was also taken to upgrade destroyers with the latest weapons; *Cockade* for instance was taken into Singapore Dockyard in March 1952 to have 'X' mounting removed and two Mark 6 'Squid' anti-submarine mortars installed in its place with their associated bomb handling room and improved sonar. She returned to the war zone in December 1952 after a work-up.

The threat of air attack from the Soviet Union or China was always present but, fortunately, there was only one such attack on a British warship. The destroyer *Comus* had covered a landing by a USN reconnaissance unit on the west coast on 21 August 1950 and was steaming about 85 miles west of Kunsan when she was attacked by two North Korean Il-10 'Beast' bombers which dived on her singly from astern.[29] The first dropped four bombs that hit the ship on the port side killing one sailor, wounding another and leaving a hole 4ft high by 8ft long on the waterline which flooded the forward boiler room. The second aircraft's aim was less accurate; it dropped its bombs ahead of the ship and all of them missed. *Comus* was able to make for Kure under her own power, escorted by her sister-ship *Consort* and a CAP of USMC fighters. Fears that this might mark the beginning of a Communist attempt to break the blockade led FO2 to order his ships off the west coast to concentrate in order to increase their anti-aircraft firepower and *Triumph* to maintain a Seafire CAP over them in daylight for the immediate future. The attack proved to be an isolated incident, however, and there were no further attacks on the carrier battle group or any other Commonwealth warship.

Command and Control

It was clear from the outset that the United States would bear the heaviest share of the fighting in Korea and, since there was an existing US command structure in nearby Japan, it was natural that the British and Commonwealth warships in the war zone should fit into it. Operational command was the most significant since the British FEF retained administrative control through its own logistical and type-support infrastructure. This was also able to support the Australian, Canadian and New Zealand ships since they and their equipment were, at the time, all of British design and origin. Personal relations between American and British officers were founded on mutual respect and remained effective and cordial throughout the war.[30] Misunderstandings and differences of outlook were inevitable but were always overcome. Many arose simply because of the difficulty found in arranging verbal contact with the American operational commanders, most of whom exercised their commands afloat. In contrast, the three British admirals who acted as FO2FES during the war all exercised their command from Sasebo in Japan, only embarking to 'get a feel' for the operational area with a small staff on relatively infrequent occasions. The chief difference between the American and British systems lay in the rigidity of the former at the time. Orders were extremely detailed and direct communication on a junior level with another Service or even another task force were not normally permitted. All communications were expected to go back up the chain of command, through the top and then back down again. The information addressees on signals did not take action until ordered to comply by their superior authority, even when it was obvious that such action would have to be taken. Practically no discretion was left to the 'man on the spot'. In the British Common-wealth command structure of the time, on the other hand, anticipation and initiative were expected and exercised. USN ships attached to the west coast task force very much appreciated the reduced reliance on signals, instructions and demands for situation reports. Relations between the USN and RN over the coming decades were to benefit greatly from the perceptions of mutual confidence that grew out of the Korean conflict.

Another specific difference between the USN and the RN is worth explaining. In the USN it was a rule that the officer in tactical command of a carrier task force must himself be a qualified aviator.[31] It was accepted that this might leave the flag officer less expert in anti-aircraft and anti-submarine screening tactics. The RN view was that any admiral, not necessarily an aviator, could command a carrier task force and that his staff would cover any shortfall in personal experience, as they would do on non-aviation matters in the USN. In fact none of the three FO2s that served in the Korean War was an aviator and this made it difficult for the Commander Seventh Fleet to understand how they could command a task force that contained two light fleet carriers. At one stage it was even suggested that the carriers should be taken out of FO2's task force and placed under the operational command of TF 77, the USN carriers that normally operated in the Sea of Japan. The RN politely vetoed this idea and operations continued as they normally did in RN carrier task forces. This difference was to become an issue in later NATO Strike Fleet operations, however.

The British Perception of the Air Interdiction Campaign in Korea

Complete interdiction of a battlefield has always proved difficult but circumstances in Korea seemed to offer special opportunities.[32] The complete blockade enforced by the overwhelming UN naval forces entirely ruled out the possibility of enemy supply by sea and the meagre rail and primitive road communications of North Korea seemed vulnerable to the UN air offensive. Additionally, important road and rail centres on the east coast were close to the shore and vulnerable to naval bombardment. Further, the vulnerability of the rail system seemed to be enhanced, as we saw earlier, by the large number of bridges and tunnels necessitated by the mountainous terrain of the east coast of northern Korea. After the Chinese offensive had been contained, the main effort of UN air operations centred on interdiction of the Communist lines of supply. This was the primary responsibility of the US 5th Air Force, supported by Allied contingents and all available naval and USMC aircraft. The efforts of the USN and USAF were never co-ordinated at theatre level due to the lack of a unified US command structure. It gradually came to be accepted, however, that the USN would deal with the east coast railway and highway systems and the USAF would deal with the west coast where it interacted with RN carrier operations. Except when circumstances dictated other temporary uses of aircraft, this policy continued for twenty months. Immense damage was unquestionably inflicted on the enemy communications systems, and movement by rail or road was confined to the hours of darkness, but the full interdiction of the battlefield was never achieved. Throughout the campaign, the Communists were always able to launch an offensive when they wished, largely because they needed far less supplies than Allied troops.

The causes of this failure, in British eyes, were primarily due to inhibitions accepted by the UN for political reasons, but tactical and operational conditions were also partly to blame. Politically, the ban on attacking Communist sources of supply in Manchuria robbed aircraft of targets that could have been decisive and the static war, accepted during the protracted armistice negotiations, enabled the

Communists to keep their strongly-fortified front lines supplied to a degree they could never have achieved in a war of movement reacting to Allied amphibious assaults. The enemy was allowed to fight on his own terms and this negated many of the advantages possessed by the Allied forces. When it was initiated in January 1951 the object of the interdiction campaign was to impede the Communist advance. Though this line of reasoning was justified at the time, it was opposed by Vice Admiral Arthur D Struble, commander of TF 77, who felt his aircraft could be used better to provide close air support for troops on the ground. Continuation of the interdiction campaign throughout the long armistice negotiations savoured dangerously of trying to win the war by the use of air power alone, while the Army and Navy were relegated to relatively static and defensive roles. It is difficult to resist the conclusion that this strategy, which certainly suited the Communists, was continued for too long and that better results would have been obtained if a more aggressive strategy had been implemented with the Allied Services working together in close co-operation to capitalise on the UN strengths. With hindsight, had the UN forces continued to exert the mobility and flexibility given to them by their command of the sea, as they had at Inchon in 1950, the enemy would have been forced into a war of movement he could not have sustained and aircraft would have played a critical part in joint operations. This stood more chance than an air interdiction campaign, on its own, of compelling the enemy to accept more satisfactory armistice conditions at an appreciably earlier date.

Logistics
The US Military Sea Transportation Service brought 95 per cent of the US troops that fought on the ground in Korea into the war zone without interruption from enemy action because of the UN command of both the sea and the air above it. In the three years of war the Service delivered five million servicemen, 52 million tons of cargo including ammunition and 22 million tons of petrol and oil. Every US soldier landing in Korea was accompanied by 5 tons of equipment and needed 64lbs of supplies per day to keep him there. For every ton of air freight flown into Korea, 270 tons were delivered by sea and 4 tons of fuel for the transport aircraft's return trip had to be brought into Korea by sea.[33]

The Royal Fleet Auxiliary (RFA) played a prominent role in keeping the carriers and all the other Commonwealth warships at sea. A total of thirteen tankers and five stores issuing ships were deployed in support of operations off Korea. When FO2 returned to Sasebo after the initial series of carrier strikes he found Admiral Brind's chief of staff, Commodore G F Burghard RN, waiting for him to discuss 'the whole gamut of needs and troubles, refit programmes, personnel and logistics'.[34] COMNAVFE generously urged the RN to make use of USN facilities in Sasebo but the principal British requirements for oil, food, stores and ammunition were well catered for by the FEF's own logistic organisation. Later in the war, when fighting intensified and pre-positioned stock in the Far East was used up, there were some delays shipping replacement stock from the UK and the carriers, for instance, had to use USN bombs with their different attachment lugs which had to be modified. There were also shortages of radio and radar valves which caused problems but overall the system worked very well and FO2 commented that the fleet logistic staff 'almost seemed to possess the power of thought reading' so well did they meet his ships' needs.

An Overview of the Carriers' Achievement

At the outset of the Korean War Admiral Andrewes said that it would be wrong to regard a single light fleet carrier as representative of what naval aviation was capable of achieving in any theatre. Even taking into account the limited nature of air and naval opposition, however, the performance of the British and Australian light fleet carriers between June 1950 and July 1953 was remarkable. The intensity of flying and the hard lessons learned throughout the long campaign, during the whole of which one ship had been deployed on station despite the recent manpower crisis, brought the ships, squadrons and their people to a high level of professionalism and efficiency that was matched in few other elements of the British armed forces. It built upon the experience of the BPF to maintain a highly-effective Fleet Air Arm that was well placed to move onto the new generation of jet aircraft and helicopters as well as the technical innovations that would revolutionise carrier aviation in the next decade.

The light fleet carriers provided the most conspicuous aspect element of the British contribution to Korea and they flew at rates which had never been achieved before. In an analysis of *Theseus'* early operations, FO2 calculated[35] that she flew 670 sorties in a given period and he compared this with an average of 585 sorties per carrier for the 1st Aircraft Carrier Squadron of the BPF over a similar period in 1945. These statistics were found to be even more impressive when the analysis revealed that the average air group of a single carrier in the BPF was 'about 54' but that *Theseus'* air group was only twenty-eight. A later analysis using figures for *Glory* or *Ocean* in 1953 would provide even more impressive statistics. The British and Australian carrier operations during the Korean conflict were admitted on all sides to be outstanding but, realistically, this level of achievement was only possible because of the lack of serious naval and air opposition. Had these existed on an appreciable scale, more carriers would have been required to form a task force capable of both offensive and defensive operations on a larger scale. This would have stretched the early post-war RN but would, nevertheless, have been possible.

It should not be forgotten that though the enemy had a large but simply equipped Army, it would have found it extremely difficult to locate and fight the carrier task forces the USN and RN could have brought into action had the need arisen.

During the Korean War the RN committed five aircraft carriers and the RAN one to the UN cause out of total of seventy-six warships committed by the Commonwealth governments to the conflict. Their achievements were the result of hard work, much improvisation and operations which had driven many ships, including the light fleet carriers, to the limit of their machinery's capability; in some cases, such as *Theseus*' catapult, it was arguably driven beyond it. The armistice signed on 27 July 1953 ended hostilities that had lasted 1128 days and involved warships from Australia, Canada, Colombia, France, the Netherlands, New Zealand, the Republic of Korea, Thailand, the UK and the USA.

The seal of royal approval was set on the achievements of the Royal and Commonwealth Navies by the following message from Her Majesty the Queen to the Board of Admiralty which was subsequently signalled to the Fleet. 'Please express to all serving in the Commonwealth Fleet my deep appreciation of the splendid service they have given throughout the fighting in Korea', signed ELIZABETH R.

3 Assistance for Commonwealth Navies

The Royal Navy had come to rely heavily on the Commonwealth for the manpower needed for the rapidly expanding number of new ships and naval air squadrons after 1941. By 1945 about 50 per cent of the Fleet Air Arm's aircrew came from Australia, Canada and New Zealand, the bulk of them serving, technically, in the reserve elements of the RAN, RCN and RNZN but spending all their mobilised time serving with the RN. It seemed logical, therefore, that the RCN and RAN should eventually operate their own carrier task forces, although it was accepted that the post-war RNZN would be too small to do so. Carriers could be lent by the RN at first to give experience but both the Australian and Canadian Governments saw that their navies would need to include carriers after the war if they were to be capable either of independent action or making a realistic contribution to a UN, Allied or Commonwealth task force. There was certainly some truth in the view that the Admiralty saw carriers operated by the RAN and RCN as a way of solving its manpower problems in 1944 but, to be fair, it also saw RAN and RCN carrier task forces as 'safe pairs of hands' that could contribute to an overall Commonwealth capability, effectively reducing the number of carriers and their air groups that the RN would need to maintain in commission itself.

Initially, the operation of escort carriers seemed to offer an attractive method of gaining experience but the terms of the Lend-Lease Agreement between the US and British Governments specifically stated that these US-built ships must remain a part of the RN and could not be handed on to a third party, even one that was part of the British Empire and also flew the White Ensign. In the longer term the new light fleet carriers provided an ideal option since they would be reasonably cheap to operate and contained many of the systems already in service in RAN and RCN cruisers and destroyers. By 1945 the RN realised that it had more of these ships under construction than it could man and operate after demobilisation without a drastic reduction in the number of other types of ship but it did plan to retain a number in service and would continue to be the design authority for the class, reducing still further the cost of ownership to the Commonwealth navies. Put simply, the large number of light fleet carriers being completed in 1945 represented too good an opportunity to miss.

The Royal Canadian Navy

After the Allied leaders' Quebec Conference in 1943 a joint RCN/RCAF committee was established to study the future potential for naval aviation in Canada. In October it recommended that 'aircraft carriers be acquired and operated by the Navy',[1] as a vital component of the RCN's ability to command the oceans adjacent to Canada, Newfoundland and Labrador. In co-operation with the RCAF it was also expected to contribute to the defence of Imperial sea communications, and to the joint defence of the oceans adjacent to North America as well as supporting national policies and interests generally. The Navy Board accepted the recommendation and factored it into its short-term plan to form a Canadian Pacific Fleet that would form a distinct national organisation but deployed operationally as a component of the BPF until the end of hostilities. In principle the Board hoped to acquire two light fleet carriers on loan during 1944 but when informed by the Admiralty that ships would not be available until 1945 an alternative scheme was considered and then adopted. The Admiralty agreed that two 'Ruler' class escort carriers would be made available to provide the RCN with carrier experience. To circumvent the Lend-Lease restriction both ships remained under RN control but their executive and seaman departments were provided by the RCN. The air department and embarked squadrons were provided by the RN, albeit with a number of New Zealand aircrew. Harmony was not helped by the differing scales of pay and daily victualling allowances paid by the RN, RCN and RNZN although this had not initially been recognised as a potential problem. The first of these ships, HMS *Nabob*, was taken over by the RN in September 1943 but spent some months in Burrard's Yard in Vancouver undergoing modifications. Her RCN sailors joined her at Esquimalt in January 1944. She underwent further modifications in Liverpool after arriving in the UK but eventually worked up with 852 (Avengers) NAS embarked in June before joining the Home Fleet. With the squadron embarked, her ship's company comprised 504 RCN, 327 RN and nine RNZN personnel.

She sailed in late August 1944 from Scapa Flow for Operation 'Goodwood', a strike by the Home Fleet's carriers on *Tirpitz* in Kaa Fjord. Bad weather interfered with the attack but *Nabob* was hit aft by an acoustic torpedo fired by *U-354* which blew a hole 50ft long by 40ft high below the waterline and bent the single propeller shaft. She was fortunate, however, in having Chief Shipwright J R Ball RCN in her complement, whose previous duty had been shoring up torpedo-damaged ships in St John's, Newfoundland. His experience helped to shore up bulkheads around the damaged area and the ship was able to return to Scapa Flow on 27 August under her own steam. Despite being down by the stern, she had even managed to fly off Avengers on an anti-submarine patrol. Unfortunately, she was found to be so badly damaged that there was insufficient capacity in UK shipyards to repair her and so she was de-commissioned on 30 September 1944 and left, unrepaired, on a mud bank on the south bank of the Firth of Forth where she was stripped of equipment for use as spares by her sister-ships.[2]

Puncher was commissioned in February 1944 and on 10 May 1944 Captain R E S Bidwell RCN assumed command. She was used initially as an aircraft ferry carrier and made several passages in convoy from New York to the UK before suffering a main gearing failure in November 1944. She was refitted and repaired on the Clyde with items removed from *Nabob*. Once repairs were complete she joined the Home Fleet in February 1945 and embarked 881 (Wildcats) and 821 (Barracudas) NAS for strike operations off the Norwegian coast. The war in Europe ended while she was refitting in the Clyde but in May and June she operated as a deck landing training carrier for 1790 and 1791 (Fireflies) NAS before having bunks and extra bathrooms fitted into the hangar for duty as a troopship. From August she carried out a number of runs between the UK, Halifax and New York with a reduced ship's company. On the first of these she carried 491 RCN and fifty WRCNS personnel home from the UK. On the last runs eastwards, she carried men and stores to man the new light fleet carrier *Warrior* which was being completed by Harland & Wolff in Belfast for loan to the RCN.

It had been intended to transfer *Ocean* and *Warrior* to the RCN on loan in 1945 but the RCN had its own manpower problems and proved unable to accept a light fleet carrier before September 1945, ruling out *Ocean* which was, therefore, manned by the RN.[3] Instead it was decided that *Warrior* and *Magnificent*, both being built by Harland & Wolff in Belfast, would be lent with *Warrior* first in 1946. *Magnificent* was a more capable ship, able to operate larger and heavier aircraft and in the event she replaced rather than augmented *Warrior* in 1948 and remained on loan to the RCN until 1957 when she was in turn replaced by her modernised sister-ship *Bonaventure* (formerly *Powerful*) which had been purchased outright by the Canadian Government. The creation of a Canadian Fleet Air Arm was helped in the Spring of 1945 by the transfer of 550 surplus RCAF pilots to the RN for service in the BPF. They travelled to the UK for training and, with the unexpectedly early end of the Pacific War, were ideally placed to join other Canadians in the formation of the RCN's first naval air squadrons. These were formed in the UK in exactly the same way as RN air squadrons, taking up the numbers of units that had been temporarily disbanded. The first of these was 803 (Seafire LIIIs) NAS which re-commissioned at RNAS Arbroath on 15 June 1945. Its aircraft flew in standard RN markings but the words 'ROYAL CANADIAN NAVY' rather than 'ROYAL NAVY' were painted on the after fuselage above the airframe number. The squadron became officially part of the RCN on 24 January 1946, the day on which HMCS *Warrior* was commissioned.[4] Another early unit was 825 NAS which

HMCS *Magnificent* in Grand Harbour, Malta during 1952. The aircraft on deck are Sea Furies and Avengers. (Author's collection)

re-commissioned for the RCN with Barracudas at RNAS Rattray on 1 July 1945. Fireflies replaced the Barracudas in November and the unit transferred formally to the RCN on the same day as 803 NAS.

By the time *Warrior* arrived in Canada a shore base would be required for disembarked naval air squadrons and a committee of RCAF and RCN senior officers was tasked make a joint plan. In October 1945 an agreement was reached which was surprising in the light of the RN's own bad experience with the joint control of air matters prior to 1937. The RCAF was to be responsible for the management of all naval shore-based aviation, including major aircraft repair, maintenance and the provision of air stores. The RCN had jurisdiction over all carrier-based activities and shore-based minor repairs and aircraft inspections. Permanent shore facilities were to be at RCAF Dartmouth in Nova Scotia where RN telegraphist air gunners had been trained during the war. By 31 March 1946 when 803 and 825 NAS disembarked from HMCS *Warrior*, an RCN Air Section had been established at the base which was shared with aircraft of the RCAF, Maritime Airways and Trans-Canada Airlines. As in the UK, however, the shortcomings and, ultimately, failure of joint control rapidly became apparent and unacceptable. Effectively the RCAF held the 'purse-strings' for the logistical support of the Fleet Air Arm but put its own priorities first, confronting the Navy with shortages in such vital items as flying clothing and general air stores. The senior naval officer described his status to higher authority as that of a 'beggar tenant' in an establishment that was in desperate need of repair.[5] For example, in January 1947 faulty heating systems in hangars 108 and 109 forced their temporary evacuation. The Government considered moving the air facility but Dartmouth had such clear advantage as a naval base that control of both the airfield and all shore-based maintenance activity was transferred to the RCN and the base commissioned as HMCS *Shearwater*, RCNAS Dartmouth on 1 December 1948.

By then there were two carrier air groups, the 18th and 19th. The latter composed the first two squadrons that had formed in the UK and the latter two new squadrons, 883 (Seafires) and 826 (Fireflies) which had commissioned in Canada. A third air group had been formed for training in May 1947 and included a fleet requirements unit, 743 NAS, with a variety of aircraft and an operational flying school. Operational flying training after the award of 'wings' was carried out at RN operational schools in the UK until the mid-1950s when the RCN moved away from using aircraft that were standardised RN types. The RCN maintained an Observer School which trained a number of RN observers during the period while the RN tried to unite pilot and observer training. From 1948 Hawker Sea Furies began to replace Seafires in the fighter squadrons and from 1951 modified Grumman Avengers specialising in anti-submarine warfare replaced the Fireflies. No Canadian carrier took part in the Korean War and, although consideration was given to embarking a Canadian Sea Fury squadron in an RN carrier, the plan came to nothing.

When *Bonaventure* came into service in 1957 she operated an air group comprising McDonnell Banshee fighters of 870 NAS and the Grumman Tracker anti-submarine aircraft of 880 NAS. The air group later included Sikorsky Whirlwind anti-submarine helicopters. It was still run very much on the lines inherited from the RN but now had a distinctly Canadian flavour and earned a high reputation for anti-submarine operations within NATO. The Banshees always operated at the margin of capability and were withdrawn in 1962 without replacement. Consideration had been given to replacing them with Douglas A-4 Skyhawks procured from the USN and deck landing trials were carried out but the Government would not agree to meet the modest cost.

In 1968 the RCN was subsumed into the joint Canadian Armed Forces (CAF), which failed to comprehend her value and despite the fact that she had only completed a 'half-life' refit in 1967, she was listed for disposal in 1969 and scrapped in 1970. Sikorsky Sea King helicopters, which had replaced the Whirlwinds in 1963, continued to be used in single-aircraft flights embarked in destroyers, flown by CAF aircrew. By 2014 the CAF had been recognised as a failure and the proud name of the RCN restored. However, the CAF legacy is that the restored RCAF still operates ship-borne helicopters which are shore-based at a heliport on the site of the former RCNAS. Government attempts to replace the Sea King have proved a costly failure since 1992 with two different types selected, millions of dollars spent and no operational aircraft to show for the effort. Part of the problem is the specification which states that the aircraft must float if they come down in Arctic seas and, beside their anti-submarine capability, must have cargo-handling equipment to suit them for a variety of tasks. None of the three major anti-submarine types in service with Western navies can meet this criteria and it is, perhaps, not being unfair to say that Canadian naval aviation lost its way after 1968 and has yet to recover.

The Royal Australian Navy

By 1945 the RAN was, arguably, a significantly less potent force than it been in 1914 or 1939. In 1914 the battlecruiser *Australia* and its supporting fleet unit constituted a balanced and powerful force and in 1939 it deployed a significant force of five modern cruisers and a number of destroyers. As the war progressed, however, naval aviation became the dominant factor in naval warfare and the RAN 'fell out of step' with modern navies[6] in that it had no tactical aircraft embarked and could not, therefore, form a viable task force on its own. Moral was high, however, and both officers and men were proud of their wartime achievements. From a professional point of view they wanted a chance to display their worth and efficiency in future and 'it was obvious throughout the fleet that this would entail the introduction of naval aviation'.[7]

The acquisition of aircraft carriers for the RAN was not without controversy, however. Early in 1944 it had already become clear to the Australian Common-wealth Naval Board (ACNB), that a carrier task group manned by the RAN would be the most effective method of contributing to the Allied offensive against Japan as well as being the logical focus of a post-war fleet.[8] Negotiations for the transfer of a new light fleet carrier and two cruisers from the RN to the RAN at no cost to the Australian Government began in a 'quiet and unofficial way'[9] and Admiral Sir Guy Royle, an RN Admiral serving as First Naval Member of the ACNB and Chief of the Naval Staff, announced the scheme at a meeting of the Advisory War Council on 21 March 1944. Unfortunately he had not discussed the matter beforehand with the other Chiefs of Staff or with Sir Frederick Sheddon, secretary of the Defence Committee. All feigned shock and the latter took his disquiet to John Curtin, the Prime Minister, who sent for Royle and reminded him that communication with the Admiralty on such matters should be through Government channels.

Sir Guy Royle continued to argue for this scheme when Curtin visited the United Kingdom for talks with the British Prime Minister, Winston Churchill. While

Churchill's arguments had considerable merit, which Curtin recognised, he gave the impression that the British were merely trying to solve their own manpower crisis by obtaining Australian sailors to commission new ships which could not otherwise be deployed in 1945.[10] The British offered two light fleet carriers on free loan, possibly *Venerable* and *Ocean*, although the exact choice of ships would have depended on completion dates and manpower availability but John Curtin continued to hold the line that the need for Australian carriers must be examined as part of a study of post-war force structures. He did eventually accept the offer in February 1945, however, four days after the BPF arrived in Sydney to an enthusiastic welcome but the war ended before the scheme could be implemented. Had it been taken forward, the ships would have been 'mix-manned' with the RAN providing the executive department and the RN the squadrons and the bulk of the air departments like the arrangement that had proved successful in the RCN-manned escort carriers. During 1945 a number of RAAF Spitfire pilots transferred to the RANVR to fly Seafires in the BPF. The scheme was cut short by the unexpectedly early end to the war on 15 August but there were many more volunteers than could be trained. Many of these would, no doubt, have found their way into the squadrons embarked in an Australian light fleet carrier. Also, judging by the experience of the BPF, there would have been many volunteers among the sailors in their air departments to transfer permanently into the RAN.

Admiral Sir Louis Hamilton relieved Sir Guy Royle in 1945. He was to be the last RN admiral seconded to Australia to act as the Chief of the Naval Staff and was determined to settle the issue of aircraft carriers for the RAN. He commissioned a study into the need for Australian naval aviation and entrusted Lieutenant Commander V A T Smith DSC RAN,[11] who had served with the RN Fleet Air Arm as an observer for much of the war, with the task. Unlike his predecessor, Sir Louis Hamilton 'cultivated' Sheddon and worked on Mr Chifley the new Prime Minister. He had to inform them that in Great Britain's difficult post-war economic circumstances it could no longer offer light fleet carriers free of charge and Australia would be expected to bear some of the burden of defending Common-wealth interests in the Pacific. Mr Chifley accepted this and agreed with Smith's recommendation that the post-war RAN should be centred on two carriers, at least one of which would always be available and capable of both defensive and offensive action in an independent task force or as part of a coalition fleet. Despite hostile opposition from the RAAF which argued that all forms of aviation should be land-based and operated only under its own control, the Australian Government finally agreed to purchase two light fleet carriers from the Admiralty as part of a five-year defence plan. After some negotiation, the Admiralty agreed to sell two ships of the *Majestic* class to Australia for the estimated build cost of one.[12] The programme cost was, therefore, £2,750,000 for the two ships plus £450,000 each for their initial outfits of stores, a total of £3,650,000 but against this could be set £427,000 raised by public subscription in Australia for a replacement after the loss of the cruiser *Sydney* in 1941. Legislation could easily apply this sum against the cost of the first of the new ships after it was decided to name it after the cruiser. Many Australian citizens were therefore able to feel that they had contributed directly to the procurement of the nation's most powerful warship and the fact that it was an aircraft carrier showed that the RAN was moving into a new era.

Despite Hamilton's hard work mistakes were made and, unfortunately, the Admiralty made no allowance in the quoted price for the improvements that would be necessary to support new generations of aircraft at a time of rapid change in both aircraft and their supporting systems. Considering the far-reaching and expensive work being undertaken in the UK at the time on projects such as the rubber landing deck[13] and steam catapult this oversight is surprising. In the early post-war years the Australian Government was suspicious of every penny spent on what some critics viewed as a large aviation component within a small navy and what appeared to be cost over-runs did not help.[14] As the Fleet Air Arm became 'Australianised' and RN influence diminished, the Five Year Defence Plan made good progress and these fears abated but they were to surface again in the Australian carrier replacement debate during the late 1970s. Arguments about procurement and cost were not simple to resolve but the concept that embarked aircraft formed a critical element in naval warfare was not, at first, obvious to the RAAF and it sought to block the procurement of the two carriers. Even after they were accepted as part of the Five Year Defence Plan in 1947, the Minister for Air insisted that the RAAF must provide the aircraft, aircrew and infrastructure. His intransigent view was all the more difficult to understand, given the success of the obvious 'role models' in Great Britain and the USA and the outcome of Commander Smith's Study which had been accepted by Government. Despite further objections from the Minister for Air that the establishment of a Fleet Air Arm in the RAN was 'not in the best interests of defence',[15] the Prime Minister accepted that the RAN's air component would wear naval uniform, be under naval operational control and backed by naval shore stations and facilities.[16] If the RAAF had had its way, *Sydney* might have started life with a nominal air group that was institutionally averse to the concept of carrier aviation and could not have done as well as she did in Korea and, perhaps, could not have deployed at all. The failure of the RAAF to recognise that aviation forms an important and legitimate part of its sister-service's operational capability left a political legacy that proved difficult to eradicate. It was particularly unfortunate that men who believed themselves to be proponents of 'air power' actively sought to eradicate the RAN's Fleet Air Arm and its ability to provide an important tactical capability in the national interest.

20 Carrier Air Group was formed for the RAN at RNAS Eglinton in Northern Ireland on 28 August 1948;[17] it comprised 805 (Sea Fury FB 11s) and 816 (Firefly FR 4s) NAS. A second air group, 21 CAG, was formed in Australia at RNAS St Merryn in April 1950 comprising 808 (Sea Fury FB 11s) and 817 (Firefly FR 5s) NAS and subsequently took passage to Australia in *Sydney*. To provide the aircrew for its new squadrons the RAN entered thirty-five ex-Second World War aviators at Flinders Naval Depot in January 1948 with the rank of Acting Lieutenant RAN.[18] Also four lieutenants from the Royal Australian Naval College, RANC, started flying training with the RN in the UK and five ex-RAAF pilots already serving on short-service commissions in the RN were transferred to the RAN. On its formation 20 CAG comprised the four lieutenants from the RANC, the first six of the aircrew who had entered Flinders in January, fifteen RN pilots, six RN observers and six aircrewmen recruited into the RAN from the RN. The air group commander and the two squadron commanding officers were both RN at first but by 1952 the only RN officers in the Australian Fleet Air Arm under the rank of commander were the small number of exchange officers retained in squadrons as a permanent feature to broaden the knowledge of tactics and ideas at unit level.

The ship that became HMAS *Sydney* 3 was laid down in Devonport Dockyard as HMS *Terrible* in April 1943 as one of sixteen 1942-design light fleet carriers,[19] part of the massive expansion of naval aviation within the RN during the latter part of

HMAS *Sydney* leaving the UK for Australia with a large number of cocooned Sea Furies and Fireflies for the RAN's new Fleet Air Arm on deck and in the hangar. (Author's collection)

the Second World War. The 1942 design was divided into two classes, the *Colossus* class of ten ships and the improved *Majestic* class of six ships which were capable of operating larger and heavier aircraft. Four ships of an even larger 1943 design were built for the RN but they were considered to be beyond the RAN's ability to man and operate in the early 1950s. The *Majestic*s were laid down slightly later; all were suspended incomplete soon after the Japanese surrender and none saw service with the RN. *Terrible* was laid up in Devonport before she was bought by the Australian Government on 3 June 1947 but work re-commenced immediately to complete her to the original design and she was handed over to the RAN in December 1948 and commissioned by Mrs J A Beasley, wife of the Australian High Commissioner in London, on 5 February 1949.[20] Her first commanding officer was Captain R R Dowling DSO RAN who maintained the very close links between the RN and RAN. Even those who worked so hard to establish an Australian carrier strike force did not realise how effective the Fleet Air Arm would become in a very short time; just over a year after her arrival in home waters, *Sydney* deployed to the Korean War with the outstanding success described in the previous chapter.

The second Australian carrier was *Majestic* herself, renamed as HMAS *Melbourne*, built by Vickers and suspended at Barrow-in-Furness after 1946. She was completed at a slower pace so that that the revolutionary new British carrier systems could be included. In the event she was virtually rebuilt to a much-improved design and when completed in November 1955 she was only the third carrier in the world to be completed with a steam catapult, angled deck and mirror landing aid fitted during build rather than retro-fitted later.[21] She too was to have a long and productive life, remaining in operation until 1982. To cover the period before *Melbourne* was completed, some years later than originally planned because of the amount of reconstruction needed to bring her up to the latest standard, the light fleet carrier *Vengeance* was lent to the RAN from November 1952. She sailed for the UK in June 1955 with the ship's company that would take over the new *Melbourne* and was returned to the RN in August. It would be difficult to imagine a closer relationship between two navies.

The light fleet carriers were undoubtedly a good choice for Australia. They were available, affordable, economical in operation and at the time of their completion both ships represented the current 'state of the art'. The completion of the second ship on a slower timescale to incorporate new technology was also a sensible move which gave the Fleet Air Arm the chance to mature. Had Australia elected to buy one of the 1943 light fleet carriers it is doubtful whether it could have been completed before 1954, a considerable delay, and it would have had a much higher 'price-tag'. It would also have been more expensive to man and operate. In an era

A 'most original forgery' on the flight deck of HMAS *Vengeance* when she escorted HM Queen Elizabeth II for part of her tour of the Commonwealth in the liner *Gothic* during 1954. (RAN)

when personnel were trained by, and interchangeable with their RN contemporaries the ships' standardised British equipment was easy to absorb and presented few operating problems[22] and this meant that attention could be focused on flying operations. The only viable alternative would have been surplus USN escort carriers of the *Commencement Bay* class and with their different machinery, systems and ammunition they might have been cheap to buy but would have been expensive to assimilate and operate. *Sydney* proved herself to be a better carrier than ships of this class such as the USS *Rendova* in operations off Korea. She was also more seaworthy and better able to adapt to subsequent development.

The Indian Navy

India was the last Commonwealth navy to adopt aircraft carriers, although a small shore-based Fleet Air Arm had been operated since independence in 1947. In 1957 the Indian Government purchased the incomplete light fleet carrier *Hercules*, a sister-ship of the vessels procured and operated by Australia and Canada. She had been built by Vickers-Armstrong on the Tyne but laid up incomplete in the Gareloch after launch. After her purchase she was towed to Harland & Wolff in Belfast for completion, capitalising on the experience gained with the modernisation and completion of *Bonaventure*. She was completed in 1961 and commissioned as INS *Vikrant*, the last of the 1942 light fleet carriers to enter service, and fitted with a steam catapult, angled deck and mirror landing aid. Her air group comprised Hawker Sea Hawk FGA 6 fighters and Breguet Alizé

HMAS *Melbourne,* seen here with a Gannet landing-on, was the only third aircraft carrier in the world to be completed with a steam catapult, angled deck and mirror landing aid rather than having them added later. (Author's collection)

anti-submarine/reconnaissance aircraft which were later joined by Westland Sea King helicopters. The IN had hoped to buy French Etendard fighters but accepted the obsolescent Sea Hawks as the RN was withdrawing them from service and offered them at a bargain price.[23] A subsequent batch of surplus Sea Hawks was bought at low cost from the Federal German Government which was replacing them with F-104 Starfighters. *Vikrant*'s ship's company and the squadrons were initially trained in the UK but, unlike Canada and Australia, India moved away from British technical management to adopt its own more nationally-centred support infrastructure. It obtained remarkable value for money from its purchases and the IN's Sea Hawks were not finally withdrawn from service until the 1980s after proving effective in a number of regional conflicts. Indian naval air squadrons were never numbered in the RN sequence but were, instead, given numbers in the 300 range. In the 1980s India became the only export customer for the Sea Harrier which replaced the Sea Hawk at modest cost. They were able to operate from *Vikrant* which was fitted with a 12-degree 'ski-jump' and subsequently from *Hermes*, renamed *Viraat*, which was purchased from the RN in 1986, again at a bargain price which included a major refit in Devonport Dockyard. She is still active in 2015 with an air group of Sea Harriers and Sea King helicopters to which a small number of Russian-built Kamov Ka-31 airborne surveillance and control helicopters have been added.

Russian influence grew significantly and in 1994 the Russian Navy offered one of its *Kiev* class aircraft carriers for sale. The offer was not immediately taken up but in 1999 the former *Admiral Gorshkov* was offered free of charge provided that the

INS *Vikrant* in 1962 shortly after her arrival in India. (Author's collection)

Indian Government paid for her to be modified to a revised design and refitted. Again this was seen as a bargain which was taken up with a contract signed in 2004 but, in this instance, the 'bargain basement' tactic proved unsuccessful. The original cost of the work was US\$ 625 million but unforeseen problems and difficulties delayed the project and the ship, renamed *Vikramaditya*, was not delivered until 2013 at a cost well over \$2 billion with several technical issues including boiler reliability unresolved. Like similar ships in the Russian and Chinese navies she uses a 'ski-jump' to operate fighters in the short take-off but arrested landing (STOBAR) mode. A new carrier built to an indigenous Indian design with Italian engineering support was launched in 2014 for planned completion in 2018. She is to be named *Vikrant* II and the Indian Navy hopes to build further carriers with catapults instead of the 'ski-jump' to give fighters greater load-carrying capability and flexibility.

The Royal New Zealand Navy

Despite the large number of New Zealand aircrew who flew with the RN in the Second World War, the post-war RNZN was not large enough to operate an aircraft carrier or form its own Fleet Air Arm and a number of New Zealanders have flown with the RN and RAN as pilots and observers. RNZN ships have operated helicopters since 1966, however, when the first *Leander* class frigate entered service. Westland Wasps were procured and flown by RNZN pilots trained in the UK with RNZAF maintenance technicians to support them. With the introduction of the ANZAC class frigates from 1997, Wasps were replaced by the Kaman SH-2G Seasprite. These too are flown by RNZN pilots and observers trained in New Zealand and supported by embarked RNZAF detachments. This arrangement is likely to continue for the foreseeable future as a further batch of Seasprites was ordered in 2014.

4 Invention, Innovation, New Aircraft and Rebuilt Ships

During the Second World War the Admiralty's Directorate of Naval Air Warfare (DNAW) introduced a monthly journal called *Flight Deck* with the first edition appearing in August 1944. On its first page there was a message from the First Sea Lord Admiral of the Fleet Sir Andrew Cunningham who said that 'the future of the Navy depends largely on a vigorous air arm and it is essential for all of us to acquire full understanding of its activities if the Navy is to maintain its great traditions of enterprise and efficiency'.[1] Vice Admiral Sir Dennis Boyd, the Fifth Sea Lord and Board member responsible for air matters, endorsed this message with his hope that the Journal would be of service 'to the Navy as a whole and particularly to those who are concerned, in any capacity, with the provision and use of aircraft which are the spearhead for the Navy's attack and defence'. Despite its importance and undoubted success, the journal ceased publication in January 1946 amid the austerity that followed the end of the war and demobilisation.

It left an important gap, however, which was filled by a revitalised *Flight Deck*, introduced as a quarterly journal by DNAW in the winter of 1952. The incumbent Fifth Sea Lord, Vice Admiral Anstice, said that the new Journal was 'to provide up-to-date information for those who fly our aeroplanes and for those who, though not aviators, are concerned with the operation of aircraft and should be aware of their capabilities. The whole of the Navy of today is included in this latter class.'[2] The First Sea Lord, Admiral Sir Rhoderick McGrigor, added that 'Progress in the air is rapid. It affects all naval activities and it is essential that all officers should fully appreciate developments and the effect they will have on naval warfare.' This edition had, as its opening article, an extract from a lecture delivered by Vice-Admiral Sir Maurice Mansergh to the Royal United Services Institute (RUSI) in 1952[3] Mansergh had previously commanded the 3rd Aircraft Carrier Squadron and, between 1949 and 1951 had been the Fifth Sea Lord and Deputy Chief of the Naval Staff responsible for air matters.

The Task of Naval Aviation

Mansergh began by stressing that aircraft had become 'part and parcel of the daily round and common task of the Navy' like guns, torpedoes, boats or 'any other manifestations of naval life'. The 'Air' was now included in the term 'Sea Power'. By 1952 the RN had emerged from the post-war manpower crisis but faced an uncertain future. British politicians focused their attention at the time the procurement of atomic weapons and the retention of powerful land forces in Germany to defend Western Europe, if necessary, against Soviet forces from behind the 'Iron Curtain' as the Cold War developed. The need for sea power to maintain trade and vital lines of communication was not forgotten but was undoubtedly given a lower priority. Mansergh's lecture to RUSI was intended to emphasise the continuing need for a powerful navy to a wide and informed audience but the fact that an extract was printed in *Flight Deck* showed the importance placed by the Admiralty on making its own officers aware of the important role sea power still had to play. Interestingly, Mansergh did not claim that naval aviation was a panacea but noted the effective achievements of RAF Coastal Command in the recent Battle of the Atlantic together with the extensive minelaying operations carried out by Bomber Command. Arguably, he even over-stated some of their achievements in order, perhaps, not to be accused of a partisan approach. The combination of land-based and carrier-borne aviation was accepted as relevant and important by the Admiralty but, as we shall see in later chapters, similar views were not held in other Government departments.

Carrier-borne aircraft were described by Mansergh as vital in the performance of three main fighting roles. In order of importance these were:

(a)   Anti-submarine warfare.
(b)   The air defence in depth of fleets at sea and convoys of merchant ships.
(c)   Air strikes against surface ships and land targets.

A further important role was identified as the tactical or close support of land forces, the task being performed very successfully by the light fleet carriers in the Korean war zone at the time, but this would have to be carried out by the aircraft designed for tasks (b) and (c) above. The role did not, therefore, merit inclusion in the list of main tasks and in addition to the fighting roles there were a number of subsidiary requirements for naval aircraft to perform including the training of aircrew and ship's companies in the use of their anti-aircraft systems.

The anti-submarine role was believed to require an aircraft with relatively long endurance, able to carry out visual and radar searches for 'snorkelling' or surfaced submarines so that they could be avoided by surface forces or attacked. The same aircraft was to be able to localise a dived submarine with sono-buoys and to attack it, when possible, with a homing torpedo or depth charges. The new Fairey Gannet was designed from the outset to be a 'hunter/killer', able both to search for and strike at an enemy submarine in the same sortie at a significant range from the carrier. Mansergh was one of the first to draw attention to the important role that was becoming apparent for helicopters in this field. He said that the board was interested in the capability being shown by these innovative aircraft as 'short-range search aircraft able to deal with the submarine that eludes the normal search and gets towards a position from which it could attack'.[4] In this role, he said, it would have to deal with submerged submarines and would have 'a sono-buoy receiver and good communications with surface craft; later it might carry an anti-submarine weapon'.

Air defence was described as the ability to hold, or seize, command of the air in areas threatened by enemy air attack and through which surface forces or convoys must pass. Mansergh broke this broad requirement down into two distinct categories. In the first he noted the need to defend convoys by destroying shadowing aircraft which might be working with submarines and a shore headquarters with the potential to order air strikes. The second involved the defence of the strike fleet by preventing weapon release by anything up to full-scale, escorted air attacks in waters that were within range of the enemy's highest-performance bomber and fighter aircraft. Attacks of this kind could be expected in all conditions of light and weather and so this second category was further divided into two. Under good weather conditions by day the Admiralty felt that pilots had less need of inter-ception aids[5] and could be brought into visual contact with the enemy by direction officers using the carrier's radar. In bad weather or at night, the fighter needed to be fitted with air-intercept radar with an observer trained as a second crew member to operate it and guide the pilot into cannon range of the target,[6] say 250 yards down to 100 yards depending on whether the target was manoeuvring.

The best aircraft for the defence of convoys was thought to be a two-seat, radar-equipped fighter of good performance but not necessarily as good as the fighters required for the air defence of the fleet. These would have to be of the highest performance and the need to intercept high-speed bombers before they could release their weapons was felt to be sufficiently obvious to need little stress. Achieving that high performance might need endurance to be sacrificed and that had led the Admiralty to consider deck-launched interception[7] rather than the maintenance of CAP. Lessons from the Pacific War had shown the need for airborne radars capable of detecting enemy attacks made beneath the fleet's radar coverage and this requirement was to be fulfilled by the transfer of fifty Skyraider airborne early warning aircraft to the RN by the USN under the NATO mutual defence assistance programme (MDAP). Although the ideal fighters for fleet air defence and convoy defence were not identical, the need to reduce the number of different aircraft types in service meant that a single type of night fighter would have to be procured for both roles and in the short term, the de Havilland Sea Venom would be used for the task. The day fighter was to be the Hawker Sea Hawk.

The strike role was the least well advanced at the time, following the cancellation of the large, specialised aircraft types in 1946. The ideal strike aircraft was to be capable of attacks on ships and land targets and also capable of the close support of military forces in amphibious operations and, when necessary, further inland. The only dedicated strike aircraft in service in 1952 was the Blackburn Firebrand and delays developing its intended successor, the Westland Wyvern, meant that it would be already be considered obsolescent when it eventually achieved operational capability.

Innovation – The 'Rubber Deck'

Deck landing trials with Sea Vampires highlighted the limitations imposed by the slow acceleration rates of early jet engines[8] and changes in both carrier technology and deck landing technique were obviously needed. Scientists predicted that the next generation of fighters designed for supersonic performance could add further problems with swept wings designed for high performance at altitude leading to much higher landing speeds. To make matters worse, 'high-speed' wings were expected to be too thin to accommodate the substantial undercarriages needed to absorb the impact velocities of heavier aircraft deck landing at unprecedented speeds. The one good feature of jet operation, apart from the obvious high-speed performance, was that they used distillate fuel with a higher flashpoint than avgas which could be stored in integral hull tanks like fuel oil, allowing much greater quantities to be stowed in carriers. That said, jet fuel was only refined in the USA at the time and had to be purchased with scarce dollars. Costs dropped, however, after the emergence of civilian aircraft, such the de Havilland Comet, when aviation turbine fuel began to be refined in the UK.

For a while in 1946–7 it seemed that if no radical solution was forthcoming the operation of jet fighters would only be possible in very small numbers. One solution that was taken very seriously came from Mr Lewis Boddington, the Head Scientist at the new Naval Aircraft Department (NAD), at the Royal Aircraft Establishment at Farnborough. He proposed transferring the pneumatic absorption of the deck landing from the aircraft to the carrier, in other words operating aircraft without undercarriages. Although extreme, his idea was based on the logic that catapults and arrester wires, the other devices that allowed short take-offs and landings, were built into the carrier and not the aircraft. It had the additional merit that undercarriage-less fighters would be some 15 per cent lighter than their conventional equivalents and this could be translated into higher performance. The obvious drawback was the inability of aircraft without wheels to move under their own power after landing either on a carrier deck or an airfield ashore. The Admiralty was sufficiently concerned about the problem that it devoted money, manpower and resources to evaluate the concept at the height of the post-war economic and manpower crisis.[9]

With the possibility that landing speeds up to 135 knots might be necessary, downwind carrier approaches were flown by Sea Vampires to evaluate the problems of deck landing control officers (DCLOs) and a flexible deck, more commonly referred to as a rubber deck, was built ashore at RAE Farnborough. Boddington proposed that aircraft flew a low, flat approach well above stalling speed to pass just over the rubber deck with the hook down. The pilot was to treat each approach as a potential miss until he felt the retardation as his hook took the single arrester wire rigged across the deck. Shore trials were flown by Lieutenant Commander Eric 'Winkle' Brown DSC AFC RN who flew a modified Vampire prototype, TG 286, and several Sea Vampire F 21s. The latter had a conventional undercarriage but were built with a strengthened fuselage capable of withstanding the impact of wheels-up landings. Judging the right height over the rubber deck which was raised about 2ft above the surrounding surface was not easy and both TG 286 and the rubber deck were damaged in one approach that dropped too low but the trials were generally sufficiently successful to move forward to sea trials.

In 1948 *Warrior*, which had recently returned to Portsmouth from loan service with the RCN, was fitted with a rubber deck made out of hosepipes laid athwartships over the conventional flight deck between the two centreline lifts; they were filled with compressed air and covered by a rubber membrane on which the aircraft landed. The surface was lubricated for landings by hosing fresh water onto it. A single USN Mark 4 arrester gear was fitted over the rubber deck with the actuating pistons situated fore and aft alongside it. It had a maximum pull-out of only 160ft which meant that a high minimum wind over the deck was required for every recovery. *Warrior*'s first rubber deck trials took place in November 1948 and the first landing was carried out by Lieutenant Commander Brown in TG 286 at an indicated air speed of 96 knots into a 35-knot wind over the deck which gave an entry speed into the wire of 61 knots. Once landed, the aircraft was lifted by 'Jumbo' the mobile crane so that its undercarriage could be lowered and it could then be manoeuvred on the conventional area of flight deck forward of the rubber deck as normal. From there it carried out a free take-off and returned to RNAS Lee-on-Solent where the trials aircraft were based. All subsequent landings were flown by Sea Vampire F21s which were heavier and capable of being launched by catapult. A DLCO, or 'batsman' as he was more commonly known, was positioned on the flight deck aft to monitor approaches and wave aircraft off if they appeared to go low. He did not give a 'cut' signal since the aircraft was intended to 'fly through' the wire. There were problems on two occasions when the arrester wire struck the aircraft's booms which forced it out of the hook. In both cases the aircraft made contact with the deck and slid along it but the application of full power allowed them to climb away safely.

Subsequent trials included landings at higher entry speeds with retardations measured between 1.8 and 3.1g and deliberate off-centre landings. On 25 November 1948 Sea Vampire VT 805 was launched by *Warrior's* BH 3 hydraulic catapult, the first time the RN had launched a jet-propelled aircraft with a nose-wheel undercarriage from one of its aircraft carriers. Further trials were carried out in March 1949; this time with two USN Mark 4 arresting gears mounted in tandem with the wire carried around the moving crossheads of both allowing a pull-out of 290ft and an entry speed up to 120 knots. Five pilots with varying degrees of experience flew the aircraft this time in addition to Lieutenant Commander Brown. The USN sent observers to witness these trials including representatives of the Military Requirements, Ship's Installation Division and the Naval Air Material Center. As late as November 1952 a classified report by these agencies spoke optimistically about the project[10] but by then it was really moribund.

A number of safe landings had demonstrated the ability of undercarriage-less aircraft to land on a flexible deck but they also demonstrated the fundamental flaw in the concept quite clearly. Conventional landings by wheeled aircraft onto straight-deck carriers averaged about two per minute at the time. At closing speeds of about 60 knots this meant that as the first aircraft took a wire, the second should be turning finals 1000 yards astern. Taking this distance as an acceptable minimum, Boddington argued that aircraft with a closing speed of 110 knots should be able to recover, theoretically, at the rate of one every 16 seconds, about four per minute. Assuming that the wave-off signal for a deck that was not yet clear was left until the following aircraft was in to 200 yards, this allowed 12 seconds to clear the rubber deck after each landing. The reality was that it took five minutes to clear each aircraft off *Warrior's* rubber deck, lifting them by crane while their under-carriages were pumped down.[11] Given the number of aircraft embarked, even in the light fleet carriers, a landing interval of five minutes was never going to be acceptable and NAD produced a number of ingenious ideas to overcome the problem but none was ever likely to be a practical success at sea. They included a hydraulically-lowered ramp forward of the rubber deck down which the aircraft could be hauled by a wire, quickly attached to a ring on its nose by an aircraft handler who ran out to it as it stopped. After the recovery the ramp would be raised to form part of the flight deck again. Another proposal was a system of wires to pull aircraft onto side lifts which would strike them down into the hangar rapidly. The least unlikely idea was to split the deck with a nylon barrier; as aircraft slithered

The problem with the 'rubber' deck and undercarriage-less aircraft is shown clearly here. Once the aircraft had come to rest, it had to be hauled onto the trolley in the foreground by a cable attached to a winch. To make matters worse, the trolley had no brakes, which made it difficult for handlers to manoeuvre. In the time it took to clear this aircraft from the landing area as many as ten conventional fighters could have landed-on and taxied into Fly 1. (Author's collection)

to a halt a handler would attach a wire cable to the nose, the barrier would be lowered and the aircraft pulled quickly forward and the barrier raised in the style of conventional straight-deck operations. Once in Fly 1, the jumbled mass of aircraft on their bellies could be sorted out in slower time, lifted by crane on to trollies and re-spotted, but this would have taken a long time. The faster recovery time would have been achieved at the expense of a very slow re-spot that would still have degraded a carrier's ability to generate sorties.

The idea of separating launch and recovery decks was the best thing to emerge from this spate of design concepts. The idea of canting the landing deck to port of the ship's centreline so that so that aircraft could be pulled off it into Fly 2 led directly to the brilliantly simple idea of the angled deck. This was a period of innovative thought like none that had gone before it and bright ideas continued with the result that the rubber deck was not finally abandoned until 1954. Some major problems were never addressed, among them the need to have rubber 'mats' available at airfields throughout the world where carrier-borne aircraft might have to divert. Another was the problem of landing undercarriage-less aircraft with pylons fitted with unexpended weapons or drop tanks which could be damaged on landing as well as ripping up the rubber deck. NAD made a final proposal in 1952[12] in an attempt to revive the concept. This suggested designing aircraft with 'taxiing wheels' which could be lowered after landing to allow the aircraft to taxi or be moved without needing trollies. The design effort required for such a unique aircraft requirement and the weight and complexity of adding an undercarriage, complete with brakes, on which it could not land, was utterly impractical and was rejected by both the RN and USN and the rubber deck experiment was officially terminated in 1954. In the event, carriers with angled decks, better aircraft design and the rapid evolution of turbo-jet engines solved what had been perceived as the major problem of landing-on high performance aircraft. Although the rubber deck experiments seem bizarre in hindsight, they certainly show the extreme lengths to which the Admiralty was prepared to go in order take its fighters into the supersonic era.

Invention – The Angled Deck, Steam Catapult and Mirror Landing Aid

Jet aircraft with their higher landing speeds needed a longer pull-out once they had taken an arrester wire and space had to be left for both conventional and nylon barriers to protect aircraft parked in Fly 1. By 1951 the amount of parking space left was becoming significantly smaller, limiting the number of aircraft that could be parked after a single land-on and thus the size of the maximum deck-load strike that any given carrier could recover in a single operation. The newer and heavier aircraft in prospect would virtually eliminate the space available for Fly 1 and so, if the RN was not to be forced to return to the clear deck techniques of the 1920s, a solution had to be found. Lateral separation with landing and parking areas alongside each other was not possible on existing ships and would call for unacceptable beam dimensions in new designs. It was a serving naval officer who came up with the simple but elegant solution. Captain D R F Campbell DSC RN was serving as the Deputy Chief Naval Representative at the Ministry of Supply (MoS), in 1951 and he was inspired by some of the concept designs put forward during the rubber deck trials in which the landing area had been offset from the centreline to allow aircraft to be pulled clear once they had landed. Campbell worked with Lewis Boddington to put forward the very practical idea of radial separation. By rotating the axis of the landing deck by a few degrees off the centreline of the ship from a point in the centre of the round-down at the after extremity of the flight deck, several positive and attractive benefits were achieved. Even a slight angle brought the forward edge of the landing area to the edge of the flight deck at a point well aft of the bows, significantly lengthening the space available to bring aircraft to rest after they caught a wire. The area to starboard formed a larger and safer Fly 1 which could be used for parking aircraft after a land-on and the sum of the length of the two areas was greater than the length of the original flight deck. Even better, the angled deck gave pilots a clear deck with no barrier in front of them since aircraft parked in Fly 1 were parked to starboard of the wingtip safety line, clear of the line of flight. If his aircraft's arrester hook missed all the wires, the pilot simply opened the throttle and climbed away for a further circuit.

The Naval Air Department at the RAE used a model of an *Illustrious* class carrier in a water tank to demonstrate the advantages of the angled deck, known initially in the RN as the 'skew deck' and in the USN as the 'canted deck'. Model fighters have been used to show the space made available in the offset Fly 1 for parking, an aircraft taking an arrester wire and even one on a stick to show it turning downwind. (Author's collection)

The concept was demonstrated by photographing a model carrier with an angled deck floating in a tank and by flying trials on *Triumph*. An angled deck was painted into place with its centreline extending from the starboard quarter to a point on the port deck edge abreast the island, angled 8 degrees to port of the ship's centreline. In February 1952 examples of all RN aircraft in service and being developed took part in flying trials which involved approaches to *Triumph*'s angled deck which terminated in low overshoots ordered by the DLCO. No actual 'touch-and-go' roller landings were carried out because of concerns that the undercarriage might snag one of the arrester wires, which were still aligned with the axial deck, and might thus cause an accident by snagging a tyre[13] but the trials were very successful. No difficulties were experienced flying circuits to the angled deck, the new constant-power approach down a steeper glide slope proved easy and pilot confidence was greatly improved by the lack of a barrier ahead of the landing area. Concerns about potential snags with drift if the wind was not quite down the angled deck and with funnel smoke were found, in practice, to be of no consequence.

The USN was kept fully informed at every stage of the new development,[14] quickly appreciated its value and adopted it immediately. Trials similar to those in *Triumph* were carried out on to a deck painted onto an *Essex* class carrier in the spring of 1952 and in the summer, another *Essex* class ship, the USS *Antietam* (CV-36), was fitted with a full 10-degree angled deck and the arrester wires re-aligned to line up across the new landing area. The first-ever arrested landing on an angled deck was carried out by her captain, Captain S G Mitchell USN, flying a North American SNJ Harvard on 12 January 1953 and a series of trials with a variety of aircraft types followed. These included a visit to Portsmouth in the autumn and RN trials which included a large number of arrested landings by operational RN aircraft. DLCOs were embarked to give height corrections for aircraft on finals and the cut for piston-engined aircraft. Known initially as the 'skew deck' in the RN and the 'canted deck' in the USN, the simpler term 'angled deck' was soon adopted by both and the concept was adopted immediately. The only delay was caused by the significant amount of dockyard work needed to build the port-side sponson that supported the forward end of the new landing area and to re-align the arrester wires. Since its invention all carriers built or modified to operate fixed-wing aircraft in every navy have been fitted with angled decks.

The second important invention of this period was also the work of a man with wartime naval experience. Commander C C Mitchell RNVR had proposed the development of a slotted-cylinder catapult to the Admiralty in the 1930s but, with the minimal requirement to catapult the light naval aircraft of the time, the existing hydraulic catapults had been deemed adequate and the idea, although recognised as sound, was not progressed. With the greatly increased weight of naval aircraft in 1945 and the prospect of even heavier jet aircraft in the near future, however, the BH 5 hydraulic catapults to be fitted in *Eagle* and the 1943 light fleet carriers were recognised as being at the end of their development potential[15] and Mitchell resumed work on his more powerful catapult. He was able to hasten development when he found that the Germans had used a similar catapult to launch V-1 'flying-bombs' and he acquired components through the British Intelligence Operational Survey Team. The result was a prototype catapult in which rams were driven along parallel cylinders by steam pressure. A cradle linked the rams so that they ran along their cylinders together and provided the structure on which the towing shuttle was fixed. This ran along a slot at flight deck level, pulling the aircraft forward by means of a wire strop which was looped at either end onto hooks on the underside of aircraft.[16] Rubber seals ran along the tops of the cylinders which were forced open by devices on the leading edges of the cradle and resealed behind it to allow its passage without significant loss of steam pressure.[17] High pressure steam was provided from the ship's boilers and stored in large accumulators at up to 4000 psi.

The hydraulic catapult had used a short piston which activated miles of wire-rope reeving in pulleys which translated the piston stroke into movement of the shuttle. Maximum acceleration was reached after less than a third of the shuttle's travel and the wire pulleys were a constant source of unserviceability. The new slotted-cylinder, or steam, catapult, on the other hand, not only had a greater energy potential but accelerated more smoothly to reach a maximum at two-thirds of the shuttle's travel. The Admiralty immediately saw the potential of the design and awarded a development contract to the Scottish engineering firm of Brown Brothers and Co which Mitchell joined when he was demobilised from the RNVR. After extensive trials with a development catapult ashore, the prototype steam catapult, BXS1, was built into a new structure on the deck of the maintenance and repair carrier *Perseus* in Rosyth Dockyard during 1951. Sea trials were carried out first with wheeled trollies known as dead loads which could be accurately weighed, controlled and increased with varying amounts of water. Next came surplus aircraft with their outer wing panels removed. These were run up to full power and then launched without a pilot at increasing fuel weights. Although not expected to fly very far, some of them flew for surprising distances before they crashed into the sea to add more aircraft to the number of wrecks on the sea bed. Finally, manned operational aircraft were launched at their maximum take-off weight. The catapult structure covered the deck as far aft as the island and, since *Perseus* had never been fitted with arrester wires, aircraft had to fly ashore to land after being launched. The aircraft had to be craned on board every day from lighters off Rosyth Dockyard.

The whole series of trials were carried out in conditions of strict secrecy and proved to be completely successful. A total of 1560 catapult launches were made

The raised structure containing the prototype BXS-1 steam catapult on *Perseus* can be seen clearly in this overhead image. A Sea Hornet is positioned on the catapult with the strop attached to the shuttle and there is a second aft of the structure with its wings folded that has not yet been manned. The aircraft parked aft are a Sturgeon, Avenger and Sea Fury. A Sea Fury parked aft of the island is partially obscured by the mast. (Author's collection)

from *Perseus*, of which 1000 were dead loads and the remainder unmanned surplus aircraft, mainly Seafires and Sea Hornets, and the balance of manned operational aircraft including Sea Vampires.[18] As with the angled deck, the USN was kept fully informed and had observers on *Perseus* throughout the sea trials. The RN made the ship available for USN sea trials and she arrived in the USA in December 1951. A further 140 launches were carried out using USN dead loads and operational aircraft;[19] the data was found to correlate well with RN reports and the USN acquired the manufacturing rights for its own steam catapult production as part of the benefits of MDAP. Work began in the USA in April 1952; the first catapult was installed at NAS Patuxent River in December 1953 and the first launch from an operational carrier took place on 1 June 1954 when the USS *Hancock* launched a Grumman S2F-1 Tracker. Despite the Admiralty's enthusiasm, however, British industry was not capable of such rapid development and the first British steam catapults went to sea in *Ark Royal* in February 1955.

The third major problem in 1951 was the recovery of jet fighters at increasingly high speeds. A Sea Vampire made a series of downwind approaches to *Illustrious* during trials which confirmed that DLCOs, no matter how experienced, were unable to appreciate errors in height or line quickly enough to signal them in time for the pilot to make corrections. The new steeper approach with power on meant that the DLCO was not even required to order the cut and so there was nothing left for him to offer although there was no replacement system in prospect.[20] Once more the solution came from a serving naval officer, Commander H C N Goodhart RN, who was Captain Campbell's assistant at the MoS. He had an engineering background and had flown Hellcat fighters during the Second World War. His solution was to place a large mirror facing aft by the port deck edge with a source light 150ft aft of it to project its light into the mirror. By tilting the mirror back slightly, an ideal pre-determined but adjustable glide slope indication was shown to pilots on final approach with the reflected 'blob' of light, soon to be known universally as the 'meatball' or simply 'the ball', in between green datum bars of projected light on either side of the mirror. If the ball appeared exactly between the datum bars, the pilot's eye was exactly on the glide slope. If it appeared high he was high and if it appeared low he was low. Reaction-time lags were reduced to those of the pilot himself and potential misinterpretation of hand signals were eliminated. By adjusting the brilliance of the source lights, the pick-up range of the mirror could be increased or decreased. In practice two or more source lights were installed so that the failure of any one would not render the sight useless.

The equipment was known as the deck landing mirror sight (DLMS), and the Admiralty tasked RAE Farnborough with the production of prototypes for evaluation ashore and at sea as soon as possible. The first mirror was installed on

A pilot's-eye view of a real angled deck, in this case *Centaur*'s. The mirror landing aid is clearly visible to the left with a black wind break shielding it. The reflected 'meatball' is slightly higher than the six datum lights, three on either side of the mirror, indicating that the photographer, probably in a helicopter, is higher than the ideal fixed-wing glide-slope. Note all the aircraft parked neatly to starboard of the wingtip safety line. (Author's collection)

Illustrious in October 1952 and comprised a convex, polished steel sheet on wooden backing with reflective metal datum bars. Whilst crude, it showed promise and a more effective sight was designed by Mr D Lean of the RAE. This comprised an aluminium-faced mirror with aft-facing green lights as datum bars and it had a gyro stabilisation system to cancel out the effect of ship pitch. It was installed on *Indomitable* in June 1953 and sea trials were carried out with landings made by a variety of operational aircraft.[21] These were witnessed by RCN, USN and USMC observers and some of the landings were flown by American as well as British pilots. The exact point where the hook would hit the deck could be selected with considerable accuracy by adjusting the tilt of the mirror and the trial proved extremely successful. The sight solved the problem of giving pilots of aircraft with high approach speeds adequate glide slope information and also meant that the number of arrester wires could be reduced from an average of twelve in 1950 to just four with complete safety, thus reducing both the amount of installed flight deck machinery and the number of technical ratings needed to maintain it. The reduction in the number of wires meant that those fitted could be sited further forward, nearer the centre of pitch and further from the round down giving greater clearance for the tail hook in rough weather. The new angled deck and mirror sight together not only made deck landing safer, they made it easier. Within the space of two years, at a time of financial and manpower stringency, the RN had carried forward a revolution in carrier operating techniques that was of as great a significance to naval warfare as the design of the revolutionary battleship *Dreadnought* fifty years before. The new inventions were adopted by every carrier navy and are still the basis of most fixed-wing operations in 2015. *Dreadnought* had rendered all her predecessors obsolete but existing carrier hulls could be re-constructed to incorporate the new technology.

Royal Navy Aircraft in 1952

The Hawker Sea Hawk had made progress by 1952 and was undergoing intensive flying trials at RNAS Ford. It was powered by a single Rolls-Royce Nene centrifugal-flow jet engine and capable of 520 knots, clean, at low level. Its primary armament comprised four 20mm front-guns in the nose under the cockpit with 200 rounds per gun and 1000lb or 500lb bombs could be carried on underwing hardpoints. Alternatively up to four 3in rockets with 60lb warheads could be carried on rails under each wing. Drop tanks could be fitted to the underwing hardpoints to extend endurance to 3 hours 50 minutes at economical speed. It was expected to be the last sub-sonic, straight-wing day fighter in naval service and the first two squadrons were to be available to replace Attackers by mid-1953.[22] Subsequently one Sea Hawk squadron was expected to be formed every three months until a total of nine operational units were in service.

The aircraft selected to replace the Sea Hawk was the Supermarine N-113D.[23] Treasury sanction was given for the MoS to procure 100 fighters to meet Specification N113 in 1952; the first was expected to fly in 1954 and the first squadron to be formed in 1956. The N113 was a swept-wing, twin-turbojet engined development of the Supermarine Type 508 and was intended to intercept enemy bombers at viable ranges when launched from a deck alert. To achieve this, its outstanding feature was to be an exceptional rate of climb in the region of 20,000ft per minute up to an operational ceiling of 49,000ft. Armament was to include two 30mm Aden cannon in the nose and, eventually, air-to-air missiles.

In the short term, the de Havilland Sea Hornet NF 21 was to be replaced in the night and all-weather fighter role by the de Havilland Sea Venom, a developed version of the Venom night fighter in service with the RAF, and built to Specification N107. Powered by a single de Havilland Ghost jet engine, the first fifty were to be built to FAW 20 standard with AI Mark 10 radar and the first prototype, WK 376, flew in April 1951. Carrier trials were carried out in *Illustrious* in July 1951 but entry into service, intended for 1953, was delayed by the discovery of weaknesses in the undercarriage and arrester hook mounting.[24] In the event the more highly developed FAW 21 was the first to embark operationally in 1955.

It was equipped with AN/APS-57 radar supplied by the USN under the MDAP and known as AI Mark 21 in RN service. The standard armament for both versions was four 20mm cannon in the nose and bombs and rockets could be carried under the wings.

In the longer term, the Admiralty had issued Specification NA38 for a more advanced two-seat, twin-engined all-weather fighter with transonic performance to the MoS in 1952 and this had been accepted and passed to de Havilland for tender action. The Admiralty had hoped that the requirement could be met by a development of the de Havilland DH 116, a comparatively small, high-performance aircraft with a single re-heated turbojet engine which was at the design study stage. By 1952, however, the Admiralty was advised by the MoS that the firm's design capacity was insufficient to cope with the work required to take the DH116 forward and it had been abandoned. As an alternative, the MoS recommended that the DH110 be considered[25] and an investigation into its possible application to meet NA38 was carried out in 1952. It proved to be a much larger aircraft, with a wingspan of 50ft against 42ft 10in and a maximum weight of 46,700lbs compared with 15,000lbs. It did, however, have the advantage that it could be stowed more densely in a hangar since, with its twin-boom layout, aircraft could be parked nose under tail. The DH110 was also expected to carry a substantial weapons load, making it suitable for the strike role. If adopted it was expected to be in service from 'about 1957' but, as with other aircraft, this was to prove optimistic since too few prototypes were procured and the firm lacked both design and testing capacity during a period of frantic activity.[26]

By 1952 the Gannet had been given 'super priority' status and 210 were on order for the RN. It was described as a 'single package' anti-submarine aircraft, able to search for submarines over a wide area with ASV-19B radar and visually, localise a target with sono-buoys and attack with a homing torpedo or depth charges. Fears that the Gannet might prove too heavy to operate from escort carriers in any future conflict led to specification M123D for a light anti-submarine aircraft which could be produced easily and economically in quantity during an emergency and operate in rough weather from small, slow carriers. Short Brothers were awarded a contract to produce a simple aircraft of rugged construction which emerged as the Seamew. Very much in the tradition of the late-war Swordfish III that operated from MAC-Ships, it was expected to fly in 1953.

The Westland Wyvern S4, the first production version of the long-delayed strike fighter, was expected to equip an operational squadron in 1953. About the same weight as a DC-3 Dakota airliner, the Wyvern was a big aircraft and it had considerable problems with engines, propeller control units and the airframe which delayed it by years. Its Armstrong Siddeley Python turbo-prop engine was actually the third power unit to be tested in its airframe. It was expected to be able to carry a single Mark 17 torpedo, three 1000lb bombs or a variety of weapons under development when it came into service.

In the longer term, Specification NA39 called for a two-seat, twin-turbojet engined strike aircraft that was eventually to emerge as the Buccaneer. It was to incorporate all the lessons of Korean operations and carry a weapon load of 4000lbs over a radius of action of 500 miles from its parent carrier. Maximum speed at sea level was to be 'at least 580 knots' and it was to be capable of attacking at extremely low level under enemy radar coverage. Preliminary discussions with the MoS informed the Admiralty that production aircraft were unlikely to reach squadrons before 1959. Another new specification, NA43, was written for an anti-submarine helicopter of about 15,000lbs maximum weight, a considerable size for 1952. It was to be capable of carrying both dipping sonar, known at the time as asdic, and a homing weapon or the equivalent weight of depth charges. Preliminary discussions with the MoS indicated that the requirement could best be met by a version of the Bristol Type 173,[27] a prototype of which was flying in 1952. The Supermarine Sea Otter biplane amphibian was withdrawn from service by 1952 and replaced in carriers and naval air stations by a licence-built version of the Sikorsky S-51 helicopter known as the Westland Dragonfly.

Aircraft supplied by the USN under MDAP arrangements continued to fill an important place in the RN, both in reality and theory since it was believed that in the event of war with the Soviet Bloc the British aircraft industry would struggle to cope with orders for the RAF and the RN would have to rely heavily on Lend-Lease American aircraft as it had in the Second World War. For this reason British carrier specifications continued to require the ability to operate USN types but new aircraft such as the Douglas A-3 Skywarrior with a wingspan of 72ft 6in and a maximum weight of 82,000lbs were viewed with alarm. The RN expected to receive 100 Grumman TBM-3E Avengers in 1953 which were to replace Barracudas and Fireflies as a stop-gap until sufficient Gannets were available. They were to be modified for the anti-submarine role to British standards by Scottish Aviation at Prestwick.

Also in 1953, the RN expected to receive twenty-five Sikorsky HO4S-3 helicopters equipped with dipping sonar which it intended to use in trials to evaluate the short range anti-submarine role and twenty Hiller helicopters to be used for pilot training. The most important aircraft delivered under MDAP was the Douglas AD-4W Skyraider which equipped the re-formed 849 NAS in July 1952 in the airborne early warning role. Known as the Skyraider AEW 1 in British service, its AN/APS-20C radar could detect a destroyer-sized surface ship at about 120 miles and a four-engined bomber in flight at about 60 miles. About fifty of

A Skyraider AEW 1 of 849B NAS lined up on *Ark Royal*'s angled deck for a free take-off. Note the huge radome for the AN/APS-20 scanner between the main undercarriage legs.

these aircraft were to be supplied, some of which were to be used as spares. The RN operated these aircraft in a very different way from the way they were used in American service. In the USN the AD-4W flew with a single pilot and one or two technicians in the rear seats who were responsible for maintaining a data link that transmitted the radar picture back to the parent carrier where it was interpreted. They could not interpret or make use of the radar picture themselves but the pilot did have a small screen in the front cockpit. In the RN, the two rear seats were occupied by specialist observers, trained as fighter controllers and able to interpret the radar picture for both surface and air searches,[28] acting in effect as a flying operations room.

Air Weapons

Work on the 30mm Aden cannon at this time centred on producing a version with a higher muzzle velocity, expected to be in the region of 2500ft per second. As a back-up in case it failed the Hispano Type 825 which had a considerably higher muzzle velocity, was kept in development. Due to the high expenditure of bombs in the Korean conflict, there was a general shortage of bombs both in the FEF and in the UK. The run-down British bomb-manufacturing industry was concentrating in 1952 on the build-up of weapons for Bomber Command's new V-Force jet bombers and so a number of bombs had to be procured from US sources. Consequently a number of types not usually met in naval service had found their way into the supply chain and had to be modified locally to fit RN aircraft suspension points. Many of these bombs were of cast, as opposed to forged,

A Wyvern S 4 of 831 NAS tensioned ready for launch on *Eagle*'s starboard catapult. It is armed with sixteen 3in rockets on underwing rails. (Author's collection)

construction and were therefore unsuitable for use against armoured or hardened targets.[29]

Three new heads for the standard 3in rocket were under development in 1952; these included the Type D anti-submarine solid head with a straight underwater trajectory, the 60lb anti-tank hollow-charge head and a 60lb anti-tank squash head. A 36-round 2in rocket launcher was adopted as a joint requirement with the RAF; initially expected to be used on the Sea Hawk, it did not in fact come into service until the 1960s. Throughout the early 1950s work continued to meet a joint Naval/Air Staff requirement for an unguided air-to-ship strike weapon which was allocated the codename 'Red Angel'. It was a development of the earlier 'Uncle Tom' rocket, had an 11.5in diameter and a 500lb warhead; it was intended for use initially by the Wyvern and later, in developed form, on the NA 39. Difficulties were experienced with the fuze and the flip-out tail fins (it was carried on the aircraft in a tube with the fins retracted). Continuous development setbacks were encountered, not the least of which was the tendency of the missile to break up on entering the water. An assessment of Red Angel's hitting probability in 1956 decided that from the optimum intended range of 5000 yards it would require a very large number of rockets to be fired at a cruiser-sized target[30] to guarantee a hit and these would require an impractically large number of strike aircraft to carry them. Red Angel was, therefore, cancelled.

An even bigger anti-ship bomb was specified in another joint Naval/Air Staff requirement and developed under the codename 'Green Cheese'. This was to be a rocket-powered bomb weighing 3300lbs at launch with a 1700lb warhead. It was to home onto radar reflections from the target which had, therefore, to be illuminated by the attacking aircraft's radar throughout the missile's time of flight until impact. Unsurprisingly, extensive sea trials found that target illumination against a cruiser-sized target was badly degraded by the sea clutter generated in seas associated with winds of Beaufort Scale 7. It was anticipated that the weapon would be carried by naval aircraft such as the Gannet and NA 39 at heights up to 18,000ft and released at a slant range of 10,000 yards from the target. RAF 'V'-bombers were expected to use the weapon and release it from heights of 50,000ft to slant ranges of 20,000 yards.[31] Despite high hopes, this weapon was also cancelled in 1956 because of 'insufficient money and scientific effort to meet the requirement'. This left the RN with obsolescent 1000lb and 500lb bombs and 3in rockets as its principal conventional anti-ship weapons for the next two decades.

Air-to-air guided weapons were also the subject of a number of Naval/Air Staff requirements which called for both active radar-guided and passive infrared homing guided missiles. There were three radar-guided weapons, the earliest and simplest of which was the Fairey Fireflash, developed under the codename 'Blue Sky'. It was a visually sighted, radar beam-riding missile intended for use by day fighters in clear weather. The missile itself was unpowered but accelerated off the launch rail by booster rockets; when these burnt out and detached the weapon slowed rapidly and had, therefore, to be fired at close range. It rode down the beam of the gun-ranging radar Mark 2 which was fitted in the RAF Hunter and the RN Scimitar so the nose of the fighter had to remain pointed at the target throughout the engagement. It was always seen as back-up for more advanced projects and, although development was completed by a joint RN/RAF trials party at RAF Valley in 1956, Blue Sky was never taken into operational service and the project was terminated.

'Red Hawk' was to be a radar-guided missile intended for carriage on high-speed fighters at heights up to 65,000ft and speeds up to Mach 2 giving the greatest possible tactical freedom to the launching aircraft before and after it was fired. From the RN perspective it was intended to break up massed attacks on the fleet by shore-based Soviet bomber regiments. Weapon aiming was to operate on a radar line of sight allied to a blind prediction sighting system and was to be possible by day or night under all weather conditions. Since Red Hawk was technically complex it was appreciated that its development would take a long time and so an interim version, codenamed 'Red Dean' was requested for use by RN and RAF all-weather fighters. This, too, was to be a radar-guided weapon but it was both large and heavy. RN interest was centred on the development of a missile with a maximum weight of 1500lbs; two missiles and their associated guidance system were expected to be installed in a developed version of the DH 110. By 1956 the missile's designers,

Vickers, had actually increased rather than reduced the missile's weight and the Admiralty had, reluctantly, to withdraw from the joint project when it was appreciated that no naval aircraft in service or projected would be capable of carrying it.[32] The Admiralty began to examine the possibility of obtaining other, more suitable, missiles that would give fighters full tactical freedom and selected the USN AIM-9A Sidewinder infrared-homing air-to-air missile for use on the Scimitar in 1957.

The most successful of the British joint missile projects was the de Havilland Firestreak, developed under the codename 'Blue Jay'. A passive-infrared guided missile, it was intended for use in the DH 110 and P177 fighters as well as in a number of RAF aircraft projects. Its guidance system had the advantage that pilots could 'fire and forget' it and did not have to track the enemy aircraft after launch but the drawback was that its sensor had to lock onto the enemy's heat signature, effectively the jet exhaust, which meant that the missile had to be fired in a cone-shaped area astern of the target at ranges between three and five miles. It had an expanding-ring warhead which cut through the target like a chainsaw as the missile passed close by the target, detonated by a sensitive fuze positioned aft of the sensor in the nose. It did not have to hit the target but, if it did, the kinetic energy of the impact would destroy most aircraft. An operational standard Firestreak hit and destroyed a drone target when first fired in 1956 and operational missiles went to sea with 893 NAS in *Victorious* during 1958. Firestreak entered service with a variety of training rounds; these including inert rounds for training magazine and weapons supply route handling parties and a practice acquisition round known as a PQR. This was a new concept intended to train aircrew in air-to-air acquisition and target tracking and it comprised the live sensor fitted into an inert missile with no motor or warhead which could be fitted to aircraft repeatedly. Apart from feeding information into the aircraft's systems, it also fed a recorder which could be used shortly after every air combat training sortie by air warfare instructors (AWI) to debrief aircrew.

Work continued on two 18in air-dropped anti-submarine homing torpedoes throughout the early 1950s. The larger of the two was the 2000lb 'Pentane' which had a speed of 30 knots and a theoretical maximum range of 6000 yards. It was intended to have a minimum detection range of 1000 yards irrespective of target noise or speed and a maximum depth of 1000ft. Development was slow and the weapon was eventually overtaken by the procurement of lighter, more effective USN torpedoes which led to Pentane's cancellation. 'Dealer B', the lighter weapon, proved more successful and was introduced into service as the Mark 30 in 1954 for use in the Gannet AS 1 and, eventually, the Whirlwind HAS 7 helicopter. It was an electrically-powered, passive acoustic homing torpedo with a length of 8ft 6in and a range of 6000 yards at 12.5 knots. Weight was only 670lb with the air tail and parachute units, intended to keep the weapon stable after release from the aircraft before it hit the water, fitted making it considerably more practical than Pentane, it had a maximum diving depth of 800ft and could be released from aircraft flying at over 300ft at speeds up to 300 knots.

On entering the water the flight in air material detached and the Mark 30 sank to a depth of 20ftbefore activating. It than set up a circular search pattern a depth of 30ft until detecting the sound of a submarine. Trials indicated a homing radius of 600 yards against an 'S' class submarine moving at 5 knots but the exact radius depended on the radiated noise caused by target speed.[33] When a sufficiently strong signal was detected the weapon automatically increased speed to 19.5 knots.[34] To avoid a stern chase developing, a small 'cone of silence' was built into the acoustic sensor in the centre of the torpedo's nose; this established a 'lead angle' whilst maintaining contact and caused the weapon to aim slightly ahead of the target until the last seconds. As a passive weapon, it also had the advantage that it could not be detected until it was in the water and actually homing on its intended target. Depth charges and rockets remained the weapons of choice for use against surfaced or snorting submarines.

The development of mines continued for some years after the Second World War and by 1954 a number of different new types were in service. These included the A Mark 12 which had 'boxed assemblies' which allowed the firing system to be changed on board a carrier, doing away with the need to embark specialised mines for individual operations. The A Mark 10 was a moored mine intended for use against minesweepers and was to be interspersed with ground mines.

Avionics

As weapons and their tactical use became more complicated in the mid-1950s, aircraft systems also became more expensive and complicated. The gyro rocket bomb sight and naval strike sight intended for use on the Wyvern and NA 39 for use with Red Angel and Green Cheese were given high priority in 1952 but eventually cancelled with those projects. Work on radar ranging for the gyro gun sight continued and was fitted in the Scimitar from 1957. Work started in 1954 on a pilot attack sight intended to give a complete blind firing/visual display allied to varying types of radar for the firing of air-to-air weapons including guided weapons. A new high-frequency radio set, ARI 18032, was introduced in 1954 with gapless cover out to 160 miles specifically for use in the Gannet. Late in the 1950s military aircraft changed from VHF to UHF short-range communications in common with the rest of NATO and a British version of the American AN/ARC 52 radio set was adopted for use.

A Gannet AS 4 of 814 NAS on anti-submarine patrol with its ASV-19B radar dome lowered. The type's large bomb bay can be seen forward of the radome. (Author's collection)

Radars were available in a considerable variety by 1954, some of the air-intercept types having been designed for the RRE at Pershore with no specific aircraft type in mind. Those of interest to the Naval Staff included ASV-19B which was fitted to the Gannet AS 1 and ASV-21, an improved version intended for use in the Gannet AS 4 from 1958. The latter had a 150 KW transmitter and a 9in ground-stabilised display on which sono-buoy beacons could be displayed. It was also intended as the target indication radar for the Green Cheese stand-off bomb. It was an 'X' band equipment with all round coverage capable of detecting a submarine snort at 12 miles in a calm sea state. AN/APS-20A was the American-designed search radar originally fitted to the Skyraider AEW 1. These sets were being upgraded to AN/APS-20C standard which was capable of detecting a destroyer-sized surface contact at 120 miles. A more powerful derivative, the AN/APS-20E was being procured to equip the future AEW aircraft which emerged as the Gannet AEW 3.

Air-intercept radars included AI Mark 10, a basic set that equipped the Sea Venom FAW 20; it was unstabilised but gave a satisfactory performance. AI Mark 17 was developed as insurance in case insufficient USN AN/APS-57 sets were provided under MDAP to equip the Sea Venom FAW 21. It was an 'S' band set with blind firing facilities and was chosen to equip the Sea Venom FAW 53 for the RAN. AI Mark 18 was a more advanced set under development under a joint Naval/Air Staff requirement; its naval application was to be in the DH 110. Progress was divided into two distinct phases, the first for the basic radar with blind fire facilities which was not taken into service and a second with addition of attack and missile firing computers which did, eventually, go into service with the Sea Vixen after 1958.

AI Mark 20 was a speculative set intended to allow single-seat fighters to carry out day and night interceptions at high altitude in clear weather. By 1954 it was realised that visual detection ranges from the cockpits of high-speed fighters at altitude were insufficient to give pilots time to get into a firing position and radar guidance for what had previously been considered as purely visual interception techniques was considered essential. AI-20 was required to be simple enough for a pilot to use without assistance from a specialised observer and was intended to complement radar interceptions when the direction officer initiated the turn onto the enemy's 6 o'clock position. The Naval Staff planned to use it in later versions of the Scimitar but, in the event, their development was cancelled in 1957.

AI Mark 21 was the UK designation allocated to the American AN/APS-57 air-intercept radar which was, itself, a simplified version of the AN/APQ-35 radar-guided fire-control system. AI 21 lacked target lock-on and blind fire capability but was an improvement over the AI 10 and was fitted to the Sea Venom FAW 21. Another speculative design was AI Mark 23 which was capable of the blind fire control of guns and missiles by the pilot in single-seat fighters. It eventually found an application in the RAF Lightning but was considered for use in developed versions of the Scimitar. Even more speculative was an investigation into the use of infrared sensors for air-intercept purposes. These were seen in the mid-1950s as having less utility than radar but did have the advantages that the necessary 'black boxes' would weigh considerably less, take up less volume and require scanners measured in inches rather than feet. These systems were all the result of joint naval and air staff requirements but there was one area where experience led the staffs to specify different equipment, the identification of friend from foe. The majority of aircraft were fitted with the AN/APX-6 transponder which was compatible with the IFF Mark 10 system fitted in HM Ships but the naval staff wanted fighters to be fitted with an air-to-air identification system, FIS-3, which was a simple cross-band equipment working with IFF-10 including simple coding. It would allow AI-fitted fighters to identify appropriate radar contacts as friendly and be of considerable value for fleet air defence work. The air staff and USN favoured 'Black Maria', FIS-4, and additional equipment had to be designed into naval aircraft to make the two systems compatible.

Flying Clothing

The rapid development of high-flying, transonic fighters in the early 1950s led to urgent joint Naval and Air Staff requirements for specialised flying clothing to replace the old, accepted equipment. These included a pressure-breathing suit to keep pilots conscious in the event of a cockpit pressurisation failure above 48,000ft. It would allow them to descend rapidly to a safe altitude and recover the aircraft to the carrier. Anti-G suits had been used during the Second World War but now found a wider application to allow fighter pilots maximum G-tolerance while manoeuvring at low level. They would eventually become universal in the form of over-trousers inflated by air pressure as 'G forces' increased, preventing blood from being forced into the lower body away from the brain. Individuals varied but anti-G suits could make a difference of 2 or 3 G before blacking out when flying to the aircraft's limits. Immersion suits intended to keep aircrew warm after ditching had become standard during Korean operations, as had the need for a cover on the new lightweight dinghy to prevent survivors from hypothermia while they waited for rescue. The rescue itself was to be assisted by a new personal radio beacon equipment known as TALBE, an acronym for tactical aircrew locator beacon equipment. This was carried in the life-saving waistcoat and, when activated, sent out a continuous wave signal on which searching aircraft could home.

Ejection seats were accepted as vital for all strike and fighter aircraft, including the Wyvern, because manual bail-out was found to be difficult, if not impossible, at high speeds and high altitudes. Early Martin-Baker models required aircrew to separate manually from the seat once it was clear of the aircraft but a new Mark 2 variant was produced from 1954 to meet a joint naval and air staff requirement for automatic separation after ejection. It had a minimum safe height at which the seat could be used of 100ft provided the aircraft had a forward speed of over 90 knots and the canopy was automatically blown clear when the pilot pulled the handle. The development of successive, improved ejection seats has continued to this day and gives aircrew the confidence to fly their aircraft to the limit in combat. Martin-Baker proved to be a world leader in the technology and its products are standardised in the RN, USN and RAF as well as many other air arms throughout the world in 2015.

The most obvious new element in the modernised range of flying clothing was the Mark 1 protective helmet. Increasing aircraft speeds in the late 1940s and early 1950s had led to accidents in which many aircrew had suffered head injuries because the familiar leather flying helmet offered no protection; effectively it was a comfortable way of holding earphones, goggles and the oxygen mask in place and little else. The new assembly, which was also adopted by the RAF, comprised an inner cloth helmet containing the earphones and attachment points for the oxygen mask or the throat microphone worn by helicopter aircrew. Over this there was a leather-lined, hard plastic helmet to protect the head against impact. Initially this was fitted with attachments for goggles but these were soon replaced by a visor on a ratchet which could be pulled down to a position just above the oxygen mask to protect the eyes against wind blast on ejecting. Usefully, tinted visors could be used to protect against the sun's glare. The Admiralty's intention was to make the wearing of protective helmets obligatory from 1955 and, despite some initial misgivings about the loss of the familiar leather-helmeted image, the change was popular with aircrew.

Rebuilt Ships

At the end of the Second World War the Admiralty's attention had been focused on new carrier designs intended to operate the new generation of aircraft. The cancellation of the *Malta* class and long delays anticipated before the surviving ships of the *Audacious* and *Hermes* class could be completed meant that the 'legacy' carriers of the *Illustrious* class would have to be extensively modernised to be of any value if they were retained in service. In the short term the *Colossus* class light fleet carriers with their greater hangar height and modern facilities were capable of operating the last generation of piston-engined fighters more efficiently economically than the fleet carriers and they continued to do so throughout the Korean conflict. All six ships of the *Illustrious* group had survived the war but some of them bore the scars of considerable damage and extensive worldwide service.[35]

Indomitable and *Implacable* were the only fleet carriers to embark operational air groups in the immediate post-war years, both having undergone limited refits to improve their capabilities. The single-hangar ships had hangars only 16ft high; *Indomitable*'s upper hangar was only 14ft high and the smaller lower hangar only 16ft. In the last two ships both hangars were only 14ft high. The first four ships could operate aircraft weighing up to 14,000lbs; the last pair aircraft up to 20,000lbs. Aircraft fuel stowage was totally inadequate to support jet operations and the small lifts of the earlier ships, intended to minimise intrusions that would weaken the armoured flight deck, were a significant limitation. Newer carriers had all been designed to operate aircraft weighing up to 30,000lbs with hangar heights of 17ft 6in and these criteria were accepted as the minimum to which the old fleet carriers should be rebuilt. The question of closed or open hangar design had been an issue that had delayed the design of the *Malta* class but by 1947 the naval staff accepted that the closed option represented the better design philosophy. The decision was influenced by the USN shift to closed designs after experience with typhoons in the Pacific during 1945 and the conclusions drawn from the Bikini Atoll atomic bomb tests in 1946 which clearly demonstrated that aircraft needed to be protected from the blast effect of a distant atomic explosion.

A committee under the chairmanship of Rear Admiral G N Oliver, ACNS (Air), considered reconstruction issues and came firmly to the conclusion that only a full modernisation could be justified since this would give the ships a further twenty years of operational life which would keep them effective 'into the mid-1960s for about half the cost of a new carrier' for each ship. It was hoped that all six ships could be rebuilt in the order *Formidable, Victorious, Indomitable, Illustrious, Implacable* and *Indefatigable*, but the committee noted that some had a considerable number of unrectified defects that would complicate their reconstruction. In 1947 the committee recommended the initial full reconstruction of *Formidable* and *Victorious* to the Admiralty Board, describing the end result as resembling 'a fast, armoured, *Hermes* type' capable of operating forty-eight aircraft. Board approval was given in January 1948 after Treasury sanction which concurred with the presumption that the modification of existing ships represented better value for money than new construction in the short term. Detailed work on the design, which would have to involve dismantling the hull down to hangar deck level and building a 'new' ship on top of the old lower hull, began in February 1948 and was not completed until June 1950. By then both ships had been surveyed and it had been found that *Formidable* had a distorted flight deck, propeller shaft defects and a

Victorious shortly after the completion of her modernisation in 1958. A Skyraider is lined up on the angled deck for a free take-off and Sea Venoms are parked close to the island and in Fly 4 to port of the angled deck right aft. Sea Venoms were small and much easier to park than their larger replacements. (Author's collection)

considerable amount of internal structure that had been damaged by Kamikaze hits and fire in 1945 but only hastily repaired or painted over. Since March 1947 she had been left in un-maintained reserve and her hull was found to have deteriorated significantly as a consequence. In 1950, therefore, it was decided to modernise *Victorious* first. She had been running as a training ship until recently and her hull was found to be in far better shape.[36]

There were good reasons why ships from the early group of the *Illustrious* class were chosen first. Apart from the fact that that they were the oldest ships, there were three of them and design drawings for reconstruction would, therefore, apply to several hulls. Similarly the last group comprised two ships, making them a more a more attractive prospect; drawings for *Indomitable* would only have applied to the one hull. The impact of the new carrier technology on *Victorious*' reconstruction also had a considerable impact and the design had to be re-cast several times to incorporate steam catapults, a fully-angled deck, mirror landing aids and the large Type 984 three-dimensional radar and its associated comprehensive display system. *Eagle*, *Ark Royal* and three of the 1943 light fleet carriers, *Albion*, *Bulwark* and *Centaur*, were all completed to interim standards which meant that by 1956 *Victorious* had to be completed since she was the only ship designed to take all the new equipment in its optimal form. She was too important to cancel but her reconstruction took eight years and cost more than a new ship would have done. No other ships of her class were rebuilt although *Eagle* was modernised since she was too large and valuable a hull to discard and the 1943 light fleet carrier *Hermes* was rebuilt on the slipway to a design similar to *Victorious*. Plans to modernise the remaining 1943 light fleet carriers to a standard similar to *Hermes* were discarded after the defence review in 1957, although by then *Centaur* had been fitted with steam catapults. Her two sisters, *Albion* and *Bulwark*, were modified into commando helicopter carriers and both were to give valuable service in the 1960s.

5 'Cold War', NATO and the Middle East

The years after 1945 saw the RN matched against a new threat as the relationship between the Western Powers and the Soviet Union deteriorated. Its ability to react to that threat was constrained by limited funds, the post-war manpower crisis and the need to develop and absorb new and emerging technologies.[1] There were many analysts who believed that the atomic bombs dropped on Hiroshima and Nagasaki in 1945 had rendered all conventional forces, especially navies, obsolete and that the concentration of ships into task forces or convoys merely provided more suitable targets for atomic weapons dropped from land-based bombers. In reality, however, the early atomic bombs were not available in large numbers.[2] Numbers were so limited, in fact, that if war had broken out before 1952, the newly-formed USAF Strategic Air Command (SAC), planned to use the few atomic bombs that it did have in an opening shock attack against the Soviet Union to be followed by a conventional bombing campaign using the weapons and tactics of the Second World War. The supply of weapons-grade uranium took a considerable time to build up and for this reason the USAF strongly opposed USN plans for nuclear-powered submarines because the provision of material for their fuel would slow the rate at which bombs could be manufactured.

The Cold War

Early in 1948 the Communist takeover in Czechoslovakia stimulated a sense of imminent crisis in the West[3] which was heightened in June when Soviet forces tried to cut off the Allied sectors of occupied Berlin which lay many miles to the east of what had already been referred to by Churchill as the 'Iron Curtain'. The subsequent Berlin Air Lift by Allied transport aircraft carried food and fuel into West Berlin for over a year before a negotiated settlement ended the immediate crisis. The British Cabinet's Defence Committee held a series of urgent meetings throughout 1948 to consider the national response. They decided that the economic reconstruction of the nation must come first but that the UK must be sufficiently strong at sea and in the air to act as a deterrent to a hot war and to provide a foundation for fighting the Cold War at a political level. The North Atlantic Treaty

Organisation (NATO), was formed in the same year to counter the possible threat of a conventional attack on Western Europe by the Soviet Union. Significantly this was the first time that the world's two largest navies, the USN and RN, had joined a peacetime alliance to act together against a potential aggressor and the alliance was named after the ocean that linked the member states together. The chiefs of staff were asked for their views but the recently-appointed Minister of Defence A V Alexander, who had been the wartime First Lord of the Admiralty, put forward his own less expensive proposals for the size of the fleet that was to be retained in commission and these were the ones accepted by the Cabinet. His decision not to retain battleships in commission led to the scrapping of some famous old ships including *Nelson*, *Renown* and *Queen Elizabeth* and the gradual reduction of the *King George V* class to reserve after a spell in the Home Fleet Training Squadron.

Throughout the Cold War, Allied intelligence agencies had a tendency to over-estimate Soviet capability but, despite this, the view was taken in 1948 that the danger of an all-out war in the next five years was small. By 1957, however, the Soviet Union was expected to have created a greatly increased arsenal of nuclear weapons together with the means to deliver them. By then the threat of war was expected to be grave and British re-armament with weapons reflecting new technologies would be needed. Since some years would elapse before the period of maximum danger, government policy tended to concentrate on the longer-term development of weapons systems that were believed to offer the most effective means of fighting a major conflict after 1957. In the short term, the armed forces in general, including the RN strike fleet, were to make do with adequate aircraft and ships procured in minimal numbers and to 'skip a generation' of development. If, by miscalculation or design, war was forced on Britain before then, the nation would have to fight with such forces and weapons as it possessed.[4] The Government's top defence priority at this time was stated to be the creation of a medium bomber force equipped with nuclear weapons as quickly as possible; second priority was the reconstruction of the RN with powerful air and anti-submarine elements to oppose Soviet surface warships and submarines in the North Atlantic.

A war against the Soviet Bloc in the late 1940s or early 1950s would almost certainly have seen nuclear weapons used from the outset but they were neither powerful enough nor numerous enough to win the conflict outright. They would, instead, have changed the way in which a largely conventional war would have been fought and the period up to 1952 can be thought of as an initial phase of the Cold War. SAC calculated, probably very optimistically, that it would take it a minimum of six weeks for a bombing campaign to force the Soviet Union to halt a conventional attack against Western Europe and allow the Allies to dictate the terms for a ceasefire and subsequent peace settlement. Large conventional forces were still required to hold ground and buy time for the bomber offensive to gain momentum. Powerful navies were still required to fight convoys across the Atlantic with reinforcements, ammunition and food. In this phase the USA gradually built up its nuclear arsenal to the extent that such weapons could be used tactically as well as strategically. The Soviet Union had nowhere near the same number of nuclear weapons in 1952 and was deterred from making a conventional attack against NATO in Europe by the threat of 'massive' US nuclear retaliation. The first British atomic bomb was detonated in the frigate *Plym* near Monte Bello island off the remote north-west coast of Australia in 1952.

While nuclear weapons caught the popular imagination and would have changed the manner in which a largely conventional war would be fought, other new technologies had a greater short-term impact. These included fast submarines, jet fighters and guided weapons. Each of these, in their own way, rendered obsolete large numbers of warships that had successfully fought the recent war and required countermeasures that would be time-consuming and expensive to develop. All of the threats needed to be detected, intercepted and destroyed over large areas of ocean and carrier-borne aircraft were recognised as the most effective and economical method of achieving this aim, reinforcing the importance of naval aviation to the modernised RN. Of interest, it was soon appreciated that all three of these new threats were difficult to counter in the final stages of an attack on a task force or convoy and that they would more effectively countered 'at source' by destroying submarine bases and the airfields from which aircraft could attack the fleet. At the very least, fleet fighters would need to destroy aircraft carrying guided missiles before they reached a position from which they could detect the fleet and launch them.

Political Theories and a Series of Defence Studies

In the latter part of 1948 an Inter-Service working party was set up under the chairmanship of Edmund Harwood, a senior civil servant who had spent the war years in the Ministry of Food and was considered expert in the achievement of economy. The RN representative was Rear Admiral Charles Lambe, who had commanded the aircraft carrier *Illustrious* in the BPF and was to be a future First Sea Lord. The committee considered the role to be played by the armed forces in the years from 1950 to 1953 and took as its baseline the expenditure ceiling placed on the armed forces' budgets for that period by the Treasury, £700 million. At the time the UK was spending 10.8 per cent of its gross domestic product (GDP), on defence compared with about 3.8 per cent by the USA.[5] The report was submitted to the Minister of Defence in February 1949 and recommended that the UK must continue to meet its existing commitments and wage the Cold War effectively.

Beyond that it confirmed the existing priorities by recommending that some new weapons should be procured as limited insurance against the possibility of accidental war in the short term but maximum effort should be devoted to developing longer-term weapons against the more likely threat of war in 1957 or soon after. Harwood placed the greatest emphasis on the RN capability to defend sea communications to the UK, perhaps naturally given his wartime experience with food imports, and it was taken for granted there would be American support from the outset of a major war. The Review also recommended drastic reductions in the number of ships deployed outside the UK in the Far East, Middle East, Mediterranean and West Indies. This was seen as a risky policy by Alexander and the Chiefs of Staff, however, who argued that the withdrawal of support for Commonwealth countries would place them at risk from Communist influence. In July 1949, therefore, a further working party was established under the chairman-ship of Sir Harold Parker, Permanent Secretary at the Ministry of Defence.[6]

The result of this committee's deliberations was a recommendation that led to a scheme for a 'revised, restricted fleet' of adequate shape and size to meet the RN's wide-ranging tasks. It was accepted in turn by the Admiralty Board, Ministry of Defence and Cabinet in late 1949 and represented the status quo in 1950 when the Korean War broke out. *Eagle* and *Ark Royal* plus the four 1943 light fleet carriers were to be completed and it was hoped, optimistically, to have them in service by 1952. There was also to be a modest expansion in the size of the air groups available for embarkation in them. The decision, recommended by successive studies, to insure against short-term conflict led to production orders for some aircraft that had only been expected to fly in prototype form. These included the Supermarine Attacker, sixty-three of which were ordered to contract 6/Acft/2822/CB.7(b) on 29 October 1948.[7] Subsequent batches were ordered in small numbers but it is worth noting that the Admiralty's slow procurement of new aircraft types was not due, as some critics have claimed, to a lack of interest in aviation but rather to an attempt to keep pace with the strategy and cost ceiling required by the Ministry of Defence. The Sea Venom was ordered as a short-term priority to replace the obsolescent Sea Hornet in the night fighter role although interest remained in a longer-term 'definitive' night fighter.

The Korean War and the return of Churchill as Prime Minister led to a further study of British defence policy in 1952. The exercise began with a meeting of the Chiefs of Staff[8] at the Royal Naval College Greenwich in February 1952. Significant input was also made by Sir Ian Jacob, formerly the military assistant secretary to the War Cabinet during the Second World War, who had subsequently become Director General of the BBC. Churchill demanded[9] his appointment to the Ministry of Defence as chief staff officer. He was released by the BBC as the chiefs of staff produced their initial draft and, on reading through it, felt that it was too obviously an uneasy compromise between the Services, with the mark of three different authors. He asked for the chiefs and their secretary, Brigadier F W Ewbank, to produce a more coherent document that could be put before the Prime Minister. Discussion about a revised draft continued through the spring; Sir Pierson Dixon of the Foreign Office became involved and the first part of the revised paper was amended on his advice. The result was a document known as the Global Strategy Paper which set in context the Conservative government's defence policy until the next review which was planned for 1957.

The Paper contained three principal objectives, the first of which, 'to provide the forces required to protect our worldwide interests in the Cold War', was straight-forward and implied an emphasis on conventional peacekeeping and limited war forces. The second was also logical and required little argument: 'to build up with our allies in NATO forces of a strength and composition likely to provide a reliable deterrent against aggression'. It was the third that was most open to argument about interpretation although the stated objective 'to make reasonable preparations for a hot war should it break out' seemed straightforward enough. By then the first phase of the Cold War was ending as the USA had built up a sufficiently large stockpile of nuclear weapons to plan on using them for tactical, as well as strategic, strikes. The Soviet Union exploded its first atomic weapon in 1949, some years earlier than expected by the Western powers but it was still unlikely that a sufficient stockpile of nuclear weapons would be ready before 1957. In 1952 the USA exploded its first hydrogen bomb and work on similar weapons was being carried out in the UK and Soviet Union. At first these weapons were massive and only large bombers such as the B-36 or B-52 could carry them, but work to reduce their size continued as a matter of the highest priority.[10] The first US production H-bombs appeared in 1954 and SAC stockpiles increased steadily. The Soviet Union surprised the West by detonating a prototype H-bomb in 1953 although this was a crude device and it took several years to produce operational bombs in quantity. The first British H-bomb was not detonated until 1958.

The period between 1952 and the later 1950s constituted a second phase of the Cold War in which Western governments calculated that the large stockpile of atomic bombs and the growing number of H-bombs were capable not just of inflicting major damage on the Soviet Union but of destroying it. At the same Soviet medium bombers and intermediate-range missiles were capable of destroying the UK and most of western Europe although few Soviet systems had the capability to reach the USA. A war between the West and the Soviet Union, therefore, was no longer seen as a nuclear exchange followed by a prolonged period of conventional warfare but came to be seen as a single, mass-destructive strike against the Soviet Union using the resources available at the outbreak of war whilst using such resources as there were left to counter the riposte. The term 'mutually-assured destruction' came into use and adequately described this concept. A war that would end in days, possibly even hours, meant that there would be no need for reinforcements or convoys to bring them across the Atlantic. The creation of the H-bomb led to renewed questions about the need for conventional weapons and the global strategy paper was already out of date. Rather than wait, the Government ordered a new review of UK defence which evolved into the radical review described in the next chapter.

The Royal Navy in 1954

While all this political argument was going on, the RN had emerged from the years of manpower crisis and was playing a major part in the British war effort in Korea. The dockyards were full of warships, although many of these were wartime hulls laid up in low-category reserve. Many more ships were retained in dispersed reserve bases at harbours and shipyards up and down the country. These would have been required in a prolonged war but there was no need for them in a short nuclear exchange. The following figures[11] give an idea of the size of the RN in February 1954 as the first phase of the Cold War ended:

Type	Active	Trials/Training	Reserve/Refit
Battleships	*Vanguard*		*Anson*
			Howe
			Duke of York
			King George V
Carriers	*Eagle*	*Illustrious*	*Victorious*
	Glory	*Indefatigable*	*Indomitable*
	Warrior	*Implacable*	*Ocean*
		Triumph	*Theseus*
		*Perseus**	*Centaur*
Cruisers	10	1	15
Destroyers	26	3	71
Frigates	33	21	115
Submarines	37	20	
Minesweepers	38	16	146

* Ferry/helicopter carrier

The number of ships operating on 'trials and training' duties demonstrates the Admiralty's success in keeping ships running with reduced complements so that they could be brought forward rapidly for operational service if needed in the danger period expected after 1957. *Triumph*, for instance, had replaced the cruiser *Devonshire* as the training ship for cadets from the Britannia Royal Naval College, Dartmouth. Extra accommodation, classrooms and a gunroom were built into the forward and central hangars but a flight of Boulton Paul Balliol trainers was embarked and struck down into the after hangar. Capable of both catapult launch and arrested landing, these aircraft were used to give air experience to cadets, an ideal arrangement in the new air age but one that proved too expensive to sustain and frigates took over the training task in 1956. *Implacable* and *Indefatigable* had been kept running in the Home Fleet Training Squadron to maintain them in satisfactory condition for modernisation but by 1954 it was recognised that work on the scale required was neither technically nor financially feasible with *Victorious* still some years from completion. *Ocean* and *Theseus*, both far cheaper to run, were modified for service as training ships. Several light fleet carriers were being completed for the RAN and RCN but *Hercules*[12] and *Leviathan*[13] were laid up incomplete.

Soviet Threats to be Countered

The Cold War threats that the RN had to face came in all three elements; *Sverdlov* class cruisers on the surface, medium bombers of the Soviet Naval Air Force including the Tupolev Tu-16 'Badger' in the air and 'W' class submarines below the surface. The *Sverdlov* class cruisers were designed with noticeable influence from captured German technology and Allied intelligence was aware that large numbers were under construction with the first vessels launched in 1950.[14] Eventually seventeen were launched but only fourteen were completed for active service. They were armed with twelve 5.9in guns in four triple turrets, twelve 3.9in guns in six twin turrets, thirty-two 37mm anti-aircraft guns and ten 21in torpedo tubes in two quintuple mountings. They had mine-rails on the quarterdeck as a standard fitting and were reputedly able to carry up to 250 mines although what other weapons would have to be sacrificed when the full load was carried was never clearly understood in the West. Powerful machinery of 130,000shp gave a maximum speed of 34 knots and they had a complement of just over 1000. These were clearly powerful ships but little was known about them until 1953 when *Sverdlov* attended the Coronation Review at Spithead and one of her sister-ships visited Sweden.

Given the recent wartime experience of the German attack on shipping, the Admiralty had to assume that these vessels were intended, if a 'shooting war' broke out, to sever the Atlantic link between America and the UK by attacking convoys. The RN could not hope to retain enough cruisers in service to seek them out and engage them individually and so the threat posed by the growing number of new Soviet cruisers gave added impetus to the requirement for a new generation of carrier-borne aircraft to find them and attack them from long ranges. The new surface-search capability offered by the Skyraider AEW 1 was obviously critically important and impetus was added to the development of the NA-39 strike aircraft.

Whilst Wyverns could attack with conventional bombs and rockets, it would take a large number of them to score sufficient hits to neutralise a *Sverdlov*. Airborne torpedoes remained an option but closing in to 1000 yards when opposed by radar-laid medium-calibre gunfire appeared to be an increasingly suicidal method of attack. The need to sink or badly damage a 19,000-ton cruiser with the minimum number of attack aircraft meant that they had to be equipped with the most accurate weapons delivery system available. The NA-39 specification required the aircraft to use its search radar to provide data for an accurate toss-bombing technique that would allow bombs to be released beyond the maximum effective range of the target's anti-aircraft guns.[15] As the potential for the UK to produce a relatively small, tactical nuclear bomb became apparent in the mid-1950s, the resulting Red Beard weapon was added to the specification. Using the standard toss-bombing technique, a single Red Beard could destroy or severely incapacitate an enemy cruiser even if it missed by several hundred yards.

The Admiralty was also concerned that some protection would need to be given to naval task forces that did not include an aircraft carrier. This is why *Vanguard* was retained in commission and some of the *King George V* class retained at reasonably short notice into the early 1950s, to provide heavy, radar-laid gunfire far beyond the range of a *Sverdlov*. The wartime cruisers also had some value as escorts and as flagships on the various naval stations around the world. Both battleships and cruisers were expensive to run, however, and their numbers declined rapidly through the 1950s as re-equipment programmes had to be funded. The Soviet Navy also retained battleships into the early 1950s. Two dated from 1914 and the third was the former Italian *Giulio Cesare*, ceded to the Soviet Union under the terms of the Italian peace treaty in 1949. None of them were regarded as mechanically reliable by Western intelligence agencies. Over 100 new 'Kotlin' and *Skoriy* class destroyers were being completed in this period, giving the Soviet Union a considerable sea-going fleet which was numerically larger than the Royal Navy but much less capable in terms of striking power. The US Navy remained pre-eminent in terms of both size and it ability to strike targets at sea and on land.

German U-boats with high underwater speed went into service too late in the Second World War to affect the Battle of the Atlantic but their technology was acquired by the Soviet Navy and applied to a new generation of submarines. From 1950 'W' class submarines were being built in a number of yards across the Soviet Union; by the late 1950s more than 170 were in service. They were known to be supplemented by an improved 'Z' class with twenty in service by 1960. Again the Allies looked back to the threat posed by German U-boats and assumed that the Soviet Union planned to use this large force for an attack on Allied shipping. With the wisdom of hindsight it is now believed that, together with the *Sverdlov* class cruisers, the 'W' class submarines were intended more to protect the homeland against attack by the Allied carrier strike and amphibious forces that had so impressed the Soviet leadership in 1945 than to launch an attack on Western trade. Stalin had presumed that with nuclear weapons and such powerful, mobile forces at their disposal, Western leaders must be considering a pre-emptive attack on the Soviet Union before it recovered from the Second World War. Whatever their true purpose, the huge submarine-building programme produced boats that could have severed Europe's 'lifeline' across the Atlantic in the event of open hostilities if they were not effectively countered.

The 'W' class had a dived displacement of 1180 tons and were armed with six 21in torpedo tubes.[16] They had German-designed diesel engines and electric motors that gave a surface speed of 17 knots and a dived speed of 15 knots for short bursts. All of them were fitted with 'snort' (snorkel) masts that allowed them to run their diesels at periscope depth, either to charge their batteries or to achieve higher underwater speed than could be sustained on the electric motors alone. It was the high dived speed that worried the Admiralty since it created relatively broad limiting lines of submerged approach, inside which boats would be able to get into an attacking position on a convoy. The best anti-submarine vessels of the Second World War were the RN 'Loch' class but these ships had a maximum speed of only 18.5 knots and would be hard-pressed to get into an attacking position on a 'W' class boat, even with their ahead-throwing anti-submarine mortars. It is easy to see why the Type 15 and 16 destroyer conversions were given such high priority since they gave dedicated anti-submarine warfare vessels with a speed in excess of 30 knots. By the mid-1950s the new Type 12 anti-submarine frigates with their advanced sensors and weapons were given a high production priority despite the expense of their construction.

The Tupolev TU-16, codenamed 'Badger' by NATO,[17] was used by both the Soviet Air Force and Navy. The Navy used the 'Badger B' variant which could carry up to 20,000lbs of free-falling weapons in an internal bomb bay over a radius of action of about 1000 miles. Of greater concern, it could also be armed with two KS-1 Komet air-to-surface missiles known to NATO as the AS-1 'Kennel'. These were carried on pylons under the outboard wings and were effectively small swept-wing aeroplanes using MiG-15 technology, powered by a small turbojet engine and armed with a 1000lb warhead. They can be thought of as early cruise missiles. The parent aircraft would fly at high level, up to 38,000ft, and search for target ships with radar. Once a target was located, the 'Badger' would home on it and launch one or both 'Kennels' at it at the weapon's maximum range of 50nm. Initially the 'Kennel' would fly on the bearing of launch using an inertial navigation system. Its own radar searched ahead and once it had locked onto a radar echo it controlled the terminal attack phase until impact. The system was relatively crude in that neither the 'Badger' nor its missiles could positively identify a target; if they were hoping to hit a high-value unit within a task force they could only choose the largest radar echo and hope. To compensate for this shortcoming, Soviet Naval Air Force units practised attacks in regimental streams of twelve aircraft, all of which attacked on roughly the same bearing and fired their missiles together in salvoes intended to saturate the defences. 'Badgers' did not enter large-scale service until the second half of the 1950s and were one of the major reasons for developing the improved generation of fighters intended for service from 1957. The Sea Hawk/Sea Venom generation had only a marginal excess of speed over the 'Badger' and would have been hard-pressed to intercept them before weapon release. They would have been capable of engaging the missiles after launch but in the congested battle space of a regimental attack, success could not have been guaranteed without a large number of fighters. The 'Badger' itself had a maximum speed of 540 knots at low level, Mach 0.75 at 38,000ft and a maximum all-up weight of 170,000lbs.[18]

Task forces and convoy defences would have had the advantage of defence in depth in the open sea. Incoming bombers would have been detected first by airborne early warning aircraft, then by the long-range air-warning radars fitted in carriers and other large warships. First to engage would be the fighters vectored from their CAP stations who would try to break up or destroy the bomber stream; after missile launch warships would attempt to jam their radars or deceive them with chaff and then open fire with medium and then short-range guns inside 7000 yards. Ships fitted with Mark 6 directors and ammunition with variable-time (VT) fuzes would stand a good chance of shooting down the early subsonic missiles which flew on a steady course and speed; older ships with wartime HACS directors would not have been effective and there was no money to upgrade the hundreds of destroyers and frigates laid up in reserve with more modern systems. In the mid-1950s Western intelligence agencies believed that the Soviet Union was developing several larger bombers capable of long-range open-ocean surveillance. One of these emerged as the Tupolev TU-20 'Bear', a large bomber which was unusual in having swept wings and four turbo-prop engines. It had a wingspan of 163ft, a maximum all-up weight of 370,000lbs and a radius of action of about 3000 miles.[19] The 'D' variant was developed for the Soviet Navy in the early 1960s and is still in service more than sixty years later.

NATO Exercises

I do not intend to describe every exercise or every British aircraft carrier's participation in them but the following examples give a good idea of RN strike fleet operations in support of NATO during this period.

Exercise 'Castanets' in June 1952 involved the warships and aircraft of nine member nations and covered a large area of the North Atlantic. *Indomitable* served as flagship of Rear Admiral Caspar John CB, Flag Officer Heavy Squadron, Home Fleet.[20] She had 820 and 826 (Firefly AS 6s) and 809 (Sea Hornet NF21s) NAS embarked plus the first RN Westland Dragonfly HAR 1 detachment to act as a ship's SAR Flight. She was joined by HMCS *Magnificent* with 871 (Sea Fury FB 11s) and 881 (Avenger TBM-3s) NAS embarked and between them the two ships formed a carrier task group. The emphasis in this group was anti-submarine and night fighter operations in defence of a convoy. The two carriers sustained operations around the clock, aided by the short summer nights but the weather was often unpleasant and favoured the enemy. The convoy phase was followed by a simulated offensive against a known submarine transit area. Sono-buoys were deployed effectively and co-operation with surface ships in accordance with the new NATO doctrine resulted in several 'attacks' on submarines that were assessed as 'kills' by the exercise umpires. This phase reflected well on the aircrew of *Indomitable* since they had only one opportunity to practice against a live submarine before the exercise. 'Castanets' also involved command and control, live firing and tactical phases in which Captain W J W Woods DSO* RN of *Indomitable* strove to get his whole ship's company involved. He was pleased to note in his ROP that the first submarine sighting of the exercise was made by Boy Signalman Wilmhouse who had only been on board for two weeks. The starboard forward 4.5in battery earned a high reputation by shooting down a towed drogue target off Portland with their first salvo during the live weapon training period.

Eagle, fresh from sea trials, working up exercises and deck landing trials with new types of aircraft took part in 'Castanets' as a strike carrier with 800 and 803 (Attacker FB 1s), 827 (Firebrand TF 5s) and 814 (Firefly AS 6s) NAS embarked. Successful strikes were flown against a number of targets and, as the largest carrier ever built for the RN at the time, she attracted a number of visitors who wanted to see the ship in operation. The most significant 'bag' on a single day included the First Lord of the Admiralty, the Secretary of State for Air, the Minister of Supply and the Flag Officer Air (Home).

Exercise 'Mainbrace' in September 1952 was the largest peacetime naval exercise ever held and the fact that it was held so soon after 'Castanets' underlines NATO concern that a high degree of readiness needed to be demonstrated to counter a potential Soviet attack on Western Europe. Overall command was exercised by Admiral McCormick USN, Supreme Allied Commander Atlantic. The RN task force was under the command of Admiral Sir George Creasy CB CBE DSO MVO, Commander-in-Chief Home Fleet and Commander, NATO Forces North-East Atlantic, who flew his flag in the battleship *Vanguard*. USN ships included the aircraft carriers *Franklin D Roosevelt*, *Wasp* and *Wright* and the battleship *Wisconsin*.

By then *Eagle* had replaced *Indomitable* as flagship of the Home Fleet's Heavy Squadron. She was not yet considered fully worked-up but embarked the same air group with the addition of 812 (Firefly AS 6s) and two aircraft from 849 (Skyraider AEW 1s) NAS. Bad weather curtailed some of the planned sorties but valuable lessons were learned that helped to bring the ship's company to full operational efficiency. The exercise was intended to demonstrate the ability of the NATO nations to work together seamlessly and was split into two phases. The first involved escorting a convoy of reinforcements across the Atlantic from west to east, followed by a second in which 1500 US Marines were landed on the Jutland peninsula to reassure the Scandinavian countries that they were not being ignored by NATO and that they could be defended against aggression. This phase ended with the strike fleet providing maximum effort to support NATO land forces in Norway and Denmark in the worst of the weather. The exercise was considered to be a success and demonstrated that the strike fleet could not only neutralise the 'enemy' surface fleet and submarines but also continue to provide realistic air support for forces ashore when land bases were closed by weather or simulated enemy air attacks. The post-exercise critique, or 'wash-up' as such meetings are commonly known, was held in *Eagle*'s upper hangar in Oslo and was honoured by the presence of His Majesty King Haakon of Norway[21] and Crown Prince Olav. Also present were General Matthew B Ridgeway USA, who had replaced General Eisenhower as Supreme Allied Commander Europe (SACEUR), in May 1952 and Admiral Sir Patrick Brind, Commander-in-Chief Allied Forces Northern Europe. Two hundred officers from eight nations attended the wash-up and the fact that *Eagle* was chosen as the venue shows how the maritime dimension was central to early NATO thinking. Sea-based forces could concentrate anywhere on the European littoral to counter aggression and the major investment by the Soviet Union in counter-maritime strategy shows respect for this capability. Regrettably it was not as well understood by Western politicians, especially those in the UK who took sea control for granted without realising that it had to be gained and maintained.

Theseus, a light fleet carrier recently returned from Korean operations, joined another carrier task force during 'Mainbrace', operating with HMCS *Magnificent* and the escort carrier USS *Mindoro*. *Theseus* had 804 (Sea Fury FB 11s), 820 and 826 (Firefly AS 6s) NAS embarked[22] and *Magnificent* had the same air group she had operated in 'Castanets'. In the first phase of the exercise this task force escorted a convoy to Bergen from Rosyth. A submarine attack carried out inside May Island was disallowed by umpires as it was outside the designated exercise area but there were a number of air attacks from 'enemy' shore bases. Flying continued despite

A storm range on *Eagle*'s flight deck during the Home Fleet spring cruise in 1953. The aircraft are Firefly AS 6s of 814 NAS and a single Skyraider of 849A NAS. Note that the cockpit covers of the forward two Fireflies have been blown off and the cockpit canopy of the left-hand aircraft has blown open, allowing considerable amounts of salt water to get in and ruin equipment. (Author's collection)

bad weather and produced several submarine contacts. In the second phase, the task force escorted the amphibious force to Denmark and covered their landings. *Magnificent*'s Avengers were awarded a submarine 'kill' at night which underscored their high state of training. When *Theseus* disembarked 804 NAS at the end of the exercise, her flight deck team showed their efficiency by catapulting nine Sea Furies with an average interval of 36.2 seconds between them, an RN record. The value of running carriers in non-operational roles with reduced ship's companies that could be brought back into full operation in an emergency was demonstrated by *Illustrious*, the trials and training carrier. On 30 August 1952 she embarked the Royal Netherlands Navy's 860 (Sea Fury FB 11) NAS for 'Mainbrace'. They were joined by 824 (Firefly AS 6) NAS on 3 September. HMS *Triumph*, the deck landing training carrier, also took part with Firefly FR 4s of 767 NAS embarked.

Other RN Carrier Activity in this Period

The early 1950s saw Anglo-Egyptian relations deteriorate and one of the sources of friction was the large British garrison maintained in Egypt to defend the Suez Canal Zone. The British Army had been deployed in Egypt since the nineteenth

826 NAS Avengers over HMCS *Magnificent* during exercises with the Canadian Atlantic Fleet. (Author's collection)

century and had undoubtedly been a stabilising factor in Middle East politics. Despite defending Egypt against the Turks in the First World War and the Germans and Italians in the second, growing Arab nationalism during this period made the British position less tenable. In 1947 British forces were withdrawn from Cairo and other regional centres into the Canal Zone itself and a year later British forces left Palestine when the new state of Israel was created.[23] However, most of the oil used by Britain came from the Middle East and passed through the Suez Canal and so the British continued to regard the defence of the canal as being of critical importance; its disruption or closure would mean tankers having to travel by the long sea route around Africa. Fervent nationalists in Egypt saw the defeat of its army by Israel in 1949 and the continued occupation of the Canal Zone by the British as equal humiliations. In October 1951 the Egyptian Government unilaterally abrogated the 1936 Anglo-Egyptian Treaty which formed the basis of the British presence[24] and a period of violent protest began in the British-occupied areas. The canal was owned by a joint Anglo-French company and the cruiser *Gambia* was sent to Port Said to protect British interests and other warships secured the southern end. A system of patrols by boats and landing craft along the canal was instituted and the Chiefs of Staff formulated a contingency plan for military intervention in Egypt if the situation got out of hand, codenamed 'Rodeo'. It involved two phases; the first involved moving troops from the Canal Zone into Cairo and the second deploying troops from Cyprus into Alexandria. Both were intended to protect British lives and interests. In January 1952 British forces were involved in an incident with the Egyptian Police in Ismailia and riots broke out in Cairo. 'Rodeo' was ordered to come to 48 hours' notice but, faced with the reality of the situation, the Chiefs of Staff were advised by senior officers on the spot that the Egyptian armed forces would resist, leaving foreign civilians to the mercy of armed mobs in places where they could not be reached and, potentially, there was the prospect of attacks the canal itself by Egyptian armed forces. The scope of 'Rodeo' was, therefore, reduced to an armed evacuation of British and Commonwealth citizens.

In July 1952 King Farouk was overthrown by a military coup and his infant son Ahmed Fuad was named King although real power lay with a Military Council under General Neguib. In June 1953 Neguib deposed the young king and declared himself president of a new Egyptian Republic. In 1954 Egypt and the UK signed an agreement that British troops would leave the Canal Zone by June 1956, although Britain retained the use of its large supply depot at Ismailia to support action in the event of external aggression against Turkey or the Arab League unless that aggression came from Israel. The depot was to be run by civilians with no uniformed presence. Neguib himself was deposed in November 1954 by a new military council led by Colonel Gamal Abdel Nasser who assumed presidential powers although he did not actually become president until 23 June 1956 after an election in which voting was compulsory but he was the only candidate.[25] The Suez Crisis of 1956 will be described in a later chapter.

British aircraft carriers were involved in a number of differing roles as the situation in the Middle East unfolded during this period. In June 1951 *Warrior* and *Triumph* ferried the Army's 16 Parachute Brigade and much of its equipment from the UK to Cyprus.[26] In November 1951 *Illustrious* and *Triumph* ferried the British 3rd Infantry Division and much of its equipment from Portsmouth to Cyprus as part of a build-up of capability in the region. In January 1952, during the fighting in Ismailia, *Ocean* was held in the eastern Mediterranean with 802 (Sea Fury FB 11s) and 825 (Firefly FR 5s) NAS embarked as part of a Mediterranean Fleet task force which also included the cruisers *Glasgow* and *Euryalus* to prepare for the defence and evacuation of British nationals if it became necessary. When the situation eased she passed through the Suez Canal to join the FEF and replace *Glory* for operations in the Korean War zone. HMS *Glory* demonstrated how interlocked strike fleet operations had become when she returned to the Mediterranean after *Ocean* relieved her. In July she was operating in the eastern Mediterranean with 807 and 898 (Sea Fury FB 11s) and 810 (Firefly FR 5s) NAS embarked. She was in Istanbul with HMCS *Magnificent* on an official visit when the crisis over King Farouk's departure broke and she sailed at short notice to join a concentration off Cyprus intended to cope with any eventuality. The crisis eased and in October she sailed for the Far East to relieve *Ocean*. The British Government considered the presence of an aircraft carrier in the Mediterranean Fleet to be critically important and several ships were deployed on the station. *Indomitable* detached from the Home Fleet to the Mediterranean in January 1953 with 804 (Sea Fury FB 11s), 820 and 826 (Firefly AS 6s) NAS embarked. Unfortunately on 3 February 1953 an explosion destroyed the aircraft oxygen generation plant, killing eight men and wounding many more. Since she was near the end of her projected operational life, no repairs were carried out and the compartment was filled with concrete. After returning to the UK she took part in the Coronation Review at Spithead and then paid off into low-category reserve at Rosyth. *Theseus* re-commissioned after a post-Korean refit in January 1952 and alternated between the Home and Mediterranean Fleets until October 1954 when she was modified to relieve *Implacable* as flagship of the Home Fleet Training Squadron. She was in the eastern Mediterranean in September 1953 when Cyprus suffered an earthquake and formed part of the RN task force assembled off the island to give support to the civilian population.

Although the Middle East featured strongly in the news bulletins of this period, carriers also played a significant part in RN operations all over the world. In

Perseus in use as a ferry carrier in 1952, seen being loaded in Southampton with cocooned Sea Furies for the FEF on deck together with an array of trucks, buses and even private cars. A Whirlwind HAR 21 of 848 NAS is landing on the clear space aft. The ship ferried the unit to RNAS Sembawang in Singapore for operations in Malaya. (Author's collection)

October 1953 *Implacable* carried a battalion of the Argyle & Sutherland Highlanders in a high-speed transit from Devonport to Trinidad as part of a British reinforcement of the region following unrest in British Guyana. In March 1954 *Triumph* was ordered to Algiers in support of the destroyer *Saintes* which was standing by the burning British troopship *Empire Windrush*. A month later, in April, *Eagle*, escorted by *Daring*, searched for wreckage from a de Havilland Comet airliner which had gone missing during a flight from Rome to Cairo. Several bodies were found and recovered. In July 1954 the ferry carrier *Perseus* carried relief supplies for Korean children from Singapore Naval Base. In August 1954 *Warrior* was serving in the FEF with 811 (Sea Fury FB 11s) and 825 (Firefly AS 5s) NAS embarked and had relieved HMAS *Sydney* on operations off Korea to monitor the ceasefire. On 25 August she was tasked to evacuate refugees from North to South Vietnam following a request to the British Government from the Prime Minister of Vietnam. Hong Kong Dockyard fitted bunk beds and extra heads and washing facilities into the hangar and she sailed for Vietnam on 31 August 1954. The evacuation began on 4 September and by 13 September she had evacuated 3000 civilian refugees. Three babies were born at sea with the help of the ship's medical staff. She returned to Hong Kong Dockyard for the removal of the extra accommodation arrangements and then sailed for the UK. In October 1954 *Warrior* was awarded a Special Unit Citation by the President of Vietnam for her humanitarian work. In October 1954 the new light fleet carrier *Centaur*, which had recently joined the Mediterranean Fleet, withdrew the last British troops from Trieste where a small occupation force had been maintained since the end of the Second World War. She was the first British carrier to be fitted with an interim angled deck, fitted shortly after her completion and she operated a transitional air group comprising 806 (Sea Hawk FB 3s), 810 (Sea Fury FB 11s) and 820 (Avenger AS 4s) NAS. Early in 1955 she carried out combined exercises with the US Sixth Fleet, reinforcing the close links forged between the two navies in the Pacific in 1945 and in Korea. By then the RN had adopted the USN system of signals for its batsmen as part of a standardised system which was used across NATO in British, American, Canadian, French and Dutch carriers. The same system was adopted by the Royal Australian Navy.

Naval air squadrons themselves continued to demonstrate versatility, underlining the fact that they could work perfectly well when disembarked to a shore base. In 1955 the British command in Cyprus began Operation 'Apollo' which was intended to prevent ships from smuggling arms onto the island for EOKA terrorists who were engaged in an insurrection against British rule. 847 (Gannet AS 1s) NAS was commissioned specifically to carry out daily patrols from Nicosia in support of warships operating off the coast, a task which continued until 1959 when the unit

In August 1954 *Warrior* was tasked to evacuate refugees from North to South Vietnam following a request to the British Government by the Prime Minister of South Vietnam. This is the scene in her hangar in early September as she evacuated 3000 refugees. Her air group was disembarked but note the spare Firefly main planes and propellers still secured to the bulkheads. (Author's collection)

flew back to the UK to disband. In October 1952 the RN re-commissioned 848 NAS at RNAS Gosport with ten Sikorsky Whirlwind HAS 21 helicopters provided by the USN under MDAP, to become the first operational helicopter unit in the RN. With their sonars removed and troop seats fitted, the squadron deployed to RNAS Sembawang, Singapore in *Perseus* and worked up as the first 'commando' squadron. It was employed on support operations for the security forces fighting the communist insurrection in Malaya. 848 NAS moved to an advanced base near Kuala Lumpur in February 1953[27] and brought unprecedented mobility to military units operating in the jungle, for which the unit was awarded the Boyd Trophy for 1953. Operations continued until 848 NAS was de-commissioned in December 1956. In February 1953 there was severe flooding on the east coast of the UK and in Holland. RN helicopters deployed to both locations and were used extensively on humanitarian relief operations; the first time that helicopters were used for this sort of task. The commanding officer of 705 (Dragonfly HAR 1s) NAS at RNAS Gosport was subsequently awarded the MBE for leading the operations and co-ordinating the work of a number of helicopters operating from widely-spaced forward operating locations.

Operational and Administrative Control of Naval Aviation

The Admiralty was not just a government department responsible for the administration of the Navy. Until 1964 it was the operational centre from which orders and instructions were given to the various fleet commanders. A civilian politician known as the First Lord was head of the department but by the early 1950s he had ceased to be a cabinet member. All matters of national policy and budget had, therefore, to be referred to the Minister of Defence for ultimate approval, if necessary at Cabinet level. The operational and professional head of the Royal Navy was the First Sea Lord (1SL) and Chief of the Naval Staff, responsible for directing the Commanders-in-Chief of the three major fleets and various Commands and Stations at home and overseas to implement agreed Government policy. The Admiralty Board member responsible for naval aviation matters was the Fifth Sea Lord (5SL), also known as the Deputy Chief of the Naval Staff, with additional responsibility for the development of tactics and operational capability across the fleet. Under 5SL there were various Admiralty departments responsible for naval air matters. These included the Directorate of Naval Air Warfare (DNAW), and the Directorate of Naval Air Organisation and Training (DAOT), both headed by senior captains, RN. A third captain, the Adviser on Aircraft Accidents (AAA), was responsible directly to 5SL on all matters of flight safety in the 1950s but this task was eventually absorbed into DNAW. The design and development of aircraft carriers, like all warships, was the responsibility of the Third Sea Lord (3SL), also known by the historic title of Controller. As with every other Branch in the RN, naval air personnel were the responsibility of the Second Sea Lord (2SL), and his Department. By the early 1950s the RN had been in full administrative and operational control of its air element for over a decade, had expanded it rapidly to fight a global war and contracted it in the subsequent demobilisation. The administrative and operational systems were well understood and worked effectively.

The procurement of new aircraft and weapons for all three Services was the responsibility of the MoS, and within that organisation the senior RN representative was known as the Vice-Controller (Air) and Chief Naval Representative MOS/Chief of Naval Air Equipment.[28] He took direction from both 5SL and the Controller and had responsibility for ensuring that the MOS fully understood naval staff requirements and acted on them effectively. He had three departments under him, the Directorate of Air Equipment and Naval Photography (DAE), the Directorate of Aircraft Maintenance and Repair (DAMR), and the Directorate of Naval Aircraft Development and Production MoS (DNDP). DAMR was headed by a Rear Admiral (E), the other two by captains, RN. When the MoS ceased to exist, this group of directorates became part of the naval staff under a rear admiral

Examples of the first generation of RN jets in formation, photographed from a Meteor T 7. Nearest the camera is a Sea Hawk, probably an F 1, then an Attacker FB 1, Sea Vampire F 20 and a Meteor T 7. (Author's collection)

with the title Director General Aircraft (Navy) (DGA(N)), retaining the same directorates.[29] In 1951 5SL was a vice admiral and the Vice Controller (Air) was a rear admiral.

Operational command of carrier strike forces came under the Commanders-in-Chief of the Home, Mediterranean and Far East Fleets in which they served, through their Flag Officers Second-in-Command. As carrier deployments came to be less rigid and the ships were no longer operated in formalised aircraft carrier squadrons, the post of Flag Officer Aircraft Carriers (FOAC), was introduced with worldwide responsibility. He administered all carriers in commission and took operational command of a task force, when necessary. He took over responsibility for working up ships and naval air squadrons to operational efficiency and for setting standards and practices to be achieved by all carriers and their embarked squadrons from the Flag Officer Air (Home). The Cs-in-C of the Home and Mediterranean Fleets in 1951 were admirals, that of the FEF, a vice admiral. FOAC could be a junior vice admiral or a senior rear admiral. The relevant fleet also directed the tasks of naval air stations within their areas. Carriers were not normally allocated to overseas stations such as the West Indies or South Atlantic but could be deployed for a specific operation under FOAC or the nearest FO2.

Day-to-day administrative control of naval carrier strike forces throughout the RN was the responsibility of the Flag Officer Air (Home), a vice admiral in 1951, who could give advice and support as necessary to overseas fleets and stations. He directed the work to be carried out by the trials carriers and oversaw an organisation split into three sub-commands, each run by a rear admiral. The first two were the Flag Officer Ground Training (FOGT), responsible for the naval air stations at which technical training of officers, artificers, air mechanics and naval airmen were carried out and the Flag Officer Flying Training (FOFT). The latter was responsible for all the air stations at which advanced and operational flying took place,[30] the output of aircrew from the training 'pipeline' to meet the needs of operational squadrons including, when necessary, the ability to surge numbers in order to form new squadrons quickly in an emergency. FOFT was also responsible for the tasking of the training carrier. The third sub-command was headed by a rear admiral (E) known as the Rear Admiral Reserve Aircraft (RARA), whose reserve aircraft organisation underpinned the worldwide operation of naval aircraft and covered a wide range of disparate tasks.[31] These included:

(a) The maintenance of a substantial reserve of aircraft and engines at varying degrees of readiness, both long and short-term, so that peacetime and emergency requirements could be met with the minimum of delay.

(b) Fulfilling the function of Air Equipment Authority including the provision of replacement aircraft for those damaged, lost or due for major overhaul; for re-arming existing naval air squadrons and for the formation of new squadrons.

(c) Administration of the repair of aircraft and engines using the factories of manufacturers and contractors, naval air yards and RN Mobile Repair Units.

(d) Bringing into service new aircraft types direct from the manufacturers, testing and equipping them for the roles in which they were required.

(e) Preparing aircraft and engines for shipment to overseas fleets and stations and receiving shipments from abroad.

(f) The maintenance of records covering all naval aircraft and engines throughout their life from receipt to disposal.

All this work was co-ordinated from RNAS Arbroath and involved AHUs at RN Air Stations Abbotsinch, Anthorn, Culham and Stretton together with civilian-manned RN Air Yards at Fleetlands, Donibristle and Belfast. Reserve aircraft were very different from the ships held in the inactive reserve fleet. All aircraft not actually allocated to a squadron were classified as reserve and this included brand new machines straight off the production line. The great majority were in a 'live' state although a proportion were 'embalmed' for long-term storage. Admiralty policy was to keep aircraft establishments small by flying a relatively small number of aircraft in the front line as intensively as possible. When anything more than a minor repair was required by an aircraft, it was withdrawn from the unit and replaced. The policy that flying units should concentrate on flying their aircraft gave RARA's sub-command the high pressure technical task of repairing, modifying, equipping and issuing aircraft to support the flying task. The maintenance of operational capability was achieved by providing the right replacements at the right time in the right place. The sub-command was required to maintain sufficient aircraft to meet the heavy demands of a national emergency and from that it naturally followed that normal peacetime requirements could be met.

Reserve aircraft were maintained in good condition by the 'throughput' process under which every aircraft, except those 'embalmed', was brought up to full operational standard and test flown at least once a year. Most aircraft were held in hangars in a preserved state that reduced deterioration. They were inspected weekly, monthly, quarterly, half-yearly and annually and any deterioration was immediately rectified. After a year in storage, aircraft were de-preserved, modifications and special technical instructions (STI), issued in the previous twelve months were embodied, the guns butt-tested and the compass swung. When all faults were corrected the aircraft was test flown by a fully-qualified maintenance test pilot, usually a lieutenant or lieutenant commander (E) (P). Any snags found in the air were rectified and further check flights carried out until the aircraft was signed off as being at operational standard. It was then considered available for issue to a user unit after which it was either despatched at once or held in a pool of serviceable aircraft which were inspected and test-flown weekly. About eighty aircraft underwent this process every month in 1952. Some aircraft were placed in long-term storage by 'embalming', a process similar to the 'cocooning' of gun mountings on warships in the reserve fleet. In this instance aircraft were completely sprayed to become encased in an impervious 'skin', inside which the air was kept dry by desiccants to prevent corrosion. The 'skin' was inspected and the desiccant renewed periodically to maintain the aircraft in good condition. Modification could be carried out but involved removal of a part of the 'skin' and re-embalming it, so modification and STI embodiment was usually held until the aircraft was brought forward and the complete 'skin' removed.

New aircraft were flown into an AHU by a ferry pilot without much of their Admiralty-supplied operational equipment. The latest modifications were also usually missing as the manufacturer could not hold up the production line to

A cocooned Sea Fury FB 11, VX 758, shortly after being delivered in Australia for the RAN. Note the dates when the aircraft was inhibited and then 'embalmed' written on the coating so that it could be removed at the due date at the latest. (RAN)

embody them. They were, therefore checked immediately to see that the contractor had supplied all the equipment for which he was responsible and then all the operational equipment required to meet the Admiralty Equipment Standard for that type was fitted (guns, radar etc). By then guns would have been butt-tested and the compass swung. A full functional test flight was carried out, after which the aircraft could be allotted to the serviceable pool. Once allotted to a squadron, aircraft remained with it until they became surplus to its establishment or it required reconditioning at the end of its planned hours-based 'life'. It would also have to be replaced if it suffered damage beyond the capacity of the squadron or a mobile repair unit to repair or if it became a total loss. Repairs were the responsibility of the repair organisation within the air yards. Replacement aircraft were provided to squadrons from the serviceable pool, those being brought forward from storage or from the receipt procedure. In 1950 the number of aircraft issued to squadrons from RARA's organisation totalled 859.

RARA's sub-command included the allotment control organisation to meet the demands of the Admiralty, FO Air (Home) and the Fleets. A total of 1900 aircraft and 1500 engines were allotted during 1950 and the despatch of aircraft, engines and equipment to foreign stations formed a significant part of the sub-commands work. In the UK aircraft were ferried from contractors to Receipt & Despatch

Units (RDU), at two of the AHUs; from RDUs to other AHUs if necessary and from them to operational and training naval air stations and repair yards. They were also ferried from air yards to AHUs. The work was carried out by a civilian contractor who employed sixteen pilots for the task and their movement about the country to pick up aircraft was facilitated by the use of two light transport aircraft lent by the Admiralty for the purpose. In an average year there were some 1500 ferry flights, all co-ordinated by a central ferry control office in RARA's headquarters. The civilian ferry pilots flew under naval regulations except those covering familiarisation on new types.

Aircraft that could not be flown were moved by one of three Naval Aircraft Transport & Salvage Units (NATSU). One of these was based at RNAS Abbotsinch, another at RNAS Worthy Down and a third, slightly smaller than the first two, at RNAS Eglinton in Northern Ireland. Their transport was the responsibility of civilian drivers but naval air mechanics dismantled aircraft and prepared them for movement. Salvaging crashed aircraft was a particularly specialised operation that often required considerable initiative since no two crash-sites were the same. The majority of aircraft for overseas shipment were embarked in the Glasgow area and there was some sensitivity caused by the berths needing to be used for commercial shipping. In one instance seventy-two aircraft were embarked in a carrier in 3 hours 30 minutes after close co-operation between drivers, handling and sling-fitting parties and the crane drivers. Disembarkation was usually carried out in Portsmouth, with aircraft being placed onto lighters. During 1950, the NATSUs moved 832 aircraft, 1823 aircraft engines and 1186 miscellaneous loads. They loaded 155 aircraft onto aircraft carriers and off-loaded 232 aircraft from them. NATSU vehicles travelled a total of 1,074,746 miles.

6 A Royal Occasion and the Radical Review

From the Admiralty's initial interest in constructing a prototype rigid airship in 1908 onwards, the integral part of the RN that operates aircraft has had to undergo a number of politically-inspired transformations and has had many different names.

The Importance of Identity

The handful of pioneer naval aviators at Barrow-in-Furness and Eastchurch had no separate title but on 13 April 1912[1] the government of the day centralised all British military flying activities into to the newly-created Royal Flying Corps (RFC), which comprised Naval and Military Wings together with a Central Flying School. The Military Wing was capable of operating on land to provide reconnaissance support for the BEF but the Naval Wing was not yet able to operate regularly from ships at sea and the development of specialised naval operations drew the Naval Wing away from its land-based counterpart. Its potential was demonstrated in the 1913 fleet manoeuvres and the closer integration of aircraft with fleet activities led to the Naval Wing being officially renamed as the Royal Naval Air Service (RNAS), in July 1914. By 1918 it led the world in the development of naval aviation and even fulfilled the original Naval Wing's commitment to support the RFC ashore when requested to do so. This was not taken into account, however, in 1918 when the Government inflicted another political change on the RN when it amalgamated the RNAS and RFC to form a 'unified' and 'independent' Royal Air Force (RAF).

Although it was only in existence for the last few weeks of the First World War, the RAF rapidly showed that it lacked interest in naval operations and its own political independence split naval operations[2] into disparate entities controlled by separate naval and air staffs. Initially the groups of aircraft, aircrew and mechanics embarked in aircraft carriers, battleships and cruisers were known as 'RAF Contingents in His Majesty's Ships'. This cumbersome title proved to be as unpopular as the initial RAF outlook that any pilot could fly any aircraft on land or from a ship. This proved not to be the case and naval aviation suffered from having to train a through-put of new pilots who then returned to shore-based duties as soon as they became proficient. The situation reached a crisis point in 1924 but the Government still refused to return the control of naval aviation to the Admiralty. Compromise was reached after discussions between Admiral Keyes and Air Chief Marshal Trenchard[3] in 1924. The Trenchard/Keyes Agreement, as it subsequently became known, resulted in a joint administration of naval aviation with the RN taking operational command of embarked units and the RAF retaining responsibility for shore administration and the procurement of new aircraft and engines. To provide greater continuity of personnel, 70 per cent of pilots, all observers, all telegraphist air gunners and all flight deck handling parties were to be provided by the RN and 30 per cent of pilots together with all maintenance personnel were to be provided by the RAF. To distinguish the new jointly-administered force from the earlier contingents, the Admiralty adopted the name Fleet Air Arm for it and it was known as such from 1924 onwards. Unfortunately, the term only applied to that part of naval aviation that embarked in ships; shore-based aircraft formed what came to be known as Coastal Command of the RAF, a title that revealed its limited scope. Whereas the RNAS had operated aircraft on naval duties from both ships and land bases, the advent of the RAF had split that structure in two. By 1937 it was so obvious that split control was not working that even politicians became aware of it and the Minister for Defence Co-ordination, Sir Thomas Inskip, an eminent QC,[4] was instructed to investigate the matter and make recommendations. He found that 'dual control' had been a failure that had caused the RN to lose its world leadership and observed that naval aircraft were not passengers in a convenient vessel but an essential part of a naval weapons system. He accepted the Admiralty's case that naval aircrew should have the same background and training as other naval officers and ratings and gave instructions[5] in July 1937 that the Fleet Air Arm was to be handed over to full RN control within two years.[6] With Air Ministry co-operation the hand-over was completed by May 1939 but, unfortunately, only applied to the Fleet Air Arm. Coastal Command remained a part of the RAF although from 1941 it came under Admiralty operational control to fight the Battle of the Atlantic more effectively.

Unsurprisingly, the Admiralty wanted to mark its recovery of the full control of embarked naval aviation with a changed identity to emphasise the fact that it was, once more, a fully-integrated part of the RN. It was re-named as the Air Branch of the Royal Navy[7] and the term Fleet Air Arm was officially dropped. A number of schemes were introduced to expand pilot numbers since there were insufficient general service officers available. These included short-service officers recruited for a fixed number of years who wore straight RN sleeve lace with an 'A' in the executive curl indicating that they were Air specialists who were not qualified for sea command. General service officers who were qualified for sea command had no 'A' in the curl but both wore their 'Wings' badge over the curl of the left sleeve lace. After September 1939 expediency led to the majority of wartime pilots being recruited as members of the RNVR who wore 'wavy' sleeve lace with an 'A' in the curl to indicate the Air Branch.[8] Early members of the RNVR Air Branch had been hastily trained but by 1945 many were decorated lieutenant commanders in command of naval air squadrons who knew more about air warfare than their longer-serving general service colleagues. Many transferred to the RN after the end of the war and the 'A' was dropped from the curl of the sleeve lace of all RN officers but retained by the RNVR. Both official and unofficial names continued in use throughout the Second World War, many of the older men referring to the organisation as the 'Fleet Air Arm' and the younger RNVR men referring to themselves as 'Branch Types'. The situation was resolved in the Coronation year, 1953, when the Admiralty Board decided to discontinue the name 'Air Branch' and re-title naval aviation as the 'Fleet Air Arm of the Royal Navy'. Signal 240805Z/May/53 certainly shows that this move was popular with the more senior officers and the name has continued into the present century in the RN and RAN.[9] Although popular, the term Fleet Air Arm is not widely understood by the British public in 2015 and I have often been asked whether I served in the Royal Navy or the Fleet Air Arm. I am not convinced that reversion to the older name was such a good idea as there is certainly less ambiguity in 'Air Branch of the RN'. There is no going back on the change, however, and Fleet Air Arm certainly has the merit of longevity even if the public are not sure what it is.

The Coronation Review of the Fleet

Reviews of the Fleet on important occasions had taken place in the anchorage at Spithead for centuries. The Review that took place on the eve of war in July 1914 had contained fifty-nine battleships although the pre-dreadnoughts were no longer capable of playing a viable part in the Grand Fleet which was ordered to its war base at Scapa Flow in the Orkney Islands by the First Lord of the Admiralty Winston Churchill after the event. HMS *Argus*, the world's first true aircraft carrier, took part in the 1924 Review and King George VI's Coronation Review in 1937 included five aircraft carriers. The Coronation Review assembled for Queen Elizabeth II on Monday 15 June 1953 included only one battleship, *Vanguard*, but there were nine aircraft carriers in Line 'F' with her.[10] The official souvenir programme[11] noted that this was a fleet devised to implement 'those many lessons that the last war taught, and designed to give effect to the modern weapons and aids that that the advance in scientific achievement has provided'. Critics noted that five of the carriers were non-operational and were soon to be withdrawn from

'Carrier Row', 'F' Line at the Coronation Review of the Fleet by Her Majesty Queen Elizabeth II on 15 June 1953 looking east to west. *Eagle* is nearest the camera and beyond her are *Indomitable, Implacable, Indefatigable, Illustrious, Theseus,* HMCS *Magnificent,* HMAS *Sydney* and *Perseus*. (Author's collection)

service but, to be fair, there were five new carriers under construction in British shipyards and *Victorious* was being reconstructed to the most advanced design. All previous Reviews had contained a mixture of the new and the old and this one was no exception.

As in the past, the RN Hydrographic Department had had planned the anchorage in considerable detail and every vessel was allocated a designated anchor position in the main Lines 'A' to 'M' with a number of smaller Lines for minor vessels. Care had to be taken that there was sufficient space for each ship to swing to its anchor with the tide and that there was sufficient water under every keel at low tide. Several of the ships came from the Reserve Fleet, including the cruisers

Dido and *Cleopatra*, three destroyers, three frigates and a submarine depot ship but since it was the function of the large reserve organisation at the time to keep a number of ships at short notice for mobilisation in the event of war, their inclusion was both practical and sensible. The vast array of ships included over 200 warships from the RN, RAN, RCN, RNZN, Royal Pakistan Navy and the Indian Navy plus numerous foreign ships including the USS *Baltimore*, the French *Montcalm*, the Soviet *Sverdlov* and the Swedish *Göta Lejon*. There were also ships representing the Royal Fleet Auxiliary, Trinity House, the Commissioners for Northern Lights, the Commissioners for Irish Lights, HM Customs, an ocean weather ship, the Merchant Navy, the Fishing Fleet and the Royal National Lifeboat Institution.

On the day of the Review, the Fleet dressed overall at 08.00 and Her Majesty Queen Elizabeth II used HMS *Surprise* as a temporary Royal Yacht.[12] She was normally employed as a Commander-in-Chief's despatch vessel on the Mediterranean Station but was refitted for Coronation duty with the removal of the twin 4in gun mounting in 'B' position and the substitution of an inspecting dais. During the morning Her Majesty the Queen and the Duke of Edinburgh received

In addition to her own ship's company, HMAS *Sydney* also carried the Australian and New Zealand Army and Air Force contingents to the Coronation in 1953. She is seen her with sailors, soldiers and airmen manning the deck appropriately *en route* to the UK. (Sea Power Centre – Australia)

the Board of Admiralty and senior flag officers on board *Surprise* and then held a luncheon party at 13.00. At 14.35 other members of the Royal Family, including HM The Queen Mother, embarked in *Surprise* and she sailed at 15.00. Preceded by the Trinity House vessel *Patricia* and escorted by the frigate *Redpole* which was acting as the Admiralty Yacht, *Surprise* made her way towards the lines of ships. As they approached the Review Fleet, a Royal Salute was fired and *Surprise* entered the Review Lines at 15.30. The Royal Yacht and Admiralty yacht were followed by *Starling* with the Board of Admiralty guests, *Fleetwood* with the C-in-C Portsmouth's guests and *Helmsdale* with the Lord Mayor of Portsmouth, the Mayor of Gosport and their guests. Government guests followed in the merchant ships *Orcades*, *Pretoria Castle* and *Strathnaver* and Admiralty staff in the motor vessels *Brading* and *Southsea*. A novel feature was the construction of grandstand seating on the flight deck of *Perseus* that allowed invited guests to view the day's whole spectacle. Once the Review of the lines of ships was complete, *Surprise* anchored at the head of 'E' Line at 17.10 and at 17.35 the Fly Past by naval aircraft began. The day was still not complete, however, and at 18.30 HM The Queen hosted a sherry party on *Surprise* followed at 20.30 by dinner on board *Vanguard* with the Fleet's commanding officers; a memorable occasion for those who were present. At 22.30 the Fleet was illuminated by lights and at 22.40 there was a firework display. The following morning, Tuesday 16 June 1952, *Surprise* returned to South Railway jetty in Portsmouth Dockyard and HM The Queen and the Duke of Edinburgh returned to London in the Royal Train.

From a strike fleet perspective, the ability to launch and control 300 naval aircraft, varying from helicopters to jet fighters, to arrive over the Royal Yacht on time to the second and in the correct order was one of the day's more memorable aspects. Like the surface fleet, the aircraft demonstrated a period of change with thirty-two squadrons of piston-engined aircraft which were approaching obsolescence, eight squadrons of the new jet fighters and representatives of the new helicopter types and the Gannet turbo-prop. The Fly Past was led by Rear Admiral W T Couchman OBE DSC in a Sea Vampire and seven of the forty naval air squadrons taking part were provided by the RNVR Air Branch, a reflection of both the organisation's numbers and its ability to generate aircraft when required. Squadrons were also provided by the RAN and RCN, disembarked from their carriers anchored in Line 'F'.

A total of 327 naval aircraft took part and it was realised early in the planning process that several naval air stations would have to be involved in the launching, control and recovery of so many aircraft which varied from helicopters to a variety of piston-engined types and jet fighters. They were, therefore, dispersed to four naval air stations. RNAS Ford took eight jet fighter squadrons, RNAS Gosport

Naval Air Squadrons in order of Fly Past with names of Commanding Officers

Admiral's Flight	Rear Admiral W T Couchman OBE DSC
705 NAS	Lieutenant Commander H R Spedding RN
781 NAS	Lieutenant Commander D L Stirling RN
771 NAS	Lieutenant Commander R Pridham-Wippell RN
796 NAS	Lieutenant Commander J S Barnes RN
750 NAS	Lieutenant Commander E F Pritchard RN
766B NAS	Lieutenant Commander D W Winterton RN
737 NAS	Lieutenant Commander J L W Thomson RN
719 NAS	Lieutenant Commander R A W Blake RN
812 NAS	Lieutenant Commander J M Culbertson RN
814 NAS	Lieutenant Commander S W Birse OBE DSC RN
817 NAS	Lieutenant Commander A L Oakley DFC RAN
820 NAS	Lieutenant Commander G C Hathway RN
824 NAS	Lieutenant Commander O G W Hutchinson RN
825 NAS	Lieutenant Commander R P Keogh RN
826 NAS	Lieutenant Commander J W Powell DSC RN
1830 NAS	A/Lieutenant Commander (A) R C Read RNVR
1840 NAS	A/Lieutenant Commander (A) A P D Simms RNVR
1841 NAS	Lieutenant Commander (A) K H Tickle RNVR
776A NAS	Lieutenant Commander M A Birrell DSC RN
1833 NAS	A/Lieutenant Commander (A) B W Vigrass RNVR
849 NAS	Lieutenant Commander J D Treacher RN
738 NAS	Lieutenant Commander H J Abraham RN
802 NAS	Lieutenant Commander D M Steer RN
804 NAS	Lieutenant Commander J R Routley RN
871 NAS	Lieutenant R Heath RCN
1831 NAS	A/Lieutenant Commander (A) W A Storey RNVR
1832 NAS	Lieutenant Commander (A) G R Willcocks DSC RNVR
1835 NAS	A/Lieutenant Commander (A) G M Rutherford MBE DSC RNVR
728 NAS	Lieutenant Commander P C S Bagley RN
809 NAS	Lieutenant Commander E M Frazer RN
815 NAS	Lieutenant Commander L P Dunne DSC RN
881 NAS	Lieutenant Commander W H I Atkinson DSC RN
Gannet Flight	
759 NAS	Lieutenant Commander D R O Price DFC RN
736 NAS	Lieutenant A R Rawbone AFC RN
800 NAS	Lieutenant Commander R W Kearsley RN
803 NAS	Lieutenant Commander J M Glaser DSC RN
806 NAS	Lieutenant Commander P C S Chilton RN
Prototype Fighter Flight	

took the helicopters and two piston-engined squadrons, RNAS Culham took seven piston-engined squadrons and RNAS Lee-on-Solent took the greatest share with twenty-three piston-engined squadrons. Lee-on-Solent, the headquarters of the Fleet Air Arm, had the most need for carefully considered organisation and its part is worth describing in more detail. Each squadron was briefed before leaving its home base with a time to arrive at Lee and both marshalling parties and refuelling

Aircraft ranged tightly on a runway at RNAS Lee-on-Solent ready to launch for the Coronation Review Fly Past. The aircraft in the foreground are Fireflies, the type that participated in the largest number. (Author's collection)

facilities were programmed around these. All the aircraft taking part were parked three abreast on runway 11/29, leaving room for refuelling bowsers to move between aircraft. A full dress rehearsal was carried out on Saturday 13 June and both during this and the real event on 15 June, radio discipline had to be carefully implemented. Only the leader of the first squadron called for taxi clearance, all subsequent units taxied in their turn after him. If any aircraft went unserviceable while taxi-ing, pilots were briefed to pull off the perimeter track onto the grass and handling parties were placed at strategic points to help them. If an aircraft became unserviceable at the marshalling point, pilots were briefed to give the runway controller a thumbs-down signal and then taxi down the runway as fast as possible, clearing it at the upwind end to avoid any interruption in the flow of aircraft taking off.[13] There was a continuous stream take-off with aircraft using alternate sides of the runway to avoid the slipstream of the aircraft ahead; once airborne they turned to starboard and proceeded to their briefed squadron form-up areas where they tucked into formation and joined the stream. If an aircraft became unserviceable after take-off, pilots were briefed to remain airborne if they could to land back at Lee after the stream take-off. If they could not stay airborne, pilots were briefed to land at RNAS Gosport or RAF Thorney Island depending on the degree of emergency, Gosport being nearer but smaller. After the Fly Past, a stream landing of each squadron in rotation was briefed with initial homing to nominated holding positions and heights. From these, the squadrons were called in to land according to a fixed order and squadrons had practiced recoveries with an interval of only 20 seconds between aircraft. So that there was no break in the process, three heights were allocated over the airfield; when called in squadrons first joined a high wait at 1500ft. When it was clear, they moved down to the low wait at 1000ft and then into the circuit at 500ft. As soon as it was clear to do so, they followed the squadron ahead to land. If any pilots missed their approach to land, they were briefed to fly a tight circuit to join up at the end of their squadron or to hold clear until called in to land after the main stream. The worst thing that could happen would be a crash during landing that would block the runway. If this happened, a second runway control van was positioned ready so that another runway could be used. Throughout the rehearsal and during the Review itself, a search and rescue helicopter was held at immediate notice at RNAS Gosport.

Each squadron was to fly eight aircraft in the Fly Past[14] so they flew off nine and the spare pilots were briefed to land back at Lee, or to return to their parent air stations if they had the endurance, after the stream take-off if they were not required. A civilian air traffic control officer was positioned at Lee to co-ordinate activities with the Southampton Control Zone and liaison worked very well. After the Review some squadrons flew directly to their parent air stations but the majority returned to land at Lee. There were twelve waiting positions, including the high and low waits and the circuit itself dispersed clockwise around the airfield. As squadrons landed, those behind them were ordered to advance position to the next wait. On the day of the Review the average interval between the 196 aircraft taking off from Lee-on-Solent was 11 seconds. The average interval between the 111 aircraft that landed afterwards was 17.4 seconds; better than the 20 seconds achieved in the rehearsal. The balance of eighty-five aircraft flew direct to their parent air stations once they were released. At RNAS Ford, sixty-seven jet aircraft were launched in less than five minutes and landed on after the Review in only nine minutes. All in all, the Coronation Review Fly Past on 15 June 1953 was an impressive achievement. The author of the souvenir brochure emphasised the completely naval nature of the Fly Past and stated on page 49 that 'they are all naval aircraft, flown and maintained entirely by naval officers, ratings and WRNS'.

The Review at Spithead was not the only RN flying event to mark the Coronation, however. HMS *Ocean* was asked to carry out a fly past near the front line in Korea on Coronation Day itself, 2 June 1953, by the British Naval Liaison Officer (BNLO), in Korea. There were some mixed feelings about the idea until it was learnt that the fly past was to be eight miles south of the lines in relatively safe air space. Conveniently, *Ocean* was due to finish her current war patrol on 30 May and planned to fly off fourteen Sea Furies of 807 NAS to RAAF Iwakuni for the task while she was on passage to Sasebo; these were all that could be spared from inter-patrol maintenance. Unfortunately fog prevented their disembarkation and she entered Sasebo on 31 May with the aircraft still on board. When the fog cleared on 1 June, *Ocean* launched thirteen Sea Furies using RATOG, while she was moored to a buoy; a fourteenth aircraft went unserviceable before launch. This was the first time that such a launch had been carried out in harbour. Unknown to 807 NAS or *Ocean*, however, the BNLO had, on hearing that the aircraft were stuck on board, asked 2 Squadron of the South African Air Force to carry out the fly past with its F-86 Sabre jet fighters. On learning that 807 had in fact got ashore to Iwakuni, he requested them to carry out the fly past after all once the Sabres had cleared the area.[15] Weather on 2 June was good and 807 crossed the Sea of Japan to arrive south of the front line just as the sabres departed. They made their first pass in an 'E' formation from east to west, followed by an 'R' formation from west to east and then carried out a line-astern 'beat up' of Commonwealth positions on the ground which, unfortunately, caused three Army staff cars to collide with each other as their drivers watched the aircraft. Somewhat more formally, all Commonwealth warships in Sasebo dressed overall on 2 June 1953 and a parade was held in *Ocean*'s hangar.[16]

The Radical Defence Review

With the end of the Korean War, government attention turned once more to the reduction of defence expenditure and an attempt to face the new reality of

The Review Fleet illuminated at night, seen from HMAS *Sydney*. (Sea Power Centre – Australia)

thermonuclear weapons. The armistice that ended the fighting in Korea was signed on 27 July 1953 at Panmunjon at 10.00 local time and came into effect twelve hours later. On the same day the British Cabinet met to discuss the need for a review of defence programmes to determine whether any reductions in addition to those already recommended could be made and 'also to consider what further reductions might be secured in expenditure on defence during 1955'.[17] The initial report[18] laid down the priorities to be met by the armed forces and looked for economies that would 'have the effect of reducing defence expenditure in 1955 below £1550 million, without making provision for the cost of the occupation forces in Germany'. This was the figure proposed by the Chancellor of the Exchequer, R A Butler. The review listed three priorities which were in general agreement with those accepted by the Chiefs of Staff. These were:

(i)   The minimum forces necessary to carry out essential Commonwealth commitments in peacetime.
(ii) Forces which would directly assist us in surviving the supreme opening phase of a Third World War.
(iii) Subject to the essential needs of the first two categories – forces which, though making no direct contribution to our survival in the opening phase of a major war, would be essential in the ensuing period of less intensive warfare.

Expenditure on forces which did not fall into any of these categories was, as far as was practicable, to be brought to an end.

By then, it was clear that Duncan Sandys, the Minister of Supply, was the main influence opposed to the Admiralty in the Cabinet.[19] His position in charge of aircraft procurement gave him a powerful voice, as did his relationship with the Prime Minister[20] and despite briefings to the contrary by the Admiralty he argued that strategic bombers and air defence fighters for the RAF should have first call on the restricted defence budget. Butler followed the arguments but informed Lord Alexander that the absolute maximum sum that could be spent on defence in the 1955–6 budget would be £1650 million and this was to be taken as a ceiling figure for subsequent years. Out of this sum the Ministry of Defence proposed to allocate only £360 million to the Admiralty, only two-thirds of the sums that were to be allocated to the other Services. As discussions continued through the autumn some surprising points of view emerged. Sandys had concentrated his attack on aircraft carriers, their embarked aircraft and the large reserves of aircraft maintained by the RN to support the front-line squadrons. He also criticised cruisers, stating his belief that they were 'nice to have' but he thought they would be of little value in the opening shock of a nuclear war. Surprisingly Churchill, who had suffered a stroke and only recently returned to health, expressed a desire to see a significant reserve fleet kept in existence, criticising Admiralty plans to save money by scrapping battleships as being 'penny wise and pound foolish'. Three of the *King George V* class battleships were by then in extended reserve in the Gareloch and one was kept in preservation by operation at Devonport as a back-up for *Vanguard*: 13,000 rounds of 14in ammunition for them was held in naval armament depots at a cost of about £1 million per year. The maintenance tasks needed to keep these big ships safe required about 900 men. Their disposal would not save large sums but if the fleet was to be drastically reduced they were significant. At the same time four of the *Illustrious* group armoured carriers were being reduced to extended reserve and being replaced by light fleet carriers in non-operational tasks. Churchill's statements also introduced another new phrase to the terminology of the Cold War when he referred to the period of 'broken-backed' warfare[21] that would follow a nuclear exchange. This period was expected to include a mixture of nuclear and conventional conflict in which the very survival of the UK might depend on the RN's ability to fight relief convoys and reinforcements across the Atlantic. The weakness of this argument lay in the implied maintenance of a reserve fleet of elderly and expensive battleships which would take considerable effort and manpower to re-commission.

An important element of the Admiralty structure in the 1950s and early 1960s was 'M' Branch, a civilian-manned department that advised the First Lord on

The end of an era, the battleship *King George V* laid up in the Gareloch in 1957; note the carefully-cocooned guns, turrets and directors. Only months after this photograph was taken the four ships of this class were scrapped during 1958. (T Ferrers-Walker Collection via Maritime Books)

strategy and doctrinal matters. Its head in 1953 was Philip Newell, a brilliant mind who was able to write short, cogent arguments of considerable value. During the discussions over the radical review he made the point that as the mutually assured destruction of a nuclear exchange became more probable with the ever-expanding number of weapons on both sides, war between the great powers would be constrained to a conventional level, probably through surrogates or 'client nations'. Unlike many who allowed dogma to cloud their judgement, his vision was both accurate and well thought-out. Rear Admiral Sir Anthony Buzzard, the Director of Naval Intelligence, put forward a similar view when he expressed doubt that the massive first strike by the SAC would result in a knock-out blow that would prevent the large Soviet Navy from seizing control of the Atlantic if insufficient forces were left to oppose it. The appearance of the *Sverdlov* class cruisers and large numbers of 'W' class submarines added weight to this argument.

The First Sea Lord, Admiral Sir Rhoderick McGrigor, understood these arguments but took them a logical step further. The NA 39 had been specified as

Admiral Sir Rhoderick McGrigor GCB DSO LLD, the First Sea Lord in 1953. He was promoted to Admiral of the Fleet on 1 May 1953. (Author's collection)

a '*Sverdlov*-killer' and there was no doubt that modernised carrier task forces would form the ideal battle-fleet to oppose them. The generation of new aircraft planned for the late 1950s would be required to counter the Soviet Naval Air Force, cruisers and submarines that would contest control of the Atlantic and any fleet without them would be incapable of defending the UK's sea communications or even playing a viable part in NATO operations. Ironically it was the need to search out economies and reduce the fleet to smaller numbers of ships with core capabilities that led the Admiralty Board to concentrate on a carrier strike fleet capable of operations in the NATO area. By 1953 the Mediterranean was no longer seen as the pivotal theatre and, as we saw in the early NATO exercises, British carriers formed

A Seamew AS 1 seen seconds after catching number 1 wire on *Warrior* during deck landing trials. (Author's collection)

Carrier Strike Group 2 of the NATO alliance. They had a significant advantage over the USN carriers of Strike Group 1 that they could be in action in defence of European NATO days or even weeks before the Americans could arrive in strength. NATO strike operations also led McGrigor to the conclusion that the NA 39 would need to carry a tactical nuclear weapon to guarantee the destruction of a *Sverdlov*. Therefore, given its projected radius of action of over 400 miles and high speed at 200ft, below the enemy radar horizon, an NA 39 would be perfectly capable of attacking an enemy naval base to destroy enemy ships, submarines and aircraft at source together with their ammunition, infrastructure and support. NA 39s may not have been specified for the land attack role but they would be perfectly capable of carrying it out. In fact, the RN requirement for the aircraft to attack at high speed and low level arguably made it a far more effective platform than the medium bomber force being developed at great expense for Bomber Command which would comprise aircraft only able to bomb from high level where they were vulnerable to radar-guided interception by fighters and missiles.

Sandys spoke out against carrier strike and the Cabinet asked the First Lord, James Thomas,[22] to provide a definition of the roles of aircraft carriers in both peace and war. He made a strong case for the use of fleet carriers for offensive operations and for the defence of naval forces and convoys outside the range of land-based fighters. Light fleet carriers were to be used for the air and anti-submarine defence of convoys and shipping in the open ocean with the NA 32, which became the Short Seamew, intended for operation from these ships. The paper also made much of the many peacetime roles carried out by carriers, not the least of which was their ability to carry large numbers of marines or other troops and their equipment over large distances at high speed. As discussion continued, Sandys rather defeated his own argument when he stressed that a major reason for funding the RAF's medium bomber force was to gain commensurate influence over USAF bombing strategy. Newell briefed the First Lord that if this was the case, there was equal merit at considerably less expense in having influence over the NATO carrier striking fleet's AJ-1 Savage and A-3D Skywarrior nuclear bombers. The Admiralty's firm conviction was emphasised by the conclusion of the First Lord's statement in which he spoke of '. . . the disastrous results which would follow if, in spite of the strategic need, fleet carriers were abolished from the Royal Navy. In the eyes of the rest of the world we would cease to be a major naval power'. To this he added that 'I must ask you to bear in mind the effect of this on the morale of the Royal Navy and on its confidence in any Board of Admiralty which agreed to such a measure'.[23] At one stage arguments over the need for the Fleet Air Arm looked like degenerating into the sort of bitter controversy that had characterised the bomber versus battleship arguments of the 1930s and the more recent B-36 versus carrier controversy in the USA. However, in December 1953 McGrigor and Air Chief Marshal Sir William Dickson GCB KBE DSO AFC,[24] the Chief of the Air Staff (CAS), met and agreed, for the time being, a settlement that formed the basis of Ministry of Defence policy. The two Chiefs agreed that the re-equipment of Bomber Command envisaged by the Government could not substitute for the strike fleet without substantial reinforcement. Even if it were reinforced, it could not guarantee to carry out attacks on northern Soviet air bases. They even agreed that a carrier strike force might be more effective against northern targets and that carrier-borne aircraft might be more suited to laying mines in northern waters. They further agreed that 'a contribution of two fleet carriers was a small price to pay for having a say in the employment of the NATO Strike Fleet'. Having built the carriers, it was 'wasteful not to use them'.[25]

Towards the end of 1953 there was some criticism in both Parliament and the press that the Admiralty lacked sufficient vision to cope with new technologies and the changing strategic situation. In strong rebuttal of these views, the Admiralty produced a paper entitled 'The Navy of the Future'[26] in early 1954 which began by stating that the role of the RN remained what it always had been, to use the sea to impose the UK's will on an enemy, to deny its use to that enemy and to prevent his interference with sea communications. Although traditional, these tasks would be undertaken by an array of new technologies and these were expected to include nuclear weapons for use on carrier-borne aircraft, anti-aircraft missiles, VTOL fighters operating from a smaller generation of aircraft carriers and anti-submarine helicopters operating from a range of warships. Interestingly the paper included thoughts on 'seaborne ballistic rocket launchers', including submarines that could be used as part of a nuclear first strike but gave little emphasis to amphibious warfare beyond hoping, eventually, to replace the existing ships with adequate replacements. The Admiralty showed its lack of faith in Bomber Command's new medium bomber force by noting the 'increasing vulnerability of large bombers at high altitude' and the number of targets that would be outside the force's radius of action. A realistic nuclear strategy, the Admiralty affirmed, needed to exploit attacks by low-flying strike aircraft supported by fighters launched from aircraft carrier strike forces far out at sea. This was certainly a forward-looking and well-thought-out paper that showed that the Admiralty had ideas in advance of the RAF and even the US armed forces at the time; no other air arm was considering the use of specialised low-level attack aircraft to evade detection by enemy radar in 1954. Both RAF and USAAF strategic bomber forces thought themselves to be capable of operating above Soviet air defences until 1 May 1960 when a U-2 spy plane was shot down by a salvo of SA-2 'Guideline' anti-aircraft missiles over Sverdlovsk in the Urals.[27] Both made attempts to adopt low-flying tactics with large bombers that had not been designed for it but by then the NA 39 Buccaneer was already flying and would soon enter service with RN strike squadrons.

The Radical Review was still not over, however. In June 1954 the Cabinet agreed to fund a British thermonuclear weapons programme and set up a new defence review under Lord Swinton, the Commonwealth Secretary, who had been the Air Minister responsible for the massive expansion of the RAF in the 1930s. Duncan Sandys also brought his anti-carrier view to the reviewing committee together with Nigel Birch, parliamentary secretary to the Ministry of Defence[28] who had, until recently been at the Air Ministry where he had argued that the new RAF 'V'-bomber force could provide such offensive air capability as would be needed by all three Services in addition to their nuclear strike role. Depressingly, Swinton chose to undo all the recent progress made by the Admiralty by including in his

Indomitable was withdrawn from service shortly after the Coronation Review at Spithead when she was only twelve years old. It was too expensive and complicated to modernise her or to employ her as a commando carrier and she is seen here being towed to Rosyth in 1954. A year after that she was sold for scrap. (T Ferrers-Walker Collection via Maritime Books)

report to Parliament the statements that the Fleet Air Arm appeared to impose a burden of cost disproportionate to its results[29] and that the role of the aircraft carrier was 'already restricted by the ever-increasing range of shore-based aircraft'. No evidence to substantiate these outrageous statements was put forward and both were counter-factual.

The Admiralty responded with a paper entitled 'Defence Policy – The Fleet Air Arm' in which the First Lord and First Sea Lord refuted those 'expressions of opinion and recommendations which are not in accordance with the views of the Board of Admiralty'.[30] Adoption of the Swinton Report would have had a devastating effect on the RN and so Admiral McGrigor was asked to brief the Cabinet in person.[31] His success was the most important achievement of his time as 1SL and he spoke succinctly about the strike fleet's role protecting shipping from the rapidly expanding Soviet Navy. He reminded Cabinet that the Americans, who bore the brunt of NATO defence, had asked for three British strike carriers with full air groups and argued that the least the UK could do would be to provide two. The British fleet would have to fight the Soviet Navy alone until the USN strike fleet arrived and, he emphasised, without its own strike carriers it could not do so. Given its existence and availability at short notice, McGrigor pointed out that the RN strike fleet was capable of achieving other things, including playing an important role in the defence of Norway against amphibious attack. But he stressed its primary role was to defeat the Soviet Fleet and its bases. Lastly, he offered a reduction of about £3.5 million in the cost of maintaining reserve aircraft for the Fleet Air Arm in addition to the £25 million cuts across the whole RN ordered by the review thus far.

Swinton's committee now appeared rather isolated with a new Minister of Defence, Harold Macmillan, and a new Minister of Supply, Selwyn Lloyd, both of whom accepted the Admiralty's arguments. Churchill, the Prime Minister, was not prepared to press for the adoption of Swinton's proposals if the Minister of Defence was prepared to explore, with the Admiralty, alternative means of securing savings in naval expenditure. In October Macmillan rang Thomas, the First Lord, after the latter had retired to bed, to say that he had accepted the Admiralty's case. He subsequently published a Ministry of Defence Paper[32] which confirmed the commitment of two fleet carriers to the NATO strike fleet with their considerable capacities for self-defence in Cold War or open hostilities. It endorsed the Admiralty's fears about loss of morale should the fleet carriers be removed and described as 'uncertain' the view that land-based aircraft could fulfil the tasks of

The new *Ark Royal* gave a considerable boost to the RN carrier strike fleet after she was commissioned in 1955. She was the first carrier in the world to be completed with the angled deck, steam catapults and mirror landing aids rather than their being added after entering service. She also had a side-lift on the port side amidships which only served the upper hangar. She is seen here in May 1957 after P1 and P2 4.5in gun mountings had been removed from the port side forward to allow the angled deck to be lengthened. The aircraft on deck are Sea Hawks and Sea Venoms parked in Fly 1 after a recovery. (Author's collection)

their air groups. Their removal would, therefore, constitute 'a course of action which would be most damaging to the authority of the Fleet and the prestige of Great Britain'. Such a blow was not worth the sum of money that might be saved by the measure.

There were losers in this latest round of savings, however. The Explanatory Statement on the 1955–6 Navy Estimates stated that whereas in the past a large fleet of ships had been kept in reserve in various states of readiness. The emphasis now was to be put on retaining a reserve fleet that contained only the ships that could be maintained at the highest standard of readiness, fit for the roles in which they would be used. A year later, the 1956–7 Explanatory Statement went a stage further and noted that the modern fleet was now built around the concept of the battle group with carriers and their multi-purpose squadrons of aircraft as its most important element. The reserve fleet had been re-organised to retain the most efficient ships for the least amount of money and manpower. It was considered too expensive to bring the remaining ships up to the most modern standards and keep them up to date. The best of them were to be made available to foreign navies and the remainder were to be scrapped. Within four years the latter category included the five un-modernised fleet carriers of the *Illustrious* group and the four battleships of the *King George V* class. Despite hopes that she could be maintained in commission as an anti-*Sverdlov* and anti-aircraft gun battery in support of a carrier battle group, the last battleship *Vanguard* proved to be too expensive to run on and she was reduced to reserve.

In addition to the light fleet carriers on operational and training duties, others were kept active as trooping and ferry carriers. This is *Vengeance* in 1952 loaded with stores and vehicles on a trooping run in 1952. (Author's collection)

7 The Suez Crisis

In the decade after the end of the Second World War successive British defence reviews had focused on all-out nuclear war and little emphasis had been placed on amphibious operations, surprisingly perhaps, given the outstanding example of what they could achieve at Inchon in 1950. British Army Commandos had all been disbanded in 1946, leaving the Royal Marines as the UK's only commando force. 3 Commando Brigade RM included 40, 42 and 45 RM Commandos and was designated to act as the UK's spearhead amphibious force with a small number of tank landing ships (LST) and craft (LCT), maintained in commission for training although the opportunities to do so in any significant numbers were rare. The Brigade lacked armour, artillery, field engineers and other important elements, however, and these would have to be provided by the Army for a full-scale, brigade-sized operation.[1] A number of wartime LSTs and LCTs were also maintained in long-term reserve by the Admiralty to provide a brigade lift, agreed by the Chiefs-of-Staff as their basic requirement should an amphibious operation be required. This seemed a far cry from the huge amphibious forces that had contributed so much to the D-Day assault on Normandy only ten years earlier but the contemporary emphasis on a short, sharp nuclear exchange illustrates the extent to which politicians had lost sight of any other form of conflict. The very real possibility that British armed forces might have to fight in the national interest against a non-nuclear opponent at short notice had been given very little priority and this shortcoming became clear in the summer of 1956.

Background to the Suez Crisis

While theories on how Britain's future defence policy should be balanced were being argued over in Whitehall, there were a number of areas throughout the world where there was a risk that conventional conflict could act as a 'trigger' for a major nuclear war. Successive British defence reviews had been seduced by the 'bomber lobby' theory that the threat of a devastating nuclear exchange would prevent conflict but overlooked the fact that if left unchecked, 'brushfire' wars could escalate to the point where nuclear strikes became far more likely. Capable conventional forces were required to extinguish the 'brushfires' but the 'V'-bombers and inter-continental ballistic missiles (ICBM) had little to offer in any scenarios short of all-out war.

The prospects for peace in 1955 were not good. In Poland workers had confronted the Communist authorities in Poznan and in Hungary discontentment with the Communists was moving towards an uprising that broke out in 1956. France had relinquished Indo-China after the Geneva Armistice Agreement that followed its crushing defeat by the Viet-Minh at Dien Bien Phu in 1954 and was now involved in a war against a nationalist insurrection in Algeria. The UK was fighting against communist guerrillas in Malaya, trying to maintain order in Cyprus where Greek and Turkish Cypriot factions were fighting each other and in curbing the activities of the Mau-Mau in Kenya. There was still the possibility of a resumption of the conflict between Nationalist and Communist China; in 1954 a Nationalist frigate was sunk by Communist warships and in 1955 US fighters shot down several Communist MiG-15s which had attacked them in international airspace off Formosa. Winston Churchill had finally retired in April 1955, replaced by his Foreign Secretary Anthony Eden who saw himself as an international mediator. He had put a great deal of personal effort into the Geneva meetings that had ended the fighting in Indo-China.[2]

The situation in the Middle East had deteriorated and was just as serious. The British garrison in the Suez Canal Zone had been drawn down since the 1954 Agreement and the last British Army units left Port Said in June 1956, ending an occupation that had lasted for over seventy years.[3] There was growing hostility between Egypt and Iraq as both sought regional leadership but enmity towards the new state of Israel was a unifying bond between the Arab states. Both countries sought to buy modern weapons from the West but, for a variety of reasons, proposed deals were not carried forward. In August 1955, however, a deal was signed between Egypt and Czechoslovakia, then a Soviet satellite-state, for the supply of MiG-15 fighters, Ilyushin Il-28 bombers, T-34 tanks, SU-100 self-propelled artillery, conventional artillery, rocket launchers, Czech-pattern rifles and mortars. These secured Egypt's military re-equipment programme and Nasser adopted a more aggressive stance against Israel. The first MiGs arrived in the Soviet freighter *Stalingrad* in October 1955 and were taken to the airfield at Almaza where they were assembled by Czech Air Force technicians. Egyptian Air Force technicians were hurriedly trained and took over the work from November. The assembly of Il-28s followed. Egypt and Syria established a joint military command at this time and both countries received large shipments of Soviet-made equipment. In 1950 the UK, France and the USA had agreed to seek an arms balance between Israel and Egypt and, in the event of aggression by either side that crossed the borders agreed in the 1948 Armistice, they would 'take common counsel' over what action to take.[4] Once the British garrison left the Canal Zone, however, there were no Allied forces near enough to forestall any sudden move by either state. In the event, the French supplied sixty Mystère IVA fighters to Israel as a counter to the Egyptian MiG-15s.

In 1955 the Americans brokered a mutual defence organisation that evolved into the Central Treaty Organisation (CENTO). Its basis was the Baghdad Pact, signed between Iraq and Turkey in February 1955. Later in the year the UK, Iran and Pakistan joined as full members. The USA provided military and economic support but never became a full member of the council. Egypt and Syria were opposed to CENTO and their relations with member nations continued to deteriorate. Egyptian Radio's 'Voice of the Arabs' broadcasts were intended to foster discontent in Aden, Algeria and other places where Western interests were concentrated. Another contentious issue was the Egyptian request for a loan to build the Aswan High Dam, Nasser's most cherished project. The British Government believed by early 1956 that Egypt was playing the West against the Soviet Union to see who would make the better offer. By May it was rumoured that the Soviets were prepared to offer an interest-free loan of £50 million but the UK and USA doubted that Egypt could afford to repay such a loan, even without the interest, and withdrew from negotiations. To Nasser's surprise the Soviet Foreign Minister, Dmitri Shepilov, announced on 22 July 1955 that the Soviet Union had never offered to finance the dam. That left Nasser with only one potential source of new revenue, the Anglo-French Suez Canal Company.

Nasser was declared President of Egypt on 24 June 1956. On the evening of 26 July he followed recent public gatherings celebrating the British withdrawal to give a three-hour-long speech to a vast crowd gathered in the Liberation Square of Alexandria in which he announced the Egyptian Government's decision to nationalise the Suez Canal Company. His use of the name 'de Lesseps' gave the signal to seize the company's offices in Egypt and he ordered all employees of the company, including British and French nationals, to remain at their posts. Martial law was declared throughout the Canal Zone. The cruiser *Jamaica* was in Alexandria harbour at the time on a friendly visit. Thousands of Egyptians ran through the streets from Liberation Square to the harbour shouting anti-British slogans and the cruiser went to action stations for a period when it looked as if she would be attacked. She sailed shortly afterwards. The Prime Minister Anthony Eden was telephoned by the Foreign Office after he had retired to bed that night and informed of developments. Despite his reputation as a mediator, Eden took the view that appeasement had failed to stop Hitler in the 1930s and that force would be required to stop Nasser now. The Suez Canal was regarded as a vital link with

Middle East oil supplies and most of the UK and Europe's trade with the Far East passed through it. Besides the obvious issues of ownership, management and compensation, the canal's total operation by Egyptian authorities raised another issue because the canal had already been closed to Israeli vessels for several years and there were fears that Nasser would pick and choose which ships could pass through it. From the outset the British and French Governments considered military action to restore the canal to its legal owners and to ensure its use by the international community.[5] As the UK and France studied their military options in the days after nationalisation, the full extent of the UK's military unpreparedness for an unexpected conventional conflict became only too apparent. This chapter will describe the operation from the point of view of the RN carrier strike fleet but reference will be made to military operations as they affected, and were affected by, carrier operations.

The Available Strike Fleet and its Reinforcement

Eagle was the only aircraft carrier in the Mediterranean Fleet at the end of July 1956.[6] She was reinforced by *Bulwark* which was able to transition easily from tasking as the trials and training carrier to embark three Sea Hawk squadrons before deploying to the Mediterranean in August. She had demonstrated her operational capability in 1955 by embarking two Sea Hawk and an Avenger NAS for the Home Fleet's summer cruise. A third carrier, *Albion*, had begun a short refit in Portsmouth in May but its completion was hastened forward to allow her to deploy to the Mediterranean Fleet in September.[7] The two light fleet carriers of the Home Fleet Training squadron, *Ocean* and *Theseus*, were deployed slightly later to act as commando-assault helicopter carriers. The RN carriers operated under FOAC, Vice Admiral M L Power DSO, who flew his flag in *Eagle*.

There were two French carriers in the Mediterranean, both of which joined the strike fleet for operations off Egypt. They were the *Arromanches*[8] and *La Fayette*[9] and served under Admiral Yves Caron FN. Military action against Egypt was given the codename Operation 'Musketeer' and its initiation was ordered by the Allied Commander-in-Chief's Signal 310550Z October 56. The naval task force was activated in turn by the C-in-C Mediterranean's Signal 310730Z October 56. The carrier strike group, including the French carriers, was designated as Task Group (TG) 345.4 and the helicopter carriers as TG 345.9.

Eagle preparing to launch a massive strike range of Sea Venoms, Sea Hawks and Wyverns while working up off Malta on 10 October 1956. (Author's collection)

Carrier Strike Groups and their Embarked NAS – October 1956

HMS *Eagle*	Captain H C D MacLean DSC RN	
830 NAS	9 Wyvern S4	Lt Cdr C V Howard RN
892 NAS	8 Sea Venom FAW 21	Lt Cdr M H J Petrie RN
893 NAS	9 Sea Venom FAW 21	Lt Cdr M W Henley DSC RN
897 NAS	12 Sea Hawk FGA 6	Lt Cdr A R Rawbone AFC RN
899 NAS	12 Sea Hawk FGA 6	Lt Cdr A B B Clark RN
849A NAS	4 Skyraider AEW 1	Lt Cdr B J Williams RN
Ship's SAR Flight	2 Whirlwind HAR 3	Lt Cdr J H Summerlee RN
HMS *Bulwark*	Captain R M Smeeton MBE RN	
804 NAS	11 Sea Hawk FGA 6	Lt Cdr R V B Kettle RN
810 NAS	10 Sea Hawk FGA 4	Lt Cdr P M Lamb DSC AFC RN
895 NAS	12 Sea Hawk FB 3	Lt Cdr J Morris-Jones RN
Ship's Flight	2 Avenger AS 5	
SAR Flight	3 Dragonfly HR 4	
HMS *Albion*	Captain J M Villiers OBE RN	
800 NAS	12 Sea Hawk FGA 6	Lt Cdr J D Russell RN
802 NAS	11 Sea Hawk FB 3	Lt Cdr R L Eveleigh RN
809 NAS	9 Sea Venom FAW 21	Lt Cdr R A Shilcock RN
849C NAS	4 Skyraider AEW 1	Lt Cdr D A Fuller RN
Ship's SAR Flight	2 Whirlwind HAR 3	
HMS *Theseus*	Captain E F Pizey DSO RN	
845 NAS	8 Whirlwind HAS 22	Lt Cdr J C Jacob RN
	2 Whirlwind HAR 3	
HMS *Ocean*	Captain I W T Beloe DSC RN	
Joint Helicopter Unit	6 Whirlwind HAR 2	Lt Col J F T Scott RA
	6 Sycamore HR 14	
French Carriers		
FNS *Arromanches*	Capt de V Bailleux	
Flotille 14F	18 Corsair F4U-7	Lt de V Cremer
Flotille 15F	18 Corsair F4U-7	Lt de V Degerman
23S Escadrille	HUP-2	
FNS *La Fayette*		
Flotille 9F	10 Avenger TBN-3	Lt de V Bros
23S Escadrille	HUP-2	Lt de V Sarreau

The Politics behind Operation 'Musketeer'

In his speech on 26 July 1956 Nasser claimed that Egypt received an income of only £1 million from the Compagnie Universelle du Canal Maritime de Suez's annual revenue of over £30 million, despite the fact that by 1956 the day-to-day running of the canal was largely carried out by Egyptian personnel. He claimed that if Egypt received the entire revenue the Government could finance the Aswan High Dam project without a foreign loan. The nationalisation was denounced as a flagrant violation of international law in London and Paris; the US Government seized Egyptian assets but the Soviet Union warned that the affair must be settled peacefully.[10] Nasser gave assurances that the canal would remain open despite its closure to Israeli-flagged vessels and the dubious legality of the Company's facilities being seized by Egyptian troops. An international conference was convened in London on 16 August at which the French delegates favoured military action against Egypt, the British agreed that force might be necessary but hesitated to commit to it and the USA and the Soviet Union sought a delay for further discussion. The conference broke up on 23 August with an agreement to send a five-man international committee to Egypt led by Robert Menzies, the Prime Minister of Australia. It was to demand the establishment of an international company to run the canal. Menzies arrived in Cairo on 2 September 1956 but the proposed international company was flatly rejected by Nasser and nothing further came from this approach. Eden's next move was to write to President Eisenhower of the USA proposing that the matter be referred to the UN Security Council and seeking justification for a military operation to recover the canal. He described nationalisation of the canal as the opening gambit in a campaign planned by Nasser to expel Western influence and commercial interests from Arab countries. If he was allowed to get away with it, Eden claimed, Egypt would stimulate revolutions in Saudi Arabia, Jordan, Syria and Iraq. British and US intelligence agencies were already aware that Egypt was attempting to undermine the government in Iraq, considered in 1956 to be the most stable, progressive and pro-Western Arab nation, with agents and broadcasts on Egyptian radio. However, US presidential elections were due on 6 November 1956 and Eisenhower was not prepared to jeopardise his campaign by becoming involved in a foreign conflict that the US electorate would find it hard to understand. He refused to support the increasingly forceful British and French position.

The Egyptians, naturally, saw the position entirely differently. They believed themselves to be victims of British imperialism, with revenue that should rightly have come into their economy being used to swell the profits of Western-owned companies. Nasser was not regarded as a despotic villain in his own country but as a national hero. His refusal to negotiate proved to be flawed, however, and he made three major errors of judgement. He underestimated both the depth of French resentment over Egyptian support for the Algerian independence movement and the absolute importance attached to the Suez Canal by the British. Last, and most importantly, he failed to consider the unlikely possibility that Israel would form an alliance with the UK and France to take co-ordinated military action. He was probably not aware of Eden's personal animosity but might have been aware from the British press that his actions were being compared to those of Hitler in the years of appeasement before 1939. Secret negotiations between France and Israel, without British or American knowledge, had begun as early as April 1956. By late October 1956, the British had become involved in these talks and an Israeli mission[11] flew to Paris in French military aircraft to finalise arrangements with British and French officials. The discussions took place at Sèvres, where the French Minister of Defence had a villa. United in opposition to the new regime in Egypt, the three nations actually made unusual allies in every other way. The British wanted to preserve the freedom of traffic using the Suez Canal and to re-affirm their long-standing position of influence in the Middle East; if necessary they were prepared to do this with Nasser if he were prepared to co-operate. France also wanted free movement through the Canal but wanted to topple Nasser, a man seen as the leading enemy of France in Algeria. The Israeli delegation would much rather have acted militarily against Egypt alone but lacked the strength to do so.

The agreed plan, signed by representatives of Great Britain, France and Israel, was for Israel to launch an attack against Egypt across the Sinai Peninsula toward the Suez Canal on 29 October 1956. On 30 October the British and French Governments were to issue an ultimatum that conflict close to the Suez Canal was not acceptable and call on both sides to withdraw 15km from it. Israel was to agree to the ultimatum but Egypt was expected to refuse and thus give Great Britain and France an excuse to land troops at the northern entrance the canal with the object seizing the Canal Zone. To ensure that the Egyptian Air Force could not oppose the landings and subsequent movements, it was to be destroyed.[12] It was hoped that the defeat of the newly re-equipped Egyptian armed forces and resumption of international control of the canal would lead to the overthrow of Nasser and his regime and that a pro-Western regime would follow it. The signed document reflected little credit on the British Government and was kept secret for many years.[13] Its last sentence actually contravened the existing Anglo-Jordanian Treaty by stating that if Jordan attacked Israel during the period of the agreement, the British government would not come to Jordan's assistance. By October 1956 Admiral Lord Louis Mountbatten had become First Sea Lord and he was quick to observe that Britain had put itself into a difficult position. If Israel were to attack Jordan, it could call on both Britain and the USA for assistance. If the British Government refused to provide it and supported Israel but the USA supported Jordan, British and US forces could find themselves on opposing sides. The situation for the British forces stationed in Jordan for its defence were about to become extremely difficult. At best their presence became questionable overnight; at worst they were the outnumbered representatives of a nation that would be accused of betraying Jordan and the Arab world. President Eisenhower and the US Government were not informed of the secret agreement and no thought seems to have been given to the possibility that the Soviet Union might back Egypt to enhance its standing with the Arabs. Little thought was given to how the landing of Anglo-French forces in Egypt might be reported in the world's press, not least in Arab countries across North Africa and the Middle East where anti-Western feeling was likely to become intense. The hastily thought-out scenario of an Israeli attack and 'withdrawal' to a line only 15km east of the canal would leave virtually the whole of the Sinai Peninsula in Israeli hands. Throughout the Arabic-speaking world this would be seen as a disaster, with Nasser more likely to be portrayed as a martyr for Arab nationalism than a despot who should be removed from power. When he was eventually consulted, President Eisenhower took the advice of his Secretary of State, John Foster Dulles, and refused to lend American support to a military operation. With hindsight, it can be seen that Eden's decision not to appease Nasser and to use force to regain control of the canal was not only ill-considered, it alienated people who would have supported a negotiated settlement in which Britain could have played a leading role. As it was, Commonwealth countries, Arab states and influential members of the UN all found themselves opposed to the Anglo-French use of force.

Military Options and Preparations

Once the government of the United Kingdom decided that it might resort to the use of force, the armed forces had to prepare options to meet the politicians' agenda. *Eagle* was the only strike asset in the Mediterranean that was fully worked-up and ready for action but the UK and France both had military garrisons and modest air forces in North Africa and the Middle East in 1956. Few of them were trained or immediately available for a major amphibious operation, however. About 10,000 British troops were committed to operations against EOKA terrorists in Cyprus during the summer of 1956. These included two Royal Marines Commandos and two battalions of the Army's 16 Parachute Brigade. These deployments had interfered with regular training and the marines were no longer in current amphibious warfare practice; the parachute battalions had no recent airborne assault training and there were no British or French transport aircraft in the Eastern Mediterranean theatre. The British 10th Armoured Division was based in Libya and the 10th Hussars with their tanks were based in Jordan but since both were in Arab countries, their use to attack Egypt would inevitably lead to dangerous repercussions and was not considered practical. The RAF in the Middle East had several squadrons of Venom fighter-bombers, one of which was based in Jordan to protect against an attack by Israel.

Initially the name chosen for the operation was 'Hannibal' after the Carthaginian general that attacked Rome and it was thought in London that the word was the same in both English and French. Orders went out that all British military vehicles were to be painted in sand-coloured camouflage with the letter 'H' conspicuous on the front and rear. Too late it was learnt that the French name was 'Annibal' and the plans were re-named as Operation 'Musketeer' which was the same in both languages. Changing thousands of 'H' lettered vehicles to 'M' was too difficult and the 'H' remained, giving cynics the chance to make jokes about vehicles marked 'H' for 'Hegypt'.[14] Early plans envisaged a landing at Alexandria to give the Allies immediate access to a deep-water port but were changed in September when it was appreciated that access from there to the Suez Canal would have to be across the easily-defended Nile delta with its numerous bridges. If the stated aim of the assault was to take control of the canal the best place to land would be at Port Said, allowing immediate access to the canal with the potential for rapid progress along it to secure the Canal Zone. At the first Chiefs of Staff meeting in early August Lord Mountbatten is reputed to have said that a battle group based on *Eagle* could land marines to seize the canal immediately before opposition groups had a chance to consider the situation. This proposal had obvious merit but the other Chiefs of Staff refused to accept it because such a small landing force might be overwhelmed if the Egyptian Army opposed it effectively. Building up the sort of force required would take months and so delay was accepted as inevitable from the outset.

On 2 August 1956 a number of Army reservists were called up by Royal Proclamation, the discharge of regular soldiers who had completed their terms of service was halted and the return of National Servicemen from overseas garrisons was suspended. British forces had garrison commitments in Germany, the Middle East and Far East and their removal was not practical in the short term so it was decided in August to use the 3rd Infantry Division, based in the UK, augmented by an armoured brigade comprising 1st and 6th Royal Tank Regiments (RTR). None of the units was up to its full war complement but the Chiefs of Staff agreed in August that seizure of the Suez Canal would require an assault force of about 40,000 British and 30,000 French troops. The two Commandos were withdrawn from Cyprus and the re-formed 3 Commando Brigade RM carried out extensive amphibious training in Malta. 16 Parachute Brigade was also brought, hastily, up to operational standard. I do not intend to describe all the difficulties encountered in moving such a large expeditionary force to the Eastern Mediterranean but the problems encountered by 1 and 6 RTR are illustrative of the British lack of preparedness for short-notice action in 1956. Both units were split between a number of locations, some of them in Germany but most in the UK, and some squadrons at low readiness had no tanks at all. Drawing tanks, weapons and equipment from depots throughout the UK was time-consuming and many of the issues were outdated, unserviceable or both. A number of tanks still lacked radio aerials and ammunition racks when they were embarked. Transporting Centurion tanks to embarkation ports at Southampton and Portland proved to be far from straightforward. They were too heavy to travel by rail and the Army had sold off the majority of its low-loading tank transporters. Pickford's removal firm was contracted to move them but its men worked to strict union rules and movement of the brigade from depots to docks was painfully slow. 6 RTR eventually sailed for Malta on 4 September; 1 RTR not until a month later. Valuable training time was lost. A large number of tank landing ships and craft had been retained after 1945 in reserve but only two of each type were in operational service in 1956. Twelve more were brought forward from reserve by dockyards by the end of October. Cyprus was the nearest base but it lacked a deep-water port and so the amphibious assault units and shipping assembled in Malta. British and French airborne assault forces gathered on Cyprus where three airfields[15] hosted air force bomber, fighter, photographic-reconnaissance and transport units from the two nations.

Despite the impressive claims made for it during the Radical Defence Review, Bomber Command proved to lack flexibility, mobility and the common sense required to overcome unexpected obstacles. Twenty-four Vickers Valiants, the first of the RAF's new 'V'-Bombers, were deployed from RAF Marham to RAF Luqa in October. Their maintenance personnel needed a large number of transport aircraft to move them from the UK to Malta and the quantities of fuel and bombs they required needed a number of ships and the sea control to move them safely, factors few bomber theorists had taken into account. The eventual air force build-up was centred on three airfields in Cyprus and three in Malta,[16] and by October the British element comprised a total of twenty-four Valiants, ninety-eight Canberras, forty-seven Venoms, twenty-eight Hunters, twenty-four Meteors, twenty Valettas, fourteen Hastings and the Shackletons normally resident at Luqa. The French element comprised thirty-six F-84F, ten RF-84F, forty Noratlas and five Dakotas. Both the military and air components of the expeditionary force had a British officer in overall command with a French deputy, reflecting the input made by the two nations. The Hunters were intended to provide some air defence for the bases since it was realised that Cyprus in particular, only 30 minutes flying time from Egypt and with virtually no defence it depth, was desperately vulnerable to a pre-emptive Egyptian strike. The first strike on Egypt was to be made by RAF bombers but from the outset poor planning and the lack of liaison between the RAF's own Commands rendered the operation ineffective and wasted valuable resources.

The officer commanding RAF Marham where the Victors were based[17] was the designated bomber wing commander at Malta. He was ordered by Bomber Command in the UK to carry out an attack on specified Egyptian airfields on the night of Saturday 31 October 1956. Unfortunately the order was not repeated to the Air Officer in Command at Malta who was responsible to the RAF's Middle East Air Force, (MEAF). The air headquarters in Malta was closed because it was a Saturday and no-one seems to have informed it that a war was due to start on that day. The AOC, when contacted, refused to allow the bomb dumps to be opened without higher authority. Eventually and despite protests by armed RAF police who took orders from the AOC, Bomber Command personnel broke down the gates to gain access to sufficient bombs to arm their aircraft for operations that night. Until that Saturday afternoon the bomber crews had no idea whether they were expected to attack Israel or Egypt:[18] when the targets were confirmed they had to be analysed, briefings carried out and navigational preparations made in some haste. The first night's attacks were to be carried out in separate raids on Egyptian airfields. For some reason, Bomber Command ordered the bombing runs to be carried out at 30,000ft so that the targets could be seen more clearly rather than 40,000ft at which the aircrews had been trained and had always practised. With no experience of bombing at this lower altitude it is hardly surprisingly that inaccurate results were achieved. The first raid was intended to hit Cairo West airfield but after the Valiants had set heading from Malta, the Air Ministry in London learnt that the US Government had concentrated American civilians at the airfield and was in the process of flying them out of the war zone. A personal signal from the Chief of the Air Staff to the bomber wing commander in Malta succeeding in aborting the raid and the Valiants were recalled. The tightly packed airfields had to cope with subsequent raids taxiing out to take off fully armed while the first wave returned early, having to drop its bombs into the sea. The Malta Wing Canberras were hastily re-briefed to attack Almaza airfield which was to be marked with flares by pathfinder Canberras from Cyprus. Unfortunately, in the haste to find and mark a new target the wrong airfield was attacked[19] and the aircraft dropped their bombs on Cairo International Airport, not Almaza. This was hardly an impressive start to the night bombing campaign but the subsequent official report was able to state that 'fortunately, the presence of Russian-made aircraft of the Egyptian Air Force on Cairo International was later established'. Of course, none of them had been hit by the air raid. Subsequent raids on 31 October attacked Almaza, Kabrit, Abu Sueir and Inchas. British and French photographic reconnaissance (PR), sorties on the morning of 1 November, however, found that the bombing raids had been almost totally ineffective with the aircraft parked around the various airfields all left intact. One of the RAF's PR Canberras was intercepted and slightly damaged by an Egyptian MiG-15. On the morning of 1 November 1956 the Egyptian Air Force was believed to have about 300 aircraft of which the following were operational:

Fayid
26 Meteor F4/8
10 Vampire FB 52

Kabrit
27 MiG-15
Abu Sueir
15 MiG-15
Kasfareet
18 Vampire FB 52
Luxor
20 Il-28
Almaza
15 MiG-15
6 MiG-17
20 C-47
20 C-46
5 Meteor NF 13
20 Il-14
Cairo West
15 Vampire FB 52
Dekheila[20]
Light aircraft
Inchas
29 Il-28

There were also a number of Lancaster bombers of uncertain serviceability.

On 29 October 1956 Israel fulfilled its part of the Sèvres Agreement by launching an attack on the Sinai Peninsula. Prime Minister Ben-Gurion cabled President Eisenhower to say that his government 'would be failing in its essential duty if it were not to take all necessary measures' to prevent the elimination of Israel by force. The die was cast but despite the obvious build-up of Allied forces in Cyprus, the Egyptians seemed unaware that action was imminent. Having looked at some of the background, I will now describe the Allied Fleet's task force organisation and then the RN carrier strike fleet's part in action, looking first at summaries of the individual carriers' operations, to give their slightly differing perspectives, and then at their overall effectiveness.

Task Force Organisation

The command structure for Operation 'Musketeer' placed a British officer in charge of each naval, army and air force element with a French deputy. General Sir Charles Keightley GCB GBE DSO was appointed as overall commander-in-chief with Vice Admiral d'Escadre P Barjot as both his deputy and as commander of all

French forces committed to the operation.[21] The command structure of the naval forces was as follows:

Task Force 345, the naval task force was commanded by Vice Admiral L F Durnford Slater CB, the Flag Officer Second-in-Command Mediterranean Fleet. His deputy was Rear Admiral P Lancelot who commanded the French naval forces. The task force was divided into a number of task groups. These were:

TG 345.4 – the carrier strike group commanded by Vice Admiral M L Power CB CBE DSO, the Flag Officer Aircraft Carriers.

TG 345.9 – the assault helicopter carrier group under Rear Admiral G B Sayer CB DSC.

TG 345.5 – the support force under Rear Admiral D E Holland-Martin DSO DSC*.

Vice Admiral Manley Power CB CBE DSO*, Flag Officer Aircraft Carriers, who flew his flag in *Eagle* throughout Operation 'Musketeer'.

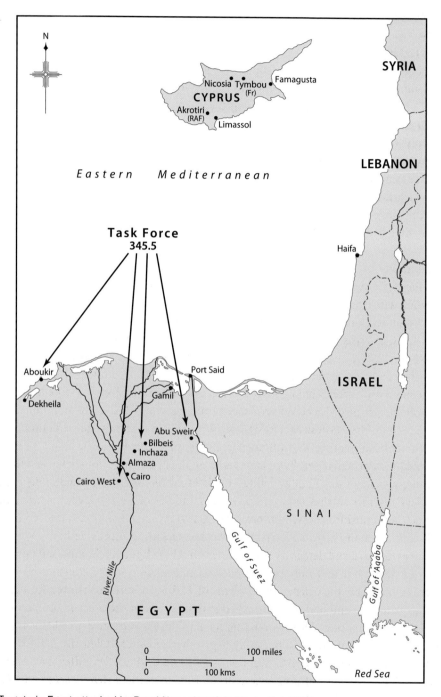

Targets in Egypt attacked by Royal Navy aircraft in November 1956.

TG 345.2 – the amphibious assault force under Commodore R deL Brooke DSO DSC* RN.

TG 345.7 – the minesweeping group under Captain J H Walwyn OBE RN.

A second RN task force, designated **TF 324,** operated in the Red Sea under Captain J G Hamilton RN, the Senior Officer Red Sea Group.

The carrier strike operations during the short operational phase of Operation 'Musketeer' can be divided into three phases. The first was the neutralisation of enemy aircraft in the air and on the ground. Then came attacks against enemy armour, mechanised vehicles; all immediate forms of army support and softening of the beachhead before the amphibious assault. Third came close air support for the parachute landings and the subsequent amphibious assault at Port Said. All three phases were completed with conspicuous success with carrier-borne aircraft providing 83 per cent of the successful tactical missions.

HMS *Eagle*

In the early summer of 1956 *Eagle* followed the normal Mediterranean Fleet routine with exercises, several of them with the US Sixth Fleet, interspersed with port visits to Istanbul, Lebanon and Naples and self-maintenance periods in Malta. As the Suez crisis developed 893 NAS flew its Sea Venoms out from the UK to replace 812 NAS which disembarked its Gannets to RNAS Hal Far. Both Sea Hawk squadrons carried out an intensive period of night operations using Hal Far as a spare deck after which all pilots were able to operate from the deck at night. Emphasis was also placed on armament training with live strafing, bombing and rocketing on the Maltese ranges by day and night. Pilots also practised bombardment spotting, tactical and photographic reconnaissance and close air support techniques. Particular emphasis was placed on the night launch of strikes and their subsequent form up. This was aided by fitting a retractable, aft-facing light on leaders' aircraft so that they could be seen and formed on quickly.[22] The night launch was considered essential because the first strikes were to be launched over 100 miles from the Egyptian coast with the fleet operating silently without radar or radio at first to avoid detection and counter-attack by Egyptian bombers. After the first strikes, radar and radio would be used as normal and the launch positions were to be nearer the coast. The Wyverns of 830 NAS were not cleared for night deck operations and had to be launched in daylight, after the other strike aircraft.

The Mediterranean Fleet worked up its amphibious warfare capabilities in the areas and ranges around Malta during September and aircraft flew simulated close air support missions as well as reconnaissance and CAP sorties. After that, *Eagle* and *Bulwark* carried out exercises with the French carriers *Arromanches* and *La Fayette* and visited Toulon where discussions on tactics to be used in Operation

'Musketeer' were held with French officers. By October 1956 *Eagle*, her air group and ship's company felt able to undertake any task they might be given at short notice[23] but to ensure that she was ready for protracted operations if necessary, she carried out a short self-maintenance period in Gibraltar Dockyard. After a brief stop in Malta she sailed for the Eastern Mediterranean on 29 October and carried out what was described as a 'gentle flying programme'.[24] Unfortunately a catastrophic failure occurred in the starboard catapult while Lieutenant L E Middleton RN was being launched in Sea Hawk XE 441,[25] reducing the ship to one catapult as it could not be repaired at sea. Briefings were carried out on 30 October and the aircrew were issued with khaki uniform, side-arms, escape maps and equipment. As with their contemporaries ashore, there was some surprise when it was learnt that the target was to be Egypt, not Israel. In accordance with a last-

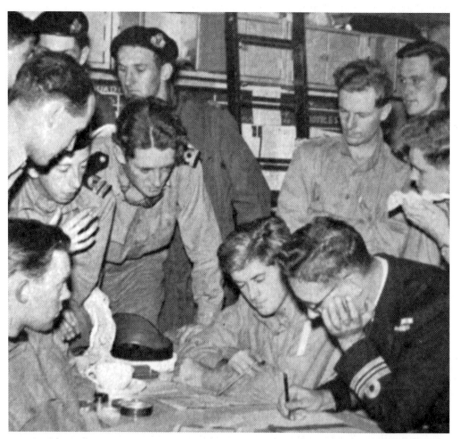

Lieutenant Middleton (seated, second from the right) and other members of 897 NAS being de-briefed after a sortie by Instructor Lieutenant Commander Winterbottom RN of *Eagle*'s intelligence team. (Author's collection)

minute decision, the aircraft were all painted with black and yellow recognition stripes, each 12in wide, three yellow and two black on their wings and fuselage. Apparently the original idea was for French aircraft to have black and yellow stripes and the British black and white to further enhance recognition. However, the signal was somewhat ambiguous, time was short and in the end all Allied aircraft, British and French, had black and yellow stripes. A replenishment at sea (RAS) to top up furnace fuel oil (FFO) and avcat was carried out on Tuesday 30 October and from dawn until dusk on Wednesday 31 October AEW patrols and fighter CAPS were kept airborne. Radar showed the air raids heading towards Egypt from Malta and Cyprus throughout the night.

Phase 1 of the carrier strike operations began on 1 November when dawn strikes were flown by Sea Hawks and Sea Venoms against Inchas airfield. Aircraft were armed with only their 20mm cannon and carried out the type of accurate, low-level strafing runs perfected in BPF and Korean operations. A CAP of Sea Venoms was maintained over *Eagle*. Subsequent strikes were flown against airfields at Bilbeis, Dekheila and Cairo West, co-ordinated with strikes by Venoms from Cyprus. Wyverns armed with single 1000lb bombs attacked Dekheila and scored direct hits on the runway intersections during the second series of attacks. Priority was then given to attacks by Sea Hawks on the blockship *Akka* which was located in Lake Timsah, apparently loaded with cement and scrap iron ready to be sunk in the canal in order to block it. Hits were achieved with bombs and solid-head 3in rockets but the Egyptians were still able to tow the ship into the canal and sink it. A better solution might have been to attack the tug attached to *Akka* with 20mm cannon fire but this was refused on the grounds that it was manned by civilians. By 2 November it was clear that the Egyptian Air Force had been eliminated and attention began to shift towards Phase 2 with an attack on Huckstep Camp to the east of Cairo where there were large dumps of new vehicles and equipment for the Egyptian Army. Considerable damage was done with bombs, rockets and cannon. During one of the last attacks on Almaza airfield, Sea Venom WW 281 of 893 NAS was hit by anti-aircraft fire and suffered a complete hydraulic failure which prevented the undercarriage from being lowered. Lieutenant Commander J Wilcox RN made a successful wheels-up landing on *Eagle* but his observer, Flying Officer R C Olding RAF, was seriously injured and had to have his left leg amputated above the knee.

By Saturday 3 November small strikes were still being sent to work over the airfields and ensure that no serviceable aircraft had survived Phase 1 but the main weight of attack was directed against Gamil Bridge which carried the main coastal road and railway line from Port Said to Damietta and the west. It was a steel girder bridge and, whilst it was soon damaged, it proved difficult to destroy by dive-bombing. Success was eventually achieved with a low-flying 'lay-down' technique

Sea Venom WW 281, side-number 095, of 893 NAS coming to rest on its belly having successfully caught one of *Eagle*'s arrester wires despite damage by anti-aircraft fire during an attack on Almeza airfield which had prevented the undercarriage from being lowered. (Author's collection)

in which the bombs were released shortly before the aircraft overflew the bridge to hit the sluice gates structure under it 'like darts' into a dart board. Fuzes with a 20-second delay ensured that aircraft were clear before detonation but one Wyvern was shot down by anti-aircraft fire. Lieutenant D F McCarthy RN jettisoned his bombs and headed out to sea but his aircraft, WN 330, was on fire and he was forced to eject about three miles off Port Said where he was shelled by shore batteries.[26] These were strafed by Sea Hawks and soon stopped firing and a section of Sea Hawks was maintained overhead to defend McCarthy. He was rescued after 75 minutes in the water by Whirlwind XG581 from *Eagle* flown by Lieutenant P Bailey RN. At the time this was the longest SAR mission carried out by an RN helicopter. By the end of the day, one-third of the bridge from the west end had been destroyed and the approach to Port Said along which Egyptian reinforcements must come from the west had been cut off. One interesting aspect of the attack was the poor intelligence provided to the fleet by the British targeting authorities who had stated that it was a swing bridge. Photographic analysis in *Eagle* showed that it clearly was not and led to the change of attack method.[27] During this phase the largely ineffective high-level bombing by Victors and Canberras continued at night in the optimistic belief, still held by the bomber lobby, despite the experience of Korea and the Second World War, that the enemy would quickly be frightened into submission.

Eagle withdrew from the operating area on Sunday 4 November to RAS liquids and the opportunity was taken to allow as much aircraft maintenance as possible to keep the maximum number of aircraft available. Phase 3 of the operation began with the landing of British and French paratroops in the Port Said area on Monday 5 November and *Eagle*'s fighters provided a 'cab-rank' of aircraft over the British positions from dawn ready to provide close air support on request. Helicopters were flown into Gamil airfield which had been quickly seized by British airborne forces, to deliver medical supplies and ferry British and French casualties out to the

A Sea Hawk FGA 6 of 899 NAS about to be launched from *Eagle*'s port catapult armed with cannon and 3in rocket projectiles with 60lb warheads. Note the staining around the cannon muzzles under the cockpit showing that they have been fired recently, probably on the previous sortie. The man running away from the aircraft is a flight deck engineer or 'badger' who has just attached the launch strop between the aircraft and the catapult shuttle. It has not yet been tensioned. The man sitting at left is working with the catapult control position or 'howdah' and he is sitting to avoid being blown over by jet blast when the aircraft is launched. (Author's collection)

fleet. The amphibious assault on Port Said was carried out on Tuesday 6 November and included the world's first operational vertical envelopment flown by helicopters from *Ocean* and *Theseus*. Again *Eagle*'s fighters flew close air support and one aircraft was shot down while strafing El Quantara and Lieutenant D F Mills RN, the pilot, ejected safely and landed on the east side of the canal. A CAP was maintained over him which 'discouraged' several vehicles which set out in his direction until a Whirlwind and its fighter escort arrived from *Eagle* to rescue him.

A second Wyvern was hit by anti-aircraft fire while carrying out an attack on the Port Said Coast Guard barracks. Lieutenant Commander W H Cowling RN, the senior pilot of 830 NAS, managed to fly his damaged aircraft back to the fleet and ejected safely. He was picked up after only a minute in the water. That night a ceasefire was agreed which ended military operations before the canal had been seized. On the morning of Wednesday 7 November *Eagle* transferred the remaining casualties to *Theseus*, transferred FOAC to *Bulwark* and then left the operating area for Malta from where she resumed her peacetime tasking. During her participation in Operation 'Musketeer', *Eagle*'s aircraft carried out 621 launches on the port catapult and expended seventy-two 1000lb bombs, 157 500lb bombs, 1488 3in rocket projectiles and 88,000 rounds of 20mm ammunition.

HMS *Bulwark*

In the summer of 1956 *Bulwark* had enjoyed a break from her trials and training duties to embark 809 (Sea Venom FAW 21s) and 824 (Gannet AS 1s) NAS for a fortnight's deck landing operational training. However, during severe gales whilst off the Scilly Isles on 28 July she was ordered to return to Portsmouth, disembark the two squadrons and make preparations to embark an air group of Sea Hawks. She entered harbour on 30 July 1956 with instructions to make all necessary preparations for operational service, including the loading of stores and ammunition. In August she embarked 804, 810 and 895 NAS and sailed for the Mediterranean. 804 was a newly-formed unit with Sea Hawk FGA 6s; 810 had been serving in the Far East in *Albion*, also with Sea Hawk FGA 6s, and had returned to the UK in May. It was to have been disbanded later in the year but this was postponed so that it could be embarked in *Bulwark*. 895 Squadron re-formed in April, initially with Sea Hawk FGA 6s but after *Bulwark*'s arrival in the Mediterranean, it exchanged its aircraft with 897 NAS and from October it operated Sea Hawk FB 3s. *Bulwark* carried out what was described in her ROP as a 'crowded and eventful' work-up[28] which included night operations and extensive live firings against Filfla rock in the Malta ranges.

Bulwark's aircraft took part in the initial dawn strike on Cairo West airfield on 1 November 1956 and this confirmed the technique for subsequent operations in

Phase 1. The pre-launch briefing gave adequate information about the target, including its defences; the tactical approach to and withdrawal from the target area and the aim of the mission. The attack was carefully timed to arrive over the target 10 minutes before sunrise and the ideal approach would have been at extremely low level from the darkest part of the horizon in the west towards the lighter horizon in the east.[29] However, photographic reconnaissance information showed aircraft parked on the day before in a north/south line and so a compromise approach was briefed. Aircraft dived over the desert to the south-west of the airfield on a north-easterly heading and left the target at ground level, flying right over the anti-aircraft positions so that guns would have to traverse rapidly to track their targets. The attack was made as a strafing dive with pilots briefed to select one target and make only one pass. The approach began at 90 degrees to the attack line with pilots turning to port for their strafing runs. Outside sections crossed over the inside sections on the order 'attack' to strafe the port hard standings; the inside sections strafed the starboard hard standings giving an overall attack on a broad front that would be difficult for gunners to engage. One flight was briefed to provide fighter escort to and from the target and would have engaged defending fighters over the target had it been necessary to do so.

Accurate navigation was essential and the route was pre-planned with timings marked in seconds. After launch full use was made of the ship's radar to give back bearings and distances *en route* for a calculation of ground speed. There was an initial lack of meteorological information for the target area and to cover every eventuality, two Sea Venoms were briefed to rendezvous with the strike so that, if necessary, they could lead it in through cloud with their radar. In the event the weather proved to be fine so although they joined up as briefed, they were not needed. The initial join-up after a night launch was crucial and was practised often in the weeks prior to the campaign. The leader flew straight ahead for two minutes after catapult launch and then made a rate one turn of 180 degrees onto the downwind leg. Aircraft in his flight 'cut the corner' to join him in close formation and he set heading for the target when he reached a position two miles on the port beam of the ship. The leader then switched on a rear-facing red landing lamp which extended from the radio access panel[30] and climbed on a vector to a position 40nm distant at 20,000ft. The second and third flights carried out the same procedure and the second flight leader also switched on a rearward-facing light. At the rendezvous the leading flight made one orbit to pick up the second flight and the two then made a second orbit to pick up the third. The rear-facing lamps were visible through and arc of about 30 degrees for 40 miles. On the first attack six Il 28s were destroyed in flames, three more appeared damaged and a single Lancaster destroyed. It was noted that only concentrated fire in the shallow dives exploded these aircraft. Surprise achieved a comparative immunity from anti-aircraft fire during the approach. On the withdrawal the Sea Hawks were too low for the depression of the enemy guns. Ninety-nine per cent of all enemy shells seemed to detonate astern of the aircraft. Subsequent attacks on Almaza, Inchas and Bilbeis confirmed that if a second attacking pass had to be made, it should be on a different direction from the first and, if possible, two aircraft should be detached to strafe the guns seconds before the attack. Generally, no target was attacked twice unless it was absolutely necessary to do so. When more than one strike was scheduled at the same time over different targets, it was important to have separate frequencies so that flight leaders could maintain control of their aircraft and give split-second orders without interference. Good post-strike photographs were essential to show whether re-strikes were needed. At the start of a strafing dive it was often impossible to see if the target was

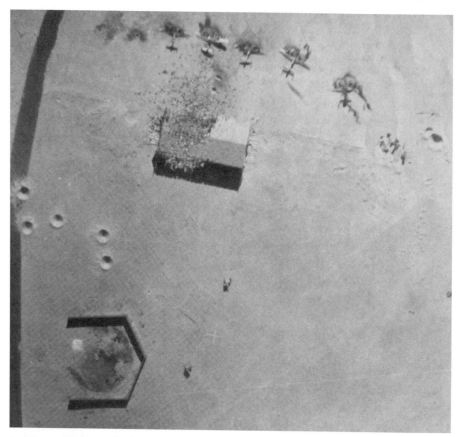

A strike assessment photograph showing burnt-out Lancaster bombers of the EAF and a hangar that had been damaged by strafing and bombing attacks on Cairo West airfield. (Author's collection)

a burnt-out wreck or a serviceable aircraft and once committed, there was no changing of targets unless they were adjacent and close.

Phase 2 began for *Bulwark*'s Sea Hawks with an armed reconnaissance of the Ismailia to Tel-el-Kebir road. For this phase six squash-head 3in rockets were carried by all aircraft and these, together with their launcher-rails, reduced the aircraft's radius of action by about 15 miles and its rate of climb very considerably. No immediate target was seen but a large area was covered and the majority of hits on aircraft by small-arms fire occurred during this phase. Although increasingly unlikely, there was always the possibility that reconnaissance aircraft could be attacked by enemy fighters. For this reason, these missions were flown by flights of four aircraft, one section staying low to carry out the reconnaissance and the other staying higher to give mutual cover. At the half-way point they swapped so that no armament was wasted and fuel was evenly used. Low-level work significantly reduced the Sea Hawk's radius of action, especially when carrying external weapons, but on the other hand land-based fighters from Cyprus lacked the endurance to even carry out these missions so the naval fighters played a critical role. Later sorties along the road found enemy tanks sheltering in the shadows of trees and these were attacked with rockets from a shallow, 15-degree dive. Soft-skinned vehicles were often carefully positioned between buses, private cars or company petrol lorries and so, for humanitarian reasons, these were ignored. Sometimes lorries were found pulled over to the side of the road and these were strafed effectively despite small-arms fire. The squash-head rockets had a devastating effect on armoured vehicles but strafing was better for lorries. The effects of rocket attacks were not always obvious to the pilots who fired them and loitering at low level to look for signs of damage was not a good idea so it was found to be advisable to have a PR section on call to witness and photograph results.

For Phase 3 the Sea Hawks were armed either with rockets or 500lb bombs as well as their four 20mm cannon. With these the aircraft had about 30 minutes available on a 'cab rank' waiting to give close air support when requested for troops on the ground. The three British carriers operated independent cycles of operation so that aircraft were maintained over the target area continuously throughout the day. An eight-aircraft sortie was the accepted number, usually controlled by senior division leaders but they flew in two divisions of four aircraft. Leaders were adept at allocating targets to the division or section that was nearest to the target or best armed to achieve its destruction, factors not easily appreciated by the forward air control (FAC) teams on the ground. When not on target, aircraft maintained loose formation at 10,000ft with minimum engine rpm to conserve fuel. A wide variety of targets was engaged during this phase including SU-100 self-propelled artillery dug into positions in a cemetery, concrete pill-boxes, a coast-guard building that had become a strongpoint and soft-skinned vehicles. When no immediate targets were available, aircraft carried out road reconnaissance after checking with the FAC team that this would be their best employment. Fortunately there were usually more aircraft available on the 'cab rank' than targets for them to attack but by the end of the operation supplies of large-scale maps were running low in the task force. CAP sorties were maintained over the fleet throughout 'Musketeer' but there was no enemy 'trade' for them to intercept. On one occasion the CAP leader identified three Egyptian fast patrol boats at sea in mist which was dispersing 30 miles off Alexandria. A strike was directed towards them which sank two and damaged the third. Despite its damage, it managed to pick up survivors and was left alone to carry them back to shore.

Maintenance procedures worked well and high serviceability continued throughout the operation. Aircraft were pooled into a 'garage' scheme rather than maintained by the individual squadrons and this worked well without any loss of competitive spirit. The technical ratings were always keen to hear what their aircraft were doing and seemed to work more effectively when they were kept 'in the picture'. Once concentrated flying began the aircraft seemed to stay serviceable, giving credence to the adage that the more you fly aircraft the more serviceable they remain. 'Maincheck' examinations called for by the number of hours flown were postponed and, in the opinion of *Bulwark*'s Commander (AE), this added to their serviceability rather than detracted from it. Many local repair schemes were carried out on aircraft hit by shrapnel or bullets; these all stood up to rigorous tests and reflect great credit on the ingenuity of the officers and ratings who carried them out. The operation of an all-Sea Hawk air group undoubtedly simplified the ship's operations, both on the flight deck and in the hangar. Within the constraints of their armament fit the aircraft also flew similar sortie lengths. During the six days of operations against Egyptian targets *Bulwark*'s aircraft flew 580 sorties and she remained with the Mediterranean Fleet for the rest of November as a precaution. In December she returned to the UK and underwent a refit in Portsmouth Dockyard after which she joined the Home Fleet in May 1957 as an operational carrier. The trials and training task was taken over by *Warrior* which had completed a major modernisation in late 1956.

HMS *Albion*

When the Suez crisis began in July 1956 *Albion* was undergoing a planned refit in Portsmouth following service in the FEF that had ended in May. The refit was shortened and she embarked 800 (Sea Hawk FGA 6s) and 802 (Sea Hawk FB 3s), 809 (Sea Venom FAW 21s) and 849C (Skyraider AEW 1s) NAS to join the Mediterranean Fleet to work up in September. 800 NAS had served in *Ark Royal* earlier in the year but she was undergoing a major refit when the crisis began and the unit embarked in *Albion* on 15 September. 802 NAS had re-commissioned at RNAS Lossiemouth in February 1956 and carried out deck landing training in *Bulwark* in June as part of its work-up for operational service. It also joined *Albion* on 15 September. 809 NAS had re-commissioned at RNAS Yeovilton and was carrying out deck landing practice in *Bulwark* when the crisis began. It joined *Albion* on 15 September. 849C NAS had been part of *Albion*'s air group in 1955 but had been based ashore for most of 1956 before joining the new air group on 15 September.[31]

Albion and her squadrons had carried out an intensive work-up in the Malta areas using RNAS Hal Far as a spare deck after her arrival in the Mediterranean. She sailed for the operational area on 29 October together, but not in company, with *Eagle* and *Bulwark*. They proceeded at high speed to the east with their escorts and arrived in a position about 150 miles off the Nile delta on 31 October. During the passage night launches and form-ups were practised twice, once individually and once in company with the other carriers. Action stations were sounded when unidentified radar contacts were detected but in every case these proved to be friendly or did not close the force. CAPs were maintained during daylight hours and after dark contrails and radar contacts showed the RAF bomber forces *en route* to attack Egypt. From 05.20 onwards on 1 November 1956 *Albion* launched her first strike. It comprised eight Sea Hawks led by Lieutenant Commander Eveleigh, the commanding officer of 802 NAS, and four Sea Venoms led by Lieutenant Commander Shilcock, the commanding officer of 809 NAS. The target was the airfield at Almaza, six miles east of Cairo and 130 miles distant from the fleet. MiG-15s, Il-28s and transport aircraft were known to be based there and the aim was to destroy them on the ground.[32] The strike went according to plan with negligible interference from the light anti-aircraft positions sited around the airfield. Two MiG-15s took off just before the strike arrived but came nowhere near the British aircraft and appeared to fly away to the south. Throughout 1 November strikes of eight or twelve aircraft continued to be launched on a one hour and five minute cycle. They climbed to 20,000ft on vectors toward their targets and then let down on track with their navigation aided by radar bearings and distances passed from the ship's aircraft direction team. Aircraft on the ground were strafed with cannon fire after which the strike aircraft retired from the target area 'on the deck' at 400 knots until they reached the coast. Once they went 'feet wet' they throttled back to conserve fuel and climbed to 5000ft. A tactic developed by the BPF was continued in which returning strikes flew over a picket destroyer which visually identified them before they entered the CAP and gun defence zones and checked that they were not being followed out to the fleet by hostile aircraft. The 'one pass and away' principle was strictly adhered to until it was realised that in some places defences were non-existent. At Bilbeis, the Egyptian air training college, for instance, there were no defences at all. Here twelve Sea Hawks found about 100 Chipmunk, Harvard and other training aircraft parked around the airfield in three groups; they set up a race track pattern and strafed aircraft until either expenditure of all their ammunition or shortage of fuel forced aircraft to return. By the end of the first day *Albion*'s aircraft were estimated to have destroyed twenty-eight aircraft on the ground and damaged a further forty-seven.

Day 2 of the operation on 2 November began with further strikes on airfields but as fewer viable targets were found on them Phase 2 began in the afternoon with attacks on a large concentration of tanks and soft-skinned vehicles at Huckstep barracks. Lieutenant Commander Russell, the commanding officer of 800 NAS, used rockets for the first time in the operation and destroyed a number of tanks. 802 Squadron's Sea Hawk FB 3s could not be fitted with rockets and used their front-guns to strafe and set fire to columns of soft-skinned vehicles. As the day progressed, it was noticed that anti-aircraft fire increased in intensity and accuracy but it still proved to be only a deterrent rather than a real threat. Other than a few dents the only significant damage was to an aircraft drop tank. On 3 November 1956 *Albion* left the task group and moved north to refuel and replenish before rejoining the other carriers on Sunday 4 November. The targets allocated to her aircraft were mainly in preparation for the assault phase and gun emplacements at Port Said were attacked four times. A dawn strike was carried out by 802 NAS on Almaza to ensure that no enemy aircraft had been flown into it and during this an anti-aircraft shell burst over Sub Lieutenant Clarke's cockpit canopy which completely shattered. He recovered safely to the ship and, in view of the recent introduction of hard flying helmets, much was made of the fact that a sliver of Perspex had stuck in his helmet but he had not noticed. A flock of birds took off in front of Lieutenant Worth as he left the target; one of them hit the starboard intake and caused considerable damage but he, too, made it safely back to the ship. Arguably birds in the delta caused as much damage as anti-aircraft gunfire. The Sea Venoms of 809 NAS were employed both on CAP and strike duties.

Following the airborne assault on 5 November and the amphibious assault on 6 November all possible aircraft were employed on the 'cab-rank' to provide close air support for the ground forces and a continuous CAP was maintained. Aircraft were maintained over Port Said and Port Fuad throughout daylight hours with 800 and 809 NAS armed with 3in rockets as well as their four 20mm cannon. 802 NAS' FB 3s used their cannon effectively against troops on the ground, soft-skinned vehicles and buildings. 802 NAS also did all *Albion*'s photographic reconnaissance work with cameras fitted inside modified drop tanks. During operations on 6 November

Lieutenant Stuart Jervis' Sea Hawk blew up after being hit by anti-aircraft fire off Port Said but he managed to eject successfully and was picked up by a sea-boat from the amphibious headquarters ship *Meon*. 849C NAS spent the early part of the operation flying airborne early warning barrier patrols between the task group and the shore to detect any enemy aircraft that might try to attack the fleet by flying below the ship's radar horizon. When the airfield at Gamil was taken by British airborne forces, however, they had sufficient serviceable aircraft to take on other tasks which included taking water, medical supplies and even 1000 cans of beer ashore for the paratroops while the airfield was still under fire from enemy snipers.

Albion's two helicopters flew throughout the daylight hours, the two pilots flying nearly 40 hours each between 31 October and 7 November.[33] They flew plane-guard duties near the deck during every launch and recovery and played an important part in evacuating seriously wounded soldiers from Gamil airfield to the carriers for

Albion's Ship's Flight Whirlwind HAR 3 helicopter bringing casualties back to the ship on 5 November 1956. (Author's collection)

medical treatment. On their trips to the shore they carried water, gasoline, medical supplies and batteries for the FAC radios. At night, even when there was no moon, they delivered operation orders for the next day around the fleet; the first time this task had been carried out by helicopters rather than sea-boats. *Albion's* ROP for 'Musketeer'[34] emphasised that the operation had shown the speed and mobility of an aircraft carrier task force which had taken the aircraft, their logistic and tactical support to the scene of action at high speed to carry out any task required of it in action. When the ship left FOAC's operational control on 29 November, the command was delighted to receive a typically understated signal from Admiral Power that said '*Albion's* work-up is now completed'. She had been operating continuously at sea for thirty-one days, flying over 1000 sorties in November and 2000 since arriving in the Mediterranean, all of them without accident. She remained in the Mediterranean Fleet until March 1957 when she joined the Home Fleet with 824 NAS (Gannet AS 1s) added to her air group.

Helicopter-borne Assault from the Sea

Between October 1952 and December 1956 848 (Whirlwind HAR 21) NAS had operated ashore in support of military forces against Communist insurgents in Malaya. Its personnel had learnt a great deal about the tactical use of helicopters and it was logical to consider using helicopters to land marines from aircraft carriers as the next step but the idea was not immediately taken forward in the UK because of the low priority given to amphibious warfare by the Ministry of Defence. In the USA, however, funding was provided to convert an escort carrier, the USS *Thetis Bay* (CVE-90), into a helicopter-carrying amphibious assault ship to test the theory of what the US Marine Corps called 'vertical envelopment', the landing of forces over the shoreline directly onto their objectives inland. The conversion took place in San Francisco Naval Shipyard between June 1955 and July 1956.[35] Her completion was, thus, very much headline news at the time the Suez crisis developed and her plans were made available to the Admiralty. Re-designated CVHA-1 when she re-joined the fleet she was capable of operating twenty HRS Marine helicopters. The catapults, lifts and arrester wires were removed and a new, larger lift sited right aft[36] with the structure aft of it cut away to allow the helicopters to overhang the after lift edge. She was considered to be an experimental ship and so the accommodation for the embarked force was somewhat austere, but she was capable of carrying thirty-eight officers and 900 enlisted marines in addition to her ship's company of 540.[37] Marine accommodation was sited at the forward end of the former hangar with the helicopters aft. Light vehicles, such as jeeps, that could be carried by the helicopters as an underslung load were parked on the starboard side of the flight

A bomb bursting during an attack on Gamil bridge. While this bomb missed the bridge, it did hit and damage a nearby radar station. (Author's collection)

deck clear of helicopter operations. As the situation deteriorated after Nasser nationalised the Suez Canal in July 1956 there was no time for a similar conversion but the RN did have two carriers that were employed on non-flying duties immediately available. *Ocean* and *Theseus* were both in commission and serving with the Home Fleet Training Squadron.

HM Ships Ocean *and* Theseus
Within 48 hours of the canal's seizure both ships were ordered from Portland to their home ports to land trainees and prepare the accommodation in the former hangar for the embarkation of troops. On 5 August *Theseus* left Portsmouth with 16th Independent Parachute Brigade embarked, a deck park of vehicles secured by ringbolts hastily welded to the flight deck and hundreds of tons of ammunition and stores stowed away in the former bomb rooms. *Ocean* sailed from Plymouth on

7 August with the 1st Army Group, Royal Artillery embarked, comprising the 21st and 50th Medium Artillery Regiments embarked with their guns, vehicles and stores lashed to the deck and a quantity of ammunition and stores in the bomb rooms and magazines.[38] Both forces were landed in Cyprus where there was no deep-water port at the time and so the ships anchored off shore and the vehicles were lowered by ships' cranes and 'Jumbo' the mobile crane onto self-propelled lighters. Chutes were manufactured that allowed stores and ammunition to be slid down into the lighters from flight-deck level in 2.5 seconds. The noon temperature was 35 degrees Centigrade in the shade and so much of the manual work of disembarkation was done at night. Even before the ships were cleared of their outbound troops, they began to embark 3 Commando Brigade Royal Marines. 45 Commando together with their vehicles and stores embarked in *Theseus*; 40 Commando plus the Headquarters Unit, vehicles and stores in *Ocean*. Both had been in Cyprus for a year on operations against EOKA terrorists and they were to be taken to Malta where they would carry out an intensive amphibious warfare work-up to prepare them for Operation 'Musketeer'. Shortly before the ships sailed the Governor of Cyprus, Field Marshal Sir John Harding, came on board to thank the commando units for their work on the island.

In September 1956 the Admiralty decided to carry out a trial to find the best manner of operating a large force of helicopters from the two light fleet carriers with the aim of landing a Commando of 450 men on an objective up to 15 miles from the ship. Once the optimum methods were identified the ships were to work up in the shortest possible time to reach operational efficiency. Rear Admiral Sayer, Flag Officer Training Squadron, was re-designated Flag Officer Helicopter Force, flying his flag in *Ocean*. The designated helicopter units were 845 NAS with eight Whirlwind HAS 22s and two HAR 3s which had previously been evaluating helicopter anti-submarine tactics at a number of naval air stations ashore and was now to embark in *Ocean*. Fortunately the squadron had carried out a short period of deck landing training in *Ocean* and *Theseus* during June 1956. *Theseus* was to embark the Joint Helicopter Unit (JHU), from RAF Middle Wallop. It was equipped with six Whirlwind HAR 2 and six Sycamore Mark 14 helicopters and was tasked with developing assault and support helicopter operations for land-based military operations; it had a mixture of Army and RAF pilots. In order to operate them the ships' avgas systems had to be restored to operational use by dockyard technicians, wiring to Flyco, the flight deck lighting and the briefing rooms had to be restored to operational capability and Air Departments had to be appointed and drafted to the ships.[39]

The initial trials evaluated helicopter operations with the ship at anchor and under way, night ranging and striking down, the calculation of maximum relative winds for rotor starting and stopping, the ideal formation for assault flights and the best way of refuelling on deck.[40] Emplaning and deplaning drills had to be perfected to get fully-equipped commandos from their messdecks deep in the ship to their aircraft on the flight deck in the shortest time. These evolutions seem straightforward and obvious now but at the time they represented a novel form of warfare that had to be learned quickly with no margin for error. The two ships had seen recent service as operational carriers but the training role had required guard rails to be fixed to the flight deck and a lot of instructional material and extra accommodation fitted into the hangar. Much of this had to be removed together with some of the ringbolts fitted in August, although a number were still required to lash down the commandos' equipment. The operation of a mixture of Whirlwinds and Sycamores from one of the ships had its own problems but the most immediate need was to train twenty Army and RAF pilots to deck land under a variety of conditions and their maintenance personnel to be effective at sea. Overall they were enthusiastic and coped very well. The work-up after the trial was shrouded in secrecy and exercise areas were carefully selected to keep the task group out of sight of land. A 22-helicopter formation manoeuvring in the middle of the English Channel must have surprised the crews of a number of fishing vessels. The trials were completed in two weeks and the JHU demonstrated its newly acquired skills by showing that it could land-on its twelve helicopters, refuel them, embark sticks of troops and launch again in the space of nine minutes. On completion of the trials, the squadrons disembarked to their parent air stations and the ships returned to their home ports.

In October the squadrons were ordered to re-embark. For reasons that were no doubt clear at the time but have subsequently become obscure, they changed ships; 845 NAS embarking in *Theseus* and the JHU in *Ocean*. Vehicles and stores were loaded and secured to the flight decks and the ships sailed for Malta. Whilst on passage the opportunity was taken to work up the ships' flight deck parties with their new squadrons and to practice the weighing of stores and movement of vehicles. Once they arrived in Malta helicopter loading and performance trials were carried out with the assistance of men from 45 Commando, the unit selected to carry out the helicopter-borne assault if it was ordered. The two ships sailed from Malta on 3 November with the Commando and its equipment divided between the two ships. The remainder of 3 Commando Brigade was embarked in conventional landing craft from which they attacked over the beaches. Brigadier R W Madoc OBE ADC RM, commanding officer of the Brigade, was embarked in the Landing Craft (Headquarters) ship *Meon*. 40 Commando under Lieutenant Colonel D G Tweedie MBE RM landed on Red Beach from the LSTs *Striker* and *Reggio*; 42 Commando under Lieutenant Colonel P L Norcock OBE RM landed on Green

Whirlwind HAS 22s of 845 NAS on *Ocean* during the early work-up phase of Operation 'Musketeer'. (Author's collection)

Beach from the LSTs *Anzio* and *Suvla*. Communications for the whole force were centred on the destroyer depot ship *Tyne* which acted as the combined headquarters ship. She sailed from Limassol in Cyprus on 4 November to be in a position 30 miles north of Port Said when the airborne assault took place. From that date onwards Air Marshal Barnett co-ordinated air operations from *Tyne*, partly through signal traffic with the air operations centre at RAF Episkopi in Cyprus and partly through a daily directive to FOAC. General Sir Hugh Stockwell, the land force commander, was also embarked in *Tyne* but his French deputy, General Andre Beaufre, embarked in the French depot ship *Gustave Zédé*.

Whilst 'Musketeer' was still in the planning stage, consideration had been given to using helicopter-borne commandos to seize bridges and other key targets but, after discussion, these ideas were considered by the majority to be too bold and it was decided to hold 45 Commando and the helicopters as a 'floating reserve'. Two operational orders had been issued with the appropriate one to be selected at short notice before an assault was ordered. The first called for a massed assault by all the helicopters into a known, large landing zone (LZ), and the second stream landings by divisions of six helicopters into a small LZ. The second order also required the use of a reconnaissance helicopter to identify the best LZ. This was an undesirable feature but would be unavoidable in the confused situation after the initial landings. By the evening of 5 November 1956 *Ocean* and *Theseus* were off Port Said. The helicopters were all ranged on deck and pre-weighed loads were placed ready alongside the marked emplaning points. Less favourable weather might have made preparations more difficult but the weather throughout Operation 'Musketeer' was perfect. Shortly before dawn on 6 November the two carriers anchored in the swept channel in a position 8.5 miles off Port Said where personnel gathered, waiting, on the flight deck had a grandstand view of the initial bombardment and conventional landings over the beach. The shore bombardment was limited to 4.5in shells from destroyers to limit civilian casualties and damage to property. *Decoy*, *Duchess*, *Diamond* and *Chaplet* between them fired 1063 rounds between 04.03 and 07.54.

Concerns grew in *Ocean* and *Theseus* that their commandos would not, after all, be ordered into action but at 07.41 the executive signal was received stating that 3 Commando Brigade required the first wave of helicopters immediately at LZ map reference GR 73999512. Operation Order Number 2 was to be used. Eighteen minutes later a Whirlwind of 845 NAS landed Lieutenant Colonel N H Tailyour RM, the commanding officer of 45 Commando, with his headquarters and LZ control team at the selected LZ. This was a sports stadium which stood out in the smoke and flames of the assault area. However, as the pilot took off a bullet hit one of his thumbs and he realised that both his aircraft and the men he had just landed were under enemy small-arms fire. Gallantly he turned back, landed and picked up the marines, some of whom had been wounded by this stage, and set them down next to the de Lesseps statue. He then radioed the details of the new LZ to the helicopter divisions which were already airborne and orbiting the carriers, and the first operational helicopter assault in history began. By 10.21 845 NAS and the JHU had landed 415 RM commandos, three anti-tank guns, four mortars and 15 tons of ammunition at the LZ. The reconnaissance helicopter was found to have thirty bullet holes which rendered it 'very unserviceable' and a Sycamore crashed on *Ocean*'s flight deck after suffering an engine failure on take-off. Fortunately there were no injuries to its crew, passengers or the flight deck party. Once it was established ashore, however, 45 Commando had the misfortune to suffer casualties in a 'friendly fire' incident.[41] The Joint Fire Support Committee (JFSC), in *Meon* ordered aircraft from a 'cab-rank' to attack an enemy gun that was firing on British ships. A division of three Wyverns of 830 NAS was called down and their leader was informed that the gun was near a mosque with two minarets with British troops 400 yards to the east; he was given the map reference and repeated it correctly. The leader found an anti-tank gun near the mosque but reported that he thought it might be British; he was ordered to continue with the attack, however. The pilot of the third aircraft reported that he could see troops on a nearby road and gave the JFSC the map reference and then strafed them with cannon fire. The men under fire were British and 45 Commando suffered sixteen casualties including the commanding officer and Major Long, the intelligence officer. Two members of an air control team were also injured. A ground liaison officer who had established an observation post on the roof of a police station on the west bank of the canal saw the attack developing and tried to call the Wyverns to tell them to abort on the ground attack common radio channel but could not establish contact. A subsequent enquiry found that attempts to pinpoint the target by the JFSC were confusing as there were several similar mosques south of the beach. The JFSC had used maps of a different scale to those carried by the pilots and should have handed control of the attack to an air control team on the spot. It was considered likely that the pilots thought that they were being given orders by an air control team in contact with the enemy and not directly from the JFSC in *Meon*. They had queried the target several times before being ordered to attack and no blame was attached to the Wyvern division for the errors that led to the incident.

Whirlwinds of 845 NAS running in to carry out the first operational airborne commando assault in history. Note the landing craft moving towards the beach on the right of the picture and the smoke burning from fires on shore. The photograph was taken from the 20mm Oerlikon gun position on the starboard side of an LCT Mark 8's bridge structure. The wire rails in the immediately in the foreground were a crude way of preventing the gun from firing into the ship's own structure when tracking a target quickly. (Author's collection)

A somewhat 'posed' photograph of the Joint Helicopter Unit disembarking from *Ocean* to Gamil airfield, intended for the media. There are five Sycamores and a single Whirlwind in the formation. Note how crowded the anchorage off Port Said had become by this stage. (Author's collection)

After the assault phase, helicopters continued to fly on a variety of tasks. The most important of these was casualty evacuation and the ROP cites the unusual case of a marine who, having left *Ocean* by helicopter, was wounded shortly after landing, evacuated back to the ship and was in a bed in the sick bay only 20 minutes after his original take-off. The ship was, by then, close inshore and so this should not be considered a normal occurrence for amphibious operations. Other tasks included support for the movement of RAF Regiment and airfield control contingents into Gamil to open up the airfield and the movement of senior officers from all Services to various strategic locations. Urgent stores and ammunition were flown ashore in large quantities and mail from ships was collected and distributed. Total flying for 6 November 1956 amounted to the landing of 479 marines and 20 tons of stores and ammunition with a total of 194 deck landings. The JHU subsequently disembarked to Gamil and *Theseus* sailed for Malta on 7 November. *Ocean* sailed a day later; both ships had a number of casualties embarked. Their ship's companies were largely proud of an innovative task that had been well executed.

The low priority given to amphibious warfare by British defence planners prior to 1956 had undoubtedly led to a lack of adequate understanding of the potentially crucial role that helicopters could play in an amphibious assault. Neither *Ocean* nor *Theseus* was adequately equipped to get the best out of the vertical envelopment role and their helicopters were certainly not the best available but the important things to note are that they were capable of the role and they were available at short notice. A lack of confidence in such a novel form of warfare led to them being seen initially as a floating reserve but their successful assault, albeit against limited opposition, showed what could be achieved and helicopter assault emerged from Operation 'Musketeer' as one of the biggest lessons for the future. Admiral Mountbatten (1SL), with his background in Combined Operations, was quick to seize on the importance of this capability and saw that it evolved very quickly into an important element of strike fleet operations. Tactics against both opposed and unopposed landings became the subject of an intense period of study over the next four years. Analysis of the assault phase of 'Musketeer' highlighted the conclusion that forces based in fixed locations intended for use in a global conflict were far from ideal for a short-notice 'brushfire' conflict like the Suez crisis where speed of reaction was essential. It summed up the general feeling by stating[42] that 'the main conclusion that can be drawn from the assault side of this successful operation is that if we require to have a "fire brigade" ready to deal with the conflagrations that are liable to break out suddenly, it is no good waiting for the fire to start before pulling the engine out from the back of the barn. Like its counterpart ashore the fire engine must be polished and ready and the crew handy.'

The Importance of RNAS Hal Far in Malta

The RN air station at Hal Far in Malta played an important role throughout the Suez crisis both as a spare deck and work-up base for the strike carriers and by administering ranges and danger areas. At one stage while *Eagle* and *Bulwark* were in harbour there were ten naval air squadrons disembarked to the air station in addition to the resident 728 NAS, a fleet requirements unit, and VP-11, a squadron of US Navy maritime patrol aircraft based permanently at Hal Far. When a bomber offensive against Egypt was ordered as part of 'Musketeer', a number of RAF Bomber Command Canberra squadrons were deployed to Hal Far; the Valiant units being deployed to RAF Luqa. Considerable quantities of bombs and fuel had to be supplied continuously to both airfields in order to keep them in action. Once the strike and assault phases began, Hal Far's major naval commitment was to maintain a supply of serviceable replacement aircraft to the squadrons embarked in the carriers. Replacements were flown out from the UK via France with speed and efficiency and then ferried forward to the fleet.[43]

Operation 'Toreador'

Task Group 324, centred on the cruiser *Newfoundland* was positioned in the Red Sea and activated on 31 October 1956 to protect British and neutral shipping approaching the Suez Canal from the south.[44] In addition to the cruiser, it comprised the destroyer *Diana*, the frigates *Crane* and *Modeste* and the RFA Tanker *Wave Sovereign*; two French frigates, *La Perouse* and *Gazelle*, were available in Djibouti if required. On 31 October *Newfoundland* and *Diana* were entering the Gulf of Suez after sunset, nine miles north of Ras Gharib when a darkened ship was detected astern of a group of merchant vessels. Both British warships were at action stations and Captain Hamilton brought them onto a course parallel to the darkened vessel with their main armament trained on it. The range had closed to only seven cables[45] when a 20in signalling lamp on *Newfoundland* was used to illuminate the ship which was immediately identified as the Egyptian frigate *Domiat*.[46] Captain Hamilton's instructions were to capture rather than sink Egyptian warships and he signalled 'Stop or I fire'. *Domiat* acknowledged and slowed at first but then increased speed and, to her ship's company's credit, trained her two 4in guns on her larger adversary. Captain Hamilton had little choice but to order fire to be opened and *Newfoundland* engaged with her main armament of 6in guns, secondary 4in guns and even 40mm Bofors guns at 01.20. The first salvo hit *Domiat* on the waterline and she was subsequently hit repeatedly before capsizing at 01.35 and sinking a few minutes later, the cruiser had checked fire at 01.30 and lowered a whaler which picked up two men. *Diana* was ordered to search for survivors and picked up six officers and sixty men. Unfortunately, at 03.00 two unidentified ships were detected to the north-west and she was ordered to break off rescue operations even though there were still men in the water near her. Throughout the unequal action the British sailors had felt considerable sympathy for their Egyptian counterparts, many of whom had been trained in the UK, and who were clearly doing their duty. Most of the survivors appeared to be unaware that Great Britain and Egypt were at war and some even offered to join the RN as cooks or stewards! A number of wounded were treated in *Diana* by her surgeon who used the wardroom as an emergency operating theatre to amputate a badly wounded man's leg. *Newfoundland* had been hit by two 4in shells which had killed a Chinese steward and wounded five of the ship's company, none of them seriously. *Diana* had engaged the target briefly with her forward turrets but suffered no damage.

In daylight the task group could have been at risk if attacked by Egyptian Il-28 bombers since it lacked its own air cover but the engagement with *Domiat* showed that gun-armed cruisers still had a part to play in giving a modern strike fleet defence in depth against a variety of threats. Throughout the night action Captain

Hamilton's principle concern had been that Egyptian fast patrol boats might have engaged his force at high speed from different directions. That is why he had his ships closed up at action stations after sunset and why he ordered *Diana* to cease rescue operations and close him when unidentified radar contacts were detected although, in the event, they proved not to be hostile and there were no Egyptian attacks on the task group. *Crane* patrolled the approaches to the Gulf of Aqaba and *Modeste* patrolled the southern end of the Gulf of Suez. On 3 November Israeli forces were moving south down the Sinai Peninsula and *Crane* witnessed a tank battle ashore from a position just off the Enterprise Channel as she went to dusk action stations. Five aircraft were seen over the battle which suddenly turned towards the ship in line ahead formation. At first they were thought to be Egyptian MiG-15s but then identified as Israeli Air Force Mystères. *Crane* had a Union flag painted on her upper deck, hoisted battle ensigns and turned south-east at her top speed of 17 knots into the growing twilight. Despite these measures, the Israeli fighters appear to have thought the ship was the Egyptian frigate *Tarik*, *Crane*'s former sister-ship *Whimbrel*, and attacked her with rockets and bombs. Once under attack, *Crane* opened fire on the aircraft, shot one down and damaged a second. With the wisdom of hindsight, placing a vessel that was identical to an Egyptian unit so close to Israeli forces was not a good idea and the incident certainly highlighted the task group's vulnerability if Egyptian aircraft had been used aggressively. The ship suffered a number of casualties but none of them were fatal and she managed to carry out repairs that kept her in the operational area until she left for more permanent repairs in Singapore. Overall the task group had achieved its aim of protecting shipping in the Red Sea and had acted decisively when necessary.

The Ceasefire

There had been international condemnation of the Anglo-French action at Suez, however, and the lack of American support virtually guaranteed the two nations' isolation. At meetings of the UN Security Council the British and French delegates used their veto twice; once against a US resolution and once against a Soviet resolution. On 2 November 1956 the UN General Assembly called for a ceasefire and there were many who spoke of the Anglo-French assault as resembling the Soviet seizure of Budapest and the overthrow of the Hungarian Government which had happened on 4 November. With a run on the pound, no support from the US Government and threats from the Soviet Union which cast itself as the protector of Arab interests in order to further its own aims in the Middle East, the Allies had little option but to agree a ceasefire. When senior officers gathered in *Tyne* on the evening of 6 November they were surprised to hear on the BBC news that a ceasefire had been agreed for 23.59Z[47] that night. This was followed shortly afterwards by a signal from London that confirmed the ceasefire and required the Allies to hand over to a UN Force as soon as it was in position. As might be imagined, the message was received with some surprise and General Stockwell ordered troops to head down the canal as fast as possible. By 23.59Z they had reached El Cap, 23 miles south of Port Said but by then the Egyptians had effectively closed the canal by sinking a number of blockships that would take a considerable time to remove.

Operation 'Musketeer' itself can be considered a military success but the three-month delay between the canal's nationalisation and Allied intervention had virtually guaranteed its political failure. The operation might have been ill-fated and ill-timed but the aspect of it that stood out above all others was the complete success of both the fixed and rotary-wing carrier operations. They had done everything asked of them and more, maintained an excellent sortie rate with minimal accidents but most importantly, they had shown themselves capable of rapid intervention in 'peacetime' emergencies. Strike and helicopter carriers had shown that they formed the essential core of a British rapid intervention capability.

Carrier Operations Analysed

Early in the operation the carriers operated in Area Alpha inside a 35-mile radius circle with its centre about 330 degrees 95nm from Port Said. The British carriers normally kept to the southern part and the French to the north. On 4 November the carriers moved nearer to the coast; the British to Area Delta, the French to Area Charlie, both circles of 20 miles radius about 70 miles from Port Said. Two submarines were stationed 12 miles off the Egyptian coast for SAR duties. Picket destroyers were stationed about 40 miles south-west of the centre of Area Alpha but these were withdrawn on the second day when the possibility of enemy air attack appeared negligible. The underway replenishment group operated for most of the time 40 to 60 miles north of the carriers.[48] Each carrier was allocated a sector within a seven-mile radius circle based on the task group guide and operated independently with its own anti-aircraft escorts. The formation axis was maintained more or less into wind.

The dawn strikes on 1 November were launched when the carriers were approximately 135 miles from their targets. The maximum practical radius of action for Sea Hawks fitted with long-range tanks was 150nm when carrying bombs and 160nm with front guns only; the carriers were, therefore, operating close to their maximum radius of action and any attack that caused delays in recovery could have had serious consequences. The French carriers flew anti-submarine patrols on 1 November and made two attacks on Egyptian warships. Strikes were also carried out against road traffic, airfields and close air support missions were flown in support of French ground forces.

The daily number of sorties flown by fixed-wing naval aircraft was as follows

Date	Eagle	Albion	Bulwark	British Total	French Total
1 Nov	135	93	124	352	27
2 Nov	125	66	105	296	28
3 Nov	113	RAS	91	204	30
4 Nov	4/RAS	80	93	177	RAS
5 Nov	124	91	101	316	45
6 Nov	120	85	66	271	36

The average number of sorties per operational day, in round figures, was 120 for *Eagle*, eighty-five for *Albion* and ninety-five for *Bulwark*. Flying operations were facilitated by good weather and the lack of serious Egyptian opposition. It was possible to ferry replacement aircraft onto the carriers from land bases after their preparation at Hal Far. On the other hand, sorties were limited by problems with the BH 5 catapult which was operating near the limit of its capability. *Eagle's* starboard catapult was unserviceable throughout the operation and *Bulwark* had both catapults unserviceable during part of the morning of 6 November and one unserviceable for part of every day except 1 November. *Albion* was reduced to a single catapult for most of 4 November. At least thirty sorties were probably lost to this cause, but the problems make the final result all the more creditable. The fact that *Bulwark* flew more sorties than *Albion* can be put down to her larger, all Sea Hawk air group.

The number of helicopter sorties flown by the strike carriers was as follows

Carrier	Sorties	Flying Hours
Eagle	75	44
Albion	130	68
Bulwark	96	48
Arromanches	32	22
La Fayette	38	27

Land-based aircraft flew a number of tactical sorties. In addition to those flown by transport aircraft, maritime patrol and photographic reconnaissance aircraft in the operational area there were 398 sorties by bombers from Bomber Command and 722 ground-attack sorties by fighters. Of these roughly 300 were flown by French F-84Fs and the remainder by RAF Venoms from Cyprus.

Fifty-five carrier-borne aircraft were airborne at one time during the dawn strikes on 1 November, about forty was a normal number for subsequent strike operations.

On most days there were about ten aircraft on CAP and four on AEW or other reconnaissance tasks and six fighters held on deck ready to reinforce the CAP if needed. Throughout the operation the three British strike carriers staggered their launch and recovery times so that they did not coincide. The best operating cycle represented a compromise between conflicting requirements, especially for the carriers operating a variety of aircraft types. Throughout the action against Egypt, 65 minutes was used as the planned cycle time. This was best suited to the Sea Hawks and Sea Venoms that formed the bulk of the air groups. It was also compatible with attacks on the Egyptian airfields from a position about 60 miles off shore. Even allowing for the catapult problems some very good launching and recovery intervals were achieved. On average these were

Aircraft	Launching interval in seconds		Landing interval in seconds
	Two catapults	One catapult	
Sea Hawk	32	52	34
Sea Venom	34	57	36
Wyvern	40	70	46

The number and types of sortie flown by British carrier-borne aircraft also makes an interesting comparison as the operation moved through its phases. They were as follows

Date	Strike	'Cab-Rank' Armed Recce	Recce	PR	CAP	AEW	Transport	Total
1 Nov	209	0	0	2	15	114	11	1	352
2 Nov	191	0	0	2	9	82	10	2	296
3 Nov	83	0	61	7	4	42	5	2	204
4 Nov	120	0	0	0	12	34	5	6	177
5 Nov	61	196	11	0	0	37	5	6	316
6 Nov	55	142	35	7	15	10	4	3	271

Armed Recce = armed reconnaissance

Recce = reconnaissance

PR = photographic reconnaissance

Overall the utilisation of naval aircraft during the air offensive must be regarded as excellent, especially when compared with that for land-based ground-attack aircraft. The RN deployed about one-third of the tactical fighters involved in Operation 'Musketeer' but flew about two-thirds of the effective strike and ground attack missions because of the better positioning of their mobile bases. There were a number of targets that RAF Venoms based in Cyprus could not reach. Even then the task group could have done better with a few more pilots and the Admiralty's operational research department believed that pilot availability was a limiting factor

Bulwark moored in Grand Harbour, Malta, after Operation 'Musketeer', carrying out ceremonial divisions inspected by FOAC with thirty-two Sea Hawks of 804, 810 and 895 NAS 'fallen in' with their identification stripes aligned immaculately. Note that the ship is flying her paying-off pennant. (Author's collection)

in the utilisation of aircraft, even though some pilots flew four sorties during several of the days in action. Operation 'Musketeer' had been a humiliating failure for British and French politicians and had revealed weaknesses in the Army and RAF abilities to generate mobile forces quickly and deploy them where they were needed. The carrier strike force, on the other hand, had shown itself again to be available, efficient and capable of a wide range of missions despite being equipped with aircraft that were far from being the best of their kind. In reading through my background notes for this chapter I was interested to see the number of other factors that have to be woven into the story of the carrier strike fleet and I deduce from this that the fleet had a vital role to play across the whole spectrum of warfare.

There was no element of the British armed forces involved in the Suez campaign which did not benefit from the presence of the carriers with all their diverse capabilities and none of the other arms could have carried out their tasks as well, or even at all in many cases, without them.

Operation 'Harridan'

After the ceasefire came into effect at midnight on 6 November 1956 British and French forces continued to hold the positions they had taken at Port Said and along the Suez Canal. *Albion* remained at sea in the operational area and flew nightly Skyraider reconnaissance sorties to ensure that no Egyptian activity threatened the support ships anchored off shore and Sea Venoms were kept on armed deck alert in case they were needed. By day Sea Hawks flew CAP sorties and carried out communications exercises with Army contact teams ashore, ready to provide close air support if needed and to provide a continuing show of force. On 29 November she left the area after 31 days continuously at sea for a self-maintenance period in Malta. Between 6 and 29 November the UN Assembly debated what to do next and it was decided to deploy a peacekeeping force to prevent a recurrence of violence as the British and French forces left. On 11 December *Albion* sailed to support Operation 'Harridan', the Allied withdrawal from Egypt,[49] and joined *Eagle* off Cyprus to be ready to provide air cover if it should become necessary. While she operated in the eastern Mediterranean she was visited by Lord Hailsham, the First Lord of the Admiralty, and Sir John Lang, the Secretary to the Admiralty. The withdrawal was completed on 23 December without a recurrence of fighting and *Albion* withdrew to Malta for a refit. She arrived in Grand Harbour on Christmas Day, effectively ending the RN carrier strike fleet involvement in the Suez crisis.

8 New Equipment and Another Defence Review

When *Victorious* emerged from her reconstruction in Portsmouth Dockyard in 1958 the RN could reasonably claim that she was the best-equipped aircraft carrier in the world. Although smaller than the new USN *Forrestal* class super-carriers, she was capable of embarking all British naval aircraft in service and development, including the Blackburn Buccaneer, in significant numbers.[1] She was the first British carrier to be fitted with a full 8-degree angled deck, steam catapults, mirror landing aids, the Type 984 three-dimensional air-defence radar and its associated comprehensive display system (CDS). Her new Mark 13 arrester gear had a constant pull-out regardless of aircraft type and weight. *Victorious* was the first British carrier fitted with magazine arrangements designed to embark nuclear weapons, the 2000lb 'Red Beard' which could be carried by Scimitars and Sea Vixens when they entered service, and the first to have magazines and workshops to support guided weapons, initially the air-to-air de Havilland Firestreak carried by Sea Venoms and Sea Vixens.

Victorious after modernisation and as she appeared when I served in her during 1966. The aircraft on deck include Buccaneer S 2s, a Sea Vixen, a Gannet COD 4 and two Whirlwind HAR 9s which were used briefly in the SAR role. (Author's collection)

Display Systems used in Carrier Operations Rooms

Ark Royal, completed in 1955, had been the world's first carrier completed with steam catapults, mirror landing aids and an angled deck built in during construction, as distinct from retro-fitted after completion but her angled deck was an interim application, set at only 4.5 degrees off the centreline. Her operations and air defence rooms also relied on a basic form of air plot compilation in which radar plot ratings 'told' contacts from their radar plan position indicators (PPI), to others who drew them on a large Perspex screen, where they could be seen by direction officers, fighter controllers and the command team. So that they did not obscure the picture, the plotters had to write on the back of the screen, constantly updating the positions of friendly and hostile aircraft. Next to the plot screens were Perspex lists on which information about strike, CAP and AEW aircraft was kept up to date together with unidentified and hostile tracks together with their allocated track numbers. Again the information had to be written from the back so that it could be read easily from the front, requiring radar plot ratings to learn to write backwards in capitals, a skill the author learnt as a midshipman and has, for some obscure reason, retained. This system was a step beyond that used by the BPF during the Second World War and was known as JW Compilation after the type of PPI generally used. Radar information came from Type 982 which resembled a horizontal hay-rake and gave accurate information in azimuth out to 90nm and Type 983 which resembled a vertical half-moon and could be rotated up and down to give accurate height information out to nearly the same range.

The CDS system introduced in *Victorious* was more effective by several orders of magnitude.[2] The system relied on the three-dimensional radar Type 984 with its distinctive 'dustbin'-shaped protective cover for the aerial array mounted on the forward part of the island. Direction officers and fighter controllers accessed the system through individual consoles, each with its own PPI screen. There was also a large Perspex air plot on one bulkhead to give everyone a an easy reference point as the air battle developed and, as cynics pointed out, to keep the art of backwards writing alive, and a prominent electronic tote on another bulkhead on which track details were entered by plotters with keyboards rather like the totes at railway stations that tell you train destinations and stopping points. The air defence room (ADR), in which the CDS consoles were fitted was kept in semi-darkness so that the screens could be seen clearly as they could not be used in full daylight. It was the information displayed on the PPIs that was revolutionary for the time, all accessed through a switch panel to the left of the screen. The operator could select one of four functions; these were the raw Type 984 radar picture, the raw picture plus identification friend or foe, IFF; IFF alone or electronic writing. In the last, a

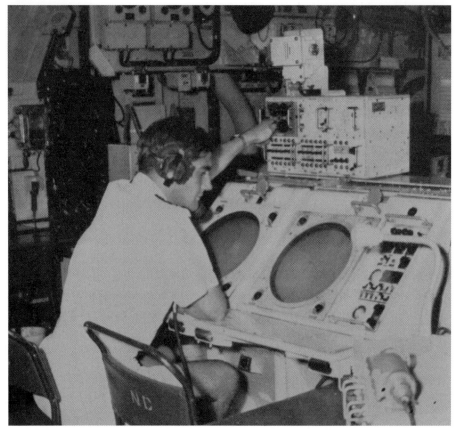

The Staff Direction Officer's position in *Victorious*' CDS-fitted aircraft direction room. (Author's collection)

computer replaced the raw radar image and IFF with a rate-aided display of information. For example

    36 . 36

    24 30

The small dot shows the position of the contact and the top left number is its track identification. The top right is the electronic store number and in this example they are the same. The extreme left bottom number shows the contact's primary category, known as the 'pricat' and the number next to it shows its secondary category or 'secat'. In this example pricat 2 shows the contact to be a hostile aircraft or 'bogey' that is unopposed. The secat 4 next to it shows that the ship's electronic warfare sensors have detected it operating its radar in the attack mode. The numbers at bottom right show the aircraft height in thousands of feet, referred to as 'angels', in this case angels 30 is 30,000ft. At a glance, a direction officer can tell from this contact that it is an unopposed 'bogey' at 30,000ft which has locked its weapon system onto the ship and the range can be seen from distance of its position from the PPI centre. It is, therefore, an urgent priority for interception. By making the appropriate switches on their control panels when electronic writing is selected, direction officers can select only the pricats that they want to see; for instance pricat 2 unopposed 'bogeys' and pricat 6 CAP fighters on call. If a target is allocated to a fighter controller these pricats would be changed to 3 for a 'bogey' being engaged and 7 for a CAP fighter carrying out an interception. The direction officer would type these changes into the computer when ordering the interception and check that the numbers had changed. Electronic writing could be transmitted using a system known as digital plot transmission (DPT), between CDS-fitted carriers and, from the early 1960s, 'County' class destroyers and 'Battle' class radar picket destroyers. Other vital information could be received from Skyraider and later Gannet AEW 3 aircraft, the latter being the type flown by the author. Observers in the aircraft could use their own AN/APS-20F radar to direct strikes, carry out interceptions and give warnings of low-level attacks that were using the earth's curvature to fly under the Type 984 beams beyond the radar horizon. They could also transmit their radar picture to a PPI in the ADR using a digital transmission system known as 'Bellhop'. Picket destroyers stationed up-threat could also transmit early warning of hostile aircraft and check that returning strikes were not being followed by hostile aircraft, a procedure known as 'de-lousing'.

Type 984 itself was the first British radar to give long-range cover out to 200 miles together with a height-finding capability in a single set. It transmitted its energy in six beams which were shaped by a 'honeycomb'-like lens at the front of the 'dustbin' aerial. These swept an area of sky from sea level up to 60,000ft and when a contact was picked up the height-finder's display showed him which beam it was in. For this function, each of the top five beams had its own cathode ray tube (CRT); energy in each beam rippled from bottom to top, isolating the target within the beam and allowing the height-finder to obtain an accurate height, to within 1000ft from the appropriate CRT. He would then type this into the computer for display in the electronic writing mode. The sixth, lowest, beam was a long range, early warning beam capable of detecting a bomber-sized contact above the radar horizon out to 200 miles.

The New Generation of Aircraft

The first of the new generation of aircraft to enter service was the Supermarine Scimitar F 1 which had been designed to meet RN specification N113D.[3] By the time it entered service in 1958 it had taken over a decade to evolve from a series of earlier specifications, the first of which had been written in 1947. At that time the Admiralty had been fascinated by the concept of aircraft without undercarriages landing on a flexible deck and specification N9/47 had been issued by the Ministry of Supply on the Navy's behalf for a high-performance fighter with no under-carriage capable of landing routinely on rubber decks. The winning design was the revolutionary Supermarine Type 505 which had two Rolls-Royce AJ-65 axial-flow turbojets,[4] thin un-swept wings and a 'vee' or butterfly-form tailplane, in which the surfaces acted as both rudder and elevator, intended to keep the surfaces clear of the jet exhaust. The Type 505 never flew but with the high thrust of its two engines, lightweight structure and thin wings it was potentially capable of exceeding the speed of sound in level flight with a maximum speed at altitude of Mach 1.2.

Trials in *Warrior* revealed the fundamental flaw in the concept, however, since aircraft had to be moved by crane onto a trolley once they had landed, greatly extending recovery times to an unacceptable 5 minutes between aircraft. The specification was revised, therefore, to call for a retractable tricycle undercarriage but this resulted in a fundamental re-design that became the Type 508. The undercarriage and its hydraulic actuating mechanism resulted in a 15 per cent increase in the design's weight and thicker wings had to be designed to incorporate the main oleos. This led to increased drag and, as a result, the 508 was not capable of exceeding the speed of sound in level flight although the higher lift coefficient at low speed improved its take-off and landing performance.[5] Three prototypes were ordered and the first, VX 133, flew in August 1951 at the Aeroplane & Armament Experimental Establishment at Boscombe Down and subsequently carried out deck landing trials on *Eagle* in June 1952. The second prototype was built to a modified design identified as the Type 529 by Supermarine although, externally, it resembled the Type 508. The design of the third prototype, VX 138, was radically modified, however, and had swept wings and a conventional tailplane, rudder and an all-moving tailplane. This further development was designated the Type 525 and it flew for the first time in April 1954. It was appreci-ated from the outset that the swept wings would significantly increase the landing speed above the figure considered acceptable by the Admiralty but Supermarine developed leading edge flaps and a system of bleed-air from the engines blown over the flaps to smooth the boundary layer and reduce the landing speed to within acceptable limits. VX 138 first flew in April 1954 without the boundary layer control but it was eventually fitted in early 1955. Unfortunately the aircraft crashed before this system could be fully evaluated, causing a significant delay to the development programme.

By this time Supermarine had been selected by the Ministry of Supply to evolve this series of development aircraft into a naval fighter to meet specification N113D.

Two prototypes were ordered, later increased to three after the loss of VX 138, and the first of these, WT 854, flew for the first time in January 1956. The production aircraft was given the Supermarine designation Type 544 although it was usually referred to as the N113 until it was given the name Scimitar in 1957. During the type's protracted development, its role changed from day fighter to strike aircraft although it retained the four 30mm Aden cannon originally specified. It had evolved from a concept designed shortly after the Second World War before supersonic flight was fully understood through a change of role and, rather than the 'advanced' type intended for use at the 'time of maximum danger' of war with the Soviet Union, it proved to be a transitional type that was already rendered obsolescent by its early design origins. Its 'thick' wing produced drag which prevented it from exceeding the speed of sound in level flight despite the high thrust of its two Avon engines. That thickness was partially due to the need to house the undercarriage but also because the original specification called for the aircraft to be capable of carrying out a free take-off from a carrier flight deck without the need for catapult assistance. The Scimitar was the last RN aircraft to have such a specification and it only ever carried out a free take-off once, with a very light fuel load, to prove that it could! To a large extent its change of role reflected the fact that day fighters without radar no longer made viable interceptor fighters. A Scimitar opening from a CAP station at 540 knots towards a Soviet bomber closing the fleet at similar speed would be closing its target at 18nm a minute; at altitude the pilot was unlikely to see his target at much more than 10nm. In 30 seconds or less he would have to identify it and judge his turn perfectly to get into a position 250 yards astern of the enemy aircraft to stand a chance of hitting it with his front guns. Most Soviet bombers of the period had tail guns so he would be under fire as he did so. This would have been a big, almost impossible, ask and as the RN Tactical School had appreciated, only radar-equipped fighters with air-to-air guided missiles operating within a sophisticated radar environment would be viable by the late 1950s.

Obsolescence in its originally-intended role and the retention of some outdated elements in its specification were the Scimitar's weaknesses but it did have some considerable strengths. It offered a huge increase in performance over the Sea Hawks that it replaced, was the first RN aircraft to enter service with swept wings and the first to fly at supersonic speed, albeit in a shallow dive.[6] It was the first to have transonic area-ruling applied to the fuselage and the first British fighter to feature blown flaps and, most importantly, it was the first to carry a tactical nuclear weapon and the first to be equipped to carry air-to-ground guided missiles. Each of its four under-wing pylons could carry 2000lbs of weapons, fuel tanks or a podded flight refuelling hose and drogue unit that allowed Scimitars to act as tankers to extend the radius of action of other strike aircraft. Scimitars were all fitted with a refuelling probe in the nose that allowed them to receive fuel. On the other hand, the Scimitar was the last RN fighter to enter service without radar although it did have a Mark 2 gun-ranging system for its four 30mm cannon which gave the pilot an accurate sight picture in his head-up display for firing. The guns were retained because of their devastating effect on small warships, soft-skinned vehicles and aircraft, although the Scimitar had to close to within a few hundred yards of its target to achieve it. The basic nose cone could be removed and replaced an alternative fitted with an F-95 camera controlled by the pilot to give the aircraft a respectable reconnaissance capability. The only Scimitar mark to enter service was the F 1; 100 were originally ordered but twenty-four were subsequently cancelled when Buccaneers began to enter service with a far more impressive strike capability. After their entry into service, Scimitars were modified to carry USN-designed Sidewinder air-to-air missiles to give them a limited intercept capability to back up Sea Vixens against regimental-scale attacks in daylight.

The first Scimitar F 1 unit was 703X NAS at RNAS Ford commissioned for trials in August 1957. It was followed by the first operational unit, 803 NAS, at RNAS Lossiemouth in June 1958. The last unit, 800B NAS, which specialised in in-flight refuelling to support the Buccaneers in *Eagle*, disbanded in 1966. The type was popular with pilots but not with engineers who found it difficult to maintain, another result of its conception as a prototype and convoluted design history. Components were difficult to locate, remove and replace and there were many apocryphal stories of long-armed or thin-fingered air mechanics retained for long periods in embarked squadrons because of their ability to get at things. Scimitars also leaked excessively from fuel and hydraulic lines in the hangar and on deck and had constantly to be supplied with drip trays and even dustbins to collect the leakage.

The Scimitar F 1 was 55ft 3in long and had a wingspan of 37ft 2in. Its height of 17ft 4in meant that it had only 2in clearance under the standard hangar deck heads of British carriers, making it a tight fight and great care had to be taken when handling it to avoid any obstructions. Its maximum weight was 34,200lbs fully loaded and it was powered by two Rolls-Royce Avon 202 turbojets, each delivering 11,250lbs of thrust at low-level. Maximum speed was 640 knots, Mach 0.96, at sea level and Mach 0.992 at 30,000ft.[7] Its radius of action depended on the amount of fuel carried in external drop tanks but with a single nuclear store and refuelling in flight from another Scimitar it could exceed 600nm. The climb from sea level to 45,000ft took only six minutes, better than many contemporary supersonic fighters. Supermarine proposed several improved versions which were never taken forward. These included the Type 562 with AI-23 radar and the two-seat Type 564 tactical strike version with Gyron Junior engines and Ferranti Blue Parrot radar. All had

A Scimitar of 800B NAS in the tanker role being prepared for launch from *Eagle*'s waist catapult. The large refuelling pod can be seen on the inboard starboard pylon. (Author's collection)

some merit but with newer types such as the Buccaneer in development, they were recognised as no longer offering relevant capability. Apart from the Intensive Flying Trials Unit (IFTU), Scimitars equipped five operational naval air squadrons and one training unit.[8]

The second fighter to enter service in the late 1950s was also the result of a long and complicated design process. De Havilland put forward design proposals in 1946 for an advanced fighter, given their project number DH 110, which could be used in the all-weather fighter and long-range strike-fighter roles by both the RN and RAF. A succession of specifications were written around the proposal which included N40/46 for a carrier-borne all-weather fighter armed with 30mm cannon and F44/46 for a 'de-navalised' RAF version. Two prototypes of the land-based version were ordered in 1949 with the first, WG 236 flying in 1951. It was lost during a display at the SBAC Show[9] at Farnborough in 1952, killing twenty-nine spectators, the pilot John Derry and his observer Tony Richards, when it broke up due to airframe failure caused by a combination of high roll rate and acceleration at low altitude. The second prototype was grounded until June 1953 by which time the RAF had lost interest in the project and ordered the Gloster Javelin.

The Admiralty had also lost interest in the DH 110 because the need for a jet-powered night fighter to replace the Sea Hornet was becoming urgent and a navalised version of the RAF Venom NF 2 was developed to meet RN specification N107. The resulting Sea Venom FAW 21/22 served successfully until 1961. Despite its success, the Sea Venom was always considered to be an interim design that was

A Sea Venom FAW 21 of 809 NAS photographed shortly after landing on *Albion*. Sea Venom squadrons painted their tip tanks in different colours and patterns so that their aircraft were easily recognisable. (Author's collection)

unable to counter the high-speed bomber attacks that the Soviet Naval Air Force was expected to be capable of mounting from the late 1950s.[10] The Admiralty issued a naval staff requirement, NA 38, in 1952 which was incorporated into the Ministry of Supply specification N131T for a Sea Venom replacement with supersonic performance. De Havilland proposed a design it designated the DH 116 powered by a single Rolls-Royce Avon RA-14 with reheat that would give a maximum speed of Mach 1.01 at 30,000ft. It would have had a maximum weight of 21,400lbs and was to be armed initially with two 30mm cannon and 2in air-to-air rocket projectiles. Developed versions were to be compatible with Red Dean and Blue Jay (Firestreak) air-to-air missiles. A wooden mock-up was made at the firm's Christchurch factory[11] which showed a cockpit similar to the Sea Venom but the twin-boom arrangement was replaced by a conventional fuselage with thin swept wings.[12] No other firm was asked to compete with the DH 116 which was known by the Ministry of Supply, unofficially, as the 'Super Venom'.

The project died in December 1952, however, when embarrassed de Havilland executives admitted to the Admiralty that they lacked the design staff to take the DH 116 forward, leaving the RN with no planned long-term all-weather fighter. The Ministry of Supply took the view that a navalised DH 110 was the only aircraft that could be offered without the considerable delay of going out to tender and thus the only one that could meet the Navy's timescale. A 1946 design that pre-dated the Sea Venom was, therefore, selected to replace it in the late 1950s. The most surprising aspect of this peculiar selection process is that the original DH 110 needed a complete re-design to meet the Admiralty's NA38 requirement for a carrier-borne all weather fighter. Only 10 per cent of the DH 110 structure was carried forward into the Sea Vixen FAW 1 and so the shortage of design staff had just as much impact on this project as it would have done on the DH 116. An order was placed in February 1954 for a semi-navalised DH 110 Mark 20X prototype[13] followed in January 1955 by an order for twenty-one development aircraft and fifty-seven production FAW 1s. The re-design included folding wings with hydraulic operation, a modified nose with a pointed radome to house the AI-18 radar with its large, hydraulically-powered scanner dish, replacement of the original engines with Avon 208s, each delivering 11,250lbs of thrust[14] and considerable internal re-arrangement to accommodate role equipment. In the original DH 110, engine removal had been through the bottom of the fuselage but in the Sea Vixen they were removed through the top in order to use the overhead gantries fitted in RN hangars. The name Sea Vixen was adopted in 1957 and the first production aircraft flew in 1957. It was a large aircraft with twin booms; the pilot's cockpit was offset to port and the observer sat in a space to the right at a lower level, known colloquially as the 'coal-hole', under a hatch that was flush with the upper surface of the fuselage. The observer had a small window on his starboard side but the stygian gloom of his cockpit was deemed necessary because the AI-18 display could not be seen clearly in daylight and since the aircraft had originally been expected to operate at night or in bad weather, an outside view was not considered essential.[15] The contribution that the observer could make to a dogfight in daylight, as demonstrated in the Sea Venom, was not considered worth the high cost of modification.

During the development process the original gun armament was removed as it was thought to be of little use against high-flying bombers and the Sea Vixen became the first British fighter to enter service with an all-missile armament. Like its contemporary the Scimitar, this type was a mixture of old and new technology. It combined an elderly fuselage with systems that were designed to operate within a sophisticated air-defence environment. Although the FAW designation was retained, Sea Vixens were the only fighters embarked in the carriers of their era

A Sea Vixen FAW 1 landing on *Ark Royal*. (Author's collection)

since radar was essential even in clear air mass interceptions at altitude. Production totalled 143 including sixty-seven that were up-graded from FAW 1 to FAW 2 standard with provision for four Red Top air-to-air missiles and extra fuel in the extended booms. The Red Top, originally Firestreak Mark 4, was an infrared homing air-to-air missile that was sufficiently sensitive to engage supersonic targets head-on rather than having to turn in astern of them to acquire the exhaust plume from their engines. All Sea Vixens could be fitted to carry Red Beard nuclear bombs, Bullpup air-to-surface missiles and conventional bombs as well as 2in and 3in rocket projectiles to back up Scimitars and later Buccaneers if necessary. The latter included 'Gloworm' variants with flare heads which could be used to illuminate targets at night. The Sea Vixen intensive flying trials unit, 700Y NAS, formed in November 1958 and 892 NAS, the first operational unit, formed in July 1959 somewhat later than originally hoped; both at RNAS Yeovilton. Sea Vixens were large aircraft with a maximum launch weight of 46,750lbs, a length of 53ft 6in and a wingspan of 50ft. At the peak of its operational service there were four operational squadrons and a single training unit,[16] all shore-based at RNAS Yeovilton when they were not at sea.

Less glamorous than the fighters but an equally important member of the modernised carrier air groups was the Fairey Gannet AEW 3. Once the Gannet AS 1 and the T 2 training version were in operational service the Admiralty

Two Gannet AEW 3s of 849D NAS from *Eagle* photographed from a third. The Gannet had two engines and was designed to allow one to be shut down alternately to conserve fuel while on patrol. Note that 071 has its left-hand engine shut down with the rear propeller it drove feathered. 072 has its right-hand engine shut down and the forward propeller that it drove feathered. (Author's collection)

instructed Fairey to begin work on an airborne early warning variant to replace the piston-engined Douglas Skyraider and the designation AEW 3 was applied to it. It soon became apparent that a radical re-design was required, however, and the only common structures used by both the anti-submarine and AEW variants were the outer wing sections. The fuselage was completely re-designed to incorporate the more powerful ASMD-8 Double Mamba 112 engine developing 3875hp and the AN/APS-20F radar with its scanner under the fuselage aft of the nose wheel bay. To provide ample clearance for the radome the undercarriage legs were longer so that the aircraft sat higher above the ground overall and unlike in the earlier marks the engine exhausts had to be sited forward of the wing so that they were clear of the radar electronics to avoid overheating them. The two observers were seated side-by-side in a cockpit above the trailing edge of the wing accessed by hatches with 'bubble' windows. Electronics were fitted over the observers who could not, therefore, have ejection seats although both had parachutes. The single pilot sat in a high cockpit 'up front' with a good view ahead and to the sides; an ejection seat could have been installed for the pilot but it was decided early in the development process to limit pilots to a method of bailing out that was similar to that of the observers. A modification, introduced after the Gannet AEW 3 entered service, substituted an underwater-escape seat which was intended to blow the pilot clear of the cockpit by compressed air as the aircraft sank after a ditching. The seat could be 'fired' by the pilot pulling a handle as in an ejection seat or operate automatically when hydrostatic switches aft of the seat were flooded as the aircraft sank. It was never known to work in the advertised manner in aircraft that ditched.

The radar was a developed version of the type fitted in the Skyraider, made under licence in the UK, and it offered long-range detection of both ships and aircraft. Each observer had a 5in PPI which was ground-stabilised and could adjust the radar performance to suit his particular task although the left-hand observer was the senior of the two and had over-riding control when necessary. Later versions of the radar had moving target indication, MTI, that allowed low-level contacts to be seen through the sea clutter at the centre of the screen. In the event of an emergency, both hatches could be blown off, allowing the observers to tumble out to the side with their parachutes. Minimum safe height for a bale-out was about 800ft from an aircraft that was level, rather more for an aircraft that was descending. Communications included two UHF sets and one long-range HF set and a small 'bomb-bay' aft of the scanner could be loaded with markers and smoke floats. A production order was placed in 1956 for a single prototype, XJ 440, and forty-three production aircraft. The prototype flew in August 1958 piloted by Peter Twiss and was subsequently used for aerodynamic work that culminated in deck landing trials in *Centaur* during November. Operational trials by three production aircraft were carried out in *Victorious* during 1959 and the AEW 3 went into operational service from 1960. The IFTU was formed at RNAS Culdrose as 700G NAS in 1959 but the Gannet AEW 3 only equipped one front-line unit, 849 NAS, which was shore-based at RN Air Stations Culdrose, Brawdy and lastly Lossiemouth. The squadron comprised a Headquarters Flight responsible for tactical development and training and four carrier-based flights identified as '849A', '849B', '849C' and '849D', each of which acted as an autonomous unit with its own commanding officer. The last AEW 3, XR 433, was delivered in June 1963 but when the carrier force was run down the number of flights was reduced from 1966 onwards. The last flight, 849B, in which I served, ran on until the last carrier capable of operating it, *Ark Royal*, was withdrawn from service and disbanded early in 1979. Gannet AEW 3s had a maximum launch weight of 26,000lb,[17] a wingspan of 54ft 4in and a length of 43ft 11in including the hook which protruded aft of the rudder when retracted. A single pylon could be fitted under each wing to which could be attached a 100-gallon drop tank, a mail pod, a Palouste starter or a 'G-dropper' which contained a dinghy and other survival equipment for dropping to help survivors in the water when they were located[18] on an SAR mission. The

Palouste was a small gas turbine that generated high-pressure air that was used to start Gannets, Sea Vixens, Scimitars, Buccaneers and Phantoms. They were built into aerodynamic pods that were fitted with retractable wheels for movement about the flight deck starting up ranged aircraft but, with the wheels folded away, they could be fitted to Gannet pylons and flown ashore to start other aircraft that had diverted for whatever reason. A hose connected the Palouste to the aircraft that was to be started and a Gannet fitted with a Palouste could even start itself.

The development of helicopters in a variety of roles will be covered in the next chapter.

NA 32 – an 'Affordable' Anti-submarine Project that was Cancelled

The rapid expansion of the Soviet submarine fleet after 1945 led to calls within the Admiralty for a simple and therefore, it was assumed, cheap anti-submarine aircraft that could be procured in large numbers. It was to be capable of operation from escort carriers with minimal deck space in almost any weather and the idea clearly stemmed from the Swordfish operations from MAC-Ships during 1944–5. The Gannet was in priority development at the time and was to be capable of both searching for submarines and carrying a variety of weapons to attack them in a single sortie. It was obviously going to be expensive but any attempt to cut cost and complexity would dramatically limit performance. There were also some officers in the Admiralty who had concerns about the ability of the Gannet to operate from 1942 light fleet carriers. This opinion was surprising because the last six ships, the *Majestic* class, were capable of launching aircraft up to 24,000lbs and recovering aircraft up to 20,000lbs and the earlier ships were modified to bring them up to this standard. The maximum launch weight of a Gannet AS 4 was 21,600lbs[19] and its landing weight 3000lbs less even if it had not used any weapons. Gannets operated successfully from HMAS *Melbourne* for fifteen years and *Glory* operated a flight of Skyraider AEW 1s with a maximum weight of 25,000lbs[20] in 1953. By 1950 there was only one escort carrier (CVE) left and the brunt of convoy escort work would have to be borne by light fleet carriers, although the USN had retained a number of CVEs in reserve and the Admiralty would have expected several to be loaned to the RN as they had been during the recent war.[21]

By 1951 the Admiralty's idea of a light anti-submarine aircraft were formalised in Specification NA 32 which led to Ministry of Supply Specification M123 for a simple aircraft capable of operating in all but the worst weather conditions. Since there were no CVEs in reserve and Gannets were to be procured in sufficient numbers to operate from the existing operational carriers, NA 32 was obviously intended as a mobilisation reinforcement factor for use in a general war[22] and would, thus, be vulnerable to the succession of defence reviews that examined the

RN role in a major war. It was hoped to attract foreign sales, however, from NATO countries that could not afford anything better but this rather naive ambition came to nothing. The design selected for development was the Short SB 6 and a contract for two prototypes was awarded in 1952. It was an odd looking aircraft powered by a single Armstrong-Siddeley Mamba turboprop and its one positive feature was the location of the two cockpits high above the wing to give the pilot an excellent view for deck landing. For simplicity the SB 6, later named the Seamew, had a fixed undercarriage; a tricycle undercarriage would have been better but the nose oleo would have interfered with the radar scanner which was sited under the fuselage aft of the engine. A tailwheel-type undercarriage was adopted which would have made the aircraft dangerous to ditch as it would have nosed over as soon as the wheels hit the water.[23] From the outset, the Seamew proved to be a very difficult aircraft to fly and the first prototype, XA 209, crashed on its first flight and had to undergo extensive repair. The flying controls were always found to be unsatisfactory and a series of modifications including fixed leading-edge slats and slots in the outer ends of the flaps alleviated but failed to resolve the problems. The second prototype was fitted with operational equipment and carried out deck landing trials in the trials carrier *Bulwark* in 1955. By then the Admiralty had decided that anti-submarine helicopters represented the long-term future and, despite being in successful front-line service, Gannet production numbers were being cut back.

It is difficult to see why interest in the Seamew continued but it did. Perhaps it was bolstered by interest from RAF Coastal Command which considered the type as a supplement to its long-range Lancasters and Shackletons. A modified version, the Seamew MR 2 was developed which deleted the equipment necessary for deck landing but retained folding wings, albeit without their hydraulic folding mechanism.[24] In February 1955 sixty production Seamews were ordered, comprising thirty AS 1s for the RN and thirty MR 2s for the RAF, with the former given priority. The Admiralty planned to use the Seamew to replace the Avenger in RNVR air squadrons and an IFTU for the type was formed at RNAS Lossiemouth in November 1956. Two aircraft carried out an operational evaluation in the new trials carrier *Warrior* during which over 200 take-offs and landings were carried including a number of catapult launches. By then the RAF had cancelled its batch of Seamews after only four had been built; three of these were converted to AS 1s and the last undertook a forlorn sales tour in Italy, Yugoslavia and Germany which evinced no interest. It crashed during a display at Sydenham after its return, killing W J Runciman, Short's chief test pilot.[25] The project finally ended in March 1957 when the RNVR Air Branch was disbanded after another defence review. There was now no requirement for the Seamew and production was terminated; the seven that had been delivered to the RN were stored at Lossiemouth and eventually scrapped.

Eleven others were completed but never delivered and they, too, were eventually scrapped. The most surprising thing about the Seamew project is that it continued for as long as it did for no very sensible reason that I have been able to discover.

NA 47 – the Cancelled Rocket Fighter

Air-breathing turbojet engines suffer from the fact that their power falls away in proportion to the density of the surrounding atmosphere[26] with the result that above 45,000ft a typical jet engine delivers only about 20 per cent of the thrust it produces at sea level. This shortcoming places limits on fighters' maximum speed, acceleration and their ability to sustain high-G turns and, since this was the altitude at which fleet fighters were expected to have to engage Soviet bombers, a solution was an important consideration in the early 1950s. At the time Saunders Roe were looking at new ideas to replace their traditional reliance on flying-boat construction and the firm proposed the radical concept of a mixed powerplant fighter which used a turbojet for take-off, landing and low-level flight combined with a rocket which gave a phenomenal rate of climb and performance at high altitude. Rockets give increased performance in thinner air because the lower back-pressure on the combustion chamber means that the motor's exhaust can achieve a higher level of thrust, reducing the time taken for a rocket-powered fighter to accelerate from Mach 0.8 to Mach 2 at altitude by as much as 90 per cent. Because rocket performance continues to increase with altitude, a rocket or mixed-power fighter would have a considerable advantage over a conventional aircraft and have a far higher service ceiling with five to ten times greater agility at extreme heights. Rockets had their drawbacks, of course; they needed far greater quantities of fuel than jet engines and the choice of oxidant was critically important. The RAE view was that liquid oxygen (LOX), was ideal because it was cheap and easy to make. Against this it boiled at minus 183° Celsius so the liquid could only be pumped into the aircraft in the last few minutes before take-off and the aircraft systems would have to be heated to prevent them from freezing solid. From a carrier operating viewpoint there was also the problem that fire in an aircraft containing large quantities of LOX would be extremely difficult to extinguish.

Maurice Brennan, deputy chief designer and project engineer for the mixed power fighter at Saunders Roe, understood that LOX posed too many problems and held out for high test peroxide (HTP). The Sprite rocket motor was developed by de Havilland to boost the take-off performance of the Comet airliner in hot and high conditions and this used a fine mesh of silver as a catalyst to form a jet of steam and oxygen to deliver thrust. As there was no combustion it was referred to as a 'cold' rocket but this motor was developed into the Spectre in which kerosene was injected into the decomposing HTP to create 10,000lbs of thrust, sufficient to

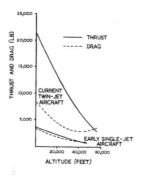

Variation of thrust and drag
with altitude of typical jet
aircraft

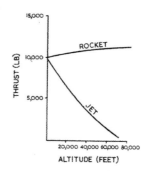

Variation of rocket and
jet thrusts with altitude

The deck-launched intercept technique
proposed for the Saunders Roe SR-177

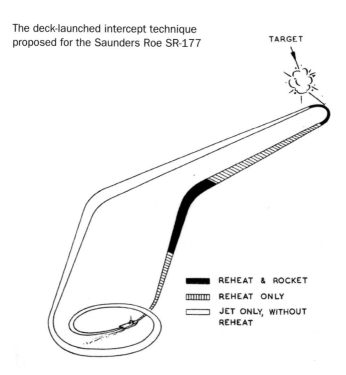

Rocket thrust increases slightly with altitude while jet thrust decreases.

give a mixed-power fighter outstanding performance at altitude. Low level performance was to be provided by a de Havilland Gyron Junior engine developing 14,000lbs of thrust with reheat. The mixed-power concept showed considerable promise and the RAF ordered two aircraft designated by Saunders Roe as the SR 53 to meet Specification F 124D. Whilst intended to be operational, the SR 53 was hamstrung by the otherwise mediocrity of its specification which lacked an air-interception radar. This shortcoming had been apparent to Saunders Roe from the outset but the Air Staff had failed to appreciate that with a closing rate of one mile every three seconds against a supersonic target, initial detection and the turn in to attack a target at high level would be almost impossible for any pilot to judge visually. The SR 53 flew successfully and proved the concept but Saunders Roe proposed a more powerful, radar-equipped fighter and it was this that drew the Admiralty's attention.

The men responsible were Captain (later Vice Admiral) F H E Hopkins who was DNAW and Captain (later Vice Admiral) Ievers his deputy, together with Lewis Boddington, Director of RN Aircraft Research and Development at the RAE. The same three had been responsible for specification NA 39 that led to the Buccaneer and they believed this aircraft to be even more important. Through them, the Admiralty issued specification NA 47 for a naval version of the proposed fighter and, shortly afterwards, the Air Staff issued their own specification OR 337. The design was considered so important that no time was to be lost with competitive tender and both versions were to be built to a common design given the Ministry of Supply designation F 177D, although the naval version was to have a stronger undercarriage and tail-hook; unusually Saunders Roe adopted the latter number and the project became known as the SR-177. In September 1956 Saunders Roe received an order for twenty-seven aircraft of which nine were for common development, nine for the RN and nine for the RAF. A project team headed by a Commander RN was established and the highest priority was allocated to the work. There was considerable interest from the Federal German Government which sent a team to the UK to follow the development. The SR 177 was the first fighter in history that was designed to be built for multiple customers with as little difference as possible between versions. The remarkable ability of DNAW at the Admiralty and Assistant Chief of the Air Staff (Operational Requirements) (ACAS(OR)) in the Air Ministry to agree a near-common specification for two un-penalised versions of this supersonic, multi-role fighter was an outstanding achievement that has yet to be matched. The RN planned to buy 150 SR-177s and the RAF at least that number as an initial batch with more to follow. The German Luftwaffe planned to procure 600 as replacements for the F-84 and F-86 and the German Navy was keen to add at least another 100 to that total as a Sea Hawk replacement. Briefings

A model of the RN version of the SR-177 made by Saunders Roe in 1957. Photographs
of it were released to the press and caused considerable excitement among those who
knew what they were looking at because it was fitted with accurate representations
of the Firestreak 4/Red Top air-to-air missile which was still classified at the time.
(Author's collection)

were also given to evaluation teams from the USN and USAF; there was, literally,
no other aircraft like it at the time.

The SR-177 was a far bigger project than Saunders Roe could handle alone and
a number of other firms were brought in as partners. Marshalls at Cambridge were
to make the wings and Armstrong Whitworth at Baginton was to undertake
production assembly and flight testing of components made throughout the UK.
Both engines were designed and built by de Havilland. In its final iteration the
design included underwing pylons for a variety of weapons including nuclear and
conventional bombs, air-to-surface rockets and drop tanks. A single Red Top infrared homing air-to-air missile could be fitted to each wingtip.[27] Production aircraft
would have had a wingspan of only 30ft which meant that folding was not required
and maximum weight was 28,000lbs. The wing was an outstanding achievement
because of its very simplicity, unlike the complicated designs in many contemporary
fighters. Model tests in a wind tunnel proved that it offered good low-speed

performance for a carrier landing but was capable of speeds well beyond Mach 2 at high level. Maximum speed at altitude was to be Mach 2.35. The turbojet engine was a de Havilland Gyron Junior PS 50 delivering 14,000lbs of thrust with reheat; the rocket motor was a de Havilland Spectre 5A delivering 10,000lbs of thrust for up to seven minutes at full power. Endurance using both after a fast climb and a single combat was over 1.5 hours but would obviously vary depending on the actual rate at which fuel had been used. Maximum altitude was to be 67,000ft although dynamic excursions considerably beyond this were possible. Time to 60,000ft from a catapult launch was estimated to be just over three minutes and at the top of the climb it was to be possible to accelerate from Mach 1.4 to Mach 2 in 66 seconds. The SR-177's spectacular performance can best be appreciated by a comparison with the only British-designed supersonic fighter to serve with the RAF, the English Electric Lightning. An SR-177 was calculated to be capable of accelerating from Mach 0.9 to Mach 1.6 in 70 seconds whilst in a five-mile radius turn at 50,000ft. The Lightning, generally regarded as an impressive high-performance fighter, albeit lacking in endurance, was incapable of level flight at 50,000ft and acceleration from Mach 0.9 to Mach 1.6 at its ceiling took 200 seconds straight and level. Any turn of less than 15-mile radius at high altitude caused the Lightning's speed to wash off.

Early in its development it was realised that the SR-177's HTP tanks could be cleaned and used to carry avcat for the single turbojet, giving it a long-range strike potential with stores mounted on external pylons. A neat, folding in-flight refuelling probe was fitted to the left side of the fuselage and the airframe was designed to be immensely strong with many components machined from solid blocks of aluminium. The wing had four spars, each pinned at the thickest point to four fuselage frames carved out of DTD 683 alloy. Such was the interest generated by the SR-177 that the Ministry of Aviation, which had by then replaced the Ministry of Supply, took the unusual step of releasing pictures of a model, before the first flight, which was published in *Flight* magazine on 18 October 1957. The editorial staff were delighted to see that the model had Red Top missiles on the wing tips which were on the Ministry's 'Most Secret' list at the time.

Eagle's modernisation was designed around a projected air group of twelve NA 39 Buccaneers, ten Sea Vixens, twelve SR-177s, fourteen Gannets and two SAR helicopters. HTP had to be stowed in exceptionally clean facilities and four pure aluminium tanks were installed in the space formerly occupied by the forward 4.5in magazines. Special aluminium pipes were designed to carry the fluid to the flight deck[28] and special rubber protective suits were designed for refuelling crews. Several million pounds was spent on perfecting methods of replenishing HTP and sea and storage tanks for it in replenishment tankers. It was not to be, however. In the defence review described later in this chapter the new Minister of Defence, Duncan

Sandys, arbitrarily cancelled the RAF version in April 1957 because of his privately-held belief, unsupported by professional advice, that the RAF was 'unlikely to require' any manned aircraft beyond the English Electric P-1B, which became the Lightning, or the 'V'-bombers.[29] Work on the naval version continued with urgency until August 1957 when, without warning or consultation with the Admiralty, Sandys announced while on a visit to the Weapons Research Establishment at Woomera in South Australia that he had now decided to cancel the RN version of the SR-177 as well. The German Air Force and Navy were not told and were left wondering what on earth had happened. Both subsequently bought the American Lockheed F-104G Starfighter in large numbers. So did other NATO countries including Canada, Italy, Belgium, Holland and Turkey. The Admiralty was appalled and Lewis Boddington said subsequently that if the Minister had told them of his desire to axe a naval programme, they would have elected to lose the NA 39 because the SR-177 was considered to be more important. There was no public outcry. By the late 1950s aircraft were complicated and difficult to progress from the drawing board but the Ministry of Supply and the Ministry of Aviation that succeeded it were calling for new designs at the rate of about fifteen per year, far more than the industry could cope with[30] or the Services absorb. Of 121 major British projects in the decade 1948 to 1958, 113 were cancelled once their cost and complexity became clear;[31] to both politicians and the public cancellation had become normal. We will never know whether the SR-177 would have been successful in service but the balance of probability is that it would. The basic design of the airframe was certainly better than the majority of its contemporaries. Its designed performance was outstanding and even if HTP had proved too difficult to use in the long term, the rapid advance of turbojet technology would have enabled the aircraft to perform well as a more conventional strike fighter. In conversations with officers who had served in DNAW at the time I found that many held the view that Sandys did not dare to look 1SL, Admiral Mountbatten, in the eye to tell him the SR-177 was cancelled, hence the announcement in Australia. Whether this was true or not, it was certainly the case that by the time he got back to the UK it was too late to argue or attempt to change his decision.

Strike Weapons

The major problem in strike warfare had always been the inherent delivery error, the distance by which the average bomb dropped by the average aircraft with an average pilot would miss a given target. This was known operationally as the circular error of probability (CEP). This figure was used by strike planners to work out the number of aircraft required to deal with any particular target and the result was frequently larger than the number of aircraft available in a given carrier so that

An inert Red Beard round fitted to a Sea Vixen FAW 1 for handling trials. Note how low the bottom of the dummy weapon is, only inches clear of the ground, hence the concerns about deck landing with it in place. (Author's collection)

multiple strikes would be needed. Two possible solutions were to produce a weapon with a bigger 'bang' or to reduce the CEP significantly. Red Beard represented the first approach and Bullpup the second, but conventional bombs and rocket projectiles were still available in large quantities and were both cheap and politically uncomplicated to use so they were to continue in service for several decades.

Red Beard

The development of a relatively small tactical nuclear weapon coincided with the entry into RN service of the second generation strike fighters capable of carrying it. It was known officially as the Bomb HE 2000lb Mark 2 Number 2 or more simply as the 'Target Marker Bomb', a description intended to disguise its true identity. It actually weighed 1750lbs and had a composite core consisting of weapons-grade plutonium and uranium 235. Two were detonated at Maralinga in Australia, one in September and one in October 1956, to prove the weapon's design and it was produced in two versions; a Mark 1 with a yield of 15 kilotons and a more powerful Mark 2. About 150 were issued to the RAF for use in Canberra and 'V'-bombers and thirty-five were issued to the RN. Typically five were deployed in each strike carrier commencing with *Victorious*, possibly as early as 1959, stored in specially-equipped air-conditioned, bomb rooms. Clearance to launch Scimitars with live Red Beards in 'conditions of emergency' was given by the Controller of Aircraft in 1961 but excluded any arrested landing because of fears that the 28in diameter weapon on its pylon might strike the deck as the aircraft was arrested to a standstill.[32] By 1963 clearance to launch Scimitars, Sea Vixens and Buccaneers with live Mark 2 Red Beards had been issued for *Victorious*, *Hermes*, *Ark Royal*, *Centaur* and *Eagle*.[33] The Mark 2 version had more safety features and was designed for the low-altitude bombing system (LABS) (see below). A single Red Beard would have been carried on an underwing pylon by Scimitars and Sea Vixens, balanced by a 200-gallon fuel tank under the other wing. which would have been close to the weight of the bomb when full. Both the bomb and the empty drop tank would be released in the LABS manoeuvre to leave the aircraft 'clean' with less drag for the return flight to the carrier. Buccaneers carried the weapon in their internal bomb bays.

A retarded version of Red Beard for low-level use, tentatively referred to as the Mark 3, was requested by the Admiralty but never developed since, although Red Beard was specified as a joint weapon, in practical terms the RN relied completely on the RAF for its development and at that time the RAF had no interest in anything but high-level bombing. The weapon had twin radar fuzes, both activated by a barometric switch after release to minimise the time in which enemy countermeasures could disable them. If for any reason an air burst triggered by the radar fuzes failed, there were back-up graze and contact fuzes to detonate the bomb on impact. Sea Vixens as well as Scimitars were fitted with the wiring and LABS computers to carry Red Beard, the latter as a back-up in case insufficient Scimitars were available. Usually four or five aircraft in each squadron were fitted with all the modifications needed to carry Red Beard and perform LABS attack profiles. Simulated loadings and attacks were often carried out to keep armourers and aircrew in current practice. Inert 'shapes' were flown for training from RN air stations ashore but the real weapon was never flown from the deck. The Admiralty saw Red Beard primarily in tactical terms, capable of destroying a raiding cruiser with the minimum number of aircraft or neutralising enemy ports and airfields before their inhabitants could sortie to interfere with Allied operations. Of course it also had a strategic use and nuclear-armed RN strike aircraft were capable of attacking the Soviet Union from any direction including from the Barents Sea, North Atlantic, Mediterranean and the Far East. As such they added greatly to the British nuclear deterrent since the West's Cold War opponents never knew from where a naval strike could hit them. This capability was under-rated by politicians who focused mainly on the 'V'-force with its well-known, vulnerable bases on land from which aircraft had only a limited choice of attacking routes.

Bullpup

The alternative way of improving the CEP was to produce more accurate weapons. The idea of using 'smart' weapons was not new; the Germans had developed examples in the Second World War and the British destroyer *Inglefield* had been sunk by a German Hs 293A glider-bomb off Anzio on 25 February 1943. By 1958 the American AGM-12B Bullpup, designed to meet a USN specification, offered

A Bullpup air-to-ground missile fitted on the inboard starboard pylon of a Scimitar F 1 of 803 NAS from *Hermes*. (Author's collection)

a practical and affordable air-to-ground missile which was adopted by the RN and a number of NATO countries although not, surprisingly, by the RAF. Bullpup had its origins in the Korean War where the USN saw the need for a bomb that could be guided accurately to its target from an aircraft that would remain beyond the range of small-calibre guns.[34] It would still, of course, be within range of anti-aircraft missiles. Later versions of Bullpup included the AGM-12D with interchangeable conventional and nuclear warheads but these were not procured for the RN. The version used by the RN had the advantage over earlier generations of missile that it could be handled like a round of ammunition and could be fitted to the aircraft with no need for system checks. The weapon weighed 570lbs and came in three parts; the centre contained a 250lb explosive warhead actuated by an electrically-operated tail fuze and the after section contained either a solid or pre-filled liquid rocket motor depending on manufacture date with two flares which were used by the strike aircraft pilot to track the missile while it was in flight. The four fixed wings were mounted to this section. The front section contained the guidance receiver, the actuator assembly for the moving, canard wings, a nitrogen bottle to provide power for them, a gyro to indicate the vertical[35] and a thermal battery to provide electrical power. The last item was becoming standard in US missile design as it had a long shelf life and it comprised an electrically-initiated 'squib' which ignited a heat energy catalyst which, in turn, melted dry electrolyte which activated the battery.

Scimitars were wired to carry three Bullpups, Sea Vixens two. To engage a target the pilot had first to locate it and then maintain visual contact, no easy task under fire. Once it was thus 'acquired', he would dive towards it within wide limitations of dive angle and speed[36] and fire the missile. When the short firing sequence was complete, the motor fired and the pilot would see the missile appear in the lower part of his field of view together with a lot of smoke. When this subsided he would know that the motor had burnt out and that he could start guiding the weapon down the sight line. The object was to keep the flares aligned with the target by moving a missile control switch with his right thumb which meant having to fly the aircraft for a short period with the left hand, something strike pilots had to get used to. The control switch acted in the normal sense for up/down and left/right and as soon as the missile was seen to detonate the pilot was free to break away. Training with live rounds was too expensive and so a ground simulator was provided to give pilots experience and a 'feel' for the switch sequences and guidance techniques. After a satisfactory standard was achieved, pilots were allowed one live missile firing. Like many of the USN missiles produced in the late 1950s, Bullpup was not perfect but it was robust and offered a quantifiable improvements over the weapons used in the Korean and Suez conflicts.

Bombs

500lb bombs were retained in service but the new generation of aircraft were mainly armed with 1000lb medium-capacity (MC) bombs for conventional operations. Their explosive filling amounted to about half the weapon's weight and the machined steel casing the remainder.[37] Most bombs used by the RN were fuzed at the tail to prevent the detonator from being initiated and, consequently, the bomb from exploding until a predetermined time after impact. This meant that the bomb would detonate inside a ship, or a hardened target on land, where it would do most damage. Against small warships, un-armoured vehicles and troops in the field, bombs could be fitted with a VT fuze, effectively a tiny radar which would give an air burst at a pre-determined height. For strikes against enemy airfields considerable delays, up to 24 hours, could be selected so that bombs would continue to detonate while repair gangs tried to make good earlier damage.

Rockets

The new generation of aircraft were capable of carrying the old 3in rockets with a variety of warheads but new 2in rockets carried in aerodynamic pods fitted to under wing pylons were under development. These were intended to have greater range than guns and to replace them in both air-to-air and air-to-ground applications. Development was not as rapid as had been expected but they did come into service from the early 1960s.

Low-Altitude Bombing System (LABS)

If strike aircraft approached their targets at high altitude they would be detected

Two-inch rocket projectiles being fired from a pod fitted under a Sea Vixen FAW 1's port wing. The store on the inboard port pylon is a Firestreak acquisition round. (Author's collection)

early by radar and intercepted. Since Korea the RN had elected to approach targets at low level to stay under the enemy radar coverage until the last moment but if a nuclear bomb was dropped using the conventional shallow dive technique, the attacking aircraft would be engulfed in the fireball and destroyed along with its pilot when the weapon detonated. The RAF continued to use high-level bombing techniques which gave the aircraft time to get clear while the weapon fell but left it desperately vulnerable to fighters and anti-aircraft missiles.[38] Both the USN and RN had been developing 'loft' or 'toss-bombing' techniques that allowed strike aircraft to pull up from low level and toss a nuclear bomb some miles ahead with reasonable accuracy while the strike aircraft turned and got clear. The low-altitude bombing system (LABS), consisted of an analogue computer that fed information to the pilot's LABS Indicator and the weapon release mechanism. Two methods could be selected, 'normal' and 'alternate', both of which basically resembled initiating a high-G loop. In the normal manoeuvre the Scimitar would be guided to an initial point (IP), some miles short of a target ship by an AEW aircraft and given a heading from it towards the ship. Against a land target the pilot would have selected an easily identified IP and marked it on his target map. Once over the IP the pilot pressed a button or trigger and commenced an IP to target run following indications from the indicator. At a further point, closer to but still short of the target, known as the pull-up point (PUP), the pilot would pull up into a loop following the LABS indicator. The indicator ensured that he flew an accurate loop pulling the right amount of 'G' and at exactly the right moment the bomb would be released automatically at a preset angle of climb; the release was indicated by a light on the indicator and the aircraft could get away. The best advice was to continue the loop on instruments and then roll upright when pointing away from the target. It was best to concentrate on instruments rather than looking out of the cockpit to prevent disorientation and, in the case of a real strike, being blinded by the flash as the bomb detonated.

The other manoeuvre was known as the 'alternate' or 'over the shoulder' attack by the RN and the 'idiot loop' by the USN. It could be used where there was no AEW aircraft to direct the strike onto a ship or no suitable IP ashore. In this instance the pilot selected 'alternate' on the LABS and used the target as the PUP, flying directly over it from any direction. Instead of the bomb being released at the start of the climb, the alternate circuit operated at an angle just past the vertical and the bomb was thrown into a higher but shorter trajectory. Apart from the obvious disadvantage of having to overfly the target, this method allowed less time for the strike aircraft to get away but it was said to be sufficient and strike pilots had to believe that it was. Thankfully, nobody had to try it for real. New strike pilots attended a course on LABS at the Air Weapons Group, HMS *Excellent* at Whale Island in Portsmouth before joining their squadrons at RNAS Lossiemouth and the pilots who regularly flew the LABS-fitted aircraft practised the technique frequently to maintain currency. There was a lot for the pilot to do in the planning stage including the choice of height and speed for the approach, timing from the IP to the PUP and the amount of 'G' to be pulled. Tables were used to calculate and then set the optimum angles of release. The requirement for accurate instrument flying added a new dimension to the annual checks that all pilots had to undergo.

Air-to-Air Weapons

We have seen that guns were no longer considered to be adequate for high-altitude, high-speed interception and so, from 1949 several British guided weapons were developed that were intended to enable fighters to engage targets at longer ranges with greater flexibility. The Fairey Fireflash was the first but while it achieved limited success, it was never put into full production and never equipped a front-line unit. It used reflections off the target from the fighter's gun-ranging radar to provide a 'beam' down which the missile flew to hit the target. Two boosters attached to the missile's nose[39] accelerated it to Mach 2 off the rail and it then glided to the target. It had a limited range of only about 1000 yards but the fighter had to be positioned directly astern of the target which had to be held in the centre of the pilot's gunsight until impact, severely limiting his options. It was not a 'fire and forget' weapon and hardly justified the cost of its development but it did at least give the British armed forces and industry early experience of missile technology.

Another dead-end project was the Red Dean radar-guided air-to-air missile which was, latterly, developed by Vickers and was intended for use in the Sea Vixen. Solutions to a succession of problems made the missile and its control avionics bigger and heavier with the result that the Naval Staff had reluctantly withdrawn from the joint operational requirement in 1956.[40] A comparison with the USN Sparrow III radar-guided missile which equipped the F3H Demon and F4H Phantom II and weighed only 400lb showed how far behind the world leaders the British industry had become by this stage, largely because of a lack of investment. One British joint project, however, did prove successful and went into production and service with the RN and RAF. It was the de Havilland Blue Jay which evolved into the Firestreak.

Firestreak

The de Havilland Firestreak was an infrared homing air-to-air missile with a true 'fire and forget' capability. The missile weighed 300lb and had a solid-propellant rocket motor; it was designed to home onto the heat plume astern of a jet aircraft and after lock-on it could be fired from a position in a 'cone' about 20 degrees either side of the target's centreline out to a maximum range of about 5nm depending on the heat signature of the target engine. Unlike simpler American missiles, Firestreak required a considerable avionic interface with the aircraft it was fitted to. It also required a number of checks to be performed after removal from a magazine before being fitted to the aircraft. The complete weapon system included the aircraft radar, AI-18 in the Sea Vixen FAW 1, which found the target and provided range, range-rate and target position information and the dynamic reference system which provided roll, pitch and heading information to the missile.[41] The aircraft was also fitted with missile-control equipment and a pilot attack sight (PAS), which displayed the aiming mark together with the signals which indicated that the missile had acquired the target and when it was within range. The missile-

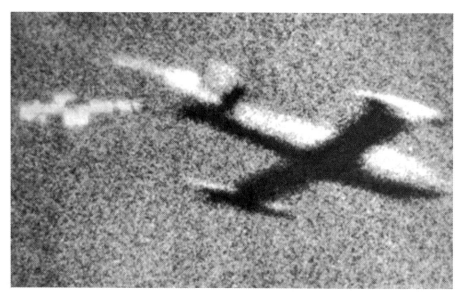

A very poor image but a fascinating one. It was taken at long-range by a target-tracking camera at the WRE Woomera in Australia and shows the moment of impact as a Firestreak missile made a perfect hit on the heat-emitting jet pipe of a Jindivik pilotless target aircraft. (Author's collection)

control equipment provided Firestreak with electrical supplies while it was on the pylon, altitude information, the 'ready to fire' signal to the PAS and the firing pulse itself, hot air for control surfaces and cold air with ammonia for cooling the electronics. Within the control equipment there were a number of safety circuits that prevented missiles from being fired before they had acquired the target and to prevent the aircraft being left with an asymmetric load of two missiles (the Sea Vixen was designed to carry four). Even this brief summary shows how the weapon system's components were closely interdependent and very complex, although their end product was simply to tell the pilot when to pull the trigger.

Development firings of Firestreak were carried out at the Weapons Research Establishment (WRE) Woomera in Australia by a joint services trials team in which there was an RN pilot but the first firings under operational conditions were carried out from *Victorious*. When she sailed for the Mediterranean in September 1958, three of 893 NAS's Sea Venom FAW 21s had been modified with avionics and a pylon under each wing to carry a total of two Firestreaks. Their task was to gain data on the acquisition phase of guided weapon interceptions and to work up the standard of flying and missile preparation to enable *Victorious* to launch guided weapon carrying aircraft. 893 was the first operational British fighter squadron to deploy with air-to-air guided missiles.[42] The missile workshops on the ship had been given the first priority and had been fitted with test consoles, some of them unproven, that had not yet been fitted in the air electrical school at RNAS Lee-on-Solent. As a result, none of the maintenance ratings had seen them before and techniques had to be learnt on the job. Missiles were embarked shortly before the ship sailed and these had to be assembled and tested. The first missiles were flown three weeks after the ship left the UK.

The squadron decided to restrict flying these aircraft to four nominated pilots in order to provide greater continuity in reporting and the commanding officer, Lieutenant Commander E V H Manuel RN, carried out the first catapult launch and arrested landing with two missiles fitted. The group found that with the missiles on their pylons the aircraft was 'somewhat un-aerobatic' and had a different centre of gravity which needed to be compensated for with ballast weights but otherwise demonstrated no handling difficulties. The aircraft's extra weight limited the maximum fuel on landing to 1000lbs and 400lbs was found to be the optimum. (With full fuel including the tip tanks the Sea Venom's capacity was 3696lbs.[43]) The sortie lengths were constrained at first to land on with diversion fuel for RNAS Hal Far but as confidence increased normal non-diversion recoveries were used.

A Firestreak-armed Sea Venom of 893 NAS on *Victorious'* starboard catapult about to be launched for trials of the weapon off Malta. (Author's collection)

The first trials consisted of familiarisation sorties for the four pilots in the acquisition phase of a Firestreak attack, carrying acquisition training missiles which were the same size and shape as a live round but contained only the homing system. Other Sea Venoms were used as targets and flew at differing heights and speeds against a variety of cloud backgrounds. These proved generally successful and the missile's seeker acquired the relatively low amplitude of infrared radiation produced by the single de Havilland Ghost engine at sufficiently long ranges to permit representative attacks to be made and the missile to be 'fired' within the specified range bracket. Airspeed, height, time of acquisition and time of 'firing' were all captured by automatic recorders in the Firestreak aircraft and this data was used by AWI to de-brief sorties.

By the end of November sufficient flying had been done to commence live firings and these were planned in close liaison with 728B NAS at RNAS Hal Far which operated Firefly U8 and U9 unmanned drones as targets. A series of firing trial rehearsals were carried out from *Victorious* in which dummy attacks were made on manned Fireflies with Skyraiders of 849B NAS providing range surveillance. 728B's direction officer controlled the whole exercise from Hal Far and the Fireflies were fitted with artificial heat sources to simulate the radiation pattern of a jet aircraft and were flown at about 10,000ft.[44] The drone's low speed was not ideal and made the interception somewhat more difficult than a faster target would have done. The Sea Venoms flew at Mach 0.7 throughout the interception. The first live firings were planned for early December but were delayed by bad weather and a temperamental drone. Once the drone was airborne it was shepherded by a manned Firefly to an area some 15 miles from Malta where it was put into a racetrack pattern. The Sea Venom was then launched from *Victorious* and vectored to a run-in point 12 miles away. When the fighter's observer gained AI radar contact, it got into a position astern of the target and made visual contact with both the shepherd aircraft and the drone; the shepherd was told to break away and with the positively identified target now in front of him the pilot ensured that he was in the correct range bracket and pressed the trigger. After this there was a short delay of about a second while the missile locked onto the target, developed its own firing voltage and fired. The Sea Venom could then break away leaving the missile to home unaided.

Firestreak was fitted with a proximity fuze so that even a near miss would result in the target's destruction. For the purposes of this trial and to minimise the expenditure of drones, the normal explosive warhead was replaced by a magnesium flash head which would show up well on recording cameras but inflict minimal damage on the drone. Of course, if the missile hit the drone it would break up and the fighters were briefed to break away at a minimum range of 1500 yards. Cameras were fitted in the Firefly's wingtips and in the nose of each Sea Venom. These showed missile bursts that would have been within the lethal distance for a war-shot missile on all but one occasion. If the drone survived the shepherd took it back to Hal Far where a pilot on the ground took over control to land it on the runway. During the trial period opportunities were taken to intercept other military aircraft operating from Malta with acquisition rounds and it was found that Canberra bombers could be detected at long ranges. Overall it was found that the system was viable but complicated. The Sea Venom firings demonstrated that it worked but they had not used Firestreak in realistic engagements against fleeting or snap targets from a variety of angles; they had been feeling their way in a new form of air warfare.

By mid-1959 700Y NAS, the Sea Vixen FAW 1 IFTU at RNAS Yeovilton, had considerable concerns about Firestreak. The aircraft itself was late entering service and there were a number of maintenance and rectification issues to be resolved before the first operational unit, 892 NAS, was due to go to sea in February 1960. At first the missile weapon system could not be made to work satisfactorily in the Sea Vixen because it was so complex. Each element was dependent on the next so that targets were only acquired infrequently. Fault-finding was found to be a difficult and lengthy process as the whole system had to be tested and the test equipment itself was often found to be faulty. With the wisdom of hindsight, we can probably deduce that much of the problem lay with the technicians' lack of familiarity with the equipment and the inadequacy of the training package provided by the manufacturer. Whatever the reasons, there were genuine concerns that 892 would go to sea without its primary armament unless steps were taken to improve reliability and DNAW decided to split the squadron into two flights with different aims once it had been commissioned and had absorbed 700Y. 892A NAS embarked in *Ark Royal* in March 1960 to gain embarked experience flying the new aircraft at sea. 892B remained at Yeovilton with four aircraft, two crews and 30 per cent of the squadron's maintenance ratings.

892B was tasked with demonstrating what availability could realistically be achieved with the Sea Vixen/Firestreak weapons system and to make recommendations on how this could be improved. It is worth mentioning that at about this time 870 NAS, a Royal Canadian Navy F2H Banshee unit armed with the USN-designed Sidewinder air-to-air missiles, disembarked to Yeovilton. It is fair to say that RN pilots were most impressed with the simplicity and effectiveness of Sidewinder and the RCN pilots were taken aback by the complexity and complication of Firestreak. Before 892B began flying, their aircraft underwent a modification programme at RNAY Sydenham that was expected to provide easier servicing for both aircraft and missiles.[45] Flying with the modified aircraft began in early 1960, following a carefully-applied training period to get the best out of the tuning and testing procedures. Rationalised servicing and maintenance schedules were developed which resulted in reduced times for routine testing and markedly improved serviceability. Several technical faults in the system and its servicing came to light and were promptly rectified. By March 1960 serviceability had improved so much that the two crews were each flying over 50 hours a month and were unable to cope with the amount of flying that could be achieved. Other crews were borrowed from 766 NAS the Sea Vixen training unit. DNAW welcomed the improvement but noted that it had been achieved by a small, tightly-knit unit with a clearly-defined task; new squadrons would need to be allowed time to gain that experience and confidence. The weapon system still absorbed 10 per cent of the effort needed to maintain the Sea Vixen in service but that was deemed acceptable although 10 per cent of the work on twelve aircraft represented a lot of man-hours. Had the weapon system not been considered acceptable the only possibility was to procure the American Sidewinder for the Sea Vixen until the Red Top, originally Firestreak 4, came into service on the Sea Vixen FAW 2. Further development to drastically simplify Firestreak was not considered justifiable in 1960. DNAW felt that this fully automatic system left very little under the control of the pilot and imposed inflexibility in combat which prevented the use of the missile to its full potential with the result that a chance shot at a faster aircraft might be missed. Some of that inflexibility came from the fact that Firestreak could only be used in the stern quadrant of targets which would inevitably becoming towards the fleet and hence the CAP station. Since the Sea Vixen was subsonic the problem of getting it into an ideal firing position was made more difficult. If the observer ordered the turn five seconds late, for instance, in a displaced head-on attack the aircraft would finish 1.5 miles astern of the ideal firing position against a target that might be faster than the fighter.

Interception Technique

The aim of an interception with a Firestreak-armed Sea Vixen FAW 1 approaching from ahead of the target was to judge the turn-in on the target in order to finish in a position on the inner side of the firing bracket astern of the target. A small height difference was unimportant and could be taken out by the missile which had a very good 'snap-up' capability against high-flying targets. The interception was divided into three phases, the approach, the turn and the attack. The first of these was the responsibility of a direction officer in the carrier's ADR or an observer in an AEW aircraft who would direct the fighter towards its target with sufficient accuracy for the observer to search for it with his AI radar. As soon as the observer gained a lock on he would call 'Judy' and take over the interception. If the pilot saw the target he would call 'Tally-Ho' but would still rely on a radar lock-on for the weapon system to work. A continuous flow of information from the fighter controller on height, speed and heading was essential as it was unlikely that a target would fly straight and level for long; once 'Judy' was called, however, the controller handed over control of the interception to the observer and remained silent unless lock-on was lost and a call for 'more help' made. It was very difficult for observers to judge the turn-in point and corrections might have to be made in the turn. At extreme altitude where the Sea Vixen might already be turning to its limit this could pose a problem. In the final stage the pilot took control of the interception and tracked the target indicator spot in his PAS, making adjustments of height and speed to get within the missile firing bracket when the ready to fire signal lit up and he could press the trigger. Constant, concentrated practice by fighter pilots and observers, AEW observers and direction officers was necessary to avoid getting into either the embarrassing position ahead of the target during the turn or the hopeless position too far astern. If an incorrect height was given by the ADR the target may not be found at all. This sounds straightforward but it must be remembered that unlike RAF fighters, the Sea Vixen had other important roles including strike and close air support which had to be practised as well. With fewer second-generation jets embarked in carriers, it was essential that they all performed as well as possible in every kind of action.

By late 1960 the RN had an effective missile-armed fighter in service and development work was proceeding on the Sea Vixen FAW 2 which was to be armed with the Red Top missile capable of engaging a supersonic target from ahead. It has to be said, however, that the British armed forces were slow to accept 'collision-course' interception techniques in which the target was engaged from ahead. The RN lacked the financial resources to develop such a system on its own and British industry in the 1950s would have struggled to perfect it but the RAF attitude that such a system was not practical did not help. From 1952 the USAF deployed squadrons of F-86D fighters around the world, one of which was at RAF Manston in Kent. This was equipped with an AI radar and a fire-control computer which directed the single-seat fighter straight at the target from any angle including right ahead, fired a volley of unguided air-to-air rockets at the appropriate moment and instructed the pilot to break clear.

Sidewinder

The larger, more complicated aircraft embarked from 1958 reduced the overall number of aircraft available within a carrier air group and DNAW sought ways in which the Scimitar's very limited interception capability could be enhanced to back up the Sea Vixen when necessary. They were armed with four 30mm Aden cannon with a practical maximum range of 800 yards against aircraft and could carry 2in rocket pods on underwing pylons which offered the slightly better range of 1200 yards but there was an obvious requirement for an air-to-air guided missile. Firestreak had to be ruled out because the Scimitar had no AI radar and lacked the space to fit the weapon system's 'black boxes' inside the fuselage. However, the USN equivalent, the AIM-9 Sidewinder, appeared to be an ideal choice and the decision was taken in 1960 to procure a batch for use on Scimitars.[46] The missile was designed by the Naval Ordnance Test Station, China Lake and proved in USN service to be a simple, reliable and effective weapon that required minimal testing. It was easy to assemble and was treated in all respects as a round of ammunition. Like Firestreak it was a passive infrared homing missile with slightly inferior performance; it was 9ft long and weighed only 160lbs. The basic component was the standard American 5in rocket motor; wings were attached to the motor casing and fitted with 'rollerons', essentially wheels which were rotated by the airflow to act as gyros that limited the missile's rate of roll. Attached to the front of this was a 25lb fragmenting warhead which was effective out to 30ft. The explosive content was designed to cut the case into a large number of small fragments that blew out at high velocity and initiation was by impact or proximity fuzes. If the missile missed its target it self-destructed itself after 24 seconds. Ahead of the warhead was the guidance and control package at the front of the missile which contained a gyro-stabilised homing 'eye'. When an infrared source appeared within its field of view, an infrared sensitive cell produced a signal which kept the 'eye' lined up on the target and operated the electro-mechanical valves which controlled the canard control surfaces fitted to this section of the missile. Power for the actuators was provided by a gas generator and this gas was also used to drive a turbo-alternator which produced the missile's electrical power. Sidewinders were loaded onto a launcher which was fitted to an adaptor which mated with the Scimitar's standard underwing pylons. The launcher contained a power-pack which received aircraft power and supplied the correct voltages for warming up the weapon; a firing sequence unit and amplifiers which injected the homing 'eye' signal into the pilot's headset to provide him with acquisition information. The normal aircraft wiring was utilised in all but a small number of cases by cutting into existing pylon cables and providing a choice of two plugs, one for the existing armament options and one for Sidewinder. The aircraft modification, therefore, did not take long to carry out and was very simple.

Scimitars could carry two Sidewinders, one under each wing, and before flight the pilot selected each in turn and the ground crew shone a torch at the missile 'eye'. If all was well the pilot would hear a 'growl' in his earphones and that was all the pre-flight check that was required. During flight the gyro ran all the time with the homing 'eye' aligned to the missile axis and missile electrics received warm-up power when it was selected by the pilot. In a normal interception the pilot would sight the enemy aircraft visually, manoeuvre to get into the firing bracket and place the fixed cross in his gunsight at the target. In due course, the weapon would 'growl' to show that it had seen the infrared source, the pilot would check that he was within the firing envelope and weapon-release 'G' limitations and then pull the trigger.[47] The missile gyro was then un-caged, the 'eye' locked onto the target, the gas generator provided electrical and mechanical power and the motor was fired. Sidewinder followed a proportional navigation course to its target and stood a good chance of success. Another of Sidewinder's advantages was that pilots could be trained to use it quickly because it was so simple. After a single introductory lecture, they carried out a series of procedure runs with an acquisition round which lacked the motor and warhead. It was not really necessary to back this up with live firings but several a year were carried out by front-line squadrons to keep operational techniques up to scratch and to prove that missiles from production batches remained serviceable after storage in magazines.

Another Defence Review

On 9 January 1957 Anthony Eden resigned as a direct result of the Suez debacle and handed over the office of Prime Minister to Harold Macmillan who made Duncan Sandys his Minister of Defence with instructions to carry out a complete review of British Defence Policy.[48] Admiral Mountbatten immediately tasked the naval staff to refine the arguments for retaining a powerful carrier strike force and, overall, they found Sandys prepared to listen to arguments that were supported by facts and figures put forward in a clear and logical way. Another factor in the Admiralty's favour was Macmillan's wish to repair the damage caused to the British 'special relationship' with the USA by Eden's recent action in the Middle East. Overt British commitment to Allied maritime operations in the Atlantic was a good way of achieving this and would counter-balance the big cuts planned to reduce military and air forces based in Germany. Sandys now thought it possible that a period of conventional warfare at sea might precede the use of nuclear weapons or that a nuclear exchange might not prove decisive, either eventuality requiring an offensive strike fleet to secure sea control. An RN carrier strike force together with modern ASW hunter-killer groups with reduced emphasis on convoy escort in the NATO area would be welcomed by the Americans and cost less than the prolonged preservation of the large, obsolescent fleet of escort vessels held in reserve since 1945. Another factor that worked in favour of the naval staff's arguments was the obvious utility of carrier task forces as a source of deployable air power in limited wars and peacekeeping missions in which the use of nuclear weapons was neither credible nor relevant.[49] The Suez operation, although politically misguided, had emphatically demonstrated the strength of this argument. Overseas bases could no longer be relied upon and Ceylon had already ordered the East Indies Station to leave its principle base at Trincomalee as a direct result of the Suez affair. The potential for amphibious forces that could be deployed from helicopter carriers also evolved rapidly after the example set at Suez because Arab countries banned the over-flight of their territory by British military aircraft, thus creating a 'barrier' that limited the usefulness of air-portable infantry based in the UK and Cyprus.

The Review itself[50] was unusual in that Sandys wrote much of himself in some haste, relying largely on his own firmly-held views but backed up by his chief scientific adviser Sir Frederick Brundrett. Mountbatten revelled in his arguments with Sandys and was ably backed up 2SL, Admiral Sir Charles Lambe, who eventually succeeded him as 1SL. Arguably, Mountbatten's greatest achievement was his success in convincing Sandys that the Navy had a key role to play in the suppression of limited or 'brushfire' wars which the application of carrier-borne aircraft, amphibious forces and their escorts could prevent from escalating. The contents of Sandys' Review were approved in basic form at a weekend meeting of ministers at Chequers on 23 February 1957. A series of further drafts followed and the contents were revealed to Allies, especially the USA. The final draft was approved by Cabinet on 28 March and placed before Parliament on 4 April 1957. A contribution to Allied deterrence and resistance to aggression was to be the first priority followed by defence of Great Britain's colonial possessions and the ability to carry out limited operations overseas.

Sandys described the Navy's role in total war as 'somewhat uncertain' but admitted the possibility that 'the nuclear battle might not prove immediately decisive, and in that event it would be of great importance to defend Atlantic communications against submarine attack.[51] Whilst this statement seemed slightly equivocal, the subsequent paragraphs revealed that the Admiralty had done extremely well explaining its case for limited war operations and peacekeeping. Under the heading 'Sea Power', Sandys' Review stated that the Royal Navy with its integral force of Royal Marines Commandos provided an effective means of bringing power rapidly to bear in peacetime emergencies or limited hostilities and the relevance of carrier strike groups was emphasised by the statement that 'in modern conditions the role of the aircraft carrier, which is in effect a mobile air station, becomes increasingly significant' and carrier groups were to form the main deployment pattern of the future RN. These were to comprise carriers with a relatively small number of better-equipped escorts. The *King George V* class battleships and the majority of cruisers would be scrapped immediately, as would the armoured carriers that had proved too costly to modernise. *Vanguard*, the last battleship, had been placed in reserve in 1955 and would go to the scrapyard herself in 1960. Effort was to be concentrated on the larger carriers and the 1942 light fleet carriers would be scrapped rather than modernised and *Warrior*, the only ship of this class to have been modernised for service in the RN, was to be placed on the sales list.

The Review stated that the RN would maintain a balanced strike force in the Far East, centred on a carrier task force but with a powerful amphibious force constantly available for use in emergencies. It was specifically stated that the types of ship required for the limited war role were exactly the same as those required for total war, reflecting the new reality that the Soviet Union was equipping sympathetic states with modern equipment. The gift of a *Sverdlov* class cruiser and several missile-armed fast patrol boats to Indonesia were examples that showed that elderly or second-rate equipment was no longer acceptable for low-intensity warfare. The Review did make the RN suffer some painful cuts but considerably fewer than the other services. Notable among these was the loss of the RNVR air squadrons as part of a general reduction of reserve forces reflecting the contemporary belief that there would be no time or requirement for a general mobilisation in the event of total war. It also reflected the end of National Service which had become the primary source of new recruits for the Air Branch of the RNVR. Whilst this may have been the case, Korea had shown the need for a reserve of aircrew to back up the front-line squadrons in prolonged conventional conflict and it would have given better use of a valuable resource to revise rather than remove the reserves. A new RNR Air Branch was created in the 1980s comprising volunteer former RN aircrew who could be mobilised when required to supplement or replace aircrew in regular naval air squadrons. The other significant loss was the SR-177 strike fighter described earlier which was cancelled arbitrarily by Sandys after the Review. Apparently he felt that the Scimitar and Sea Vixen together with the NA 39 Buccaneer which remained in development were good enough to meet the Navy's needs until the next defence review, projected for the mid-1960s. In this instance the British lost an aircraft with a potentially very good performance and considerable export potential and Sandys was undoubtedly wrong in both his decision to cancel and his method of doing it. There was another aspect of Sandys' Review that passed almost un-noticed at the time but was to cause difficulty in the future. He wanted the RN and RAF to co-operate in procuring a single nuclear strike aircraft for the future.[52] The NA 39 was almost ready to fly but the Air Staff considered it to be inadequate for RAF use and had no interest in adopting it, asking instead for a larger and more complicated aircraft with strategic capability that evolved into the TSR2.

After the Review the Admiralty produced a Paper which explained its new doctrine, emphasising the importance of limited war or 'brushfire' operations;

making the point that aircraft carriers were of central importance in carrying out this role and explaining the synergy between strike aircraft, assault helicopters and a new generation of amphibious warfare vessels. The doctrine was endorsed by the Chiefs of Staff and presented to Sandys who considered it to be 'a major advance in Admiralty thinking' with which he was well pleased.[53] Some arguments over detail did continue into the autumn, however, and these were solved by Mountbatten in his own inimitable way by inviting Sandys to stay at his house at Broadlands. Sandys pressed the case for the carriers deployed in the Atlantic to have air groups specialising in anti-submarine warfare and Mountbatten conceded the point in return for a navy with a manpower ceiling of 88,000 men. He probably knew that this was a hollow gesture, however, since the decision had already been taken to run down the Gannet force in favour of anti-submarine helicopters and the implementation of Sandys' proposal would take some years, by which time he would have moved on. The stratagem worked and no more was heard of the proposal. The evolution of helicopters and helicopter carriers will be described in the next chapter.

Mountbatten's other success at this time was to obtain Sandys' approval for the conversion of *Bulwark*, which was not to be retained as a fixed-wing carrier, into a commando carrier. Suez had proved the concept of vertical envelopment and the ship's conversion was accepted enthusiastically by a number of agencies. The Treasury was happy as the cost of conversion was considerably less than the price of a new ship; the War Office approved of the idea because it expected to be able to deploy Army formations as part of the new amphibious task force and even the Air Staff welcomed it at the time because it reduced their own need to procure helicopters and transport aircraft although they later regretted this early enthusiasm and changed their minds. The Royal Marines were delighted to find themselves as the focus of operational planning, especially since with the withdrawal of large numbers of battleships and cruisers from service they had lost their traditional role of providing large embarked detachments and crews for some of the main armament. 42 RM Commando was re-formed in 1959 for service in *Bulwark* and 41 RM Commando was re-formed in 1960. Two new landing platforms, dock, were projected to replace the elderly tank landing ships and craft in the Amphibious Warfare Squadron. By the end of 1957 Mountbatten was able to write to his illustrious predecessor as 1SL, Admiral of the Fleet Lord Chatfield, and say that 'it looks as though Duncan Sandys means to give us a reasonable deal – better than the Army or RAF'.[54] By and large he was correct and the 1957 Defence Review formed the basis of RN strike force doctrine for the next decade.

9 Helicopters and Helicopter Carriers

The decade after 1945 saw an increasing number of helicopters used by the Royal Navy in a variety of roles. The earliest practical type had been the American Sikorsky R-4 which first flew in 1943 and subsequently carried out a series of deck landing experiments on a wooden flight deck erected for the purpose on the tanker ss *Bunker Hill* off the eastern United States.[1] Their success led to the establishment of a joint board to carry forward the development of helicopters in the Allied navies. A total of sixty-seven R-4s, named Hoverfly in British service, were procured for the RN and in 1943 one of them was embarked in the ss *Daghestan* off the north-eastern US coast for a practical demonstration of its potential usefulness in convoy defence. It was flown by Lieutenant (A) A Bristow RNVR, the first Fleet Air Arm helicopter pilot, and operated off a wooden deck that was 90ft long by 40ft wide. As a practical precaution the aircraft was fitted with pontoon floats in case it came down in the sea after an engine failure. The R-4 was 47ft 11in long and had a rotor diameter of 38ft so it fitted comfortably on the deck and could, with caution, land across it or at an angle between ahead and athwartships with the aircraft's nose into the relative wind. The maximum take-off weight was only 2600lbs and the R-4 was distinctly under-powered with its single 245hp Franklin engine so its usefulness was limited to visual searches for surfaced U-boats in the immediate vicinity of a convoy but the trial did at least show that helicopters could operate from ships other than carriers that were fitted with small flight decks. Two R-4s were subsequently embarked in the ship for an operational convoy across the Atlantic, but extremely rough weather limited the amount of flying they achieved.

In 1946 the 'River' class frigate *Helmsdale* was fitted with a small flight deck aft and carried out a series of successful experiments to evaluate the use of helicopters as part of a small ship's weapons system. Again the pilot was Lieutenant Bristow who, by then, had transferred to a permanent commission in the RN. These showed that while the Hoverfly could realistically only operate with a pilot and an observer with a pair of binoculars on sorties of reasonable length, the potential for a more powerful helicopter able to carry both sensors and weapons was exciting. There were many immediate tasks for helicopters, however, including combat search and rescue (SAR) and the transfer of passengers between ships working up in home waters. In the late 1940s amphibian Supermarine Sea Otters were used in the SAR

A Hoverfly HAR 1, the RN's first practical helicopter type, being pushed into the water at Portland Naval base on a trolley. It is fitted with floats, rather than a wheeled undercarriage, that allowed it to float after a ditching. (Author's collection)

role because they could land, but not necessarily take-off, in the open sea to rescue ditched aircrew. The USN Sikorsky S-51 had performed well in this role during the Korean War and several had been detached to RN and RAN carriers as more efficient replacements for Sea Otters. Westland procured a licence to build the S-51 in the UK and seventy-two were manufactured for the RN, named Dragonfly in British service, with a series of upgraded marks. The HAR 1 had composite blades and the HAR 3 had metal blades and a hydraulic servo-control flight control system.[2] The engine in both versions was a 550hp Alvis Leonides 50; length was 57ft 6in and maximum weight 5870lbs.

Search and Rescue Capability

USN S-51s had proved that the type could fly behind enemy lines, recover 'downed' aircrew and return them to safety at one of a number of specialised forward bases. The first RN Dragonfly SAR detachment went to sea in *Indomitable* in January 1951 and by 1953 fifteen RN air stations, beginning with RNAS Lossiemouth, had Dragonfly SAR Flights. The first live rescue by a British-built RN helicopter took place on 14 May 1951 when *Glory*'s Dragonfly recovered Stoker McPherson who had fallen overboard. The carrier flights' primary task, however, was to hover close to the deck during daylight operations to recover aircrew who ditched close to the ship. *Glory*'s Dragonfly recovered four ditched pilots and four others from behind enemy lines during the ship's operations off Korea. The HAR 3 had a hydraulically-powered winch and, with a crew of pilot and winch-man, had enough disposable lift to rescue two wet aircrew from the water using either a net or a hook and under-arm strop. Whilst this sufficed for the aircraft of the Korean War era, it was not good enough when the three-seat Skyraider came into service and the Dragonfly was never expected to be more than an interim type. Helicopters were also used for a number of fleet requirements tasks and 771 NAS included a Flight of seven Hoverflies in the early post-war years. In May 1947 these were transferred to a re-commissioned 705 NAS which became the main authority for all RN helicopter operations including the training of pilots, aircrewmen and maintenance ratings. The commanding officer was also responsible for the evaluation of new helicopter types and for giving advice to DNAW on statements of requirements for helicopters.[3] When 706 NAS was formed in 1953 to evaluate helicopters in the anti-submarine role, 705 lost part of its tasking and subsequently specialised as a training and SAR unit.

705 NAS helicopters played an important part in flood relief operations in Holland during February 1953. An initial call for assistance had come from RAF Manston at 06.30 on 1 February 1953 to rescue a number of people who were trapped on the eastern end of the Isle of Sheppey by the disastrous east coast floods. Two helicopters were airborne by 07.40 but by the time they arrived the

A Dragonfly HAR 3 of RNAS Lossiemouth Station Flight; the rotor is turning and the aircrewman appears to be carrying out a winch check with a third crew member. (Author's collection)

A Dragonfly of 705 NAS operating over flooded farmland in Holland during 1953. (Author's collection)

people had been rescued by boats. The result of the gales and high tides in Holland soon became apparent, however, with high loss of life and 100,000 people needing evacuation.[4] The Dutch authorities appealed to the UK for helicopter assistance and on 2 February four Dragonflies took off for Woensdrecht in Holland at 09.40.[5] Their first task, after briefing, was to fly radio operators and their equipment to strategic positions in the flooded areas to feed back information since all other forms of communication had been severed. The detachment settled into a routine using Gilze-Rijen as a main base overnight with Woensdrecht as a forward operating base by day. All passenger seats and non-essential equipment were removed so that the helicopters had the maximum disposable lift and more radio operators were deployed after which the crews searched for people in distress. They were appalled at the area of devastation but were disconcerted to find that, after landing in a village where help was obviously needed, the RN aircrew could not make themselves understood. The problem was solved by using a number of young, English-speaking Dutch naval officers who flew out with the helicopters and briefed the survivors after landing. They briefed people on how to get into a strop or enter the helicopter and were even lowered by winch to clear obstacles from potential landing sites. Often they had to stay in flooded villages because helicopters could not return to pick them up before dark.

On 3 February 1953, five more helicopters arrived from 705 NAS's base at RNAS Gosport and joined the work of rescue. By the end of the day the nine Dragonflies had flown 63 hours and rescued 200 people. A number of landing sites had been established, mostly on roads on top of dykes, jetties by canals and churchyards. On 4 February more radios were distributed together with supplies of food and medicine and then searches were resumed. They were supported by an RN Avro Anson which made frequent trips back to Gosport and all 705's helicopters listened out on a 'naval cross country' radio frequency that enabled them to call for assistance when evacuating a village. Until then the RN helicopters were the only ones in operation but from that day they were joined by other British, American and Belgian helicopters and a Dutch naval Dragonfly. Rescue operations continued until 7 February by which time the squadron had flown 229 hours and rescued 734 people, three dogs and a cat. The flooding had weakened the principal dykes on the mainland and there were fears that further flooding might follow the exceptionally high tides forecast for 15/16 February and so 705 NAS was asked to maintain a presence until 19 February. Three Dragonflies were allocated until 14 February when the whole squadron came to readiness. During this period they flew a number of government officials, dyke engineers and doctors about and had the honour of flying Queen Juliana twice and Prince Bernhardt once to see the damage from the air.

Fortunately there were no westerly winds and the high tides did not cause the further problems that had been feared. The commanding officer, Lieutenant Commander H R Spedding RN was awarded the MBE and one of his aircrewmen the BEM for these operations and it is interesting to note that the squadron deployed ten pilots to Holland, three of whom had not yet completed their helicopter conversion course. The aircraft left in the UK also carried out valuable work. Three Dragonflies were temporarily based at RAF West Malling in Kent and used to transport vital supplies and senior government officials. Between 2 February and 16 February the three pilots flew 106 hours.

Anti-submarine Warfare

The development in the USA of lightweight sonar sets capable of lowering a transducer into the water from a helicopter hovering 40–50ft above the surface stimulated considerable interest in the USN and RN from the early 1950s.[6] The Sikorsky S-55, which replaced the S-51 in production, was capable of lifting a dipping sonar with a pilot, sonar operator and fuel enough for a reasonable sortie length but could not carry a weapon as well. The USN, therefore, operated them in hunter/killer pairs; one with a sonar and one with a weapon in sorties of short duration. This was clearly inefficient and required large numbers of aircraft to be

A Whirlwind HAS 7 of 737 NAS from RNAS Portland in a hover 40ft above the surface lowering its sonar transducer into the water. The depth of the transducer could be varied above or below thermal layers to track submarines more effectively than sonars fitted to surface ships and the system proved to be a big step forward in anti-submarine operations. The top surface of the helicopter was painted yellow so that it could be seen by other aircraft while it was motionless in the hover, both for safety and to allow the range and bearing of a submarine from the 'hover datum' to be estimated for an attack. (Author's collection)

embarked that were not easily interchangeable between roles; it was likely that more weapon-carrying 'killers' would be available than the more complex 'hunters'. Designated the HO4S, the type saw limited operational use with the USN and was mainly used to develop anti-submarine doctrine and tactics. The first helicopter designed specifically for anti-submarine warfare was the Bell Model 61, designated the HSL-1 by the USN, which won a design competition in 1950. It was a tandem-rotor design powered by a single 2400hp Pratt and Whitney R-2800-50 engine and had a maximum weight of 26,500lbs. It was intended to carry air-to-surface missiles as well as a dipping sonar. The first prototype flew in March 1953 but development proved to be protracted and deliveries to the first squadron, HU-1, were not made until 1957. A production contract for seventy-eight had been placed in 1953 but by 1956 more effective and advanced helicopter designs were emerging and production ended after only fifty aircraft.[7] The design's initial promise was limited by the lack of a flight-control system that would have allowed it to operate effectively at night or in bad weather. The Admiralty ordered eighteen HSL-1s for evaluation in 1953 but the contract was cancelled in 1954 as part of the series of defence reviews that followed the end of the Korean War. A British type was selected to replace it, the Bristol Type 191, a tandem-rotor derivative of the Type 173 which had been intended for commercial use. The Type 191 was to be powered by two 550hp Alvis Leonides engines, was 55ft 2in long and both rotors had a diameter of 48ft 7in. Maximum weight was to be 11,000lbs which would have allowed it to carry both sonar and a torpedo or depth charges. The Type 192 was to be a transport helicopter for the RAF and did eventually enter service in 1961 as the turbine-engined Belvedere. The Type 193 was to have been a slightly modified 191 for service in the RCN. The Admiralty ordered sixty-eight Type 191s in April 1956 despite fears that such a large helicopter could not easily be integrated on conventional carriers' decks with fixed-wing operations. The 191 was cancelled after the 1957 Defence Review and the RCN version was cancelled shortly afterwards. Attention then focused on an anglicised version of the Sikorsky S-58 which was to be built under licence in the UK as the Westland Wessex. It will be described in a later chapter.

While these plans had come to nothing, the RN did gain practical anti-submarine helicopter experience from 1952 onwards with fifteen Sikorsky HO4S-1 helicopters equipped with dipping sonar made available by the USN under MDAP funding. These were given the name Whirlwind in British service and this version was designated the HAS 22. 706 NAS was re-commissioned in September 1953 at RNAS Gosport to evaluate them in the anti-submarine role and also spent time embarked on *Perseus*, which was employed as a helicopter carrier, and at RNAS Eglinton from where exercises were carried out with the Joint Anti-Submarine School based at Londonderry. These trials proved so successful that the unit was re-designated on 15 March 1954 as a front-line unit, 845 NAS. It re-embarked in *Perseus* in April for passage to RNAS Hal Far in Malta where it continued to develop helicopter anti-submarine tactics with detachments operating from time to time in *Centaur*, *Albion* and *Eagle*. 845 NAS returned to the UK to disband in October 1955 but re-formed in November for a further series of trials. During this commission, as we saw in a previous chapter, the unit operated without its sonar in the commando assault role from *Theseus* during the brief Suez campaign, demonstrating still further the flexibility of embarked helicopter units. In 1957 845 NAS re-equipped with the Westland-built Whirlwind HAS 7 and embarked in *Bulwark*. This was the first time that a helicopter squadron had formed part of a strike carrier's air group and, while the unit itself was considered fully operational, its embarkation was seen as an evolutionary test to see how successfully helicopters could be integrated into the carrier's fixed-wing operating cycle.

The Westland Whirlwind HAS 7 was procured to give an interim capability while the larger, all-weather Wessex was developed, following the cancellation the earlier types intended for front-line use. It used the licence-built airframe of the Sikorsky S-55 but replaced its 700hp Wright R-1300-3 Cyclone with a British 750hp Alvis Leonides. It was 41ft 8in long and had a rotor diameter of 53ft. Maximum weight was 7800lb. The Leonides engine proved to be the type's biggest problem, however, since it was designed as a conventional engine to be fitted to the wing of a fixed-wing aircraft like the Sea Prince, to rotate a propeller with its crank-shaft horizontal. Its lubrication system was designed accordingly but in the Whirlwind it was mounted with what would have been its rear at the bottom with what would have been the propeller shaft at the top rotating the drive shaft to the main rotor gearbox. This caused lubrication problems that led to frequent engine failures and the HAS 7 was often grounded for modifications to be implemented, the longest of which lasted from April to November 1959.

Whirlwinds were also effective in the commando assault role. Sticks of five Royal Marines can be seen here running out to Whirlwind HAS 7s of 848 NAS on *Bulwark* during her early trials as a commando carrier. They are painted in sand colour for desert operations. (Author's collection)

Commando Assault

MDAP funds also made ten utility versions of the S-55 available to the RN in 1952 and in October these were used to re-commission 848 NAS at RNAS Gosport as the RN's first operational helicopter unit. These aircraft were designated as the Whirlwind HAR 21 and the unit embarked in *Perseus* for passage to RNAS Sembawang in Singapore, arriving in January 1953 to undertake operations against Communist terrorists in Malaya. The unit was also tasked with determining the limitations placed on the performance of this type of helicopter by the hot and humid conditions found in the Malayan jungle. Work-up training included cross-country navigation using indistinct rivers, jungle paths and other topographical details to fix position over the featureless jungle. Troop drills were practised using Gurkha soldiers from the local garrisons. In flight the aircrew wore jungle-green bush-jackets and long trousers with jungle boots. Every pilot and observer had a personal 9mm Browning automatic pistol carried in a holster on the right hip so as not to interfere with the collective pitch controls to the left of the seats and a Sten Gun in a cockpit stowage. They each had a haversack in the main cabin which contained a poncho, jungle knife, 24-hour ration pack, first-aid kit and water. Several casualty evacuations were carried out at first but during Operation 'Eagle', an attack on a large enemy camp near Labis in Johore at the end of the month, an SAS troop was asked to clear an area big enough for supplies to be dropped to them. A survey, when the SAS had finished their task, found the clearing big enough for a Whirlwind to land in and two of 848 NAS's helicopters shuttled twenty-three men and 2500lbs of equipment out of the jungle considerably more quickly than they could have moved on foot. During this operation the aircraft had to be refuelled frequently from four-gallon cans at a forward operating base and this became a standard feature of operations as fuel in the aircraft itself had to be kept to a minimum to allow it to achieve the maximum lift. The aircrew became adept at pinpoint navigation and were tasked to drop leaflets on small villages that would be missed by drops from high-flying fixed-wing aircraft. A small group of Whirlwinds operated from a forward operating base near Kuala Lumpur with the remainder at Sembawang and both groups specialised in the insertion of small forces both as pathfinders for paratroopers dropped from Valettas of the Far East Air Force, (FEAF), and as strike forces to intercept terrorists located in a specific place.

Operation 'Bahadur', at the end of February 1953, involved eight Whirlwinds which flew seventy-five Gurkhas into an LZ that had been located by an Army Auster carrying an 848 NAS pilot.[8] The first lift carried a squadron observer who aided subsequent operations by indicating the strength and direction of the wind with smoke and placing fluorescent panels on the ground. In March 848 NAS contributed significantly to the first brigade-scale operation during which men from four battalions were inserted into LZs in western Pahang with 650 troops landed in 183 sorties together with 4000lbs of ammunition and equipment. The value of helicopters in the rapid deployment of troops had been clearly demonstrated and the majority of the tactics subsequently used by the RN Commando Helicopter Force (CHF), evolved from the work of 848 NAS in Malaya. The squadron was awarded the Boyd Trophy for 1953. The Whirlwind HAR 21 proved to be a reliable aircraft despite the trying conditions it operated in and at no time was 848 prevented from supplying the number of aircraft requested by the land forces. All the helicopters were fitted initially with USN AN/ARC 5 radios but these had only four channels and could not operate on certain operational frequencies used in Malaya. They were, therefore, fitted with British TR 1934 VHF sets and the ARC 5s discarded. The ability of assault helicopters to communicate with land forces and other agencies in a commando assault was to be an important consideration as amphibious warfare tactics evolved.

The Evolution of Helicopter Carriers

The Admiralty had followed the development of anti-submarine helicopters with interest and noted their success at a Board meeting held in October 1955 in which a paper by 5SL was discussed. This explained that the helicopter was now 'firmly established as an anti-submarine aircraft and its development has reached a stage where we can say with some confidence that it is likely to replace fixed-wing aircraft entirely'.[9] Despite some misgivings about the interoperability of fixed and rotary-winged aircraft, the Board accepted this view and agreed that the five anti-submarine squadrons should be re-equipped with helicopters from 1957 onwards. They also agreed that production of the Gannet could be curtailed as a savings measure because of its shorter than expected life in service. The transition was to be complete by 1960 when the more capable all-weather Wessex was expected to come into service. Surprisingly, in view of this decision, the Seamew continued in development for another two years. The risk that helicopters might fail and the Gannet have to be put back into production was regarded as slight and worth taking.

The possibility of operating support carriers (CVS), like some of the older USN *Essex* class equipped with mainly anti-submarine aircraft, had been considered but rejected since the older British armoured fleet carriers would have been too expensive to operate and the 1942 light fleet carriers, while cheaper to operate, were thought at the time to be coming to the end of their useful lives.[10] Money was extremely tight and the Board had recently failed to gain approval from the government for a new fleet carrier to be built between 1958 and 1963. It seemed logical, therefore, to concentrate anti-submarine helicopters in the existing

The RN quickly found a number of uses for its new helicopters. A Whirlwind HAS 22 is seen here winching a senior officer off the forecastle of a frigate for transfer to another vessel. (Author's collection)

operational carriers. This view also accorded with the naval staff's view that airborne anti-submarine assets were intended mainly for the defence of the carrier while it carried out its primary function of operating strike aircraft and fighters. Other navies, including the US, Australian, Canadian and Dutch, elected to operate both fixed and rotary-wing anti-submarine aircraft in order to provide an area capability as well as defence in depth for a task force. The British could not afford separate support carriers to do this and, with the increased size of the new generation of strike fighters, had insufficient deck space to operate every type of aircraft it wanted. The retention of fixed-wing anti-submarine aircraft beyond 1960 at the latest was, therefore, a capability the RN could not afford. The main drawback with this approach was that Whirlwinds were initially regarded as difficult to incorporate into fixed-wing operating cycles. FOAC, Rear Admiral A R Pedder, had strong views on the subject and had stated that helicopters could not operate from fleet carriers without seriously degrading their ability to operate fighters. His view was regarded as extreme and was not accepted by the Board but trials were ordered to investigate the problem and recommend solutions. These culminated in the re-commissioning of 845 NAS with Whirlwind HAS 7s in 1957 and its embarkation in *Bulwark* as part of a strike air group with Sea Hawks, Sea Venoms and Skyraiders. The deployment proved to be very successful and, overall, the Whirlwinds were recognised as adding flexibility to the carriers' capabilities, some of which will be described in the next chapter. Other carriers followed this trend and the last anti-submarine Gannet squadron, 810 NAS which had been embarked in *Centaur*, disbanded in July 1960. Despite its overall success, the Whirlwind was admittedly not an easy type to operate. When its rotors were turning it took up a lot of space and wind gusts made rotors 'sail' close to the deck causing danger to handlers and others. The blades had to be folded manually and this was a difficult task in strong, gusty wind conditions. The evolution took time and often involved placing the helicopter on one of the lifts and lowering it partially to allow the men 'walking' the blades aft to their folded position to gain easier access. These were difficulties that a professional team could overcome, however, not insuperable problems.

To achieve the light airframe weight needed for vertical take-off and sorties that would spend much of their time in the hover, Westland built their version of the Whirlwind with extensive use of magnesium alloy, a lighter metal than the aircraft-grade aluminium used in the original S-55 by Sikorsky. Unfortunately, magnesium alloy reacted with salt water to give rapid decomposition[11] and frequent inspections were necessary to see that corrosion had not affected the fuselage structure. The HAS 7 had insufficient power to lift both the sonar and a weapon and had to operate in hunter/killer pairs where one was fitted with the sonar and the other a weapon, usually a Mark 30 homing torpedo which was carried in a recess under the centre of the fuselage. The type's most obvious drawback was its single, unreliable piston engine which required carriers to embark volatile avgas in specially protected tanks long after most other naval aircraft, including the Gannet that the Whirlwind replaced, had been designed to use avcat with its higher flashpoint.[12] On the credit side, it was accepted that dipping sonar represented the best way of defending the carrier against submarines that might otherwise have penetrated the surface screen to get within torpedo range. Since they operated close to the carrier, even the hunter/killer concept was not as bad as it seemed at first since a single torpedo-armed helicopter could be held on deck or in an airborne holding position in higher threat states to attack a contact gained by one of the sonar-equipped helicopters on the screen. The requirement to train a large number of helicopter pilots to man the enlarged rotary-wing anti-submarine force presented some problems at first but these were overcome by converting Gannet pilots and observers and by increasing the numbers of aircrew recruited for short-service commissions. The Whirlwind

HAS 7 only served in front-line squadrons for four years but it proved to be a viable aircraft that laid the foundation for the much more capable Wessex which came into service from 1961.

The Admiralty Board policy for implementing the 1957 Defence Review was known as the '88 Plan'[13] which proposed a gradual reduction of major units in the operational fleet to:

> Four aircraft carriers deploying three air groups
> Three cruisers
> Forty-nine destroyers and frigates
> Thirty-one submarines[14]

In addition there was to be an amphibious strike force including the two 1943 light fleet carriers *Bulwark* and *Albion*, now considered to be surplus to the fixed-wing carrier requirement and to be modified for use as commando carriers, and the two projected LPDs. Significantly, there was no provision for helicopter carriers, either by converting existing 1942 light fleet carriers or with new construction. Despite the earlier misgivings, it was already accepted that anti-submarine helicopters would form part of the three operational embarked carrier air groups. The 1959 costing of the '88 Fleet' still made no mention of helicopter carriers. It showed a gradual reduction in expenditure until 1964 after which there would be a sharp and sustained rise. However, with the increasing complexity of the new generation of aircraft together with their weapons and systems, it was suggested for the first time that a case could be made for removing the helicopters to another ship and running the three operational carriers as specialised strike carriers (CVA), rather than general-purpose carriers. However, the government requirement for a single carrier to be maintained permanently in the FEF and the need for the other two ships in the operational fleet to replace or augment it at short notice emphasised the need for standardised air groups that were capable of flexible deployment. Sandys' preference for the carriers in the Atlantic to operate anti-submarine air groups was seen to be impractical and was quietly dropped as Mountbatten had expected. This logical outlook was complicated on 1 April 1960, however, when the Controller, Admiral Sir Peter Reid, and the Deputy Chief of the Naval Staff (DCNS), Vice Admiral L G Durlacher, circulated a memorandum[15] that put forward the concept of a new type of ship to deploy the new single-package Wessex helicopters, freeing the carriers to operate Scimitars, Sea Vixens and AEW Gannets. Surprisingly, at this stage, the memorandum stated at paragraph 2 that 'fixed and rotary wing cannot be operated from the same flight deck simultaneously and one or the other of the types must, therefore, suffer a reduction in availability'. Since helicopters did not require elaborate launching, landing or direction assets, whereas the fixed-wing aircraft did, it was argued that helicopters should be displaced from the carriers. The memorandum was deeply flawed on a number of counts. It made no mention of the fact that Whirlwind HAS 7 helicopters had already replaced the Gannet AS 4 in all the front-line anti-submarine squadrons and had operated with success as part of the flexible air groups in *Victorious*, *Ark Royal*, *Albion*, *Bulwark* and *Centaur*. The authors could also have mentioned that if the helicopters were to be removed from carrier air groups, space was actually available for anti-submarine Gannets to give distant cover that the helicopters could not achieve and which could have added night and all-weather dimensions to the ships' strike capability. There were certainly enough aircraft available in 1960 to form three four- or six-aircraft squadrons[16] but there were hardly enough Scimitars, Sea Vixens or aircrew trained on them to expand these units to fill the space vacated by helicopters. Most important of all, however, the memorandum failed to take into account the vital contribution now made by helicopters to the last-ditch defence of the carrier against submarine attack. No mention was made of the need for extra resources to provide sophisticated aircraft workshops and the men to man them in the helicopter ships as well as the carriers. From the outset, the Wessex was a sophisticated aircraft with a complex flight control system and experience showed all too plainly that its successors were likely to be even more technically advanced. Surprisingly, no mention was made of embarking anti-submarine helicopters in *Bulwark* and *Albion* on a regular basis or making wider use of these ships, despite the fact that they were declared to NATO as having a secondary ASW capability after conversion to the LPH role. The memorandum was, thus, full of ill-considered shortcomings but the authors did at least recognise that in a navy committed to the '88 Plan', other ships and projects would have to be sacrificed if these new warships were built.

The memorandum proposed that the helicopter ships should be built as large destroyers and an annex was prepared by DG Ships to illustrate two potential designs, both intended to operate eight Wessex helicopters, a number that was considered to be the smallest tactical unit capable of maintaining two helicopters on continuous screening operations. The first would have been a ship of 5900 tons with a single 3in 70 calibre twin mounting and two Seacat missile launchers in addition to the flight deck. The unit cost was estimated to be £11.3 million. The second was a more sophisticated ship of 6200 tons to be fitted with Seaslug Mark 2 surface-to-air missile system which had not, at that time, been authorised for development, at an estimated unit cost of £13.5 million. Since these ships did not form part of the '88 Plan', tables were produced to show that if construction of the projected 'County' class guided-missile destroyers (DLG) 07 to 10 were to be postponed for two years, money could be found for the helicopter ships and the men to man them initially but made no mention of what would happen after the two years if the four DLGs were eventually to be built. The Admiralty Board discussed these proposals at its meeting on 7 April 1960[17] and the case for helicopter ships was argued strongly by DCNS who believed that they would be flexible units in their own right, able to operate without support from frigates or even outside a carrier task force if necessary. The First Lord, Lord Carrington, was not convinced and made a number of telling points against the concept. He said that there was little chance of the Navy being allocated either extra manpower or extra money for them and, therefore, helicopter ships could only be procured by cancelling other projects which had already received Board approval. Moreover, the Future Policy Committee tasked with making plans to implement the recent defence review had laid less emphasis on anti-submarine operations in a global war and more on limited war operations in line with the new Government policy. He felt that helicopter ships would be difficult to justify against this scenario, would be of questionable value in limited war and, critically, might even weaken the argument for the replacement, or even retention of the fixed-wing aircraft carriers. He was undoubtedly right and neither the Controller nor DCNS appear to have given thought to the wider implications of their proposal. The Board should have rejected the matter then but there were traditional elements that regretted the recent reduction in the number of cruisers that had served as flagships on foreign stations and as gun batteries in carrier task groups. The Board decided that it did not feel justified in putting the case for helicopter ships before the Ministry of Defence but contradicted this decision by asking for a further paper giving the cost, and other implications, of building helicopter ships to cruiser standards and directing that the 1960 costing exercise should include alternative assumptions with and without helicopters ships.

At their meeting on 20 May 1960, the Board discussed Memorandum 1334 from DCNS and VCNS described how helicopter ships could undertake the traditional roles of cruisers. The un-dated memorandum[18] explained at some length how a construction programme for these ships could be costed and examined five different schemes. Among them the *Tiger* class cruisers, *Belfast*, DLGs 07 to 10 and a number of extant destroyers and frigates were considered for delay or deletion without modernisation to fund five helicopter cruisers. Two sets of design characteristics were offered; the first with Seaslug and Seacat but no guns would have displaced 8600 tons with a cost estimated at £16.39 million including the first outfit of missiles and stores but excluding the eight Wessex helicopters. The second added a 4.5in Mark 6 gunnery system which increased the tonnage to 9100 and the cost to £17.44 million. To give comparisons, contemporary Navy Estimates stated that the conventional cruiser *Tiger* delivered in 1959 cost £13.1 million and DLG-01, *Devonshire*, cost £14.08 million.[19] Both designs would need to be escorted rather than acting as escorts themselves and a speed of only 26 knots had to be accepted as the best that could be achieved with steam machinery of 40,000shp. The Board felt that a higher speed was desirable but the extra expense could not be justified, a decision that was difficult to comprehend since these ships would have to work with carrier task forces capable of 28 to 30 knots if they were to embark helicopters taken from carrier air groups as originally proposed. Both designs were intended to embark eight Wessex helicopters and would be fitted out to Grade II flagship standard. Alternative costings for various schemes were shown in appendices labelled A to D; all four methods found savings in the near term but added considerable cost to the programme after 1966, the critical years of high expenditure during which the replacement carriers were to be funded together with new escort vessels to replace the remaining wartime hulls.

A further Board meeting on 28 July discussed these and other issues. DCNS maintained his view that such ships would be 'useful' in both hot and cold war situations[20] and, by assuming the anti-submarine helicopter task, he felt that they would improve the efficient operation of strike aircraft from the carriers. He admitted, however, that the helicopter ships would add to the size of the escort force needed to screen them in addition to the carriers in a task force operating in an area of high submarine threat. Again, cogent arguments were deployed against these helicopter ships and it was recognised that there might be considerable difficulty in obtaining approval for their construction from the Ministry of Defence and the Treasury. The problem of manning such ships could not, easily, be solved since it was still far from clear that the ships already authorised under the '88 Plan' could be manned. Lord Carrington added another contentious aspect to the debate at this stage by stating that he did not like the term 'helicopter ship'. At his suggestion the term 'escort cruiser' was substituted and adopted by the Board for further planning. The Board ended this series of discussions by agreeing that escort cruisers would be 'desirable' and asked DG Ships for outline drawings to be prepared for presentation in 1961. The Board also agreed that the concept could be mentioned to the Ministry of Defence but there was to be no suggestion that the Board had formally decided to seek approval to build. That step was to await discussion of drawings in due course but in the meantime the escort cruiser was to be described as 'valuable for its own versatile capabilities and not depending for its justification simply, or even predominantly, on the carriage of anti-submarine helicopters'. In a few months the proposal had changed from a simple helicopter-carrying destroyer intended to relieve carriers of the complication of operating mixed fixed and rotary-wing air groups into a cruiser capable of independent operations in which the operation of helicopters was not even the primary role among several. It is difficult to see the project as anything but an

Helicopters were also evaluated for light salvage operations; a Whirlwind HAR 3 is seen here towing the coastal minesweeper *Gavinton*. For a time the RN considered using helicopters to replace minesweepers by towing sleds fitted with acoustic and magnetic systems to detonate influence mines. The concept was not taken forward in the UK but was developed and used by the USN. (Author's collection)

attempt to replace the 18,000-ton GW96A cruiser project that had been cancelled in the 1957 Defence Review. The Board that had fought so hard through successive defence reviews to retain aircraft carriers and their balanced air groups of strike aircraft, fighters and helicopters was now putting their replacement in jeopardy by supporting another expensive major warship project. In addition to the major cost of its own construction programme which must be added to that of new carriers, the proposed escort cruiser would have the effect of weakening the general purpose capability of the carrier air groups and making them more vulnerable to submarine attack without their own defensive helicopters. The cost of a future carrier task force would be increased significantly by the need to include an escort cruiser as well as DLGs, air-direction destroyers and anti-submarine frigates even in limited war situations.

Fortunately it was recognised within M1 Division, the element of the Admiralty secretariat that supported the naval operational staff. Its head, K T Nash, advised that without careful management the escort cruiser argument could fatally weaken the case for the replacement carrier programme. Senior members of the secretariat warned the Board that they could expect to be 'sharply questioned' on the subject by ministers. Until 1960 the new carrier design had been thought of as a CV, supporting a general-purpose air group capable of performing a range of naval functions that included strike warfare. From now on it was to be described as a strike carrier (CVA), with a focus on the operation of long-range strike aircraft and fighters. This more specialised role and the perceived overlap with the RAF bomber force would be very much more difficult to justify politically and, as the Board should have predicted, Harold Watkinson the new Minister of Defence, was becoming alarmed at the large and expensive naval building programme that was emerging for the mid to late 1960s. The Admiralty's latest plan required £250 million in excess of the '88 Plan' as it had been accepted in the 1958 costings. He asked the First Lord to explain the situation at a meeting on 29 September 1960 at which 1SL, the Controller and DCNS were also present.[21] A wide range of projects including carrier replacement, nuclear submarines, assault ships, frigates and an ice patrol ship were discussed in addition to the escort cruisers and it should be noted that all of these, except the nuclear submarines, were to be capable of embarking helicopters, weakening still further the argument in favour of specialised helicopter cruisers. The First Lord explained that the agreed programme included ten DLGs, of which four had already been ordered and two were awaiting confirmation. Escort cruisers, if it was decided to proceed with them after the study of staff requirements, would replace the last four DLGs. It was implied, but not stated, that other savings would need to be found to cover the additional cost of the escort cruisers. The Minister of Defence asked the Admiralty to consult more deeply with his Ministry and put forward firm, costed proposals for the escort cruiser as soon as possible. To his credit, Lord Carrington asked the Minister for an early decision on the carrier replacement programme, hoping to order the first ship in 1963 in order to spread the cost more evenly through the planning period and reduce the burden in the later, over-committed years. Despite the sense in the obvious merit of this approach, the Minister refused. His Government had accepted the continued operation of the existing carrier force but had yet to agree, fully, to its long-term replacement. This could explain one of the reasons why the SR-177 had been cancelled, Sandys had seen it as a long-term project, stretching beyond the life of the existing carriers. Carrington also mentioned the Board's belief that the new carriers would require a new generation of aircraft and was the first to propose that they should be developed jointly with the RAF. The Government was clearly not yet ready to confirm orders for new carriers and the Board should have heeded the warnings from M1 Division; unfortunately it failed to do so.

In the autumn of 1960 DG Ships had some spare capacity and moved quickly to study various design options for escort cruisers in advance of a clearly defined staff target. Attention concentrated on ships with a speed of 26 knots 'deep and dirty' with facilities to support up to eight Wessex helicopters. Design series 6 looked at ships up to 460ft in length displacing 5900 tons. Series 9 introduced missile armament but in the absence of a British surface-to-surface guided weapon and with no decision to adopt the USN Tartar system, Seaslug was assumed. Design 9C could carry twenty-eight missiles, sixteen of which were in knocked-down component parts (KDC) that would require assembly before launch, on 6400 tons with a speed of 26 knots. Hangar height was only 16ft 6in and the deck was only stressed for the Wessex HAS 1 at 12,600lbs maximum weight, leaving absolutely no margin at all for future growth. Following the Future Requirements Committee's recommendation that provision should be made for the USN HSS-2 Sea King (which was eventually to be procured for the RN as a Wessex replacement), this design was upgraded to 9D with a hangar height of 18ft 6in and decks stressed to take 26,000lbs. Again, there was no margin for growth beyond these figures in the life of the ship. Design 9E represented a further development of these Seaslug-armed ships with the superstructure offset to starboard as an island in order to maximise the amount of flight deck available. A port side sponson allowed four helicopter operating spots to be used simultaneously and the tonnage of this version rose to 6730 tons. Designs 6 and 9 had concentrated on ships designed to destroyer standards but following the Board decision to upgrade these ships to cruiser standards, a further series of studies were set in train.

The best of these was Design series 21 and 21H.2A was a cruiser with an offset island like 9E but with armoured protection around machinery spaces and magazines, a twin 4.5in Mark 6 gun system directed by MRS 3 on the island facing aft and Seaslug missile stowage increased to forty-four, although only twelve of these were ready-use. Length was increased to 535ft on a displacement of 9500 tons. Study 21J.2 added a second 4.5in mounting on a displacement of 9700 tons and study 21K placed the Seaslug launcher aft like that in the DLGs with the gun mountings forward, apparently a more complicated arrangement that increased the tonnage to 9,850. Study 21L.2 took the same armament as 21J.2 but introduced more powerful machinery of 60,000shp to give a speed of 28.5 knots, increasing the tonnage to 10,250. All these studies had a radius of action of 4500nm at 20 knots.[22]

The Defence Secretary's stricture that plans for escort cruisers should be laid before him as soon as possible led to a series of papers that looked into ways and means of manning, funding and assimilating such ships into the programme. In addition to delaying DLGs 07 to 10, delays to the modernisation of the cruiser *Swiftsure* in Chatham Dockyard and of the first four (DC current) *Daring* class destroyers were considered together with reductions in the escort force that included paying off five 'Ca' class destroyers[23] and all four *Leopard* class anti-aircraft frigates into operational reserve. It would have been politically too embarrassing to admit that the three *Tiger* class cruisers, the first of which had only entered service in 1959, with their obsolescent gun armament were of little value to a modern task force and these plans envisaged their retention for about ten years after which they could be quietly discarded.

The Board decided, at its meeting of 20 October 1960, to plan for a force of five cruisers by 1967–8 including the three *Tiger*s, two of which would be in operational reserve at any one time.[24] *Swiftsure* was to be scrapped and *Belfast* reduced to reserve. The two escort cruisers were eventually to be followed by three more, paid for by further delays to DLGs 07 to 10, by refitting rather than modernising the DC *Daring*s and by limiting frigate construction. A design that had no clear purpose, lacked versatility and actually detracted from the potential of the Navy's central carrier replacement programme seemed to have become the focus of attention. At best, the Board would be 'sharply questioned' about what now appeared to be a change in its policy, at worst the Air Ministry would mount determined opposition to specialised strike carriers that appeared to encroach on the role of their medium bomber force and politicians might not accept the naval case. So much had been won in 1957; now there was a lot to lose.

In October 1960 DAOT was asked how many extra strike/fighter aircraft could be embarked in the existing carriers if eight Wessex helicopters were to be removed from each of them. The reply was far from positive and shows the complete lack of enthusiasm for the escort cruiser in the air element of the naval staff.[25] After some years of experience, the value of anti-submarine helicopters in defending the carriers and as part of general-purpose air groups had been recognised. The extra numbers put forward were:

Eagle	1
Victorious	3
Ark Royal	1
Hermes	2
Centaur	1

Quite why the larger *Eagle* and *Ark Royal* with their large double hangars could take less than the smaller ships with single-deck hangars was not made clear although later papers refer to a 'rule of thumb' that the space required to stow ten Wessex equated very roughly to three Buccaneers. To man the extra fixed-wing aircraft required to fill the space made available by the removal of helicopters, ten aircrew and eighty maintenance ratings plus a suitable margin would have to be added to the Vote A strength of the RN. Annual intakes of pilots and observers would have to be increased, putting strain on the operational training squadrons. An additional buy of Buccaneers and Sea Vixens would be necessary to support the enlarged front-line and training squadrons. Furthermore, an increase in Vote A strength would also be necessary to provide air staffs and supporting elements in the escort cruisers in addition to those already serving in the carriers. The author of the document made it clear that he was opposed to the concept of escort cruisers and was putting into print every argument he could summon against them.

A draft case for the escort cruisers was prepared by M1 Division and circulated within the Admiralty for comment on 14 December 1960.[26] It began by saying that the importance of aircraft carriers <u>and</u> cruisers was increasing as the number of overseas bases was reduced but made no comment on the fact that a second major warship project would have to be developed in the mid-1960s and in the tight prevailing financial climate, this would be extremely difficult. The document went on to say that to make the best use of carriers in what would today be described as the power-projection role without prejudicing the Fleet Air Arm's contribution to anti-submarine warfare, escort cruisers would embark the helicopters removed from carrier air groups. These new ships would have the additional advantage of ensuring that what were described as the desirable characteristics of cruisers were to be embodied in the new escort cruisers. They were described in somewhat vague detail as being of 'about 10,000 tons' with cruiser qualities of endurance and self-maintenance, to be armed with Seaslug 2 which was now authorised for development, guns for shore bombardment and the ability to operate eight Wessex. Complement, excluding the air personnel, was to be 'about 600' and cost 'some £20 million'. Apart from the guns the design had no anti-surface ship capability and would have to rely on carrier-borne aircraft for airborne early warning, area reconnaissance, surface warfare and anti-aircraft defence in depth. Since Seaslug was a beam-riding weapon it only offered a single channel of fire; once its controlling Type 901 radar had locked on to a target and a missile had been fired, no other target could be engaged until the first target was hit. Thus while Seaslug had a capability against shadowing aircraft at medium to high level within its effective range, it could not engage the majority of targets in a regimental type of attack and the task force would rely on carrier-borne fighters, DLGs and Seacat-armed escorts for defence in depth.

Escort cruisers might have made it easier to operate the decks of carriers without mixing fixed and rotary-wing flying but by 1961 both the operations departments and the flight deck handling parties were well used to launching helicopters in the intervals between fixed-wing launch and recovery cycles. The larger, second generation jets meant that there were fewer aircraft in launches and helicopters could land at the extremities of the deck, if necessary while the ship was out of wind, to keep clear of them. The operation of mixed air groups had become a well-drilled routine that, unfortunately, protagonists of the escort cruiser seemed to be unaware of. For this reason DNAW, Captain Vincent-Jones, openly opposed the escort cruiser in his response to M1's draft case.[27] He reminded the Staff that when first proposed the helicopter ship had been described as providing anti-submarine defence for carriers with the helicopters removed from their air groups in order to make them more efficient in the strike role. Even in a limited war situation, therefore, the helicopter ship would have to operate as part of a carrier task force and, at nearly half the cost of a new carrier, it would be a high-value target in its own right. The eight Wessex helicopters would have two valuable units to defend rather than one and would be that much less efficient. That number of helicopters had been specified as the minimum required to keep two airborne continuously to screen the carrier. The introduction of an escort cruiser that would also need to be protected would need a significant increase in the number of embarked helicopters and, consequently in the size of the ship to operate and maintain them if the helicopters were required to boost the defences of a larger task force. DNAW confirmed the extent to which helicopters were now accepted as an important element of a general-purpose air group by saying that they 'added to the carriers' ability to support military forces ashore' and 'provided a wide range of flexible, tactical air power far removed from land bases'. The USN HSS-2 Sea King would, he felt, boost this capability still further if it were purchased as a Wessex replacement in due course. He made two other interesting general comments, firstly that escort cruisers might have a useful potential for the carriage[28] of VTOL aircraft or hovercraft 'should such projects come to fruition' and second that they might have limited capability in the amphibious role. No attempt was made to amplify these comments or to say how commandos, once landed by helicopter, could be supported. In summary, DNAW felt that the value of escort cruisers was, at best, theoretical and recommended that it would be better to wait until the new generation of carriers was approved and then see how best to support them with escorts rather than commit to the construction of expensive ships that 'might not ideally complement the carriers' and might even compromise plans for their procurement. This was excellent advice and, with hindsight, there can be little doubt that some elements of the naval staff wanted a flagship that was emerging as an alternative to a carrier, not as part of its escort. DNAW was not alone in recommending delay until after the carrier programme was authorised.

Captain Martell, the Director of Tactical and Weapons Policy (DTWP), pointed out in his reply to the M1 draft[29] that the naval staff had accepted one of the concepts at the heart of the 1957 Defence Review that surface-to-air guided weapons would take over the task of fleet air defence from fighters. With hindsight we know that this did not happen for decades to come but in 1961 it was felt that it might happen 'soon'. DTWP believed, therefore, if surface-to-air missile ships were to be procured for operation with the new carriers, it would be best to wait and see what form these ships would take before deciding on the design of a type that would interact with them. DTWP also stated that, since it appeared that both anti-aircraft and anti-submarine defence appeared likely to be undertaken by ships other than the carriers themselves from the mid-1960s, there was logic in placing both capabilities in a single hull, the escort cruiser. He failed to mention that there was even greater logic in placing both capabilities in the single hull of the carrier itself, thus saving the cost of the cruiser and the requirement for men to man it. Acceptance of this philosophy would, in his opinion, place more emphasis on air defence than anti-submarine warfare. Delay would be advantageous as the design of the escort cruiser would have to be re-cast and it might, then, be possible to arm it with the Seaslug replacement system, CF 299, which was to evolve into Sea Dart. He added that such a delay would allow DLGs 07 to 10 to be completed in order to keep escort numbers up to strength.

For different reasons, the naval staff had shown a lack of commitment to the escort cruiser concept and recommended delay. The project had no clear aim from the outset and had consequently accumulated objectives that metamorphosed it into a cruiser design which had many features in common with the design that had been cancelled in the Defence Review. It was a backward-looking concept that had little relevance to the new reality of carrier task forces supporting amphibious operations in 'brushfire' or limited war situations. The Board should have seen this and terminated the project, indicating to ministers their clear intention to remain within financial and manpower targets but they did not. M1 Division sought to clarify the increasingly obscure rationale for the escort cruiser by circulating a questionnaire around the operational naval staff divisions[30] which asked basic questions about the potential roles and capabilities of the new type of warship. The resultant answers showed a predictable spread of opinion overall but the staff were unanimous in stating that removing anti-submarine helicopters from the carrier air groups was a very bad idea. The escort cruiser had become an open threat to the replacement carrier programme.

DNAW took the firm line that the new generation of carriers must be designed to embark at least eight anti-submarine helicopters for their own defence. Any carried in escort cruisers would, therefore, be in addition to those embarked in the carriers' air groups with all the extra expense that this would entail. He added, bolstering his earlier arguments, that the space occupied by helicopters was not large and that it would be unwise to remove the capability they offered. Their retention in new carrier designs would certainly not make them unacceptably large and expensive. It was implied, but not stated, that the construction of escort cruisers would be an expensive addition to task forces. The Director of Plans, Captain Ashmore, described the utility cruisers could offer to the operational fleet and mentioned their ability to operate for long periods independent of base support, good endurance, command and control facilities and the ability to support ships smaller than themselves. Surprisingly he also wrote of their ability to carry troops to a trouble spot but made no mention of how they would be supported once ashore. These comments would have been appropriate in the 1930s but in 1961 they are difficult to comprehend. Most of the cruiser's traditional tasks on foreign stations had already been taken over by frigates which had a similar cruising performance but were far cheaper to man and run. Aircraft carriers had far better command and control facilities and were able to monitor the battle space in three dimensions. Cruiser fire-control systems were obsolescent and their guns of little value against the quality of air attack expected from the Soviet Union and its client states in the late 1960s. The new commando carriers, able both to land and sustain military forces ashore with helicopters and landing craft, were the obvious means of carrying military force to a trouble spot. DN Plans' backward-looking and ill-considered comments were blurring not just the case for new carriers but also that for the new amphibious ships. His statements about cruiser endurance are particularly hard to comprehend. For instance the fleet carrier *Victorious* had an economical endurance of 11,080nm at 13 knots and the light fleet carrier *Glory* 9390nm at the same speed. The cruiser *Swiftsure*, a half-sister of *Tiger* completed to the original design, only had an economical endurance of 6350nm at 11 knots and *Belfast*, the largest cruiser left in service in 1960, had figures of 7440nm at 13 knots.[31]

Captain Symonds, the Director of Undersea Warfare, was absent when the questionnaire was circulated but Commander Griffiths, the Assistant Director, added to the muddled thinking about the escort cruiser's potential. He recommended that there should be two different types of cruiser, a larger type for open-ocean fleet operations and a smaller type for more limited operations, perhaps as part of support groups. On balance, however, whilst he believed that the escort cruiser had some attractive features, it was not an economical way of operating our limited number of anti-submarine helicopters and could not be regarded as more essential than the large carrier. DTWP agreed that carriers must continue to operate eight helicopters for their own defence since the advent of nuclear submarines meant that evasion alone was no longer sufficient for carriers to defend themselves against the underwater threat. Surprisingly, he believed that commando carriers might prove to be a short-lived experiment and agreed with DN Plan's view that cruisers might be necessary to carry troops in the mid-1970s. Given these answers, M1 Division drew up a draft Paper which outlined the capabilities now seen as desirable in the escort cruiser.[32] These included the ability to operate at long range from a base and to handle 'any situation that may be encountered or require to be dealt with'. Operational versatility demanded a variety of weapons, helicopters and 'a capacity for carrying troops and stores for emergencies'. High speed was needed to cover, quickly, the long distances implicit in long-range operations. As a Grade II flagship, this concept was far-removed from the original proposal for a helicopter ship and was clearly intended to operate at some distance away from a carrier as an alternative flagship. It had become a 'versatile, independent unit armed with Seaslug 2, a bombardment gun system, nine Wessex helicopters, a full communications outfit, space for a flag officer and his staff together with space for an appreciable number of troops and their vehicles and impedimenta'. The design might even be capable of 'ferrying' a small number of VTOL aircraft, although there was no elaboration about what this statement might mean, thus becoming 'an extremely potent and impressive cold and limited war weapon'. Such a ship would be of about 10,500 tons with a complement of 1043. Three such ships were to be available to the active fleet, thus four would have to be ordered and, ultimately, a fifth to cover long refit periods. The lack of a surface warfare capability commensurate with the size and value of the ship does not seem to have caused concern at the time and nor does its vulnerability to regimental Soviet air attack outside a carrier task force. The escort cruiser seemed to have developed its own momentum and it is almost as if the recent defence review had not happened.

It is interesting to note that M1's description exactly fitted the PF-57 design rated as a *croiser porte-helicopteres* by the French Navy. Laid down in 1957, one example was built and completed in 1963. It was named *La Resolue* at first but re-named *Jeanne d'Arc* when an older cruiser of that name was discarded. The design included a flight deck and hangar capable of operating up to eight Sikorsky S-58 helicopters,[33] a twin Masurca surface-to-air guided weapon system and four 3.9in guns for shore bombardment on a hull of 10,000 tons. Speed was 26.5 knots, achieved with machinery of 40,000shp and the complement was 1050. A battalion of 700 men and light equipment could be embarked for short periods. I have not been able to ascertain evidence of any collaboration between the escort cruiser and PH-57 but the similarity is too striking to be entirely coincidental. The Italian Navy also built helicopter cruisers from 1958 onwards but these were smaller ships, armed with the USN Terrier missile system, which only operated from three to six helicopters depending on their size. Despite the disparity in helicopter numbers, these ships were more closely comparable with the British 'County' class DLGs than with the proposed escort cruiser. Neither navy operated or could afford to operate aircraft carriers similar to those both planned and projected by the RN during this period and ships of this sort have to be considered as hybrids that attempted to impose minimal aviation facilities onto a small hull that was, as far as possible, traditional in design. Even the USN devoted some effort to evaluating the possibility of fitting flight decks over the quarterdecks of *Iowa* class battleships brought out of reserve but never proceeded with such an expensive project.

By mid-1961 the escort cruiser sketch requirement had absorbed most of the weapons and capabilities projected for the cancelled RN 1950s cruiser and cruiser/destroyer projects and had clearly been influenced by PH-57. Judged by these criteria, the three *Tiger* class cruisers, which had only just been accepted into service, were obsolete and their use for anything other than 'showing the flag' was open to question. Despite the lack of enthusiasm within the Naval Staff, the Board decided to continue with the escort cruiser project, a presentation was made to the Minister of Defence in May 1961 and it was endorsed by the Chiefs of Staff Committee in December.[34] The agreed requirement was for ships that could deploy anti-submarine helicopters to the best operational advantage in addition to those embarked for self-defence in the carriers; contribute to building up the surface-to-air guided weapon defences of the fleet and to provide ships with the command facilities, versatility and long endurance of the cruiser. The Chiefs of Staff Plan 'Strategy for the Sixties'[35] called for a fleet strength of seven cruisers, including the three *Tiger*s which were to be kept in operational reserve as back-up to the four new escort cruisers, one being reduced to reserve as each new cruiser joined the fleet. The first long-term costing for escort cruisers appeared in LTC 62 for an order expected to be in July 1966 after the necessary design work was finished and for completion in July 1970. The plan soon had to be amended, however, as an economy measure which underlined how wide of the mark the project had always been. In order to reduce the size of the projected 1965/66 defence budget, it was decided to dispose of the *Tiger*s rather than keep them in reserve to save the cost of their long refits and maintenance. By late 1962 it was obvious that the staff of DG Ships was struggling to cope with its heavy load of design work and the escort cruiser design had to be delayed by at least two years. Further delay followed the UK government's decision to procure the Polaris submarine-launched strategic missile system in 1963. It had been assumed in Whitehall that Polaris would, eventually, be procured but not until after the new generation of aircraft carriers and escort cruisers were built and in service. Until then RAF 'V'-bombers

The cruiser *Tiger,* seen here, and her sister-ship *Blake* were expensively modified with hangars and small flight decks to operate up to four anti-submarine helicopters. A Sea King is seen here on finals to land; although two circles are painted on the deck, there was, actually, only room for a single helicopter to land at a time. The two circles merely offered alternate spots, the after one allowing some parking space just outside the hangar doors. (Author's collection)

equipped with the US Skybolt air-launched ballistic missile system were expected to provide the UK independent nuclear deterrent until the mid-1970s. The unilateral decision by the USA to cancel Skybolt and the UK Government's decision to replace the 'V'-bombers with British nuclear submarines armed with Polaris by 1968 changed everything.

An Interim Solution
In 1963 the Fleet Requirements Committee expressed concern at the lack of anti-submarine helicopters the RN could actually deploy in the NATO area where

other navies seemed to be outpacing the UK in their development and use. With two of the three operational carriers now committed to the FEF the basic problem was the reduction in carrier numbers after the last defence review with only one helicopter squadron, in the third carrier, available for the Home and Medi-terranean Fleets to train with. In a memorandum for the Admiralty Board dated 18 October 1963, VCNS put forward a number of suggestions for increasing the number of embarked helicopters. He noted that there had been three separate representations from commanders at sea within the past eight months but explained that the RN would have difficulty in expanding the anti-submarine force in the short-term future due to its inability to recruit and train sufficient helicopter pilots. The creation of the commando helicopter force and plans to put Wasp and Wessex flights into large numbers of frigates and destroyers had already caused large increases in the necessary annual intakes of pilots. Further expansion would be expensive and strain the training organisation to its limit. A secondary factor would be the need to procure more helicopters, including the more sophisticated Wessex HAS 3 which was due to replace the HAS 1, with no compensating reductions. Treasury approval could not be assumed without a hard fight and might not be won even then. This weak area had not been addressed in the arguments in support of the escort cruiser project.

Despite these limitations, four schemes were considered to fill the perceived gap before the first escort cruiser was expected to join the fleet in about 1973. These were either to construct new helicopter ships; build repeats of the RFA *Engadine* modified for service as warships; convert the *Tiger* class cruisers to operate helicopters or to embark anti-submarine helicopter squadrons in commando carriers on a regular basis. The first scheme was immediately discounted because the lack of design effort to take the escort cruisers forward would have prevented any work on them, even if the ships were built to mercantile standards. The second scheme was rejected because clones of *Engadine*, which had originally been designed as an RFA to provide the cheapest flight deck at sea for helicopter aircrew training, would have needed extensive re-design before they would have been suitable for fleet use, putting them into the same category as the first scheme. In an ideal world, anti-submarine helicopters in both cruisers and commando carriers would have been viable but there were insufficient aircrew and aircraft for both. The latter had large flight decks and space for workshops, magazines and accom-modation to support an anti-submarine unit but their deployment pattern had, necessarily, to be centred on amphibious operations in the Far East. Despite the advantage of having their own embarked, defensive anti-submarine helicopters if this option were adopted, the commando carriers would, therefore, make little impact on the number of helicopters available in the NATO area. The recommended solution, therefore, was to modify the *Tiger*s to operate four helicopters each. The delay in building the escort cruisers meant that they would have to remain in service and would, therefore, need to undergo a long refit. The opportunity could be taken to remove the after twin 6in gun turret and replace it with a hangar and flight deck for an increase in refit cost from about £3.5 million to about £5 million. The result could at best be described as a poor compromise and the ships would have too few guns to be of any use in the anti-surface or anti-aircraft roles, too few helicopters to maintain two on the screen continuously and command and control facilities that were inadequate when compared with aircraft carriers. With a ship's company of 885 officers and men they could realistically be described as a liability rather than an asset.

The limited design work for the *Tiger* class conversions was believed to be available within the dockyards which had capacity to start work in 1965, 1966 and 1967 for completion, it was hoped, in 1966, 1967 and 1968. Conversion was recommended to the Board and accepted at their meeting on 24 January 1964[36] as offering the fleets west of Suez an anti-submarine helicopter capability at what was thought to be a modest cost. It was assumed that Treasury agreement for the conversions would be forthcoming but this proved not to be the case. The Admiralty was 'sharply questioned' about the intended lives of these ships after conversion. None of them was more than five years old but *Blake*, the newest, had already been reduced to reserve after only one commission. The Treasury wanted to see a viable return of service for the cost of conversion and so it was decided to plan for a life of eight to nine years after the long refit. The Admiralty decided to prolong the delay of two years for the first escort cruiser and defer the first order until 'about the middle of 1970'. Although not stated, this accepted de facto that the escort cruisers, if they were ever built, would replace rather than augment the *Tiger*s. Since she was already out of service, *Blake* was taken in hand first and was to have been followed by *Lion* and then *Tiger*. The Treasury, however, refused to sanction the conversion of all three ships and fought each one in turn. Only *Blake* and *Tiger* were ever converted; both conversions took longer than expected and the latter cost nearly three times the original estimate. Put another way, it cost 25 per cent of the projected cost of the new carrier CVA-01 to convert *Tiger* but she could only operate four helicopters and had mediocre command, control and communications facilities.

The Relationship between Helicopter Ships and the Replacement Carrier Project

There can be no doubt that the Admiralty Board's enthusiasm for the helicopter ship/escort cruiser adversely affected its own plan to build a new generation of aircraft carriers. It did so both directly and indirectly. Directly because the removal

A wasted opportunity. *Perseus*, seen here in 1952, had far more to offer as a helicopter carrier than the cruiser conversions and could have operated helicopters up to Sea King size in large numbers, as could her half-sisters *Magnificent* and *Leviathan*. She would have needed to be fitted with an effective anti-submarine and surface plot operations room but this would not have been unreasonably expensive. (Author's collection)

of anti-submarine helicopters from the carrier air groups in the early concept studies appeared to require a total package that included two big hulls instead of one to provide the same capability. Even after the decision that anti-submarine helicopters for the cruisers would have to be procured in addition to those in the carriers, the name 'escort cruiser' was ill-conceived and implied that carriers had become so vulnerable to submarine attack that they required a massive investment in escort ships to protect them. The alternative, championed by DNAW, was to put the anti-aircraft and anti-submarine missile systems, Sea Dart and Ikara, in the carrier itself as the ship most likely to be attacked in a task force. Whilst this drove up the price of the carrier, it removed the cost of an escort cruiser and its manpower.

DN Plan's enthusiasm for cruisers is all the more incomprehensible since, in 1955, the Naval Staff had rejected the feasibility of support carriers (CVS), in the belief that they were too expensive to operate alongside the larger strike carriers. The 1957 Defence Review had cancelled a new missile-armed cruiser design because its construction was considered too expensive to justify given the ship's limited operational value. After 1960, however, the Admiralty Board seems to have gone to extraordinary lengths to project the construction of a number of less capable but more expensive cruisers. It is difficult to understand why no thought was given to using the 1942 light fleet carrier *Magnificent*. She was placed on the Disposal List in 1961, after loan service with the RCN, when only thirteen years old but was not scrapped until 1965. With no structural alteration she could have out-performed the much vaunted long-range capability of any RN cruiser and could have operated up to thirty Wessex,[37] but would have needed changes to her operations room and magazines during a refit that would still have been less complex than that carried out on the *Tigers*. She would have been a far more effective emergency troop carrier as her sister-ships *Ocean* and *Theseus* had shown at Suez. To me, the 'blindness' that led to these versatile ships being ignored is one of the great mysteries of this period.

Indirectly the escort cruiser project led to the designation of the new carrier as a strike carrier, or CVA in the NATO system. To the majority of politicians, who hardly understood the detail of naval affairs, this apparently reduced the ship's usefulness to nuclear strike and little else. Nothing could be further from the truth and, as we shall see in a later chapter, CVA-01 would have been one of the most versatile ships ever built for the RN but when the Admiralty Board placed great emphasis on the escort cruiser's potential as a flagship on independent operations during a period of financial restraint, politicians could be forgiven for assuming that they represented a viable alternative to aircraft carriers for commanding and executing three-dimensional operations on, over, under and from the sea. This they certainly were not and the continued references to 'maintaining the desirable qualities of cruisers' are difficult to understand. Aircraft carriers had fighting qualities better adapted to modern war at all levels of intensity and continued to demonstrate them. The rapidly declining usefulness of cruisers had been starkly illustrated by the virtual extinction of the type with a rate of decline faster than all other types of warship between 1955 and 1963. Helicopter ships were not cheap alternatives to carriers. At this time, the Board seems not to have fully understood that after 1957 Great Britain had scope for only one major shipbuilding project and, for a variety of good reasons, that should have been a new generation of aircraft carriers. The opportunity to make use of several 'flat top' hulls that still had many years of life left in them was a missed opportunity that could hardly have evoked greater opposition from the Treasury than the 'botched' *Tiger* class conversion and would have allowed ships of far greater value to be commissioned and used.

10 A Range of Carrier Operations

As we saw in the last chapter, some senior members of the Naval Staff had found it difficult to comprehend the Royal Navy's new role and had yearned for the days when cruisers policed the Empire. Fortunately, the operational divisions within the Admiralty and the deployed fleets had no such difficulty. Task forces centred on aircraft carriers demonstrated their value, deterred conflict, projected power in limited war situations and carried out the traditional peacetime tasks of sea power. The following examples demonstrate carriers' effectiveness in a variety of unexpected situations that required rapid responses, often providing the ideal solution when no other British asset was capable of operation.

Lebanon and Jordan, 1958

The aftermath of the 1956 Suez Crisis left the Middle East unstable and the weakened British position in the region led to an expansion of Communist political influence. The USA attempted to fill the vacuum with what it termed the 'Eisenhower Doctrine' in 1957. This offered to 'protect the territorial integrity and political independence' of nations that requested 'aid against overt armed aggression from any nation controlled by international communism'.[1] King Hussein of Jordan dismissed his government in April 1957 when it threatened to seek Soviet aid and, supported by loyal Bedouin forces, he appealed to the USA for help. In order to 'avoid that chaos Moscow hopes to exploit',[2] the US Sixth Fleet cruised off Beirut in a display of regional strength and the US Government offered King Hussein $10 million in aid which was accepted immediately. In February 1958 the situation became more complex when Presidents Nasser of Egypt and Kuwatly of Syria announced the union of their countries to form the United Arab Republic (UAR). Days later Jordan and Iraq responded by forming the Arab Federation with King Feisal as its head, although both kings retained sovereignty within their own country; both were denounced as traitors to the Arab cause by Nasser. Between these two combinations, the Lebanon with its partially Christian population remained unattached. It had, however, a substantial opposition party that criticised President Chamoun for taking US aid which was compared

Two 897 NAS Sea Hawks orbiting *Eagle* in her low wait position, photographed from a third. Note the plane-guard Whirlwind to starboard of the ship's island. There is a launch in progress with a Sea Hawk taxiing onto the port catapult and manned Sea Venoms aft; when it is complete, *Eagle* will adjust her course to put the wind down the angled deck and these aircraft will land-on. (Author's collection)

unfavourably with the Soviet aid which was, by then, pouring into the UAR. On 13 May 1958 the Lebanese Foreign Minister informed the US, British and French ambassadors that his country would call for military assistance if it was attacked. Both the British Mediterranean Fleet and the US Sixth Fleet were ordered to adopt a heightened state of readiness and deployed units to the eastern Mediterranean. In order to preserve secrecy, the movement of the British amphibious warfare squadron from Malta to Cyprus was declared to be part of the NATO Exercise 'Medflex Fort'. The same cover was used to explain the move of *Ark Royal* with her task force to the east 'with all convenient despatch as soon as possible under cover plan with the utmost secrecy'.[3] The RN subsequently maintained a carrier task force, which varied in composition from time to time, in the eastern Mediterranean for the next five and a half months except for a short period at the beginning of July. *Eagle* subsequently replaced *Ark Royal*, flying the flag of Vice Admiral A N C Bingley, FOAC, who assumed command of British maritime forces in the area.

British and US contingency plans were drawn up in the expectation of a formal request to defend the Lebanon against aggression and were given the codename Operation 'Blue Bat'. The plan anticipated landing US Marines over the beach to secure Beirut airport after which British troops would be flown in from Cyprus. Air support for both elements would be provided by fighters from British and US aircraft carriers. However, in June 1958 the United Nations Assembly discussed the situation in the Middle East and arrived at a consensus opinion that the use of force would not become necessary. Unfortunately FOAC shared this opinion and sent *Eagle* back to Malta for a self-maintenance period. She was, thus, off station when the crisis broke on 14 July 1958. With ruthless speed and efficiency, the Iraqi Brigadier Kassem and his 19th Brigade murdered the young King Feisal and his family, the former Regent Abdul Illah and Nuri-as-Said, the pro-British but autocratic Prime Minister, and an Iraqi Republic was announced immediately. On 15 July President Chamoun of the Lebanon made an urgent appeal to the USA for military aid and President Eisenhower agreed to land American forces 'to protect American lives and, by their presence, to encourage the Lebanese Government in defence of its sovereignty and integrity'.[4] On 16 July King Hussein asked the British Charge d'Affaires in Amman for military aid and the British Government agreed to provide it. Operation 'Blue Bat' was set in motion by the US Sixth Fleet but was now a purely American venture in defence of the Lebanon. London and Washington agreed that any international criticism of the intervention would be best shared and so the target for the British airlift of troops was transferred to Amman in Jordan, a task given the new name Operation 'Fortitude'. It was to involve 16 Parachute Brigade Group which would be flown from Cyprus in RAF transport aircraft but, unlike the Lebanon, Jordan had no Mediterranean coast and political permission would be required for the aircraft to over-fly neutral territory.

Eagle sailed from Malta with all despatch but her maximum speed was limited initially because the maintenance carried out on her boilers had not yet been completed. This prevented her from arriving in the operational area until after the first attempt to airlift troops. Critics of sea power might feel tempted to claim that land-locked fighters could have been flown into Akrotiri in Cyprus from the UK but they would miss one of the most fundamental advantages of carrier-borne aircraft. *Eagle* arrived at the scene with a fully-functioning maintenance organisation, fuel, ammunition and a command system able to use her balanced air group to the best advantage. She also had a fully-functioning RFA logistic support system on station and was able to position herself in the ideal place to operate her aircraft close to the scene of action, clear of adverse weather and able to react quickly to any unexpected eventuality. Land-locked fighters in Cyprus would have lacked all of these advantages and would have had to operate at the limit of their radius of action, reducing their usefulness and time of reaction.

The first attempted airlift to Jordan took place on 17 July 1958 and followed a route from Nicosia in Cyprus to Cape Pyla, thence through the American amphibious objective area to Lod in Israel, over which they were to turn east for Amman. As the leading aircraft approached Amman, however, they were ordered to turn back by the British Government because permission had not been granted for the over-flight of Israel. However, the first five aircraft went ahead and landed Brigadier Pearson and his small advance party while the remainder turned back and landed in Cyprus. A diplomatic argument between the British and Israeli Governments led to permission being granted for the airlift to resume on 18 July, the day *Eagle* returned to the operational area south-east of Cyprus. Her air group comprised 806 (Sea Hawk FGA 6s) NAS; 894 (Sea Venom FAW 22s) NAS; 849A (Skyraider AEW 1s) NAS; 814 (Gannet AS 4s) NAS and two Whirlwind SAR helicopters.[5] Just before sunset on 18 July *Eagle* landed on 802 NAS (Sea Hawk FB 5s) which had flown out from the UK to reinforce the air group via Dijon, Pratica di Mare, El Adem and Akrotiri in 36 hours. The carrier took up an operating area centred some 50nm to seaward of Haifa, well to the south of the American operating area.

The first British airlift had fighter cover from USN CAPs in the American amphibious area but had flown on alone near Israel. FOAC's chief of staff was flown from *Eagle* to a meeting at the British Joint Headquarters in Cyprus at which it was decided that RAF fighters would provide day escort for the transport aircraft in the vicinity of Cyprus and *Eagle*'s fighters would provide day and night protection from the point where the transport aircraft entered the American air defence sector to the point where they went 'feet dry' over Israel. The airlift to move 16 Brigade lasted for five days, throughout which the aircraft were protected by *Eagle*'s fighters. By day two sections of Sea Hawks patrolled near the transport route and a third maintained CAP over the radar picket frigate *Salisbury* which was stationed 50nm south of *Eagle* between the task force and the Egyptian coast. By night one section of Sea Venoms was maintained on a CAP positioned to be able to defend both the airlift and the task force if necessary. Skyraiders maintained a radar 'barrier' over *Salisbury* with instructions to search for fast attack craft, referred to as 'E-boats', and low-flying aircraft heading towards the force. Gannets flew on an anti-submarine patrol 40nm square around the task force against the potential threat posed by Soviet submarines based in Albania. During this critical five-day period, *Eagle* flew 388 operational fighter sorties and the Gannets and Skyraiders a further 112 reconnaissance sorties. Unfortunately, RAF transport aircraft at this period were not fitted with IFF equipment making them difficult to identify positively in what was often very crowded airspace. Two hundred and eight aircraft were intercepted and identified by fighters, 121 of which proved to be Allied transport aircraft. Of the remainder, seven were UAR military aircraft, fourteen were UAR civil aircraft and seven were Israeli military aircraft. Fifty-nine others were miscellaneous civil aircraft going about their lawful business.[6] For part of this period there was an American airlift flying US citizens out of Beirut. It followed a route parallel to the British one but inshore of it and was also protected by *Eagle*'s fighters until 22 July when the movement of Allied aircraft by day ended and the task force withdrew to the Cyprus area to rest, replenish and prepare for further action.

The US operation in the Lebanon was on a larger scale but also relied on a forward maritime presence for its successful conclusion. An Army rapid reaction force comprising two battle groups based in Germany had been nominated for the defence of the Lebanon but there was only sufficient USAF air transport in Europe to move one at a time and then only by a long and circuitous route avoiding communist territory to Adana in Turkey, the nearest US base to Beirut. The USAF tactical fighters and strike aircraft allocated to support 'Blue Bat' were based in the USA and faced both transatlantic and trans-European flights to deploy to Adana. They also needed large numbers of transport aircraft to carry their maintenance personnel, support equipment and ammunition into the theatre. The Sixth Fleet comprised two strike carriers, one anti-submarine carrier and three amphibious squadrons, each with a USMC battalion landing team of about 1800 marines embarked. One of the latter was south of Cyprus, only 12 hours steaming from Beirut, and was ordered to land its men at Beirut at 15.00 on 15 July at exactly the time when President Eisenhower publicly announced US intervention. The marines were supported by eleven FJ-4 Fury fighters and AD-2 strike aircraft which launched from the USS *Essex* off Greece and refuelled at a British airfield on Cyprus in order to be over the landing beaches at exactly the right time. The marines secured Beirut airport an hour after landing and the remaining battalions landed as they arrived on 16 and 18 July.[7] A fourth USMC battalion landing team flew from the USA in Marine Corps aircraft and landed at Beirut on 18 July. The US Army and Air Force units began to arrive in the Lebanon on 19 July but they could not be effective for some weeks until their vehicles, ammunition and stores arrived by sea. *Essex* continued to fly support missions until 20 August, supported from 18 July by the USS *Saratoga*. Other carriers were sailed from the USA to reinforce the Sixth Fleet while these two carriers were committed to operations in Lebanon. The prompt Allied moves stabilised the situation in the Lebanon and Jordan before fighting broke out, although it must be admitted that the military forces ashore would have been hard pressed if attacked. British and US carrier task forces were maintained in the eastern Mediterranean until the crisis passed and troops were withdrawn in October. 16 Brigade in Jordan was lightly equipped and, had the Jordanian Army's armoured corps rebelled against its government, would have been totally reliant on carrier-borne aircraft for close air support. The Commander-in-Chief Mediterranean Fleet, Admiral Sir Charles Lambe, signalled the Admiralty on the subject, emphasising that 'nobody else can give the Army in Jordan much

Albion sailing from Portsmouth for the Mediterranean in 1958 with 42 RM Commando and a number of vehicles embarked as a contingency reinforcement for the theatre. (Author's collection)

help'.[8] The presence of aircraft carriers to provide a dominating presence over the eastern Mediterranean and cover land operations from the sea can justifiably be said to have been fundamental to the whole Allied effort.

The protection of these airlifts and the Allied troops once they were deployed were not the only examples of how the RN's new limited war strategy influenced events on land in 1958. The threat of revolution was present throughout the Middle East and warships were involved in moving Royal Marines and other forces to protect British and Commonwealth interests in Libya, the Persian Gulf and the Arabian peninsula. A number of carriers showed their versatility by ferrying troops and their vehicles over large distances.[9] *Albion* was working up in the UK in early June when it was decided to use her to ferry 42 RM Commando to the Mediterranean. She disembarked her air group, and entered Portsmouth Dockyard to have 1000 extra ring-bolts welded to her flight deck to allow the Commando's vehicles to be lashed on deck for the transit. Her air group flew out to RNAS Hal Far and *Albion* landed the marines in Malta before having the extra ring-bolts removed in the Dockyard before re-embarking her aircraft.[10] She relieved *Eagle* for a short spell before resuming her planned deployment to the FEF. Her sister-ship

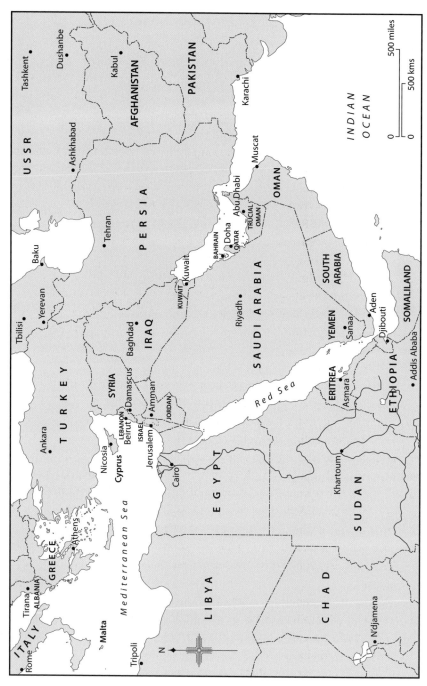

Lebanon, Jordan and Kuwait.

Bulwark was in Mombasa in mid-July and she also made a significant contribution. Her aircraft flew strike missions against rebel forces in Oman, and she ferried an Army battalion from Kenya to Aden from where it was deployed to Aqaba in Jordan. On her way back to the UK she too relieved *Eagle* for a spell. Despite the two reliefs, *Eagle* reported that in the ninety-five days since she had left the UK she had only been alongside and able to give shore leave on seventeen days. Throughout the series of crises in 1958, three British and three USN carriers had played a key role in the military measures that had stopped the spread of revolution and brought a period of stability to the Middle East. They achieved their aim and, significantly, neither the UAR or any other potentially hostile power had come even close to preventing them from doing so. Two quotations are worth noting on completion of the carrier strike fleet's contribution to Operation 'Fortitude'. FOAC, Vice Admiral Bingley, stressed in his ROP that 'it is of the greatest importance that our slender allowance of aircraft carriers should be kept up to a state of maintenance and training which will ensure that they are available for the many demands which they alone can meet'.[11] Admiral Mountbatten, the First Sea Lord, was obviously delighted at the successful implementation of his limited war strategy and said that 'the Navy is completely mobile, flexible, versatile. And so, you see, it has got an enduring and vital function.'[12]

Bulwark and the *Melika* Salvage, 1958

In the early part of 1958 *Bulwark* had been serving in the FEF with an air group that comprised 801 (Sea Hawk FGA 6s), 891 (Sea Venom FAW 22s), 849D (Skyraider AEW 1s) and 845 (Whirlwind HAS 7s) NAS; the latter unit being the first operational anti-submarine helicopter squadron embarked as part of a general purpose air group. She was held in the Aden area throughout August and September 1958 to be on hand if the situation in the Persian Gulf deteriorated and ready for any other contingency and the opportunity was taken to strike at Talib insurgents in the Jabal Akhdar, a mountain range in Oman.[13] The RAF had been attacking targets in the area and proved helpful in providing background intelligence and local area briefings. Operations began on 12 September when forty-four sorties were flown and particular success was achieved with variable time-fused 500lb bombs.

However, on 13 September a distress message was received which said that the Liberian tanker *Melika* had collided with the French tanker *Fernand Gilabert* off Masira Island and both ships were on fire. There was clearly a threat to the lives of both crews who had abandoned ship and *Bulwark* recovered the dawn strike and headed towards the burning ships. Other tankers were near the scene and had rescued survivors, many of whom were seriously injured and these were transferred

Bulwark passing a tow line to the damaged tanker *Melika* while the frigate *Chichester* stands by to assist if necessary. Aircraft on deck include Sea Hawks, Sea Venoms and a single Whirlwind HAS 7 ranged forward ready to start up and launch at short notice. This commission proved that fixed and rotary-wing aircraft could work successfully together in a wide range of operations. (Author's collection)

to *Bulwark* by helicopter where they could receive initial medical attention. Many were flown to the RAF base at Masira and then on to Bahrain. Salvage parties led by *Bulwark*'s First Lieutenant were flown to *Melika* by helicopter and managed to extinguish the fires supported by further helicopter sorties that brought foam, hoses and salvage equipment across. *Bulwark* then took *Melika* in tow with the frigate *Puma* keeping her steady with a wire attached aft. It took seven days to tow her into Muscat and every day 845 NAS helicopters flew parties across to help make the ship safe including volunteer aircrew who cleaned the tanker's port boiler. They were subsequently awarded with 'honorary stokers' badges' by *Bulwark*'s Commander (E). Helicopters had also flown a party led by *Bulwark*'s Commander to *Fernand Gilabert* and once her fires were extinguished she was towed to Karachi by *Loch Killisport* supported by *St Brides Bay*. Once *Melika* was safely anchored, *Bulwark*'s air group carried out one more session of strikes against the Talib before passing through the Suez Canal to relieve *Eagle* off Cyprus. 845 NAS was subsequently awarded the 1958 Boyd Trophy in recognition of its efforts in support of the salvage operation. The squadron had demonstrated not only that it could operate successfully alongside fixed-wing aircraft but also that it could make a valuable contribution to overall carrier capability. *Bulwark* showed her versatility in October by landing her fixed-wing squadrons to RNAS Hal Far in Malta, from where they flew back to the UK. She kept 845 on board and turned over 'East of Suez' material and information to *Albion* which was to relieve her in the FEF after the interruption caused by the operations in the Eastern Mediterranean. That task completed, she embarked 42 RM Commando and their vehicles to return them to the UK now that the immediate crisis was over. This was her last commission as a strike carrier and on her return to the UK in November she was placed in Portsmouth Dockyard hands for conversion to a dedicated commando carrier with the removal of all fixed-wing operating equipment.[14]

Kuwait, 1961

Kuwait is a small, independent sheikhdom in the north-west corner of the Persian Gulf which has northern and western frontiers with Iraq. Its southern boundary adjoins the Saudi-Arabian province of Hasa. Until 1899 it was nominally part of the Turkish province of Basra but in that year its Ruler signed an agreement that granted Great Britain the right to manage its foreign relations. Oil production began in 1946 and a refinery and deep water port were constructed at Mina al Ahmadi. Increasing wealth and enhanced status led the Ruler to request freedom from British control but after the Iraqi revolution in 1958 there were fears that General Kassem would make a forcible attempt to seize Kuwait.[15] Despite these, the British Government agreed in 1960, in principle, to end the agreement and on 19 June 1961 the right to manage its own foreign affairs was formally restored to Kuwait. From 1958 a reinforced Theatre Plan[16] was prepared to defend Kuwait against Iraqi attack should it become necessary. It was finalised under the codename Operation 'Vantage' and kept constantly up to date to reflect changes in the forces available. Major changes in the intervention plan were made in December 1960,[17] taking note of the increased number of RAF transport aircraft available and the re-deployment of the RN Amphibious Warfare Squadron from Malta to Bahrain in the Persian Gulf. Preparations included keeping the LST *Striker* loaded with a half-squadron of Centurion tanks and other tanks were stockpiled for British use in Kuwait. Artillery was stockpiled in Bahrain and units listed for 'Vantage' were nominally at four days' notice to move. The intended presence of the first commando carrier, *Bulwark*, in the Middle East during 1961 was considered by the planners to be a bonus but they did not think of issuing her with operation orders for 'Vantage'.

When the British Government ended its 1899 agreement with Kuwait it gave an assurance that military assistance against Iraqi aggression would be given if Kuwait were to request it,[18] but just such an emergency came far more quickly than anticipated on 26 June 1961 when General Kassem claimed Kuwait as Iraqi territory. On the evening of 28 June the British Chiefs of Staff ordered that forces allocated to Operation 'Vantage' should be brought to the early stages of readiness. Because there had been no formal request for help at that stage, however, they did not give the executive order to implement the contingency plan and this omission was to cause confusion in the early hours of the crisis. Critically, *Bulwark*, which had recently re-commissioned after her conversion into a commando carrier, was at Karachi with 42 RM Commando and 848 (Whirlwind HAS 7s) NAS embarked. She had been intended to carry out hot weather trials during exercises in Sharjah and Muscat and then proceed to Kuwait for a goodwill visit[19] but the Admiralty ordered her to proceed with despatch directly to Kuwait.[20] Detailed 'Vantage' instructions were sent to her in a series of signals that began to flood in as she left Karachi. The commanding officer of 42 RM Commando and his staff officer operations had, however, already flown ahead to the British joint headquarters in Bahrain to discuss details of the hot weather trials and they were briefed on both the plan and the unfolding problems with its implementation. Within hours *Bulwark*'s position changed from 'bonus' to 'spearhead' as the staff in theatre realised her value. Other strike fleet movements followed quickly and the carrier *Victorious* which was on passage from Singapore to Hong Kong with her destroyer screen was ordered to make a fast passage to the Gulf. *Centaur*, in Gibraltar, was ordered to cancel a planned visit to the USA and proceed to the Gulf at high speed.

The Emir of Kuwait formally requested British protection on 30 June 1961 and the C-in-C Middle East, Lieutenant General Sir Charles Harrington assessed that his minimum requirement was two infantry battalions, two armoured squadrons and two RAF fighter/ground attack squadrons to be in place by dawn on 2 July. Operation 'Vantage' orders had anticipated a four-day build-up of British forces airlifted from the UK and Cyprus in Kuwait after the contingency plan had been ordered. The Chiefs of Staff's failure to order its implementation meant that nothing had been done to implement the contingency plan's requirement for international planning to establish the military air bridge and, hence, it could not begin. The rapid movement of troops by air was entirely subject to approval being obtained by the Foreign Office for military aircraft to overfly neutral countries along one of three routes from the west to Kuwait. The shortest at 3500nm needed permission to fly over Turkey and Iran. An intermediate route at 5000nm needed permission to cross Libya and Sudan and the longest route at 7000nm needed permission to cross Nigeria and the Congo. Without the order for 'Vantage's' implementation, none of these had been requested on 30 June and all needed a minimum of three days for full diplomatic clearance under normal circumstances.

The Turkish Government refused permission on 30 June and the first aircraft had to fly from the UK to Aden via Libya and Sudan. British troops in Cyprus intended for 'Vantage' were effectively isolated but the situation was partially resolved by the reinforcement of the RAF MEAF by aircraft from the RAF FEAF, and the timely offer of transport aircraft by the Royal Rhodesian Air Force.

While all this was going on, *Bulwark* closed the Bahrain Light Vessel at 01.00 on 1 July 1961 and launched two helicopters to pick up the commanding officer of 42 Commando and his staff officer from RAF Muharraq. Unfortunately they encountered severe sandstorms and high winds and had to be recalled to the carrier, leaving the two officers to make their own way to Kuwait. The diversion to Bahrain had delayed *Bulwark* but she proceeded to Kuwait at high speed and arrived in the late forenoon of 1 July, taking up a position 11nm east of the incomplete Kuwait New Airfield. Shortly before the first serials were launched, the CO and SOO of 42 Commando arrived on board in a Kuwaiti helicopter that had been sent to collect them. They were able to pass on the latest briefing that the Marines were to be landed at the airfield and not disposed at the defence positions on the border as had been ordered by signal. 848 NAS helicopters deployed 42 RM Commando ashore during the afternoon of 1 July, exactly 24 hours after the formal request for aid had been made. They did so despite a 35-knot 'Shemal' wind blowing from the north-west and visibility that was reduced to less than a mile in the blown sand. The Kuwaiti helicopter guided the first waves to the new airfield which proved not to be at the grid reference that had been signalled to the ship. Worse, the maps with which the ship had been issued proved to be out of date and did not show the navigational features of modern Kuwait;[21] accurate maps had to be obtained from the Kuwaiti authorities. Kuwait New Airfield was just that; its runways, taxi tracks and parking aprons were complete but it had no finished buildings or air traffic control. By the late afternoon 42 Commando had been deployed ashore and were ready, if necessary to defend the airfield. Most of 848's pilots had flown in desert condition before but none had experienced the temperatures up to 45° Centigrade found in Kuwait, nor the continuous dust storm maintained by the 'Shemal'. A naval helicopter control team was landed in the first wave and this provided air traffic control at the new airfield until an RAF air traffic control organisation was established on 3 July.

Bulwark settled immediately into a variety of roles which included co-ordination of the air defence organisation, provision of the base from which assault helicopter operations were planned and the logistic support base for the Commando's operations ashore. The early flying was carried out with the ship at anchor since the 'Shemal' gave sufficient wind over the deck to allow launches at maximum weight but the amount of dust and sand in the atmosphere caused severe visibility problems. As soon as the commandos and their initial supplies were ashore, *Bulwark* moved to a position off Kuwait City where the Amphibious Warfare Squadron was unloading tanks and other vehicles and used a 'rhino' ferry to land vehicles, equipment and supplies for 42 Commando overnight. The RAF wing of Hunter FGA 9s, comprising 8 and 208 Squadrons, flew into the airport from Bahrain followed by transport aircraft that carried their maintenance personnel, support equipment and stocks of ammunition. Other important reinforcements at the new airfield included 78 and 152 Squadrons of the RAF which flew Scottish Aviation twin Pioneer aircraft. They were used to fly supplies up to the forward area. Together with the Army Air Corps Taylorcraft Austers attached to the Brigade headquarters, they were able to use a light aircraft landing strip at Al Jahara. 24 Brigade set up its headquarters alongside the Kuwaiti HQ in a Police Post on the southern fringe of Al Jahara and the air support operations centre (ASOC), was eventually established alongside it. Once RAF and Headquarters units were flown in from Bahrain, the MEAF transport aircraft were able to join the airlift of military units from Aden. Initially an ad hoc arrangement was established with 42 Commando forward air controllers calling the Hunter squadron at the new airport directly with requests for aircraft and the pilots checking in with *Bulwark* as they got airborne. On completion of their task they carried out practice interceptions under the control of *Bulwark*'s direction officers which, after a few teething problems, worked well. By day two, the RAF had established an air traffic control organisation in the new airfield and the ASOC began to function but *Bulwark* remained the focal point of air defence operations.

The C-in-C Middle East juggled the land forces at his disposal to give a second infantry unit alongside 42 Commando as quickly as possible. Two companies of Coldstream Guards were ordered from Bahrain to Kuwait and 45 RM Commando and the personnel of an armoured car regiment were ordered from Aden to Kuwait but by the evening of 1 July only the heavy armoured strength had met the numbers called for in the 'Vantage' plan. This was due to the stockpile of tanks in the Amphibious Warfare Squadron's LSTs, the stockpile in Kuwait itself and the fortuitous presence in Theatre of two squadrons of Dragoon Guards who were carrying out a routine change-over of standby personnel. The Guards arrived in the evening of 1 July and took over the defence of the airport from 42 Commando which was reinforced by the RM Detachment from the frigate *Loch Alvie* and moved up to the border to join the Kuwaiti Army in its defensive positions along the Mutla Ridge. The helicopter control team then moved forward to support 42 Commando from a forward operating base (FOB), commanded by *Bulwark*'s Commander 'Air'. All helicopter movements were carefully controlled and pilots kept informed of other movements in their area. Given the low visibility in the frequent sandstorms this was an important aspect of operations but when 42 Commando fell back to operate as a mobile reserve from Shuwaik Barracks, the helicopter control team and FOB moved with it leaving no positive control for helicopter operations near the front line. The need for helicopter support and control had proved to be another 'grey area' in the 'Vantage' plan that needed to be improved for future operations.

Loch Alvie stood by in the best position to provide naval gunfire support for the troops ashore and was the only artillery available at this opening phase of the crisis. There were no military radars in Kuwait and so all air warning and fighter direction was carried out by *Bulwark* which managed to maintain a non-stop air plot in its operations room, albeit with gaps in cover caused by her close proximity to the land. The RAF Hunters lacked sufficient numbers to maintain a standing CAP so they were held at alert on the ground and launched when necessary to investigate suspicious contacts. Interceptions had to be carried out by the visual sighting of targets since the aircraft were simple day fighters with no AI radar and their only air-to-air weapons were 30mm cannon. The air defence task was made more difficult by the lack of modern IFF in the Hunters and RAF transport aircraft flying into Kuwait. A pre-positioned Type 787 ground radar station was flown into Kuwait from Bahrain early in the operation but could not be brought into operation until 16 July when it was finally set to work by technicians flown out from the UK for the purpose. This made the Type 960 air-warning radar in *Bulwark* all the more important and the importance of having ships fitted with fully-functioning air-defence radars as key elements of a rapid-reaction task force was one of the most important lessons derived from the Kuwait operation.[22]

Bulwark moved to Mina al Ahmadi on 2 July where arrangements had been made to refuel her. Thereafter until 12 July 1961 she followed a routine of remaining at sea during the night to reduce the risk of any attack being mounted by the Iraqi fast patrol boats that were known to be based in the Shatt al Arab. She usually anchored off Kuwait during the day. Throughout the crisis, *Bulwark* provided direct logistical support to the Royal Marines as well as maintaining command and control of the air defence organisation. In addition to functioning as a large helicopter base she also functioned as a 'fuel dump', 'magazine' and 'supply depot' for items as diverse as toilet paper, barbed wire and replacement combat clothing, all of which were stored on board in bulk. 848 NAS helicopters were able to move water, fresh bread and other creature comforts from *Bulwark* up to 42 Commando on the Mutla Ridge on an hourly basis in stark contrast to the lack of support that Army formations had to endure. Having been flown in at short notice with only the equipment the men stood up in, these lacked both

848 NAS Whirlwinds landing sticks of Royal Marines in the Kuwait desert. (Author's collection)

logistic support and the vehicles with which to move it. Nothing highlights the differences between air and sea lift as starkly as a close study of the first phase of Operation 'Vantage'.

45 RM Commando was flown into Kuwait from Aden on 2 July together with the Hussars to operate armoured cars brought from Bahrain by the Army LST *Empire Skua*.[23] By then, the Turkish Government had changed its mind and agreed to permit the over-flight of its territory by RAF transport aircraft but the first British troops, 2nd Battalion Parachute Regiment, did not leave Cyprus until the evening of 2 July. Even then, air movements were complicated by the fact that movements personnel and technical staff who would normally have been early arrivals in theatre to 'activate the route' had been left in Cyprus because of the urgent priority given to combat formations. Their absence was another impact of the failure to give the executive order for 'Vantage' at the appropriate time and was to cause problems of organisation and transport aircraft turn-round at the air-head. The movement of 2 Para took two nights and the unit did not reach its full strength until 5 July by which time another infantry battalion had been flown in from Kenya. The latter unit relieved 42 Commando on the Mutla Ridge on 7 July and a second battalion from Kenya relieved 45 Commando on 9 July. Another important arrival on 2 July had been the Landing Ship (Headquarters) *Meon*[24] which berthed alongside the new Kuwait jetty and established herself as a Joint Services communication and signal relay centre. Her arrival was timely as there were no significant Army or RAF communications in Kuwait. Her complement included both RN communications staff and 601 Signal Troop, Royal Corps of Signals and they set up command links between Task Force 317, the RN warships gathered in the northern Gulf, Kuwait New Airfield and 24 Brigade which was

An 848 NAS forward operating base in Kuwait. Note the air-portable RM Citroen 2CV by the group to the right, the only vehicle that could be lifted by a Whirlwind. (Author's collection)

assuming its planned 'Vantage' task. In effect, *Meon* became the focal point for all 'Vantage' communications and the Flag Officer Middle East (FOME) repeatedly stressed her importance in his ROP.[25] Other ships of the Amphibious Warfare Squadron made major contributions from 2 July including the delivery of ammunition and other freight loads together with armoured cars from the Bahrain stockpile in *Striker*, *Bastion* and *Redoubt*. The C-in-C Middle East and the General commanding Middle East Land Forces moved the Headquarters from Aden to Bahrain on 2 July in order to be nearer the scene of action.

Important lessons were learnt about how best to operate a commando carrier during an intervention of this nature. Most important of these was the realisation that the ship must have deployable facilities that could be landed to support helicopters operating from a FOB. 848 NAS extemporised a mobile refuelling rig consisting of a pump and streamline filters fitted onto a Citroen 2CV and as tents, cooking and washing facilities were set up it became clear that a small organisation similar to a wartime MONAB would be required.[26] It was also found that greater emphasis needed to be placed on forward maintenance so that minor defects could be dealt with to keep the maximum number of aircraft flying. After five days ashore 848 NAS moved back on board and once the Army and RAF were firmly established ashore it was decided to re-embark 42 Commando. After the defensive positions were well established, *Bulwark* began to organise rest facilities on board so that 200 troops at a time could be brought out to the ship to rest and relax in her air-conditioned spaces and wash. The ship's company showed many kindnesses

Victorious, together with *Bulwark* and *Centaur*, formed a critically important element of the British ability to defend Kuwait in 1961. Her 'package' of Scimitar and Sea Vixen fighters, Gannet AEW aircraft and a sophisticated air control environment comprising Type 984 radar, CDS and communications would have been impossible for the Iraqi forces to counter. (Author's collection)

and the Army began to refer to '*Bulwark* Butlins' as a key element in the maintenance of morale.[27]

The RN had been particularly annoyed by the lack of informed press coverage on naval, and especially naval air, matters during both the 1956 Suez Crisis and the Malayan Emergency and steps were taken to put this right with press facilities on several ships and 848 NAS was tasked with helping BBC News to film events and put them into perspective. Another interesting aspect of the operation was that some RN members of the joint ASOC were flown out from the UK in commercial flights to get into theatre as soon as possible without waiting for the military airlift which was fully-committed at first to combat units. Lieutenant Commander W A Tofts AFC RN was put on a commercial flight which stopped to refuel in Rome, Amman and Baghdad! Despite spending some hours in Baghdad and having to show his passport he was, fortunately, not arrested.

Victorious arrived with her escorts on 9 July and immediately took over the tasks of air defence, close air support of land forces and command of TF 317. Her air group comprised 803 (Scimitar F1s), 892 (Sea Vixen FAW 1s), 849B (Gannet AEW

It was extremely hot in the Northern Gulf off Kuwait. This contemporary PR photograph shows chefs on *Victorious* frying eggs on the flight deck to prove the point. Unfortunately the eggs were contaminated by the non-slip paint and were, therefore, well-cooked but inedible. (Author's collection)

3s) and 825 (Whirlwind HAS 7s) NAS.[28] Rear Admiral J B Frewen, Flag Officer Second-in-Command Far East Station (FO2FES), and the ship's operations officer had flown ashore to Singapore by Gannet as the ship passed so that they could be briefed on the situation in Kuwait and handed operational orders. Once they landed back on the ship there was no more flying until she arrived in the Gulf. FO2 was flown off in another Gannet to Bahrain on 9 July to get the latest information. By that time the intelligence appreciation of the situation was that Iraqi troop movements near the border no longer appeared aggressive[29] but there was concern that an offensive might still be launched on 15 July, Iraq's national day. FO2FES assumed the duty of CTF 317 from 9 July 1961 and *Victorious* settled into a routine of four days continuous flying followed by two days of replenishment and maintenance but at any time during the latter she could resume air operations within an hour if there was an Iraqi attack.

The high ambient temperatures and low surface wind at sea by this stage, combined with *Victorious'* relatively short catapults, constrained the Scimitar's ability to launch with maximum fuel and sorties were limited to 40 minutes, mostly spent at low level. In view of the short distances involved this was acceptable and the primary offensive weapons were 2in rockets and 30mm Aden cannon. Their limited ability to carry 1000lb bombs was mitigated by a UK Government ban on their use for counter-offensive action. By 31 July *Victorious* had been at sea without a break for thirty-six days when she was relieved by *Centaur*. After a brief hand-over, which included an inter-carrier 'sports day' on *Centaur's* flight deck, FO2FES transferred his flag to her and *Victorious* left for a visit to Mombasa. After the visit, she was deployed to Zanzibar where two of 825 NAS's Whirlwinds were landed to help the police deal with an outbreak of civil unrest. 803 NAS's Scimitars helped by flying at low level over 'dissident' villages at police request. *Centaur's* air group comprised 807 (Scimitar F 1s), 893 (Sea Vixen FAW 1s), 849A (Gannet AEW 3s) and 824 (Whirlwind HAS 7s) NAS[30] and both she and her escorting destroyers remained off Kuwait ready to give strike, air defence, close air support and naval gunfire support to the forces ashore. By 15 August it was clear that the threat of invasion had passed and British forces were gradually withdrawn.

Both FOME and FO2FES drew attention in their reports to the need to improve communications. As the flagship of TF 317, *Victorious* was handling 80 per cent of the signal traffic even before she arrived in the Gulf and her communications staff had only just been able to cope.[31] Admiral Frewen noted that the 'Vantage' communications plan had been designed to cover a short but intensive operation and was over-complicated for the protracted, uneventful operation that actually happened. The plan was simplified on 28 July and, thereafter, *Centaur's* statistics showed an average of 151 signals a day passing through her bridge wireless office compared with the 352 a day handled by *Victorious* in early July. Difficulties had been experienced in communicating with freighting RFAs and in replenishing War Office LSTs since neither carried cryptographic material at the time. FOME wrote a comprehensive report on the communication aspects of Operation 'Vantage' and concluded that the lack of an established joint organisation and procedure was felt seriously ashore. FO2FES drew similar conclusions and, after commenting on the inter-service muddle in the early stages with regard to call-signs and address groups, he recommended the appointment of joint signals officers in future, to be responsible to the joint command. Overall, 'Vantage' was successful in that it deterred an Iraqi invasion of Kuwait and it had certainly shown that both aircraft carriers and commando carriers had a critical part to play in suppressing aggression before it could escalate into major conflict. Mountbatten and his staff had got that element of the new defence policy absolutely right and, at the time, the politicians realised it. Even the press got the message largely right. There was a negative side, however. The Kuwait Crisis had been an excellent test of Great Britain's ability to deploy its limited armed forces to deal with the threatened outbreak of a limited or 'brushfire' war. The emergency and the need to deal with it had been foreseen several years earlier and operational plans had been drafted and kept up-to-date. No other emergency had complicated the issue and yet, overall, the operational plan had been found wanting in some of its basic assumptions. Superficially, the movement of troops by RAF transport aircraft had seemed a prompt way of delivering military power to a trouble spot but in practice this had proved not to be the case for a variety of reasons. The flights themselves had been thrown into disarray too easily and, in this instance, the failure to order a timely D-Day and the authorisation of flights over neutral territory had dislocated the early movements. More importantly, when airlifted troops did arrive they were not combat fit, had only the equipment they stood up in with no logistic support and suffered badly from the extreme heat and sandstorms. The commanding officer of 42 RM Commando noted in his ROP that his had been 'the only fully equipped unit ashore for at least seven days'[32] and that it had been 'the envy of other unit commanders'. The key point here was that *Bulwark* had delivered 42 Commando ready for battle, acclimatised and with its own transport and self-contained supply organisation and assault helicopter support. The freedom of the sea meant that the movement of a commando carrier to a trouble spot as part of a naval task force was possible when it was clearly not possible to move land and air forces in any other way. The vital contribution made by *Bulwark* and her commando group and the need for strike carriers to provide air defence over both land and sea together with the in-built infrastructure to maintain operations for a considerable period had shown themselves to be the key elements in any operation of this nature. Without them, Operation 'Vantage' could have been a disaster if serious opposition had been encountered on the ground and in the air.

The East African Mutiny, 1964

Zanzibar and Kenya were granted independence from British colonial rule in November 1963. Tanganyika had been independent since 1961. The three new nations had democratically-elected governments and were committed to peaceful progress and their small national armies had evolved from battalions of the former Kings East African Rifles. However, on 12 January 1964 the African population of Zanzibar revolted against the Arabs and Asians who held power on the prosperous island and murdered a number of them. The British High Commissioner was trapped in his residence and was unable to communicate with London. On hearing the news the British C-in-C Middle East, Lieutenant General Sir Charles Harrington, ordered preparations to protect British lives and property. The survey ship *Owen* and the frigate *Rhyl* were ordered to stand by off Zanzibar and Rear Admiral J Scotland, the FOME, ordered the aircraft carrier *Centaur* which was

Centaur on her way to East Africa on 24 January 1964. The Ferret armoured cars and a Land Rover of 16/5 Lancers can be seen parked on the starboard side of Fly 1, leaving the port catapult clear for use if necessary. Crates of ammunition and stores can be seen in Fly 2 by the island and 892 NAS Sea Vixen FAW 1s are parked on deck to make room in the hangar available for the Royal Marines of 45 Commando to sleep and prepare their weapons. There is a Gannet AEW 3 aft of the island in Fly 3 and two RAF Belvedere helicopters are parked right aft. (Author's collection)

anchored off Aden to embark 600 men of 45 RM Commando which was based in Aden. No alongside berth was available and so the carrier had to embark the men, twenty-four Land Rovers and 70 tons of stores and ammunition by lighter while anchored a considerable distance offshore. She also embarked five Ferret armoured cars and personnel of the 16/5th Lancers, hundreds of cans of vehicle fuel (mogas) and two Belvedere helicopters of 26 Squadron RAF from RAF Khormaksar. All of this in addition to her air group which, by then, comprised 892 (Sea Vixen FAW 2s), 849B (Gannet AEW 3s) and 815 (Wessex HAS 1s) NAS.[33] From the order to embark to weighing anchor and sailing only 13 hours elapsed and *Centaur* sailed from Aden at midnight on 20 January 1964 with the destroyer *Cambrian* in company. Recently employed on counter-insurgency operations in the Radfan mountains, 45 Commando had no recent amphibious warfare experience or training.

Commando stores were secured on the starboard side of *Centaur*'s flight deck, forward of the island in Fly 1. Vehicles were parked along the extreme starboard edge of Fly 1, leaving the port catapult clear to launch fixed-wing aircraft should it prove to be necessary. The Belvederes were too big to strike down into the hangar and their blades could not be folded so they were parked at the after end of the flight deck. Most of *Centaur*'s own aircraft were parked on deck with covers on to allow space for the marines to sleep in the hangar but space was kept on deck for the marines to keep fit in. A plan, known as 'Sardine Stations' was prepared to allow for the operation of the Sea Vixens and Gannets. If it was needed, marines, vehicles and stores were to be struck down into the hangar and the six Wessex and two Belvedere helicopters were to be launched to hover alongside while fixed-wing launches and recoveries were in progress; any rotary-wing aircraft that went unserviceable would have to be dealt with as and when the problem occurred.[34] Fortunately the need for a fixed-wing launch did not arise until after the embarked force had been landed. While *Centaur* was on passage the sonars were removed from the Wessex helicopters which would be required to operate in the assault role; another clear advantage of having helicopters as part of a general-purpose carrier air group.[35]

On 20 January 1964 men of the Tanganyikan Rifles mutinied in Dar-es-Salaam and rioted in the city, terrorising the population.[36] Two days later soldiers mutinied in Uganda and British troops were flown in to restore order at the request of the Ugandan Government. In Kenya, President Kenyatta asked the British Government for support from the British Army units still stationed in the country and these quelled a mutiny by the 11th Battalion of the Kenyan Army on 24 January. At sea in *Centaur* her commanding officer, Captain T M P StJ Steiner RN and the commanding officer of 45 Commando, Lieutenant Colonel T M P Stevens RM, set up three planning teams that covered aspects of intelligence, assault including logistics and communications. With no knowledge of how the embarked force would be used, they concentrated on essentials and prepared simple, flexible procedures that could land marines in the Wessex helicopters. As *Centaur* arrived off Dar-es-Salaam she received a signal from the C-in-C Middle East instructing her to 'disarm Tanganyikan Army Colito Barracks soonest'. President Nyerere asked the British Government for military assistance at 23.00 on 24 January 1964. At midnight Brigadier Sholto-Douglas, the former commander of the Tanganyikan Army, was brought off shore by boat and reported a second night of rioting, looting and killing in Dar-es-Salaam. By then it was 01.00 on 25 January and swift action was clearly necessary to save the lives of innocent civilians. Captain Steiner

Centaur's deck range seen from aft, showing the two Belvederes clearly. They were too big for the lifts, even if their rotor blades were removed, but the Wessex helicopters were kept in the hangar as long as possible. (Author's collection)

decided to take Colito Barracks at dawn, only five hours away and to avoid courting delay he acted on the authority he had been given without seeking advice from London. The essence of his plan was speed, surprise and an overwhelming display of force.[37] Marines were to be landed in a sports field alongside the barracks and *Cambrian's* guns would be used together with strike aircraft if necessary. It was considered essential to minimise casualties among the mutineers and their families and so *Cambrian* was ordered to lay down a diversionary bombardment on an uninhabited area to the north of the barracks, no easy task in a tideway with no forward observer to spot the fall of shot. The plan was deliberately kept simple and a briefing was held at 03.30; the helicopter flying programme was the only element that was written down.

At 06.10 on 25 January 1964, seven hours after British aid was requested, Wessex helicopters of 815 NAS landed Z Company of 45 RM Commando at Colito Barracks. There was an initial show of resistance but after an anti-tank missile was fired into the guardroom, the mutineers surrendered. Many ran into the bush and were shepherded back by a hovering helicopter with the pilot pointing his pistol at them through the cockpit window. At 11.00 *Centaur* moved into harbour and requisitioned tugs and lighters onto which vehicles and stores were unloaded by crane. She also landed her own marine detachment. Armed parties were sent to Taboora, 340 miles inland, where the mutinous 2nd Battalion was disarmed. By then *Centaur* had returned to sea and launched Sea Vixens which flew over Taboora in case a show of force was needed. Other mutineers were disarmed at Natchingwea after British troops were flown in from Kenya by RAF transport aircraft escorted by 892 NAS Sea Vixens.

By a happy coincidence 26 January is Australia Day and the Australian High Commissioner in Dar-es-Salaam held an official reception to mark the occasion and the rapid return of peace to the streets. *Centaur* showed that there are many ways in which a carrier can actively influence events on land by parading her RM Band to beat retreat, marking the end of a very successful reception. An air display was organised over the city a day later. Within hours of President Nyerere's call for help the mutiny was over, order had been restored and the authority of his Government re-established. Only two mutineers had been killed, both in the guardroom when the missile hit it; there were no British casualties. *Centaur* and *Cambrian* sailed shortly afterwards to continue their general service commissions in the FEF.

This operation had shown the latent capability of even a small carrier to deal, effectively, with a limited war situation which might very well have escalated without its prompt and imaginatively led intervention. In all the operations described in this chapter several factors stand out. Firstly the ability of the RN to project power over the land and in the air from ships at sea proved to be the enabler that had ensured success, showing that for all the criticism levelled at it, Duncan Sandys' 1957 Defence Review had got this aspect right and that the RN had got the right equipment. On the other hand, the value of military airlift had proved disappointing and had failed to provide troops when needed that were either ready to fight immediately or suitably equipped. They still needed a seaborne lift to provide bulk fuel, supplies, vehicles and ammunition. Also worth bearing in mind was the fact that none of the potential adversaries had been able to deter the Navy from projecting power and sustaining it for long periods but both they and others could disrupt an airlift if they chose to. For those with eyes capable of seeing, *Centaur*'s action in the East African Mutinies had shown that strike carriers, besides providing a balanced deployment of British power and resolve, were capable of deploying the Army and RAF to the scene of the action quickly and in a way that would not, otherwise, be open to them in an emergency that required prompt action.

Bulwark launching a range of aircraft. Sea Venoms are positioned on the two catapults, more Sea Venoms and Sea Hawks are positioned amidships with Gannets right aft. (Author's collection)

11 The Evolution of Strike Warfare

By the late 1950s British aircraft carriers and their embarked air groups were powerful strike forces capable of moving over large distances quickly and striking effectively at targets on, beneath and above the surface of the sea and far inland using aircraft of differing characteristics that were capable of secondary uses that were not always obvious to politicians. The ships contained the means to command and control air operations and support aircraft with maintenance facilities, weapons, fuel and logistic support. In other words they were ready for action the minute they arrived and did not have to wait for the manpower and logistic 'tail' to catch up by air or sea lift. Commando carriers had added to this capability with their ability to land a highly-capable military force from the sea, to provide it with assault and logistic transport and, above all, to sustain it in action from the outset in a way that air transport could not achieve without considerably more aircraft and bases.

To some politicians, however, it appeared that the RN was beginning to replicate the role of the RAF but this point of view does not stand up to rational analysis. From its inception the RAF had concentrated on what came to be seen as the classic role of land-based air power, exemplified by Bomber Command: long-range attack according to a fixed and pre-planned schedule against fixed targets that were not time sensitive. Bombers could operate over long distances but only spent a few minutes, or even seconds, over their targets and could not, therefore, react well to changed target priorities or circumstances. Naval aviation was, and is, significantly different in that has evolved on the basis of striking with time-sensitive information at targets, such as ships, that move. Pre-assigned target schedules were of little use to naval strike aircraft and what mattered more was the ability to operate relatively close to potential targets so that aircraft could react quickly to changed priorities and spend as much time as possible near the target area. That is why naval aircraft did so well in Korea, Suez, the Eastern Mediterranean and the Kuwait Crisis in the campaigns described thus far. No other British military aircraft at the time could have done what they did, as well as they did; they were not competing with anyone, just doing a very effective job.

By 1960 British strike carriers had demonstrated three significant virtues. They could operate relatively close to a scene of operations, finding clear weather when necessary, and generate a large number of sorties with a relatively small number of aircraft against a range of time-sensitive targets:[1] if necessary striking at several different, mobile targets at once after they had been located. The second virtue, demonstrated in East Africa, was the ability to carry a joint or 'all arms' force such military formations and their vehicles or RAF helicopters into an operation that they could not otherwise have reached. The third virtue is more subtle but just as important. Foreign governments do not always support the actions of the United Kingdom and its allies and may not allow the use of bases or flights over their territories by combat or transport aircraft that are intended to take hostile action against a third party. Experience has shown that vetoes of this kind have been less likely when a British carrier strike force was present in the open sea and operations could proceed anyway with or without such permission.[2] To replicate the capability of a carrier task force a land-based air force would have to distribute aircraft among a number of different bases. The transfer between bases of their people, ammunition, logistics, fuel and command structures would not be easy and could well involve most, if not all, of the nation's transport capability. By 1960 the Scimitar F 1, Sea Vixen FAW 1, Gannet AEW 3 and Whirlwind HAS 7 were in squadron service at sea but a new generation of aircraft was being developed for the Royal Navy which proved to be among the most successful British military aircraft of the post-1945 era.

The Blackburn Buccaneer

Developed to meet Admiralty Specification NA 39 for a carrier-borne, low-level strike aircraft with a considerable radius of action, the Blackburn Buccaneer survived Duncan Sandys' defence review because he accepted the Naval Staff's view that that strike capability was a vital part of the complete RN weapons system, without which the fleet could no longer expect to operate in the face of sophisticated opposition. Until 1960 the RAF continued to fund improvements to its medium bomber force to increase the height at which the 'V'-bombers could penetrate enemy airspace but when, on 1 May 1960, a U-2 reconnaissance plane was shot down over Sverdlovsk in the Soviet Union by an SA-2 'Guideline' surface-to-air missile (SAM), system it was immediately obvious that high altitude no longer gave any protection against SAM systems and the USAF, RAF and other air forces began to practice low-level operations with aircraft that were unsuited to them. By then, far-seeing members of the Naval Staff with experience gained in the Korean War had already written the NA 39 specification for a strike aircraft capable of attacking under enemy radar coverage at very low level and prototypes

A Buccaneer S 1 of 801 NAS being struck down on *Ark Royal*'s forward lift, nose aft. It is painted in the type's original white anti-radiation finish. (Author's collection)

had been flying for two years. In retrospect it appears that these officers were years ahead of any other Western organisation and the aircraft they asked for emerged as the outstanding strike aircraft of its generation.[3] Blackburn was one of a number of companies that were asked to submit tenders; it had a long history of producing naval aircraft but its most recent product, the Firebrand, could best be described as mediocre and many pilots had worse adjectives to describe it. It, in turn, had been replaced by the unspectacular Wyvern which NA 39 was to replace. Blackburn's design team led by B P Laight had been studying the possibility of producing a naval all-weather fighter but had no major project on hand at the time. Having studied the Admiralty requirement, Blackburn allocated their project number B-103 to the aircraft and carefully considered what would have to be a remarkable solution to a most difficult specification.

Most organisations were mesmerised by the attraction of supersonic speed at the time but this would burn too much fuel to be attractive for NA 39 and would make it difficult to follow contours over land beside causing buffeting that would be too severe for the crew to stand for long periods. It soon became apparent that the design had to be optimised to operate in a clearly defined 'window' below an enemy radar horizon, ideally 200ft above the surface or less on the approach to the target. Beyond Mach 1.0 there would be too much buffeting for the crew to stand at this height and so Mach 0.9 would be a realistic penetration speed. Below 100ft it would be difficult for pilots to 'hug the surface' over land and so these parameters defined the point at which NA 39 would excel. In order to meet the range requirement, total engine thrust had to be kept to the minimum necessary for flight at low-level close the speed of sound. To meet the limitations of overall size and maximum weight imposed by the existing RN carriers the airframe had to be compact with the smallest wing size possible, a factor that would have the secondary bonus of helping to reduce gust response at the aircraft's operating height. All these parameters led Blackburn to design a relatively small aircraft with a high lift-coefficient wing and high-subsonic performance. Jet deflection was considered to achieve maximum lift but Blackburn found that blowing smooth air over the entire wings' surfaces to prevent airflow 'break-away' at low speeds would allow a small wing to give greater lift than a larger conventional wing.[4] Blackburn found that a full-span slit along the wing trailing edges gave 50 per cent more lift than any alternative scheme and blown flaps and 'drooped' ailerons increased lift still further but increased the aircraft's pitching moment dramatically, demanding exceptionally high tailplane power to counter it. Again, blowing provided the answer and the B 103 had a control surface mounted high on the tailplane which had leading edge blowing and its own training edge flap interconnected with the high-lift system. The wing leading edge was blown and this solved the anti-icing problem without detracting from maximum lift. The final shape and size of the wing was determined by the take-off case with landing a close second. The resulting shape was found to be eminently suitable for high-speed flight at extremely low-level.

Two engines would give a margin of safety in the event of action damage or a single failure but would burn substantially more fuel than a single powerplant. Most of the B 103's rival designs had proposed Avon or Sapphire turbojets with their high fuel consumption at low level but Blackburn, by then a member of the Hawker Siddeley Group, elected to use the much lighter and more economical de Havilland Gyron Junior engine. This met the requirement for high-speed cruise and was modified to provide the large amount of air bleed required. It was only just sufficient for take-off but the Admiralty accepted this limitation as short take-off and landing performance was built into the carriers. Overshooting after a single engine recovery, however, if an arrester wire was not caught was considered marginal and aircraft that had lost an engine invariably recovered into a rigged nylon safety barrier. The new area-rule technique was rather crudely applied, giving rise to the distinctive bulge aft of the wing trailing edge but at least this provided plenty of space for equipment. Because high power was needed on both engines

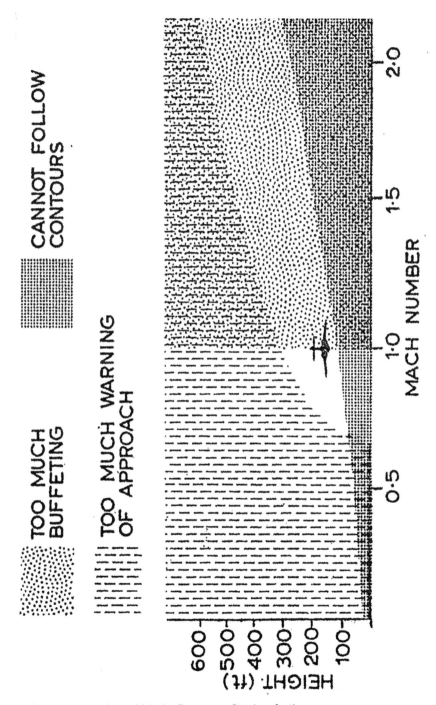

The design parameters into which the Buccaneer fitted perfectly.

during the approach to land, large clamshell airbrakes formed the rear end of the fuselage and greatly increased the profile drag when open. An overshoot, when necessary, was achieved as much by closing the airbrakes as by opening the throttles for the remainder of their travel. The airframe construction was exceptionally strong, with skins manufactured from machined aluminium sheet with spars and ribs milled from solid forgings. Particular attention was paid to the carriage of weapons and their release from the internal bomb bay was studied with care. After examining several schemes, Laight and his team designed a rotating door with the outside flush with the bottom of the aircraft and the bombs attached on its inside. In order to minimise transient effects, the door revolved rapidly through 180 degrees, placing the bombs in free stream air so that they were less likely to tumble like weapons dropped out of a conventional bomb bay. The door could be removed by un-shipping the hinge pins and hydraulic jacks, so that it could easily be replaced by a reconnaissance pack with cameras or a long-range fuel tank plumbed into the aircraft system.

Avionics included a Ferranti Blue Parrot radar in the nose which provided ground mapping, surface-search, terrain-warning and weapon-delivery functions and which formed part of an integrated system with pilot's attack sight, the autopilot and the LABS computer. Wide-band homing sensors were fitted near the wing tips so that the observer could detect radar transmissions from a target ship and home on them. By judging their strength he could advise the pilot when to drop down to low level in order to remain undetected beneath the enemy radar horizon.[5] Both the radar and wideband homer displays were in the observer's cockpit situated aft of the pilot under a continuous, clear canopy that represented a huge improvement over the cramped cockpits in the Sea Vixen. Both pilot and observer had Martin-Baker Mark 4MS ejection seats which could be used at ground level with no forward air speed and, if the canopy could not be released, could eject the occupant safely through the Perspex. Both seats could be fired underwater if necessary. To provide the observer with some forward view, the pilot's seat was 2in to port of the centreline and the observer's 2in to starboard and slightly higher. The observer controlled weapon selection and the Buccaneer could carry any strike weapon in naval service from the Red Beard nuclear bomb, through Bullpup and 2in rocket pods to 1000lb bombs. Late in the development process wiring for AIM-9 Sidewinder was added to the pylons to give a limited self-defence capability against enemy fighters.

While the Buccaneer was being developed Rolls-Royce developed an advanced turbofan engine as a private venture intended originally for the civil aviation industry.[6] It was named the Spey[7] and was found by chance to suit the Buccaneer perfectly, increasing both performance and radius of action by a considerable

The large range of weapons that could be carried by the Buccaneer S 2 shown in front of an aircraft of 736 NAS at RNAS Lossiemouth. The large bomb in the centre is a Red Beard, flanked by 1000lb bombs on either side. Beyond them are a bomb-bay photographic pack on the right and an auxiliary bomb-bay fuel tank on the left. Other stores include Bullpup and Sidewinder missiles, a refuelling pod, drop tanks, 2in rockets and 'Glow-worm' illuminant rockets. Later stores such as Martel would be added to this impressive list. (Author's collection)

margin. Development of a Spey-powered Buccaneer S 2 proceeded rapidly while the S 1 was brought into service. A development batch of twenty Buccaneers was ordered in July 1955[8] to Ministry of Supply specification M-148T, showing that at last the procurement organisation had realised that a sophisticated modern aircraft with its complicated avionics and weapons system could not be evaluated by using a small number of hand-made prototypes. This large batch allowed the aircraft to be built to production-line standards and different aspects of the test programme to be carried out concurrently.[9] The first flight was made on schedule on 30 April 1958 by XK 486 and the Admiralty was astute enough to 'freeze' the design so that development was not slowed by constant changes and revisions. The first nine

A Buccaneer S 2 of 800 NAS from *Eagle* executing a long-toss manoeuvre releasing eight 1000lb bombs. The last one, on the starboard outer pylon is about to release and the bomb-bay remains open having released the first four bombs. (Author's collection)

aircraft were essentially prototypes and were used by Blackburn and de Havilland for airframe and engine development work. Subsequent airframes were pre-production aircraft with full systems, folding wings and bomb bays used for service trials and clearances. The first deck landings took place on *Victorious* in January 1960 and the name Buccaneer was officially approved in August 1960 and the RN intensive flying trials flight, designated 700Z NAS was formed at RNAS Lossiemouth in March 1961. The first S 2 flew in 1964 and in April 1965 a further IFTU, 700B NAS was formed to introduce the type. The last S 2 was delivered to the RN in 1968. Buccaneers served with a training unit, 736 NAS and four front-line squadrons, 800, 801, 803 and 809 NAS; the lower numbers reflecting the reduced number of carriers in service as well as the cost and complexity of the aircraft compared with its predecessors. The S 1 certainly proved to be under-powered in service and even with catapult launch its maximum all-up weight was restricted, especially in the high temperatures encountered in the Far East. The problem was alleviated in *Eagle* by embarking a specialised Scimitar tanker unit,

A Buccaneer S 2 of 809 NAS at the moment of launch from *Ark Royal's* bow catapult. Note the strop falling away from the aircraft. The store under the starboard wing is a Martel missile control pod. (Author's collection)

800B NAS, which allowed armed Buccaneer S 1s to be launched with weapons but a low fuel state and then 'filled up' once safely airborne. *Victorious* lacked the space to embark a tanker unit and had to achieve a compromise between fuel and weapons[10] with a number of Buccaneers fitted as tankers; the Commander Far East Fleet (COMFEF), urged the Admiralty to hasten the type's clearance to carry 500lb bombs as a more practical weapon than the 1000lb bomb. The S 2 entered operational service with 801 NAS in *Victorious* during 1966[11] and proved to be the outstanding strike aircraft of its generation.

The Westland Wessex

The first British-designed anti-submarine helicopter was the Bristol Type 191 and sixty-eight were ordered for the RN in April 1956. A similar number, given the type number 193, were ordered for the RCN at the same time.[12] With tandem rotors driven by free-power turbines which had not yet been fully developed the 191 would have been an expensive and technically complex aircraft to develop. Thirty feet longer than a Sea King, even with the blades folded, it would have been a huge aircraft to handle on deck and even though the rotor diameter was smaller, there were two of them. The 191 was probably what FOAC had in mind when he said that helicopters could not be integrated into strike carrier operations; despite the fact that the 191 was cancelled in the 1957 Defence Review, he may have feared that subsequent designs would be as big or bigger. Admiralty studies after 1957 resulted in a decision to procure a derivative of the Sikorsky S-58 powered by a single Napier Gazelle free power turbine. The S-58, designated the HSS-1 by the USN, had been in service with the US Navy and Marine Corps as an anti-submarine and assault helicopter since 1955, powered by a single Wright R-1820 radial piston engine developing 1525hp. Like the Whirlwind, the HSS-1 had a limited capability and had to operate in pairs, one with a sonar and one with a weapon. The USN wanted a single helicopter that could combine these roles and in December 1957 began to develop the superb Sea King.

The Admiralty's choice of an obsolescent airframe, albeit with a new engine, to meet its long-term anti-submarine requirement was therefore very conservative but capitalised on the type's acceptable dimensions, Westland's proven ability to build Sikorsky designs under licence and British research into free-power turbine technology. Development of what was to become the Westland Wessex began with the signing of a licence agreement and the purchase of an S-58 airframe, XL 722, in May 1957. It was fitted experimentally with a Napier Gazelle and used as a pattern for the manufacture of further aircraft in the UK. The first Westland-built Wessex flew in June 1958. Despite the use of a proven airframe, development was slow because the Admiralty specified a sophisticated flight control system (FCS) in addition to the new engine and its controls. Thus equipped it was to be the first anti-submarine helicopter in the world to be capable of day, night and all-weather operation with dipping sonar; but not for long, as the USN introduced the vastly more capable SH-3 Sea King only a few months after the Wessex in 1961. The Gazelle engine delivered 1450shp and was both smaller and lighter than the Wright R-1820 in the S-58, bringing a number of benefits. First it gave sufficient power to take-off with a weapon as well as a reasonable fuel load and was thus able to operate as both hunter and killer in a single sortie; secondly its smaller dimensions allowed many of the Louis Newmark FCS 'black boxes' to be fitted in the nose bay with easy access through large inspection panels. Its principle sensor was the Type 194 dipping sonar. The airframe was narrow and could be packed densely in hangars although, unfortunately, much use was made of an aluminium alloy containing magnesium in the fuselage skin, making it vulnerable to salt-water corrosion. The gas turbine engine meant that volatile avgas need not be stored in carriers any more although the Gazelle was started by aviation iso propyl nitrate (AVPIN), a liquid with such unpleasant properties that it was stowed in canisters on rafts with quick-release couplings by the deck edge so that they could be ditched over the side if there were any risk of fire. Compared with the piston engines in earlier helicopters, the Wessex was quieter and more robust for embarked operations. It was the aircraft around which the 1960 designs for helicopter/escort cruisers were centred.[13]

A Wessex HU 5 of 845 NAS from *Bulwark* launching an SS-11 air-to-surface missile over the Borneo jungle. (Author's collection)

The Wessex IFTU was commissioned as 700H NAS at RNAS Culdrose in June 1960 and the first operational unit, 815 NAS, formed a year later in July 1961 for service in *Ark Royal*. The Wessex rapidly replaced the Whirlwind in both anti-submarine and, with the sonar removed, commando squadrons. A total of 129 Wessex HAS 1 were built and they equipped 814, 815, 819, 820, 824, 826 and 829 NAS for anti-submarine duties, 845, 846, 847 and 848 NAS for commando assault duties and 700H, 700V, 706, 707, 737, 771, 772 and 781 NAS for second-line and training duties. Despite its modest design origins, the Wessex could genuinely be called a successful aircraft that filled a number of disparate roles well. It was a joint project and Marks 2 and 4 were applied to versions used by the RAF for troop transport and the Royal Flight.

Developments continued after the Wessex HAS 1 entered service. These included the HU 5 commando assault variant in which two Rolls-Royce Gnome engines replaced the single Napier Gazelle giving it the capability to carry underslung loads up to 3000lbs under most conditions or up to sixteen fully-equipped marines on internal seats along the sides of the cabin. One hundred of this version were built

A Wessex HU 5 of 848 NAS from *Albion* carrying a 105mm pack howitzer from 29 Commando Light Regiment Royal Artillery as an underslung load. The Wessex was a huge advance over the Whirlwind and could easily carry loads of 3000lbs including guns, ammunition and lightweight Land Rovers over reasonable distances. (Author's collection)

and the version re-equipped 845 NAS in 1966, followed by the other commando units. It remained in service until the early 1980s. The Wessex HAS 3, an improved anti-submarine version was markedly less successful. Three HAS 3 were built from scratch and forty-three others converted from HAS 1s. This mark featured a surface-search radar mounted in a dorsal radome from which it could 'see' to the sides and rear but not directly ahead through the main rotor gearbox. It also had the much-improved Type 195 pulse-doppler dipping sonar and an improved FCS which was capable of manoeuvring the aircraft through the jump cycle from hover to hover to lower the sonar body into the water without the pilots' hands on the controls by day or night in any weather. The Gazelle engine was slightly uprated to 1600shp but this was not enough to compensate for the increased weight of the new equipment. The HAS 3 had fuel for a nominal 90 minutes flight but in the temperatures found in the Far East, this was seldom possible. Endurance could be extended by fitting a 98-gallon drop tank to one of the two weapons pylons but this extra weight precluded the carriage of a weapon and prevented the HAS 3 from operating as a hunter/killer like the HAS 1. The Wessex HAS 3 represented an attempt to 'put a quart into a pint pot' and the type only served briefly in *Eagle*,

Hermes, the two *Tiger* class cruiser conversions and the 'County' class destroyers in which space for a flight deck and hangar substituted for the two Mark 10 mortars in the early design proposals. Despite the high hopes entertained for it, the HAS 3 was of very limited operational use and it was soon replaced by an anglicised version of the Sea King that will be described in a later chapter.

The Search for a Gannet AEW 3 Replacement

When it entered service, the Gannet AEW 3 was expected to be an interim type and its radar, which had evolved from a design first flown in 1944, was certainly near the end of its development potential. Naval Air Staff Requirement 6166 was produced by the Admiralty in the early 1960s to examine a range options for a long-term carrier-borne AEW aircraft. It is worth noting that that a similar concept appraisal by the USN at this time led to production of the E-2A Hawkeye which, in highly-developed form, is still in production and service with the USN in 2015. One possible outcome from NASR 6166 was a new frequency-modulated interrupted continuous wave, FMICW, radar with a completely new airframe to carry it.[14] This was expected to cost in excess of £80 million to develop at 1965 prices,[15] leading to a unit cost of £3.2 million each for a production run of forty aircraft. The RAF was not interested in AEW at the time[16] and so few, if any, other customers for such an aircraft were considered likely. This sum was expected to be unacceptable to the Ministry of Defence and Treasury so cheaper options were considered. The most likely solution, had the Government not decided to scrap carriers, was a further major re-design of the Fairey Gannet to carry an AN/APS-82 radar in a new rotodome over the fuselage. This was the radar developed for the USN E-1B Tracer AEW aircraft which had entered service in 1960. Again it would have represented a conservative approach but would have been another evolutionary step beyond the AN/APS-20. The cheapest solution was a re-opened Gannet AEW 3 production line giving a unit cost of £0.5 million each for a run of forty aircraft with moving target indication and other minor improvements to the radar.

The Search for a Joint Strike Fighter Design

There is a widely-held belief that joint projects were forced on the Admiralty and Air Ministry by political pressure and that the two departments found it difficult to agree combined requirements. At best this is a gross over-simplification and there were many successful joint projects in the 1950s. Examples include all nuclear and conventional air weapons, sensors including radars and sono-buoys and a number of aircraft projects including the Hornet/Sea Hornet, Venom/Sea Venom, Dragonfly, Whirlwind and Wessex. The SR-177 rocket fighter was a successful project with compromises on both sides that showed great promise until Duncan

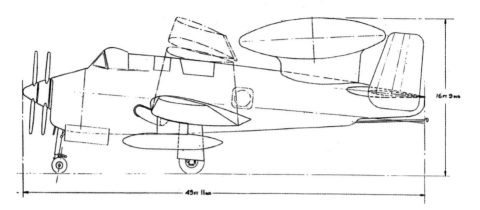

A side view of the projected Gannet AEW 7 with the AN/APS-82 radar scanner in a pod over the fuselage and a re-designed tail. Had the carrier replacement programme gone ahead in 1966 as planned, this was the most likely AEW aircraft to have replaced the AEW 3 for the new ships at an affordable development cost. (Author's collection)

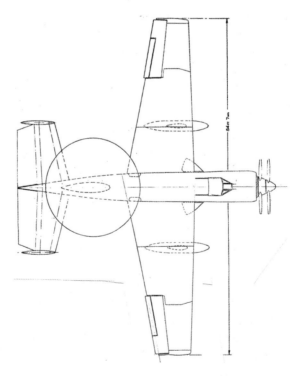

Overhead view of the projected Gannet AEW 7 on which a significant amount of development work was carried out. It would have required more powerful engines than the earlier variant. (Author's collection)

Sandys insisted on its cancellation. Its 'death throes' make an interesting comparison with later politicians' statements on the need for joint aircraft projects. As we saw in an earlier chapter, Duncan Sandys announced the cancellation of the SR-177 while he was on a visit to Woomera in Australia. At the time the Ministry of Aviation had five prototypes close to completion, two Services that wanted the aircraft and German interest in procuring the type. The Minister did all he could to save the project and a bizarre period followed in which the MOD, with Treasury support, tried to terminate the project and the Ministry of Aviation tried to keep it alive with small infusions of cash to prevent the Germans from finding out what was happening. It was finally cancelled in 1958. The Admiralty had viewed the SR-177 with enthusiasm and regarded the Sea Vixen as a 'second-best' option based on an outdated design with little or no development potential. Consideration was given to developing a two-seat, radar-equipped Scimitar but the dangerous politics involved in trying to develop this whilst keeping the order for Sea Vixens alive until the modified Scimitar was proved viable killed the project in its early stages.[17] From 1958 the Naval Staff had to seek a new high-performance strike fighter capable of countering the sort of threat the Soviet Union was believed to be developing but it had insufficient money to proceed alone; it had to have a partner. When Lord Carrington called on the Minister of Defence in September 1960 to discuss future RN procurement plans he stressed, among other things, the importance of new collaborative projects to provide a new strike fighter for the future generation of aircraft carriers and for their weapons and sensors. He re-stated his case in a letter[18] in which he stated that 'the Admiralty will co-operate in every way with the Air Ministry in trying to frame requirements for new aircraft, so that one basic type of aircraft can be used by both services'. On 1 May 1961 Peter Thorneycroft, the Minister of Aviation, had minuted that 'much work was now being done on the formulation of an operational requirement for an RAF and RN aircraft to follow the TSR 2 and Buccaneer and efforts are being made to define the requirements in such a way that they could be met by one basic type of aircraft'.[19] Harold Watkinson replied on 1 June that he had informed the Chairman of the Defence Research Policy Committee (DRPC), that he was 'not prepared to deviate from the policy of having one development to meet the needs of both services'.[20] The First Lord of the Admiralty, the Secretary of State for Air and he were, he said, 'all at one mind about this'.

In May 1960 the First Sea Lord, Admiral Sir Charles Lambe, had a severe heart attack and was forced to resign. Lord Carrington asked Admiral Sir Caspar John, VCNS at the time, to take over immediately; Lambe had already recommended John as his successor and had planned to hand over in 1962 but his health prevented him from serving his full term, and sadly he died on 29 August 1960.

Caspar John was the outstanding officer of his generation and the first naval pilot to become 1SL; his experience and knowledge were to be severely tested by political manoeuvring during his term of office since, by then, the Ministry of Supply had evolved into the Ministry of Aviation and had its own ideas on aircraft procurement. It wanted to see two new British inventions put into production and sought to 'massage' Service requirements to obtain political approval and funding. Unfortunately, it was far from clear that the UK had the money to continue with TSR 2 development and to launch two further advanced military types incorporating new and unproven technology. The first invention was the swivelling-nozzle Bristol Siddeley BS-53 Pegasus engine which, when installed in the Hawker P 1127 prototype, gave it the ability to take off and land vertically and even to hover. It could, of course, get airborne at a higher maximum weight with a conventional, rolling take off and then, having burnt off fuel to reduce weight, land vertically in a confined space. The acronym for this capability was VTOL for vertical take-off and landing at first but once the operational impracticality of vertical take-off became understood it was changed to STOVL for short take-off and vertical landing. Several P 1127 technology demonstration aircraft had been ordered by the Ministry of Aviation and the situation was complicated by the fact that the BS-53 had been developed with American funding and the new German Luftwaffe was interested in an improved version as a close-support aircraft. The second invention was the variable-geometry wing, commonly known as the 'swing-wing' which the Ministry of Aviation wanted to see applied to the Buccaneer/TSR 2 replacement aircraft. This was a very much more complex, and thus expensive, concept than P 1127.

In June 1960 the Air Ministry was pressed to accept a simple, low-cost, short-range, less elaborate close support aircraft to meet a portion of the roles originally contemplated in Operational Requirement 345 for the TSR 2 which was proving very expensive to develop. This supplementary type was to be subsonic with a radius of action of about 200nm and operable from basic airstrips near any potential combat zone and the Chiefs of Staff agreed that the P 1127, which had not yet flown, offered the best hope of meeting this requirement.[21] The RAF undertook to procure thirty aircraft and the first prototype, XP 831, achieved hovering flight, a few inches off the ground, in October 1960 and the second prototype, XP 836, flew conventionally for the first time in July 1961. Events moved forward quickly thereafter and a meeting was held in the Ministry of Defence on 29 November 1961 to discuss progress. It was chaired by Harold Watkinson and both Sir Solly Zuckerman, Chief Scientific Adviser to the MOD and Air Chief Marshall Sir Thomas Pike, Chief of the Air Staff were present. The RN was not asked to send a representative. Urgency was lent to the meeting by a United States offer to fund six P 1127s for evaluation if Great Britain and Germany undertook to fund six each. Watkinson started by observing that: 'A tripartite sharing of the P 1127 development programme would ensure that the BS 53 engine was developed and exploited and there seemed to be a good chance of the P 1127, either in its present or in a developed form (or possibly both) becoming an operational aircraft within NATO.'[22]

Julian Amery, Secretary of State for Air, then made a game-changing statement which was not challenged by anyone present. He said that, while the Air Ministry would stand by its undertaking to buy up to thirty aircraft for the RAF 'if this was necessary to ensure that the German Air Force adopted the P 1127', the RAF 'did not regard the P 1127 as an acceptable aircraft with which to equip front-line squadrons. It would be subsonic and would not survive in an operational environment.'[23] Air Chief Marshal Pike went even further than Amery and added his belief that no European country other than Germany would want the P 1127. 'It would be of no use for any operational purpose' and he felt that the German Air Staff held similar views to his own about the need for a supersonic aircraft. He ended by saying that 'they would equip with the P 1127 only if ordered to do so' and doubted, when it came to the point, that they would in fact buy it. Zuckerman believed that further development of P 1127 would assist the development of a supersonic VTOL close-support aircraft and observed that American interest stemmed from their desire to gain experience quickly in this relatively unknown field. The inexpensive close-support aircraft agreed in 1960 to complement OR 345 had suddenly been transformed into an expensive and sophisticated supersonic strike fighter; nobody present seems to have noticed.

On 4 December, the day the minutes of this meeting arrived in the Admiralty, K T Nash, the Head of M1 Division, did notice. In a single-page briefing written that afternoon for 1SL and the Naval Staff[24] he accepted that 'it seemed good sense to go on with the Hawker Siddeley project' and that the proposal to go forward with American and German involvement 'could hardly be opposed'. His second paragraph, however, was a damning indictment of the way in which a supersonic close-support aircraft had slipped into focus. Nash noted that 'it seems improper as well as unfair that the Minister should in this same paper stake the Air Ministry's claim to a supersonic close-support aircraft; indeed he seems to make any approval of his proposals for the P 1127 dependent on their not prejudicing that claim'. So far as he knew, 'the Chiefs of Staff have not declared that there is any operational need for a supersonic close-support aircraft'. He noted that it was also clear from the Minister's minutes that 'the relative claims of such a project on the country's R & D resources have not yet been considered by the DRPC'. Nash reminded the First Lord that when the Air Ministry had campaigned for TSR 2 development 'they let it be believed by one and all that the complementary aircraft for close support of the Army would be a relatively cheap and simple aircraft' and that P 1127 would be acceptable. Since getting the TSR 2 'they have gone back completely on this and are now saying that supersonic speed is indispensable to survival in the mid-1960s'. He ended by recommending that continued development of P 1127 should be supported but that 'there can be no consideration of the idea of a supersonic close-support aircraft for the RAF unless and until the matter has cleared the COS and DRPC hurdles'.

The momentum behind a supersonic VTOL close-support aircraft was, by then, probably unstoppable, however, because NATO had issued basic military requirement (NBMR) 3, for such an aircraft with proposals to be offered by December. It was assumed in London, rather optimistically as it transpired, that the winning design would attract export orders to become standard NATO equipment. The contemporary NBMR 4 called for a VTOL transport aircraft capable of landing in rough areas close to a battlefield in order to support NBMR 3 'in the field'. Britain also had a contender for this, the Armstrong Whitworth Type 681, that was to become an early casualty in Harold Wilson's first round of cuts. The Cabinet Defence Committee met on 6 December 1961 at Admiralty House to consider Watkinson's Memorandum about the continued development of the P 1127. The familiar arguments were repeated and Amery expressed concern that P 1127 should not prejudice the development of a supersonic aircraft. The Air Ministry remained prepared to buy thirty aircraft if they were needed to 'clinch' overseas sales but saw no operational value in the aircraft.[25] The Minister of Defence was invited to proceed with negotiations for procuring eighteen tripartite evaluation aircraft for the UK, USA and West Germany. The committee also 'took note' that the Minister of Defence would in due course submit proposals for developing a supersonic close-support aircraft, taking into account the requirements of the RN and RAF. The First Lord's comments had at least achieved that much. There can be no doubt, however, that politicians had become mesmerised by the Air Staff's attempts to win replacement aircraft for some of the projects that had been cancelled in 1957. Their thoughts were centred on fixed bases in Germany, the Mediterranean and the Middle and Far East with the small 'packets' of air power based in them. The Government's own Defence Policy documents had stressed the diminishing number of overseas bases and the need for mobility but this does not seem to have influenced Air Staff thinking and, again, nobody in the Cabinet seemed to notice.

The second invention, variable-geometry wings, also excited the Ministry of Aviation which sought funding for two research aircraft in February 1962 at a cost of £10 million to £15 million. In a Loose Minute to 1SL dated 2 March 1962,[26]

Nash mentions correspondence between the Treasury and M1 Branch about the joint Naval/Air Staff Requirement OR 346/355 for a variable geometry strike-fighter project with which the Ministry of Aviation hoped to replace the Sea Vixen at first and then, after further development, the Buccaneer and TSR 2 in the mid-1970s. It is interesting looking back on the relevant documents, with the wisdom of hindsight, to see that staff officers who had seen operational service in Corsairs, Sea Furies and Sea Hawks still thought of an aircraft's operational life in terms of a few years and expected the dramatic developments that occurred between 1946 and 1956 to continue. OR 346 never achieved the same political focus as the supersonic close-support aircraft and was clouded by cost over-runs, delays and ultimately the cancellation of TSR 2 which it was partly intended to replace. This extraordinary requirement called for an aircraft with a maximum speed in excess of Mach 2.5 at high altitude but a landing speed on an aircraft carrier, achieved with variable-geometry wings, of only 80 knots. It was to have all-weather intercept and strike capability, in the latter role armed with 10,000lbs of bombs over a radius of action of 1300nm. Maximum launch weight from a carrier was to be 50,000lbs.[27] Both Vickers and de Havilland worked on concepts and sketched a variety of designs which still appear futuristic fifty years later. Some had four engines and some claimed STOVL capability but these 'paper planes' clearly showed what the naval and air staffs expected a Joint Strike Fighter look like. The Ministry of Defence and Treasury took a more limited view and the project was an early casualty when Harold Wilson's Labour government was elected in 1964.[28]

The Hawker Siddeley P 1154

In December 1961 Lord Mountbatten played a critical part in the selection of a new strike fighter aircraft to a joint design in a paper entitled 'Future Aircraft Carrier Policy' intended to support Harold Watkinson's stance.[29] In it, he stated that 'an effort should be made to produce a common fighter/ground attack aircraft with supersonic performance on the lines envisaged NBMR 3. Such an aircraft might be introduced into service in 1969/70.' It would, he felt, have the decided disadvantage that its strike capability, particularly as regards radius of action at only 400nm, would be limited but on the other hand 'would provide a carrier-borne supersonic fighter at a considerably earlier date than is otherwise likely'. He made no comment on why NBMR 3 rather than OR 346 was chosen as the base-line but the implication drawn from the paper is that the former was expected to be short-term, affordable with export sales potential and the latter was long-term, likely to be very expensive and un-saleable abroad.

NBMR 3 called for a relatively simple, robust aircraft with supersonic capability that took advantage of emerging technology to deliver VTOL performance from rough landing strips. It was to be a ground-attack aircraft with a day fighter capability in a clear air mass, intended to fight the sort of land battle that NATO envisaged in central Europe. The planners hoped that it could be based near the forward edge of the battle area like a helicopter but failed to give sufficient thought to the scale of logistics, command and control and recovery systems needed by a strike fighter to be effective[30] or the vulnerability of aircraft on the ground to conventional artillery, rocket or air attack. Besides military considerations there were political ones; NATO had no money to buy the aircraft that won NBMR 3, that would be a national consideration and the British contender, a supersonic derivative of the P 1127 designated the P 1154, was likely to be expensive. In the event the competition was extended beyond December 1961 and even then, NATO hedged its bets by declaring the Hawker Siddeley P 1154 and the French Dassault Mirage IIIV[31] joint winners. Neither of them ever went into production. The relevance of the P 1154 to the RN is that the development lobby had pushed the Navy into a corner. TSR 2 was suffering a protracted development process of unexpectedly high cost at the time and, although it may well have emerged as an outstanding aircraft, there was only enough money to develop one other fast jet project in the UK and the Ministries of Defence and Aviation had, between them,

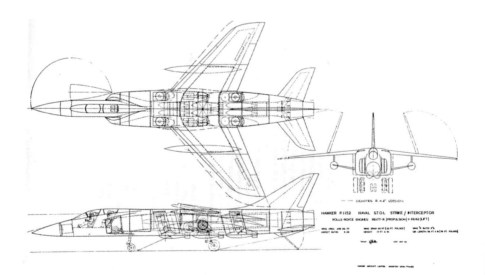

Some idea of the aircraft that would have been needed to meet specification AW 406 can be gathered from this 1961 Hawker-Siddeley sketch design for an RN strike fighter designated the P 1152. It has hardpoints for a catapult launch strop and an arrester hook; a single, re-heated engine for normal flight and four lift engines for slow-speed deck landings. Note the six semi-recessed 1000lb bombs for the strike role. (Author's collection)

decided it should be the supersonic close-support aircraft that the RAF had now decided that it must have. Mountbatten probably grasped the unpalatable truth that in the contemporary political climate, despite the RN's recent series of successful actions, the choice was probably between a modified P 1154 or nothing as a Sea Vixen replacement. The agreement to procure eighteen tripartite evaluation P 1127s led to the formation of a joint UK/US/German evaluation unit at RAF West Raynham, Norfolk in October 1964. The RN was not invited to participate and, to be fair, the Naval Staff probably saw little value in examining such a mediocre aircraft with the Buccaneer already in operational service. The US Navy did, however, send a pilot to participate. The tripartite aircraft were given the name Kestrel. They proved to have a radius of action under 200nm with two 1000lb bombs after a short, rolling take-off; the aircraft could not take off vertically with any weapons or anything like full fuel. It had no radar, no guns, no missiles and the only navigation aid was TACAN.[32] The Kestrel was subsonic and only capable of realistic operation by day in a clear air mass. NBMR 3, of course, wanted more than this and the Admiralty Board, which had agreed that it would do all it could to support a joint project, hoped that concessions would be made to meet its own requirements.

Naval and Air Staff aspirations for the developed aircraft were contained in Naval/Air Staff Requirement 356 produced in 1963.[33] It contained three sections; a preamble that explained the importance of it being a joint project; Part 1 which outlined the RAF requirement and stated that in order to meet the Hunter replacement deadline of 1968, a design very close to NBMR 3[34] would have to be accepted. Part 2 contained the RN requirement AW 406 which had been drawn up in 1962 to cover either OR 346 or P 1154/NBMR 3, whichever was taken forward. It continued to focus on the intelligence community's warnings of a supersonic bomber threat in the 1970s comprising aircraft equipped with stand-off missiles. A briefing for the Chiefs of Staff Planning Committee was also prepared and circulated on 5 June 1963.[35] This looked at the wider air defence picture including the defence of the UK, NATO operations in Europe, including Berlin, British commitments in bases around the world and the RN requirement. The same requirement for RN P 1154s appeared in both documents. What the RN wanted was a fighter capable of intercepting a Mach 2.5 target at 65,000ft in all weathers. It was to have development potential against Mach 3 targets at 80,000ft to meet projected threats during the aircraft's service life and must have an 'adequate' performance against both fast and slow targets at low level and in an environment degraded by enemy electronic countermeasures. The destruction of high- or low-level threats with air-to-air guided missiles capable of engaging targets at heights considerably above or below the fighter was considered to be 'acceptable'. If a suitable missile, such as GDA 103(T), had not completed development by 1970, four Red Top infrared homing missiles would suffice as an interim armament giving a possible double attack capability; two missiles being fired on each attack to give a 90 per cent kill probability. The new fighter was to have sufficient fuel to loiter on a CAP station 100nm from the carrier for 2.5 hours with an engagement five minutes before the end of that time. The Naval Staff was prepared to accept the radius of action that was found to be possible with the fuel needed for the fighter mission. Weapon load was to be 4000lbs and it was stipulated that the run in for the last 100nm to the target was to be flown at Mach 0.92 at less than 500ft above sea level. A crew of two was considered to be essential to make the best use of an integrated weapon system based around a pulse-doppler radar and missile-control computer. An automatic test facility for aircraft maintenance on deck was also considered important. The Naval Staff saw no need for VTOL performance – that was provided by the carriers' steam catapults and arrester wires – but would accept it if the RAF insisted on it. Catapult launch would use a 'tow bar' fixed to the aircraft's nose oleo, exactly the same as the one being developed for future USN carrier aircraft.

This was a requirement for a far more sophisticated aircraft than the NBMR 3 design that the Air Staff was now prepared to accept. Surprisingly the Ministry of Aviation, which had pushed hard for the acquisition of a more sophisticated P 1127, now dragged its heals and put obstacles in the way of any modification to the basic P 1154. One has to feel sympathy for the Hawker design team under Ralph Hooper who had worked hard to produce a simple strike fighter to meet NBMR 3. They had never been fully funded by the UK Government and had moved forward in a series of steps funded by holding contracts, each of only a few months duration. Now they were confronted with an unrealistic political directive that forced the Naval Staff to seek 'modifications' to the design that included a second crew member, a ton of avionics and a performance envelope way beyond that for which the airframe had been designed. The Naval Staff also deserves some sympathy for doing its best to procure a fighter capable of meeting the threat that the Chiefs of Staff and Ministry of Defence had accepted as likely from the mid-1970s. A team from DNAW led by Captain E M Brown CBE DSC AFC RN visited the Hawker Project Office in April 1962 to discuss the NBMR 3's suitability as a Sea Vixen replacement. The results were not encouraging although Captain Brown observed that the P 1154 would be light enough to operate from the existing carriers.[36] OR 346, which was still seen as a possible alternative at the time, could only have operated from the new carriers, leaving *Eagle*, *Hermes* and *Ark Royal* with Sea Vixens 'well into the Seventies'. Ralph Hooper noted that the naval requirement added at least 2000lb to the maximum weight of the NBMR 3 design

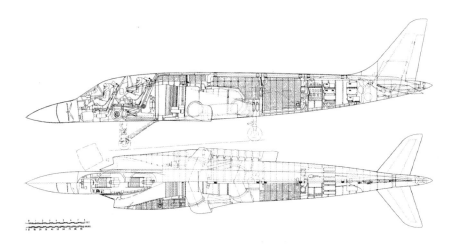

A sketch design showing the RN version of the P 1154 design as it stood in 1963. Note the avionics racks near the tail, a configuration made necessary by the need to balance the radar scanner and two crewmembers in the nose. Disposables such as fuel and weapons were positioned about the aircraft's centre of gravity in the hover to allow vertical landing. (Author's collection)

and doubled the armament load. To meet the CAP requirement there needed to be at least a 50 per cent increase in fuel capacity[37] which would have to be in the form of drop tanks. There was more; a larger wing was probably desirable to meet the cruise requirement and to carry external fuel and missiles. The most difficult problem was achieving an adequate balance for vertical landing with the weight of the radar and the two crew members in the nose. Hooper believed that the naval requirement could only be approached with a 70 per cent re-design of the P 1154; a big change to make for the small production run likely to result. He noted in parenthesis that total production of the Sea Vixen and Scimitar had only amounted to about 120 and eighty aircraft respectively[38] so that the new and very much more expensive aircraft might not exceed a production run of fifty to seventy aircraft. Hooper concluded that unless the Naval Staff could relax their requirements considerably, it was completely unrealistic to attempt to modify an existing low-level, land-based, VTOL ground-attack aircraft design to perform the high-altitude, ship-based patrol/interceptor role.

It has to be asked, if he could see that after two hours of discussion, why couldn't Harold Watkinson or Julian Amery, the politicians responsible for the nation's defence and aircraft industry? From the start, the idea of a common airframe performing virtually every fast-jet role was doomed. The performance required in each of the two primary roles simply could not be reconciled with the combination of airframe and engine chosen by politicians to meet them and money was wasted trying. Volumes could be written about the attempts during 1963 to find a common design. Each study reduced the Naval Staff's expectation of interceptor capability still further below the requirement that had originally been specified. I have selected two papers which illustrate the P 1154's failure;[39] there are many others which serve only to reinforce the point. In the first,[40] Sir Solly Zuckerman compared the parameters accepted by the Naval and Air Staffs on 10 July 1963 with the performance actually being offered by the Ministry of Aviation in early October. CAP endurance (doppler radar version) had dropped from 1.57 to 1.3 hours; maximum speed had dropped from Mach 1.86 to Mach 1.65. Strike radius of action with a 2000lb bomb load was down from 540nm to 430nm and with a 4000lb bomb load from 450nm to 330nm. K T Nash followed this comparison with a summary of the project for Board members which included an eight-page Annex.[41] He started by noting that AW 406 had been drawn up by the Naval Staff to meet a directive by the Chiefs of Staff to produce a common inter-Service aircraft based on NBMR 3. The key phrase was 'based on' because it meant that the Navy had to modify the ideal requirement it had outlined in OR 346 to conform with the basic characteristics of the NBMR. This had the effect of forcing a number of changes on the RN view of an affordable and capable Sea Vixen replacement. These were:

(a) Acceptance of a single-engine layout. This was unpalatable in view of the operating environment and accident statistics proving the increased safety factor inherent in twin-engined aircraft.

(b) Acceptance of VTOL capability. This was not required by the RN which already possessed in its catapults and arrester gear the most efficient STOL system in existence. The penalty of VTOL was heavy in terms of operational payload and cost.

(c) Degradation of fighter capability by a reduction in CAP endurance and detection range from 90nm to 60nm.

(d) Degradation of strike capability by a reduction in the achievable radius of action.

These were damning criticisms but more followed in later pages. Among these were the late discovery that manoeuvrability in the high-altitude interceptor role had been revealed as critically low by the Ministry of Aviation after the July agreement and doubts about the compatibility of the aircraft's bicycle landing gear with deck operations which the Ministry could not allay.[42] Nash finished the brief by stating that 'the RN has fallen over backwards to co-operate in this common aircraft exercise but it is crystal clear that the P 1154 is not the vehicle to provide

A model of the P 1154 produced by Hawker-Siddeley in 1963. Note the USN-style 'nose-tow' catapult launch arm fitted on the nose oleo and the tricycle undercarriage. (Author's collection)

the solution. It is felt, therefore, that the exercise should be pursued, but on a different tack.' The P 1154 debacle left more than one legacy, however, the first of which was the name selected for it; the RAF version of the P 1154 was to have been named the Harrier and the RN version the Sea Harrier. Both were to be used for the production derivatives of the P 1127 described in a later chapter. The second was less tangible but worth mentioning. The plethora of aircraft project cancellations that followed the 1957 Defence Review left Rolls-Royce with no fast-jet applications for their engines; the Buccaneer, P 1154 and TSR 2 had engines designed by de Havilland and Bristol Siddeley. Rolls-Royce applied considerable pressure to the Ministry of Aviation in an attempt to change this and even proposed a twin-Spey version of the P 1154 with crossover puffer-jet ducts to give a measure of control for a short landing in the event of a single-engine failure. Even politicians were able to see that a version with a bigger wing, two engines and a two-seat cockpit could hardly be described as an airframe with anything in common with NBMR 3 and the idea was never taken forward.

Despite the P 1154's obvious failure, Admiral F H E Hopkins, the DCNS, warned his Board colleagues that they should proceed with caution, given the political enthusiasm for a joint project. After commenting[43] on a report by the Directorate of Operational Research (DOR), which had cast doubt over the aircraft's ability to achieve, in speed and acceleration, a sufficiently high kill rate against the supersonic stand-off attacker, he warned his colleagues that the RN was virtually committed to the joint fighter. It should be opposed only if it did not represent a sufficient advance over the Sea Vixen and 'rocking the boat' while the carrier replacement programme hung in the balance might not be the best idea. After discussion, the Board took the view that the best way forward was to try to persuade the Chief of the Air Staff that the P 1154 suited neither role and, therefore, neither Service and should be terminated. Given the perceived urgent need to replace the Hunter, Air Staff support for such a stance was lukewarm and conditioned by the RAF's own internal arguments about whether a close-support aircraft should be simple or sophisticated, supersonic or not. In the end the RN objected alone and its version of the P 1154 was cancelled in February 1964. There is a well-known adage in the engineering world that 'the function dictates the form'. The fundamental problem as far as the P 1154 was concerned was the form never even came close to reflecting the function and it reflects little credit on Harold Watkinson or Julian Amery that they did not accept the fact early in the project's life and take a sensible look at the service requirements. Sydney Camm, Hawker's famous chief designer, is said to have observed that no VTOL fighter would win export orders until it matched the performance of the McDonnell Phantom II. If he really did say it, he was right.

The McDonnell Phantom II

While Hawker Siddeley struggled with the politically-inspired P 1154, the US Navy had developed and introduced the Phantom into service and the contrast between its background and that of the British aircraft could hardly be greater. James S McDonnell had started his aircraft company at St Louis, Missouri, in July 1939 with a small office and a staff of one secretary. With the stimulus of war he gathered an innovative team that eventually specialised in designing and building jet aircraft and he won a USN contract to produce what became the first jet fighter to be designed to operate from a carrier. It first flew in January 1945 and was developed into the FH-1 Phantom which saw successful but limited service and was followed by a more powerful derivative, the F2H Banshee, which first flew in 1947 and achieved a production run of 895 aircraft. It saw service with the USN and RCN and was not finally retired until the 1960s. It successor, the F3H Demon, flew in 1951 and subsequently became the first fighter to be armed with guided missiles. Once the F-101 Voodoo entered service with the USAF in 1954, McDonnell's reputation in the design of supersonic fighters was second to none and so he was intensely disappointed when Chance Vought won a USN contract for a supersonic day fighter with the F8U Crusader. McDonnell might have diversified into other types of aircraft but he decided, bravely, to go ahead with a private venture 'all-can-do' fighter, even though there was no requirement for such an aircraft from any of the US armed services.

The project was given the name Phantom II in 1954; naval opinion was canvassed and a wooden mock-up was built to show what the new aircraft would look like. It lacked internal detail but showed a twin-engined, single-seat, radar-equipped strike fighter with four 20mm cannon and eleven under-wing hardpoints for weapons mounted on pylons. It was to be capable of carrying every weapon in the USN inventory and the engines were to be Wright J65s, licence-built versions of the British Armstrong-Siddeley Sapphire, giving an estimated maximum speed of Mach 1.5 at high altitude. The mock-up was so impressive that the USN ordered two technology demonstration airframes in November 1954. They were to be attack aircraft, originally designated AH-1 and General Electric J79 turbojets were to be substituted for the J65s. There was still no official requirement for the aircraft, however, but that changed in 1955 when officers from the US Navy Chief of Naval Operations (CNO) and Bureau of Aircraft (BuAir) Departments travelled to St Louis and gave the project the focus it needed in a meeting that is reputed to have lasted less than an hour. It was now to be a fleet fighter capable of two hours on CAP 250nm from a carrier armed with radar-guided and infrared-homing missiles but no guns. A second crewmember, known as a radar-intercept officer (RIO), was to be added to work the advanced radar and to help with the high pilot work-load. The choice of J79 engines was confirmed and the under-wing hardpoints retained giving a most impressive attack capability that would be better than most of the aircraft designed for the role. The designation was changed to F4H and prototypes were ordered in May 1955. The production specification was accepted in July 1955, only weeks after the one-hour meeting, a major achievement when one considers the complexity of the design. The first XF4H-1 flew at Edwards Air Force Base in California in May 1958. Official recognition brought the Phantom into a more normal US procurement regime and the USN placed a competitive contract with Chance Vought, both as insurance against technical failure of the F4H and to examine a different engineering solution to the same staff requirement. The resulting rival design was the XF8U-3 Crusader III which fell short of the F4H's armament and radius of action. A Navy preliminary evaluation confirmed the Phantom's superiority but it is a measure of the strength of the US aircraft industry in the 1950s that a design as good as the XF8U-3 could be rejected and not put into production. Twenty-three development and twenty-four production Phantoms were ordered in December 1958 and, during the course of development flying, the aircraft was found to have such exceptional performance that the USN decided to attempt a number of world records with production aircraft. Among those successfully captured were records for absolute height, times to various heights, 310-mile (500km) and 62-mile (100km) closed circuits, low-altitude and absolute air speed records. The aircraft were standard Phantoms except for the aircraft that won the absolute speed record which was fitted with a water-injection system to cool the incoming air ahead of the compressors. The first operational Phantoms were delivered to US Navy squadron VF-101, the 'Grim Reapers', in 1960.

By 1961 the USAF was forced to take notice of the F4H and carried out a series of competitive evaluations against a range of aircraft types in its own inventory. They found that the F4H was a better interceptor and carried a bigger weapon load further than any tactical aircraft in the Air Force. It had clear potential as a tactical reconnaissance aircraft and demonstrated better serviceability, in terms of maintenance hours per flying hour, than any of the aircraft it was evaluated against. A decision was taken to procure the Phantom as the principle weapons system of Tactical Air Command (TAC). At first it was given the USAF designation F-110A[44] but when the standardised Department of Defence designation system was introduced in 1962 the designation F-4 was adopted by all three US armed services that operated the type; the early Navy and Marine Corps versions were designated as the F-4A and F-4B. The first USAF variant was the F-4C, a minimal-change version of the 'B'. The electrifying performance of the Phantom clearly gave it export potential, it was exactly what the RN wanted as a Sea Vixen replacement and the Admiralty lobbied hard to get it throughout 1963. When the British Government finally relented in 1964 and cancelled the RN version of the P 1154,[45] an agreement was reached to procure 140 Phantoms directly from McDonnell at a cost initially estimated at £45 million for the first batch of sixty aircraft. By 1964 the USN was funding the development of an improved, F-4J, version of the Phantom and this would have been the logical choice for the RN, procured 'off the shelf' with minimal development cost. Even this simple logic proved too difficult, however, and the same Government that had cancelled projects and run down the aviation industry now insisted that British firms participate in the Phantom project. Rolls-Royce had proposed a Spey-powered F-4 for the US armed forces in 1962 but McDonnell had dismissed the concept as being too expensive and complicated to implement for the theoretical benefits that might accrue. Now, however, Rolls-Royce managed to convince the Ministry of Aviation that Speys would give increased power to facilitate Phantom operations from the smaller decks of British carriers. Re-heated Speys of a new design that had never been tested or flown were specified for the British Phantom which was designated the F-4K by the US authorities. The USN sponsored Westinghouse AN/AWG-10 pulse-doppler radar designed for the F-4J was built under a licence agreement in the UK by Ferranti as the AN/AWG-11 and most of the cockpit avionics were of British manufacture. The outer wings were constructed by Shorts at their Belfast factory and the rear fuselage and tailplane were made by the British Aircraft Corporation at Preston. In all, about half the aircraft content and structure was British but all the components were flown to St Louis for assembly, adding to the higher unit price tag for the F-4K when compared with a F-4J.[46] The Spey was heavier, wider, but shorter than the J-79 and their installation meant that the entire after fuselage had to be re-

A close-up photograph of an RN trial Phantom crossing *Eagle*'s round-down. Its hook is up so the aircraft is going to do a touch-and-go roller landing. (Author's collection)

designed; the revised shape greatly increased airframe drag and was to lead to a lower overall performance than the F-4J. The Speys also needed intakes that were 20 per cent bigger than those in the US-engined aircraft to cope with the greater mass flow of air they required, contributing yet more to the increased drag.[47] Although the standard Spey 101 turbofan had proved a great success in the Buccaneer S 2, Rolls-Royce found a reliable, reheated derivative extremely difficult to achieve and this caused delays and further increases in cost. Engaging reheat quickly for a carrier overshoot proved particularly difficult and a special variant, the Spey 203 with fast light-up augmentation, had to be developed before the F-4K could be cleared for carrier operation. Even when the aircraft, designated the Phantom FG 1 in UK service, was cleared for use an engine life as little as 20 hours was not uncommon and there were frequent failures.[48]

Apart from its engines, the RN Phantom had several other unique features. The Spey nozzles were nearer the fuselage skin and hotter than those of the J-79 so titanium had to be used extensively on the after fuselage to prevent it, literally, from melting. The USN F-4J had a nose oleo that extended by 20in to give an optimal

A Phantom FG 1 of 892 NAS from *Ark Royal* firing an AIM-9 Sidewinder air-to-air missile. (Author's collection)

attitude during catapult launch. To improve the performance off the shorter British catapults the F-4K doubled that extension to 40in, reducing the end-speed required by 10 knots. Like the Buccaneer, the British Phantom had 'blown' flaps and drooped ailerons but it also had a tailplane with an inverted slat on the leading edge to optimise airflow over it and, hence, its performance. All of these modifications increased the airframe weight and British Phantoms had to have stronger undercarriages than all other Phantom versions and stronger tail-hooks than the USN versions. The unit cost of a Phantom FG 1 had to include the cost of all this development which was unique to the UK requirement and by 1968 it was more than double that of an F-4J. One of the arguments in favour of fitting Speys was to allow the type to operate from relatively small British carriers but subsequent calculation showed that Phantoms could never realistically have operated from *Hermes*. To 'rub salt' into this self-inflicted wound, standard USN F-4Js could, and often did during cross-deck operations in exercises, launch and recover to *Ark Royal* and *Eagle* with no problem. For all the extra cost and the delay, the RN ended up with a Sea Vixen replacement which was more expensive than it need have been, with less performance than the USN version but with slightly greater endurance.

Originally the RN planned to commission five Phantom FG 1 NASs as one-for-one replacements for the Sea Vixen but the government decision to cancel CVA-01 in 1966 and the subsequent decision to run down the carrier force reduced this number drastically. The order for them was reduced to fifty-two but twenty-eight of these were diverted to the RAF and only twenty-four ever entered service with the RN. Despite its over-complicated and muddled background the aircraft was a success in service and represented a huge improvement over its predecessor. It must be admitted, however, that even this remarkable aircraft did not meet the full AW 406 requirement but since the supersonic Soviet bombers predicted by the intelligence community never materialised this proved not to be such a problem as it might have been. The first aircraft arrived at the Fighter School at RNAS Yeovilton on 25 April 1968, a great achievement by McDonnell considering the changes they had been forced to make to their design. *Ark Royal* had not completed her modernisation when 892 NAS worked up and so the unit embarked in the USS *Saratoga* in the Mediterranean for a week during October 1969,[49] demonstrating the continuing ability of the two navies to work closely together. Throughout the F-4K project the USN had done a lot to help; a number of pilots and observers had been sent to the US to fly in US Navy Phantom units and gain experience on the type, a practical form of help that was to be repeated fifty years later by a new generation.

In the end three naval air squadrons operated the Phantom; 700P the IFTU, 767 the training unit at Yeovilton and 892 which embarked in the rebuilt *Ark Royal*. 892 NAS commissioned in March 1969 and its aircraft featured a large omega on their tails because they were expected to be the last fighter squadron to form for the RN. It operated from *Ark Royal* until she was withdrawn from service in 1978 and 892 Phantoms were frequently photographed intercepting Soviet naval bombers over the Atlantic and Mediterranean during NATO exercises. The type's ability to carry four radar-guided Sparrow in addition to four infrared-guided air-to-air missiles and a wide range of strike weapons gave it a unique edge over all other fighters. On CAP it could engage multiple targets before having to return to the carrier to re-arm and on strike missions it could defend both itself and the Buccaneers against sophisticated opposition. The Phantom FG 1 was 'wired' to carry the WE 177 tactical nuclear bomb and Bullpup air-to-surface missiles and at night it could carry Lepus flares and rockets or bombs to attack targets they illuminated. It was arguably the most capable fighter operated by the RN in its first century of fighter operations. Of interest, the arguments over aircraft procurement led the RAF to take a fundamental look at the aircraft it needed to replace the obsolescent force of Hunters and Canberras in its tactical squadrons. The Phantom was in service with the USAF Tactical Air Command and was now on order for the RN. Suddenly the day fighter/ground attack community's insistence on a simple NBMR 3 type of aircraft in 1963 seemed a very dated concept and when the P 1154 was finally cancelled in 1965 the RAF obtained approval to procure a Spey-powered F-4 similar to the F-4K but without the carrier operating features. It was designated

Some, but by no means all, of the weapons that could be carried by the Phantom FG 1. Sparrow and Sidewinder air-to-air missiles, 750lb bombs and 2in rocket projectiles are visible in this photograph of a 767 NAS aircraft at RNAS Yeovilton. (Author's collection)

the F-4M and aircraft began to arrive in the UK in 1968. The RN and RAF were, thus, both operating a common strike fighter that suited both their needs and proved a success in service. What a tragedy that the politicians had insisted on a completely unsuitable design in the first place and had not studied what industry had to offer. The Ministry of Aviation's role in the P 1154 saga caused it to suffer a loss of government confidence from which it was never to recover.[50]

Lessons Learned

The harsh truth at the root of this troubled period was that after the 1957 Defence Review the Government had adopted a holistic view of defence in which it had assumed that the RAF had the most experience of air matters and, thus, the best advice to give. Unfortunately for the other two services, this was not the case and this metonymy[51] led to both the RN and Army being severely hampered in their ability to carry out the tasks successive governments expected them to fulfil. The Air Staff still worked in very compartmentalised 'role shops' that lacked the vision to look at aviation as a whole and found it difficult to think in terms of how things might be done rather than how they 'always had been done'. Realisation that the Phantom was a better aircraft, after the Navy bought it, eventually drew them into a more rational approach but by then it was too late to achieve what should have

A Phantom at the moment of launch from *Ark Royal*. Note the Wessex HAR 1 plane-guard helicopter hovering alongside. (Author's collection)

been the aim in the first place. Ralph Hooper had put his finger right on the problem in April 1962 when he observed that a production run of fifty to seventy aircraft for the RN was not a big enough project to justify the cost of design and development. What the Navy needed was a partner able to share the risk and cost of a larger production run. This so nearly happened with the Saunders Roe SR-177 because the RAF fighter community saw the aircraft as a single-role aircraft that fitted their limited requirement. It had happened with the Westland Wessex and a number of aircraft weapon projects. It had failed completely with the Hawker Siddeley P 1154 because the RAF day fighter/ground attack community could see nothing outside a basic Hunter replacement and the Air Staff were happy to follow a political lead with a small procurement that might lead to export orders for British industry. Basically the RN had wanted a good all-round fighter to meet the AW 406 Requirement that had been agreed by the Chiefs of Staff. The USN had been astute enough to seize the opportunity to procure just such an aircraft from McDonnell but the RN no longer had the luxury to 'go it alone' like that after 1957. It was actually very lucky to get the Buccaneer and had the Admiralty not 'frozen' the design to meet the tight deadline, it might well have been cancelled by uncomprehending politicians. The RN and RAF could both have had F-4Js at a fraction of the cost of the Spey-powered Phantom if more sensible views had prevailed in Whitehall or even a British equivalent. The Air Staff had taken a very narrow view of its close-support requirement and failed to act responsibly when told to act as a partner by government. This was not the first time and nor was it to be the last; as in the Second World War when the RN found itself isolated in seeking the carrier-borne aircraft it needed, it had turned to the USN and found a partner that was willing and able to help.

The other lesson was that the Ministry of Aviation had become too focused on its own development projects and was no longer listening to or advising the armed services in the way that it should. Having evolved from the Ministries of Aircraft Production and then Supply, it was supposed to provide aircraft to meet operational specifications, not dictate what was to be built to explore technology or win export orders. Mountbatten's suggestion that NBMR 3 might be a quick way to get a supersonic fighter to sea proved to have unfortunate consequences and must, with the wisdom of hindsight, be seen as ill-considered. The Naval Staff which had done so well to focus on the strike fleet's ability to counter outbreaks of local conflict and stimulate political enthusiasm for strike carriers, commando carriers and their supporting task forces which were at constant readiness had found itself mired in a bruising political argument about equipment replacement.

A Phantom of 892 NAS ready to launch from *Ark Royal*'s waist catapult with the full 40in nose oleo extension. Note the water-cooled jet blast deflector aft of the aircraft and the flight deck officer with his flag raised ready to order the launch. (Author's collection)

12 Brunei and the Indonesian Confrontation

From the late 1950s the Royal Navy changed the way in which aircraft carriers and other types of warship were commissioned and deployed. Before these changes ships were manned by sailors from the port divisions at Devonport, Portsmouth and Chatham; Fleet Air Arm ratings were drafted to appropriate ships from the FAA Barracks at RNAS Lee-on-Solent near Gosport. This system was time-honoured but wasteful in that each barracks had to retain a pool of manpower and training facilities to ensure that men of the correct skills were available when needed. The ships in commission were allocated to specific fleets for their time in commission, usually about two years, and operated with other ships from that fleet's main base, with Malta and Singapore being typical examples. At the end of a commission the ship would return to its UK base port for refit and its ship's company would be dispersed to the barracks for training, advancement and re-drafting. After the refit a completely new ship's company would be formed to work the ship up to operational efficiency from scratch. Similar methods were used to commission naval air squadrons for a particular carrier commission and they would be de-commissioned when the carrier went into refit.

After the series of defence reviews described above, manpower economies had to be found and more efficient methods of operating the strike fleet brought into use. The first major change was the general service commission in which carriers would spend time with the Home, Mediterranean and Far East Fleets during a single commission. With the reduced number of carriers available and the Government directive that one was to be constantly available in the Far East to give stability at a time when an increasing number of British colonies were being granted independence, this meant that individual carrier programmes had to be tightly interlocked. A typical carrier would commission in the UK, take part in a NATO exercise after successfully completing its operational readiness inspection (ORI), move to the Far East for a period of about nine months and then, once relieved, operate west of Suez until its next refit was due. Typically, the hand-over between carriers on task in the Far East took place off Aden. This new system had the merit that ships and their air groups became familiar with their likely areas of operation throughout the world without spending an inordinate length of time away from home. It was the capability that remained in a specified area, not necessarily the same ship for long periods. From a joint operations perspective, however, this new method of operation proved difficult for the other two Services to comprehend. The Army and RAF retained a fixed-base mentality with small garrisons of British power in such places as Gibraltar, Malta, Aden, Bahrain, Singapore and Hong Kong. In each of these a small number of static Army and RAF units spent long periods 'under orders' to defend the base, supported in some cases by a flotilla of mine-countermeasures vessels and patrol boats. A carrier task force would visit the base every few months for exercises with the garrison but military officers ashore feared that if the carrier was absent it would not be available if the base were to be threatened. This mentality can best be described a feeling that only fixed defences manned by a permanent garrison under orders could be relied upon for the defence of a specific place. It ran completely contrary to the Government's new policy of mobility and reduced reliance on fixed bases and is worth mentioning because it is a feeling that is still, surprisingly, detectable in senior Army and RAF officers in the second decade of the twenty-first century. The decades that British troops have remained in Germany after the end of the Cold War despite cuts to make 'peace dividend' savings are a case in point that I find difficult to understand. Other changes in the way ships were manned soon followed and centralised drafting replaced port drafting with a single pool of manpower administered by the Commodore Naval Drafting (CND), who had his headquarters in Haslemere[1] and ensured that adequate trained manpower was available for ships as they commissioned. With no requirement to maintain separate schools at Devonport and Chatham, these were closed, leaving only the main gunnery, torpedo, radar plot/direction and communications training establishments around Portsmouth. Another change soon followed in the early 1960s which had been enabled by centralised drafting; this was the 'trickle draft' in which ships no longer commissioned for set periods but remained in commission for considerably longer periods, even during a small refit. Instead of the whole ship's company leaving at the end of two years, small groups changed every few months but never more than one third of the total. Critics were quick to point out that this might prevent ships from maintaining peak efficiency but on the other hand they had to concede that they would never have to start from scratch with an entirely new team. Newcomers were rapidly assimilated into the ship's company and able to 'find their feet' more quickly and effectively. Overall the system worked well. The need to integrate carrier programmes to ensure that they all reached a common standard of operation and were in the right place at the right time needed the concentrated effort of a single staff and so flag officers 'Air' in the various fleets were replaced by a single FOAC, with a headquarters at Fort Southwick just outside Portsmouth. A permanent staff here worked out the carrier programme to meet Government and Admiralty requirements and FOAC himself embarked when necessary to command carrier task forces in operations and to conduct ORIs when necessary. Liaison with the staff of the Flag Officer Naval Flying Training (FONFT), at RNAS Yeovilton was necessary to ensure the flow of trained and worked-up naval air squadrons to the carriers as they came out of the refit cycle. The new system worked well but the emergence of the two commando carriers after 1960 added to the amount of staff planning required since one of these had to be permanently available in the FEF and the staff of the Commandant General Royal Marines (CGRM), had to ensure that a full Commando with its supporting arms had to be available for the deployed ship. Unlike the conventional carriers, commando carriers were not declared to NATO in their amphibious role and so the two ships worked watch and watch about in the Far East to ensure that one was always available at need. This commitment and the ships' ability to meet it was soon to be tested.

HMS *Albion*

The second commando carrier, *Albion*, was commissioned in Portsmouth Naval Base on 1 August 1962 in the presence of HRH Prince Philip, Duke of Edinburgh. She sailed on 7 August to begin her work-up with 845 (Wessex HAS 1s) and 846 (Whirlwind HAS 7s) embarked, both of which had sand-coloured camouflage and operated with their sonar equipment removed in the commando-assault role. She sailed for the Far East on 3 November 1962 with 41 RM Commando embarked in addition to the squadrons. The opportunity was taken to take part in Exercise 'Sandfly' in the Homs region of Libya with the local British garrison, during which 846 NAS disembarked to operate from a forward operating base (FOB) ashore. 845 NAS carried out a number of live firings with Nord SS11 wire-guided anti-tank missiles and became competent with these and both fixed and door-mounted machine guns in the defence-suppression role. After passing through the Suez Canal and arriving in Aden, *Albion* relieved *Bulwark* as the commando carrier on station[2] and exchanged 40 RM Commando for 41 besides taking over several tons of operational stores and ammunition. *Bulwark* then sailed for the UK to give Christmas leave. Another training period, Exercise 'First Call', followed in the area 60 miles north of Mombasa. 40 Commando was new to the role of helicopter-borne assault and intensive training soon brought the unit up to the required standard. Again 846 NAS disembarked to a FOB 12nm north-west of Malindi and were used as 'pathfinders' for the Wessex, tactical troop lifts and reconnaissance. After that *Albion* sailed to Mombasa for a planned visit which ended on 5 December 1962 when she sailed for Singapore.

The Brunei Insurrection, 1962

In 1961 Tunku Abdul Rahman, the Prime Minister of Malaya, which had gained its independence from Great Britain in 1957, proposed the formation of an economic and political union comprising Malaya, Singapore,[3] North Borneo, Brunei and Sarawak. President Sukarno of Indonesia had wanted to absorb these territories into a confederation of Indonesian states, however, and funded organisations that opposed the establishment of Malaysia. On 8 December 1962 the 4000-strong North Kalimantan National Army (NKNA), which was backed by Indonesia, launched an insurrection in Brunei[4] under its leader Yassin Affendi. They seized the British Resident and his staff at Limbang in Sarawak and attacked the Sultan of Brunei's palace as well as several centres of population including Tutong, Seria, Bangar and several oilfields. The British commander in the area, Major General Walter Walker, responded immediately by flying a Gurkha unit from Singapore to Brunei City where they engaged the NKNA, taking 800 prisoners for the loss of one officer killed and seven Gurkhas wounded. HQ 3 Commando Brigade in Singapore reacted by flying in 'L' Company of 42 RM Commando to Brunei where it arrived on 10 December under the command of Captain Jeremy Moore MC RM. On arrival they were ordered to proceed up-river to rescue the British hostages in Limbang. Two minesweepers, *Fiskerton* and *Chawton*, from 6 MS in Singapore under Lieutenant Commander Jeremy Black RN had arrived with two requisitioned flat-bottomed lighters which were used to transport the marines up-river. At dawn on 13 December they attacked the NKNA positions on the waterfront and in the main street and managed to rescue all the hostages for the loss of five Royal Marines killed and seven wounded. Thirty-five NKNA soldiers were killed and many more wounded or taken prisoner. Other British movements followed quickly. The destroyer *Cavalier* embarked troops from the Queen's Own Highlanders in Singapore, and after a high-speed passage, landed them in Labuan where they took control of Seria. The minesweepers *Wilkieston* and *Woolaston* supported by *Woodbridge Haven* provided a presence at Kuching in Sarawak and the RFAs *Gold Ranger* and *Wave Sovereign* fulfilled the same function in Labuan. The remainder of 42 Commando liberated Bangar when it arrived but unfortunately by then six hostages had been beheaded by the rebels. The cruiser *Tiger* landed a battalion of the Royal Green Jackets and other reinforcements were brought in by the despatch vessel *Alert*.

On 9 December 1962 *Albion* was ordered to increase speed and proceed to Singapore with all despatch. She arrived at 16.30 on 13 December and immediately took on fuel, stores and ammunition; she embarked HQ 3 Commando Brigade and disembarked 29 Commando Regiment RA since there was no perceived role for them in Brunei. She sailed at 21.30, arrived off Kuching on the afternoon of the following day[5] and flew 40 Commando ashore. Stores, vehicles and ammunition were ferried ashore using *Albion*'s four assault landing craft, the *Alert* and a collection of local small craft that were quickly requisitioned for the purpose. For the next three weeks *Albion* steamed at high speed up and down the coast of Northern Borneo, using her helicopters to provide reconnaissance information, tactical troop-lift, food, stores and ammunition for the troops ashore. The squadron maintenance personnel, supported by the ship's Air Engineering Department (AED), worked around the clock to keep the helicopters serviceable and in operation. On 15 December 1962 all six Whirlwinds of 846 NAS were disembarked to Brunei and *Albion*'s RM landing craft unit, 9 Assault Squadron RM, was deployed to ferry stores and ammunition up rivers to sustain inland operations. 845 NAS Wessex moved Commandos, Gurkhas and other troops rapidly about the country searching for the NKNA.

845 and 846 NAS lifted a variety of troops from RM Commandos to Gurkhas; many of the latter had no previous experience of helicopter-borne operations and had to be instructed quickly and carefully in technique, tactics and safety precautions. Stores flown ashore ranged from fuel to food, bullets to beer and everything in between. Large numbers of captured insurgents were flown out to the ship, including dead and wounded to be processed. Several of the latter underwent surgery in the ship's operating theatre. One Whirlwind pilot had fifteen rebels stand up and surrender as he flew over them, a situation that had not been covered in his prior training; he landed, had them disarmed and arranged for them to be returned to the ship and processed. Two Whirlwinds were damaged while operating ashore; one hit a tree with its tail rotor while landing in a clearing and the other crashed in a paddy field after an engine failure. Both aircraft were stripped and then lifted out by RAF Belvedere helicopters of 66 Squadron, first to Brunei airstrip and then out to *Albion*. Over the Christmas period 845 NAS Wessex helicopters flew Christmas dinners to the Commandos and 846 NAS ashore. A number of Christmas cakes were baked and delivered to every British unit ashore. On 5 January 1963 *Albion* re-embarked 846 NAS and 40 RM Commando and disembarked six Wessex of 845 NAS to Labuan and on 8 January she left the Borneo coast for a short self-maintenance period in Singapore Dockyard.

By the end of December 1962 Royal Marines and other troops operating as small search and strike teams had killed forty NKNA insurgents and captured 3500 more. *Albion*'s helicopters, later supplemented by RAF helicopters based ashore, proved to be a key factor in providing forces on the ground with eyes, tactical mobility and firepower and the ship itself had proved to be a vital factor in providing land forces with logistic support. Conceived as an assault ship along the lines pioneered by *Ocean* and *Theseus* at Suez, *Albion* had proved, like her sister-ship *Bulwark* in

Kuwait, to be far more capable than that and had become an essential element of the UK's rapid reaction forces. Most of the insurgents were located and arrested by April 1963 and their leader Affendi himself was found in a hiding place near Limbang on 18 May. His capture effectively ended this 'brushfire' conflict and showed just how effective the UK's new maritime strike fleet was in bringing force to bear quickly from the sea.

The Confrontation with Indonesia, 1963–1966

In January 1957 the UK signed the Anglo-Malayan Defence Treaty which committed it to the external defence of the former colony.[6] This commitment continued into 1963 when it became obvious that there would be substantial Indonesian opposition to the formation of Malaysia, a union between Malaya and the former British territories in Borneo. Tension was heightened by the transfer to Indonesia by the Soviet Union of the *Sverdlov* class cruiser *Ordzhonikidze* in October 1962. She was re-named *Irian* and the Indonesian Deputy Chief of Naval Staff spoke confidently about the prospect of a second cruiser being transferred and a third being converted into an aircraft carrier in a Soviet shipyard.[7] The later transfers never happened but two 'Riga' class frigates were transferred with *Irian* to supplement five *Skoryi* class destroyers and six 'W' class submarines that had been purchased from Poland in 1959. The Indonesian Naval Air Arm had a single squadron of Gannet AS 4 anti-submarine strike aircraft but in any conflict with the UK could not expect to obtain spares or support for them. The Air Force had also been re-equipped with a substantial number of Soviet aircraft obtained at bargain prices. These included MiG-17, 19 and 21 fighters, Ilyushin Il-28 and Tupolev Tu-16 bombers and a number of transport aircraft and helicopters. The purchase price had not included spares backing and only limited training support with the result that aircraft had to be 'cannibalised' for spares and few could be maintained in any sort of operational condition.[8] The problem was exacerbated by the number of different types in service, including ex-American P-51D Mustang fighters and B-26 Invader bombers, and the distances between various bases.

While steps towards the formal creation of Malaysia took place in London and Kuala Lumpur, the Indonesian Government announced a policy of 'Confrontation' against the new state on 20 January 1963.[9] As the British forces ended the insurrection in Brunei, regular Indonesian Army units began raids against Sarawak and Sabah in North Borneo. After delays to allow the UN to conduct referenda in Sarawak and Sabah, the Federation of Malaysia formally came into being on 16 September 1963 as a democratic monarchy under the Yang di-Pertuan Agong as Head of State. *Albion* had continued to operate off the coast of Borneo as a floating logistic base for British operations and in addition to rotating the Royal Marines of 40 and 42 Commandos into the front line, she deployed the 2/10th battalion of the Gurkha Rifles to Borneo. Other military units including the SAS saw action but the Royal Marines and Gurkhas bore the brunt of the fighting along the jungle border supported by *Albion*'s two helicopter squadrons which gave them the mobility the enemy did not have. The Confrontation had occasional flashpoints such as an attack by the Indonesian Army on Tebedu, the capital of Sarawak, in April 1963 in which several policemen were killed in their police station and an attack on a frontier post in June during which five Gurkhas were killed. Overall, however, confrontation became a war of infiltration, patrol and ambush. The threat to Singapore and the Malay peninsula was countered by a layered defence with minesweepers and other inshore vessels backed up by larger warships. The FEF was reinforced to deter any attempt by the Indonesians to use their Navy in support of amphibious assaults on Malaysia or British bases and at one point in 1963 *Ark Royal*, *Hermes* and *Centaur* were all in the Far East. A series of large Commonwealth naval exercises in the 'Jet' and 'Fotex' series added HMAS *Melbourne* to the strike fleet's potential and deterred the Indonesian Navy from playing any serious part in the Confrontation. 'Fotex 63' was the largest gathering of Commonwealth warships for a single purpose since the Korean War. As the new state of Malaysia came into being Indonesian mobs attacked British citizens in Jakarta and the British embassy was destroyed by fire.[10] In response Western aid was suspended and President Sukarno sought assistance from Communist China. 845 and 846 NAS rotated their aircraft and aircrew through long-standing detachments at Sibu and Nangga Gaat. By June 1963 they had completed 3500 operational sorties. Indonesian raids were launched against Malaysia by sea and air; those by sea were almost all detected, intercepted and driven off. Indonesian paratroops dropped into Malaysia were rounded up with relative ease, arrested and interned. General walker was appointed as the Joint Director of Operations in Borneo and routinely had two naval helicopter squadrons and six minesweepers under his command. He decided that the increased level of enemy violence required further British reinforcement in Borneo and *Albion* showed another facet of her usefulness by making a fast passage to Tobruk where she embarked RAF Belvedere and Whirlwind helicopters and ferried them quickly to Singapore where they were prepared for operational service, another example of the RAF relying on a carrier to get its aircraft into action in a timely manner. While she was in the naval base unloading them Indonesian forces attacked Long Jawi in Sarawak. *Albion* sailed immediately and as soon as the Wessex detachment of 845 NAS was in range they were flown ashore to pick up sticks of Gurkhas which were taken to Long Jawi. They took the Indonesians completely by surprise and in the ensuing battle over forty of the enemy were killed and the remainder captured. Whirlwinds of 846 NAS based ashore carried out an assault with Gurkhas that defeated an Indonesian attack on Simanggang. By November the six Whirlwinds of 846 NAS had flown 3184 operational sorties in Borneo. In early 1964 *Albion* was relieved in the FEF by *Bulwark* but some of her helicopters remained in theatre.

The Passage of the Lombok Strait

In September 1964 *Victorious* visited Western Australia with her escort destroyers *Cavendish* and *Caesar* and COMFEF decided to make a further statement of British resolve by sailing her back to Singapore through the narrow Lombok Strait east of Bali. This would have the double benefit of demonstrating the 'right of innocent passage' through international waters and showing that the RN was confident it could deal with any threat the Indonesian Navy and Air Force might try to mount against it. Before the passage the guided-missile destroyer *Hampshire* and the frigates *Dido* and *Berwick* joined the task force and when the passage was made on 12 September the ships were at action stations with guns manned and loaded. The Indonesian Navy tried to block the passage by declaring that naval exercises were to take place in the strait but in the event *Victorious* and her consorts passed through unchallenged. An Indonesian submarine was seen on the surface and gun crews were ordered to open fire if it showed any hostile intent but it tactfully exchanged identities and wished the British force good day. The strike fleet had emphasised its complete dominance over the Indonesian fleet and, in doing so, had deterred the enemy from escalating the conflict any further. By the end of 1964 the Indonesians were estimated to have 22,000 men on the Malaysian border in Borneo but General Walker obtained political authority to launch operations across the border 'in hot pursuit' of the enemy. The enemy were taken completely by surprise and began to scale back operations after a series of defeats. Although the Confrontation did not finally end until 1966, British victory was never in doubt. The whole thing had been kept below the level of all-out conflict by the powerful presence of the British strike fleet and the number of Royal Marines and other forces on the ground had been kept low by the mobility and logistical support given to them by the commando carriers. In a speech to the House of Commons after the Confrontation, Dennis Healey the Defence Secretary claimed that its successful termination would be recorded in history 'as one of the most efficient uses of military force in the history of the world'.[11]

846 NAS in Borneo

846 NAS disembarked to Kuching on 15 December 1962 and spent much of the next year ashore in Borneo, alternating with rest periods at RNAS Sembawang in Singapore. Its bases during the period were:

Wessex HU 5 'G' of 848 NAS from *Albion* lifting off after landing a Gurkha patrol on a hilltop landing pad in Borneo built by Royal Engineers. (Author's collection)

15 December 1962	Kuching
5 January 1963	*Albion*
10 January 1963	Sembawang
1 February 1963	*Albion*
7 February 1963	Labuan
20 February 1963	*Albion*
19 March 1963	Brunei Airport

13 April 1963	Kuching
18 May 1963	Sembawang
1 June 1963	Kuching
30 June 1963	*Albion*
19 August 1963	Kuching
10 November 1963	*Albion*
22 December 1963	Kai Tak
12 January 1964	Tawau
12 October 1964	*Bulwark*
19 October 1964	Disbanded at RNAS Sembawang[12]

The squadron's operations ashore were packed with incident and operating an obsolescent helicopter with a single piston engine over the jungle was not without danger, regardless of the enemy's actions. On one occasion the Senior Pilot, Lieutenant Commander P J Williams RN, with Lieutenant D M Carr RN as his number 2 was carrying out a routine stores lift between Tepoi and Tebedu when three Indonesian aircraft were seen. A single B-25 Mitchell bomber flew over the helicopters at about 1000ft and two P-51 Mustang fighters carried out a series of dives over the jungle; as the helicopters emerged out of a mountain pass the Indonesians saw them and immediately retreated across the border. The Whirlwind's cartridge starter system was notoriously unreliable and had, frequently, to be changed. One detachment managed to start aircraft 'O' on three occasions by hand-turning the engine until it fired like a wartime Swordfish. In another incident involving the Senior Pilot, his aircraft lost power while he was roping a patrol of Gurkhas into an ambush position on top of a ridge. The aircraft sank to the ground and, fortunately, a tree stump became imbedded in the base of the engine which prevented the aircraft from rolling down the steep slope.[13] A second aircraft was close by, also roping down Gurkhas, and Lieutenant Commander Williams managed climb up the rope into the cabin, no mean achievement, and fly back to base where he organised a salvage effort. The next day an engineering team was roped down which stripped the aircraft, the rotor head and other components being winched out by other Whirlwinds. Once it was light enough the aircraft was lifted out by an RAF Belvedere helicopter of 66 Squadron which took it to Engkillili where it was repaired by squadron mechanics in only 70 hours. Many of the sorties flown by 846 NAS were medical evacuations to Kuching hospital in support of the local population which remained staunchly opposed to Indonesia. These included a number of pregnant women and this 'hearts and minds' effort played its part in defeating the confrontation. 846 NAS was eventually replaced in Borneo by an RAF Whirlwind unit.

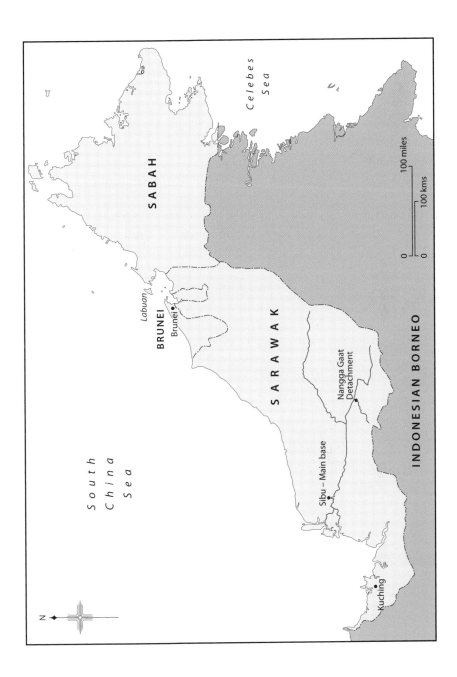

The operational area in North Borneo during Confrontation.

RNAS Nangga Gaat

Situated at the junction of the Gaat and Baleh rivers, the RN FOB at Nangga Gaat was 35nm up-river from Kapit from where an adequate supply of fuel and supplies were brought daily by longboat. The area was cleared of trees by Gurkha engineers and 845 NAS personnel; helicopters from the base were able to cover the whole flying task for the eastern half of Sarawak's Third Division, the western half being covered from the civil airport at Sibu. Squadron personnel lived in bamboo and atap long-huts like those used by the Iban natives which proved to be surprisingly comfortable. At first cooking was carried out over wood fires and washing was done in the river but the Gurkha engineers made continuous improvements which eventually included showers and semi-permanent field kitchens. The base also boasted the Anchor Inn, claimed to be the only 'authentic' British pub in Borneo[14] which did a roaring trade every night filled with 845 NAS personnel, Ibans and Gurkhas. The sailors tended to wear sarongs in the evening, Ibans wore shorts and

An aerial view of the RN FOB at Nangga Gaat in Borneo with Wessex HAS 1s of 845 NAS on three spots and a fourth Wessex approaching along the river to land on the vacant spot. Note the number of trees that have been felled by Gurkha engineers to make helicopter operations at the base safe. (Author's collection)

Gurkhas could be identified by their lack of tattoos. 'The Gaat', as it was known, had a supply of electricity, generously provided from his generator by the Temong-Gong Jugah, paramount chief of the Ibans. This allowed frequent film shows with the very latest titles[15] despatched by the FEF to maintain morale. The Far East premiere of the James Bond film *From Russia With Love* took place in the Anchor Inn on Christmas Eve 1963 to an appreciative audience of sailors, Ibans and Gurkhas. At first Nangga Gaat was expected to be a temporary facility but as it became obvious that confrontation would continue for some time, a series of improvements were made. I have never met anyone who served there who does not look back on the experience with nostalgia and enormous pride in a job well done.

845 NAS in Borneo

When *Albion* returned to Singapore at the end of the Brunei rebellion, half of 845 NAS's aircraft were left in Borneo and lessons were learned about how to man and operate a commando squadron that still have value in the second decade of the twenty-first century. Fortunately, when it re-commissioned as a commando helicopter unit in April 1962 the manpower allocated to 845 NAS had taken into account the likely need to operate remote detachments ashore with a fair degree of autonomy. Planning was based on basic flights of four aircraft since it was considered unlikely that fewer aircraft would operate on their own for long periods and the need for larger numbers could be extrapolated upwards from the basic numbers.[16] Each detachment was treated as a mini-squadron with its own senior rates in each technical branch, a detachment CPO, domestic and technical stores rates and regulators. A technical officer, answering to the detachment commander was responsible for aircraft maintenance, stores backing and the ratings' divisional work. Since the detachments would have to look after themselves, it was appreciated from the outset that the squadron needed to include cooks, sick berth attendants, writers, a photographer and aircraft handlers to move aircraft and operate the unit vehicles. The whole squadron was trained in the use of small arms and was to be capable of defending its FOB against light scales of enemy attack but an infantry unit was usually close by to defend against enemy attacks in strength across the border. Surprisingly, in 1963–4 there was no formalised commando aircrewman branch and squadron personnel were trained 'on the job' to take charge of the troops, passengers and stores that occupied the rear cabin. This was soon recognised as an oversight and a more formalised Aircrewman Branch was introduced.

Ideally there should have been a complete outfit of spare parts and equipment for every detachment but this never proved possible due to the lack of space both ashore and on board. Communications had to be good enough to ensure that, at

Wessex HAS 1s of 845 NAS at Nangga Gaat. Note the fuel drums next to each spot to help the quick refuelling of aircraft between sorties and the large pile by the river. Fuel drums were brought up every day by lighters. (Author's collection)

all times, replacement components could be forwarded to the detachment if needed to fix unserviceable aircraft. In general, the skilled and intelligent application of what was available together with careful planning and excellent knowledge of the Wessex and its systems meant that aircraft availability in the forward detachments seldom dropped as low as 80 per cent and was usually much higher. Aircraft were divided between larger bases such as Sibu and FOBs such as Nangga Gaat and the RN flexible servicing system worked well. Each aircraft was cleared of all major servicing requirements due in the following seven days, flown to the FOB and one was brought back that required attention; there was often a daily changeover when things were running smoothly and this was used to advantage. Changeovers were arranged so that the outbound aircraft would depart in the morning and the returning aircraft fly back in the evening to provide the 'bus service' required by operations. In eighteen months of operations ashore, 845 NAS never failed to deliver a promised flight. Non-routine maintenance had to be dealt with as and when it was required and, whenever possible, the aircraft was flown out to the rear HQ. If the defect was too serious to fly with, a repair team was sent to the FOB; this had to consist of the minimum number of men to do the job and the pilots all became proficient in helping the mechanics with a range of tasks.

Perhaps the most exacting maintenance task was the replacement of an engine fuel control metering unit, something that was usually done by its manufacturer in a clinically-clean laboratory. In Borneo it was done under a parachute draped over the front of the Wessex, under which the mechanics sweated profusely. As each fuel connection was broken, the halves were blanked with polythene from old stores wrappings. Fitting the replacement took a long time because extreme care had to be taken to ensure that polythene, sand and sweat did not get into the components. After such a change a full-power engine run secured to a tie-down base was required but in 1964–5 there was no such base in Borneo. The ingenious solution to this problem was to cram the cabin full of so many sailors, Ibans and Gurkhas that the aircraft would be too heavy to lift off the ground. Engine power was increased carefully as far as the risk of ground resonance would allow and the likelihood of full power being available was assessed from performance graphs drawn from the lower range as far as it had got. The crammers were then ordered out and the pilot, encouraged by the presence of an engineer sitting next to him, took off and hovered. If this was satisfactory he made a test flight during which the

Wessex HU 5 'Q' of 848 NAS lifting off from 3 Spot at Nangga Gaat. The aircraft has weapon-carrying panniers attached by the main oleos but no weapons are fitted to them. (Author's collection)

aircraft carried out a full-power climb. The system worked well in practice and it was seldom necessary for more than a few minor adjustments to be made before the aircraft was declared serviceable.

By mid-1964 845 NAS maintained a rear link in Singapore and two detachments totalling eight aircraft in Borneo which covered about 25,000 square miles of jungle. Fleet Air Arm 'firsts' were achieved by using Wessex as 'gunships' to fire SS11 wire-guided air-to-surface missiles at enemy positions and 0.5in machine guns fitted as 'front guns' on special weapons panniers. The aircraft in Borneo had flown approximately five million passenger miles in support of Borneo operations and it was a great relief when *Bulwark* joined the FEF with the remainder of the squadron and six new Wessex to expand the size of the unit. This meant that some could take part in SEATO Exercise 'Ligtas' while the Borneo commitment was still being met. An idea of the squadron's activities is best shown by the detachment record:

2 November 1962	*Albion*
14 December 1962	Kuching
7 January 1963	*Albion*
10 January 1963	Sembawang detachment to 12 February 1963
12 February 1963	Sembawang
9 April 1963	Kuching detachment to 27 July 1963
17 April 1963	*Albion*
18 August 1963	Labuan detachment to 30 September 1963
19 August 1963	Sibu detachment to 8 September 1963
26 September 1963	Sibu detachment to 23 June 1965
30 September 1963	Kuching detachment to 15 December 1963
1 October 1963	Belaga detachment to 1 November 1963
1 November 1963	Nangga Gaat detachment to 23 June 1965
29 January 1964	*Albion*
10 March 1964	Semangyang detachment to 4 June 1964
23 June 1965	*Bulwark*
3 September 1965	RNAS Culdrose

The Role of the Commando Carrier in More Detail

The deployed power that backed up all Commonwealth operations during the Confrontation was undoubtedly the carrier task force which was always capable, if necessary, of destroying both the Indonesian fleet and shore-based air forces. Fortunately it never had to do so but the other, newer element of the RN strike fleet, the commando carrier and its helicopters, did have to operate at nearly full stretch throughout this period. From May 1964 the twin-engined Wessex HU 5, designed specifically for commando assault operations began to replace both the Wessex HAS 1 and the Whirlwind HAS 7 and proved particularly suited to the role. The Kuwait Crisis in 1961 and a series of exercises in the Mediterranean, Middle and Far East had shown how effective commando carriers were in the assault role with an embarked RM Commando but the Confrontation showed that these ships had even wider utility. As we saw in an earlier chapter, some members of the naval staff had failed to comprehend the full meaning of the post-1957 change toward a fleet capable of containing 'brushfire' wars; they had over-estimated the value of traditional warship types and underestimated the value of amphibious helicopter carriers. In part, this was probably due to an assumption that the post-colonial operations would only affect Great Britain as emerging states such as Malaysia gained their independence. In reality, the UK found that it could not just 'walk away' from responsibility and the need for forces capable of rapid intervention in situations that affected its own security and that of allies and Commonwealth partners was to continue for a considerable time. It still continues in 2015.

By 1965 the commando helicopter squadrons were large units organised into four flights. Two of these were usually committed at any one time to anti-Confrontation operations in Borneo while the remainder were embarked for use in other amphibious operations and exercises. The flights were rotated so that all pilots were kept up-to-date with the amphibious assault role as well as sharing the operational flying from Sibu and Nangga Gaat.[17] Jungle warfare was recognised as being extremely hard on all the forces committed to it and all arms were rotated out of Borneo after an average of three months' activity. Changing the infantry in the front line that frequently would have been a major logistical problem without commando ship support and these roulements came to form an important part of the commando carrier tasking, notwithstanding the fact that they often needed to be carried out in areas that were quite different from those in which the detached helicopters were operating. A comparison with the important but diverse role played by *Unicorn* during the Korean War is interesting and shows that the role of a big deck 'support-ship' in limited-war operations was an important element of fleet capability that should have been recognised earlier than it was. The two flights of Wessex HU 5s embarked in the deployed commando carrier proved capable of flying in a replacement battalion with its supporting arms and withdrawing the unit it replaced in a single day. The short voyages from and to Singapore gave the outgoing and incoming units time to focus, prepare and recover as necessary.

Another role that had not been anticipated was the movement of Army and RAF light aircraft. De Havilland Beavers of the Army Air Corps and RAF Scottish Aviation Pioneers were used extensively over areas of jungle near the border, operating from improvised clearings prepared by Army engineers. These had regularly to be exchanged with aircraft from Singapore for maintenance purposes and would have had to be dismantled, crated and shipped both ways. Instead the pilots of both Services proved able, with a little training, to land on the commando carrier and to take off, greatly easing the rotation of their aircraft and also reducing the number that needed to be available in theatre. Although it was originally presumed that only Royal Marines could operate effectively from these ships, operations in Borneo demonstrated that any Commonwealth infantry battalion could be deployed with success in low-intensity operations. *Albion* demonstrated that even a Malaysian battalion in which very few people spoke English could be deployed to a satisfactory standard after a few days training.[18] Commando carriers worked to a carefully-planned operational tempo during which they were frequently off the coast of Borneo to rotate the flights and land stores and supplies into Sibu. Tied in with this, the ships provided troop, vehicle and helicopter transport, using their assault landing craft and pontoons as well as the Wessex helicopters to embark and disembark men, equipment and vehicles; the latter including 3-ton trucks and light armoured cars. Military stores such as food, ammunition, fuel and water could be carried in considerable bulk for forward issue by helicopter to troops in the front line. Commando carriers acted as a mobile base in support of the front line, providing casualty-evacuation, medical, laundry, workshops, rest and recreation in an air-conditioned environment and a host of other facilities that could not easily be provided ashore. While concentrating on activities ashore, the commando ship was still able to support the naval task force off the coast with aircraft able to operate in the medium anti-submarine torpedo carrying helicopter (MATCH) role and against enemy fast attack craft with SS11 missiles. As in the Kuwait operation, aircraft direction and task force control were also important functions that might have to be undertaken in support of tri-Service activities for considerable periods. In late 1965 the command team in *Albion* observed that many of her activities were joint in nature and that all members of the ship's company had to understand other arms' problems and work out how best to anticipate them and provide solutions. If added justification were needed for the commando carrier concept, they felt that no other warship in peacetime was tasked so constantly in its primary operational role.

Wessex HU 5

The Wessex HU 5 differed from the HAS 1 in having two Rolls-Royce Gnome free-power turbines, each developing 1320shp and an improved transmission that allowed an increased maximum weight of 13,600lbs. It was capable of carrying up to sixteen fully-equipped marines or under-slung loads up to 3000lbs depending on the aircraft fuel state and the ambient conditions. The prototype, XS 241, first flew in May 1963 and the IFTU, 700V Flight, formed at RNAS Culdrose in December 1963. 848 NAS re-formed with the type in May 1964 and 845 operated the type from January 1966. Two other front-line RN units operated the Wessex HU 5, 846 NAS from July 1968 and 847 NAS from March 1969.

A 'posed' PR photograph showing a Wessex HAS 1 of 845 NAS over *Albion*. Other Wessex and Whirlwinds are ranged on deck. Both types were painted in a sand-coloured camouflage during the early 1960s and were identified by individual letters rather than numbers, a practice continued by the Commando Helicopter Force in the twenty-first century. (Author's collection)

Bulwark's Achievements during the Confrontation

In early 1964 *Bulwark* replaced *Albion* as the commando carrier on station in the FEF. Her roles were to provide and sustain a major contribution to the helicopter effort in support of the operations by land forces in Borneo on the frontier between Malaysia and Indonesia and, whilst doing that, to maintain the capability to embark a Royal Marines Commando and land it in the assault role at short notice. By September 1965 the ship had spent 18 months in the Far East and had steamed

Bulwark using her port crane to support the refuelling hose while she replenishes the coastal minesweeper *Woolaston* during operations off Borneo. Whirlwinds of 846 NAS are ranged on deck. (Author's collection)

83,729nm. Her helicopters had flown for 11,905 hours and carried 19,992 passengers and 1872 vehicles. In doing so they had carried out 8546 deck landings. 845 NAS reflected the two roles by maintaining seven Wessex, two Whirlwinds and a Hiller in Borneo and nine Wessex with two Hillers[19] permanently embarked in the ship.[20] The seven Wessex in Borneo supported the Second and Third Divisions of Sarawak, an area approximately the size of Scotland, flying on average 350 hours a month from the main base at Sibu and the FOB at Nangga Gaat. The ship's versatility was demonstrated in early March 1965 when she ferried twelve RAF Whirlwind helicopters, four Army Air Corps Sioux helicopters, two RAF Pioneer aircraft and Royal Engineers' plant for preparing jungle airstrips, including an earth-grader and a gravel crusher, and delivered them to various destinations in Borneo. Later in the same month she took part in the large and impressive Commonwealth Exercise 'Fotex 65' with *Victorious*, *Eagle* and *Melbourne*. A detachment of 845 NAS had operated from Nangga Gaat for over two years when 848 NAS took over from it on 23 June 1965. The Squadron was awarded the Boyd Trophy for its defence of Malaysia during 1964 but the naval personnel were particularly moved by the many gifts given to them by the native Iban people from all over the Third Division. These included home-dyed and woven blankets, beautifully-decorated parangs[21] and a delicately-carved wooden hornbill to name but a few. The Iban people also collected sufficient money from local longhouses to erect a permanent memorial to the RN personnel who had been killed defending their country against aggression and it would be fair to say that the 'hearts and minds' success of the naval helicopter squadrons played a considerable part in ensuring the successful outcome of Confrontation operations.

848 NAS Operations in Borneo

848 NAS operated ashore from Sibu and Nangga Gaat until September 1965 when RAF helicopters of 110 Squadron took over this task and 848 moved to Labuan until the end of the Confrontation in 1966. The improved lifting performance of the Wessex HU 5 and its twin-engined reliability were both found to be a great asset in jungle operations. A pattern had evolved in which two or three Wessex would leave Nangga Gaat or Sibu and proceed on a round of jungle clearings, dropping stores or radio parts, photographing an area of interest or exchanging a patrol on the ground. The increased payload allowed 848 NAS to do in a single trip, what might have taken the Wessex 1 two or more. There was a real feeling of sadness when Nangga Gaat was left for the last time since 'anyone who worked there, for however short a time, became instantly attached to the place'.[22] There was a real sense of a vital job being done efficiently under difficult circumstances and the way in which sailors 'bonded' with the local population that they were defending is

A view of the 'FOTEX 65' aircraft carriers in line taken from *Eagle*. Next astern is *Bulwark*, then HMAS *Melbourne,* then *Victorious*. Aircraft on deck in the foreground are a Sea Vixen FAW 2 of 899 NAS, Scimitar F 1s of 800B NAS and a Wessex HAS 1 of 820 NAS. (Author's collection)

particularly noteworthy. Borneo was not just one of the early successes of the British aim to contain regional conflict, it was also a role model against which other campaigns can be judged.

By the end of 1965 it was clear that the Indonesians could not hope to succeed in their original aim of toppling the new state of Malaysia but operations continued into 1966. In March of that year elements a Gurkha battalion ambushed an Indonesian force in Sarawak and captured thirty-seven of the enemy for no loss to themselves. Hostilities continued on a smaller scale right up to 11 August 1966 when Malaysia and Indonesia signed a peace treaty in Bangkok after several months of negotiation.[23] Prompt action followed by a sustained and effective presence had preserved the independence of Malaysia and, in doing so, had demonstrated the effectiveness of helicopters to give mobility to small parties of troops operating in difficult terrain. As in Korea the operations gave a legacy of highly-skilled professional personnel who were capable of turning their hands to oppose aggression or cope with disasters anywhere on earth using the equipment available at short notice with the minimum of fuss. The commando helicopter squadrons became important elements of the RN strike force and are still known in the second decade of the twenty-first century as 'Junglies', testimony to their work in Borneo all those years ago. 848 NAS detachments were:

12 March 1965	*Albion*
28 April 1965	Sembawang
23 May 1965	Sibu to 18 September 1965
	Nangga Gaat to 15 September 1965
12 July 1965	Bario to 5 August 1966
20 September 1965	Labuan to 5 August 1966

Albion in the FEF with Wessex HAS 1s of 845 NAS and Whirlwind HAS 7s of 846 NAS on deck. Commando vehicles are parked aft. Note the two landing craft, vehicles and personnel, at davits on the port quarter. There are two others on the starboard side. (Author's collection)

13 The British Nuclear Deterrent and the End of the Admiralty Era

Successive British governments during the 1950s saw nuclear deterrence as the cornerstone of the nation's defence policy but the most effective and affordable form for it to take eluded the policymakers for more than a decade. At first it had been funded in addition to considerable conventional forces but the development of thermonuclear weapons made conventional warfare between the West and the Soviet Bloc seem an improbable scenario and non-nuclear forces were drastically reduced in size. By the end of the decade it had become obvious that Great Britain could no longer afford both a credible nuclear force and large conventional forces based around the world. Considerable sums were spent on nuclear weapons and the means to deliver them, by no means all of it wisely, and these were bound to have an impact on the RN strike fleet and other largely conventional forces. In this chapter I will give a brief description of the development of the British nuclear deterrent so that decisions to fund a succession of delivery systems can be compared with the carrier strike force and its effective operations. The eventual, sensible, decision to move away from a manned bomber force marked the 'death knell' of the RAF's original ambition to create a new form of warfare that would be conducted by aircraft operating independently from the other two Services and left it struggling to justify its very existence. In consequence unnecessary arguments began in Whitehall over the form that British conventional and nuclear defence should take and they continue to this day. At the height of these arguments the Admiralty was subsumed into a newly structured Ministry of Defence and this change obviously had an effect on the way the naval case was argued.

The British Nuclear Deterrent

London had been the first city in the world to be attacked by both cruise and ballistic missiles, the notorious German V-1 and V-2 weapons, in 1944–5. Given this experience of a new form of warfare, the first British plans for a nuclear delivery system appear in retrospect to be surprisingly unimaginative. Captain S W Roskill RN, later to write the official history of the War at Sea, had been the British naval representative at the US Bikini Atoll nuclear tests in 1946 and had been impressed with what he saw. In his report he stressed Britain's vulnerability to a nuclear device detonated in a major port after delivery in an 'innocent-looking' merchant ship. The detonation of Britain's first atom bomb in the frigate *Plym* off Monte Bello island in 1952 reflected some concern that a ship might be used as a delivery vehicle[1] but RAF Bomber Command had a large force of conventional bombers operating from fixed bases in the UK and, since the first British operational nuclear weapons would be both large and heavy, bombers were accepted as the most obvious delivery system. A number of firms were given design contracts for new bombers in the late 1940s that were seen at the time as being futuristic but which were to become much less so during their lengthy periods of development. All of them were designed to meet the requirements of Specification B35/46 which sought an aircraft which would have twice the speed and operational height of the Avro Lincoln, an enlarged development of the wartime Lancaster. Three designs were taken forward, each encompassing differing degrees of complexity and the original intention was to fly all three in prototype form, select the best and place a production contract for it. In the event, regardless of the extra cost involved, all three were given production contracts and saw service with Bomber Command. Despite a Ministry of Supply Memorandum issued on 5 November 1954 that predicted that Soviet air defences would improve rapidly by

Valiant B 1s at RAF Gaydon; they were faster and could fly higher but their weapon systems offered little advance over the Washingtons, Lincolns and Lancasters they replaced. (Author's collection)

1960 to a point where they would have the capability to make high-level attacks on Soviet targets with free-fall bombs prohibitively dangerous, considerable sums were spent on all three bomber types to increase their operating altitudes. Known generically as the 'V'-bombers, all three had names beginning with the letter 'V'.[2] First to enter service was the Vickers Valiant in 1954. It had a maximum speed of Mach 0.84; a service ceiling of 56,000ft and a range with a nuclear weapon of just over 2000 miles. One hundred and four Valiants were built in the basic B 1 version with two sub-types modified for use as photographic reconnaissance aircraft and in-flight refuelling tankers, the first aircraft of this kind to be used by the RAF. Interestingly, considering the contemporary RN interest in low-level strike under enemy radar coverage which led to the Buccaneer, Vickers produced a private venture B 2 version of the Valiant which had wings stressed for low-level flight. Despite its success in trials, Bomber Command saw no use for it and no orders were placed for a production run.[3]

The next medium bomber designed to meet B35/46 was the Avro Vulcan which featured a large delta wing with an unbroken sweep angle of 52 degrees. For the time this was an advanced concept but development by the run-down British aircraft industry was slow and a production contract was not signed until 1952. It was found that the original wing design caused buffeting during the application of G-forces at high altitude near the aircraft's performance limit. This posed a fatigue problem and the wing was redesigned with the leading edge sweep angle reduced by 10 degrees at half span and increased further outboard. The first production aircraft flew in 1955 and the first operational squadron formed with the Vulcan B 1 in 1957. The type was armed with a single free-fall nuclear weapon or up to twenty-one 1000lb bombs and was capable of flying at Mach 0.92 at 50,000ft over a radius of action of 1700 miles. Development intended to improve high-altitude performance continued and a B 2 version flew for the first time in 1957. It had more powerful Bristol Siddeley Olympus engines and a redesigned wing to give a cruising speed of Mach 0.97 at up to 65,000ft. The first unit equipped with the B 2 was declared operational in 1960.

The last 'V'-bomber to enter service was the Handley-Page Victor. It was arguably the most advanced of the three with a unique crescent wing planform with which a constant critical mach number was maintained from root to tip by graduated sweepback but there were concerns about the ability of Handley Page to develop its new design. The first prototype flew in late 1952 but crashed in 1954 due to a fatigue failure which led to the break-up of the tailplane during a low-level run. The first squadron to be equipped with the Victor B 1 was declared operational in 1958 but, as with the Vulcan, considerable further development was funded to improve the aircraft's high-altitude performance. This resulted in the B 2 version with more

A Victor B 2 in the landing pattern with a Blue Steel in its bomb-bay. Note that the missile's lower fin has folded to port as the aircraft's wheels were lowered to give adequate ground clearance; it was still not good though, despite this feature. (Author's collection)

powerful Rolls-Royce Conway engines and a wing of increased area, giving a service ceiling of over 60,000ft but the type did not enter operational service until 1962 by which time it was obsolescent in its designed role. Maximum speed at this altitude was Mach 0.95 and the type had a radius of action in excess of 2000 miles. Like the Valiant, the Victor was produced in photographic and tanker versions as well as the basic bomber variant. It had a considerably better conventional performance than the Vulcan and could carry up to thirty-five 1000lb bombs as an alternative to the nuclear weapon. When the Victor was withdrawn from the bombing role, a number were converted for use as in-flight refuelling tankers and continued in service with the RAF into the 1990s. By 1964 the RAF finally accepted that bombers attacking the Soviet Union at high-level would no longer be viable and the 'V' force was switched to low-level penetration techniques for which the aircraft had not been designed. The Valiant squadrons had been declared to NATO as a tactical strike force for low-level operations when the aircraft were replaced in the deterrent role by Vulcans and Victors but it was found that several aircraft had suffered fatigue cracks in their wing spars during 1965. The whole fleet was, therefore, grounded and then scrapped. The visible sign of the change to low level penetration was the new paint finish applied to the Vulcan and Victor aircraft. Previously they had been finished in anti-radiation gloss white overall to protect them against nuclear flash. Now the upper surfaces were painted in a high-gloss grey and green camouflage scheme intended to make them less visible to fighter pilots looking down on them from above. The lower surfaces remained white.

Blue Steel

In order to give the 'V'-bomber force some chance of penetrating Soviet defences after 1960, the Air Staff issued specification OR 1132 in 1954 for a supersonic missile capable of being launched from a bomber to carry a nuclear warhead to its designated target, allowing the bomber to turn away clear of the defences.[4] The Ministry of Supply selected Avro to design and manufacture the weapon, although it had no previous experience in this field, and the codename Blue Steel was applied, which it was to retain in operational service. It was powered by an Armstrong Siddeley Stentor liquid-fuelled rocket motor[5] which gave it a range of about 130nm. A gyro-based inertial navigation system was designed for it by Elliot Brothers which proved to be far more accurate than the system fitted to the parent bombers themselves and navigators could use the missile, plugged into the bomber, to help guide them to their release point. The liquid fuel proved to be an operational problem when Blue Steel eventually entered service since it had to be pumped into the missile by men wearing special protective suits as late as possible before take-off and the full launch preparation took up to seven hours, which hardly made it a quick-reaction weapon. The process obviously had to be complete before take-off but had also to be finished before the aircraft could be placed on four-minute alert. After flight, the missile had to be de-fuelled and have extensive checks carried out on it so it was far from being considered as a round of ammunition. Early development was compromised by the fact that the Ministry of Supply could not confirm whether the Orange Herald or Green Bamboo nuclear devices would be used as warheads and so the missile was designed to accommodate the 45in diameter implosion sphere diameter of Green Bamboo.[6] In the event however, British and US co-operation over nuclear weapons development led to an agreement that Blue Steel could be armed with Red Snow, an Anglicised derivative of the US W-28 thermonuclear warhead with a yield in the 1.1 megaton range. To hasten Blue Steel's entry into service, development rounds were flown to the WRE at Woomera in Australia for test firings actually attached to 'V'-bombers from 1960 onwards. By then Blue Steel was supposed to be in service already and the development of a more reliable Mark 2 version had to be cancelled in order to concentrate resources on the Mark 1 but it still took another three years to develop and did not finally enter service until February 1963. Even then, a total of only forty-eight Vulcans and Victors were modified to carry Blue Steel in modified bomb bays, leaving the balance of the 'V'-force to take its chances with free-fall weapons if it had to go into action. The Stentor was a two-

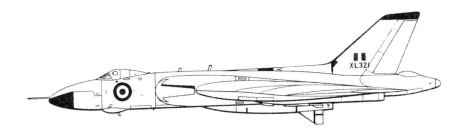

Drawing of a Vulcan B 2 with a Blue Steel Mark 1 in place. (Author's collection)

chamber rocket and after launch the first chamber would develop 24,000lbs of thrust and accelerate the missile to about Mach 1.5 on a pre-determined course. Close to the target the second chamber was fired, delivering a further 6000lbs of thrust and accelerating the missile to Mach 3 for a short period. Over the target the rocket cut out and the weapon fell to a pre-determined height at which Red Snow detonated as an air-burst. Within a year of Blue Steel's entry into service Bomber Command changed from high-level attack profiles to low-level operations and a hasty series of modifications had to be developed to allow the weapon to be released from 1000ft. Blue Steel was last flown in an operational aircraft in 1969 and was formally withdrawn from service in 1970. A Bomber Command report in 1966 is believed to have criticised Blue Steel reliability and warned that a significant number would have failed to fire when dropped.

Anglo-American Co-operation

With the entry into service of the Valiant in 1955 and British development of a thermonuclear capability the Americans were persuaded to agree closer co-operation on matters of nuclear weapons design, stockpiling and targeting. General Nathan F Twining, Chief of Staff of the US Air Force, was authorised to hold talks with his British counterpart Marshal of the Royal Air Force Sir William Dickson[7] in September 1955. These proved to be fruitful and subsequently US Secretary of Defence Charles Wilson authorised the USAF to furnish the RAF with US atomic bombs in the event of a general war and to co-ordinate the atomic strike plans of Strategic Air Command (SAC) with those of RAF Bomber Command. The result was an integrated war plan produced by Bomber Command and SAC staffs which 'took into account Bomber Command's ability to be on target in the first wave several hours in advance of the main SAC force operating from bases in the USA'.[8] In the initial plan, which was to be reviewed and amended annually, Bomber Command was allocated 106 targets but there was a significant problem that limited co-operation in that neither air force was allowed by its government to reveal the yield of the weapons allocated to specific targets and this inevitably led to duplication and wastage in some cases. Remarkably, this co-operation survived the 1956 Suez Crisis and continued until British bombers were withdrawn from the strategic nuclear role in 1968. Another aspect of co-operation was the US Project 'E' under which US nuclear weapons were provided for use by British Valiant and Canberra bombers. Mark 5 bombs were provided for the Valiant squadrons based at Marham, Waddington and Honington and Mark 7 bombs were provided for the Canberras of Bomber Command and RAF Germany.[9] The arrangement continued until 1963 for Bomber Command and 1969 for RAF Germany. However, the bombs had to be kept under US national custody and this limited the ability of Bomber Command to disperse aircraft fitted with them. This limitation became acute during the Cuban missile crisis in October 1962 when the RAF sought to arm and disperse the three SACEUR-assigned Valiant squadrons at Marham. It soon became apparent that there were insufficient USAF custodial officers to maintain control of the weapons.[10] The solution came from the Commanding General of the USAF in Europe who allowed the weapons to be handed over to the Group Captain in command of Marham, an act that exemplified the remarkable trust that had grown between the two air forces by that time.

Thor Intermediate-Range Ballistic Missiles

In another generous arrangement, subsequently codenamed Project 'Emily', the US Government agreed to 'lend' sixty Douglas Thor intermediate-range ballistic missiles (IRBM), to the UK after an agreement reached between the US President Dwight D. Eisenhower and the British Prime Minister Harold Macmillan at Bermuda in March 1957. The missiles, their specialised support equipment and training were provided at no cost to the UK but the infrastructure and units to operate the missiles were provided by RAF Bomber Command. Twenty sites, all of them former Second World War bomber airfields, were requisitioned for a second time, refurbished and they were each fitted with launch sites for three missiles. The Thor missile force formed 3 Group of Bomber Command and were 'clustered' in four areas, each comprising a master base[11] and four satellite fields.[12] The three-missile launcher unit at each airfield was formed as a squadron re-using wartime bomber squadron numbers. During the Cuban Missile Crisis fifty-nine of Bomber Command's sixty Thors were brought to operational readiness. The missile was designed and manufactured by Douglas for the USAF and was classified as an intermediate-range ballistic missile with a range of 1500 miles. When erected on its launcher it stood 65ft tall and the cylindrical body was 9ft wide. It weighed

A Thor IRBM of 77 Squadron, RAF Bomber Command, at RAF Feltwell being hoisted into the launch position in February 1960. Its shelter, part of which is visible to the right, has been moved clear on its rails and hoses for the missile's fuel and LOX supplies are connected to it via the structure to the missile's left. The 'arm' under the missile is taking its weight until it reaches the vertical. (Author's collection)

109,800lbs when fully fuelled and was powered by a single Rocketdyne LR79-NA-9 liquid-fuelled rocket motor with 150,000lbs of thrust at launch. It had a burn time of 165 seconds and the missile reached a height of 300 miles at the apogee of its ballistic trajectory. The warhead was a single W-49 thermonuclear bomb fitted into a blunt-nosed Mark 2 re-entry vehicle; it weighed 2200lbs and had a yield of 1.4 kilotons. Test firings showed that the Thor system was reliable and that the warhead had a circular error of probability of impacting within just over half a mile from a designated target. Although the missiles were painted with British roundels and operated by RAF personnel, the warheads remained in US custody and could not be fitted to the missile or launched without the approval of both the US and UK Governments.[13] The first Thor squadrons, 77, 97, 98 and 144, were declared operational at the master bases in January 1959 and the remaining sixteen between July and December 1959. RAF crews carried out twenty-one Thor training launches from Vandenberg Air Force Base in the USA between April 1959 and June 1962. One of them, codenamed 'Foreign Travel' on 6 October 1959 was witnessed by Lord and Lady Mountbatten and another, 'Clan Chattan', used the first missile returned from the UK for the purpose.

Thor's great weakness lay in its liquid-fuelled rocket motor which burnt kerosene with liquid oxygen (LOX) as an oxidant. When not at alert, the missile was stowed horizontally inside a hardened shelter fitted with wheels that ran along tracks. Propellants for each missile were stored in tanks near the launcher but since LOX boiled at normal temperatures, its supplies had constantly to be topped up. When brought to alert, the hardened shelter was retracted on its rails and the missile rotated to the vertical by a launcher arm;[14] after checks were completed the missile's tanks were filled with LOX and kerosene, the former constantly topped up until the firing button was pressed. During the whole process the missiles and their launcher units were vulnerable to a surprise attack. Given the warning time of only four minutes from the ballistic missile early warning radar at Fylingdales,[15] there was no question of launching Thors in response to a pre-emptive Soviet strike although some missiles might be got away amid the chaos and confusion around them. A small proportion of the total could be brought to fuelled alert on a daily basis, however, and potentially formed a more potent deterrent than the obsolescent 'V'-bombers with their free-fall bombs. The original agreement envisaged Thor remaining in service until 1968 by which time it was to be replaced by a British designed and built medium-range ballistic missile (MRBM). When a replacement failed to materialise and the British Government decided to procure the submarine-launched Polaris system, there seemed little point in retaining Thor in operational service as its slow reaction time was considered to render it obsolescent. It was withdrawn from service in 1963 and

A Blue Streak development missile on its handling cradle being winched from the horizontal to sit vertically in its fuelling and preparation tower at the WRE Woomera in Australia. The size of the missile can be deduced from the height of the group of men standing on the left. (Author's collection)

missiles were returned to the USA where they were mostly employed in the US space programme.

Blue Streak

The influential British Defence Research and Policy Committee (DRPC) studied the work of the German rocket scientists after 1945 and came to the firm conclusion that the UK should develop a ballistic missile system as the vehicle for carrying its nuclear deterrent. Of interest, they also recommended the development of an anti-ballistic missile system but work on this ended in the late 1950s when it was decided that ballistic missiles, once launched, were almost invulnerable to defensive measures. The cost of an anti-ballistic missile system was also found to be beyond the UK's means to develop alone. Although the resulting missile was to be built by a British firm, Anglo-American co-operation was a fundamental feature of the project from the outset. Duncan Sandys, then Minister of Supply, signed an agreement with his US equivalent in 1954 that the two nations would produce complementary missiles and share the technology that enabled them. Given his interest in missiles, Sandys must have considered this one of his most outstanding achievements. The US element of the plan evolved into the Atlas inter-continental ballistic missile; the British element evolved into the de Havilland Blue Streak MRBM.

The Air Ministry issued Operational Requirement (OR) 1139 in 1955 for a ballistic missile with a range of 2000 miles capable of carrying a thermonuclear warhead. A contract was awarded to de Havilland for design and construction and work began in 1957 once the size of the warhead was finalised. This was to have been Orange Herald, tested during the 'Grapple' series of tests at Christmas Island in 1957, and yielding 720 kilotons. By then de Havilland Propellers had signed a licence agreement with the manufacturers of Atlas, General Dynamics, that allowed the same construction technique to be used for the missile's airframe, essentially two thin tanks of liquid forming a metal-skinned tubular balloon.[16] Rolls-Royce licensed the S3 rocket motor from the Atlas, built a copy designated the RZ-1 and then refined the design to save weight. Two of the resulting RZ-2 rocket motors were to be used in Blue Streak. Orange Herald weighed about 2000lbs and to enable it to reach targets in the Soviet Union from sites in the UK and, possibly, the Middle East meant using liquid propellants as solid-fuel rocket technology had not yet reached the level of thrust required for an MRBM. Like Thor, Blue Streak's motors burnt kerosene and LOX. This posed the problem that while kerosene could be stored in the missile's tanks for prolonged periods, LOX could not[17] as it would have frozen the entire missile in a matter of hours. LOX had to be stored in special tanks, close the missile launch site, from which the liquid could be loaded in a short time. Pumping LOX on board was not considered feasible, partly because the process would be too slow and partly because pumps powered by diesel generators might not be reliable in the devastating opening minutes of a nuclear exchange. A remarkable solution was designed by de Havilland to solve the problem; 120 tons of LOX were stowed in a shockproof vacuum tank near the launcher. It slowly boiled off at atmospheric temperature but the tank was replenished economically

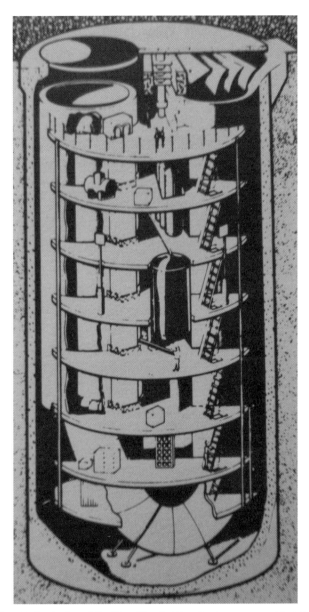

The K-11 hardened silo designed for Blue Streak. The circular armoured hatch is at the top left. The 'U-tube' at the base of the silo directed the hot exhaust gases away from the missile, up the right hand side of the silo and out to atmosphere through the curved 'fan-shapes' at the top right. The silo contained sufficient LOX to fill the missile with a considerable reserve in the tank visible at its centre; it also had its own generators and accommodation for the launching team during periods of high alert state. (Author's collection)

by re-liquefying the escaping oxygen. When the order to fire was given, 65 tons of LOX were blown on board in 3.5 minutes using the force of compressed nitrogen kept permanently stored near the missile in cylinders. At readiness Blue Streak already had 27 tons of kerosene on board in its thin-walled tanks and balancing pressures as the LOX entered the tank and the nitrogen that had pressurised it was forced out would have posed safety problems that required close attention, but de Havilland demonstrated with prototypes that it could be done and USAF Atlas and Titan ICBMs using similar technologies worked well into the 1980s.

The RAF was well aware that the major weakness of Thor was its exposed launcher position on the surface and so, from the outset, it was intended that Blue Streak would be deployed in underground silos. It was estimated in 1957 that if Blue Streak was deployed in sixty hardened silos,[18] sufficient would survive an initial Soviet attack to maintain a credible nuclear 'second strike' capability. Given de Havilland's optimism that the rapid fuelling system was viable there was also every chance that some missiles could be launched close to the four-minute warning given by the ballistic missile early warning system; the Soviet Union could certainly not rely on the possibility that no Blue Streaks could be launched from their hardened shelters. The chosen silo design was K-11 which contained an octagonal launch tube for the missile which was itself 10ft in diameter and 90ft high. Steel platforms could be lowered from the launch tube sides to the missile for inspection and maintenance and the tube was lined with acoustic panels to absorb some of the intense noise of the launch. Below the missile was a deflector or U-tube which would have forced the rocket efflux into the vertical shaft from where it would have exhausted during launch. To one side of the launch tube were the LOX and kerosene tanks together with the nitrogen cylinders for blowing the former into the missile. Above them were six floors of equipment rooms, generators, storage and accommodation, including a kitchen, for the launcher crew when they were at high alert states.[19] The silo had a 0.5in mild steel liner to protect the equipment inside it from the effects of electro-magnetic pulse from nearby nuclear explosions. Until the last seconds before firing, the whole structure was protected by a 750-ton concrete lid which ran on rails into its locking position. The designers left little to chance and powerful water jets, fed from tanks inside the silo, were fitted that would sweep the lid clear of debris before it was opened.

If the order to fire had been given, the crews of high-readiness missiles in their silos would have initiated the blowing of LOX into its tank. The target co-ordinates would already have been set but the gyros would need to be run up and stabilised, a task that took about a minute. The silo was designed to withstand anything but a direct hit by a three-megaton nuclear warhead so the balance of probability is that most would have survived the level of initial attack aimed at the UK by the

Soviet Union. After less than five minutes' preparation, individual Blue Streaks would be ready to fire; the missile crew in their blastproof accommodation inside the silo would initiate launch, the lid would unlock and retract on its rails and, seventeen seconds later, the missile would be on its way. The two rocket motors burnt for four minutes and the entire flight lasted only 20 minutes. During rocket burn the Elliot inertial navigation system compared position and velocity with the values in its data store and fed corrections to the two gimballed rocket motors which made adjustments. During its ballistic trajectory Blue Streak reached a height of 500 miles and after motor burn-out the re-entry head separated leaving the rocket body to burn up as it fell to earth. The warhead had its own small motors and one of the last instructions from the guidance system told these oddly named 'bonkers' whether or not to fire to give a precise final velocity. Seconds later, small 'squibs' were fired to tilt the warhead to the correct angle for re-entry into the atmosphere and spin it to give accuracy and stability. A heat shield protected it from burning up as it fell towards the target[20] and sensors would detonate Orange Herald high over the designated target.

A comprehensive test programme was to be carried out at the WRE at Woomera with an impact area for the inert warheads at Talgarno, south of Broome on Australia's north-west coast with costs shared between the UK and Australian governments.[21] By 1959, however, the British Government was alarmed by the soaring cost of Blue Streak. A K-11 silo was priced at £2.5 million and with over sixty projected, this aspect of the project alone would have cost £150 million. The cost of developing the missiles and their warheads and then manufacturing operational versions would have been considerably more. Sandys was unequivocal and pointed out that any 'home-grown' independent British nuclear deterrent was going to have a 'price-tag of £500 million or more'.[22] The Government set up a study group in 1959 tasked with examining the Blue Streak project, on which considerable sums of money had already been spent in the UK and Australia, and to make recommendations. The key argument was one of vulnerability; could missiles be launched before a Soviet pre-emptive strike destroyed all the Blue Streak silos? If the answer was 'yes', was the Soviet Union prepared to devote this proportion of its nuclear arsenal to destroying the British nuclear capability? It is likely that the group was 'stacked' with members known to oppose Blue Streak because its report concentrated on the vulnerability of fixed sites and decided that it was unlikely that the missiles could be launched within the four-minute warning time but, remarkably, gave the opinion that some manned 'V'-bombers could get airborne from alert in less than the four-minute warning time and thus survive a pre-emptive strike. The study group could not have known how many silos were likely to be destroyed in a Soviet first strike so the warning time was largely irrelevant; silos gave Blue Streak potential second-strike capability. Their concept that aircraft from about twenty airfields with no protection against air-burst weapons over a wide area would be less vulnerable than sixty missiles widely dispersed in hardened shelters that could only be destroyed by individual direct hits seems frankly laughable but it gave the Government the pretext it needed for cancellation. Yet again an expensive project had been started as an 'ultimate deterrent' with no though for the full cost implications or indeed whether it was the best method of achieving the Government's strategic aim. Ironically it fell to Admiral Sir Charles Lambe, 1SL, who was visiting Australia in March 1960 to inform Sir Robert Menzies that the project had been unilaterally cancelled by the British Government.[23] Bomber Command had always made it clear that it had little enthusiasm for fixed missile sites and seemed pleased that it was now able to retain its manned bombers for the foreseeable future. It had commented positively on the USAF technique of carrying out airborne deterrence flights, known as continuous airborne alert, with relays of B-52 bombers kept airborne with pre-targeted missiles. These would, it was assumed, be difficult to intercept and, when given the order, they could turn towards their briefed targets and launch their missiles as soon as they were within range. Needless to say the cost of such a system would have been considerable.

Skybolt

Operational Requirement 1159 called for a long-range stand-off missile to replace Blue Steel Mark 1 that would allow Bomber Command to carry out its own continuous airborne alerts. Avro won the design contract and proposed a ramjet-powered Blue Steel Mark 2 with a speed of Mach 3 at 70,000ft and a range of 800 miles. In 1959 it was cancelled as the cost of development began to rise alarmingly and to allow Avro to concentrate on overcoming the problems with the Mark 1 and get it into service. At the same time Harold Watkinson replaced Duncan Sandys as Secretary of Defence. He did not share his predecessor's enthusiasm for missiles, but was equally keen on Anglo-American partnership, especially if it could save the UK considerable sums in the development of new weapons. In February 1960 the US Government decided to proceed with a new project for an air-launched ballistic missile (ALBM), with a range of 1000 miles. This fitted perfectly with the USAF and RAF concept of continuous airborne alert and the cancellation of Blue Streak shortly afterwards may not have been entirely coincidental. In May 1960 the UK and US Governments agreed that the UK would purchase 100 Skybolts to be carried, initially, be re-wired Vulcan B 2 bombers[24] with one on a pylon under each wing. Bomber Command wanted replacement aircraft capable of carrying up to six Skybolts and there was intense rivalry between Hawker Siddeley which

A grainy but interesting photograph taken from the tracking camera of a chase-aircraft when a B-52G released the first Skybolt ALBM in April 1962. (Author's collection)

offered an enlarged version of the Vulcan and the British Aircraft Corporation which offered a modified version of its VC 10 transport design. Preparation of the first Vulcans went ahead quickly and an inert Skybolt was released over the West Freugh test range in Scotland in December 1961.

WS 138A, the Skybolt ALBM, was unique[25] in that it comprised an air-launched, two-stage solid-fuel ballistic missile designed to achieve high accuracy at ranges up to 1000 miles from the point at which the parent aircraft released it. Douglas was awarded a design study contract in May 1959 and a development contract in February 1960. Aerojet-General designed the propulsion system; General Electric the re-entry vehicle and Nortronics the guidance system. It navigated its way to the target using an astral seeker which compared data with an inertial platform and made corrections. Like all advanced systems, however, Skybolt encountered unforeseen development problems and both the propulsion and guidance systems failed in early live launches. In April 1962 the first live launch terminated when the second-stage rocket failed to fire. In June there was no ignition on the first stage when the second live missile was dropped and in August the third live missile veered off course and had to be destroyed. Two subsequent launches also failed and added cost and delay to the project. When the Kennedy administration replaced that of President Eisenhower, the new Secretary of Defence, Robert S McNamara, a former CEO of the Ford Motor company, showed himself to be obsessed with what he called the 'cost-effectiveness' of weapons systems. He decided that the land-based USAF Minuteman and USN submarine-launched Polaris, both of which were already operational, were the only ballistic missiles the USA needed and Skybolt's rising cost and history of failure gave him the ammunition he needed to recommend its cancellation to the President. Kennedy only viewed Skybolt from a US perspective and in December 1962 he agreed to its cancellation without even consulting the British. There was an outcry in London which surprised Kennedy and his initial reaction was an offer to transfer the whole Skybolt programme to the UK, although it would have to retain the US firms contracted for its development. Since the UK only required 100 missiles and would have to develop a new bomber to carry them this was far too expensive an option, the offer was refused and McNamara arrived in London on 11 December for talks. He suggested that Polaris could be made available to the UK under favourable terms but there was still a powerful body of opinion in the UK that favoured some form of bomber/missile combination.[26] Admiral Mountbatten had always favoured Polaris but the Admiralty Board had hoped that its procurement would follow Skybolt in the mid-1970s, giving the RN time to complete its new carrier construction programme. McNamara's meeting in London did not produce a way forward but it was agreed that Prime Minister Macmillan and President Kennedy would meet in Nassau a week later to resolve the crisis.

Polaris – the USN Project

The advantages of operating their 'V' weapons from a moving rather than a fixed static base had been obvious to the Germans and V-1 'flying bombs' had been launched experimentally from U-boats in 1945. Launching the liquid-fuelled V-2 rocket from a ship posed immense problems and was never attempted. The USN improved on V-1 technology with the Regulus 1 and 2 programmes, producing cruise missiles that could be launched from the deck of aircraft carriers or from catapults fitted to specially-modified submarines. In November 1955 the USN set up a Special Projects Office to consider the possibility of designing a ballistic missile that could be launched from a dived submarine. At first the project team considered joining the US Army in the development of a liquid-fuelled IRBM, but with a maximum weight over 100,000lbs and fuelled by LOX and kerosene the problems of fitting such a weapon into a submarine proved insuperable. Early attempts to substitute a solid-fuel rocket led to designs that increased in both size and weight.

The breakthrough came in September 1956[27] when the US Atomic Energy Commission offered a dramatic reduction in warhead size and weight, making an IRBM in the 30,000lb class a feasible proposition. Work to develop an operational weapons system began in 1957 and at first it was estimated that its entry into service would be towards the end of 1964. However, as the system's potential was appreciated and the technological hurdles were surmounted, the amount of money available to the Project Office was increased to such good effect that the USN found itself able to plan for the deployment of nine operational submarines by the end of 1961. The missile was given the name Polaris. The exact sum spent was classified but was believed to exceed $1 billion at 1958 values. Unsurprisingly, considerable opposition was levelled at the submarine-launched missile programme by the USAF which had a vested interest in preserving SAC, the creation of which had led to the creation of an 'independent' Air Force out of the former Army Air Force in 1947. As we saw above, the administration favoured Polaris rather than Skybolt and cancelled the latter in 1962.

The Polaris project office faced immense tasks in several widely disparate disciplines to achieve the operational goal. It had to oversee the design,

The first Polaris ICBM launch from a submerged submarine on 20 July 1960. The boat in question was the uss *George Washington*, name ship of the first class of SSBN to enter service with the USN. (Author's collection)

development and construction of the submarine launching vessel, the missile fire-control system, the missile navigation system and the equipment to launch the missile from a dived submarine, all of this in addition to the basic design of the Polaris airframe and its rocket motor. The submarines, designated SSBN, were to be nuclear-powered and effectively 'scaled-up' from the latest hunter/killer SSN to carry sixteen Polaris missiles stowed in vertical tubes aft of the control room. A pressure hull at least 30ft in diameter was required and this led to a low-drag hull design for the initial *George Washington* class, 380ft long with a submerged displacement of 6700 tons. The subsequent *Ethan Allen* class was 410ft long and displaced 8600 tons. The contract for *George Washington* itself was placed in June 1958; she was launched a year later and commissioned in 1960. She launched two Polaris missiles in sequence on 20 July 1960 whilst dived at a depth of 90ft in a position 30nm off Cape Canaveral in Florida. Both dummy warheads impacted in the 'prescribed area' of the Atlantic Missile Range north of Puerto Rico, 1100nm from the launch position. Firing the rocket motor inside the submarine launch tube was considered to be unsafe and so the missile was ejected by air pressure and the motor fired as it emerged above the sea surface. Extensive trials with models and full-scale missiles were carried out to prove that the system worked in most sea states. There was no means of controlling the missile as it left the launcher because it was still underwater; reliance was placed on the fact that this phase was too short to allow a major departure from the ideal and this proved to be the case. As it emerged above the sea the main propulsion motor ignited and control was achieved by deflecting the rocket efflux by devices around the nozzles which were controlled by servo-motors responding to combined autopilot and inertial guidance system commands.

SSBNs were fitted with inertial navigation platforms which made use of sensitive accelerometers mounted on a gyro-controlled stable platform to feed a precise launch position to the missile since the boat remained dived throughout its patrol and was unable to make use of radio beacons or to take star sights to fix its position. Once launched, the missile had to be able to determine any corrections made necessary by its passage through water and subsequent flight involving a 10g acceleration to 100mph in the launch tube; deceleration on the way up to the surface and then a gradual build-up of acceleration during the two stages of rocket-powered flight to over 6000mph. The missile guidance system was one of the most challenging aspects of the design and its reliability and accuracy represented the 'state-of-the-art' in 1960. The missile's attitude and trajectory were controlled by the efflux deflectors leaving speed as the only other major variable. This rose rapidly as fuel was consumed and was measured by computations from the axial acceleration. When the speed reached the required maximum value, thrust was terminated immediately so that the warhead continued on its planned path to its pre-determined target. When the warhead detached from the final propulsion stage it followed a ballistic trajectory before re-entering the atmosphere on the final leg of its flight. Aerodynamic drag caused the heat of the outer skin to rise rapidly until it glowed incandescent at up to 4000°C. The nuclear device itself and its fusing components were therefore protected by an external jacket of plastic laminate.

Polaris gave the USA a mobile deterrent fitted in platforms which could loiter in the open ocean where there was little chance of their detection by the Soviet Union. There was certainly no possibility of the Soviets destroying all the SSBNs before they had a chance to fire. The missiles themselves were reliable and could be held at readiness in large numbers in SSBNs that potentially operated thousands of miles apart. The USN gave each submarine two crews in order that they could spend the maximum amount of time deployed at sea but each crew comprised only twelve officers and 100 men in the first class and slightly less in later ships. Therefore, although the boats and missiles were expensive to procure, their operating costs with such small ship's companies were far less than SAC's vast bomber fleet. Polaris gave the USA a deterrent that was not influenced by warning or reaction times, that could not easily be intercepted or damaged by a potential enemy and which had a genuine second- or even third-strike capability after the initial exchanges in a nuclear war. It was well thought out, technologically brilliant and practical.

Polaris – the RN Project

Admiral Mountbatten had first become aware of USN interest in submarine-launched ballistic missiles in 1955, shortly after he became 1SL, when Admiral Arleigh Burke, his USN opposite number, briefed him on the project. The close relationship between Mountbatten and his contacts in the USN allowed the RN to make rapid strides in the field of nuclear-powered submarines. His agreement with Admiral Rickover, chief of the USN nuclear programme, that an American reactor could be supplied for *Dreadnought*, the first British SSN, allowed its completion three years earlier than would have been possible with a British-designed reactor. By 1958 he had negotiated an agreement that allowed two RN officers to join the Polaris Special Project Office in Washington and they were able to keep him fully informed of developments. Mountbatten himself was said to be averse in principle to the idea of an independent British nuclear deterrent but felt that, if the Government believed it to be necessary, it would eventually become a naval responsibility. Arleigh Burke made no secret in their discussions that he believed Skybolt to be 'technically feasible provided enough research and development is done on it but it is a very expensive and vulnerable system'.[28] Fortunately, in July

1960, shortly after the cancellation of Blue Streak, the Board of Admiralty had instructed the Controller, Rear Admiral Michael Le Fanu to investigate the implications of procuring Polaris for the RN if Skybolt were to fail and his clear, lucid summary was kept to hand when the Skybolt crisis broke in November 1962.

McNamara offered the British three alternatives in London on 11 November 1962. We have already seen that the first was rejected because the UK could not afford to continue with Skybolt alone. The second was to provide Britain with a number of AGM-28B Hound Dog missiles. This was an inertially-guided Mach 2 weapon with a maximum range of 690 miles powered by a single 7500lb Pratt & Whitney J52 turbojet. It weighed 9600lbs was carried on pylons under the wings of B-52 bombers. The primary purpose of its small thermonuclear warhead was to suppress Soviet air defences and allow other aircraft to attack high-priority targets. At best it would have extended the lives of the obsolescent 'V'-bombers for a few years but their retention would have been expensive and, with their American warheads, they would not have provided the UK with a credible and truly independent deterrent. Hound Dog was refused as quickly as the anglicised Skybolt. The third offer was for either Minuteman or Polaris missiles which could be fitted with British warheads and this formed the basis of a meeting between Macmillan and Kennedy with their advisors at Nassau in the Bahamas between 16 and 19 December 1962.

The exact nature of the discussion is not known but the decision to opt for Polaris was far from certain. Peter Thorneycroft, the Defence Secretary was known to favour a solution based on Bomber Command with some kind of missile. The British team also included Sir Solly Zuckerman, the Chief Scientific Advisor to the Ministry of Defence, and Admiral le Fanu who probably knew more about the Polaris project than any other member of the British group. The RAF was represented by Air Vice Marshal Christopher Hartley, the Assistant Chief of the Air Staff. Macmillan himself is believed to have seen the advantages of Polaris and favoured it over Minutemen which would have been confined to the narrow land mass of the UK with all the political ramifications over where to build the silos. There was clearly some disagreement within the British party and after the first day the Cabinet was asked to discuss the possible impact of the introduction of Polaris into the RN and cable its recommendation to the Prime Minister in Nassau. Captain John Moore RN was serving in the Admiralty Plans Division at the time and at 15.00 he was asked to prepare a paper on the subject for presentation to Lord Carrington, the First Lord, at 09.00 the next morning. He was told that he could consult anyone necessary over an open line and began by producing a list of subjects that would need analysis.[29] Rear Admiral Rufus Mackenzie[30] the Flag Officer Submarines (FOSM), and Sir Alfred Sims the Director General Ships both

Revenge, the last boat to be completed of the RN *Resolution* class SSBN. She and her sisters carried out a total of 229 patrols, the last of them in 1996. (Author's collection)

proved to be very helpful. The Resident Clerk, a senior civil servant and the duty typist were then brought into play and the first draft paper was prepared by 03.00. Moore made his deadline and gave a presentation, backed by a 27-page typed briefing, at 09.00 to the First Lord in his office. 1SL and the other Board members, except of course the Controller who was in Nassau, were present for what proved to be the initiation of the largest RN peacetime programme of the twentieth century. At 09.45 Lord Carrington and 1SL left to brief the Cabinet which decided to support the procurement of Polaris. The decision was communicated to the Prime Minister who signed the historic agreement with President Kennedy before leaving Nassau on 19 December 1962.

The agreement itself had, necessarily, to be followed by a great deal of detailed planning and in February 1963 the British Government announced that the first RN SSBN was to be on patrol in 1968. Five 7000-ton nuclear-powered submarines, each carrying sixteen Polaris A3 ballistic missiles were ordered at the same time but the fifth, for which some steel had been procured, was cancelled as an economy measure in February 1965. Two boats, *Resolution* and *Repulse*, were built by Vickers-Armstrongs at Barrow-in-Furness which acted as lead yard: the former was laid down in February 1964 and the latter in March 1965. The second pair, *Renown* and *Revenge*, were built by Cammell Laird at Birkenhead with the first laid down in June 1964 and the second in May 1965. They were 425ft long and had a dived displacement of 7500 tons. The Polaris A3 missile had a range of 2500nm enabling dived submarines to get into positions from which any target in the Soviet Union could be engaged. The USN gave the RN a great deal of assistance during the procurement phase, not least in training manpower for the rapidly expanding submarine force. All British SSBNs carried out their test and practice firings using USN range facilities. The Polaris missiles were bought outright for the RN but the warheads were designed and manufactured in the UK. The RN followed the USN practice of manning each boat on a two-crew basis to achieve the maximum operational time at sea; changeover occurred approximately every three months. *Resolution*, the first of class, began trials in June 1967 and met the Government target of being on deterrent patrol in 1968. *Revenge*, the last boat, was accepted into service in December 1969.[31] The RN stockpile of Polaris missiles was believed to be about seventy, with about fifty warheads available to them at any one time.[32] After the decision to replace Polaris with the USN submarine-launched Trident system the *Resolution* class was withdrawn from service and replaced by four *Vanguard* class SSBNs. The first to go was *Revenge* in 1992 and the last *Renown* in 1996.[33] Between 1968 and 1996 at least one British SSBN was on patrol somewhere in the world's oceans, virtually undetectable and able to retaliate when ordered if the UK was attacked by a nuclear power.

Trident

As the Polaris SSBNs drew towards the end of their operational lives it became necessary to look for a replacement system and, logically, the British Government selected the USN Trident system in July 1980. At first the Trident C4 was selected but in 1982 the UK opted, instead, for the Trident D5 missile. The missile airframes are leased from the USN and returned to the US 'pool' for maintenance in order minimise the cost of operation but the warheads are designed and manufactured in the UK. The D5 variant is a three-stage, solid-propellant rocket with a range of 7500nm and can be fitted with up to eight individual thermonuclear warheads. The greater range allows the *Vanguard* class submarines, each of which carries sixteen missiles, to hide in far greater expanses of ocean than their predecessors. Four SSBNs of this class were built, *Vanguard*, *Victorious*, *Vigilant* and *Vengeance*, all of them by Vickers Shipbuilding at Barrow-in-Furness. The first of class was completed in 1993 and fired her first missile in 1994; she carried out her first operational patrol in 1995.[34] Trident D5 was a new system that had only entered service with the USN in 1990 and, once again, the RN received considerable help from the USN in bringing the system to operational maturity. Trident remains in service with the RN in 2015 with increasingly confident talk by the UK

Vigilant, one of the four RN *Vanguard* class SSBNs. (Author's collection)

Government about ordering a replacement class of SSBNs to deploy Trident into the foreseeable future. After an expensive and not very clearly thought-through beginning, the UK's independent nuclear deterrent stabilised after 1968 into a viable force of submarine-launched missiles. If a deterrent continues to be deemed necessary, this represents the most practical and effective way of deploying it.

The End of the Admiralty

The Admiralty, as a department of state, had existed for many centuries before the events described in this book and had occupied the same offices in Whitehall since 1726. The Lords Commissioners existed to carry out the duties of the Lord High Admiral when that post was in abeyance, as it was between 1837 and 1964. The tasks of the Navy Office and Victualling Boards were absorbed into the Admiralty in 1832 but the department's core business was the administration and strategic control of fleets, the construction of new ships and the appointment and promotion of officers. The First Lord was a Cabinet member who acted as the political head of the organisation and formed its link with government. The First Sea Lord was the professional head of the RN and responsible, from 1904 when Admiral Fisher assumed the duty, for operational, as well as administrative matters. He was assisted by other Sea Lords and by 1939 these comprised the Second Sea Lord responsible for personnel matters; the Third Sea Lord or Controller responsible for the procurement of ships and weapons; the Fourth Sea Lord responsible for stores and transport and the Fifth Sea Lord responsible for naval aviation matters. A Deputy Chief of Naval Staff, Vice Chief of Naval Staff and Assistant Chief of Naval Staff also sat as Board Members together with civil servants who filled important administrative positions.

A Naval Intelligence Department (NID) was established in 1880 to advise 1SL on the growing capabilities of foreign warships. A Trade Division was established in 1902 to advise on the defence of Britain's vast mercantile shipping operations.[35] In 1904 the C-in-C of the Channel Fleet, Admiral Lord Beresford, complained about the inadequacy of the Admiralty's war plans[36] and the ensuing controversy reached the ears of the Prime Minister, Asquith, who ordered an inquiry. This recommended the establishment of a war staff and a Naval Mobilisation Division was created in 1909 to take over the planning tasks of NID and the Trade Division, eventually replacing the latter completely. Two years later the Agadir Crisis brought the UK close to war with Germany and 1SL was found to lack a sound plan for this eventuality, largely because he believed his own personal authority to be pre-eminent and that NID and the Mobilisation Division should play no more part in advising him on such matters than any other part of the Admiralty. Clearly this could not continue and Asquith appointed Winston Churchill as First Lord with the express purpose of creating a naval war staff and ensuring that it was properly employed. Churchill saw the need for three staff branches; one to acquire information; a second to develop policy and a third to put decisions into effect. A post of Chief of the War Staff was created, working under 1SL and a new Operations Division created. This was broadly the organisation that fought the first two years of the Great War but it never achieved its full potential.

Changes were made when Admiral Jellicoe became 1SL in 1916; the War Staff was re-titled the naval staff and Jellicoe assumed direct charge as Chief of the Naval Staff, CNS, in addition to his duties as 1SL. While the Admiralty Board was still held corporately responsible for the RN overall, CNS was responsible, personally, for operations direct to the First Lord. Thus he was empowered to issue orders to the fleet affecting war operations and the movement of ships in his own right. By 1918 much greater emphasis was placed on the Naval Staff's role in the operational use, not the support, of the fleet and much greater emphasis was placed on officers receiving staff training. After the Great War both the Admiralty and the Naval Staff were reduced in size but by 1923 the latter had developed into a body of professional naval officers responsible for Fleet operational control. It was organised on lines that lasted, with slight changes, for the next forty years and some aspects of it were still recognisable within the structure of the Ministry of Defence in 1997. Divisions included Operations, Plans, Naval Intelligence, Trade, Gunnery, Torpedo and Naval Aviation. The Admiralty had an excellent system for retaining records up to its demise in 1964 and a wealth of information is available in ADM files in the National Archives at Kew. Unfortunately the Ministry of Defence organisation which absorbed the Admiralty had no such satisfactory system and the RN plays little part in the identification of material that should be preserved. Lack of storage space led to wholesale destruction of papers and what remains is inadequate for studying the evolution of the Defence Staff after 1964.

The Naval Staff expanded again during the Second World War but retained a recognisable form. It played a considerable part in the formation of the Inter-Service Directorate of Combined operations when it was formed in June 1940. New Divisions such as Economic Warfare and Press were created but not retained in 1945 when the Staff was again reduced in size to administer the peacetime fleet. Between 1945 and 1964 the Admiralty Board coped well with the radical changes required by new technology, with a succession of minor conflicts at considerable distances from the UK, with the emergence of the nuclear deterrent and, not least with the threat to the RN's very existence posed by a succession of not very well thought-out defence reviews which only considered certain aspects of defence and never really understood the wide range of functions undertaken by the Navy in the national interest. With his wartime background in charge of combined operations, Admiral Mountbatten was believed to favour closer ties between the armed forces[37] and a decision was taken in 1963, while he was Chief of the Defence Staff, to amalgamate the single-Service staffs serving in the Admiralty, War Office and Air Ministry. The change took effect on 1 April 1964 and Her Majesty the Queen took the title of Lord High Admiral which was no longer to be discharged by the Lords Commissioners of the Admiralty.[38] The First Lord was re-titled as the Navy Minister and was no longer a cabinet member. The single-Service staffs were absorbed into the existing Defence Staffs; the former Joint Planning Staff became the Defence Planning Staff and a Defence Operations Staff came into existence to issue operational policy decisions and orders to the unified Commanders-in-Chief, only recently created and not destined to last much longer as the British withdrew from bases in the Middle and Far East. A Defence Operations Executive, of which ACNS became a member, supervised the Defence Operations Staff which included the Directorate of Naval Operations and Trade. Gradually the new system led to a diminution of knowledge and the wise Admiralty civil servants such as K T Nash moved to 'career development' opportunities in other government departments. Projects had to be considered on a MOD basis and it was not always possible to convince Army and RAF staff officers of the importance of the naval case. The sudden end to the Cold War in 1989 led to an 'Options for Change' defence review by the Government which did not, in fact, offer more than one option and that was a drastic reduction in the size of the conventional armed forces, including the RN. It did, however, accept that the instability that might follow the break-up of the Soviet Union would require intervention which, in some cases would involve combat rather than peacekeeping operations. Naval staff officers in the Plans Division were able to explain the part naval forces could play in these and the continuing need for access which only sea power could provide.

'Options' was followed by the 'Prospect' Study of the MOD Headquarters which caused greater amalgamation of a smaller number of staff officers into a new series Defence Directorates that had no links to their former Admiralty Divisions and this process has continued. It has become common to read about Army officers explaining the need for new air warfare destroyers and RAF officers talking about the need for pilot training before squadrons can embark in a carrier. None are masters of their subject although they may have impressive management skills and, unfortunately, it shows. Looking ahead of the point we have reached in the chronology of this book, the South Atlantic War of 1982, the Gulf War of 1991 and operations in the Former Yugoslavia in the 1990s were all to be conducted as national, joint-Service operations and command at Joint Commander level was exercised by a single-Service C-in-C appointed by the Defence Staff. Since this was likely to be the way in which future operations would be conducted, a decision was made by Government to concentrate command facilities at one permanent site where the Joint Commander could exercise operational command. In April 1996 a national Permanent Joint Principal Headquarters (PJHQ), was established at Northwood with a joint staff to be reinforced when an operation was set in train. Responsibility for military strategic direction of an operation and the allocation of forces to achieve the political objective since then has rested with the Chief of the Defence Staff. Thus the Naval Staff, acting in time of crisis, ceased to play a part in the operational direction of the RN Fleet. By 1985 the vestige of 'M' Branch was renamed as Sec(NS) and had faded to the extent that it no longer had the experience to offer advice.

In 1911 the requirement for the Board of Admiralty to be supported in its operational direction of the Fleet by a staff of experienced seafaring officers who were expert in naval matters was recognised. By 2000 the task of directing naval operations and planning the composition of the Fleet and its equipment had passed, together with decisions on strategic policy, into the hands of the Defence Staff, leaving 1SL/CNS and the few staff officers with specifically naval duties with the task of managing the RN Fleet for delivery to the operational control of PJHQ and the provision of professional advice when it is requested. Of interest, this is not the way that the USA has organised its armed forces. The Pentagon fulfils the same function as the Ministry of Defence but the USN remains a separate entity with a Civilian Secretary of the Navy (Sec NAV) at its head and a Chief of Naval Operations (CNO) who has operational control of Fleets, although a growing number of warships are allocated to joint commands for operations such as those around Africa. The American system concentrates knowledge where it is needed and, in my opinion, is the better for it. The British Government has made a virtue out of joint control which has not always been justified by results and which seems to struggle at times to find the expertise it requires. Directorates that are manned on a 'pro-rata' basis will, inevitably, tend to have a majority of Army and RAF desk officers who are not necessarily the ideal people to understand the ideal type of warship for future operations or indeed how best to use the ones we have.

14 The Cancellation of CVA-01

The impact of the British Government's decision to procure Polaris as the nation's nuclear deterrent was far-reaching and felt throughout the armed forces and industry. For the RN it began a complex programme, the largest ever undertaken in peacetime, that succeeded in sailing the first of four SSBNs on patrol in 1968 as planned. Remarkably the project delivered the submarines, missiles and warheads together with their extensive support facilities at Faslane and Coulport on time and at the predicted cost. The submarine branch had undergone significant expansion to create the eight crews and their supporting staff and a great deal of help had been received from the USN. Taken with the contemporary procurement of the Phantom as a Sea Vixen replacement and the generous facilities made available to introduce RN personnel to the new aircraft, the two programmes brought the two navies closer together and enabled the RN to maintain its status as a major force with worldwide commitments.

The RAF saw Polaris in a very different light, however. It had been created by politicians in 1918 to specialise in strategic bombing, a new form of warfare that was intended to be independent of operations by the other two Services and outside their control. Bomber Command had been at the core of RAF operations and culture but the decision to adopt a sea-based deterrent rendered it irrelevant as soon as the SSBNs were ready. Since 1957 Fighter Command had been reduced in size as it was recognised that fighters could not defend the UK against missile attack. The English Electric Lightning had been brought into service, as what was expected to be the last manned fighter, principally to defend Bomber Command's airfields for long enough to allow some aircraft to get airborne from alert in the event of a surprise Soviet attack by manned aircraft. The Command's residual NATO air defence tasks were not large and were expected to be taken over by missiles. The RAF commitment to the NATO 2nd Allied Tactical Air Force (2 ATAF) in Germany had been drastically reduced after 1957 but had now assumed greater significance if the loss of strategic deterrent responsibility was not to be a 'death sentence' for the independent Air Force. The Canberra replacement aircraft, TSR 2,[1] became the most important aircraft development for the RAF and it

386

assumed critical importance in the eyes of its sponsor Service. Senior RAF officers foresaw a very real danger in 1963 that their Service might be on the verge of disbandment at the next defence review with the residual strike fighter role passing to the Fleet Air Arm and the close-support and transport roles passing to a resurrected Royal Flying Corps within the newly-formed Army Air Corps (AAC). Suggestions by politicians that compromises should be made in future aircraft projects such as the P 1154 and variable-geometry strike aircraft to enable them to meet RN requirements and operate from carriers caused even more apprehension in the RAF and every means was taken to insist on unique designs that were not compatible with carrier-borne deployment. Since the majority of politicians assumed that the RAF had the most expert knowledge of air matters, this myopic and expensive viewpoint was never challenged and the UK's defence often suffered as a consequence.

The Background to CVA-01, the un-built *Queen Elizabeth*

A succession of new designs were put forward by the Admiralty in the 1950s, none were authorised by the Government for construction but the requirement was never formally cancelled and four new fleet carriers remained in the long-term costings under the generic title of 'guided-missile equipped aircraft carriers'. The longer their construction was delayed, however, the greater the 'bow wave' of expenditure that would be needed to replace the growing number of older carriers would become. Logically the most efficient and economical process would be to order a new ship every five to ten years in order to maintain an even cost of construction and development, a process used by the USN and subsequently accepted as ideal by the UK Government for the construction of SSNs. In 1958 DNC informed the Admiralty Board that, notwithstanding the modernisations then being carried out, the existing carrier fleet had only a finite life and that new construction would be necessary to supplement and eventually replace them at some stage. Despite the arguments over carrier size since 1944, the Naval Staff still had no firm view on the relative merits of a larger number of relatively small carriers or a smaller number of large carriers. In January 1960, therefore, the Fleet Requirements Committee (FRC) was tasked to study the question and make recommendations.[2] A wide and disparate range of numbered studies were distilled down to just six for presentation to the Board. The smallest of these was Study 27 for a 42,000-ton ship that could carry twenty-seven Buccaneer or Sea Vixen-sized aircraft with a defensive armament of Seacat missiles and the others were Studies 23D and E for ships of 48,000 tons, Study 29 for a ship of 50,000 tons, Study 24 for a ship of 55,000 tons and Study 30 for a ship of 68,000 tons. All of the larger ships were to be armed with US Tartar missile systems and would be able to carry significantly

The first artist's impression of CVA-01 released to the press in 1963. It shows the original design with an 8-degree angled deck and circles for vertical landings aft. The fixed-wing aircraft are crude representations of the P 1154. (Author's collection)

more aircraft which could be operated in worse weather and sea conditions than Study 27. It was estimated that four Study 27 carriers would cost £180 million to build compared with four Study 24 ships which were estimated to cost £240 million to build.[3] Both sums would be spread over a number of years and there were clear advantages in size. It was calculated that Study 24 could operate forty-nine aircraft compared with only twenty-seven in Study 27. This gave better value for money illustrated by a 'ship-build cost' of £1.2 million per aircraft in a single Study 24 ship but £1.6 million per aircraft in a single Study 27 ship. The decision to authorise construction rested with the Ministry of Defence and ultimately the Cabinet, both of which would of course have to be persuaded that the higher total cost of construction was affordable. The Admiralty Board, however, felt that the small percentage rise in cost for such a considerable increase in operational performance was a powerful argument that could not be ignored.

In January 1961 the Board decided that a ship of at least 48,000 tons would be needed to operate the new generation of aircraft and those expected to replace them. The Ship Characteristics Committee was instructed to work out a detailed Staff Requirement, amalgamating several of the earlier studies into a new one identified at first as Study 35. The committee was instructed to assume that the sketch design for the first ship would be approved in late 1962 and provisional orders for the hull and machinery would be placed in 1963. Building drawings were to be completed in 1965 by the lead shipyard and metal would be cut for the first ship in the same year. Launch was to be in 1967 with a trials programme commencing in 1970 for operational service from late 1971. The carrier designs in the 1950s had assumed general-purpose aircraft carriers capable of operating aircraft, including helicopters, for a wide range of fleet duties. Study 35 had one important difference, however, in that the Board decided that the new ship's primary purpose was to be strike warfare and the design was to be optimised for the operation of aircraft capable of attacking both ships and land targets with nuclear and conventional weapons. It was, therefore, allocated the NATO brevity code CVA for a strike carrier rather than CV for a general-purpose carrier or CVS for an anti-submarine support carrier. From this time onwards the project was referred to as CVA-01 with later ships of the class following as CVA-02, -03 and -04. Strike warfare might be the optimal role but a ship of this size was, of course, perfectly capable of carrying out a full range of other tasks including the operation of fighters both to escort the strike aircraft and provide air defence over large areas of sea or land and the operation of radar-equipped AEW aircraft capable of searching for air and surface targets and directing strike aircraft and fighters onto them. Significantly the Board accepted that anti-submarine helicopters added value to the air group and were vital for the close-range defence of the carrier task force against submarine attack, making the continued interest in escort cruisers at the time even more difficult to understand. With hindsight, the design actually reflected a true general purpose capability but the Board probably elected to adopt the CVA designation to impress the USN and NATO with the ship's ability to form part of the NATO Strike Fleet alongside the new USN 'super-carriers' of the *Forrestal* class. It was important, nationally, that the RN showed that it had the capability as well as the skills needed to retain command of NATO Strike Group Two and the CVA designation was one way of helping to achieve that aim. Unfortunately this subtlety was lost on British politicians and those who gave any consideration to the subject at all probably thought that the ship only had one role and that was nuclear strike.[4]

The design process and staff work intended to finalise the ship's requirement proceeded on the assumption that the new carrier was to have a displacement similar to the modernised *Eagle* at about 50,000 tons but, with a more modern and efficient hull design, would represent a significant measure of improvement. A number of further design studies were ordered to compare Study 35 with the 75,900-ton USS *Forrestal* and the 31,000-ton French *Foch* which represented the opposite extremes of new carrier construction. The former was deemed too large for existing British infrastructure to support it and too expensive to build; the latter was criticised because of doubts about its stability if all the thirty aircraft projected were embarked. Next, five more refined studies were laid before the Board, identified as Study 50 for a 50,000-ton carrier, Study 52 for a 52,000-ton ship, Study 53 for a 53,000-ton ship and Study 55 for a 55,000-ton ship. Logically, the final Study 58 was for a 58,000-ton ship. A sketch design with the best features derived from these studies emerged in April 1962 and was examined in detail by the Board. It was for a carrier that would be 890ft long at the waterline with a maximum width, including the angled deck sponson, of 177ft with a nominal displacement of 50,000 tons. After their examination, the Board asked for quick studies to be made of designs up to 60,000 tons; the implication of using commercial docks for the new carrier's maintenance and a comparison with the modernised *Eagle*. These revealed that a larger carrier would have a construction cost beyond the total that the Cabinet could be expected to authorise; refits in commercial yards would be expensive because only the Royal Dockyards had the infrastructure to support high-technology equipment such as radar and electronics but that docking might be a practical possibility. The comparison with *Eagle*, as might be expected, showed that a later design based on the growing wealth of jet operating experience would not only be more efficient but cheaper to operate than the older ship, even after its modernisation. It made the point that *Eagle* had reached the limits of its design potential and that the new design offered significant room for growth over its projected lifespan.

These quick studies confirmed that Study 53 represented the best compromise and the Board instructed Sir Alfred Sims, the Director General Ships, to develop it into a mature design to replace *Victorious* in service. Its cost was estimated at between £55 and £60 million for the first ship and the Board accepted that this had to represent a 'ceiling' figure that must not be increased by alterations and additions made during the detailed design and building processes. Study 53 was to operate an air group comprising thirty-six strike/fighter aircraft and four AEW aircraft plus six anti-submarine helicopters and two SAR helicopters. The fact that separate studies throughout the 1950s and 1960s had all arrived at the conclusion that a carrier of about 53,000 tons represented the best operational value for money indicates that this figure was a minimum, not a maximum, if the ship was to be effective through-out its planned life. The early *Illustrious* class ships had shown what could happen if ships were built with too small a margin to incorporate new developments. Ominously, however, Lord Carrington, the First Lord and the man who would

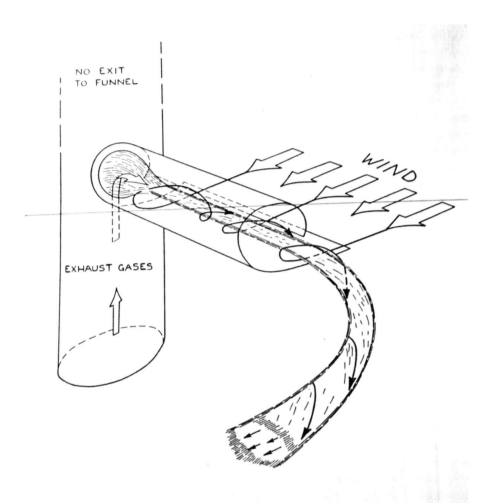

NO EXIT
TO FUNNEL

WIND

EXHAUST GASES

THIS ILLUSTRATES THE PRINCIPLE OF A HORIZONTALLY
MOUNTED CYCLONE GENERATOR AS SUGGESTED FOR A SHIP'S
INSTALLATION. FOR CLARITY THE DEVICE HAS BEEN SHOWN
TRANSPARENT.

A contemporary diagram showing the principle of how cyclone generators could be used to draw exhaust gases from a 'mack'. The concept was adopted for CVA-01. (Author's collection)

have to make the case for the new carriers to the Cabinet through the Ministry of Defence, expressed doubts. After listening to the brief on Study 53 he suggested that the Board should look again at carrier designs of about 40,000 tons capable of operating twenty-four aircraft. Clearly he was not impressed by the arguments about the cost-effectiveness of larger designs but throughout 1962 he had bowed to the professional opinions of his naval Board colleagues. It is unfortunate that he thought in terms of tonnage as the principal cost driver since by then the sophisticated electronic equipment, sensors and command facilities required in major warships of any tonnage had a major impact on cost. His uniformed colleagues obviously failed to emphasise this important point and his somewhat naive view came to be shared by a number of politicians who eventually terminated the project without ever really understanding the requirement for such a vital ship or even where the true construction costs lay.

In early 1963 there were still four new carriers in the long-term costings but the decision to procure four SSBNs to carry Polaris as the national deterrent caused a re-appraisal and the number of new carriers was reduced to three. The sketch design was approved by the Admiralty Board in July 1963 and the Cabinet approved development work on the first of class but, with the reduction to three from four as the eventual size of the carrier force, the Admiralty was told to replace both *Victorious* and *Ark Royal* with the first ship. £1.6 million was allocated to cover development and design costs but as each item fell due for payment the Treasury tried to block it, resulting in delays and further nugatory expenditure. Progress was also slowed by the fact that the Admiralty's Ship Department at Bath lacked the design staff to carry forward all the work on CVA-01 that was now required in addition to the higher-priority design work on SSBNs which had to be built and in service by 1968. Politicians accepted, without question, that these SSBNs were the optimum design to carry sixteen Polaris missiles, patrol with them for long periods and launch them when required, perhaps because of their similarity to their proven USN equivalents. Tonnage was, thus, much greater than any previous RN submarine but the Admiralty does not appear to have been asked if the boats could be built to a smaller tonnage to reduce cost, while still performing the same function. Perhaps this was a feature of the 'money is no object' attitude to the nuclear deterrent but it is unfortunate that similar comprehension of the carrier design function dictating the form was never achieved among politicians.

By 1963 no single British shipyard had facilities large enough for the new carrier and work would be required to dredge fitting-out berths and to both lengthen and widen slipways. There was a shortage of draughtsmen to prepare construction drawings and even the combined staff of two builders such as John Brown and Fairfield would still have left a shortfall in electrical specialists. Despite this, the work was achievable and the project could have proceeded, albeit at a slower pace than originally intended. Technically the ship reflected the years of careful thought that had gone into its development process. She was considered to be just too large for a two-shaft arrangement and so a three-shaft system was selected; this had the added value of redundancy in the event of action damage and allowed high speed to be maintained on two units while a third was shut down for maintenance during long periods at sea. The steam plant was the most advanced ever designed for the RN and would have run at 1000 psi and 1000° Fahrenheit. Electrical power output was to be 20,200 kW; when compared with the 8250 kW in the modernised *Eagle* showing both the limitation on upgrading an older design and the rapid contemporary increase in the need for electrical power. CVA-01 had an innovative exhaust system for the boilers with smoke carried above the island in two combined 'mast and smoke-stack' structures known as 'macks'. Vortex generators in the starboard side of these caused the smoke to be led away to starboard well clear of the flight deck. The arrangement worked well in wind-tunnel model tests. The island structure consisted of two separate blocks, each with a 'mack' carrying the exhaust gases from the separated boiler rooms; the space between the blocks was used as a 'garage' for flight-deck tractors and other equipment and had roller shutters to close it if required. Above the 'garage' the blocks were joined to give space for offices and ready rooms, giving the appearance of a single continuous island slightly larger than those on USN carriers. Radars and the TACAN aerial were carried on top of the 'macks'. The planned long-range surveillance radar was the Anglo-Dutch Type 988 'three-dimensional' array in a large and distinctive dome on top of the forward 'mack'. This was cancelled when the Dutch elected not to purchase the British Sea Dart missile system and, had she been built, CVA-01 would probably have had an improved version of the Type 984 with transistors replacing valves. The decision that, as the highest-value unit in any task force, CVA-01 should be fitted with its own defensive weapons rather than placing total reliance on escorts, proved to be one of the design's most significant cost drivers. The original design included both the CF-299 area defence missile system, later named Sea Dart, and the Ikara anti-submarine missile system developed in Australia. Both needed 'special to class' launchers and missile-handling systems as well as extensive magazine arrangements. Their removal would have led to a far more significant reduction in build cost than a reduction in tonnage since steel and its fabrication cost far less than modern radar-guided missile systems but this fact was not adequately explained to, or comprehended by, politicians. The Sea Dart launcher was similar to the version fitted in Type 82 and Type 42 destroyers but it was to be loaded horizontally from a 'travelling box' which was itself loaded from the handling system aft of the magazine and raised level with the launcher arms. Its development would not have been cheap. At first the design had no armour but it did have new and effective anti-torpedo protection based on work by NCRE. During the design development process armour was worked into Study 53/CVA-01

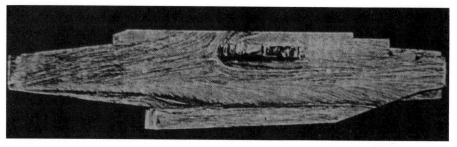

A wooden model of CVA-01; this one was used for wind-tunnel tests to evaluate the effect of wind over the deck. The grainy image from a recording camera shows the wind down the original 8 degree angled deck. (Author's collection)

which included a 3in flight deck, 3in hangar sides, 1½in bulkheads around magazines and 'splinter-proof' steel bulkheads. This took the design about 1000 tons over the politically-charged 53,000 tons but that figure was still used to describe the new carrier 'under standard operating conditions', that is with some fuel and ammunition expended. The 3.3 kV electrical distribution system would have been new to the RN and used step-down transformers.

Considerable thought went into the design of CVA-01's aviation arrangements and the hull and flight deck were, in many ways, significantly more efficient than those the USN *Nimitz* class. The large single hangar had an opening right aft through which aircraft could be moved onto the small quarterdeck to carry out engine runs and systems checks, removing the need for them to be ranged onto the flight deck where they would interfere with flying operations. There were two aircraft lifts; the forward one sited inboard but to starboard of the centreline so that it did not obtrude into the landing area. In order to save weight, it used a new 'scissors' arrangement under the platform to raise and lower it rather than the previous designs which suspended the platform from chains at the other end of which were balance weights. It was one of the few features of the CVA-01 project to be carried forward to another design, two similar lifts being fitted in each of the *Invincibles*; they proved to be problematical in service and required time, expense and development effort to be expended before they could be considered reliable. A side-lift suspended more conventionally from chains was fitted on the starboard side aft. Both lifts were specified to take a 75,000lb load. The island was designed well inboard leaving space, known as the 'Alaskan Highway', outboard of it along which aircraft could be taxied allowing a circular movement from the parking areas either aft to the side-lift to be struck down or forward to the bow catapult. Early iterations of the design had a large sponson to port to take an 8-degree angled deck but in 1962

The wooden model of CVA-01 used by DNAW to describe the advantages of the 3-degree 'parallel deck'. (Author's collection)

the Fleet Work Study Team proposed extending the sponson forward and aft in order to shift the whole landing area to port creating a parallel deck angled at only 3 degrees off the ship's centreline. This small angle was retained to ensure that aircraft that missed the arrester wires and 'bolted' would pass well clear of aircraft in Fly 1, the forward parking area. In effect the flight deck was divided into two parallel lanes with the parking area to starboard increased by 15 per cent and an unobstructed landing area to port. It would also have made recovery in poor visibility easier since aircraft would have been lined up closer to the wake for their carrier-controlled radar approach. Another advantage of the parallel deck was that the recovery area could be moved further forward than in the earlier angled deck arrangement, allowing the arrester wires to be positioned closer to the hull's centre of pitch, making recoveries in bad weather less stressful. Here again the 53,000-ton design had merit as the ship was nearly 1000ft long and less susceptible to pitch motion than a smaller, shorter ship. The simultaneous launch and recovery of aircraft in what the USN termed the 'battle flexi-deck' was entirely practical, although parking would have become tight with large numbers of aircraft in a single launch or recovery. The flight deck was to be stressed to take aircraft up to 70,000lbs.

The philosophy behind the design and the planned air group of forty-eight aircraft was that about two-thirds of the air group could be stowed in the hangar and about two-thirds could be parked on deck. This left a 'spare third' that could be filled by a squadron deployed to reinforce the carrier as 803 (Buccaneer) NAS demonstrated on *Hermes* in 1968 in the Indian Ocean. The RN also hoped that it might prove possible to embark RAF squadrons to provide a surge reinforcement capability, especially in the Far East, and successively proposed joint forces of Hawker P 1154, Buccaneer and Phantom aircraft. All were rejected by the RAF which showed no enthusiasm for operating its aircraft at sea under joint command. Interestingly, politicians never thought it necessary at the time to question this viewpoint despite the enthusiasm for joint operations that followed the creation of a unified Ministry of Defence; another example of the metonymy of the RAF and the erroneous political assumption that it must have the best knowledge of air matters. Every aspect of the design was carefully studied and modelled if necessary including the diamond-shaped flying control position or 'Flyco' which gave an unprecedentedly good view of the deck and aircraft in the visual circuit and on approach. Lighting and flight deck floodlighting for night operations were to a new design which was eventually fitted to the modernised *Ark Royal*. The two steam catapults each had a stroke of 250ft and were capable of launching a 55,000lb aircraft at an end speed of 115 knots; the longer stroke giving a smoother acceleration than the shorter stroke of earlier British steam catapult installations. Experience with *Victorious* and *Hermes* had shown that the catapult aircraft line-up equipment (CALE) installation aft of the catapults was unnecessary and it was omitted from CVA-01 but new water-cooled jet blast deflectors were designed to be positioned aft of the catapults to protect aircraft moving out of the range from the re-heated jet blast of aircraft being launched. These, too, actually saw service after two were fitted in *Ark Royal* during her modernisation. The catapults were positioned on the starboard bow to launch aircraft ranged on the starboard side and on the port waist to launch aircraft raged to port. During flexible launch and recovery operations aircraft ranged in Fly 3 could taxi forward along the 'Alaskan Highway' outboard of the island to launch from the bow catapult while aircraft landed on the angled deck, turning to taxi into Fly 2 to clear the runway. Both lifts could be used while these operations were in progress to strike down unserviceable aircraft or bring up serviceable replacements. There were four arrester wires, each capable of stopping a 40,000lb aircraft at an entry speed of 112 knots; all were of the new direct-acting design. A projector landing aid was fitted on a sponson which projected out to port from the parallel deck and a second sight with 'hi-lo' datum

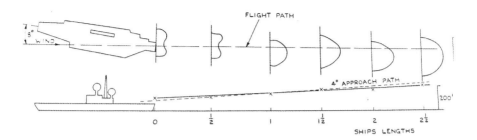

The result of extensive wind tunnel tests; a diagram showing the turbulence in the aircraft recovery area aft of the flight deck with the wind down the angled deck. (Author's collection)

bars was positioned aft of the island on the starboard side. The operations room and ADR were sited on 5 deck and a lift would have connected them to the bridge so that captain and his senior aviation and warfare officers could move quickly between the two positions if necessary. CVA-01 had fewer boats than previous British carriers; they were stowed to starboard of the Sea Dart launcher on the quarterdeck, aft of the flight deck and could be lowered into the water by the aircraft crane which was sited just aft of the side-lift, forward of the boat deck. The crane was capable of recovering a ditched but floating helicopter and lifting it onto the side-lift; it was cleared to lift 40,000lbs. The side-lift was also to be used for the movement of stores during solids RAS. For these the lift would be in the down position with the jackstay wire attached a strong point on the side of the deck above it. Stores would have been taken straight into the hangar, moved by mechanical handling equipment and struck down into dedicated stores areas using specialised lifts instead of manpower. There were four bomb lifts, each able to service both the hangar and flight deck with any air weapon in naval service from nuclear bombs and air-to-surface missiles to torpedoes and depth charges.

Design work on CVA-01 was completed on 27 January 1966 and approved by the Admiralty Board which warmly congratulated the staff of DG Ships who had achieved a great deal in a difficult period. Orders for long-lead items costing a total of £3.5 million, mainly machinery, had already been placed despite Treasury tardiness in allocating the money. The detailed plans were ready for dispatch to shipyards for the competitive tender process and the name *Queen Elizabeth* had been given Royal approval for the first-of-class although the Admiralty Board, unfortunately, elected not to announce the fact until an order was placed for the ship. CVA-02 was allocated the name *Duke of Edinburgh*, reportedly at the insistence of HM The Queen and CVA-03 was allocated the name *Prince of Wales*.

Controversy in Whitehall

The timing of the Admiralty's work on a new class of aircraft carriers coincided with a new directive on revised political assumptions produced by the Prime Minister, Harold Macmillan, in 1961.[5] Its principal points were that:

- The UK could no longer rely on using military bases or facilities in independent countries, even those in the Commonwealth, for operations which were not in full accord with their wishes. Until 1970 reliance could be placed on Gibraltar, Malta, Aden, Gan (Addu Atoll), Seychelles and Bahrain but there would be increasing restrictions on the existing bases in Libya, Cyprus, Kenya and Malaysia.
- There would be increasing difficulty in securing overflying rights for the airborne deployment of forces
- The UK would continue to maintain an independent contribution to the Western strategic nuclear deterrent.
- Intervention operations by the UK alone would be at no greater than brigade strength and it was expected that they would be conducted only when limited opposition had to be faced to establish forces ashore. Intervention in the face of heavy opposition requiring a full-scale assault was not considered feasible other than as a joint operation in co-operation with allies.

At the same time NATO policy began to shift from a nuclear 'tripwire' to a 'flexible response' strategy which gave increased emphasis to the role of conventional forces in the outbreak of a war with the Soviet Union. There was much in the new directive and NATO policy that favoured the carrier strike fleet and 1SL, Admiral Sir Charles Lambe, proposed that the only way to deploy air power effectively to meet the UK's worldwide commitments, especially those east of Suez, after British forces had withdrawn from their overseas bases was by carrier-borne aircraft. He went further, however, and explained his vision of using the carriers not just as fleet units in a mainly naval role but as floating bases in support of joint amphibious forces. He believed that they should be truly joint in character and capable of operating both RN and RAF aircraft. Shortly after making this proposal, Admiral Lambe had to retire because of ill health but his successor, Admiral Sir Caspar John, the first RN pilot to be appointed 1SL, continued with this concept and ordered studies to investigate the practicalities of its implementation. Not all Board members supported a new generation of aircraft

A side view of another early wind tunnel model of CVA-01; this one shows how effectively cyclone generators kept funnel smoke clear of the aircraft approach path aft of the ship. (Author's collection)

carriers without argument. VCNS, Vice Admiral Sir Varyl Begg, expressed doubts about the value of carriers based on his experience as FO2 FEF between 1958 and 1960, flying his flag in *Albion* and *Centaur*, both of which had obsolescent air groups of Sea Hawks, Sea Venoms, Skyraiders and Whirlwinds. He admitted that there was no alternative to a carrier if the RN were to continue to provide support for amphibious operations and military forces ashore but argued that the strike role could be provided more effectively and cheaply by submarine-launched missiles. He thought that the air defence problem could be solved by having a fleet composed entirely of submarines. These naive arguments were rejected by his Board colleagues because no strike missile that could be launched by a dived submarine existed and there could be no certainty that developing one would be cheap. A fleet composed entirely of submarines would have to be nuclear-powered and, consequently, considerably more expensive and less capable in a number of important roles than a carrier task force composed of conventional warships on the surface. The weakness of his arguments and the fact that support for military operations ashore emerged as one of the major reasons for keeping a carrier task force east of Suez led to Begg's views to be effectively sidelined.

We saw above that Lord Carrington, the First Lord, had suggested further study into a smaller carrier than Study 53 and asked the Board to consider 40,000 tons. He also wondered whether a V/STOL fighter based on the P 1127 might be acceptable but 1SL pointed out that the prototype, as flown, had a radius of action and payload considerably less than that of a Sea Hawk FGA 6 and could hardly be considered a viable type on which to base worldwide power-projection when compared with the Buccaneer or Phantom.[6] Carrington eventually bowed to the majority Board view but insisted that CVA-01 should be presented to Cabinet, through the Minister of Defence, on the broadest possible inter-Service basis and not as a purely naval weapons system. The state of the UK economy continued to be weak and the Minister of Defence was under strong pressure from the Treasury to reduce the defence budget but other Government Departments, including the Foreign Office, resisted any cuts in commitment. The Admiralty Board sought to cushion the cost of the carrier programme by presenting alternative proposals that reduced construction costs in other areas but by the autumn of 1962 the carrier programme remained the single most expensive item and became the subject of heated debate in Whitehall. In an attempt to find consensus on the matter, Lord Mountbatten, the CDS, asked the Chief of the Air Staff, Marshal of the Royal Air Force Sir Thomas Pike, to submit a paper on the case for replacing the existing carrier fleet. Whether he expected Pike to support joint carrier-borne aircraft operations or rationalise some other step towards joint operations, Mountbatten's intervention had unfortunate consequences. It gave Pike the chance to put forward untested theories in a document that can fairly be described as partisan and unreasonably prejudiced against the RN. To politicians seeking economies but careless of facts and consequences, his proposals seemed to be worth consideration.

The Chief of the Air Staff's Paper and the 'Island Strategy'

Pike observed that the cost of defence equipment, and especially aircraft, was rising faster than the defence budget and that weapons systems whose cost was disproportionate to their effectiveness, or which involved a duplication of effort could no longer be afforded. In a rational debate it would have been noted that most of his dogmatic arguments could be levelled against his own Service; what was development of the TSR 2 after the Buccaneer had just been developed and introduced into service by the RN if it was not duplication? It might be argued that the TSR 2 was better but it was still duplication. Such was the metonymy that the RAF already enjoyed that it never seemed to occur to any politician to ask this reasonable question. Pike went on to claim that the strike fleet's nuclear capability was limited in power, range and speed of deployment. This was an odd point of view that made no mention of the influence it gave over targeting and operations with US armed forces and within NATO, CENTO and SEATO. It also failed to mention that carrier-borne strike aircraft could attack targets beyond the range of Bomber Command, a capability admitted by an earlier CAS, and that the carriers were, arguably, considerably less vulnerable to a pre-emptive strike than the twenty or so fixed airfields regularly used by Bomber Command. The Soviet Union had to find them first and, as Coastal Command could have told Pike, this was not a capability that could be taken for granted in 1962.

The paper went on to make a series of partisan allegations that were not really worthy of serious debate. It claimed that in the conventional roles of protecting sea communications and supporting a military force ashore carriers could provide insufficient aircraft to produce worthwhile results. No mention was made of the fact that they might well be the only British aircraft within range of a crisis point or that the carrier could position itself to keep the maximum number of its aircraft over the operational area and could quickly re-arm and re-fuel them between sorties and launch them with fresh, newly-briefed pilots. No mention was made of Korean operations or the Suez intervention. Of course, the paper also failed to mention that aircraft operating at extreme range with air-to-air refuelling needed to be available in very large numbers, which the RAF did not have, and had none of the advantages mentioned above. Pike claimed that carriers were vulnerable, a statement that was not borne out by statistics, but made no mention of the large number of RAF airfields overrun by enemy forces during the Second World War and subsequently used by the enemy against Great Britain and her allies. Examples could be listed in France, North Africa, Malaya and the East Indies. The paper went on to produce a number of lesser but time-worn examples of RAF dogma, among them the bizarre statement that a carrier was slow-moving to deploy in comparison with aircraft. This completely missed the point that whilst military aircraft could fly quickly to a friendly airfield, they were useless until maintenance and operational support arrived in transport aircraft and bulk supplies of fuel arrived by sea, assuming that the British had sufficient sea control to do so. The transport aircraft that were flying in RAF maintenance, air traffic control and administrative staff could not be moving troops, so how could the number of combat 'boots on the ground' be built up and sustained while the RAF was fully committed to its own movement and support? A carrier arrived with its own maintenance facilities, air traffic and fighter control facilities, bulk fuel and ammunition and was ready to go into operation the minute it arrived in the operational area. Its attendant RFAs provided logistic support, if necessary for a considerable period. Reading through the Pike paper one cannot but be surprised that a senior officer made such naive and partisan statements or that anyone in the Ministry of Defence gave it sufficient credibility to use it as the basis for argument. The paper ended by making the assertion that the key to effective operations outside Europe after 1970 would be the air-delivery and subsequent supply by air of an infantry brigade group which, he claimed, could be transported for 1000 miles from a major base and sustained for one month without the need for any support from the sea. Quite how bulk supplies of fuel and ammunition were to be sustained was not explained and nor was there any attempt to explain how RAF theories could be dovetailed into joint activities with the other two Services in what would have to be very much a combined operation. The Government was keen to promote joint operations to reduce cost but, for some reason, failed to appreciate the single-Service bias in Pike's paper and thought it had something of substance to contribute.

In addition the CAS's paper, the Air Staff produced an even more unrealistic document in October 1962 that proposed an 'island strategy'. This envisaged establishing and maintaining bases on a number of islands from which intervention operations could be mounted by air up to a maximum range of 1000 miles. Apart from the need to create new overseas bases at a time when government policy was to reduce them in order to save money, the proposed strategy envisaged the use of the proposed OR 351 STOL transport aircraft with cover provided by the P 1154 V/STOL fighter. The former had not progressed beyond the requirement stage and the Air Staff can have had no idea of the likely cost of development and production so to claim its use a savings measure was, frankly, laughable. Even assuming both aircraft would eventually enter service, the strategy paper made no reference to how bulk fuel for their return flights was to be taken to the islands. Like so many theories put forward by Pike's air staff at this time, the proposal seemed to follow a pattern of stating a requirement, assuming it will come to fruition and putting it forward to rival joint operational doctrines that had been accepted by the Chiefs of Staff. The proposed islands were Aldabra, Masirah, the Cocos Islands with additional bases at Butterworth in Malaysia, Darwin in Australia and Manila in the Philippines with Ascension Island in the South Atlantic and Gan in the Indian Ocean as staging posts. Gan was actually used by the RAF as a fuelling stop for transport aircraft *en route* to the Far East and it relied on RFA tankers to supply its bulk fuel. Of course, the RAF took it for granted that the RN would be able to defend these bulk fuel and other supplies on their long ocean passages; the RAF certainly couldn't. The fundamental weaknesses of this strategy were three-fold; not all of them were on British territory and, therefore, might not be available at a time of crisis if the host nation did not agree with British action. Australia, for instance, had opposed the Anglo-French intervention at Suez in 1956 and Sri Lanka had ordered the RN to leave its base in Trincomalee after the same operation. The bases would have to be built at enormous cost, not mentioned in the strategy paper, to have an infrastructures capable of operating any aircraft, bulk storing fuel ammunition and spares and accommodating all of the men and women needed to man the base on a war footing and to operate the aircraft in addition to the brigade group while it waited to be taken into action. To be effective the bases would have to be stocked with sufficient logistical support for aircraft of different types to fly in and start operations at once, as they would do from a carrier.

Logistical support for the brigade group at the base and for the claimed month's deployment 1000nm away would also have to be immediately available. keeping stocks at this level would have been expensive but the strategy paper failed to mention how the new funding could be found. As important was the defence of the bases; if left with only a care and maintenance party when not in full use they would be open to seizure by Soviet special forces and then used against the UK. How would the UK defend its assets in Manila? Remember the air staff's adamant opposition to the P 1154 being designed with air-to-air radar and missiles and insistence that it could only be used in the fighter role by day in a clear air mass. What use would such fighters be in defence of an island base with no other British fighters, by definition, within 1000nm? Of course they would have needed a carrier and its task force to defend both the island base and the large amount of shipping needed to sustain both it and the place that was supposed to be the whole purpose of the operation, the location where the brigade group was to be landed. What the Air Staff had done, for those with the ability to think rationally, was provide an argument for the new generation of carriers. It is worth noting that one of the biggest sea battles of the Second World War, Midway, had been fought to defend an island base and it had taken the entire strength of the US Pacific Fleet, including several aircraft carriers, to do so. Pike and his staff had stressed the RAF weakness in expeditionary warfare, not its strength.

CAS's paper and the 'island strategy' proposal had ignored most of the British experience gained at such cost during the Second World War and in the unexpectedly turbulent years after it. A rebuttal was produced by 1SL, Sir Caspar John, in which he made the following points, all of which were based on actual experience rather than theory. Air-transport operations could be delayed by third-party refusal of the right to overfly their territory; the recent Kuwait crisis had been an embarrassing example of this shortcoming. No heavy military equipment or armoured vehicles could be delivered by air and movement of a whole brigade group would require a considerable and very costly increase in the number of expensive RAF transport aircraft available at short notice, especially if they were to be of the unique OR 351 STOL design. The fact that carriers were far less vulnerable than Pike had suggested was backed up by relevant statistics. 1SL went on to point out that an amphibious assault force based on ships at sea could be poised over the horizon from a potential objective for considerable periods and could still go ahead when air operations were inhibited by political considerations. If not needed, a task force at sea could sail away virtually unknown; winding down an air 'bridgehead' would be more difficult, obvious and, potentially, embarrassing. The 'island strategy' was dismissed on the grounds of cost, impracticality and the fact the sea control for the movement of supply ships would still be vital. Another point that Pike had tried to make was that the existence of carriers and their aircraft 'would not enable the RAF to dispense with a single combat aircraft'. Caspar John pointed out that the adoption of a Polaris SSBN force meant that there would no longer be a requirement to launch nuclear strike by either carrier or land-based aircraft. Large numbers of aircraft in both Bomber and Fighter Commands, if not the Commands themselves, could be dispensed with and this was the nub of the argument. The RAF felt that it had to fight for its survival and had chosen not to join the joint operations proposed by the RN and accepted by the Chiefs of Staff and Government but to fight for a continued independent role.

CAS's paper had hardly mentioned the importance of carriers in one of the RN's most vital roles, the protection of shipping, trade and British interests worldwide. In Caspar John's response, this important role was mentioned but not stressed, perhaps because the naval staff took it for granted. It was pointed out, however, that without carrier-borne fixed-wing aircraft the Navy would be unable to carry out either surveillance or reconnaissance and would be severely constrained in both anti-surface vessel operations and in defence against air attack. One difference between the arguments that was that while the RAF claimed, with no supporting evidence or basis in fact, that land-based aircraft could perform every task everywhere, the RN never saw itself carrying out every airborne task and, therefore, never claimed that carrier-borne aircraft would be able to do so. Long-standing commitments ashore such the RAF tactical air force based in Germany and the major bases in Singapore and Bahrain were obviously better performed by air force units which did not require mobility. Although rational enquiry should have exposed them, the RAF claims carried considerable weight with politicians because the unknown costs were hidden whereas the unit cost of replacement carriers was

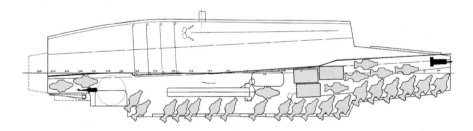

A 1965 drawing of CVA-01's flight deck showing the number of aircraft that could be parked on the flight deck while still keeping the landing area clear for recoveries or launches using the waist catapult. The three boxes represent the dimensions allowed for the Gannet AEW 3 replacement which would probably have been the Gannet AEW 7 as explained in a previous chapter. The black object at the bow is 'Jumbo' the crane. Note that there is still room in Fly 2 to park more aircraft. (Author's collection)

obvious. Unfortunately the increasingly acrimonious debate tended to polarise arguments and the wide range of carrier capabilities tended to be obscured as specific aspects were compared with land-based aircraft capability. After Sir Charles Lambe's initiative in 1961 the Naval case had tended to justify the need for carriers in terms of their joint-Service intervention capability and had sought close co-operation with the RAF. A great deal of original thought went into studies that looked into the practical implications of joint operations,[7] culminating in a report to 1SL by two recent FOACs, Admirals Smeeton and Hopkins, presented on 15 November 1961. They expressed the consensus opinion that until a common aircraft could be developed and brought into service, the only prospect for an RAF contribution to embarked aviation was the formation, with naval aircraft such as the Sea Vixen and Buccaneer, of an air group or individual squadrons to be manned and maintained by the RAF in addition to the RN's existing front-line units. The administrative difficulties would have been considerable but not insuperable given goodwill. The units could, of course, operate successfully ashore but since they would come under naval command when embarked it was felt that the proposal was unlikely to be attractive to the Air Ministry.

The early prospects for a common strike fighter seemed poor in late 1961. The bright prospects for the joint Saunders Roe SR-177 had been dashed by Duncan Sandys in 1958 and, as we saw in an earlier chapter, the political choice of the Hawker P 1154 to fit widely disparate roles proved to be a failure. The Buccaneer was only just entering RN service but, while it was clearly a far superior aircraft to the obsolete Canberra, the RAF refused to consider procuring a batch and remained fully committed to the development of the TSR 2. Buccaneers could operate from ashore[8] as readily as from carriers but there was no prospect of the TSR 2 being 'navalised';[9] in any case, in 1961 neither type was expected to be replaced before the mid-1970s at the earliest. The Navy did want a supersonic all-weather interceptor fighter to replace the Sea Vixen in the early 1970s and issued OR 346 to cover it but whether the RAF could be persuaded to participate in such as project was open to question. The new Hawker Siddeley Group[10] was stimulated by the political interest in a joint design and set up an advanced projects group, APG, to study the concept. It spoke to both the naval and staff staffs about the prospect of a joint Buccaneer, Sea Vixen and TSR 2 replacement design but 'it soon became apparent that the requirements of the two Services were incompatible. The TSR 2 successor would be too large and too late for the RN and the naval fighter requirement was too soon and, possibly not sophisticated enough for the RAF.' To make matters worse, while the naval staff requirement was well known and clearly stated, the air staff had not yet formalised its view on a TSR 2 replacement and was unwilling to discuss details.

After the exchange of views between the naval and air staffs over the carrier replacement programme, Mountbatten asked the CAS to comment on the type of aircraft carrier he would envisage to fulfil the major roles upon which the chiefs of staff all agreed, the safeguarding of the sea delivery of Army equipment and the close support of land forces in an expeditionary operation against light opposition. Pike took the view that VTOL close support/fighter aircraft would be suitable and could be operated either by the RN or RAF. The aircraft he had in mind was the Hawker Siddeley P 1154. He described it, inaccurately, as 'requiring' an interception role, whereas in fact the requirement stated that such a capability was 'desirable' provided that it did not interfere with the primary mission. One can see, however, that this proposal gave Mountbatten the idea that such an aircraft could be joint and could provide a supersonic fighter to replace the Sea Vixen in the right time frame. As always, the devil proved to be in the detail. Interestingly Pike proposed that these aircraft should be operated from 'commando-type carriers' and used a phrase that has echoed through the corridors of the Ministry of Defence ever since. He said that 'in the interests of operational flexibility and economy, however, it is both undesirable and unnecessary that [these aircraft] should be regarded as part of the permanent complement of the fleet'. This was a statement that paid no regard to the Inskip Award of 1937 and showed no understanding of the training and acquired skill required to achieve operational efficiency in an embarked squadron. He went on to bring the Admiralty Board's ill-considered thinking on escort cruisers into his argument by stressing the Air Ministry's view that there was no need for a fleet carrier since the increasing range of land-based bombers made the operation of strike aircraft from carriers unnecessary. By dispensing with the carrier-borne long-range strike role,[11] the commando carriers could be freed to operate a number of VTOL close-support fighters with the assault forces displaced into the new LPDs and escort cruisers with their tactical helicopters. He did not mention where the vital anti-submarine helicopters were to go.

Effectively, Pike was proposing a 'dual-purpose carrier' or CV and, given his antagonistic stance towards aircraft carriers as a generic group, his proposals were remarkably generous. He proposed replacing the existing fleet and commando carriers with 40,000-ton ships capable of operating twenty-four STOVL strike fighters and four AEW aircraft. He even accepted that the ship could be fitted with catapults and arrester wires for the AEW aircraft, making the 'cross-deck' operation of a wide variety of Allied carrier-borne aircraft possible. ASW helicopters were not mentioned but, given the tonnage, an embarked squadron of six would surely have been possible. CAS's proposal failed to make clear whether the 40,000-ton recommendation referred to standard displacement or full load, the latter including full fuel, armament stores and aircraft; probably because the air staff did not appreciate that there was a difference. Since the usual convention was to make reference to standard tonnage, the proposed dual-purpose carrier, or CV, was a very substantial ship, closely comparable to the modernised *Eagle* which had a standard displacement of 43,000 tons and a full load displacement of 50,786 tons. *Hermes*, which operated a small but effective air group that included Scimitars, Sea Vixens, Gannets and Wessex, had a standard displacement of only 23,900 tons but had no margin for growth through her expected life. It is of interest that Lord Carrington also chose 40,000 tons as his target figure and it would be fascinating to learn what discussions led him to that figure since there appears to be no written record. The air staff's carrier proposal can now be seen as the greatest missed opportunity of this controversial period. The naval staff failed to recognise the 'hostage to fortune' that had been offered to them, just as the air staff failed to realise that fleet carrier capability stemmed from the design and equipment of the ship, not the individual aircraft types embarked at any given time. A new carrier of 40,000 tons standard displacement had the <u>potential</u> to act as a strike carrier even if long-range strike aircraft were not embarked. Some stature with the USN and within NATO might be lost but this could be negotiated when the new ships entered service. It was the RN's nuclear-armed strike aircraft that the CAS and the air staff sought to eliminate, not the carriers themselves, which were agreed to have a wide range of roles when they operated a general-purpose tactical air group.

It would seem that arguments about the replacement carrier design had been distilled down to a difference of 13,000 tons, largely steelwork since both large and small carriers would have had have the same sensors and command facilities if they were to be effective; workshops, magazines and machinery would reflect the lower tonnage and considerable cost could have been saved by not fitting Sea Dart and Ikara, relying on CAP fighters and escorts for a layered defence against air and submarine attack. Taking the average cost of steel in 1961 as £100 per ton, the structural difference between the two concepts was about £1.3 million exclusive of the cost of fabrication. This sum does not seem excessive but it could allow arguments to swing both ways. In Study 53 the Admiralty Board had devised a ship that offered the best value for money and lowest hull cost per embarked aircraft; it had a good margin for growth through its projected life. A smaller hull offered less value for money but the initial outlay was significantly less, especially if guided weapons were omitted, and if the Cabinet, Treasury and Chiefs of Staff baulked at the higher outlay the 40,000-ton carrier had to be an attractive option that deserved to be taken seriously. A high outlay to procure a better product was only going to be possible if the nation could afford it and a growing body of political opinion felt that it could not, especially once the Polaris project got under way. The Admiralty Board's inflexible adherence to a large design that offered better value for money but a higher 'price-tag' was to have lethal consequences.

The Naval Staff officers tasked with analysing the Air Staff paper defended the RN long-range strike capability strenuously and stressed the cost-effectiveness of the Buccaneer against the TSR 2.[12] They also questioned the air staff claim that enemy air opposition could be eliminated on the ground by long-range bombers before any expeditionary operation began and the need for specialised high-performance fighters was re-stated. NBMR 3, they pointed out, had only a secondary air-to-air capability although they accepted that the type could operate 'at will from either carriers or shore bases when available'.[13] They rightly regarded as 'unsound' the idea that STOVL fighter squadrons need not form part of the permanent resources of the fleet because 'these will, in any case, have to spend much of their time embarked in carriers'. They felt that a 40,000-ton carrier was too large to act as a commando carrier and should, instead, be designated as a 'close-support carrier'.[14] Altogether the Naval Staff raised sixty-five points of contention with the Air Staff's ten-page paper but 1SL's response to Mountbatten in December 1961 did not go into great detail and nor did it criticise CAS's paper on land-based air power. The strategic value of the carrier strike force was re-stated and its role defined in somewhat limited fashion as the 'air support of land or maritime forces in places or at times when shore-based aircraft cannot do so, either adequately or at all'.[15] It left unsaid that aircraft were now vital to virtually every aspect of naval as well as strike warfare and that without embarked aircraft the RN might find itself unable to act against even a third-rate naval power. 1SL recognised three factors that would limit the size of a future carrier; the ratio between cost and the number of aircraft to be embarked; the need to balance expenditure between various fleet capabilities and the physical size of existing dry docks. Given these considerations he, too, envisaged a ship about the size of *Eagle*.

A Proposed Solution

Given the divergence of opinion that had followed his request that CAS and 1SL put forward their views, Mountbatten asked the Chief of the General Staff (CGS), Field Marshal Sir Francis Festing, to propose a solution. He had been the British military commander during the 1956 Suez operation and was fully conversant with the capabilities that expeditionary forces could expect from both carrier and land-based tactical aircraft. Fully briefed by both the Naval and Air Staffs he actually wrote two papers, one covering the remainder of the 1960s and one focused on the 1970s. In the first he accepted that the existing carrier fleet would meet any likely requirement during the first decade. After 1970 he stated firmly that it was neither necessary nor desirable to stake everything on land- or carrier-based aircraft since both had to be available.[16] During the 1960s, he stated, 'any deployment of tactical air power overseas must take full advantage of the qualities of flexibility, mobility and substantial independence of shore bases which aircraft carriers can offer'. For the brigade-sized operations envisaged East of Suez, he recommended that no more than four strike/light bomber squadrons were required and this number could be achieved by embarking two squadrons in the two carriers likely to be deployed into that area and two further squadrons at either end of the area, Aden and Singapore, to provide reinforcements trained for deck landing and maintaining embarked proficiency by rotation between the ships. Each carrier would also embark a fighter squadron and the only non-carrier-capable high-performance aircraft should be two all-weather fighter squadrons for the defence of the major bases. The primary benefit of such deployments would, he believed, be the withdrawal from service of three RAF squadrons and part of a fourth together with their administrative and logistical support.[17] Moreover, the nuclear strike capability of the carriers would honour the UK's commitment to SEATO without having to store the weapons ashore; thus avoiding possible embarrassment to HMG or the host nation.[18] Festing regarded it as 'unfortunate' that differing RN and RAF requirements had resulted in the Buccaneer and TSR 2 emerging with significant differences but, while he accepted that the technically more sophisticated TSR 2 would be needed in the NATO area in the 1970s, he did not consider that its performance would be essential East of Suez and recommended that the Buccaneer should be adopted as a common aircraft with a consequent reduction in TSR 2 procurement.[19] This represented a potentially large saving as, at the time, production TSR 2s were expected to cost three times as much as a Buccaneer.[20] In the longer term, he hoped that a single aircraft design might be developed to replace both the TSR 2 and the Buccaneer, although he recognised that it was too far ahead to visualise late 1970s operational requirements in any theatre with accuracy.

With regard to aircraft carriers themselves, Festing made it clear that he had not accepted CAS's argument over the existing commando carriers. He stated emphatically that 'it has been accepted that a commando ship cannot be satis-factorily adapted to carry out the additional task of operating modern fixed-wing aircraft in the close support and strike roles. It is also common ground that we need an aircraft carrier distinct from the commando ship and this fact must be recognised.'[21] Significantly, when I researched material for the naval staff history from which parts of this chapter have been derived, I was unable to find many responses from the Naval Staff, probably because the final paper was so close to the Admiralty viewpoint that there was no perceived need to refute it. The Air Ministry's reaction also proved difficult to examine but there can be little doubt as to the impact of Field Marshal Festing's study report. Once it had been digested, Mountbatten discussed its findings in committee with the Chiefs of Staff. On 20

December 1961 he minuted the results of their discussion to the Minister of Defence, Harold Watkinson, and his words are significant enough[22] to be quoted at length. Underlining, where shown, reflects emphases added to the original document by an unknown member of the naval staff who prepared it for circulation within the Admiralty. Lord Mountbatten informed the minister that:

1. We are now agreed that since the extent to which reliance can be placed in the next twenty years or so on fixed bases is at best very uncertain and we may in this period be faced with having no land bases between the UK and Australia, there will be a need for aircraft carriers to provide floating airfields from which British air power can be operated irrespective of whether this power is provided by the Royal Air Force or Fleet Air Arm. We are also agreed that the proposal to combine the functions of a commando carrier and aircraft carrier in one ship is not practicable.

2. We consider that in addition to providing air defence for itself and for seaborne forces the carrier must also be capable of operating aircraft to meet the requirements for air support of the Army and for tactical strike and reconnaissance.

3. It is difficult to foresee exactly what type of aircraft will be necessary to operate from the future carriers or in what numbers. There is, however, a general tendency for aircraft to become larger and heavier. In view of this and since there is a clear requirement for an aircraft carrier replacement programme we consider it would be only prudent to provide carriers which would afford the maximum flexibility and aircraft capacity within the limits of our present docking facilities etc. This would mean the size of the replacement carriers would be in the order of that of the existing *Ark Royal* class.

4. We have also considered what should be our policy as regards the provision of future aircraft and are agreed that it should be our aim to provide, as soon as possible, aircraft common to the Fleet Air Arm and Royal Air Force for the roles of fighter, ground attack, strike and reconnaissance. If Royal Air Force crews are to be capable of operating from either a land or a floating base this will mean that such aircraft must be capable of vertical take-off and landing, or at least of very short take-off and landing, in order to obviate the necessity for the crews to be trained and kept in practice in operating from aircraft carriers.

5. We consider that the most important step would be to attempt to produce a joint operational requirement for a common aircraft to replace OR 354, the TSR 2 replacement, and OR 346, the Buccaneer replacement. This aircraft should, if

possible, meet the joint requirements for the fighter/ground attack/strike/ reconnaissance roles.[23] If such an aircraft proved impracticable we would aim to produce joint ORs for two common aircraft, one to fill the fighter/ground attack role, the other strike reconnaissance roles. The object should be to produce the aircraft not later than the time scale 1975-77.

6. In the interim and as a first step towards achieving this aim an effort should be made to produce a common fighter/ground attack aircraft with a supersonic performance on the lines envisaged in the NATO NBMR 3. Such an aircraft might be introduced into service about 1969/70. It would have the decided advantage that its strike capability, particularly as regards radius of action (400nm), would be limited but on the other hand would provide a carrier-borne supersonic fighter at a considerably earlier date than is otherwise likely.[24]

By 1962, therefore, the Chiefs of Staff had agreed that a carrier replacement programme was necessary and that the most cost-effective design had merit. Watkinson and Carrington pondered CDS's minute for a month before submitting their own joint memorandum to the Cabinet Defence Committee, putting forward the arguments for a new carrier to replace *Victorious* in 1970. They recommended that a design study should be put in hand and long-lead items funded, up to an expenditure of £1.6 million during the next three years for a 'carrier of the future'. They stated that 'it is already clear that this ship will not be a fleet carrier in the sense of a capital ship designed for global war. It will be designed as a floating airfield capable of operating Royal Navy or Royal Air Force aircraft. The Chiefs of Staff have agreed that we should aim to provide, as soon as possible, aircraft common to the RN and RAF for the roles of fighter, ground attack, strike and reconnaissance.' For the present, a new carrier had broad agreement but now the sticking point, and the next round of argument concerned the design and development of a common aircraft. Following CDS's advice, Harold Watkinson chose the Hawker P 1154 and another series of divisive inter-Service arguments followed which were described a previous chapter. Eventually the RN selected the McDonnell F-4H Phantom II, describing it to the cabinet as less risky and cheaper alternative to the P 1154. The RAF subsequently followed this lead.

The Cancellation of CVA-01

Just before its summer recess in 1963, Mr Thorneycroft announced that the Cabinet had decided to order a single new aircraft carrier for the RN to replace both *Victorious* and *Ark Royal*. The lives of *Eagle* and *Hermes* could, with refits, be extended until about 1980[25] and the new ship would form part of a force of three ships that would 'ensure that the Fleet Air Arm can maintain its role at least until

1980'.[26] Thorneycroft stated detailed design work for the new ship would follow with an order to be placed by competitive tender in 1965. A few weeks after this positive statement, Admiral Sir David Luce replaced Sir Caspar John as 1SL. This project was still slowed by argument and differences of opinion, however, and on 3 January 1964, Luce was forced to write to Mountbatten complaining about the attitude of the Treasury.[27] In his letter he wrote that,

> Since the Cabinet decided last July to build a new carrier we (the Ministry of Defence and the Admiralty) have been in continuous negotiation with the Treasury about the placing of certain extra-mural research and design contracts, without which we cannot get on with implementing the Government's decision. We also wanted sanction, though less urgently, for ordering long-lead items. After a great deal of whittling down in the discussions between officials, we said we would accept for the moment that only nine particular development and design contracts should be placed at once, amounting to £600,000 in all; we would re-open next April the question of the next lot of development and design contracts, and of contracts for the long-lead items. This was the package deal agreed between our officials. The Chief Secretary, however, has refused his sanction even to this. The Minister of Defence after a final talk with the Chief Secretary on Wednesday decided that he cannot tolerate any further delay and he has proposed to the Prime Minister that the matter should be thrashed out in the Cabinet.

The result was that some funding was made available but design work was delayed and competitive tender would not be possible until 1966.

In October 1964 Harold Wilson became Prime Minister after a narrow general election victory and set in train a major review of defence with the aim of reducing expenditure to an absolute maximum figure of £2 billion by 1969/70. Since much of the argument about re-equipment had centred on the provision of air power in support of expeditionary operations East of Suez, the study group was directed to examine the requirement for fixed-wing aircraft in maritime operations with especial regard to the economics of carrier and land-based aircraft. Whilst the study was in its preliminary stages, a number of RAF aircraft projects were cancelled including the TSR 2, P 1154 and the HS 681 STOVL transport. The RAF now pinned its hopes on the acquisition of the American F-111A strike fighter which was believed to have an excellent low-level strike capability at long range. A meeting at Chequers in June 1965[28] sought to reduce commitments in order to cut the cost of defence. For the RN this meant a reduction of presence in the Mediterranean, withdrawal from the Caribbean and South Atlantic, withdrawal from Aden, a

The artist's impression of CVA-01's final design. The original hangs by the desk in my study at which I am typing this book. Note the cyclone generator stubs poking out to starboard of the two 'macks' and the Phantom taxiing forward onto the 'Alaskan Highway'. (Author's collection)

reduction of commitments in the Gulf and an overall reduction of intervention capability and commitments in the Far East after the end of the Confrontation. There was to be a 20 per cent reduction in the size of the surface fleet, but for the moment the strike carrier fleet survived. The Overseas Defence Committee was tasked, in August 1965, 'to examine the choice between land -based and seaborne air power', a statement it initially regarded as unfortunate as it implied that one or the other must go but it became clear that to meet the Government's target this was indeed the case. Dennis Healey, the Defence Secretary, called for further reviews and both 1SL and CAS provided statements. There was little new to say but 1SL explained the crushing loss of capability that a Navy without aircraft carriers would suffer.

The Chief Scientific Adviser to the MOD, Sir Solly Zuckerman, produced a paper in September 1965 which was refreshingly impartial.[29] In it he expressed serious misgivings about the RAF's untried and untested assertions and said that if the Government felt that it could not afford carriers, it should not be deluded into thinking that their capabilities could be replaced by buying a few extra aircraft for the RAF. The Secretary of State called for a further round of studies and 'moved the goalposts' by stating that British forces would only be retained in the Far East for a peacekeeping role. No limited wars would be undertaken without allies and the remaining bases in the region should not be considered as permanent. The USN sought to help at this point by offering the USS *Shangri La* to the RN. 1SL regarded this kind offer as a short-term palliative rather than a solution and, since the ship was older than any of the RN carrier fleet and had very different command and control arrangements, the offer was politely refused. Throughout this difficult period the Navy Minister,[30] Christopher Mayhew, and 1SL continued to support the CVA-01 project despite the fact it seemed, by then, to have to compete with a combination of opposing arguments, nearly all of them self-centred, ill-considered or ill-founded. On 26 January Healey went on a tour of Commonwealth and Allied nations to forewarn them on the effect of the defence review on the UK's defence posture. His itinerary included Washington, Canberra, Singapore, Kuala Lumpur and Bahrain. On 7 February he chaired a meeting of the MOD's Admiralty Board and explained that CVA-01 would not be built, partially on financial grounds and partially on what he mistakenly described as operational grounds. He put forward his personal view that that carriers had been useful for the operational tasks that had arisen during the previous decade, but had not been essential. This gross distortion of fact ignored the essential role played by RN carrier-borne aircraft in Korea, Suez, Jordan/Lebanon, the Kuwait Crisis and the critical role being played by the strike fleet in the Confrontation against Indonesia. As if this was not bad enough he ended by saying that he found it difficult to devise a scenario in which the carrier was essential but among the plethora of studies that he had ordered there was one. One paper had specifically noted that shore-based air cover could not be provided for the defence of the Falkland Islands but, with his customary lack of comprehension, Healey had rejected it. On 14 February 1966 the Cabinet formally decided to terminate the project to build CVA-01 and endorsed the MOD recommendation to procure fifty-six F-111A strike aircraft. Mayhew, the Navy Minister, resigned on 19 February and Admiral Sir David Luce resigned on 22 February, the first 1SL to resign on a matter of publicly-stated principle. The former was replaced by J P W Mallalieu and the latter by Admiral Sir Varyl Begg, who, it will be recalled had never been a supporter of carriers. In *Vanguard to Trident*, Eric Grove described the decision to abandon CVA-01 as 'perhaps the most traumatic shock to the RN of the entire post-war period'.[31] If anything this was an understatement and I vividly remember the shock when I and other officers were told about the decision. Until then we had been told that while the RN might no longer be the largest navy in the world, our Government would continue to ensure that it was the best equipped. After February 1966 that was no longer to be the case.

Even the Statement on the 1966 Defence Review[32] was ineptly handled and badly edited. Part 1, the Defence Review, stated that 'experience and study have shown that only one type of operation exists for which carriers and carrier-borne aircraft would be indispensable: that is the landing, or withdrawal, of troops against sophisticated opposition outside the range of land-based air cover. It is only realistic to recognise that we, unaided by our allies, could not expect to undertake operations of this character in the 1970s – even if we could afford a larger carrier force.' I will refer back to this pusillanimous statement in a later chapter. Part II,[33] on the other hand, stated under the heading Royal Navy General Purpose Combat Forces that 'the aircraft carrier is the most important element of the Fleet for offensive action against an enemy at sea or ashore and makes a large contribution to the defence of seaborne forces. It <u>can also</u>[34] play an important part in operations where local air superiority has to be gained and maintained and offensive support of ground forces is required.' The two contradictory statements are hardly the outcome of a rational review and reflect little credit on the expanded MOD in its first full year of operation. The latter statement was probably written before 14 February and reflects the Navy's whole argument which was couched in tones that were reasonable and which never made extravagant claims based on untested theories. The Cabinet's decision to cancel CVA-01 was based on a growing financial crisis that eventually led to the pound being devalued. Advised that land-based aircraft could fulfil the national requirement, Ministers, who should have known better, accepted the RAF proposals at their unproven face value, thinking them to be a cheaper but viable alternative. Their successors subsequently found the flaws in the RAF concept when British forces did have to carry out an opposed landing, without allies and outside the range of land-based aircraft in 1982.

The British economy continued to decline after 1966 and without orders for merchant ships, the Government's decision not to build a new generation of aircraft carriers proved to be a 'death sentence' for the shipyards on the upper Clyde who could have used the project to help modernise their facilities and survive. By 1970 Harold Wilson's government had spent more money trying to 'prop up' the shipbuilding industry, without success, than it would have spent on CVA-01. Perhaps building a new generation of aircraft carriers might only have delayed the end for some yards but at least the taxpayer would have acquired something vitally important for the money. In 1968 more cuts became necessary and it was announced that the UK would withdraw from the Far East in 1971 and concentrate its forces in the NATO area. The F-111A, latterly the lynchpin of arguments against the carrier, was cancelled and the RAF finally accepted a small batch of new-build Buccaneers as a Canberra replacement. Many others were taken over from the RN as the carrier force was run down. The type proved very effective and popular with its crews. By the 1980s the RAF found itself with two principal tactical aircraft, the Phantom and the Buccaneer, both designed to naval specifications which had been strenuously opposed by the air staff.

15 Rundown of the Carrier Force

When he put forward the Navy's case during the 'radical' defence review of 1953, the First Sea Lord, Admiral of the Fleet Sir Rhoderick McGrigor, had spoken of 'the disastrous results which would follow if, in spite of the strategic need, fleet carriers were abolished from the RN'. He emphasised the fact that 'in the eyes of the rest of the world we would cease to be a major naval power' and asked the review body 'to bear in mind the effect on the morale of the Navy and on its confidence in any Board of Admiralty which agreed to such a measure'.[1] Subsequent Boards were united in keeping faith with this concept, although some members had clearly not realised that their arguments in favour of various cruiser options had weakened the central argument. In August 1963 Sir David Luce outlined the Board's philosophy in a letter to commanders-in-chief and flag officers,[2] in which he explained its view that carriers and a viable Fleet Air Arm must continue to be integral parts of the fleet. He began by explaining to the thirteen recipients that it had proved impossible to keep them up-to-date with the latest thinking in Whitehall because 'the pace has been so hot, with the direction and ground of attack shifting so radically and so frequently, that any papers we might have sent out were apt to have been overtaken by events almost before you got them'. Once the Government had announced its intention of building a new carrier, however, he felt the Board's opinions to be more firmly based. The letter included several annexes which emphasised the basic arguments that had proved why the RN must have carriers if the nation and the RN were to be able to meet the Army support requirement overseas and 'if the RN is to be able to safeguard our worldwide maritime interests'. It is greatly to his credit that Sir David Luce resigned after the cancellation of CVA-01 and, given the traumatic change to the RN's long-term plans, it is arguable that the whole Board should have resigned with him.

The Search for Alternatives
One appendix to 1SL's 1963 letter had examined the possibility of opting for an alternative future Navy without carriers and its content now seemed particularly relevant. Such a radical change was found by the study group to risk abandoning a field in which the UK had the advantage over every potential enemy. The UK

continued to lead the world in fixed-wing naval air power and, while it might be smaller than the USN, it had earned the Americans' long-lasting respect.[3] The appendix noted emphatically that to stand a chance of countering either the Soviet Navy or a smaller 'client' navy equipped with Soviet weapons the RN would have to undertake the rapid and expensive development of very long-range surface-to-surface (SSGW) and surface-to-air guided weapons (SAGW). Neither would be effective without organic AEW aircraft to locate their targets 'over the horizon' and neither could, realistically, be operated from any ship in service or projected with the RN. A new type of 'battlecruiser' would be required which would have to be equipped with advanced sensors, command facilities and communications. It would be expensive and would lack many of the flexible qualities of aircraft carriers. Even if fixed-wing aircraft were to be discarded for political reasons, the question of how to operate large numbers of embarked helicopters in the anti-submarine, commando assault and, potentially, AEW roles would remain. The authors ended by observing that the role of carriers[4] 'is essentially offensive and apart from destroying the enemy as he comes in to attack, a high priority will be accorded, whenever the political situation allows, to the destruction of enemy air, surface and submarine units and supporting installations at airfields and bases'. None of this would be possible without carriers. Polaris missiles were not mentioned but their use from the deployed

Vice Admiral Sir Richard Janvrin KCB DSC, a former commanding officer, saluting *Victorious* as she began her last journey on 11 July 1969. He is in the rear cockpit of Swordfish LS 326 which was, at the time, the last airworthy example of the type. (Author's collection)

SSBNs, when they entered service, could only be considered for static targets on the Allied list that were not time-sensitive but they could not be used realistically against tactical targets like the bombs from strike aircraft.

A number of factors had arguably made the impact of CVA-01's cancellation more devastating than previous new carrier construction projects which had been delayed or cancelled since 1951. None of these had ended the RN's carrier strike capability because there had been a number of hulls under construction left over from the emergency war programme and, whilst not ideal, these were adequate for the task. Some had been capable of modernisation to an acceptable standard but by 1963 there were no more. Undoubtedly the Admiralty had over-stated the urgency of the carrier replacement programme in order to stimulate new construction and, having done so, there was no easy way of claiming, after February 1966, that the need was not quite as urgent as had been claimed. Worse still, with the expanded role of the Ministry of Defence after April 1964, the naval staff was no longer the focus of attention when new projects were discussed; it now formed only a small part of a much larger defence staff and all the same arguments against carriers came to the surface again. The new 1SL, Sir Varyl Begg, immediately showed himself to be part of the problem, not the solution, when he took office. It will be remembered that he had not been a supporter of carriers and now he added to the RN's pain by instituting a Future Fleet Working Party (FFWP), which was instructed to investigate the possibility of creating a fleet without aircraft carriers by the mid-1970s when the existing ships were expected to reach the end of their useful lives. The existing plan[5] showed *Victorious* running on until 1971, *Eagle* undergoing a long refit between 1972 and 1973 and then running on, *Hermes* running on and *Ark Royal* due for disposal at the end of 1972. Separate assumptions were made to cover CVA-01 beginning operational deployments in 1972 (Plan X) or 1973 (Plan Y). By the time this plan was prepared it had already been decided to discard *Centaur* which was only twelve years old. The RN strike fleet now faced opposition from a lethal combination comprising a 1SL who seemed unaware that the last twenty-one years of naval development had happened, a MOD that had had little or no practical knowledge of anything naval and an air staff that was determined to preserve the independence of its land-based bomber force against all arguments. The RN was fortunate to have men such as Le Fanu and Hopkins to fight for what they knew to be the right policy.

The FFWP immediately found itself in an impossible situation for exactly the reasons put forward in 1SL's 1963 paper. A Government that had cancelled CVA-01 for the stated reason that the defence budget could not afford it was hardly likely to offer an even larger sum of money to begin the urgent development of new SSGW, SAGW and new 'battlecruisers' to deploy them. Without AEW aircraft both types of missile would be limited to line-of-sight engagements with only minimal warning of low-flying attackers that flew below the radar horizon, exactly the type of attack the RN had perfected with the Buccaneer for use against Soviet cruisers that lacked their own air cover.[6] Without fighters the fleet would have no defence against shadowing aircraft which remained outside missile range and would be unable to destroy missile-firing aircraft, like those used by the Soviet Navy and its smaller 'clones', before they launched their weapons. Without fixed-wing assets the RN would be unable to probe beyond the range of small, embarked helicopters which would be desperately vulnerable when located by missile-armed enemy warships.

Asked for comment on the importance of having some form of embarked aviation capability in the future fleet, DNAW took a line in March 1966[7] that differed significantly from the arguments that had been deployed in support of CVA-01. Days after her cancellation, Captain R D Lygo RN, the deputy director of DNAW, wrote that 'progress in aeronautics was such that future aircraft were likely to reduce in weight and complexity for any given staff requirement'.[8] In the same document Lygo stated that AEW was the most important embarked role and that, notwithstanding DNAW's earlier opposition to the procurement of Hawker P 1154 STOVL strike fighters, aircraft like it were now seen as 'having the potential to carry out their roles successfully from ships other than aircraft carriers'. The trauma of CVA-01's cancellation and the negative attitude of the new 1SL meant that naval members of the defence staff could no longer attempt to re-open the question of a new carrier, they were fighting for anything they could get and if that was to be a small ship with STOVL fighters then so be it. By 1966 work by DG Ships on the SSBN project was sufficiently far advanced to allow work to begin at Foxhill on new sketch designs. The FFWP acted as the conduit for a number of proposed new ship designs which drew together several roles in an attempt to keep the budget within the existing long-term costings (LTC) but provide viable warships. All of them were loosely described as cruisers with a qualifying adjective.

Sketch Designs for a 'Commando Cruiser'

As early as 11 March 1966 the RN Directorate of Tactics and Weapons Policy forwarded a paper[9] that proposed a 'commando cruiser'. Four escort cruisers and two replacement commando carriers remained in the LTC agreed by the MOD and it was felt that if the two requirements were drawn together, six ships could be procured that would be capable of carrying either an embarked commando force and its associated helicopters or an air group comprising a mixture of A/S, AEW and missile-carrying helicopters, probably Sea Kings. For the first time, serious consideration was given to the potential for embarking STOVL fighters that could be exchanged for helicopters on a one-for-one basis. By May 1966 FFWP had commissioned studies into the alternative assumption of embarking a 'self-contained air strike and reconnaissance capability' comprising six P 1127 Kestrel derivatives in each of the six commando/escort cruisers. Work was also funded to evaluate the possibility of fitting AEW radar into helicopters such as the Sea King or, surprisingly, the large Chinook that was just entering service with the US Army. A staff target for the commando cruiser was prepared hastily by the end of March 1966 and sketch designs were presented to the FFWP in April. It was found that the requirement to operate and support STOVL strike fighters, even in modest numbers, had driven up the tonnage considerably beyond that envisaged for the 'base-line' escort cruiser. The first sketch was for a ship of 15,000 tons with a small but conventional flight deck and a hangar that formed part of a large starboard-side island. It was to be capable of housing six Sea Kings or four P 1127 Kestrel fighters with two SAR helicopters. The choice of a hangar within the island limited the number of aircraft that could be embarked but allowed a large amount of mess deck space under the flight deck for a commando group of up to 600 men. It was immediately obvious that besides being too small, the aviation arrangements were not practical. With the hangar doors open, jet and rotor downwash from aircraft operations would have made working in the hangar extremely difficult. In some ways the design resembled a very scaled-down CVA-01 but with a relatively larger island to incorporate the hangar. Like the cancelled carrier there was a large radome intended for Type 988 'Broomstick' radar which was itself soon to be cancelled. There was to be a Sea Dart launcher aft, a 4.5in Mark 8 gun forward of the island and a Sea Wolf launcher on the after part of the island. The flight deck was to be 645ft long[10] and 100ft wide at its widest point abeam the island. In addition to its sophisticated radar and weapon fit, the sketch included Type 182, 184 and 185 sonars. Steam machinery of 60,000hp derived from that of CVA-01 was intended to give a maximum speed of 28 knots six months out of dry dock. The design included the capability to act as a Grade II flagship and cost, at 1966 prices, was estimated at 'about £30 million' or half the estimated cost of CVA-01.

The design gave the FFWP cause for considerable thought. The various roles stipulated in such haste could not be carried out concurrently in such a small hull. If such a ship were deployed in the commando role their limited helicopter numbers and lack of landing craft and support facilities[11] would put them at a grave disadvantage compared with the light fleet carrier conversions that they would replace and which had good qualities in all these areas. In the STOVL fighter role they would be very expensive ships for the modest capability they deployed. The missile and gun armament put them in the destroyer category but the sketch design had no anti-submarine weapon, other than those carried by helicopters when operating in the ASW role. When operating in the commando or fighter roles they would have no A/S defence and would need surface escorts to screen them. This sketch design revealed that the originators of the concept did not really know, in a very literal sense, what they were talking about; the commando cruisers, if they had been built, would have given very little capability in return for their high cost. Begg's negative attitude added to the trauma of CVA-01's cancellation by his insistence that aircraft carriers had become so big and expensive that 'only the United States could afford them'. Nobody in the MOD commented on the fact that the three commando/escort cruisers that would have to operate together to give a balanced capability with an estimated £90 million build cost would still fall far short of the capability offered by a single CVA-01-type carrier at an estimated £60 million build cost.

After considering the initial commando cruiser sketch design, the FFWP ordered further work to produce a design that overcame its many obvious weaknesses. The major changes in requirement were an increase in the number of aircraft that could be embarked from six to eighteen and an increase in the size of the embarked commando force to 650. Bizarrely, however, 325 of these were to be accommodated to full RN standards and the remaining 325 in basic, bunk-only accommodation. Quite how this was meant to allow a military force to poise over the horizon from a potential target whilst retaining their fitness was never made clear. Even the full number was far short of the number that could be carried in the existing light fleet carrier conversions. The extra aircraft were to be accommodated in a 'half hangar'

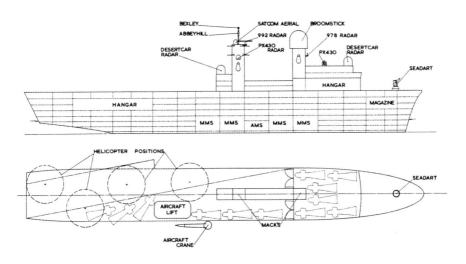

A 1966 sketch design for a commando cruiser that could not be mistaken for an aircraft carrier. It would have been unnecessarily impractical to operate. (Author's collection)

on 4 deck under the after part of the flight deck, capable of taking six Sea Kings or Kestrels, in addition to the island hangar alongside the flight deck. It would need a lift to range and strike down aircraft and this would have been positioned at the aftermost part of the flight deck and stressed to take loads up to 30,000lbs. The change negated the original point of the island hangar which had been to remove the need for lifts to penetrate the flight deck, however, the new after deck lift meant that the Sea Dart launcher had to be moved forward. Enlarging the sketch design gave the opportunity to incorporate armour protection around the machinery and increase the fuel stowage to meet the staff target of a 'fast deployment' capability. This was defined as the ability to steam for 5000 miles non-stop at 25 knots.[12] These changes forced the sketch design up to 17,000 tons and the projected build cost to 'about £38 million'. The air group was envisaged as comprising six ASW Sea Kings, four AEW/electronic warfare Sea Kings and eight surface strike/search Sea Kings equipped with the projected Martel air-to-surface missile. In the medium term the strike Sea Kings were to be replaced by eight Kestrel strike fighters. Six aircraft were to be struck down into each of the two hangars and six more retained in a deck park. At least this enlarged design had a more balanced capability but when it was shown to Begg he criticised it as looking 'too much like an aircraft carrier' and said that therefore it was not acceptable. DG Ships responded by stressing that function dictates form and since the proposed ship, unlike any other in the future fleet, was intended to operate a number of aircraft it had been given the ideal form

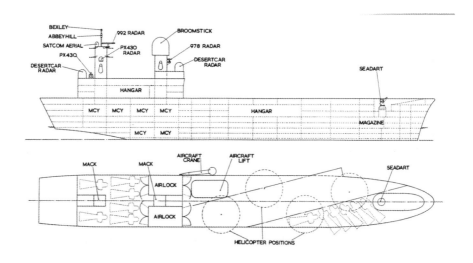

An even worse 'non-carrier like' commando cruiser sketch design from 1966. (Author's collection)

for the purpose. This response was not accepted and, through the FFWP, Begg ordered further studies of ships that could not be mistaken for aircraft carriers. Sketch designs were offered by a Ship Department that was clearly embarrassed offering ships with superstructures on the centreline aft, amidships and forward. All of them avoided the hard-won lessons of the past, had higher projected build costs and offered less operational capability than the 'carrier-form' hull. They must represent the design 'nadir' for the Navy that had invented the aircraft carrier itself, the angled deck, steam catapult and the mirror landing aid.

A More Rational Alternative from DG Ships

On its own initiative, the Ship Department produced a simple design for a commando carrier of about 20,000 tons with a hull built to mercantile standards which was intended to establish a base-line size and cost for a ship intended to meet the primary purpose of deploying a commando group efficiently. It was to be 'inexpensive' with none of the command or weapons systems specified for the commando cruiser, all of which could be built into another hull with the primary purpose of carrying them making both ships more efficient in their primary roles. The basic hull form was derived from a design to Lloyd's rules that had been developed, prior to its cancellation in the 1966 Defence Review, for a submarine depot ship. A small, starboard-side island was included for command and control with a combined 'mast and smokestack' or 'mack' arrangement for the exhaust gases from the steam machinery. Both were derived from CVA-01 technology in a last attempt to gain some benefit from the expenditure on her development. The single-shaft machinery would have developed 25,000shp giving 20 knots at full load displacement six months out of dry dock and was designed to give an endurance of 5000nm. Hangars under the flight deck had space for nineteen Wessex HU 5 assault helicopters with two lifts, one at the forward extremity of the forward hangar and one at the after extremity of the after hangar. Both were of the 'scissors' type designed for CVA-01 and both were offset to starboard leaving the runway centreline clear for potential rolling take-offs by Kestrel-type STOVL fighters. Between the two hangars there was a vehicle garage with a lower deck-head height than the main hangar capable of holding thirty-two Land Rovers and sixteen trailers; access to it would have been through the hangars. Trucks and other large vehicles could be stowed on the flight deck as in the light fleet carrier conversions *Albion* and *Bulwark*.

In order to keep the hull as close as possible to that of the base-line depot ship, sponsons were not included at the deck edge but had the design been taken forward they could have been for relatively little extra expense. There was space on the flight deck for eight Sea King-sized helicopters to run on spots concurrently and four

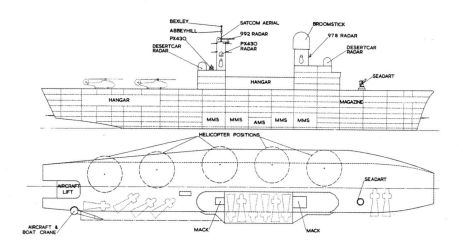

One of the more practical, if small, 1966 commando cruiser sketch designs that shows the gradual evolution towards *Invincible*. (Author's collection)

landing craft (vehicles and personnel) could have been fitted to davits either side of the flight deck aft. Accommodation was proposed for a ship's company of about 500 and a full commando group of up to 900 Royal Marines, all of it to full RN standards, allowing for a prolonged period poised at sea if necessary. The design concept harked back to the successful 1942 light fleet carriers with a capability that approximated very closely to the US Navy's *Iwo Jima* LPH class; DG Ships estimated its build cost at about £20 million. Unlike the FFWP's commando cruisers, this sketch design had focus and it was the most practical design to emerge from this period of frantic effort but, unfortunately, it was not taken forward. Nor was the commando cruiser and the FFWP focused its attention on the fact that the existing strike carrier force was to be phased out in the mid-1970s. The *Tiger* class helicopter cruisers were embarrassingly short of both command and aviation facilities and their guns were obsolete. Something urgent needed to be done to provide replacements and the working party became only too well aware of the number of capabilities inherent in aircraft carriers that had been taken for granted and on which the RN relied completely for its ability to operate effectively in contemporary warfare. The escort cruiser project had not been cancelled but had been moribund since design work on the SSBN force had taken greater priority. The FFWP now focused its attention on the 1963 design but had to take into account the fact that it had been designed to supplement the carrier strike fleet, not to replace it. Something bigger and better would be required and the term 'command cruiser' came to be used to describe the ship that would be needed to act as a flagship from which to control the largely frigate navy that was anticipated in the 1970s. A series of studies followed which evolved into the *Invincible* class which will be described in Chapter 17.

The Costing of Warship Projects

Having been instructed to start work with the precept that aircraft carriers had grown so alarmingly expensive that the UK would never be able to afford such ships again, it would be fair to say that the FFWP was shocked by some of the construction costs estimated by DG Ships for the alternative concepts they put forward. For much of the previous decade the Admiralty Board had focussed its attention on the replacement carrier project but had not paid sufficient attention to the fact that the cost of every type of warship had increased significantly in recent years. This was largely due to the dramatic increase in the number of technologically-advanced systems now being fitted throughout the fleet; radar, communications, guided missiles and the early forms of computer-assisted command systems. Politicians, including Lord Carrington while he was First Lord, still tended to equate tonnage with cost and it seems that many senior officers including Varyl Begg had also not fully understood the change. DG Ships became increasingly concerned that the FFWP's attempts to specify 'cheap' alternatives to

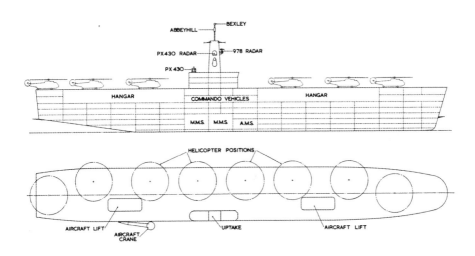

The DG Ships 1966 sketch design for an affordable and practical commando carrier. Unfortunately it was not taken forward. (Author's collection)

aircraft carriers lacked focus, included every kind of weapon and could only be described as expensive and impractical. The surprised reaction to every cost estimate caused DG ships to give a formal presentation to the Controller on 12 July 1968 in which it was stated that:

> It has been made abundantly clear to us in recent years that our predictions of unit cost for projected new ship designs cause both pain and surprise to Board members. The pain obviously arises from high costs versus limited budgets. The surprise shows a lack of common ground between Board members and ourselves in terms of judging the potential costliness of a given warship concept as a whole and of individual features of that concept both in an absolute sense and in comparison with other designs and with merchant ship types. Some of this may be due to diverging mental pictures of the ship package to which the cost is attached. This is a highly unsatisfactory state of affairs to both sides and it is our earnest hope this afternoon to clear away some of this difficulty.[13]

The catalyst was that design work was about to begin in earnest on the projected command cruiser and, if this was to be effective it had to be based on a sound analysis and understanding of where costs lay. CVA-01 had been a cost-effective design; it certainly had a big 'price-tag' but the nation got a lot of capability for it. At any one time it could operate in anti-surface, anti-submarine, anti-air warfare and strike-at-source missions against enemy bases while acting as a national command and control centre during combat operations or any kind of emergency. A full list of capabilities would be a long one. Any alternative command ship would have to be fitted with the same radars, command systems and communications and would, arguably, need more guided weapons systems to counter the lack of defence in depth that fighters would have given and to provide some sort of anti-surface vessel capability. Anti-submarine helicopters would still have to be operated in some numbers and the lack of fixed-wing AEW aircraft would have to be compensated for by more specially-designed helicopters. Such an alternative ship was never going to be 'cheap' and given the need for an efficient flight deck to operate helicopters around the clock the biggest difference was always going to be size, especially internal volume and the steel to encapsulate it. There had to be a wider understanding that the systems were more expensive than the structure. A secondary factor was that CVA-01 had already been designed and developed; the 'package' was ready to go out for competitive tender and build. The 'clean sheet of paper' designs being discussed by the FFWP would have to undergo some years of system development before they were ready and this would be reflected in the cost. There was no simple solution to the problem highlighted by DG Ships but it was decided that his department would, in future, inform the Board through the planning staff of the likely cost implications of warship planning assumptions in more detail than previously. The process was to start with the command cruiser project described below.

A Crisis of Confidence in the RN

Sir Varyl Begg had a deep-rooted love for the RN but had felt that his primary objective as 1SL was to face up to what he believed to be political reality. The weakness in this stance was that the politicians' view of the Navy and the weapons it needed to fulfil its purpose was deeply flawed. Put simply, he had chosen to impose political will on a Service that had taken aircraft carriers for granted[14] rather than fight for the existence of the ships that the modern Navy had been built up around. His own lack of conviction about the capability of carriers should have been balanced by listening to the knowledge, experience and advice of his expert colleagues. He did not do so but, to his credit, he did become aware that the Navy was undergoing a crisis of confidence that he would be unable to resolve. He could have continued as 1SL until 1969 but decided to stand down in 1968. His replacement, Admiral Sir Michael Le Fanu, took over on 12 August 1968; a former captain of *Eagle*, Controller and a staunch advocate of aircraft carriers, he was enormously popular and was expected to achieve great things. When his appointment was announced in February 1968 the officers of 759 NAS, the RN advanced flying training unit at RNAS Brawdy equipped with Hawker Hunter T8s, sent him a valentine card which revealed the high hopes the RN had for him. It said 'O mighty one whose august power will shield us all in danger's hour, this Service save, nor let decline and be our own true valentine!'[15] He was well aware of these hopes but said in a letter to a friend that 'I fear a lot of people expect me to work miracles and unscramble miscellaneous messes. It won't be that way, the powers of the Board in general and the First Sea Lord in particular have been badly eroded but of course I'll do my best.'[16] He was certainly able to steer the plethora of cruiser designs away from the smaller, un-focused and less capable ships towards larger designs with an unobstructed flight deck and starboard-side island that would be capable of operating STOVL fighters. Throughout these turbulent years Admiral Sir Frank Hopkins had been a tower of strength for the practical cause of embarked aviation, first as DNAW and then as 5SL/DCNS under a succession of 1SLs. His support for 'carrier-shaped' ships must have been particularly difficult to sustain in the Varyl Begg years.

This is probably the right point to reflect on whether the Admiralty was right to hold out for a large, 'cost-effective' carrier in 1966 or whether it should have put forward alternative assumptions for smaller STOVL carriers. In my opinion the Admiralty did follow the right path but could perhaps have been more politically aware than it was. It is an unfortunate fact that politicians will invariably take the option that offers the smallest short-term capital outlay. Long-term economy will only benefit a subsequent Parliament and is, unfortunately, therefore of little concern. Every previous British carrier design had been hampered by restrictions of tonnage, size and cost imposed mainly for political reasons. This had limited their ability to 'grow' and incorporate new aircraft and systems; the worst example being the fleet carrier *Indefatigable* which only saw two years of operational service because of its low hangar height. The new carrier design had offered real value for money in that it had ability to operate every type of aircraft in RN service, sufficient capacity to absorb every likely new type throughout its projected lifetime and the ability to command and control naval task forces. Its AEW aircraft would have been vital throughout the spectrum of warfare and were a type of aircraft that the RAF did not possess and, arguably, was not even aware that it needed until the RN paid for it to modify a handful of obsolete Shackletons for this role. With the wisdom of hindsight many analysts have pointed out that the Admiralty would have been better off if it had sought to buy smaller carriers to operate derivatives of the Hawker P 1127 since this is what it eventually did. This entirely misses the point that the P 1127 had yet to be developed to offer an effective all-weather fighter capability and a small carrier would have offered nothing like the range of capabilities that the larger CVA-01 offered. The smaller ship would have had little margin for growth and would have been 'hostage' to P 1127-sized aircraft for its entire life as, indeed, the *Invincible* class was to be. In 1966 the British Government had not yet decided to withdraw all its forces from the Middle and Far East; on the contrary, it was still talking about the importance of the British contribution to stability in the region and strike carriers with their associated Royal Marines Commandos offered the best means of achieving it. The political wrangles over whether land-based or sea-based strike jets offered the 'cheapest' means of deployment obscured the enormous value of carriers and their ability to deal with unexpected emergencies. The Admiralty was right to push for the carrier design that it felt offered the best value for money; the subsequent mistake was to think, as Varyl Begg insisted that the RN must do, that carriers would no longer be allowed and that some alternative form of warship must be found. If a smaller carrier had been offered in 1966, it would possibly have been approved but after cancellation there was no reason not to fall back on less expensive options but these would have to be realistic, like the DG Ships' 20,000-ton commando carrier, made cheaper by the removal of systems, not structure weight and volume. The concept that aircraft carriers were, somehow, subject to cost escalation that other warships were not was completely misplaced but it took a long time to expose this fallacy and discuss the real merits of carriers as the basis of both fleet and joint operations.

The Rundown of the Existing Carriers

Ministry of Defence policy after 1966, which the RN had to accept, was that the existing carriers would have to run on until the mid-1970s because there was nothing to replace them. They were, however, regarded as a 'wasting asset' and such money as was available should be focused on designing an alternative form of warship with some of the carrier's capabilities which could be accommodated within a reduced defence budget. The first ship to go was *Victorious*, which had been intended to remain in operational service until 1971. She had been serving in the FEF and sailed from Singapore in May 1967 to return to the UK for a short refit but had been retained off Malta during the Arab/Israeli 'Six Day War';[17] an example, if another were needed, of the option for intervention that a self-contained carrier task force gave the Government. In the event the British Government decided not to intervene and *Victorious* arrived in Portsmouth in June to begin the planned refit. This had nearly been completed on 11 November 1967 when a fire broke out in Number 13 Mess on the gallery deck, caused by a tea urn that had been left switched on and had boiled dry. It caused the death of CPO J C Nicol and minor damage to structure and wiring. The refit, including repairs to the fire damage, could still have been completed on time but the Government seized on the opportunity to dispose of the ship immediately. The re-commissioning ceremony which had been planned for 24 November 1967 was replaced by a ship's company families day. Those of us who had served in her were shocked by the suddenness of her withdrawal from service and unable to comprehend why such an effective and famous ship could go in this way. On 5 December the immaculately-painted ship was cold-moved from 'D' Lock to Middle Slip jetty where she was de-stored and stripped of useful equipment and on 13 March 1968 the White Ensign was lowered for the last time at sunset in a ceremony attended by former commanding officers. Aircraft of her 801 and 893 NAS flew over the ship in salute. Having taken the decision to dispose of her, the MOD moved swiftly to end the embarrassment of seeing this fine ship moored close to the dockyard and she was sold to ship breakers on 11 July. When she was towed out of Portsmouth, Vice Admiral H R B Janvrin, a former captain and now Flag Officer Naval Air Command (FONAC), flew over her in the last airworthy Swordfish torpedo-bomber and saluted the fine old ship. Her loss did little to improve the fleet's morale.

There was no money to modernise *Centaur* and she had already been taken out of service in 1965 when only twelve years old. Despite the fact that she could have been refitted as a CVS to operate up to thirty Sea King-sized helicopters she was only retained, with a small administrative ship's company of her own, to act as an accommodation ship for carriers in refit, first *Victorious* in 1965/66[18] and then, after being towed to Devonport, *Eagle* in 1966. After being used as a tender to the RN

Barracks in Devonport she was towed back to Portsmouth and used as an accommodation ship for *Hermes'* refit. By 1970 she was back in Devonport but her material state had deteriorated significantly and she was placed on the disposal list. In August 1972 she was sold to ship breakers and towed to Cairnryan in Wigtownshire where she was broken up for scrap. What a waste of an asset! She had far greater potential than the *Tiger* class cruisers and in addition to anti-submarine helicopters, with her steam catapults she could have operated Gannet AEW aircraft for more than another decade.

Hermes was the newest of the strike carriers, having only been completed in 1959, and it was decided to convert her into a commando carrier after 1970. That conversion went ahead and she emerged from Devonport Dockyard in her new role in 1973 but, unlike her half-sisters *Bulwark* and *Albion*,[19] she operated a squadron of anti-submarine Sea Kings in addition to the Wessex assault helicopters. Unlike the commando cruiser sketch designs, however, she showed the enormous advantage of internal volume and was subsequently refitted with a computer-assisted command system and a ski-jump to enable her to operate Sea Harrier STOVL fighters after 1981. Despite political criticism that she was too small to be a viable CVA in 1966, she actually showed herself to be a viable design that proved to be of critical importance in 1982. In 1986 she was sold to India and renamed *Viraat*. In 2015 she is still in service and operating Indian Navy Sea Harriers and Sea Kings fifty-six years after she first entered service with the RN. That must represent an outstanding return on the original investment for her construction.

Perhaps the saddest loss was the recently-modernised *Eagle*, the first ship in the RN to be fitted with action data automation (ADA), a computerised command system. She had the three-dimensional Type 984 radar like *Hermes* and *Victorious* and steam catapults capable of launching 50,000lbs at end speeds up to 105 knots. One of her arrester wires was modified to allow her to recover Phantoms during the type's sea trials but she would have needed the remainder to be modified to operate Phantoms on a regular basis. She would also have needed modifications to her workshops to support Phantoms and their missiles. *Eagle* had been intended to remain in operational service until at least 1980 but she needed a refit in 1971. *Ark Royal* had just undergone a refit to allow her to operate Phantoms as well as Buccaneers, Gannets and Sea Kings but she had not been modernised in any other way. She lacked a modern command system, Type 984 radar and all the other advantages that *Eagle* offered and, worse, during the long years in which virtually no work had been done on her hull during her protracted build,[20] much of her wiring and machinery had deteriorated, leaving her in a poor physical state. Indeed, this fact had been used as an argument for the need for CVA-01 to replace her as soon as possible. *Eagle* was recognised as the better ship but the money to refit her was not immediately available and the MOD felt that after the money spent on *Ark Royal*'s Phantom refit she could not immediately be paid off. In 1970 the decision was taken, therefore, to delete *Eagle* and retain *Ark Royal*. As a short-term excuse it was claimed that paying off *Ark Royal* while *Eagle* was in refit would have left a gap in carrier capability but when only one carrier remained there would in any case be gaps while it was refitted and this argument never seemed very convincing. *Eagle* arrived back in Portsmouth from the FEF for the last time in January 1972 flying a 450ft long paying-off pennant. She was paid off after de-storing and towed to Devonport where she was laid up off Cremyll in the River Tamar to be used a source of spares for *Ark Royal*. She was eventually sold for scrap and towed to Cairnryan in September 1978. *Ark Royal* was intended to run until 1972 at first, then 1974. However, the US Government had the majority of its carriers committed to the conflict in Vietnam at this time and was unable to meet its NATO commitment to the strike fleet in the Atlantic. It therefore put considerable pressure on the UK to maintain *Ark Royal* in commission for as long as possible to fill the gap. She continued to operate in the Atlantic with frequent exercises with the USN and NATO throughout the 1970s, giving the RN a credible strike capability while the new *Invincible* class ships and the Sea Harrier were developed and built. She paid off for the last time in February 1979 and, after a spell moored off Cremyll where *Eagle* had lain, she was towed away to be scrapped at Cairnryan in September 1980.

The Possibility of Retaining the Existing Carriers was Considered
In 1970 the Conservative Party won a general election and formed a new government under Edward Heath. In their election manifesto they had said that the Labour Party had been wrong to do away with the carrier strike fleet as it represented a major investment in UK defence that could not easily be replaced. It is probable that they had begun to appreciate the high cost of replacement options and were seeking an inexpensive compromise. The MOD was asked to evaluate the

Surrounded by tugs, *Victorious* moves away from Portsmouth for the long tow to the breaker's yard at Faslane. (Author's collection)

Centaur alongside the breaker's yard at Cairnryan in 1972.

possibility of running on the existing carrier fleet to 1979, a date that seemed to represent the limit of long-term defence planning at the time. The answer had to be given quickly in order that a clear statement on the way forward could be given during the Parliamentary Debate on the Navy Estimates in the late spring and considerable staff effort was devoted to it for several weeks. Taken at face value, the arguments in favour of retaining the carriers in service were overwhelming but they were fatally weakened, on closer examination, by the costing assumptions laid down by the new government. First there was to be no question of building a new carrier, making the whole evaluation an exercise in managing what the politicians saw as a wasting asset. *Eagle* and *Ark Royal* were to remain in operation until 1979 but *Hermes* was still to undergo conversion into a commando carrier from 1970. *Victorious* had already been scrapped and *Centaur*, which would have needed a major restorative refit, was not considered for retention. To these bleak caveats others were added that all the existing Phantom and Buccaneer aircraft were to be handed over to the RAF in accordance with the 1966 Defence Review,[21] leaving the RN with Gannet AEW aircraft and obsolescent Sea Vixens as its only embarked fixed-wing aircraft. Funds would have to be found to buy new aircraft. As bad, the afloat-support ships that had supported the carrier force and the dockyard capacity that had maintained them were still to be taken as savings measures and would have to be 'bought back' into the Navy estimates to keep *Eagle* and *Ark Royal* viable. Stores and spare parts would have to be procured to replace those passed on the RAF.[22] *Albion* and *Bulwark* were taken to be amphibious ships and were not, therefore, included in this study. The latter eventually showed the inherent flexibility of the light fleet carrier hull by operating in her last years as a

Hermes saw extensive service after her conversion to a support carrier. She is seen here with Sea Harrier FRS 1s and Sea King HAS 5s on deck, carrying out the acceptance trials on her new 'ski-jump' that I ran in 1981. Note the mobile deck approach projector sight that was positioned at the forward edge of the former angled deck to demonstrate its effectiveness for Sea Harrier recoveries. The runway is actually angled 1 degree to starboard.

CVS with both Sea King ASW and Wessex assault helicopters embarked. In 1979 consideration was even given to fitting her with a ski-jump to operate Sea Harriers like *Hermes*.

These were crippling reservations which offered no real solution to the ultimate need to re-provide within a decade the core capabilities around which the RN had been constructed since 1945. The MOD was informed that the design effort to plan *Eagle*'s refit and the conversion of *Hermes* together with the planned re-provision of stores and support would be large and expensive undertakings. After a great deal of consideration, as we have seen, the MOD decided to retain *Ark Royal* in service with a minimal number of Phantoms and Buccaneers until well into the 1970s and to discard *Eagle*. This decision made little sense and the relatively small sum to retain *Eagle* and a viable air group for her would have bought time and provided a capability that no other member of NATO except the USA could offer, giving the UK a powerful bargaining position that a small number of troops, tanks and fighters on the NATO central front in Germany could never do. Most NATO nations could recruit and provide a small army but at the time only Great Britain and the USA could provide sea power when and where it was needed, giving the Alliance flexibility if hostilities began and significant bargaining power in its planning process. By 1969 the MOD estimated that it had spent a little over £30

Ark Royal passing the forlorn hulk of *Eagle* in 1975. After de-commissioning, *Eagle* was laid up off Cremyll in the River Tamar, just south of Devonport Dockyard, until she, too, was broken off for scrap in 1978. (Author's collection)

million on *Ark Royal*'s Phantom refit and something over £15 million converting *Tiger* and *Blake* to operate helicopters. Considerable sums from a different budget were being spent to provide work in the Upper Clyde shipyards which had no orders. Against these figures, £60 million for CVA-01 does not seem to have been so great a sum and the Government's decision not to proceed with it must be recognised as an mistake based on advice from an air staff that was entirely ignorant of strike fleet capabilities and operating methods together with its own narrow understanding of what was, in reality, a much wider picture.

After All the Talk, What would Replace the Carriers and their Air Groups?

By 1968 Harold Wilson's government had been forced to admit that making drastic reductions in the size of the armed forces would not reduce the budget deficit and the momentous decision was taken that major commitments would have to go. It was decided that British forces would be withdrawn from Aden, the Persian Gulf and, most significantly, from the Far East by 1971. Bases in Aden, Bahrain and Singapore would be closed and the dockyard in Singapore sold off. The decision was an obvious example of the UK's declining wealth and influence that caused considerable unease in the Commonwealth and among Britain's allies. It further impacted on the RN because many of the pro-carrier arguments had been based on the provision of an expeditionary warfare capability 'East of Suez'. The value of carriers to operations in the Atlantic, including those practised every year by the NATO strike fleet, had been considered too obvious to stress but should have been argued more forcefully since, from 1971 the only major British commitment was to be within NATO, maintaining the British Army of the Rhine and its supporting RAF tactical air force. There were not many politicians who gave much thought to NATO and most of those that did assumed that the role of navies, if there was one, was to support the re-supply across the Atlantic of Alliance armies fighting a desperate battle on the central front in Germany against massed Soviet ground forces before any conflict became nuclear. It was assumed that the USN would provide escort forces in the western Atlantic and that a token force of RN nuclear submarines and frigates with the ability to operate some helicopters would suffice to meet the residual task in that part of the north-eastern Atlantic and English Channel that remained a British responsibility. The ships that had formed the balanced FEF, such as aircraft carriers and fleet destroyers, could be dispensed with and most of them were. Token air cover for the surface escorts could be provided by land-based RAF squadrons from airfields in the UK; after all that was what the RAF had said it could do in all the Whitehall arguments for the previous decade. Politicians failed to notice a discrepancy in RAF plans to provide air support to its sister-Services, however. Cover over the Atlantic was to be provided

A harbinger of the future. A prototype P 1127 operating with Wessex HU 5s on *Bulwark* during the trials carried out in 1966. The P 1127 is carrying out a rolling take-off on the former angled deck and the four Wessex in Fly 1 have all started one of their two engines; towing arms attached to their tail wheels will allow the tractors to pull them quickly onto launch spots as soon as the P 1127 is clear. Once there, they will start their second engines, engage rotors and be quickly airborne. This trial proved that fighters and helicopters could work effectively and safely together. *Bulwark* continued in service throughout the 1970s as a helicopter carrier. (Author's collection)

out to 500nm, if necessary using air-to-air refuelling to keep fighters on CAP stations near designated surface warships. Looking to the east rather than the west a similar radius of action from airfields in East Anglia would take strike fighters as far as Berlin, a long way east of the NATO central front but, here, the RAF insisted that its tactical aircraft must be based in Germany, close to the scene of action so that they could respond quickly and return to base frequently to be re-fuelled and re-armed. Response times and replenishment did not seem to be important over the sea but perhaps no-one outside the RN cared. Even as close to the UK as 500nm maintaining one land-based fighter over a task force would have been expensive and two would be a realistic minimum requirement; with one on task there would have been one more in transit outbound and one returning to base with three others preparing to repeat the cycle. An entire squadron would, therefore, have to be dedicated to the task of maintaining one CAP station. Tanker aircraft would have to be dedicated to its support because the failure of one to arrive on task could lead to the loss of all the airborne fighters when they ran out of fuel a long way from home. Throughout their sorties the fighters would rely on direction officers in the ships they were to support for command, control and communications. There was, of course, the obvious point that if a fighter had fired all its weapons there was no point in refuelling it to remain on the CAP station since there was nothing further it could do but its relief would not arrive until its planned time and the tanker might have other tasks before returning to it. Long-range fighter support over a task force was soon realised to be an expensive and very inflexible business. Strike aircraft would have had similar problems finding their targets and AEW would be crucial to the effective operation of any aircraft with the fleet. Unfortunately, the RAF had no interest in AEW at the time and relied on land-based radars for the ground-controlled interception tactics of its UK-based fighters. By the late 1960s most of remaining fighter squadrons were equipped with the short-range English Electric Lightning which had been designed for the point defence of small areas in the UK and in overseas bases. Operating it even a short distance out to sea would tie up most of the RAF's meagre tanker assets for long

What should have been. A trials Phantom from Boscombe Down on *Eagle*'s waist catapult. The hold-back is attached but 'badgers' are holding the launch strop which has not been tensioned. The launch is evidently intended to examine the effect of higher aircraft weight as the Phantom is loaded with inert 1000lb bombs, an easy and practical way of progressively and accurately increasing aircraft weight between launches. (Author's collection)

periods. The obsolescent Gloster Javelin was withdrawn from service in 1968. Successive defence reviews had significantly reduced the number of aircraft available and the order for fifty-six American F-111s on which the RAF had based its claims for long-range strike capability was now cancelled on economic grounds. Bomber, Fighter and later Coastal Commands were amalgamated into a new Strike Command which deployed three small groups, one each for strike aircraft, fighters and maritime patrol aircraft.

Within days of CVA-01's cancellation DNAW had put a series of papers before the FFWP that examined ways of re-providing the critical capability of AEW after the fleet carriers were withdrawn. Several VTOL options capable of operation from 'cruisers' were examined and four separate papers were put forward on one day, 30 March 1966, that examined different options.[23] These included studies of commercial VTOL transport aircraft that might be modified with AEW radar to replace the Gannet AEW 3. Several appeared to offer potential at the time but actually went no further, among them the Canadair CL 84 and the LTV-Hiller-Ryan XC-142A. Both of these were prototype tilt-rotor aircraft intended to carry passengers. DNAW thought that, after development, both might be able to launch vertically from a small 'cruiser-sized' deck with a Gannet-sized crew of three, fuel for three hours' endurance and a version of the USN AN/APS-82 radar fitted in the carrier-borne Grumman E-1 Tracer AEW aircraft. The XC-142A[24] had actually flown in prototype transport form but with a wingspan of 67ft 6in and a launch weight of 44,500lbs without radar or military equipment it would have been difficult to operate from *Ark Royal* and *Eagle* and almost impossible from the sort of decks that the FFWP had in mind. The Canadian CL-84 was smaller and lighter but that meant that it would have been critically tight on the ability to carry the fuel, crew and role equipment required; in all probability it could not have done so. Neither proposal was affordable or in any way realistic. Neither type saw production in any form. If these suggestions were impractical, DNAW's Paper 3 was even less so; it looked in some depth at the German Dornier DO-31 transport technology demonstration aircraft. This combined two Rolls-Royce Pegasus[25] vectored-thrust engines to give both lift and forward thrust with two banks of vertical lift engines, one at each wingtip containing four engines each, a combined total of ten engines at full power being required for a vertical take-off! It could have carried all that was required for the AEW role but with a launch weight of 58,400lbs, a wingspan of 64ft and a height of 25ft 9in it would have been a monster to operate from anything but the largest of aircraft carriers. The cost of replacing the Gannet AEW 3 with an aircraft that could operate from ships other than carriers was proving to be excessive and, for those who gave the matter realistic thought, highlighted the fact that the theoretical savings achieved by building ships with small flight decks was more than offset by the cost of the specialised aircraft that would be needed to operate effectively from them. The same group of studies also examined the use of helicopters in the AEW role with the twin-rotor Boeing CH-47 Chinook, designed as a troop transport for the US Army, somewhat surprisingly receiving the most attention. This would also have required a big-deck ship since it had a length of 98ft 3in with both rotors turning and had a launch weight of 33,000lbs. It would have needed modifications to provide power-folding for its rotor blades and to make the airframe suitable for life in the salt-laden, corrosive atmosphere found at sea. None of the sketch cruiser designs had lifts or hangars big enough to take it and even CVA-01 would have found it difficult to operate on a regular basis. The 1966 studies concluded that VTOL and STOL aircraft for the AEW role, including helicopters, were feasible but would be very expensive. In consequence, if procured, they would be unique to the RN since no other organisation would consider them to be cost-effective. The cheapest option, by far, was to put the Gannet back into production and retain ships capable of operating it. Prior to 1966 a development of the Gannet with the AN/APS-82 radar designated as the Gannet AEW 7 had been proposed as an interim replacement for the AEW 3. It would have been a low-risk, low-cost development that would have been an invaluable asset in 1982.

Despite its perceived importance, the RN was eventually forced to give up the embarked AEW role when 849 NAS was disbanded after *Ark Royal* was withdrawn from service in 1979. The interim solution decided upon after 1968 was to begin scrapping Gannets and fit their radars into redundant RAF Shackleton MR 2 aircraft[26] together with other role equipment. This was carried out at RN expense since the RAF 'had no requirement for the AEW role'.[27] RAF aircrew were trained by 849 NAS at RNAS Lossiemouth to full AEW observer standard and this also involved them being trained as fighter controllers so that they could direct strike aircraft and fighters in operations over the sea. The RAF's 8 Squadron was re-formed in 1972 with twelve Shackleton AEW 2 aircraft; several RN pilots and observers served in the unit to help bring it up to operational standards. It formed part of Strike Command although, initially, most of its tasking was in support of naval operations and exercises. RAF interest grew rapidly, however, once its own people started flying in the role and fighter squadrons in the UK saw the value of AEW in support of their interceptions over the large sea areas within the UK air defence region. The RAF now sought further development of the frequency-modulated interrupted continuous wave radar that the RN had requested under Naval Air Staff target 6166 for a Gannet replacement system and large sums of money were spent on the failed Nimrod AEW 3 projected and the subsequent procurement, in large numbers of the Boeing E-3A airborne warning and control aircraft. These projects are beyond the scope of this work but they illustrate that, when it was prepared to listen, the RAF had much to learn from Fleet Air Arm operational capability.

The Government decision to run down the carrier strike fleet forced the RN to plan a reduction in the structure of the Fleet Air Arm that come into effect from 1969. Some of these were obvious to the wider public, some less so. The RN Air Stations at Lossiemouth, Brawdy, Hal Far in Malta and Sembawang in Singapore were to be closed and handed over to the RAF, or, in the latter case the embryonic Singapore Armed Forces. Arbroath was to become a Royal Marines' base and the technical training that had been carried out there moved to Lee-on-Solent. The RN Air Yard at Sydenham in Belfast was to close. The squadrons retained to form *Ark Royal*'s air group were to move to RAF bases in 1972 where they were to operate, when disembarked, alongside the former RN Phantoms and Buccaneers used by the RAF to support naval operations in addition to their other tasks. Thus 809 NAS moved to RAF Honington where it operated alongside 12 Squadron RAF and 892 NAS moved to RAF Leuchars where it operated alongside 43 Squadron RAF. 849 NAS[28] was at RNAS Lossiemouth and remained there as a lodger unit after the RAF took over the airfield. The 'new' RAF Shackleton AEW unit, 8 Squadron RAF, moved to Lossiemouth in 1972. Command and control arrangements were complicated. They obviously worked well when the squadrons were embarked in *Ark Royal* as the whole package formed part of the operational fleet under the orders of its C-in-C. When disembarked the squadrons were supposed to come under the day-to-day operational control of RAF Strike Command although Fleet could still 'request' their use in naval exercises, trials and training periods. This arrangement proved to be somewhat ramshackle in practice because the disparate groups that made up Strike Command only thought in terms of what their own single-purpose squadrons were tasked to do. They appeared to be embarrassed by the broad range of capabilities the naval squadrons showed themselves to be capable of deploying in RAF air defence exercises.[29] On a personal level it was rather gratifying to see the enthusiasm with which control by 849 NAS Gannet crews was greeted by RAF air-defence fighter pilots, many of whom began to insist that AEW cover was provided when they were scrambled to investigate Soviet aircraft approaching UK airspace or even in routine 'bread and butter' air-defence exercises.

The MOD implemented other changes which affected naval aviation. Among these the storage and depot-level maintenance of all fixed-wing aircraft passed to the RAF and the RN took responsibility for all helicopter storage and maintenance using the RN Air Yards at Fleetlands and Perth. The training of RN fast jet pilots ceased in 1970, with 759 and 738 NAS disbanded. From 1972 all Phantom and Buccaneer aircrew training passed to the RAF and both 767 and 736 NAS were disbanded. From 1972 RAF pilots were appointed to fill gaps in *Ark Royal*'s air group as the number of RN pilots reduced. On a positive note, this proved to be a good example of inter-service co-operation. It is true that some RAF pilots arrived with an 'I am here to teach you how things are done' attitude which was of little value to them or the air group but the vast majority were fascinated to become part of a very different sort of flying arm with a much wider remit and opportunities to show initiative than their own Service had allowed them. They valued their experience with the Navy and benefited from it in their subsequent careers; I think many of them enjoyed being a bit different and emerged as characters not quite cast in the usual RN or RAF moulds.

While there were these successes on a personal level, senior air staff officers wanted a name to describe the new organisation that would highlight the change. The result was 'tactical air support of maritime operations' (TASMO). It involved the declaration to NATO of RAF squadrons that could be tasked to support operations in the north-eastern Atlantic. 43 Squadron was equipped with Phantom FG 1 fighters originally ordered for the RN and 12 Squadron was equipped with ex-RN Buccaneer S 2s. Both units were 'shackled' to their land-locked bases and had other day-to-day tasks to fulfil. Readers will not be surprised that we could not understand why the same aircraft had not been used to form an air group for *Eagle* in continued service. It would have given them a global, rather than local, capability but by then politicians did not want to hear about anything that could be used outside the NATO area. Of course, both units could call on RAF tankers and AEW Shackletons but both of these forces were finite and had many other commitments. Both would need to be completely committed to supporting a single Phantom on CAP station over a task force in the Atlantic. Struggling to find any positive comment that could be applied to TASMO, I suppose one could note that it provided a token capability and that was all that mattered to the UK Government at the time. It did not matter whether it actually worked in practice, it had such a low priority. There were other elements that linked with TASMO, among them what appeared to be an attempt to retain 'V'-bombers in service by finding an alternative use for them. The RAF declared that in addition to its declared role as part of the NATO tactical nuclear strike force, 27 Squadron would be tasked to use its Vulcans in what was called the 'maritime radar reconnaissance' (MRR) role. This involved the aircraft flying at very high level over the Atlantic using their radar to search for surface vessels in order to build up a surface picture. Whilst in theory this seemed useful, in practice it was noticed during major NATO war at sea exercises such as the 'Ocean Safari' series that the Vulcans were unable to find the

NATO strike fleet and had to ask where it was. Senior officers in Strike Command were said be 'furious' when the USN admiral in command of one exercise strike fleet refused to signal his fleet's position, course and speed every day. From an RAF perspective it was apparently felt that little value was gained from a war game in which their reconnaissance aircraft did not know where to look; from a sailor's perspective they learnt a great deal, because ships in the wide ocean are not easy to locate. Reconnaissance aircraft are meant to build up a picture of what is going on, not find out beforehand so that they can get publicity by taking part. From a professional sailor's point of view TASMO, and everything to do with it, was going to be ineffective if it was ever to be tested for real. In 1982 it was tested but by then the RN was able to offer a real capability that worked.

Amphibious Warfare

The commando carriers had been considered solely as amphibious units and were not therefore included in the draconian cuts that reduced the rest of the Fleet Air Arm in both scale and capability at this time. It was decided to move 3 Commando Brigade from Singapore to the UK when the FEF was disbanded and redefine its role towards tactical operations in support of NATO's flanks. For the short-term future, the ships were to survive and although 847 NAS, which had been shore-based at RNAS Sembawang in Singapore, was disbanded, 845, 846 and 848 NAS were retained, giving the Royal Marines a genuine raiding and assault capability which would have been of concern to Soviet forces had they ever attacked the NATO central front. The one weakness, of course, was the lack of fighter and close air support cover for any landing with the run-down of the carrier force. Had 3 Brigade ever gone into action from the sea it would have relied on the US Navy and Marine Corps to provide air support. The commando squadrons' shore base was moved from RNAS Culdrose to RNAS Yeovilton when the latter gave up its task as the shore base for fighter squadrons in 1972. Annual exercises were held in Turkey and the eastern Mediterranean to practice intervention operations on the southern flank of NATO, usually in the autumn. The ships, Wessex helicopters and commandos needed no modification for this scenario but the northern flank required rather more training and investment. From 1970 a series of winter training periods, given the codename Operation 'Clockwork', were set up to train a cadre of aircrew and commandos in arctic warfare techniques.[30] They were based at the Royal Norwegian Air Force base at Bardufoss during January, February and March every year but the Norwegian Government would not allow a permanent UK base on Norwegian soil. A number of changes to the Wessex HU 5 were found necessary to render them suitable for arctic, rather than temperate or jungle, operations but the aircraft and their aircrews proved adaptable and a viable capability emerged. Arguably the RN/RM arctic cadre remain among the best trained cold-weather raiding forces in existence today. The training period in Bardufoss usually led into a NATO exercise such as 'Cold Winter' with a commando carrier or LPD close to the coast. From 1972 autumn and winter exercises also took place in the vast ranges in Canada. For some reason the commando strike force survived this not very enlightened period and there was even talk of replacement ships as we have seen. Fortunately 100 Wessex HU 5 had been built before the 1966 debacle and these proved sufficient to keep the type in operational service until the mid-1980s.

Other Changes

The Hawker Hunter T8 and GA 11 fast jets that had been used in the advanced and operational training squadrons were used to form a new fleet requirements and aircraft direction training unit (FRADU), which was based at RNAS Yeovilton from 1972. It was manned by civilians and operated under civilian contract but some of the aircraft were used by the RN pilots of the RN Fixed-Wing Standards Flight.[31] It took over the task of the civilian-manned fleet requirements unit at Hurn that had flown Scimitars and the aircraft direction training unit at Yeovilton that had flown Sea Venoms. For a while FRADU operated a few Sea Vixens but they proved expensive to keep in service and the unit became an all-Hunter force from 1974. The Hunters remained on RN charge and demonstrated some flexibility after 1982 when they were wired to carry Sidewinder missiles to give them a limited operational capability when flown by RNR pilots in the 1980s. The aircraft themselves were interesting. Half the T 8s were built as such for the RN but the other half and all the GA 11s were former RAF F 4s which were purchased by the RN for their scrap value[32] when they were withdrawn from service in the late 1950s. They were used in the training role from 1962 to 1970 and then with FRADU until the early 1990s, representing excellent value for money and a shrewd use of available resources.

The anti-submarine helicopter squadrons were not, in theory, affected by the decision to run-down the carrier strike fleet but of course they were because less could be embarked without the big decks. The *Tiger* class cruisers could each carry four and the 'County' class destroyers one each but that was not enough to maintain one on task continuously. With judicious management of men and machines the squadron embarked in a cruiser might just be able to defend their own ship but they had little to offer the defence of a task force or convoy. The single helicopter embarked in the destroyers was intended to work with the similar helicopters embarked in a carrier. Without the carrier the destroyers would, arguably, have been better off with two Westland Wasps acting in the MATCH role. At least they would have been available over much longer periods than the single Wessex to act as a weapon carrier to prosecute contacts detected by the ship's active sonar. The 'County' class had no anti-submarine weapon other than the embarked helicopter. By the late 1960s it had to be accepted that the Wessex HAS 3 was a failure; too much equipment had been crammed into a small airframe. Its Type 195 dipping sonar had been a success but in the hot temperatures found in the Mediterranean and Far East the HAS 3 could not take off with full fuel and its endurance was limited to less than an hour. Even in the colder Atlantic conditions the carriage of a single torpedo limited endurance to about an hour and some squadrons reverted to the concept of flying some aircraft without sonar as weapon carriers to support those that were sonar-fitted. The decision was taken to procure a version of the USN Sea King to be built under license in the UK by Westland. It will be described in a later chapter.

Ark Royal, the only strike carrier to be run on into the 1970s. (Author's collection)

16 Capability, the Beira Patrol, Aden and Belize

While arguments continued in Whitehall, deployed carriers continued to react quickly to operational requirements ordered by the UK Government in response to unpredicted world events which were too far away or too time-sensitive for the RAF to respond to in time, or at all. Within days of the announcement that CVA-01 had been cancelled and the 1966 Defence Review's statement that 'experience and study have shown that only one type of operation exists for which carriers and carrier-borne aircraft would be indispensable: that is the landing, or withdrawal, or troops against sophisticated opposition',[1] a carrier sailed at short notice to cover the inability of the RAF to react to developments in the Indian Ocean. In this same period the new generation of naval aircraft demonstrated their impressive capabilities.

Buccaneer S 2 and Phantom FG 1 Capabilities Demonstrated

Shortly after I joined *Victorious* in 1966, she embarked 801 NAS, the first Buccaneer S 2 squadron, and demonstrated its capabilities to the press while working up in the English Channel on 3 June 1966.[2] I had by then completed my Midshipman's Fleet Board successfully and was attached to the ship's Air Department, working for Lieutenant Commander J A Neilson RN, Lieutenant Commander 'Flying' (Little 'f'). The demonstration involved launching a Buccaneer fitted with a photographic-reconnaissance pack in its bomb-bay and two 230-gallon drop tanks under the wings from a position in the south-west approaches to the English Channel. It was re-fuelled in flight by other 801 NAS Buccaneers and flew at high level over the sea for a distance of about 1000nm to Gibraltar where it let down to very low level and flew over the dockyard where it photographed a Wren holding up the latest edition of the Gibraltar daily newspaper. This task completed, it climbed back to high level and returned to the ship, being re-fuelled in flight again by another 801 NAS Buccaneer. The ship was able to follow the aircraft outbound and inbound for long distances on its Type 984 radar and an airborne Gannet AEW 3 was able to extend the picture still further.[3] The aircraft was airborne for 4 hours and 50 minutes and shortly after it landed on the film was removed and developed by the Photographic Section; dozens of prints were run off which clearly showed the Wren with her verifiable newspaper and I helped to distribute these to the press in the main briefing room. Commander 'Air', Commander Ivan Brown RN, gave a briefing which stressed the new capability that the Buccaneer S 2 offered the RN; we had just launched a state-of-the-art strike aircraft which had flown 1000nm to carry out a reconnaissance. It could equally have carried nuclear or conventional weapons which it could have dropped with what was, for the time, considerable accuracy. Obviously not every sortie would be flown at such extreme range but we all believed that this had demonstrated an impressive capability within which there were a whole range of options that would be just what the nation needed in dealing with a crisis situation such as striking at an enemy fleet at sea or supporting British interests on land. Not all the press representatives saw it that way, however, and when Commander Brown asked for questions we were somewhat surprised that the representative from *Flight* Magazine asked why the RN was not interested in the Hawker P 1127. When told that we were here to talk about the Buccaneer, not the P 1127, he persisted and so Commander Brown told him why the Navy had little interest in the VTOL prototype at the time. On 7 February 1963, he said, a prototype P 1127, XP 831, landed on *Ark Royal* while she was working up in the Lyme Bay danger area off the coast of Dorset. The aircraft had insufficient fuel to fly from Hawker's airfield at Dunsfold in Surrey to the operating area, about 120nm, so it deployed to Exeter Airport to be nearer, only about 40nm. Even then *Ark Royal* had to close the coast to within the 10 fathom line to give the aircraft sufficient fuel to return to Exeter if it could not land on. As Commander Brown pointed out that was hardly an impressive performance when compared with what the Buccaneer had just demonstrated. I have included this anecdote to illustrate the reason why the Navy was less interested in the theoretical capability of the P 1127 than the more capable aircraft it was introducing into service at the time.

I was fortunate to witness another demonstration of the Buccaneer's impressive capability two years later in August 1968 when I was serving in *Hermes* with the FEF.[4] At the time the Government had announced that that UK land and air forces would soon be withdrawn from the Far East but a naval presence would be retained as a contribution to SEATO which could be quickly reinforced if necessary. To draw attention to the RN's ability to fulfil this requirement and emphasise the importance of the Fleet Air Arm as a major component of the RN, the new 1SL, Admiral Le Fanu, flew 8000 miles in the observer's seat of an 803 NAS Buccaneer S 2 to land on *Hermes* in the eastern part of the Indian Ocean at 13.15 on 23 August 1968.[5] The aircraft was one of four that had used RAF flight refuelling tankers to fly from RNAS Lossiemouth to RAF Gan in the Maldives and, after refuelling, from there to the ship. It is a measure of Le Fanu's leadership that he had secretly travelled to Lossiemouth to undergo sufficient instruction in a Buccaneer observer's tasks to be able to give the pilot, Lieutenant Commander J Nichols, the support he needed on the long flight. He made the flight within a week of assuming his new appointment[6] and this inspired example of his leadership style did a great deal to restore morale in the Fleet Air Arm. His arrival in *Hermes* was completely unexpected on board and caused a great deal of delight.[7] 803 NAS was the Buccaneer trials, development and headquarters unit, normally shore-based at RNAS Lossiemouth but capable of reinforcing any carrier, worldwide, as this exercise had demonstrated. The RAF tankers had played a vital role and showed how important they had become to UK defence. What 803 NAS had demonstrated with their help was that high-performance aircraft could be deployed over great distances to land on a fully-equipped and armed mobile base, the carrier, to expand the number of strike aircraft or fighters on board for a particular mission or to replace aircraft lost in action. Once turned round and armed, the aircraft that landed on *Hermes* that day could have been airborne on a tactical or even strategic mission within an hour flown by fresh crews from 801 NAS that was already part of the air group. Sea Vixens or, in the near future, Phantoms could be deployed in a similar way. The merit of using carriers in this way was that the reinforcing aircraft arrived in a fully-functioning, armed and equipped base with a logistic supply organisation close at hand to re-provide fuel, ammunition, stores and food. 'Hotel' accommodation to a familiar standard was immediately available within the carrier which would form part of a heavily-defended task force. Land-based aircraft deployed to a remote airfield would have none of these benefits and would have to wait for transport aircraft to fly in everything that the aircraft needed. Bulk supplies of fuel and ammunition would still have to arrive by sea, would rely on British or Allied control of that sea and might take weeks to arrive. Defences would have to be established from scratch if they were needed and these, too, might have to come by sea. One final point worth mentioning is that after an operation of short duration, a carrier and its task force could move on to any point on the oceans of the world leaving nothing behind. Land-based aircraft deployed to a temporary base would leave a considerable 'footprint' that would have to be dismantled and returned to the UK or, in the case of runways, buildings etc, abandoned. These were some of the very significant differences between carrier-based and land-based tactical aircraft that the politicians had failed to grasp.

There is one other demonstration that is worth mentioning but it was not one I was fortunate enough to witness. 892 NAS re-commissioned with McDonnell Phantom FG 1 fighters on 31 March 1969 and worked up for service in *Ark Royal*. She had only recently emerged from her major refit, however, and was not yet ready to embark her air group so an agreement was reached with the USN that 892 NAS could embark in the USS *Saratoga* in the Mediterranean for a week in October 1969 to gain embarked experience with their new aircraft.[8] Both navies learnt from the embarkation[9] which demonstrated that Allies could embark aircraft in each other's carriers for coalition operations in the same way that Allied aircraft could be deployed to friendly air bases. The capability was to be demonstrated in the future by USN and USMC aircraft embarking in RN carriers for exercises.

Rhodesian UDI and the Beira Patrol, 1965–1966

On 11 November 1965 Ian Smith, the Prime Minister of the British Colony of Southern Rhodesia,[10] made a unilateral declaration of independence from British rule.[11] His action was condemned as illegal by the United Nations but it was left to the UK to do something about it. President Kaunda of Zambia, the former British Colony of Northern Rhodesia which had gained independence on 24 October 1964, appealed to the UK for defence against a possible Rhodesian air attack, citing the Kariba Dam as a possible target. At that time the former Royal Rhodesian Air Force deployed four operational squadrons, one each with Hawker Hunter FGA 9s and de Havilland Vampire FB 9s and two with English Electric Canberra B 2s.[12] Initially the UK Government tasked the RAF to deploy fighters to Zambia and a squadron equipped with Gloster Javelins was ordered to prepare but it had to be pointed out that, while the aircraft themselves could be deployed with reasonable haste, it would be some weeks before their support elements could arrive to provide an adequate operational capability. Worse, the aircraft were based in Cyprus and considerable difficulty was encountered in negotiating overflight clearances for the ten fighters and their supporting transport aircraft. The UK Government was

A Buccaneer S 2 of 801 NAS being launched from *Victorious'* port catapult in 1966. (Author's collection)

embarrassed by its initial inability to accede to President Kaunda's request and on 18 November *Eagle* was ordered to proceed at her best economical speed from Singapore to the East African coast. Her air group was ready to act in defence of Zambia from 28 November 1965 with the options of disembarking Sea Vixens, Gannets and Scimitars to an airfield in Zambia or operating them at long range from the carrier or a combination of both.[13] Had Rhodesia resorted to force it would have been unable to prevent strikes against military installations by aircraft from *Eagle* since, apart from anything else, its rudimentary air defence organisation would have no idea where the carrier was or from what direction its aircraft would approach. Of interest, Harold Wilson revealed that he did not really understand the RAF's argument that it could provide long-range air defence for the fleet because, when speaking to the press, he said that *Eagle*'s Sea Vixens 'would have been hard pressed by distance to have been operational in Zambia'.[14] If this was the case for carrier-borne fighters from *Eagle*, then it was also the case for land-based fighters in the UK. The RAF fighters eventually arrived on 3 December 1965 and were able to fly operational sorties some time after that. The *Times* newspaper was able to report that 'the sudden appearance of the aircraft carrier *Eagle* cruising off Tanzania emphasises the advantages and flexibility held by a carrier in the Indian Ocean'. A battalion of British troops was deployed to the airfield at Ndola in Zambia to defend the RAF Javelins if necessary.

On 20 November 1965 the UN Security Council agreed a resolution, UNSCR 217,[15] that called for an international embargo on all shipments of oil to Rhodesia. Again it was left to the UK to do something about it and Harold Wilson's Government hoped at first that a declaration of sanctions would be effective without having to implement a blockade. This proved not to be the case and by February 1966 it became obvious that oil was still arriving at the port of Beira in the Portuguese colony of Mozambique, from where it was pumped through a pipeline to land-locked Rhodesia. The port was situated mid-way through the Mozambique Channel between Madagascar and the mainland of Africa and tankers could arrive from any direction over vast stretches of ocean. Maritime patrol aircraft such as the RAF's Shackleton were equipped with radar to search large areas of sea for surface contacts but the RAF had to admit that, with no bases in the area, it would be some time before a squadron could be deployed and its support regime established. Something needed to be done at once and *Ark Royal*, which was visiting Mombasa, was ordered to sea to establish what was to become known as the Beira Patrol.[16] She sailed on 3 March 1966 and took up a position in the Mozambique Channel with her escorting frigates *Rhyl*, *Lowestoft* and later *Plymouth*.[17] The Gannet AEW 3s of 849C NAS with their powerful radar, visual search capability and good endurance on task were the primary means of

The sea area covered by the Beira Patrol.

establishing and keeping up to date a full plot of all the shipping in the area. They were assisted by the faster Sea Vixens of 890 NAS and the Scimitars of 803 NAS which could be vectored out to more distant contacts to photograph, identify and report them. The Wessex of 815 NAS were used to investigate shipping that came closer to the carrier. Flying was continuous and Gannets were maintained on task

Eagle standing by to defend Tanzania should it become necessary in November 1965. The aircraft on deck are Sea Vixen FAW 2s of 899 NAS, Buccaneer S 1s of 800 NAS, Scimitar F 1s of 800B NAS, Gannet AEW 3s of 849D NAS and Wessex HAS 1 of 820 NAS. (Author's collection)

without a break for ten days. *Ark Royal* was replenished at sea by a succession of RFA tankers and stores ships.

When interviewed by the press, *Ark Royal*'s captain, Captain M F Fell DSO DSC* RN, explained that his ship existed to 'steam vast distances quickly and then perform any operational task assigned to us, as we demonstrated during the Beira Patrols'. He added that the ship's recent presence in the Far East during the Confrontation had been 'not only a stabilising but a restraining influence' on Indonesia.[18] When she eventually left the Far East Station, Vice Admiral Sir Frank Twiss KCB DSC said that 'the *Ark* is a key figure in a world political scene of great difficulty. It should be a matter of pride that this is so and that each movement and action of the ship should count for so much.' This was another point that seemed to be escaping the bureaucrats in Whitehall at the time; carriers were spending a long time deployed at sea around the world. Literally thousands of people saw them on port visits from the USA and Canada, through Africa and the Mediterranean to Australia, New Zealand and Japan. To many these ships and their escorts were all they knew about Great Britain and they were the very embodiment of British power and prestige. Squadrons of Vulcan, Canberra, TSR 2 or F-111 bombers in their remote airfields were unlikely, ever, to achieve similar

Ark Royal on her way to the Beira Patrol in May 1966. The aircraft visible parked in Fly 1 include a Sea Vixen FAW 1 of 890 NAS and Scimitar F 1s of 803 NAS. (Author's collection)

recognition. *Ark Royal* remained on the Beira Patrol until 15 March when she was relieved by *Eagle* and returned to Singapore Dockyard for a maintenance period.[19]

Eagle was tasked with searching a vast area of sea to the east of Beira in order to identify and report all tankers which were approaching the port. She was supported by the destroyer *Cambrian* and the frigate *Plymouth* together with the RFAs *Reliant*, *Resurgant* and *Tidepool* which were themselves replenished in Mombasa. By the end of March an RAF Shackleton unit had been established in Mahajanga in Madagascar but reported that it was unable to cover the required sea areas so *Eagle*'s captain, Captain J C Y Roxburgh DSO DSC* RN, had to inform his ship's company that this patrol would be a long one as *Ark Royal*'s maintenance period in Singapore was taking longer than expected. In fact she spent seventy-one days at sea, a new record for any British warship since the age of sail, and during that time she steamed 30,000nm.[20] Her aircraft flew 1880 sorties during which they covered an area of 200,000 square miles every day locating and identifying 767 ships of which 116 were oil tankers. She was released from the Beira patrol on 30 April, handing over to the frigate *Mohawk*, and met *Ark Royal* on 4 May 1966 to transfer three Scimitars and a Gannet to bring her relief's air group up to its full complement. After leaving the Beira Patrol, Captain Roxburgh said in his ROP[21] that he placed on record his 'pride and gratitude in being the commanding officer of such men, such machines and such a ship at such a time'. Considering that many on board would have been shocked and disappointed by the recent news about the cancellation of CVA-01 and subsequent run-down of the carrier fleet, they could not have done a better job.

Ark Royal began her second period on the Beira Patrol a day later on 5 May 1966. By then flying operations to search for and track surface contacts had become a well-established routine. The Gannets of 849 'C' NAS could be used in two ways, either at low level visually identifying surface contacts themselves or at greater heights up to 20,000ft to give a greater radar horizon for controlling probe aircraft, either a Scimitar or Sea Vixen, at lower level to identify radar contacts.[22] The drawback with the latter method was that the area of radar clutter from sea returns 'under' the aircraft was commensurately larger. Although this type of flying was relatively low key and repetitive, it was not without its risks. On 10 May 1966 Gannet XL 475 was carrying out a night deck landing at about 21.30 after a four-hour surface surveillance sortie. The lower part of the nose oleo broke as the aircraft hit the deck causing the nose to pitch down, lifting the tail and causing the hook to pass over the arrester wires.[23] The aircraft went off the end of the angled deck and over the port side of the ship, hitting the water slightly left wing low seconds later. Fortunately all the crew, Lieutenants Jermy and Cullen together with Rotheram who was a Sub Lieutenant at the time, got out of the aircraft and were rescued by either the SAR helicopter or the ship's sea-boat. A Sea Vixen had been lost earlier on the same day in an incident that led to the tragic loss of its observer. Lieutenants Allan Tarver RN and John Stutchbury RN of 890 NAS had been acting as a probe to identify shipping and were returning to *Ark Royal* at high level in Sea Vixen XJ 520, side-number 014/R, when the aircraft suffered a catastrophic generator failure which sheared a fuel line, causing a massive fuel leak as well as a loss of electrical power. Tarver was still some distance away from the ship and so he shut down one engine and flew at the best speed to make use of the remaining fuel before it ran out. Meanwhile a Scimitar tanker flown by Lieutenant Munro-Davies RN was launched from *Ark Royal* as quickly as possible and was vectored onto 014, turning hard in front of it with the drogue streamed when the two aircraft met but unfortunately by then Tarver was unable to hold his aircraft steady. Losing power on his remaining engine he was descending and found it impossible to fly the Sea Vixen's probe into the drogue on the end of the fuelling hose.[24] He tried to make contact five times but then the remaining engine stopped when the aircraft finally ran out of fuel. The Sea Vixen had large wings which gave it surprisingly reasonable gliding characteristics for a fast jet but they could still not be described as good. Control was maintained flying at about 200 knots as both pilot and

A Buccaneer S 1 of 800 NAS from *Eagle* photographed by its number 2 overflying the tanker *Joanna V* off Beira to identify it in 1966. The ability of carrier-borne fast jets to probe contacts detected at long range by Gannets made the Beira Patrol far more effective that it could have been had only land-based maritime patrol aircraft been available. (Author's collection)

observer tightened their straps to prepare for ejection[25] with the carrier now visible on the horizon and Munro-Davies giving the ship a running commentary over the R/T on what he could see happening. At 6000ft Tarver ordered Stutchbury to eject but nothing happened. Having pulled the primary, face-blind, handle then the alternate, seat-pan handle, the hatch cover was still in place and the seat had not fired. Tarver then ordered Stutchbury to bale out manually while he reduced the air speed as much as possible to help him. He saw the hatch jettison and then the observer's head and shoulders appear but he was a big man and he appeared to have got stuck somehow but by now his intercom lead had become disconnected and he could not speak to him. As the aircraft approached 3000ft Tarver rolled it inverted hoping that Stutchbury would fall clear but he hung there, still trapped. A second roll had some effect, more of the observer's body emerged from the cockpit and Tarver could see him lying flat along the top of the fuselage but something was still snagging his feet. In desperation he reduced speed to about 130 knots, opened his own cockpit canopy and reached across to try and free Stutchbury's feet but to no avail, his observer appeared, by now, to be unconscious and the aircraft was close to stalling only 400ft above the sea surface. Circling overhead in his Scimitar, Munro-Davies saw Tarver's last desperate attempts to free his observer and then the Sea Vixen stalled and rolled to port before crashing into the sea. At the very last second, as it was on its side, he saw the pilot's ejection seat fire then there was a huge splash and he reported that that Tarver must have left the aircraft too late to survive. In fact he had survived; his parachute had half deployed as he hit the sea, just enough to save him and although stunned he managed to get into his dinghy. He was rescued by a Wessex helicopter and only eight minutes later he was back on board where it was found that his only injury was a strained muscle in his back. For the outstanding courage he showed trying to save his observer's life, and almost losing his own in the process, he was awarded the George Medal which was presented by Her Majesty The Queen at Buckingham Palace on 1 November 1966. *Ark Royal* remained on the Beira Patrol until 25 May when she departed to return to the UK leaving surveillance to the Shackletons which were ready at last. During this second patrol her aircraft had continually searched 12 million square miles of ocean, located and identified 500 merchant ships and steamed over 12,000nm.[26] After a year in the FEF, her next activity was NATO Exercise 'Straight Lace' in the North Atlantic during September.

The British Withdrawal from Aden, 1967–1968

Aden had been a British colony for 128 years, but, with the knowledge that the UK Government intended to grant independence after the last British forces were withdrawn from the bases there in January 1968, the colony was racked by what amounted to civil war as rival organisations fought for power whilst they continued a bombing campaign against the British. *Hermes* visited the colony in May 1967 after transiting the Suez Canal a month before it was closed by the Arab-Israeli Six Day War. Her visit coincided with the final evacuation of all British service families and subsequently she was ordered to remain in the area because of the increased tension in the region. Her aircraft flew close-support missions in support of the Army on the border with Yemen and senior officials of the Federal Government of the South Arabian Federation were taken to sea to witness a demonstration of British sea and air power. Unfortunately, little was gained as the Federal Government was rapidly losing what little control it had to two terrorist organisations; the National Liberation Front (NLF) and the Front for the Liberation of South Yemen (FLOSY). The former was already gaining the ascendant position from which was able to assume power after independence.[27] Civil disturbances and terrorist atrocities became worse as British forces were steadily pulled back to a series of defence lines throughout 1967, leaving abandoned areas in which there was heavy fighting between factions for control. During 1967 there were more than 3000 terrorist incidents in Aden resulting in the deaths of fifty-seven British servicemen with a further 325 wounded. Nineteen British civilians were also killed and over 100 wounded. By 24 September all British units were withdrawn behind the old Victorian defence works just to the north of RAF Khormaksar and the UK Government decided to bring forward the date for what was now recognised to be an evacuation under the threat of hostile action to the end of November 1967 from the previously planned date in January 1968. The withdrawal was given the codename Operation 'Magister' and it was to be covered by a powerful RN task force, designated TF 318, which was eventually to include two strike carriers, two commando carriers, the two new LPDs and a large number of destroyers and frigates. It began to assemble off Aden in October.[28]

The first to arrive was *Albion* which had steamed around the Cape from the UK with 848 (Wessex HU 5s) NAS embarked. 848 NAS Wessex were fitted with cockpit armour and machine guns and, after a briefing about the threats and local conditions, they began to fly armed patrols around the areas still held by British forces. These sorties were controlled from the operations team at Khormaksar and, for a while, they were shared with the Wessex HC 2s of 78 Squadron RAF. Both types of Wessex operated from *Albion* and ashore and proved to be usefully interchangeable.[29] *Eagle* sailed from Singapore in October and joined TF 318 in early November 1967. When she arrived the RAF began to withdraw its fighters from Khormaksar with the last leaving on 7 November. The Wessex HC 2s were taken to RAF Sharjah in the Persian Gulf by *Fearless*. Responsibility for air defence was taken over by *Eagle* and she used her Type 984 radar both to give early warning of hostile air threats and to co-ordinate and control all air operations. Buccaneers and Sea Vixens flew frequent armed air patrols over British positions. TF 318 was formally reviewed off Aden by Sir Humphrey Trevelyan, the last Governor, on 25 November who was embarked on the minesweeper *Appleton*. On completion of his review, there was a fly-past by twenty-four Wessex HU 5s and HAS 3s from 848[30] and 820 NAS[31] followed by *Eagle*'s Buccaneers, Sea Vixens and Gannets; 800, 899 and 849 'D' NAS.

The final withdrawal began at dawn on 26 November with forces pulled back from Crater City, Steamer Point and Molalla while RAF transport aircraft flew personnel out of Khormaksar. 45 RM Commando were the last element of the garrison to be taken off but Royal Marines of 42 Commando had been landed from *Albion* to cover the final phases of the departure. At 15.00 on 28 November they hauled down the Union Flag for the last time and were lifted off by 848 NAS for the short flight to *Albion*. TF 318 remained just off Aden until midnight when

Part of the RN Task Force 318 that covered the RN withdrawal of British forces from Aden in 1967. *Eagle* is to the left and *Albion* is in the centre with the LPD *Intrepid* to the right. (Author's collection)

independence was officially recognised. Some ships, including *Eagle*, then dispersed but others were brought into the area in case they were needed to support British interests. *Bulwark*, with 845 (Wessex HU 5s) NAS and 40 RM Commando embarked, replaced *Albion* and *Hermes* operated in the Persian Gulf for a period before moving to the area off Aden at the end of December 1967. After a short spell there the UK Government decided that there was not further need for a covering force and both ships reverted to their normal tasking. Operations immediately connected with the withdrawal from Aden ended officially in January 1968.

British Honduras, 1972

In January 1972 British intelligence sources led the Government to believe that there was a credible and immediate threat that Guatemalan forces were on the verge of invading British Honduras, a small colony in Central America.[32] British since the seventeenth century, the small self-governing colony had a population of about 90,000 and faced the Caribbean Sea to the east and Guatemala to the west. Its capital city was Belize, the name to be adopted by the whole country after independence, and it had a small garrison of British troops. Reinforcements on a small scale could be flown in by RAF transport aircraft but they lacked the ability to move vehicles and bulk supplies of ammunition and fuel which would have to be sent by sea.[33] Fighters could be flown into Belize airport with extensive airborne re-fuelling but it would take weeks to establish the infrastructure to support them or even turn them round after their long flight. Without maintenance and logistic support Strike Command would merely be flying in hostages to be captured by the Guatemalan Army which was obviously testing London's resolve. Its leaders probably thought that after the recent series of defence cuts, the UK lacked the will or the means to defend a remote possession and they would not be the first or the last aggressors to think so. A few extra troops were flown in with light scales of equipment and a destroyer and two frigates were sent to the area from the Atlantic but a bold and decisive step had to be taken to deter Guatemala from using force.

That step was provided by *Ark Royal* which was in mid-Atlantic on her way from the UK to exercises with the USN off Norfolk, Virginia. On 26 January she was ordered to close the Gulf of Mexico with despatch to provide visible air support for the British forces on the ground in British Honduras. She drove hard into stormy seas and sustained some damage to weather decks and fittings but preparations were made for a long-range Buccaneer sortie on 28 January to provide an air presence over Belize.[34] Timing and fuel consumption had to be carefully calculated, as did the fact that aircraft would fly very close to the sensitive south-eastern segment of the US air defence zone that faced Communist Cuba and then the island of Cuba itself. At mid-day on 28 January 1972 *Ark Royal* turned into wind and launched four Buccaneers S 2s of 809 NAS, 2 for the long-range sortie and the others as tankers to refuel them 600nm miles away from the carrier on the outbound leg. The leading aircraft of the long-range pair was flown by Lieutenant Commander Carl Davis RN, 809 NAS's commanding officer, with his observer Lieutenant Steve Park RN and the number two was flown by Lieutenant Commander Colin Walkinshaw RN and his observer Lieutenant Mike Lucas RN. Their track took them over the Bahamas and the southern extremity of Florida, carefully skirting around the unfriendly Cuban airspace and southwards down the Yucatan peninsula to Belize where they let down to low level. Then, having spent 10 minutes making themselves very obvious over British Honduras, they climbed and flew all the way back again. Over Grand Bahama and about 400nm from 'Mother' they carried out a precisely-timed rendezvous with another pair of Buccaneer tankers which gave them a further 4000lbs of fuel each, sufficient to complete their mission. When the aircraft landed-on safely, they had been airborne for just under six hours and had flown 2530nm. British intelligence sources signalled that the Guatemalans had taken note of the British strike capability and that the threatened invasion was now unlikely to happen. The Guatemalan Army Air Force was equipped with only three squadrons, all of them piston-engined aircraft that dated back to the Second World War, one each of P-51D fighters, B-26 light bombers and C-47 'Dakota' transports.[35] Neither they nor their Army

A Buccaneer S 2 of 809 NAS from *Ark Royal* photographed from its number 2 over Belize city in British Honduras in 1972. The presence of British strike aircraft able to defend the colony during this period of tension both reassured the local population that the British Government cared and immediately ended the threat of invasion when the Guatemalan Government realised that it could do nothing to oppose the carrier's powerful air group. (Author's collection)

headquarters would have had any idea where the carrier was, nor how to prevent strikes by its aircraft on their airfields and troops on the ground. Each member of the long-range crews was given a photograph of their launch by Captain J O Roberts RN, *Ark Royal*'s commanding officer, which had been printed, mounted and framed while they were airborne.

Ark Royal was ready to launch further sorties as the range closed but the UK

Government decided that they were not necessary. 809 NAS's first sortie had been enough but the ship was kept in the USN Key West exercise areas for a few days just in case the situation deteriorated again. When it did not she resumed her original programme from 2 February, beginning with a visit to New York. The carrier had demonstrated the classic use of sea power showing the right amount of force in the right place at the right time for just as long as it was needed to deter aggression. *Ark Royal* had done exactly what politicians had agreed that carriers would be very good at in the 1957 Defence Review. In the interval they seem to have forgotten and by January 1972 *Eagle* was being de-stored for disposal, *Hermes* was being converted into a more limited role as a helicopter carrier and *Ark Royal* was the only strike carrier left in service. With work proceeding on a 'through-deck cruiser' capable of operating STOVL fighters, however, there was at least the hope of revival, albeit on a smaller scale.

17 Small Carriers and Vertical Landing

After the UK Government had taken the decision to retain only one strike carrier in service and to continue with the deletion of the remainder, attention focused once more on various cruiser options. After the bruising battles of the 1960s, even the senior RN officers who believed emphatically in the value of naval aviation felt unable seek political approval to design and build a true carrier. A cruiser with a large flight deck that could evolve into a light carrier seemed to be the best option and work on sketch designs proceeded as a matter of urgency. To be fair to him, it should be noted that Admiral Varyl Begg had finally agreed the draft staff proposal for such a ship before he handed over the post of 1SL to Admiral Le Fanu. Surprisingly, in view of his recent complete lack of empathy with senior RN officers on the question of replacement carriers, Defence Secretary Dennis Healey became a staunch advocate of the cruiser project which was outlined, initially, in MOD document OPD(67)46 Annex C. On 28 June 1967 he wrote to Jim Callaghan, the Chancellor of the Exchequer,[1] putting forward a strong case for a new class of ships he referred to as command cruisers which were to replace the *Tiger* class. He pointed out that the 1966 Defence Review had contained the phrase 'we are planning a new type of ship to succeed them'[2] when referring to the run-down of the carrier force. Whilst this had not been a particularly descriptive or emphatic statement, it did at least give some room for manoeuvre. It is, perhaps, also possible that by then Healey realised the damage his Defence Review had done to the RN which could hardly hope to operate as even a second class naval force on the surface after the carriers had been retired.[3] Perhaps he had also been informed of the devastating blow the review's reduction in orders for RN warships would cause to the shipbuilding industry as orders for merchant shipping went increasingly to foreign yards.

Development of the *Invincible* class
For whatever reason, Healey now urged the naval case and described the projected command cruisers as having 'a number of capabilities which are essential if the shape of the fleet, based mainly on relatively lightly-armed frigates, is to be credible in the 1970s; in particular command and aircraft control facilities'. He explained that the new ships would also have to embark the larger anti-submarine helicopters which he expected to be 'increasingly important', especially for use against nuclear

461

submarines. He stressed the word 'essential' again when describing the vessels' three capabilities 'whether we deploy naval forces outside Europe or only within the NATO area'. This new 'single class of ships of the size of small cruisers' would, Healey stressed 'be the most cost-effective means of providing them'.[4] To offset the cost of their construction Healey was 'prepared to limit the Type 82 class of large destroyers which, at a cost of £20 million each, figured alongside a new class of cruisers in our earlier plans to the prototype ship which is now on order'. The change would, he claimed, offer savings of 'more than £200 million' in terms of new construction alone over the nine years common to the 1966 and current costings although he did not go into specific details. His letter ended by hoping that Callaghan would support his re-equipment proposals 'including the cruisers, on the understanding that the programme will continue to be discussed between our two departments as it takes firmer shape. The details of the ships can then be scrutinised in the normal way before we commit ourselves to any major expenditure on them.' Having started 'Dear Jim', the letter ended 'yours ever, Dennis'. It is interesting to note that the costings for CVA-01 and the Type 82 destroyer were seen as excessive at the time but with hindsight we can see that they were entirely reasonable for ships that were a generation removed from their less sophisticated predecessors. The realisation that it was system complexity and not tonnage that made a difference was still not widely understood outside the design world.

In the same month as Healey's letter, a series of exploratory studies began in what was now the MOD Ship Department at Foxhill in Bath. The work that Healey

Ark Royal 5 in the English Channel, shortly before entering Portsmouth for the first time on 1 July 1985. She has not yet been handed over to the RN and is, therefore, still flying the Red Ensign. A Sea Harrier FRS 1 of 899 is secured on the 'ski-jump' and a Swordfish is on the runway right aft. (Author's collection)

had lightly dismissed as taking place before 'any major expenditure' involved the professional control of the design process by four constructors, four assistant constructors and three naval engineers,[5] assisted by up to 100 Ship Department staff at Foxhill. Over ninety of the latter worked on the design for over four years together with 360 staff at Vickers Shipbuilding and Engineering at Barrow-in-Furness who carried out the detailed design work. When researching the origins of the *Invincible* class design I searched through documents held by Section NA/W1 of the Ship Department at Foxhill that were about to be disposed of and found fifty-two different sketch design options with references to others.[6] These ranged from about 8300 tons with a single-spot flight deck at the stern and a 'shed' for four helicopters like the *Tiger*s with no gun or missile armament costing about £20 million to about 18,750 tons, a hangar for nine Sea Kings or P 1127 Kestrels under the flight deck armed with Sea Dart and torpedo tubes costing about £36 million. The sketch design that was finally accepted for development was for a 19,500-ton ship with a narrow runway or 'through deck' just big enough to allow take-off by STOVL fighters and an excessively large island set to starboard of the centreline but unnecessarily far inboard from the starboard deck edge to provide stowage for boats. Surprisingly, considering some of the earlier cruiser designs which had continued the full-width flight deck right forward over the bow like an aircraft carrier, the design had an open forecastle aft of which there was a Sea Dart launcher mounted in what proved to be the most inconvenient place for both missile arcs of fire and aircraft parking forward of the island. Early studies were revised and updated by Constructors Lawrence and Austin before the final configuration was adopted.

The possibility of operating a navalised version of the P 1127, which was by then under development with the name Harrier[7] for the RAF, was included in the design studies from the outset, as was the possibility of operating a specialised AEW helicopter. Although the early sketch design referred to naval P 1127 derivatives as 'Kestrels', the version that eventually went into service with the RN was allocated the name 'Sea Harrier'[8] and this name will be used throughout the remainder of the book. In a briefing given to DG Ships and his staff in April 1968 the Controller, Admiral Sir Horace Law, gave his views on the ship that would be required which incorporated those of 1SL. He envisaged a ship with a carrier-style flight deck and a large hangar capable of operating an air group of five P 1127s, nine anti-submarine Sea Kings and three AEW Sea Kings, accepting that not all of these could be stowed in the hangar. The exact number and type of aircraft to be embarked was be capable of change on a one-for-one basis but it was already understood that fighters required a very much larger infrastructure in terms of workshops, control, carrier-controlled approach and the sheer number and variety of weapons they could carry. These were expected to include Martel air-to-surface guided missiles, Sidewinder air-to-air guided missiles, unguided 2in rockets, conventional 1000lb 'dumb' bombs, Lepus flares and 30mm Aden cannon. It was generally accepted that the *Invincible* design was about the smallest that could operate a tactically viable number of fighters which, by now, were accepted as a valuable force asset giving a layered air defence system, strike potential against both ships and land targets and a reconnaissance capability. DNAW had been able to explain that only a fighter could shoot down shadowing aircraft or enemy missile-carrying aircraft that sat just outside the range of surface-to-air guided missiles and this became widely accepted. It was also accepted, at last, that a small number of embarked fighters could maintain CAP over a task force far more economically and effectively than larger numbers of fighters operating from a remote base and relying on tanker support to reach and return from their CAP station. Surprisingly, a perceived lack of hangar space and accommodation eventually led to AEW, considered to be the most important role in 1966, being deleted from the staff requirement during the detailed design phase. Bitter experience would show just how wrong this decision was.

From the outset these were to be complex ships which needed a large internal volume but for political reasons the tonnage had to remain below 20,000. The result was a ship about the size of a 1942 light fleet carrier but with a structure of unusual lightness to enclose the envelope.[9] *Invincible* had an internal volume of 3,178,303ft³ and for comparison *Tiger* had an internal volume of 1,412,579ft³ and *Centaur* 3,248,932ft³. Weight-saving measures were achieved by the use of finite element analysis and a determined policy of using lightweight equipment such as the scissors lifts[10] which saved the weight of the counter-balances used in previous designs. Even then the weight of steel used in the ship's construction was calculated at 10,000 tons but its erection amounted to only 15 per cent of the man-hours consumed in *Invincible*'s construction. From these figures it will be readily apparent that an increase in hull size and, thus, volume with the same outfit of equipment would not cause a very large increase in steel weight or construction cost in terms of man-hours worked but could offer a dramatic improvement in the ability to operate aircraft. A decision on the choice of machinery was only made after a long debate between the advocates of advanced steam units derived from the CVA-01 design, diesel-electric options and gas turbines. Olympus gas turbines were eventually selected because of their low manpower requirement and the commonality they gave with other applications including new destroyer and frigate designs. The ability, if necessary, to change individual units at sea was also attractive but the downside of gas turbines was their requirement for intakes and exhausts of five times the cross-sectional area that would have been required for steam machinery. The resultant trunking and individual lifts for each of the four gas turbines, which were sited low in the ship, led to the hangar having a narrow centre section which limited the number of aircraft that could be struck down significantly below that of previous hangars such as that in *Hermes* or *Centaur*.

The hangar was to be 20ft high to allow plenty of height for the as-yet unknown helicopter that was expected to replace the Sea King by 1985 and a combination of design drivers gave the *Invincible* class the highest freeboard of any ship in the RN. Taken with the design's very high beam to draught ratio and modest displacement, the innovative hull caused a number of problems, not least the need to retrofit larger anchors to counteract the hull's windage. The four Rolls-Royce Olympus TM 3B gas turbines were capable of delivering a continuous 94,000shp through two shafts. At 47,000shp on each shaft this was more than any previous British warship; for comparison the equivalent shp/shaft figure for the 1955 *Ark Royal* was 38,000, *Victorious* 36,000, the battleship *Vanguard* 32,000, the battlecruiser *Hood* 36,000, the cruiser *Belfast* 20,000 and the 1952 destroyer *Daring* 27,000. All of them had much heavier, stronger and, in all but *Daring*, armoured hulls. When combined with a volumetrically-large hull of unusually lightweight construction it is easy to see why the first two ships suffered from vibration and why the third ship had to have 500 tons of steel added to the shaft area to cure the problem, a modification incorporated in the first two ships during refit. The term 'through-deck cruiser' was used to describe these ships at an early stage and brought with its some ridicule[11] but it was actually a reasonable description of the ship that had evolved from a complicated design process. It official designation was originally a command helicopter cruiser (CAH).

Naval Staff Requirement 7097

In order to hasten the preparation of detailed production drawings, the design was 'frozen' in the early 1970s. This was a practical thing to do but unfortunately coincided with a period of significant development in the aircraft types she was to operate and necessitated a number of modifications to be incorporated soon after completion of the first ship. The following comments are based on the third edition of NSR 7097, MOD Reference 22400/1 dated March 1979, about one year before the first ship's completion.[12] It was originally intended that Vickers Shipbuilding and Engineering would build all three ships at its Barrow-in-Furness shipyard and as we saw above Vickers' staff acted as lead yard in the production of drawings. For political reasons, however, the Labour Government that returned to power in 1974 decided that the second and third ships should be built by Swan Hunter on the Tyne.[13] This led to delays and an increase in cost of about £50 million[14] over the production phase of the project. The NSR was a typical product of its time and the

The original 'command cruiser' model used in DGA(N) to consider the flight deck arrangement. Note that it had no 'ski-jump'.

opening paragraphs read more like a defence review than a staff requirement. It stated that the ships were to:

- Command a task force and control the operation of land-based aircraft.
- Act as Force ASW commander of a NATO Task Group.[15]
- Operate large ASW helicopters for area ASW defence.
- Deploy area surface-to-air guided weapons.
- Deploy a surface reconnaissance capability.
- Deploy a quick-reaction contribution to limited air defence, probe and strike capability with V/STOL aircraft.

It is worth looking at the opening paragraphs because the requirements, and the order in which they were listed, led to initial limitations on the *Invincible* class and their effectiveness. The embarked Task Force Commander was expected to respond with force 'only when specifically directed' which implied that the MOD expected tight political control over activities in a confrontation with the Soviet Bloc. The NSR further 'envisaged that non-firing operations may last for up to three months, during most of which maritime contingency forces might be constituted'. If escalation continued, 'firing operations might last a further month, the last week of which would see widespread operations at an intensive level'. This tightly-specified concentration on the period of transition leading to war rather than actually carrying out a variety of combat operations ranging from 'brushfire' intervention to major conflict led to an extremely small requirement for weapons stowage. It would also seem to indicate that MOD planners thought that the post-1957 era of British involvement in low-intensity conflict was over and the only prospect of hostilities was a confrontation between the Soviet Bloc and NATO. The requirement for air weapons was listed as forty AIM-9 Sidewinder air-to-air missiles, eighteen air-to-surface guided missiles, eighteen conventional 1000lb bombs and twenty-four Lepus flares. For comparison, stowage in the volumetrically-similar *Hermes* was 750 conventional 500lb bombs and considerably more guided weapons. *Invincible* had stowage for twelve nuclear weapons, the British WE-177, which could be configured either as a strike weapon for use by Sea Harriers or as a nuclear depth bomb for use by Sea Kings or Wasps operating from ships in company. There was also stowage for fifty-four ASW torpedoes but only twenty-four conventional Mark 11 depth charges.[16] Fortunately the air weapons magazines were designed with a deck large enough to take these weapons in a single layer. At least with conventional bombs, depth charges and the containers for rockets and cannon ammunition it proved possible to increase the numbers embarked significantly by stacking them on wooden spacers in the manner of beer barrels in pub cellars. In peacetime the requirement expected the ships to 'be deployed to provide a maritime presence for exercises and training throughout the NATO area and as the flagship of task forces visiting other parts of the world'. Individual ship lives were expected to be from twenty to twenty-five years with a planned interval between refits of about four years.[17] Under peacetime conditions they were expected to spend about 50 per cent of their time at sea, considerably less than the fleet carriers had been spending throughout the previous decade. Despite the political limitation on tonnage, there was no limit on the design's overall dimensions and they were not required to transit the Panama Canal.

I joined the Director General Aircraft (Naval) Department of MOD (Navy) in 1979 as the officer responsible for inspecting the flying arrangements of the *Invincible* class to see that they met the requirement and to act as the lead for organising the tests and trials that would clear them for the operation of Sea Harriers and Sea Kings. A myth surrounded the construction phase that the incorporation of Sea Harriers into the design was an afterthought that caused problems during the build. This is not true. The possibility of operating STOVL fighters had been one of the design drivers from the outset and the 'through-deck' design had been adopted for this very reason. In 1971 the Directorate of Naval Operational Requirements (DNOR) and DNAW had sought clarification of the actual cost of incorporating STOVL fighter facilities from DG Ships as opposed to the second-best alternative of completing the ships fitted 'for but not with' these arrangements.[18] It was confirmed by the Ship Department that within the total cost per ship estimated at £44.2 million, a sum of £1.5 million was included for fixed-wing facilities and a further £0.75 for fitting out. Naval Staff Requirement 6451 for a 'maritime V/STOL aircraft' based on the Harrier GR 1 in RAF service followed in 1972. Development work by Hawker Siddeley was authorised immediately with a production contract for the first batch placed in 1975, five years before the first ship was completed, albeit later than originally intended.[19] Paragraph 5 of NSR 6451[20] specifically stated that interim decisions had been agreed to allow further work on the cruiser's design to be funded under LTC 72 provisions. Surprisingly, in view of the fact that earlier versions of the Sea King had already operated in *Eagle*, *Ark Royal*, *Hermes*, *Albion*, *Blake* and *Tiger*, most difficulty was encountered absorbing the latest version of the Sea King, the HAS 5, which had been developed after the *Invincible* design was frozen. The Sea King HAS 1 and 2 had been relatively simple aircraft incorporating the sonar and radar systems of the Wessex HAS 3 in a larger, heavier airframe designed by Sikorsky and built under licence by Westland in the UK. Trial 'Gypsum' had revealed the value of passive sonics in tracking nuclear submarines and the Sea King HAS 5 was designed to carry, dispense and monitor sono-buoys as well as the dipping sonar. This meant that *Invincible* had to modified to provide both deep and ready-use stowage for sono-buoys and a convenient route through which they could be moved to aircraft while the ship was at action stations. It proved possible to work in bulk stowage for 1200 in the first ship with a further 300 for ready use at hangar level. A bulk facility for 2000 was designed into the less-advanced second and third ships.

Another alteration made necessary by the Sea King HAS 5 was the need to incorporate a helicopter acoustic analysis unit (HAAU), to serve two functions. First was to enable the post-flight de-brief and analysis of passive sonar information that had been recorded on the Sea King's 'black box' during a sortie and second the continuation training, at sea, of sonar operators. Unfortunately the relevant section of DGA(N) sought to place the HAAU in a space designated as a training aids room as late as 1979, after *Invincible*'s original completion date when she was already late. The training aids room, as the name suggests, was used for the continuation training of aircrewman in Type 195 active sonar operation and had no operational function. The project manager at Bath refused to agree the change because he was confused by the training aspect of the existing compartment and the secondary function of the HAAU into thinking that the new equipment was of secondary, non-operational importance. In fact it was of considerable operational importance and under-pinned the Sea King HAS 5's importance as a force ASW asset. At some difficulty and cost an interim HAAU was eventually provided in *Invincible* and more refined versions in the later ships.

The 'Ski-jump'

The most significant change to the original 'through-deck' design, however, was the 'ski-jump'. Like the steam catapult, angled deck and mirror landing aid before it, the 'ski-jump' was the 'brainchild' of a serving naval officer, in this case Lieutenant Commander D R Taylor RN who had been carrying out a period of aeronautical engineering study at Southampton University for the award of an M Phil. The original *Invincible* design had envisaged launching fighters from a rolling, short take-off up to 450ft long and the runway was angled one degree to port of the ship's centreline so that aircraft would clear the protective 'zareba' around the Sea Dart launcher. By the forward edge of the flight deck[21] a Sea Harrier would, typically, have accelerated to about 90 knots and with a wind over the deck (WOD) of 20 knots this gave an end speed of 110 knots relative to the free stream air passing over the ship. This was still below the wing's stalling speed and so when he reached the bow the pilot would select the nozzles down to about 50 degrees relative to the fuselage and raise the nose slightly to give optimal wing incidence. Most of the aircraft weight would thus be borne by engine thrust but a proportion of that thrust was still directed aft and would continue to accelerate the aircraft. Once the wing's stalling speed was exceeded the pilot rotated the nozzles fully aft and the aircraft was flown like a normal fighter. This technique was practised in *Hermes* from 1977 onwards using Harrier development aircraft and prototype Sea Harriers flown by test pilots. There was insufficient engine thrust to allow the aircraft to take off vertically with full fuel and weapons but a rolling short take-off allowed the aircraft to launch from a flat deck 30 per cent heavier than the maximum weight at which vertical take-off would have been possible. The P 1127/Kestrel/Harrier/Sea Harrier series of aircraft were particularly well suited to this form of short take-off from a carrier deck since, being designed to hover before landing, they were fitted with a system of flying controls that worked when the wing was not giving lift and there were minimal forces acting on the tailplane and rudder. When the aircraft were in wing-borne flight they used conventional elevators, ailerons and rudder. When the engine exhaust nozzles were rotated below 10 degrees these surfaces continued to move but, additionally a series of 'puffer jets', fed by pipes which took high-pressure air bled from the engine were activated. These gave the pilot control authority using his conventional controls. Large control deflections took more bleed air and reduced the amount of hover thrust available causing the aircraft to descend if thrust was only marginally greater than weight. Sea Harriers were fitted with a small tank of demineralised water which could be injected into the engine to give a few seconds of optimum performance during a hover landing onto a carrier so that the aircraft could land on at a reasonable weight but, even then, fuel had to be jettisoned down to a few minutes' supply in hot conditions, leaving only a small safety margin if the landing had to be aborted for some reason. A flat deck launch, however, left the aircraft low and slow close to the surface of the sea for up to 15 seconds after launch and at night or in bad weather this was clearly not ideal. Any sort of malfunction would leave the pilot very little time to eject. Another drawback was that Sea Harriers would not always be able to achieve their full load-carrying potential from the small deck run available in *Invincible* and her sisters.

In his first paper[22] Taylor examined several ways of launching V/STOL aircraft more efficiently. These included the use of catapults and ballistas but the most elegant proposal was for a curved ramp or 'ski-jump'[23] at the forward end of the flight deck which allowed the aircraft to leave the deck after nozzle rotation at the apex of the curve at a speed which could be significantly less than that needed for a flat-deck take-off. This effect could be translated into a much shorter deck run or a higher launch weight. A 20-degree ski-jump offered a launch speed reduction of 30 knots at a given aircraft weight compared with a flat deck. At the highest aircraft weights associated with strike missions this represented a 30 per cent reduction in launch end-speed which, because the take-off deck run depends on speed squared, reduces the required deck run by about 50 per cent. At the lower short take-off weights associated with fighter missions the decreased end-speed requirement represented a 40 per cent reduction in velocity and required a deck run of only about one third of that needed for a flat deck launch. Alternatively, from a longer deck run end-speed remained comparable with that achieved with a flat deck launch; only about 4 knots being lost 'climbing the hill'. The aircraft was, thus, effectively launched with 30 knots excess end-speed and could carry 30 knots x 66lb per knot or roughly 2000lbs more payload than it could from a flat deck. Of interest, the US Marine Corps elected to retain flat decks on its amphibious carriers to allow more space for helicopter operations. Their AV-8 Harriers do, however have the advantage of a deck run nearly twice as long as that in *Invincible* but still have to accept the low, slow climb away from the deck.

A 'ski-jump' was erected at RAE Bedford made from Fairey girder bridge components and trials were carried with development Harriers and Sea Harriers. Theoretically launch performance increased with 'ski-jump' angle but in practical terms, there was an optimum end-speed corresponding with maximum launch weight. For a desired maximum launch weight there was a minimum angle, the size of which was derived from the radius which would avoid undercarriage stress becoming a limiting factor at that weight. This effectively sized the 'ski-jump' since excess load factor was proportional to end-speed squared divided by the radius of the curve. In practice, practical curve radii for the Sea Harrier was found to lie in the range 600 to 800ft. The application of Euclid's law then determined how long and how high the actual 'ski-jump' structure would be for a given exit angle. The

Ark Royal 5's 12-degree 'ski-jump' structure being lowered into place by crane at Swan Hunter's Wallsend shipyard on the Tyne. (Author's collection)

size of the structure was found to grow markedly above 12 degrees and this was a disincentive to considering bigger angles. The advantages of the 'ski-jump' were immediately apparent and work was put in hand by the ship department to evaluate its installation on *Invincible*, despite the 'frozen' design. The result was positive but cautious. The merits of installation were agreed to justify the extra cost of drawings and modification during build. From our point of view in the Ships and Bases Section of DGA(N) the advantages of the 12-degree structure were obvious but the ability to operate Sea Harriers had only been listed as number 6 in a list of six requirements for the design in NSR 7097 and DG Ships was concerned that a 'ski-jump' would significantly limit the adjacent Sea Dart mounting's arcs of fire. It was eventually agreed that a small 7-degree 'ski-jump' would be fitted, a compromise between improved Sea Harrier performance and surface-to-air guided weapon capability. The design section at Bath responsible for *Hermes*, with whom I also worked, were not constrained by a Sea Dart installation and saw the improved operation of aircraft as their priority. They went for a larger 12-degree structure which was installed during the ship's 1980 conversion in Portsmouth. This was to prove far more effective and was copied on the third ship of the *Invincible* class, *Ark Royal*. The first two ships were subsequently modified with 12-degree 'ski-jumps' during refits. It was thought at the time that research into improved 'ski-jumps' would continue and to assist with this a 'ski-jump' installed on the dummy flight deck at RNAS Yeovilton was designed to be infinitely variable at considerable cost. In the event the *Hermes* structure was found to be ideal and even the 'ski-jump' fitted in the *Queen Elizabeth* class thirty years later is similar.

The Completed Ships

As *Invincible* was fitted out I was one of a group of officers who carried out inspections that prepared the ship for subsequent harbour and sea trials.[24] It soon became obvious that we were the first to view the new ship through the eyes of practical operators rather than the theoretical planners who had argued over the design's origins. The difference in perspective was striking and it was apparent that while we wanted a ship that delivered credible fighting capability, the latter had often been more concerned with not upsetting politicians in Whitehall with demands for changes to improve the operation of aircraft. This difference in outlook manifested itself in a number of ways, among them manpower and the *Invincible* class has a fair claim to being the first attempt to produce 'lean-manned' warships into the RN. NSR 7097 Edition 3 in 1979 specified a ship's company of 926, comprising 114 officers, 239 senior ratings and 573 junior ratings based on its role with a flag staff embarked and an air group of five Sea Harrier FRS 1s and nine Sea King HAS 5s. The ship's company for the second and third ships, based on the same assumptions, rose to a total of 965 comprising 120 officers, 248 senior ratings and 597 junior ratings. The accommodation itself was to be at the highest standard yet achieved in the RN, with all officers and a proportion of senior ratings in single cabins and separate bunk and recreation spaces built into each mess for the remainder. By 1997, however, the scheme of complement for the class had risen to 1250, comprising 201 officers, 307 senior ratings and 742 junior ratings since, by then, the air group had grown to six Sea Harrier F/A 2, nine Sea King HAS 6 and three Sea King AEW 2. There were, however, only 1249 bunks available and the man without a bunk was a junior rating. These figures indicate that the original scheme of complement was kept low for political reasons but once the ships were built and had become an accepted fact, more realistic levels of manpower had to be achieved. The increase from theory to practical reality was an unprecedented 26 per cent. Surprisingly, the flag and command arrangements also had to be expanded before they could be considered good. Fortunately the high initial standard of designed accommodation lent itself to modification as soon as the first ship arrived in Portsmouth when extra bunks were immediately worked in.[25] A second bunk was built into most junior officers' cabins but more radical solutions were incorporated to house the extra men required for the Sea King AEW squadron. It was found that if Sea Kings were parked in the after hangar nose aft, there was room for a mezzanine space to be built above them to contain four- and six-berth officers' cabins. A similar mezzanine deck was installed in the forward hangar to hold bulky aircraft spares for which there had been no other space. If necessary it could be used as temporary accommodation for Royal Marines' Commandos when the ships were employed in their secondary LPH role. These modifications were eventually applied to all three ships.

The air arrangements suffered from the fact that the initial design had actually been based on outdated naval engineering standards applicable to cruisers and the design team had been encouraged at first to think in terms of 'a cruiser with an aircraft capability' rather than 'an aircraft carrier with surface-to-air missile and command capability'.[26] As the first ship neared completion at Barrow-in-Furness it was obvious that the RN was growing in confidence and the visible evidence of this came with the first ship's final coat of paint when it was seen that she had been given a pennant number with an 'R' rather than a 'C' flag superior.[27] Artists' impressions of the design in the 1970s had shown 'CAH', C 01 and other cruiser identification markings but, with the ship nearly complete and Sea Harriers already flying the RN was confident enough to allocate a pennant number in the NATO aircraft carrier range, R 05, previously carried by *Eagle*. There was no specific announcement about the change but the term command cruiser gradually faded. At last the RN had a new aircraft carrier, albeit a rather small one, and was no longer afraid to refer to it as such.

A lot of the ship's air arrangements were found to be impractical and had to be set right before the ship became operational. It had originally been hoped that Sea Harriers could use the type of helicopter glide slope indicator fitted in frigates but when this concept proved to be impossible, a prototype system of visual landing aids was installed[28] in *Invincible* and *Hermes* but proved inadequate for the demanding task of giving pilots the precise glide-slope information they needed to

A posed photograph which does, however, demonstrate that the *Invincible* class had developed into effective light carriers by 1990. The aircraft to the right is a Sea Harrier FRS 1; that to the left a Sea King AEW 2. More Sea Harriers and Sea Kings are visible on *Ark Royal* 5's deck. (Crown Copyright)

come the hover alongside a deck landing spot, especially at night or in bad weather. I was able to organise trials ashore and in *Hermes* to evaluate the use of the projector sight, used by the previous generation of fixed-wing carriers and to force through the production of a modified version to be known as the deck approach projector sight (DAPS). This proved to be ideal for the purpose and was first fitted on *Illustrious* and then *Hermes* and *Invincible* as soon as possible and on *Ark Royal* while she was under construction. I was also involved in trials of similar equipment for US Marine Corps AV-8A Harriers in the USS *Tarawa* in 1981 off San Diego. Carrier-controlled approach in conditions of low visibility was also necessary but DNAW had resisted the fitting of TACAN despite its recent use in most carriers and its retention in *Hermes* because of fears that it might give away ships' positions to enemy reconnaissance aircraft. The ship's navigation radar could be used but lacked sufficient definition in the worse conditions and a device known as microwave digital guidance equipment (MADGE), manufactured by MEL Aviation was procured. Position information was limited to a 90-degree sector astern of the ship out to 10 miles and limited to 'line of sight' reception but it was fairly secure against interception. Its use was limited at first but it later gained widespread acceptance. Sea Harriers could also use their own radar locked onto the ship to carry out a recovery in adverse conditions.

There were a number of minor defects that had to be set right quickly. Among them was the layout of the consoles in Flyco which, as built into the first ship, prevented Lieutenant Commander 'Flying' from seeing any part of the flight deck when seated in his normal position. I had to work quickly on a re-design with the relevant section at Bath and arrange for the changes to be carried out as soon as possible after the first ship arrived in Portsmouth and in due course in the later ships. *Hermes* had the large Flyco typical of all the earlier strike carriers and thus never had the same problem after her conversion to operate Sea Harriers. The two designed briefing rooms were archaic with chalk boards, minimal communications and no flight planning facilities for aircrew. Each had twenty comfortable Volvo 'truck-drivers' seats which was not a wise distribution since the fighter squadron had eight pilots and the helicopter unit about fifty aircrew. The comfortable seats had to be ripped out in the latter and replaced by benches that could just seat all the helicopter aircrew when necessary. The least satisfactory feature of the design was the flight deck and it is difficult to understand why this was so since a much better sketch design for a 20,000 tons 'suitable for conversion to VTO aircraft' had been produced in 1953 with a much better, wider deck.[29] The merit of a wide deck to allow vertical landings by fighters and helicopters at any angle across the deck when the ship was not headed into wind was clearly well understood twenty years before *Invincible* was laid down in 1973 but the message seems to have been lost. The men who started with a clean sheet of paper to design the 'command cruiser' created a very narrow deck made even narrower amidships by siting the unusually long island well inboard from the starboard deck edge. These two design factors combined to make cross-deck landings anywhere but right aft extremely difficult and, therefore, reduced the tactical flexibility that would have been possible if a design like that of 1953 had been used. The narrow design forced the *Invincible* class, like all their

During the early 1980s I took part in a number of RN and USN Sea Harrier/AV-8A trials and acted as the liaison officer on the subject in an information exchange project between the two navies. I am seen here, second from the left standing, with a trials team from the US Naval Air Systems Command on the USS *Tarawa*, LHA 1, during trials of recovery aids for the AV-8A Harrier. (Author's collection)

predecessors, to have to turn into wind for every launch and recovery. The design of the deck was made even worse by the two centreline lifts which both impinged into the STOVL runway, the forward one more so than the aft. If the forward lift was stuck down, and the scissors design proved at first to be very unreliable, it prevented Sea Harriers from using the 'ski-jump'. Despite all these niggling shortcomings, the important fact was that the RN had all three ships of the *Invincible* class. They were larger than the earlier escort and commando cruiser designs and were, therefore, able to absorb the changes and function as light fleet carriers, deserving their new NATO designation as CVS. By 1981, despite the fact that the Sea Harrier did not yet have a full release to service for the full range of weapons it could carry, the new ship and her squadrons had formed an effective team.

The Nott Defence Review

In 1979 a Conservative government under Margaret Thatcher was elected which set in train a number of studies to cut government expenditure and 'balance the books'. A defence review was completed in 1981 which decided to limit the UK's capabilities even more closely to the NATO central front in Germany. With little personal knowledge of the subject matter, the Defence Secretary, John Nott, allowed himself to be persuaded that land-based aircraft could meet the reduced requirements of a fleet that was to be composed largely of nuclear submarines and a few frigates. It was therefore announced in February 1981 that *Invincible* had been sold to the Royal Australian Navy at a reported bargain price of £175 million, believed to be less than her estimated final build cost.[30] The RAN was seeking a small carrier to replace *Melbourne* but had dismissed the *Invincible* design as being too expensive and complicated and was thinking in terms of a modified USN *Iwo Jima* class ship but could not resist the bargain price. The RAN already operated Sea Kings and had two pilots flying Sea Harriers with the RN so Sea Harriers might have been an option. I attended a meeting at the Australian High Commission in 1981 where the possibility of 801 (Sea Harrier FRS 1) NAS being lent to the RAN when the ship was handed over was discussed but no firm decision was taken. In service she would have been re-named *Australia* and would have undergone a number of changes, not least the removal of Sea Dart. In fact, however, the deal did not go through and the reason will be explained in the next chapter.

The New Aircraft
Hermes was modified with a 'ski-jump' and workshops to allow her to operate Sea Harriers from 1981 and, together with the three ships of the *Invincible* class, she operated a new generation of RN aircraft.

Westland Sea King
Despite the high hopes entertained for the Westland Wessex HAS 3, it proved to be of limited operational use because of its low endurance and, even before the first squadron entered service, a contract was placed with Westland to produce an anglicised version of the Sikorsky Sea King in June 1966. So soon after the cancellation of CVA-01 this shows the confidence the FFWP must have had in the requirement to operate large anti-submarine helicopters with the fleet. The Sea King had been developed in the USA to meet a 1957 requirement and was to evolve into one of the greatest aircraft designs of all time, designated the SH-3 by the USN. It first flew in 1959 and Westland immediately purchased a license production agreement. The fact that the Admiralty was not tempted to take advantage of this low-risk development immediately shows how critically the naval staff still viewed helicopter dimensions and weight on the small, contemporary British carrier decks.[31] The Sea King was procured belatedly after the Wessex HAS 3 had proved that a 'quart measure' of avionics, weapons and fuel could not be squeezed into the 'pint pot' of its airframe. As with the Wessex, Westland bought Sikorsky airframes to hasten development and four were delivered in October 1966. The first to fly

was XV 370 which was virtually a standard SH-3D but the subsequent airframes were fitted progressively with Rolls-Royce Gnome H1400 turboshaft engines similar to those in the Wessex HU 5. They were also fitted progressively with British equipment including the Plessey Type 195 dipping sonar, Ecko AW 391 search radar and a Louis Newmark Mark 31 automatic full-authority flight control system.[32] The latter was a simplified and more reliable derivative of the system fitted to the Wessex HAS 3. The Sea King IFTU, 700S NAS, was formed in May 1969 at RNAS Culdrose and 824 NAS, the first operational squadron, took the type to sea in *Ark Royal* from February 1970. Westland continued to develop the design and the RN took advantage of this work to move on to a HAS 2 version with both new build and conversions of the forty-eight surviving HAS 1 airframes. The work was done by RNAY Fleetlands in Gosport and the Naval Aircraft Support Unit, NASU, at RNAS Culdrose and involved fitting a strengthened transmission system and a six-bladed tail rotor, increased fuel capacity and other detail improvements. The new version was issued to 826 NAS in 1976 and the whole fleet was re-equipped by 1978. Both the HAS 1 and 2 could be armed with up to four homing torpedoes or depth charges and could be fitted with machine guns in the cargo hatch and crew entry door.

The number of different versions eventually operated by the RN bear testament to the basic soundness of the design and Sea King development subsequently broadened and achieved the political 'holy grail' of joint status in 1978 when the first Sea King HAR 3 was delivered to the RAF for SAR duties. Westland developed a version it called the 'Commando' as a private venture and sold twenty-one to Egypt and this version attracted the RN at first to augment and then replace the Wessex HU 5. Eventually sixty-six were procured and designated the Sea King HC 4 in RN service. They differed from the anti-submarine version in having fixed undercarriages[33] and local strengthening to carry heavy underslung loads such as Land Rovers or field guns. 846 NAS began to replace its Wessex with Sea Kings in 1979. During the same period a considerable amount of development went into the avionics suite of the anti-submarine version to allow it to process both active dipping and passive sonar inputs, the latter from patterns of sono-buoys that could be laid by the aircraft. Development work on the HAS 5 began in January 1979[34] and the first aircraft, a converted HAS 2, flew for the first time on 14 August 1980. Again procurement included both new-build and converted airframes with the work being done by the same organisations. The first two production HAS 5s were handed over to the RN in August and were issued to 820 NAS which began to work up with the type for service in *Invincible* as soon as she completed her trials programme. As we saw earlier, however, the HAS 5 had considerably more sophisticated systems than its predecessor and their integration into the ship's

A Sea King HAS 1 of 824 NAS from *Ark Royal* 4 screening her; it is lowering its sonar transducer into the water. (Author's collection)

operations took time to perfect. The main external difference between the HAS 2 and the HAS 5 was the larger dorsal radome to house the MEL Sea Searcher radar but internally it mounted a Marconi Lightweight Acoustic Processing and Display System (LAPADS), to display information from the 'Jezebel' sono-buoy system. Stowage was built into the after cabin for a number of sono-buoys which were dropped into the sea by hand. Another piece of equipment that was new to the RN was the magnetic anomaly detector (MAD), a system that had been used on USN fixed-wing anti-submarine aircraft for some years. This picked up variations in the earth's magnetic field caused by large metal objects underwater and, to keep it clear of interference from the helicopter itself, it was fitted in a pod, known as a 'MAD-bird' towed by a long cable astern of the aircraft. When not in use it was wound onto a drum in the starboard undercarriage sponson. Not all HAS 5s were fitted with MAD but all were fitted for-but-not-with. The system had a very short range, only about 300ft from the 'MAD-bird' under ideal conditions, so the aircraft had to fly very low. It was obviously useless as an area search tool but did have value in pinpointing the position of a shallow submarine for weapon release.

Armament remained as in the HAS 2 with Mark 46 or, later, Stingray torpedoes being standard. During the 1980s composite rotor blades began to replace the original metal ones, giving up to four times the operational life. The HAS 5 had LAPADS and sono-buoys situated in the after part of the cabin and this had the effect of moving the aircraft's centre of gravity near the after limit, especially in the hover, leading to stresses and cracks which needed frequent repair. The last anti-submarine version was the HAS 6 which introduced airframe and transmission strengthening to rectify this problem and further improvements to the sonar systems. Four new HAS 6s were built and twenty-five HAS 5s upgraded to this standard, the first being delivered to 824 NAS at RNAS Prestwick in 1988. Sea Kings eventually served with 706, 707, 737, 771, 772, 810, 819, 820, 824, 825, 826, 845, 846, 848, 849, 849A, 849B, 854 and 857 NAS and are still in service with some units in 2015 despite plans to replace them from 1980 onwards. The AEW version will be described in the next chapter in the context of the South Atlantic Conflict.

Hawker Siddeley/British Aerospace/BAE Systems Sea Harrier

RN interest in a VTOL fighter can be traced back to 1945 when the Admiralty issued a requirement for a VTO fighter capable of deck-launched interception against Japanese Kamikaze aircraft. It had envisaged such an aircraft being 'fired' up rails by a combination of rockets and a turbojet and although Fairey designed its Delta 1 around this requirement and tested it at WRE Woomera it came to nothing. Earlier in the chapter I mentioned the 1953 sketch design for a VTOL-capable carrier and early examination of the NA 39 requirement by Blackburn had considered swivelling engine nozzles to allow engine thrust to support some aircraft weight during recovery to reduce the deck landing speed. The Admiralty had shown little interest in the Tripartite evaluation of the Hawker Siddeley Kestrel FGA 1 at RAF West Raynham in 1965 but in June 1966 a prototype P 1127 was embarked in *Bulwark* for two days of trials and demonstrated that STOVL take-off and landings could be integrated very successfully with helicopter operations. Her captain, Captain D B Law MBE DSC RN, had proposed the equipment of future commando ships with 'a mixed complement of Wessex 5 and Hawker P 1127 V/STOL aircraft'[35] and stated his 'personal conviction, based on fifteen months in command of *Bulwark* that these ships are not being worked to maximum capability and that there is room for fixed-wing aircraft without denigrating the ability of the ship to land and support a Commando'. On completion of the trial he stated enthusiastically in his report to the Commander-in-Chief Plymouth[36] that 'following the most encouraging results of this trial, the proposal . . . to equip a commando ship with a mixed V/STOL and rotary-wing force merits early consideration'. He was thinking primarily in terms of close air support for the RM

During 'Release to Service' trials, scientists from the A&AEE Boscombe Down used special cameras to measure the exact end-speed of aircraft on the 'ski-jump' by timing the exposure; the result was this somewhat elongated image. This example was signed for me by Lieutenant Commander David Poole RN, the test pilot who carried out the early 'ski-jump' launch tests in *Invincible*. (Author's collection)

Commando ashore but, of course, the aircraft could have performed a number of other roles. Although their performance fell far short of the aircraft that were now being embarked in the strike carriers, they were adequate for relatively short-range close air support missions. In the end, Captain Law's enthusiasm achieved nothing because the timing was wrong. Only days after the cancellation of CVA-01, politicians saw the idea as a 'back door' way of keeping carriers and senior RN officers were too traumatised by the loss of the new carrier to begin another fight with the MOD and Government.

The idea was not lost completely, however, and as we saw earlier the FFWP took note of the possibility of embarking STOVL fighters and included them in the plethora of command/commando cruiser sketch designs. The catalyst for progress came when the cabinet approved the development of a more sophisticated version of the Kestrel FGA 1 to replace the Hunter FGA 9 as a close air support aircraft. This was to evolve into the Harrier and was to have a maximum weapons load of 5000lbs after a short take-off, podded 30mm guns and a sophisticated navigation system including a moving map display derived from the avionics designed for the aborted TSR 2. A version of the Harrier, designated the AV-8A, was procured for the US Marine Corps in 1971. With much of the development flying achieved by the P 1127 and Kestrel prototypes, Harrier development went relatively smoothly and was complete by 1969, when the first RAF squadron was formed. For what it could do, however, the Harrier was a very expensive aircraft and the initial order was for only seventy-seven. To 'hedge its bets' the RAF ordered 200 Jaguar aircraft at the same time. These were built as a joint venture with France[37] and formed the core of the RAF tactical strike force. Apart from the individual aircraft costing less than a Harrier, they had a significantly better performance. A Harrier GR 1 had a maximum take-off weight of 26,000lbs and a hi-lo-hi radius of action with a 5000lb bomb-load of 200nm. Compared with this the Jaguar GR 1 had a maximum take-off weight of 34,612lbs[38] and a hi-lo-hi radius of action of 750nm with a 10,000lb bomb-load. The Harrier certainly had a unique 'niche' capability but the aircraft's operator had to pay a high price for it. Nevertheless, a STOVL aircraft was now in service, Hawker Siddeley was enthusiastic about a maritime derivative and it was against this background that the *Invincible* class had been designed with a through deck and sufficient hangarage to support a derivative design. In 1966 DNAW forwarded papers on STOVL fighters to the FFWP that looked at various options. Deployment to destroyers and frigates was discounted because of the necessary expensive duplication of support facilities and manpower.[39] The concept of catapult launching the Sea Harrier, as proposed for the P 1154 before it, had a distinct fascination and several ideas for 'slotted-cylinder' catapults that did not need steam were discussed.[40] None of these were, in the end, taken forward.

Technology had moved a long way forward since the abortive P 1154 and it proved possible to produce a single-pilot strike fighter with a lightweight radar in the nose allied to a weapon system that fed information and primary flight data to him through a head-up display. The requirement, NSR 6451, issued in January 1972 called for an aircraft that would provide a 'quick-reaction multi-role capability

A Sea Harrier FRS 1 launching from *Ark Royal* 5's 12-degree ski-jump. Note the heat haze behind and below it showing that the nozzles have been partially lowered to generate lift. At this stage the aircraft is effectively following a ballistic trajectory until speed increases to the point where the wings generate enough lift for normal flight. (Author's collection)

for tasks which could not be met by any other ship-fitted weapons system'.[41] They included the area and point reconnaissance of surface contacts; harassment and engagement of enemy air reconnaissance and data-link aircraft; offensive action against surface ships and offensive action against airborne missile launchers. Significantly, paragraph 5 stated that 'the military payload would be significantly increased by using a short take-off run in preference to a vertical take-off. Hence the cruiser configuration.'[42] The multi-role capability was reflected in the Sea Harrier's FRS 1 designation, 'F' for fighter, 'R' for reconnaissance and 'S' for nuclear strike. Its Rolls-Royce Pegasus 104 vectored thrust turbofan was rated at 21,500lbs thrust with water injection and the aircraft's maximum weight at take-off was 26,200lbs. Its maximum weapon load was 5000lbs carried on four external under-wing hardpoints with a fifth under the fuselage. Its radius of action for a hi-lo-hi strike mission was about 300nm. Weapons that could be carried included the WE-177 600lb nuclear bomb, Sea Eagle air-to-surface missile, AIM-9L Sidewinder air-to-air missile, conventional 1000lb bombs, 2in rocket pods, 30mm Aden cannon in two under-fuselage pods each with 100 rpg and Lepus flares. A single F-95 oblique camera was fitted on the starboard side of the fuselage, just forward of the cockpit to give an important reconnaissance capability. Full-scale development was authorised in 1972, before *Invincible* was laid down in 1973, making it obvious that the new class of carrier was always intended to operate STOVL fighters, and a production contract for three development and thirty-one production Sea Harriers was placed with what was now British Aerospace in May 1975. The first aircraft to fly was XZ 450 and the IFTU, 700A NAS formed at RNAS Yeovilton in June 1979, initially with a single Sea Harrier, XZ 451. To help development two Hunter T 8s were fitted with the Sea Harrier's Ferranti Blue Fox radar in the nose and when this work was completed they were designated T 8M and used by the RN to teach pilots radar intercept techniques. Three training Harriers that lacked radar but were otherwise similar, designated Harrier T4N, were ordered and entered service with 899 NAS, the Sea Harrier headquarters and training unit at RNAS Yeovilton from 1983 together with the Hunter T 8Ms and a number of Sea Harriers. Three front-line units operated the Sea Harrier FRS 1, 800, 801 and 809 NAS.

Originally the Martel missile was specified for the air-to-surface role in both the TV-guided and anti-radar versions that had been used by the Buccaneer but by the time the Sea Harrier FRS 1 entered service it had been replaced by the BAE Systems Sea Eagle and this was the weapon that was embarked in the *Invincible* class. Armed with the Sidewinder infrared air-to-air missile the FRS 1 had no intercept capability beyond visual range or in bad weather. This shortcoming was corrected in the type's mid-life upgrade to F/A 2 standard when the Ferranti Blue Vixen pulse-doppler radar replaced the earlier equipment and the aircraft was

Two Sea Harrier F/A 2s of 801 NAS pulling into the vertical together. Note the variant's larger nose radome, an easy recognition feature that differentiated it from the FRS 1. (Crown Copyright)

fitted to carry the AIM-120 advanced air-to-air missile, AMRAAM. The problem of installing equipment into an aircraft that had to hover when it landed was highlighted by the fact that while the scanner was fitted in the nose, its 'black boxes' had to be fitted aft of the centre of gravity and the fuselage aft of the wing had to be lengthened by 18in to take them. Other weapons remained the same except that the nuclear capability was deleted in line with UK Government policy to limit its nuclear options to the Trident D 5 missiles in the SSBNs. The change in role was shown by the alteration of the designation to a USN style F/A indicating fighter and conventional attack capabilities and gave the aircraft an impressive 'swing' capability which was more advanced than any other fighter in Europe for some years.

Weapons for the New Aircraft

WE 177 – the 600lb nuclear bomb
The basic WE 177 was designed to fill the gap between Blue Steel and Polaris to give RAF 'V'-bombers a weapon that could be used in lay-down attacks after penetrating Soviet air defences at low level. It came in three versions, 'A', 'B' and 'C', with the latter two used by the RAF on strike aircraft based in the UK and Germany. The RN version was the WE 177A and it entered service in 1969. It could be used either as a strike weapon using a variety of techniques including lay-down and toss bombing or as a nuclear depth bomb (NDB), and the yield could be selected as either 0.5 kiloton or 10 kilotons. The smaller yield could be selected by armourers when the weapons was prepared for use but was intended solely for the NDB role in shallow water less than 130ft deep. The full 10-kiloton yield was intended for use in the NDB role in deep water or when the weapon was used against warships or land targets. It could be set for air burst at variable heights, burst on impact or retarded lay-down detonation when prepared for use. There was an instructional round which was externally identical but which, obviously, contained no fissile material, explosives or other hazardous components. They were used for ground training at the RN Air Weapons school at HMS *Excellent*, Whale Island, at Portsmouth and at RN Air Stations and could be flown, giving the aircrew the correct responses when selections were made but they were never dropped. WE 177A could be carried in the NDB role by the Wessex HAS 3, Wasp, Sea King and the Ikara anti-submarine missile.[43] In the surface-attack role it could be carried by the Buccaneer S 2 and Sea Harrier FRS 1.

Martel
Martel was used by 809 (Buccaneer S 2) NAS in *Ark Royal* during the 1970s and

was the base-line air-to-surface missile against which part of the magazine space in the *Invincible* class was designed. It was a joint venture designed by Hawker Siddeley in the UK and Matra in France and came in two versions intended for anti-radiation and anti-surface ship use; the former designated the AS 37 and the latter the AJ 168. The name derived from the project requirement for a Missile-Anti-radar-TELevision. It weighed 1212lbs and was 12ft 9in long and was powered by a two-stage solid-propellant rocket motor. The 330lb armour-piercing warhead was fused by an internal variable timing device shortly before impact and it had a range of about 40nm after launch from the parent aircraft. The AJ 168 was fitted with a Marconi Vidicon camera which transmitted TV imagery back to a data link pod on the launch aircraft which, in turn, transmitted control inputs from the Buccaneer's observer using a small control stick and TV screen. It flew a pre-determined mid-course flight path at medium level to allow easier target acquisition and maintenance of the control data link and then dived onto the target under the observer's control. It was therefore vulnerable to the improved anti-missile systems

Examples of some of the stores that could be carried by the Sea Harrier FRS 1 laid out on *Invincible*'s flight deck after 1983. They include 1000lb bombs, Aden cannon, drop tanks, Lepus flares and practice bombs. The aircraft itself is armed with loaded double Sidewinder pylons and gun pods. Note the temporary Vulcan Phalanx close-in weapon system positioned on the starboard after edge of the flight deck after the South Atlantic War. (Author's collection)

widely fitted after 1980. The AS 37 substituted a pre-selected 'home-on-radar' frequency for the TV guidance and was launched when an enemy radar had been detected that needed to be suppressed. If the radar was switched off it lost guidance but the enemy lost the use of the radar so it still had value. The biggest drawback with AS 37 was the fact that it only had one narrow-band homing sensor which was only selectable on deck before launch and it was therefore necessary to know what type of radar was to be attacked before take-off. It was also three times heavier than the USN equivalent AGM-45 Shrike anti-radiation missile.

Sea Eagle

Designed to meet Air Staff Target 1226 and specified in NST 6451 for use on the Sea Harrier, the BAe Systems Sea Eagle replaced Martel in service with the RN and RAF in 1985. It was a more sophisticated 'sea-skimming' fire-and-forget weapon with an active Marconi/Selex radar in the nose for target acquisition and tracking. It was powered by a Microturbo TRI 60 turbojet which gave it a range of 70nm at a speed of Mach 0.85. A C-band radar altimeter allowed the missile to fly at very low level, minimising the range at which it could be detected and making its destruction more difficult. The J-band target-seeking radar could detect targets up to 18 miles away and the missile's computer commanded a 'pop-up' manoeuvre to search for a target if required. It could also be programmed to fly 'dog-leg' attack profiles if missiles were fired in salvo. Sea Eagle had small, cruciform delta wings with smaller tail surfaces aft which provided steering. The small engine intake was under the fuselage and while the missile was on the launcher aircraft it was covered by an aerodynamic fairing which was blown clear on launch. The small warhead was shaped in a metal alloy casing to give good armour-piercing qualities and any residual turbojet fuel added to the damage effect on a warship. Unlike Martel, which required checks before launch, Sea Eagle was stored as a round of ammunition, fully fuelled, with inspections only required every two years. Its weakness, which caused it to be withdrawn from RN service when the Sea Harrier F/A 2 was retired, was that it was not possible for the launch aircraft to select a specific target in a cluttered littoral environment; the radar would lock onto the first target it detected. Sea Eagle did achieve export success, however, and was used among other applications by the Indian Navy on its Sea Harriers, Sea King helicopters and even Tupolev Tu-142 'Bear' maritime patrol aircraft.

Sidewinder

The AIM-9L Sidewinder air-to-air missile was a logical development of earlier versions of the missile that had been used by the RN on Scimitars, Buccaneers and Phantoms. The 'L' was the latest version and had only just entered service when the

Sea Harrier FRS 1 became operational. By then it was the world's most successful short-range missile and used a heat-seeking infrared guidance system that could detect targets at all angles including directly ahead. It had a maximum range of 11nm and used a solid-fuel rocket motor to achieve a speed of Mach 2.5. It weighed only 191lbs which meant that two could be carried on adaptors on each of the Sea Harrier's outboard wing pylons. Sidewinders could also be carried by the Harrier GR 1/3 and GR 5/7/9.

AMRAAM

The AIM-120 Advanced Medium Range Air to Air Missile (AMRAAM), was carried by the Sea Harrier F/A 2 and formed part of the weapon system with the Blue Vixen pulse-doppler radar. Up to four could be carried, one each on the outboard wing pylons and one each on the under-fuselage stations that would otherwise be used for the 30mm gun pods. On a typical CAP sortie an F/A 2 would probably not be fitted with guns but would carry two Sidewinders and two AMRAAM giving a wide choice of close-range and beyond-visual-range capability. All four AMRAAM could be fired simultaneously at different targets at heights from sea level to high altitude using information from the Blue Vixen in its 'track while scan' mode. The missiles received guidance information from the radar to put them into a position where their own terminal guidance radars could acquire

Sea Harrier FRS 1s of three naval air squadrons in formation. Nearest the camera is an aircraft of 800 NAS, an aircraft of 801 NAS in the middle with another of 899 NAS furthest away. The nearest and furthest aircraft are armed with AIM-9 Sidewinders. (Crown Copyright)

An AIM-120 AMRAAM being loaded onto the port wing pylon of a Sea Harrier F/A 2 by armourers. (Crown Copyright)

targets and guide the missiles to impact. The missile weighed 350lbs and gave the Sea Harrier F/A 2 an air defence capability that was arguably better than any other European fighter when it entered service.

Aden Cannon and Other Weapons

The 30mm Aden cannons were identical to those fitted in the Scimitar except that they were enclosed in neat, detachable under-fuselage pods which also contained 100 rounds of ammunition. They gave the Sea Harrier a useful back-up weapon in air combat when the missiles had been fired and a useful weapon against slow-moving aircraft, helicopters, soft-skinned vehicles and troops on the ground. The 2in rocket pods and Lepus flares were also identical to those used on earlier fighters. The standard, conventional weapon for use against ships and shore targets was the 1000lb bomb which could be fused for air, impact or delayed burst. It had been in service for many years and was reliable and effective.

18 The South Atlantic War

By the beginning of 1982 the RN carrier strike fleet had survived decades of decline, the cancellation of its replacement aircraft carrier programme, the substitution of smaller, much less capable ships and aircraft, the withdrawal from the Far East and, only a few months earlier, a Defence Review that had attempted to limit the RN to a second-class role within NATO. Despite the politicians, however, it was still capable of reacting effectively at short notice to any emergency.[1] The crisis, when it came, was centred in the South Atlantic on the Falkland Islands and their Dependencies, all of them British possessions that had been dismissed by Dennis Healey as unimportant and which had not even been mentioned by subsequent politicians in their arguments over defence requirements.

The Falkland Islands

The Falkland Islands lie some 400nm to the north-east of Cape Horn, the southernmost point of South America. The total population in 1982 was about 1800 of which the majority lived in East Falkland Island with the capital Port Stanley as the main settlement with its small airfield and harbour. West Falkland was smaller, even more sparsely inhabited and composed mainly of sheep farms. They were discovered by the Englishman John Davis in 1592 and the first recorded landing was by the British privateer John Strong in 1690 while Britain and Spain were at war.[2] The Union Flag was first raised by a landing party under Commodore John Byron RN from the frigate *Dolphin* on 23 January 1765 and the island had both a small garrison and a guard ship from 1766. A larger Spanish force took the islands after a fight in 1770, however, claiming that they were acting under the orders of Spanish colonial officials in Argentina. The British re-took the islands in 1771 and, once more established a garrison at Fort Egmont but Government economies in 1774 led to it being withdrawn. They left the Union Flag flying and a lead plaque over the door of the fort which read 'Be it known to all nations that the Falkland Islands, with this fort, the store-houses, wharfs, harbours, bays and creeks, thereunto belonging are the sole right and property of His Most Sacred Majesty King George III'. For some years there was no permanent population but American sealers, French and Spanish Colonial sailors lived on the islands for short periods. As trade grew in the early nineteenth century, the Falkland Islands began to function as a convenient coaling station and base for British ships and Letters Patent established permanent British occupation in 'Her Majesty's Settlements in the Falkland Islands and their dependencies'. The capital moved to Port Stanley in 1845 and there was a small garrison of Royal Marines. In 1879 the garrison was withdrawn as a savings measure, a decision that seemed to have become a recurring theme in London, but on 29 February 1892 the Islands were declared a full British Colony. The island of South Georgia and others, together with part of the Antarctic mainland were declared to be Falkland Island Dependencies in 1906, despite objections by Argentina. From 1908 Argentina claimed an historic right to the Falkland Islands, based on temporary settlements in the eighteenth century.

Throughout the twentieth century there had been a number of incidents but successive governments had taken it for granted that the powerful RN would be able to do something about them and deter any serious attempt at invasion. In 1955 the former netlayer *Protector* was converted into an ice patrol ship which was regularly deployed to the region in the Antarctic summer to look after British interests, replacing frigates from the South Atlantic Station that had previously

Invincible sailing from Portsmouth with the South Atlantic Task Force on 5 April 1982. (Author's collection)

carried out the task. She had a flight deck aft and hangarage for two Whirlwind helicopters, a twin 4in gun mounting forward and accommodation for a small Marine detachment. Another RM detachment, designated Naval Party 8901, was maintained at Moody Brook on East Falkland Island. In 1963 the Argentinian Government introduced a national holiday which named 'Malvinas Day', their name for the islands, and in 1964 it took the question of the islands' sovereignty to the United Nations.[3] In September of that year an Argentinian aircraft landed illegally on the racecourse at Port Stanley and one of its occupants got out and planted an Argentine flag. The frigate *Lynx* was ordered to the Falkland Islands and arrived on 14 October. She remained in the area until 11 November. A worse situation developed in February 1976 after the severing of diplomatic relations between Great Britain and Argentina when the Argentinian destroyer *Almirante Storni* fired a shot at the British research ship *Shackleton*. The frigate *Eskimo* was ordered to the area from the West Indies and proceeded with all despatch, refuelling *en route* from the RFA *Tidesurge*. Another frigate, *Chichester*, was on her way home from Hong Kong where she had been guard ship and was diverted to the area for a short time. In March Isabel Peron was ousted as head of state in Argentina by a military Junta but the situation in the South Atlantic stabilised and *Eskimo* returned to the West Indies Station in April.[4]

That stability did not last long and on 6 January 1977 an Argentinian camp was discovered on the Dependency island of South Thule by the ice patrol ship *Endurance* which had, by then, replaced *Protector*. She carried two Wasp helicopters which could be armed but the ship itself was of commercial design and had no guns. Unlike *Protector* which had been painted grey, her hull was painted red and she had white upper works. *Endurance* had part of Naval Party 8901 embarked and continued to monitor the situation while talks were initiated between the UK Foreign Office and Argentina. In September Argentine warships began to harass fishing vessels in the waters off the Falkland Islands, claiming that they were fishing illegally in Argentine waters, and in one incident there was a casualty in a Bulgarian fishing boat that was fired on by an Argentine vessel.[5] In November the Argentine Navy announced that it was to carry out exercises in waters around the Falkland Islands and the UK Joint Intelligence Committee (JIC) advised the Government that there was a credible and immediate threat to the Islands. In response, after discussions with 1SL, Admiral Sir Terence Lewin, the Government authorised Operation 'Journeyman'. Admiral Sir Henry Leach, Commander-in-Chief Fleet, sent a small task force to the South Atlantic comprising the nuclear hunter/killer submarine *Dreadnought* and the frigates *Alacrity* and *Phoebe* supported by RFAs *Olwen* and *Resurgent*. They sailed without public announcement and *Dreadnought* took up a position close to the Falkland Islands; the surface ships took up a holding position 1000nm to the north-east where they could act as a communications relay for the submarine and intervene quickly if necessary. This was a classic use of sea power where ships could poise 'over the horizon' for extended periods and then act quickly and decisively if needed or move away unnoticed without embarrassment if they were not. By 19 December it was considered that the immediate threat had reduced and the task force was withdrawn, as quietly as it had been deployed. With such frequent tests of resolve, one might have thought that politicians would have learnt the lesson but this proved not to be the case. The 1981 Defence Review decided to withdraw the ice patrol ship *Endurance*, the last outwardly visible sign of British presence in the region, as an economy measure and not replace her. To the military junta in Argentina this was immediately seen as a sign of weakness from a Government that no longer cared and they took the initial steps that were to lead to war. For many years there had been talks at junior ministerial level between the UK and Argentina in which the issue of sovereignty had become increasingly prominent. The Falkland Islanders' were British citizens, however, and it would be politically difficult not to support their views. Despite this, it was widely believed in Whitehall by the end of 1981 that the UK Government was considering a de facto transfer of sovereignty to Argentina under some sort of 'lease-back' arrangement to be discussed in talks scheduled for June 1982. The residents' rights as British citizens would be written into the agreement but the talks were destined never to take place.

The Argentinian Invasion of the Falkland Islands

General Galtieri, the President of Argentina, and his ruling junta faced economic, social and political problems at the beginning of 1982.[6] It appeared to them that the UK had lost interest in the Falkland Islands, an opinion that was strengthened by Nott's Defence Review which had announced deep cuts in the very forces that would be needed to fight a naval war at a considerable distance from the UK. They decided to seize the Falkland Islands and their dependent territories by force to divert attention away the government's problems, trusting that this would win popular acclaim at home and that there would be little that the UK could do in response. Plans were carried forward in secret and amphibious exercises were carried out on 19 March unnoticed by British intelligence. Meanwhile the British Embassy in Buenos Aires was informed that forty-one men would be employed on salvage work at the derelict whaling station in South Georgia for which a scrapping contract had been let. They were transported in the naval transport *Bahia Buen Suceso* and landed on 19 March 1982 after which they immediately raised the Argentine Flag. *Endurance*, commanded by Captain Nick Barker RN, was still on the station, however, and sailed from Port Stanley with a party of twenty Royal

Marines on board to investigate. She arrived off South Georgia with instructions from the MOD to watch but not take any action that might provoke an international incident. The Argentine Navy sent a corvette to South Georgia on 24 March and two days later a powerful task force sailed for what were described as anti-submarine exercises. The force included the aircraft carrier *Veintecinco de Mayo*, formerly HMS *Venerable* and then the Dutch *Karel Doorman* before being sold to Argentina in 1968, the two new British-built Type 42 destroyers *Hercules* and *Santisima Trinidad* and the French-built corvettes *Drummond* and *Granville*. It also contained the LST *Cabo San Antonio* with the 2nd Marine Infantry Battalion embarked which gave the real clue to the task force's intention. British intelligence coverage in the South Atlantic was no longer very effective and the UK Government did not learn of the task force until 31 March by which time the Junta had taken the fateful decision to invade and more ships joined the initial task force.

The Argentine codename for the operation was 'Rosario' and forces were divided into Task Groups 20, 40 and 60. The main invasion group, TG 40 headed for the Falkland Islands and TG 60 headed for South Georgia. TG 20 was a covering force comprising the carrier with A-4 Skyhawks and S-2 Trackers embarked escorted by the destroyers *Segui*, *Comodoro Py*, *Hipolito Bouchard* and *Piedra Buena*. The actual invasion began in the early morning darkness of 2 April 1982. A special forces unit of seventy men was landed by boat from *Santisima Trinidad* and split into two groups; the first to attack Government House and the other the RM barracks at Moody Brook. Frogmen came ashore from the submarine *Santa Fe* and seized Port Stanley airfield. Moody Brook was found to be empty as the Royal Marines had sufficient warning to set up defensive positions elsewhere. Fortunately a new detachment to replace the forty Royal Marines in Naval Party 8901 had just arrived on 30 March on board the British research ship *John Biscoe*. Rex Hunt, the Governor, ordered the old party to remain, thus doubling the size of the defending force. At 06.15 Government House was assaulted but when the officer in charge of the attackers was killed his men retreated under fire. A three-hour firefight ensued but by then Argentine troops in amphibious armoured personnel carriers were making their way ashore from *Cabo San Antonio*. Their advance on Port Stanley was checked for a while when Royal Marines scored direct hits on the leading vehicles with Carl Gustav anti-tank weapons but more troops were arriving ashore in helicopters and landing craft. The capture of the airfield by special forces allowed Argentine C-130 transports to fly in yet more troops and by late forenoon the officer in command of the Royal Marines, Major Norman RM, had to advise Rex Hunt that in view of the overwhelming number of enemy forces further resistance would serve little purpose and endanger the lives of the civilian population. The Governor, therefore, surrendered but it is very much to the Royal Marines' credit that they held

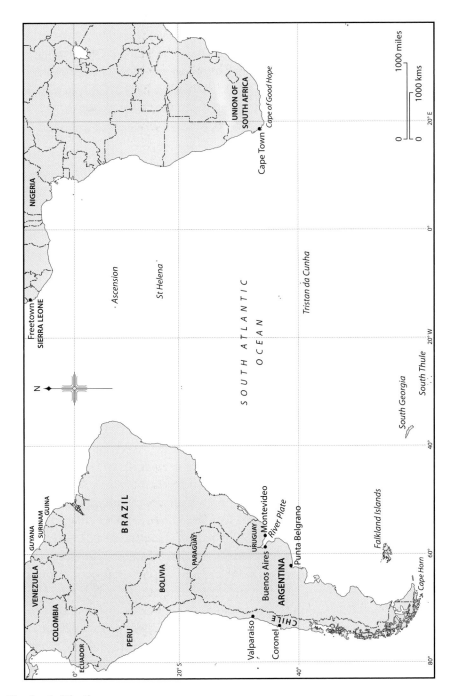

The South Atlantic.

out for so long against overwhelming odds and inflicted a number of casualties on the enemy without suffering any themselves. That evening Rex Hunt and the Royal Marines were flown to Argentina and from there back to the UK, arriving on 5 April. Eventually about 13,000 Argentine troops were deployed onto the Islands.

By 3 April the small RM detachment landed by *Endurance* at Grytviken in South Georgia was aware of the invasion that had seized the Falkland Islands and made defensive preparations. Argentine forces began to land on the island on 3 April 1982 from the naval transport *Bahia Paraiso* in Cumberland Bay and called for the RM detachment to surrender. They refused and opened fire on the helicopters that were bringing troops ashore, shooting down the first and damaging the second. *Endurance* stood off and launched one of its Wasp helicopters flown by the Flight Commander, Lieutenant Commander Tony Ellerbeck RN, to observe and report on events as they unfolded. The Argentine corvette *Guerrico* entered the Bay at this point and opened fire on the Royal Marines at close range with 40mm and 20mm guns. The narrowness of the Bay constrained her ability to manoeuvre, however, and the Marines raked her decks with machine gun fire and scored several hits with Carl Gustavs. She moved back out to sea and tried to fire with her 100mm gun but it was damaged and useless. Eventually, however, the heavily outnumbered RM detachment surrendered having made their point that South Georgia, like the Falkland Islands themselves, were British territory and would be stoutly defended.

The Reaction in London

At the time I was still serving in DGA(N) and was concerned with the completion of *Illustrious* and expanding the release to service for the Sea Harrier to operate from *Hermes* and the *Invincible* class. Shortly after the Argentine invasion of the Falkland Islands, however, my rotary-wing colleague, with whom I shared an office, suffered an injury and I had to take on his tasks as well as my own. These included the rapid formulation of staff requirements for flight decks and helicopter support infrastructure in a number of ships taken up from trade (STUFT)[7] but, except for the MV *Atlantic Conveyor*, their story falls outside the scope of this work as they were not directly concerned with the carrier strike fleet. Admiral Sir Henry Leach, the First Sea Lord, was immensely popular with the naval staff and throughout the Service. I had briefed him several times on aircraft carrier and aircraft developments and found him to be both knowledgeable and supportive. We all knew of the fight he had put up against Nott and his defence review and shared his opinion that it was conspicuous neither for its wisdom nor its statesmanship;[8] he was a man we would have followed anywhere. Some steps had been taken at the end of March as the situation deteriorated. A nuclear submarine was withdrawn from the 'Spring Train' exercises off Gibraltar, loaded with a war outfit of torpedoes and stores and dispatched to the South Atlantic, a second was made ready and consideration given to deploying a third. *Endurance*, which should have left the area, was ordered to remain and an RFA deployed from Gibraltar to support her.

On 31 March 1SL had been at the Admiralty Surface Weapons Establishment on Portsdown Hill, just north of Portsmouth, travelling in one of the two 'Admiral's barge' Wessex helicopters maintained by 771 NAS at RNAS Lee-on-Solent so that he could be recalled to the MOD quickly if necessary. There were no calls from London but on returning to his office in uniform at about 18.00 he found the latest intelligence report and a number of briefing notes. The former stated unequivocally that an Argentine invasion of the Falkland Islands was likely in the early hours of 2 April and, to his surprise, the latter advised that further naval deployments were unnecessary and undesirable. To him these papers were incompatible: there was an imminent threat to British territory that could only be reached by sea and he decided to speak to the Defence Secretary at once. It transpired that he was with the Prime Minister, Margaret Thatcher, at her office in the Houses of Parliament together with Permanent Secretaries from the MOD and FCO and a few others. He was driven there immediately, still in uniform, and was invited in. The subsequent conversation is the stuff of legend. Admiral Leach asked if there was anything he could do to help and the Prime Minister asked for his opinion on the situation. He replied that 'We must assume that the Falkland Islands will be invaded and that this will happen in the next few days'. If it did there was no way that the small garrison could put up an effective defence against the amphibious force known to be embarked in the Argentine naval task force. Nor, now, was there any deterrence that could be applied in time; therefore the islands would be captured. He added that 'Whether we take action to recover them or not is not for me to say but I would strongly advise that we did. To do so would require a very considerable naval task force with strong amphibious elements.' He believed that such a task force should be assembled 'now, without delay'. This ran counter to Nott's advice to exercise caution and not do anything that might jeopardise the talks scheduled for June but clearly struck a chord with the Prime Minister who asked if it would include *Invincible*, *Fearless* and some frigates. 1SL affirmed that it would, together with *Hermes* and *Intrepid*, which was actually being put into reserve at that moment, together with a substantial proportion of the operational destroyer/frigate force, RFAs and a number of merchant ships that would need to be taken up from trade. The whole of 3 Commando Brigade would be required, together with at least one extra Army Brigade. The Prime Minister revealed a lack of current defence knowledge by asking about *Ark Royal*, to be told that the old one was being scrapped and the new one would not be completed for another three years. Presciently, however, she asked if there would be enough air cover and Admiral

Leach explained that the whole operation would depend on the Sea Harriers embarked in *Invincible* and *Hermes* which he believed to be capable aircraft that would be 'more than a match for anything the Argentines could put up'. Every single aircraft that the RN could make operational, including those normally used for training, would be required 'to inflict sufficient attrition on arrival in the area to achieve at least local air superiority' before a British landing operation. There was considerable risk but in 1SL's opinion it was acceptable and there was no alternative. Next, the Prime Minister asked 'what about the Buccaneers and Phantoms'? She was told that they had all been transferred to the RAF when the old *Ark Royal* was paid off, they could not be operated from *Invincible* or *Hermes* and from their land bases in Scotland they had no way of reaching the theatre of operations. Quick questions and answers followed. How long would it take to assemble such a task force? About forty-eight hours for the first ships. How long would it take to reach the Falkland Islands? About three weeks. Surely you mean three days? No, three weeks, they are 8000nm away. The meeting ended with a key question 'Could we really recapture the islands if they were invaded?' Admiral Leach's reply was typical of the man: 'Yes we could and in my judgement, although it is not my business to say so, we should because if we do not, or if we pussyfoot in our actions and do not achieve complete success, in another few months we shall be living in a different country whose word counts for little.' The Prime Minister looked relieved and nodded and the die was cast; Great Britain would fight to liberate the Falkland Islands and their dependencies. As Margaret Thatcher wrote in her foreword to another book,[9] 'Once again the hour had produced the man'. The die was cast.

The Carrier Battle Group

On 3 April 1982 Margaret Thatcher announced in Parliament that a task force, designated TF 317, under the command of Admiral Fieldhouse, the Commander-in-Chief Fleet, would sail on 5 April 1982. The most conspicuous elements were the carriers *Invincible*, Captain J J Black MBE RN, and *Hermes*, Captain L E Middleton RN, which sailed from Portsmouth; a number of other warships and RFAs sailed after them from Portsmouth and Plymouth to huge cheers from crowds gathered on the seafront. There had been an uproar of protest throughout the country after the Argentine invasion and the despatch of the task force was a popular response. The ships that had been taking part in Exercise 'Spring Train' off Gibraltar were ordered to join the task force and its commander, Rear Admiral Sandy Woodward, was placed in overall command. The two commando carriers had gone[10] and 3 Commando Brigade was to deploy in the modified cruise ship *Canberra* together with the Army's 16 Parachute Brigade. The Army's 5 Brigade

Invincible with other ships of the task force. Ships in the foreground are the frigate *Andromeda* and the destroyer *Bristol*. Viewed from this angle, *Invincible*'s unhelpfully narrow deck is emphasised. (Author's collection)

was to follow in *Queen Elizabeth 2* after her conversion. The name Operation 'Corporate' was allocated to cover every aspect of the campaign. An intermediate base was established rapidly at Ascension Island, 3700 miles from the UK and roughly half-way to the Falkland Islands. It had a large runway at Wideawake Airfield that had been built by the Americans and a suitable harbour in which task force ships were stored for war. Helicopters were used extensively to transfer stores, men and ammunition between ships once they arrived. From now on I shall concentrate on the activities of the aircraft carriers and their air groups which were central to the whole campaign. The reader is recommended to study other books for wider details of the campaign[11] and there are several books about naval air aspects of Operation 'Corporate'.[12] For the following, necessarily brief, description of carrier operations in 1982 I have relied mainly on the notes I took at the time.

The statement in 1966 Defence Review that the UK 'unaided by our allies could not expect to undertake . . . the landing of troops against sophisticated opposition outside the range of land-based air cover'[13] had been exposed as the fallacious nonsense that it always was and now a British Government had decided to do just that. In order to do so it relied on one aircraft carrier that had been sold to Australia after the 1981 Defence Review and a second that the same Review had decided to withdraw from service in the near future as it had little further use.[14] Many of the men serving in the task force had had their redundancy announced on 1 April under the terms of the Review but they still turned to with a will out of respect for their Service and their colleagues. The original idea had been to sail the force under conditions of secrecy but when it was realised that this would not be possible the PR potential was used to advantage and images of the carriers sailing were seen around the world, underlining British resolve. The time taken to reach the South Atlantic was used to advantage as negotiations took place at the UN and the fleet could always have remained at sea for a long time as a latent threat or turned back; two of the advantages of sea power. It is difficult to see how a force of land-based bombers could have achieved such effective leverage.

On 2 April 1982 the commanding officers of 800 and 801 (Sea Harrier FRS 1s) NAS were ordered to prepare their aircraft, bring their personnel up to war strength and stand by to embark. The commanding officer of the Sea Harrier headquarters and training unit, 899 NAS, was ordered to support them with aircraft, pilots and maintenance personnel. Their carriers were both alongside in Portsmouth; *Invincible* was giving Easter leave to her ship's company and *Hermes* was undergoing a maintenance period. *Hermes'* 800 NAS had five Sea Harriers and took on another four from 899 NAS, two from long-term storage at the maintenance unit at RAF St Athan in South Wales and one from the A&AEE Boscombe Down. 801 NAS also had five aircraft and took on three from 899 NAS for service in *Invincible*. The 'cascade system' of recalling people from leave worked well and the squadrons were able to embark on their carriers while they were still alongside so that could sail in them on 5 April. Huge efforts successfully brought

Queen Elizabeth 2 was one of the merchant ships I was involved with and is seen here alongside in Southampton with helicopter decks fitted aft for her role as a temporary LPH. When I indicated the bulkhead where she would need to be cut back to make space for the landing spots on a constructor's drawing, men immediately ran off to light oxy-acetylene torches to start work; most MOD decisions, regrettably, take longer to implement. Swimming pools make a good basis for helicopter landing spots on cruise ships as they are designed to take the load of tons of water. (Author's collection)

Hermes out of her maintenance period, removing scaffolding, storing and bringing on board ammunition[15] and her departure on 5 April was a major achievement. She was to become Admiral Woodward's flagship when the task force 'sorted itself out' at Ascension Island. Once at sea the enhanced squadrons operated in two groups, the first commanded by Lieutenant Commander Andy Auld RN, the CO of 800 NAS, in *Hermes* and the second by Lieutenant Commander 'Sharkey' Ward AFC RN, the CO of 801 NAS, in *Invincible*. Lieutenant Commander Neil Thomas, the CO of 899 NAS acted as Force Chief Tactical Instructor (CTI), and Lieutenant Commander Tony Ogilvy, the CO-designate of 801 NAS who had joined early, became Force Air Warfare Instructor (FAWI). This highly-experienced group led the small but determined Sea Harrier force by their outstanding example. On the voyage south the aircraft were painted in an overall grey finish in place of the white and grey finish in which they had been manufactured. *Hermes*' aircraft were noticeably darker than *Invincible*'s. The embarked Sea King squadrons were 826 (Sea King HAS 5s) NAS commanded by Lieutenant Commander D J S Squier AFC RN in *Hermes* and 820 (Sea King HAS 5s) NAS commanded by Lieutenant Commander R J S Wykes-Sneyd AFC RN in *Invincible*. Their aircraft were painted dark blue but the white side numbers and words 'Royal Navy' were over-painted in black to make them less conspicuous. *Hermes* showed the big advantage of her extra volume by embarking nine Sea King HC 4s of 846 NAS commanded by Lieutenant Commander S C Thornewill RN in addition to her fighters and anti-submarine Sea Kings. The commando Sea Kings were painted in a dull green finish and in their case too, white letters were over-painted in black.

On the afternoon of 7 April 1982 Lieutenant Commander Tim Gedge RN, the former CO of 800 NAS, was ordered to leave his new 'desk job' in the MOD and to form a new Sea Harrier unit that was to become 809 NAS. It was to have as many aircraft and pilots as possible and took over most of the technical sailors left behind by 899 NAS. They were to augment and provide attrition replacements for the squadrons that had already left for the South Atlantic. It proved possible to provide eight aircraft, of which five came from storage at St Athan, two from the RN Sea Harrier Support Unit at RNAS Yeovilton and one from accelerated production at the British Aerospace factory at Dunsfold. In addition to the CO, one pilot came from the Sea Harrier simulator at Yeovilton, two came from exchange posts with the US Marine Corps and one from exchange with the Royal Australian Navy. Two experienced RAF Harrier GR 3 pilots from RAF Germany volunteered and were brought to Yeovilton to undergo a very rapid conversion course. 809 NAS aircraft were all painted in a distinctive overall light grey finish with pastel roundels and markings. This had been designed for air superiority fighters by an RAE scientist named Barley and was known as Barley Grey. It was not as effective in the

Hermes sailing from Portsmouth on 5 April. Aircraft on deck include eleven Sea Harrier FRS 1s and eighteen Sea Kings, the latter a mixture of HAS 5s and HC 4s. Both she and *Invincible* had hulls of similar internal volume but *Hermes'* bigger flight deck made her a far more capable platform. (Author's collection)

South Atlantic as the darker grey schemes on other aircraft and did not prove popular. The new squadron spent most of April working up to operational efficiency and on 25 April Lieutenant Commander Gedge landed on the VTOL pad built onto the STUFT container ship *Atlantic Conveyer* off Plymouth to prove that it could be done. It could, and having proved that the aircraft could be moved around on deck and re-fuelled, he took off vertically and flew back to Yeovilton. The ship had been taken up from trade and converted into an aircraft ferry and support ship in Devonport Dockyard in only six days. This was another of the ships with which I was associated and she was provided with a large upper-deck space sheltered by containers around the deck edge inside which aircraft could be parked, all covered in plastic to protect them against salt spray. The ship was intended to carry Sea Harriers, Wessex helicopters and RAF Harriers and Chinook helicopters into the war zone. She also carried a vast range of spare aircraft engines and other stores and weapons. It even proved possible to build in containerised bulk fuel and liquid oxygen installations to support Sea Harriers and allow one armed aircraft to be kept on deck alert that could be launched in the event of a threatened air attack. The LOX obviously boiled off continuously but given the amount installed to start with there would still have been some left in the South Atlantic.[16] On 30 April six of 809 NAS's aircraft left Yeovilton and flew to Banjul in the Gambia, refuelling in flight several times from RAF Victor tankers. After an overnight stop they flew on to Ascension Island. The remaining two aircraft followed them a day later and their deployment, using air-to-air refuelling, was similar to the deployment of the 803 NAS Buccaneers in 1968. In early May, six Harrier GR 3s of 1 Squadron RAF followed and on 6 May both 809 NAS and 1 Squadron embarked in *Atlantic Conveyor* off Ascension and sailed for the carrier battle group in the TEZ established around the Falkland Islands. A team of RN aircraft handlers had been drafted to the ship to carry out movements and ensured that the airframes being ferried could be crammed into the smallest possible space. One armed Sea Harrier was kept on the VTOL pad to provide air defence should it be necessary but its endurance after a VTO would only be about thirty minutes so a Victor tanker was kept in flight nearby to refuel it if it was launched. All eight reinforcement Sea Harriers went to *Hermes* at first, then four aircraft and pilots moved to *Invincible*. 1 Squadron went to *Hermes*, proving at last that it was possible for an RAF squadron to reinforce a carrier air group. The embarkation in *Atlantic Conveyor* was the RAF pilots' first experience of deck landing.[17] The original concept had envisaged that 1 Squadron would be used as replacements for Sea Harrier losses and that only a minimum of senior NCOs would be required to advise RN maintainers on the systems special to the Harrier GR 3. In the event the low Sea Harrier losses meant that the GR 3s were used as additions rather than replacements and so the 'specialist advisors' became non-specialist deck-hands overnight. The RAF unit flew its first mission on 20 May against a fuel storage area at Fox Bay and went on to fly a total of 126 operational missions. One aircraft was lost on armed reconnaissance over Port Howard on 21 May and a second attacking Goose Green under FAC control. Eventually a total of four Harriers were lost and four replacements were flown directly from Ascension to *Hermes* using air-to-air tanker support.

As we saw earlier, it had been clear from the outset that the Falkland Islands could not be liberated if the enemy had superiority in the air and the Sea Harriers' first duty was air defence. Against them the Argentine Air Force deployed its entire operational fleet. This comprised the six Dassault Mirage III fighters of VIII Air Brigade, thirty-one Douglas A-4B and C Skyhawk fighter-bombers of IV and V Air Brigades, nineteen Israeli Aircraft Industries Dagger fighter-bombers (essentially re-engined Mirages) of VI Air Brigade and six English Electric Canberra bombers. There were also indigenous twin-turboprop Pucara light attack aircraft, C-130 Hercules tanker/transports and a few Macchi MB-339 trainers. After the sinking of the Argentine cruiser *General Belgrano* on 2 May,[18] the carrier *25 de Mayo* returned

Lieutenant Commander Tim Gedge RN, the commanding officer of 809 NAS, landing one of his aircraft on *Atlantic Conveyor* in Plymouth Sound. Note how the containers have been used to screen the parking area aft of the landing spot and RAF Chinook helicopters have already been embarked. (Author's collection)

to harbour and stayed there, forcing her air group to operate from air stations ashore.[19] Argentine naval air squadrons deployed five Dassault Super Etendards capable of carrying Exocet missiles, only a few of which had been delivered, and eight Douglas A-4Q Skyhawks. There were also two Lockheed SP-2H Neptune maritime reconnaissance aircraft. All Argentine aircraft, therefore, had to operate at extreme range from land bases with occasional support from C-130 tankers and this put them a great disadvantage since they had to think constantly about fuel conservation. Any loss or damage to the carriers would have fatally weakened British plans and so they were operated well to the east of the Falkland Islands. Sea Harriers had to maintain CAP over the islands and sorely missed the AEW capability that had been discarded when the old *Ark Royal* had gone. Argentine aircraft soon adopted the tactic pioneered by the RN of attacking at low level, below ships' radar horizons. They also used Falkland Island terrain to mask their approach since the pulse radars fitted in most ships could not detect targets over land. It is a sad reflection that RN low-level tactics came as a surprise to some members of later-generation operations room personnel, revealing that sea training had not been as realistic as it might have been. The relatively new Sea Dart and Seawolf missile systems scored several kills but fighters proved to be by far the most effective way of inflicting attrition on the enemy.

The first RN operational strike mission since the Suez Crisis of 1956 took place on 1 May 1982 when Sea Harriers from *Hermes* attacked Port Stanley and Goose Green with top cover from *Invincible*'s aircraft. This was the first war in which reporters and camera crews sailed with a task force in large numbers and digital broadcasting techniques allowed moving pictures to be sent back to the UK in near real time[20] and this was the raid made famous when Brian Hanrahan of the BBC said 'I counted them all out and I counted them all back' when told that he could not say how many aircraft had been launched or what they had been doing. All twelve of *Hermes*' Sea Harriers had launched shortly before dawn and flew at very low level toward East Falkland. Near the coast they split into three sections, two of which attacked the airfield at Port Stanley and the other the air strip at Goose green. Four of them carried out a toss-bombing attack on the anti-aircraft positions known to surround Port Stanley; they were each armed with two air-burst and one delayed-action 1000lb bombs. Seconds after their VT-fused bombs detonated, showering the defenders in shrapnel, Lieutenant Commander Auld led his group of five Sea Harriers over the target. Between them they carried three parachute-

Those who only see aircraft carriers in harbour think them to be large enough to be conspicuous targets. Given the sort of reconnaissance capability the Argentine air arms had in 1982 they were actually very small objects in a very big sea. This is *Hermes* seen from an escorting frigate. (Author's collection)

retarded 1000lb bombs and twelve cluster-bomb containers. They had to pull up to 200ft after their high-speed, terrain-hugging approach in order to release their weapons at a height from which they would function properly. They came under fire from guns, Short Tigercat[21] and Euromissile Roland surface-to-air missiles but only one Sea Harrier was hit, the last to attack flown by Flight Lieutenant David Morgan RAF,[22] which took a 20mm round cleanly through the tailplane. After landing he was filmed by a BBC news cameraman pointing at the hole. Minutes later Lieutenant Commander 'Fred' Frederiksen RN led three Sea Harriers armed with both retarded and cluster bombs in an attack on Goose Green airstrip. They flew down Falkland Sound at wave-top height past Fanning Head before turning south-east to climb over the peat plains of Lafonia for a perfectly executed surprise attack which caught the defences completely unawares, a solitary burst from a machine-gun following the last aircraft to leave. Both attacks inflicted damage and casualties, including a Pucara of III Air Brigade and the Falkland islands Government Britten-Norman Islander light transport aircraft. Bombs had hit the runways at both targets but at Stanley they failed to penetrate the surface and the damage was quickly repaired. At Goose Green the craters were filled with earth and compacted to give a level operating surface.

While the strikes were in progress *Invincible* maintained two fighters on CAP with two more at Alert 5 on deck.[23] As the day progressed these aircraft and their successors became involved in a series of inconclusive fights in and out of cloud with Argentine Mirages and Beech Turbo-Mentors, the latter based at Port Stanley. By early afternoon, the Argentine Air Force believed that it had located where the carriers were operating and launched a series of strikes. A CAP from *Invincible* was vectored onto one of the first inbound raids by a fighter controller in the destroyer *Glamorgan* and intercepted two Mirages over San Carlos Water. Surprisingly they were not flying in battle formation and the second was flying in long trail astern of the first. Lieutenant Steve Thomas RN and Flight Lieutenant Paul Barton RAF engaged the enemy head on and the lead Mirage fired a Matra 530 missile at a range of 5nm which missed. Thomas pulled high and right, passing about 100ft over the first Mirage which turned to port and dived, giving the Sea Harrier an AIM-9 missile lock. Thomas fired and watched his missile pass close to the enemy fighter as it entered cloud. The Argentine pilot, Capitan Garcia Cuerva, was unlucky; his aircraft was damaged when the missile detonated by proximity fuze and he elected to divert to Port Stanley. As he crossed the coast he was shot down and killed by Argentine anti-aircraft fire. Barton had meanwhile positioned himself to engage the second Mirage, he got missile lock, fired at a range of about 2000 yards and saw his Sidewinder hit the target's rear fuselage. The pilot ejected and came down on the shore of West Falkland. He was the first Argentine pilot to be

Hermes' capability is shown to good effect in this photograph which shows a Sea Harrier FRS 1 and a Harrier GR 3 lined up for take-off from the runway. Seven Sea Harriers are parked in Fly 3 with a single Harrier GR 3. A Sea King HAS 5 is parked aft and a second is lifting a vertical replenishment load of stores for transfer to another ship. A fork-lift truck is visible on the port side aft that has brought the palletised loads into position for the Sea King to lift. *Invincible* could not have coped with this variety of concurrent activity on deck but still made a vital contribution to the task force. (Author's collection)

shot down in action and his aircraft was the first to be shot down by an RN fighter since Lieutenant Carmichael's MiG-15 over Korea in 1952. While this fight was in progress a CAP from *Hermes* flown by Lieutenant Martin Hale RN and Flight Lieutenant 'Bertie' Penfold RAF was directed onto two fast-moving radar contacts which turned out to be Daggers under radar control from an Argentine mobile unit sited at Port Stanley. They carried out a head-on attack diving from 35,000ft towards the Sea Harriers which were at 20,000ft. At five miles the Daggers fired two Israeli-made Shafrir missiles, one of which locked-on and began to home onto Hale's aircraft. He broke downwards and dived for cloud cover at 15,000ft but saw the missile fall away clear of him. The Daggers had not seen the second Sea Harrier, however, and turned gently across Penfold's nose with re-heat selected to disengage, thus making perfect infrared targets. He fired at 3nm against the fast-disappearing targets and hit one of them which exploded, killing the pilot. Throughout the afternoon and evening Sea Harrier CAPs were continually directed onto radar contacts and Lieutenant Commander Mike Broadwater RN and his wingman Lieutenant Alan Curtis RN intercepted three Canberras at low-level reported by the frigate *Brilliant*. Curtis fired at the left-hand bomber at a range of about 2000 yards and thought at first that had missed and so he fired a second Sidewinder but the first one had hit and the second detonated in the ensuing fireball. Neither of the Canberra's crew ejected. The other two Canberras jettisoned their bombs, blew off their wing-tip fuel tanks and broke away in opposite directions. Broadwater chased the leader and fired two Sidewinders at a range of about 4000 yards but both fell away short. Low on fuel, he had to break away and recover to his ship. On their first day in action, Sea Harriers had 'splashed' three enemy aircraft outright with a fourth badly damaged and despatched by its own side's anti-aircraft fire. It might not, in any case, have been able to fly all the way back to Argentina or even have carried out a safe landing at Port Stanley. The carriers continued to launch CAPs, continuous anti-submarine helicopter operations and strike sorties.

The next day on which air combat took place on a large scale was 21 May 1982 which was 'D' Day for the landing of 3 Commando Brigade on East Falkland from San Carlos Water.[24] On that day alone, ten enemy aircraft were destroyed with no Sea Harrier losses in air combat. Action started when Lieutenant Commander Mike Blissett RN and Lieutenant Commander Neil Thomas RN from *Hermes* arrived at their CAP station and Blissett saw four A-4 Skyhawks pass below him from left to right; he called a break to starboard and the two Sea Harriers ended up 800 yards astern of the enemy. Both pilots fired a Sidewinder and both hit their targets, one exploding and the other burning and crashing out of control. Both pilots were killed. Blissett could not get missile lock on his second target and fired out all his gun ammunition to no obvious effect. Thomas could not lock onto his second target either and stressed to *Hermes*' pilots on his return the need to fire both missiles when multiple targets appeared. Throughout the day Argentine aircraft continued to attack the warships guarding the amphibious shipping. The frigate *Brilliant* directed Lieutenant Commander 'Sharkey' Ward and Lieutenant Thomas onto fast-moving contacts as they crossed the coast from the west. They identified three Daggers as they approached and carried out a 'copy-book' attack using the Sea Harrier's low-level manoeuvrability to get behind the Argentine aircraft whose pilots had no time to recover from their surprise at being intercepted; all three were destroyed. As Ward turned to recover to *Invincible* he saw three A-4 Skyhawks heading down Falkland Sound towards a burning frigate and alerted *Brilliant* and the CAP arriving on task from *Hermes*. This was flown by Lieutenant Clive 'Spaghetti' Morrell RN and Flight Lieutenant John Leeming RAF. They dived toward the enemy aircraft, Argentine Naval Skyhawks, but were unable to intercept them before they released their 'iron' bombs on the frigate *Ardent*. Teniente de Fregata Marquez in the last Skyhawk saw Morrell's Sea Harrier drop in behind the aircraft ahead of him but was shot down by gunfire from the unseen Leeming before he could shout a warning to the others. Morrell's first Sidewinder took out the lead Skyhawk flown by Capitan de Corbeta Philippi but his second would not lock on and he had to close in and use his guns on the third Skyhawk, flown by Teniente de Navio Arca. Philippi and Arca both ejected safely.

Although nearly half its eventual total of 'kills' were on 21 May 1982, the Sea Harrier Force continued to achieve impressive results in the weeks ahead. A number of enemy aircraft were shot down by missiles and there were too many air combats to describe individually. Two, however, were sufficiently different to merit description. On 23 May Morgan and Leeming were on CAP over Grantham Sound when they caught sight of a helicopter 8000ft below them over Shag Cove. Diving to attack them they found two Pumas and what they identified as a Huey but was in fact an Agusta A-109A gunship flying as escort. The leading Puma saw Morgan as he pulled up to gain position for an attack with guns; it attempted to evade him but flew into the hillside it had been skirting round. The other two helicopters landed and their crews scrambled clear before both were destroyed by strafing runs with guns. On 1 June 'Sharkey' Ward was over Pebble Island on CAP when the frigate *Minerva*'s fighter controller detected intermittent 'skin paints'[25] to the north on his radar. Although low on fuel, Ward went to investigate, picked up the target on his own radar and began a 'tail-chase' after it, followed by Thomas, his wingman. The target was a C-130 Hercules on a reconnaissance patrol at low level which had popped up for a quick sweep with its radar, allowing the alert radar operator in *Minerva* to detect its brief radar echo. Possibly warned by the Argentine ground radar at Port Stanley, the C-130 made off at high speed and low level but was soon caught by the Sea Harriers. Worried by his low fuel state, Ward fired his first Sidewinder out of range but hit with his second. Unable to wait and see if the missile had 'splashed' such a large target he ran in to close range, emptied his guns into the target and saw it crash into the sea in flames. None of its crew survived. By this stage both pilots had only 45 gallons of fuel left[26] for their 180nm transit back to *Invincible*. Before Operation 'Corporate' this would have been considered impossible but pilots had honed their fuel-management skills by this stage to the point where both pilots were able to land-on safely. Neither had enough fuel left for a circuit in the event of a baulked approach, however.

On 25 May *Atlantic Conveyor* was 85nm north east of Cape Pembroke, moving in to disembark the helicopters and the vast array of stores which she had carried from the UK. She was hit by two Exocet missiles launched by Super Etendards

A Sea King HC 4 lifting off from *Fearless* in San Carlos Water in May 1982. Note the extemporised anti-aircraft gun position in the foreground, typical of many fitted throughout the task force. The general-purpose machine gun is loaded with a belt of ammunition and ready and the gunner has some protection from sand-bags. (Author's collection)

which were, no doubt, intended to hit the carriers. They showed the shortcoming of the first generation of sea-skimming anti-surface ship missiles in that their homing radar locked onto the first ship they detected and homed on it, in this case the unfortunate *Atlantic Conveyor*. She caught fire and subsequently sank with the loss of twelve men including her gallant captain, Ian North DSC.[27] By June the San Carlos area was sufficiently safe for Sea Harriers to be able to land on other warships such as the LPDs *Fearless* or *Intrepid* to take a quick 'suck' of fuel sufficient for a VTO and transit back to their parent carrier. The stores ship *Atlantic Causeway*, *Atlantic Conveyor*'s sister-ship arrived and brought, among a vast array of stores items, sufficient pierced steel plating to allow Royal Engineers to create a STOVL landing strip at San Carlos. In line with the RN tradition of naming its air stations after birds, the strip was unofficially named HMS *Sheathbill* after a white arctic sea-bird that wintered in the Falkland Islands. This facility soon boasted fuel and allowed CAP times to be extended with less risk to aircraft and 1 Squadron to fly close air support missions with a 'spare deck' nearby.

In order to fit within the wider subject of this work, this can only be a very brief glimpse at the operation of the carriers and their aircraft in the South Atlantic

The versatility of the Sea Harrier FRS 1 was often put to good use. This aircraft has landed on *Fearless* to take on enough fuel to return to its parent carrier after a vertical take-off. It is armed with two AIM-9L Sidewinder missiles and gun pods. (Author's collection)

Conflict. In total the Sea Harriers flew 2000 operational sorties and destroyed twenty-four enemy aircraft (including the Dagger 'finished off' by Argentine gunners) for no loss to themselves in air combat, an outstanding achievement. Unfortunately two Sea Harriers were brought down by anti-aircraft gun and missile fire and four more were lost in operational accidents. Argentine pilots nicknamed the dark-painted aircraft of the *Hermes* group the 'Black Death',[28] unknowingly reviving the tradition of the Sopwith Triplanes of Black Flight, 10 Naval Squadron,

RNAS in 1917. The key to the Sea Harrier's success in 1982 was the very high quality of the air and ground crews, many of whom had years of experience on more conventional carrier aircraft such as the Phantom, Buccaneer and Sea Vixen. The Sea Harrier was a small fighter with a 'clean' engine which did not betray its presence with a smoke trail; this was an advantage in the sort of close-in fighting to which pilots were committed with their clear air mass, infrared guided Sidewinder missile system. Another big advantage proved to be the aircraft's ability to hover alongside the carriers' centre of pitch in rough seas for several seconds, allowing the pilot to choose the best moment to move across the deck and land. The amount of deck movement in the South Atlantic would have limited the ability of more conventional aircraft to operate from carriers the size of *Hermes* or *Invincible*.[29] Following the end of hostilities, the RAF Harriers of 1 Squadron were re-roled for air defence duties and disembarked from *Hermes* to Port Stanley to remain as part of the garrison.

The lack of AEW aircraft meant that destroyers had to be deployed further up-threat than would have otherwise been necessary. To say that this put them into

Atlantic Conveyor's sister-ship *Atlantic Causeway* being fitted out as a ferry carrier in Devonport Dockyard. Her modification benefited from the experience gained working on the earlier conversion and was even more effective although it took a few days longer to complete. The roof of an enclosed shelter can be seen here under construction aft of the forecastle. (Author's collection)

The destroyer *Coventry* on fire after being hit by conventional bombs dropped by Argentine A-4 Skyhawks, aircraft that were more than two decades old at the time using weapons that were even older. The photograph was taken from one of the first RN helicopters on the scene. (Author's collection)

considerable danger would be an understatement and Captain Hart-Dyke of the Type 42 destroyer *Coventry* described their operations from his own perspective.[30] *Coventry*, *Sheffield* and *Glasgow* had formed an advanced screen to give warning of the approach of enemy aircraft. On 1 May things went decisively in the RN's favour with a number of enemy aircraft shot down by Sea Harriers and no losses in air combat. After *Sheffield* was sunk on 4 May and *Glasgow* put out of action by a bomb a week later, only *Coventry* was left. On 25 May she, too, was sunk and Captain Hart-Dyke described her loss.[31] 'We came up against a very brave and determined attack by four aircraft who sprang at us from behind the land and flew very fast and low the last 10nm or so over the sea to our position north-west of Falkland Sound. We engaged with everything we had got, from Sea Dart missiles to machine guns and even rifles, but one of the aircraft got through delivering four bombs, three of which went into the port side of the ship and exploded. However we hit at least one aircraft with guns and we learnt later that two aircraft did not get home to their bases . . . the operations room, low down in the ship where I and some thirty men were controlling the battle, was devastated by the blast and immediately filled with very black smoke.' Two Sea Harriers on CAP were trying desperately to intercept the enemy aircraft but were ordered off at the last moment to clear *Coventry*'s[32] missile arcs of fire. Hart-Dyke described the bravery of his men: 'A young officer directing the close-range guns from the very exposed position of the bridge wings did not take cover when the enemy aircraft were closing at eye-level and strafing the ship with cannon fire. He stood there for all to see and ordered the guns' crews to stay at their posts and engage the enemy until he gave the order to stop. This order was not questioned by the very young sailors manning the guns and they kept firing despite their totally exposed position. At least one aircraft was hit and two turned away by the barrage of fire.' Until 1982 it had been assumed that guns no longer had a part to play in anti-air warfare and that only missiles would be necessary. The Falklands Conflict showed that not every attacking aircraft would be equipped with stand-off missiles; that the RN might still be opposed by aircraft with 'iron' bombs in the operations it might be called on to carry out across the globe and that tracer from close-range weapons was still an effective way of putting pilots off their aim. He went on to describe a rating in the engine room who heard a thump and 'looked round to see a bomb which had come into the ship a few feet from where he was standing. He did not run but went to a telephone and reported this fact to damage control headquarters; he described the bomb, the whereabouts of the hole in the side and the nature of the damage to the machinery. The bomb then blew up as he was still talking. Miraculously he was shielded from the blast by a bit of machinery and walked out unharmed. Others were killed outright.' As the ship was abandoned, two Chief Petty Officers, 'separately and on their own initiative, revisited smoke-filled compartments' as the ship listed. One saved the life of an unconscious senior rating with burning clothes and the other led frightened young sailors to safety over a hole from which flames were issuing. Hart-Dyke expressed the feelings felt by many in the task force when he said that he could never forget the brave people in his ship who fought so well. Nor would he forget those nineteen equally brave men who lost their lives and who had also contributed so much to the battle. 'They did more than their best continuously for at least four weeks of intensive and dangerous operations . . . Our Nation, our Navy, has a priceless inheritance which has given us men of great quality who have fought so well down the ages and not least in the South Atlantic in 1982.'

Airborne Early Warning

The lack of AEW cover had proved to be one of the principal weaknesses in 1982, allowing the enemy to use the RN's own tactics against it. From the fleet's point of view, the money spent converting Shacketons to carry ex-Gannet AN/APS-20 radars was completely wasted and now that the RAF had found out what AEW was, much of their tasking was in support of UK-based fighters. The Shackleton

Later in the conflict, Sea Harriers were able to land at the temporary airstrip built at San Carlos to refuel when necessary. Two armed with Sidewinders are seen here on 13 July 1982 with an RAF Chinook. (Author's collection)

AEW 2s of the RAFs 8 Squadron were another of TASMO's failures in 1982 and as Margaret Thatcher had suddenly realised on 31 March the Phantoms, Gannets and Buccaneers that had been taken from the RN to form the RAF TASMO force would have been far more effective in a 'run-on' *Eagle.* As we saw earlier, consideration had been given to operating AEW helicopters from the *Invincible* class but the idea had been dropped because of a supposed lack of hangar space and accommodation. Fortunately Westland had put some effort into evaluating the possibility of installing suitable radars into the Sea King airframe and had retained the drawings when the project was terminated. If the RN had failed to insist on an embarked AEW after the cancellation of CVA-01, it made up for that shortcoming when the fundamental importance of the capability was remembered early in the Falklands campaign. Project LAST[33] was initiated in the second week of May 1982 when DNAW tasked DGA(N) and Ministry of Defence (Procure-ment Executive) (MOD(PE)) to carry out an urgent study into the feasibility of making available some form of AEW system in a very short timescale. A wide range of options was considered at the outset including the refurbishment of the small number of surviving Gannet AEW 3 airframes.[34] This was never really going to be a viable solution, of course, because they would have needed arrester wires and, while these could be re-fitted in *Hermes*, it could only have been done in a dockyard.[35] Once a Gannet was embarked in *Hermes* it would have been able to carry out a free take-off along the old angled deck but that was academic: it had to fly on board first. One theory was that once an airstrip ashore was captured, Gannets could be shipped out to operate from it but this too was rather a far-fetched idea. Comment on the Gannet's resurrection is included because, although it came to nothing, it shows at least that no possibility was discarded without being considered.

The most likely solution, in the short time available, was a Sea King modified to carry the Thorn/EMI ARI-5980 Searchwater radar.[36] This capitalised on the earlier study work but some means of lowering the aerial below the helicopter had to be devised to give full 360-degree coverage. This would have both structural and aerodynamic implications which would need to be taken into account in any release to service for the modified aircraft. On 13 May 1982 representatives of Westland helicopters and Thorn/EMI were invited to a meeting at the MOD to discuss the feasibility of this concept. Both firms confirmed that such a project would be possible and accepted a task to prepare a detailed study in three and a half days, to be completed by midday on Monday 17 May. They were informed that, should feasibility be proven and authority to proceed given, a Naval Staff requirement would call for the modification of two Sea King HAS 2 airframes to AEW 2 standard by 17 July 1982, some nine weeks hence. After commendable effort the firms produced a study on time which covered costing, timescales, performance and the aircraft/equipment interface. It took the naval staff a week to study the documents, after which an instruction to proceed was given. Two Sea King airframes were provided, XV 704 from MOD(PE) and XV 650 from the repair programme at RNAS Culdrose. Both became available in late May having had their Type 195 sonar removed and the cabin gutted. In addition to this new version of the Searchwater radar, ESM and additional communications had to be schemed in, together with other operational modifications. The activity at Thorn/EMI centred on producing three 'B' model radars. Design and development of a 'pallet' to house line replaceable units, LRUs, and from which the aerial would be lowered into its operating position, proceeded quickly and successfully. The first set of palletised equipment was delivered to Westland Helicopters on 26 June and the second on 15 July 1982. XV 704 was completed on 14 July and XV 650 on 23 July. In order to test the radar, the aerial had to be lowered into the deployed position and this was achieved by the simple expedient of lifting the whole aircraft by crane into a position where it was possible to run the engines, switch on electrical power and operate the radar. An EMC assessment was carried out which ensured basic safety criteria. The new system proved to be remarkably free from any problems and a short test programme followed using aircrew from Westland and the A&AEE Boscombe Down. As a result of this work, the interim Sea King AEW 2 was cleared for service use on 30 July 1982, a literally fantastic achievement.

At the time 824 NAS existed to provide detached Sea King flights to ships that had no embarked squadron of their own; it was thus well placed to provide administrative support for the fledgling AEW aircraft which became 824 'D' Flight on 14 June 1982. Preparations were made for the unit to embark in the new *Illustrious* which was to be completed early by Swan Hunter on the Tyne and commissioned at sea. She was to sail as soon as possible to replace *Invincible* in the South Atlantic. Fortuitously, sufficient ex-Gannet observers remained in the Service to make the system viable and, together with the maintenance officers and ratings, they did a three-week course on the radar at Thorn/EMI before embarking. Over 2000 items of support and test equipment had to be delivered to *Illustrious* by 30 July which had been carefully selected by DGA(N) after studying maintenance data computer readings on RAF Searchwater reliability in the Nimrod.[37] A full set of maintenance publications had been produced and printed and space for support equipment was found, somehow, in *Illustrious'* workshops. I was heavily involved in getting *Illustrious* out early and cleared to operate aircraft[38] and on 2 August, the day she sailed, an interim Release to Service was signed which enabled 824D NAS to embark. The whole project had been a remarkable effort which succeeded brilliantly thanks to the goodwill of all concerned.

Illustrious deployed with an interim AEW capability but a further eighteen months' work was needed to put the Sea King AEW 2 and its support onto a front-line basis and produce more aircraft. 849HQ NAS re-formed in November 1984 and two front-line Flights, 'A' and 'B', commissioned in 1985 for service in the two operational carriers. The need for extra workshop space overloaded the ships' original design capacity and part of the necessary facilities were installed in a 'Portacabin' wired into the hangar. From 1985 a squadron of three Sea King AEW 2s was embarked in each operational carrier and from 2008, 'A' and 'B' Flights were re-designated as 854 and 857 NAS. A further developed and very effective version of the Sea King proved to be so successful that its role designation was changed from AEW to airborne surveillance and control (ASaC). The Sea King ASaC 7 entered service in 2003 in *Ark Royal* and immediately showed its worth in the Second Gulf War.

Anti-submarine Warfare

At the beginning of the conflict the Argentine Navy had four conventional submarines; two German-designed Type 209/1s completed in 1974 and two former USN *Guppy* class completed in 1945 and sold to Argentina in 1971. There was, therefore, a credible submarine threat to the Task Force and anti-submarine helicopters flew around the clock in all weathers. For example, 820 NAS in *Invincible* flew 1560 hours in May, the equivalent of two aircraft airborne all day every day of the month. The only enemy submarine to be attacked was the *Santa Fe*, one of the two '*Guppies*' which had landed twenty Argentine Marines at Grytviken in South Georgia and then proceeded back out to sea on the surface

Hermes joined by the new *Illustrious* on her arrival back in UK waters. (Author's collection)

where it was spotted by the destroyer *Antrim*'s Wessex HAS 3 helicopter piloted by Lieutenant Commander Ian Stanley RN. He attacked it with depth charges,[39] one of which exploded close enough to cause damage which prevented the boat from diving. *Santa Fe* tried to get back into the harbour but was attacked by Wasp helicopters from *Plymouth* and *Endurance* using AS-12 missiles and machine guns which caused further damage. She eventually got back to harbour, on fire and listing to starboard, where she was secured to a jetty and abandoned.

The End of the Conflict

On 14 June 1982 white flags were seen flying over Port Stanley and the Argentine forces surrendered. Operations were still required to mop up outlying forces on West Falkland and other islands and there was the enormous challenge of disarming and processing over 10,000 prisoners and caring for the enemy wounded in addition to the British. *Hermes* was the first carrier to return to the UK with *Invincible* left on station in case Argentina broke the terms of the ceasefire agreement; she was eventually relieved by *Illustrious*[40] in August. In addition to the actions described above Sea King HC 4 and Wessex HU 5 commando helicopters had provided essential tactical mobility for the land forces. The cross-deck operations flown to prepare the amphibious forces for the eventual landing were described by the force commander as 'phenomenal'. Sea King and Wessex helicopters were fundamental to the land forces' success ashore as they deployed troops, ammunition, food and fuel forward across inhospitable terrain, often in appalling weather conditions and under enemy fire. Operation 'Corporate' had

Wessex HU 5s of 847 NAS disembarked at Navy Point, Falkland Islands, in July 1982.
(Author's collection)

been an outstanding success in which the RN and RM, supported by other forces, played the major part in achieving the national aim. This was exemplified by the speed with which TF 317 was mobilised, stored for war and sailed. Thirty-four major warships[41] were involved by the end of hostilities, four of which were sunk[42] together with the RFA LSL *Sir Galahad* and the mercantile *Atlantic Conveyor*. Research and development establishments and procurement authorities had worked around the clock to evaluate an enormous number of urgent operational requirements and innovated a variety of new systems and methods of operating in every war fighting field. British industry co-operated wholeheartedly in all these endeavours.[43] To give one example, British Aerospace worked around the clock and over weekends at a time when the workforce had just been told that all overtime was to cease because of Nott's Defence Review. The Kingston/Dunsfold Division produced some 4100 separate items for the task force, compared with about 1500 over a comparable time in normal circumstances.[44] Apart from complete Sea Harriers delivered early, the Division made and delivered pylons capable of carrying two rather than a single Sidewinder, thus doubling the fighters' armament, and chaff dispensers that could be fitted into a Sea Harrier's ventral air brake cavity. They also helped in the development of the Ferranti Inertial Navigation Reference and Attitude Equipment (FINRAE), which allowed the Harrier GR 3's systems to be aligned on a moving ship. Within the Navy's own organisations, the naval aircraft repair organisation generated fifty-eight aircraft out of reserve for all three services. The Fleet Air Arm commissioned four new squadrons from reserve aircraft: 809 NAS with Sea Harriers, 825 NAS with Sea King HAS 2s used in the commando role, and 847 and 848 NAS with Wessex HU 5s. Aircraft engines and components were repaired in very short timescales and equipment ranging from

Sea Harrier gun parts to stretcher harnesses were manufactured. It should also not be forgotten that the Director General Stores and Transport (Naval)'s organisation had stored TF 317 for war in three days without prior warning and eventually shipped over 30,000 tons of provisions, stores and ammunition to the fleet.

Returning to the carriers for a few last words about the conflict, the Sea Harrier proved to be a far better fighter in the Nation's hour of need than many outside the RN had thought possible. It had dominated the skies over the South Atlantic while the TASMO squadron personnel read about the conflict in their newspapers. The Sea Harrier had proved yet again the vital importance of having fighters that could travel to the focal point of a national crisis, complete with their supporting infrastructure in an aircraft carrier that would be ready for instant action when it arrived and stay there supported by RFAs. The Sea Harrier force earned greatness in 1982 and the Nation can look back on its achievements with pride.

Hermes back alongside in Portsmouth after 108 days at sea. Aircraft on deck include Sea Harrier FRS 1s, Sea Kings HAS 5s and HC 4s, Wessex HU 5s, a Lynx HAS 1 and a captured Argentine UH-1 Iroquois. (Author's collection)

19 A Decade of Operations

Invincible returned to Portsmouth on 17 September 1982. Since sailing on 5 April she had spent 160 days continuously at sea, a new record for a British aircraft carrier, more than doubling the previous one held by *Eagle*. Her Sea Kings had flown 3099 operational sorties and her Sea Harriers 599, with seven enemy aircraft shot down and three more probably so.[1] She was greeted by HM Queen Elizabeth II, one of whose sons, HRH Prince Andrew, had served throughout the conflict as a pilot in 820 NAS. On 1 June Malcolm Fraser, the Australian Prime Minister, wrote to Margaret Thatcher and volunteered that should her Government 'wish to re-examine the *Invincible* sale, Australia would not hold the UK to its obligation'.[2] From 7 to 13 July a team led by the Australian Defence Minister visited London to discuss the implications of the Prime Minister's letter. British politicians had suddenly remembered how important aircraft carriers were to an island nation and the delegation was informed that 'as a result of a major revision in defence planning', the UK Government had decided to retain all three *Invincible* class carriers. The Australians had been led to believe that the third ship of the *Invincible* class, *Ark Royal*, launched a year earlier by HM The Queen Mother, might yet be released to the RAN but they were now told 'quite firmly'[3] that only the 23-year-old *Hermes* would be sold when *Ark Royal* was completed. She had been offered to Australia before, in 1968, but she was now to be turned down again for the same reason; her heavy demand on manpower made her an unattractive proposition for the RAN. She was eventually sold to the Indian Navy, renamed *Viraat* and is still operational in 2015. The RAN lost its carrier capability in 1982 when *Melbourne* was de-commissioned without replacement. Interestingly, the arguments in Australia over the need for a new carrier closely mirrored those in the UK with increasingly polarised positions being taken on cost and the theory that land-based aircraft could support the fleet wherever it might be deployed. Although the Government had decided to retain all three ships of the *Invincible* class, it decided that only two of them would be operational at any one time with the third held in reserve or refit.

John Nott, the Defence Secretary, clearly had very little idea of what was going on in March 1982 and what the UK could, or should, do about it. It would be unfair to say that he was ostracised by the RN but having been in the same place on one of his visits to a ship I recall that he was not warmly received. To his credit he obviously realised his shortcomings and had offered his resignation immediately after the Argentine invasion of the Falkland Islands but Margaret Thatcher refused to accept it. However, in January 1983 he announced that he would leave politics altogether, not even standing for Parliament in the forthcoming General Election. He retired to his farm in Cornwall and was replaced by Michael Heseltine who began an almost evangelical drive towards greater unification of the armed forces and their support structure. Keith Speed, the last Navy Minister into which the post of First Lord had evolved, left and the three Service Ministers were replaced by three Ministers with individual responsibility for personnel, equipment and deployments. Since the end of the Admiralty in 1964, the naval staff and the RN support organisations had been known as MOD (Navy) and had continued to be recognisable as having evolved from Admiralty Directorates, albeit with much less power and influence. That was all to go under the Heseltine reforms. New Defence Staff Directorates were formed, based on capability with officers from all three Services and the RN support organisations such as DGST(N) were subsumed into huge new structures, in this case the Defence Logistics Organisation. The immediate effect could, reasonably, be described as chaos in the short term as people who had loyally supported the RN for decades were replaced by joint staff from any background who did not necessarily know anything about the Navy or how it operated. It took over a decade for things to settle down into a new form of normality.

Immediately after the South Atlantic War new ships and aircraft were ordered to replace those that had been lost but with the collapse of the Soviet Union in 1989 the politicians sought a 'peace dividend'. There was a widespread assumption that there would be no more conflict but, almost immediately, it became apparent that this was not the case; the Cold War had actually prevented small wars from breaking out and now that it was over conflicts that had 'simmered' came to the surface and demanded action. On 2 August 1990 Saddam Hussein invaded Kuwait, resurrecting the claim that it was Iraqi territory.[4] The UN Security Council passed Resolution 661, imposing economic sanctions against Iraq on 6 August and Resolution 662 on 9 August. The latter declared the annexation of Kuwait to be an illegal act and authorised the use of force by a coalition which eventually comprised thirty nations. At the time, Iraq had the world's fourth largest army and it took the Coalition time to build up ground forces to liberate Kuwait. The UK deployed squadrons of RAF Tornado and Jaguar aircraft which operated throughout the campaign from airfields in the region. Air Chief Marshal Sir Patrick Hine was appointed the overall UK Joint Commander with his headquarters at High

Wycombe and part of his staff at the new PJHQ at Northwood. Lieutenant General Peter de la Billière was the UK Commander 'in theatre', sharing part of the Allied Headquarters at Riyadh in Saudi Arabia. With large numbers of Allied combat aircraft in the region, the UK Government saw little point in deploying a carrier task force to add to them and an interesting argument ensued.[5] The RN wanted to deploy *Ark Royal* to use her command and control facilities to act as flagship for the large number of destroyers and frigates in the region. Politicians had clearly forgotten the arguments in the 1960s that had ended with the decision that a command cruiser was more important than an aircraft carrier. Their successors now argued that because the type of ship that had resulted, originally known as a command cruiser, was an aircraft carrier and not primarily a command ship, it was not needed. For whatever reason, no British carrier took a direct part in the conflict subsequently known as the First Gulf War but *Ark Royal* did sail from the UK on 10 January 1991 for the Eastern Mediterranean where she joined Allied warships guarding against an attack into the Mediterranean by Iraqi aircraft.[6] She led TG323.2 which included the frigates *Sheffield* and *Charybdis* together with the RFAs *Olmeda* and *Regent* and worked closely with the US Sixth Fleet ships *Virginia*, *Philippine Sea* and *Spruance*. In the event she was not required to take action but she did spend fifty-one days at sea at a high degree of readiness before returning to the UK.

Operation 'Hamden', 1991–1996

For nearly five years the RN committed warships to operations in the Adriatic in support of British and UN forces ashore in the Former Republic of Yugoslavia (FRY). The requirement evolved after the death of Marshal Tito in 1980 as the semi-autonomous regions of Yugoslavia sought independence. In 1991 Slovenia declared its independence after democratic elections and Croatia followed immediately. This left Bosnia-Herzegovina in a difficult position with increasing Serbian domination of a reduced Yugoslavia; it had a largely Muslim population but also large Serbian and Croat communities. It held a referendum in 1992 and subsequently declared independence in 1992; it was recognised as an independent state by the USA, the UK and other European Union countries. Ethnic violence erupted and the UN Security Council attempted to establish 'safe havens', one of which was Srebrenica. By 1994 fighting was serious and the UN had established a lightly-armed UN Protection Force (UNPROFOR) but it was no match for the large Serbian Army and NATO organised a Rapid Reaction Force that could be used, if necessary to protect UNPROFOR.[7] The bloody fighting ashore is outside the scope of this work but the RN soon became involved in national, UN and NATO operations in the Adriatic Sea that supported operations ashore. UN

Ark Royal in the Adriatic in 1994. Aircraft on deck include Sea Harriers FRS 1s and Sea King HAS 6s. (Author's collection)

Security Council Resolution 713 declared an arms embargo against the former Yugoslavia. UNSCR 743 created the UNPROFOR, initially for deployment in Croatia but the mandate was extended to include Bosnia later in 1992. UNSCR 757 widened trade prohibitions against the former Yugoslavia to include all items except medicine and food. The interdiction operation evolved into the NATO-led Operation 'Sharp Guard' and involved several RN destroyers and frigates between 1993 and 1996. The RN also provided support in the form of the national Operation 'Grapple' which maintained RFAs and 'B' Flight of 845 (Sea King HC 4s) NAS at Split. They provided a base for the British RRF and the potential to evacuate British forces should such a move become necessary. In January 1993 the UK Government ordered the establishment of a national task group, designated TG 612 which was to be led by an aircraft carrier. It was to remain in the Adriatic and be available at between one and ninety-six hours' notice depending on the situation ashore. Although intended to support British forces ashore if they came under attack, the TG matched similar deployments by US and French carrier task groups and routine meetings were held between their commanders to discuss activities. They shared tankers but political considerations prevented an exact matching of operational deployments. Air support had become an essential element of Allied operations after the establishment of a 'no-fly zone' over the former Yugoslavia, both to enforce UN sanctions and to provide clear skies under which UNPROFOR could be supported with re-supply and medical evacuation by helicopters. The carriers were also able to provide a show of force and close air support when called for and were able to give constant availability, unlike the NATO air bases in Italy which were frequently shrouded in mist early in the morning which prevented take-off. The embarked Sea Harriers had a number of advantages over land-based NATO aircraft; they were closer to the areas of operation and this allowed a faster turnaround between sorties. They were also effective in being able to provide air interception, close air support and reconnaissance capabilities in the same sortie with their built-in F-95 camera and a mixed weapon load. This capability was particularly appreciated by British and UN forward air controllers on the ground. By 1995 the F/A 2 version had replaced the FRS 1, giving an even more effective capability. Although no more than eight Sea Harriers had been embarked in any one carrier, they had flown more than 2200 sorties, roughly a third of all British fast-jet sorties in support of operations in the Balkans. Sea Harriers also participated in the final military stage of the Bosnian conflict when they flew as part of NATO Operation 'Deliberate Force', the bombardment of Serbian positions by aircraft and artillery. Although the RN was not a major contributor to the overall air effort in terms of numbers of aircraft, it did provide a valuable contribution with its secure, mobile and relatively weather-independent floating bases which were close to the front-line but difficult for an enemy to locate and attack. The carriers were well-placed to generate quick-reaction sorties and to fill gaps in the NATO flying programme left by fog-bound or unserviceable aircraft ashore. The latter was a particularly significant capability given UNPROFOR's vulnerable position on the ground and, at last, the carriers' achievements were noted by politicians in the UK, who also recognised that the ships could augment the numbers of aircraft and types embarked to provide flexibility. As the USA and France also demonstrated, carriers provided an essential command centre that maintained national and NATO plots; whilst themselves remaining under national operational control, they were quite capable of launching aircraft on NATO or UN tasked missions. Not least important, they were an impressive venue for the warring factions to be taken for peace talks.

The first RN carrier on task was *Ark Royal* which arrived in the Adriatic as the flagship of UKTG 612.02. She was there primarily to support British interests but in April 1993 her Sea Harriers were declared to NATO as being capable of dropping laser-guided bombs on targets that were illuminated by FAC teams on the ground. Her aircraft were tasked to take part in Operation 'Deny Flight', enforcing the 'no-fly zone' over the former Yugoslavia and were also available at short notice

A Sea Harrier F/A 2 taking part in Operation 'Deliberate Force' armed with 1000lb bombs on the outboard wing pylons. (Author's collection)

to support British and Allied ships in Adriatic against attacks by missile-carrying fast attack craft. She had to remain close to the operational area for most of the time but was occasionally released, at times of lower tension, for visits to Bari and Corfu and a short maintenance period in Malta. Whilst back in the operational area, her Sea Harriers carried out cross-deck training with the Italian Navy AV-8Bs embarked in *Garibaldi*. *Ark Royal* was relieved by *Invincible* in August 1993 and she was able to share tasking with the French carrier *Clemenceau* under a local arrangement which ensured that one of the two was always close at hand if the other took a short break. *Invincible* was, in turn, relieved by *Ark Royal* in February 1994. In addition to her normal air group, she also embarked two Sea Harrier F/A 2s of 899 NAS to prove the new variant's ability to operate at sea. From the outset her aircraft flew up to fourteen sorties a day over the former Yugoslavia and the Sea Harriers' reconnaissance capability proved extremely valuable, providing the national, NATO and UN commands with images of the movement of Serbian tanks and guns. The continued pressure of operational flying led to planned visits to Toulon and Naples being cancelled but she did carry out a short maintenance period in Piraeus in April. While she was there, Serb forces in Bosnia attacked the town of Gorazde and *Ark Royal* returned immediately to the operating area. On

16 April 1994, two of 801 NAS's Sea Harriers were tasked to attack a tank which was firing at British troops from a wooded area near the town. The lead aircraft, Vixen 23, was flown by Lieutenant Nick Richardson RN; he heard the sound of gunfire over the FAC's radio as the men on the ground tried to direct him onto the target. He and his number 2 had to descend to low-level to try to locate the targets visually, making them vulnerable to man-portable anti-aircraft missile and anti-aircraft artillery fire. They found two T-55 tanks in wooded country and carried out attacking runs but both aircraft failed to get their air-to-surface bombing systems to lock on the target and, desperate to help the men on the ground, they elected to take the risk of making a second pass. Richardson failed for a second time to get a lock and was hit by a missile which caused a massive engine fire. He retained some control of the aircraft but his number 2 called 'You've got a real bad fire man, eject!'. He did so[8] and survived the experience, eventually being found by a 'friendly' Muslim group which was fighting the Serbs. They, in turn, took him to an SAS team with which he was able to get away after some time behind enemy lines. In May *Ark Royal* demonstrated another aspect of carrier versatility by leaving the operational area for a spell, that was covered by Allied carriers, to take part in NATO Exercise 'Dynamic Impact', the largest of its kind in the Mediterranean since the end of the Cold War. It involved ninety-three warships from ten nations and her participation showed the UK's continued commitment to NATO without the enormous logistic support that would have been required to deploy an equivalent land-based 'package' of air power. After the exercise she was able to slip back into the previous routine but a ceasefire in the Bosnian conflict allowed her to follow a more relaxed profile.

Invincible arrived to replace *Ark Royal* in the Adriatic in August 1994 by which time hostilities has resumed and several Sea Harriers came under fire including two which used chaff and flares to evade missiles successfully. Christmas 1994 was spent in Malta and she was relieved by *Illustrious* in February 1995. *Illustrious* had recently undergone a major modernisation and was the first carrier to embark a squadron equipped completely with Sea Harrier F/A 2s. She spent a relatively short period in the Adriatic before being relieved by *Invincible* in June. By then NATO had taken over operations ashore on behalf of the UN. In September Bosnian Serb forces laid siege to the city of Sarajevo and *Invincible*'s aircraft joined others from the US carriers *America* and *Theodore Roosevelt* in striking at Serb-held positions around the city. During this ten-day period Sea Harriers of 800 NAS flew twenty-four bombing missions, forty-two CAP sorties and twenty-eight reconnaissance missions, helping to achieve a successful outcome when Serb forces eventually complied with UN calls to withdraw their heavy weapons from around Sarajevo. The Sea Harrier F/A 2 was widely praised for its effective multi-role capability.

A Sea Harrier F/A 2 refuelling in flight from an RAF tanker over the former Republic of Yugoslavia. (Author's collection)

During a spell away from operations, *Invincible* took part in NATO Exercise 'Infinite Courage' with the USS *America* and other Allied warships before being replaced on station by *Illustrious*. She arrived in the Adriatic in December 1995 but the situation ashore had begun to ease and on 15 February 1996 the UK task group was withdrawn from deployment although the UK Government agreed to keep a carrier at twenty-one days' notice to return. *Illustrious* became the flagship of a UKTG that crossed the Atlantic to carry out Exercise 'Purple Star', a bilateral US/UK amphibious exercise.[9] In March 1996 *Invincible* was ordered to stand by for operations in the Adriatic. In the event, the peace treaty signed between the warring factions held and she was not required. Instead, she embarked RAF Harrier GR 7s for Exercise 'Hornpipe', an evaluation of the type's ability to carry out a prolonged embarkation in a carrier with especial regard to night operations and the alignment of its navigational systems at sea. *Invincible* and *Illustrious* were jointly awarded the Wilkinson 'Sword of Peace' for their operations in the Balkan Conflict.

Operation 'Jural', 1998

In late 1997 the Iraqi dictator, Saddam Hussein refused to comply with a UN Resolution to allow weapons inspectors to search his country for weapons of mass destruction that were thought to be hidden ready for use. The Western Allies made plans to enforce the Resolution and, initially, the UK Government planned to deploy RAF Tornadoes to the Gulf but when it was found to be politically unacceptable to fly over certain countries in the area it decided instead to deploy an RN task force centred on a carrier. Yet again carriers, even small ones, had given the Government options it would not otherwise have had. *Invincible* was in the Mediterranean and was at last showing what these ships were capable of with 800 (Sea Harrier F/A 2s), 849A (Sea King AEW 2s), 814 (Sea King HAS 6s) NAS embarked plus seven Harrier GR 7s of 1 Squadron RAF.[10] The number of Sea King HAS 6s was reduced to make room for the RAF Harriers but with eight Sea Harriers the ship had a total of fifteen fast jets embarked, giving her a realistic strike potential. She entered the Gulf on 25 January 1998 and began flying operations that were integrated with shore-based aircraft and USN carrier-borne aircraft from *Nimitz*, *George Washington* and *Independence*.[11] The Sea Harriers flew for 800 hours over the Southern Iraq 'no-fly zone' as part of Operations 'Southern Watch' and 'Jural', helping to increase the pressure on Iraq to comply with the wishes of the UN. In March she was initially joined by *Illustrious* and then relieved by her and sorties continued to be flown over Sothern Iraq in some numbers. By April the RAF had managed to deploy sufficient Tornadoes to the region to take over the task on a longer term basis and *Illustrious* was withdrawn.

Invincible returned for a second period of operations, designated Operation 'Bolton II' in January 1999, this time with only the normal air group embarked and no RAF Harriers. Her Sea Harriers joined US aircraft flying missions over southern Iraq but to give them the maximum time on task she had to operate well

Pilots of 800 NAS manning their Sea Harrier F/A 2s on *Invincible* during operations in the Adriatic. (Author's collection)

to the north of the American task force, within close range of Iraqi air and surface threats. The destroyer *Newcastle* and the frigate *Cumberland* remained in close company and AEW Sea Kings flew continuously to maintain an air and surface picture. Operations continued until April when *Invincible* left the Gulf to return to the UK.

Operation Magellan, 1999
On her way back to the UK, *Invincible* was diverted to the Ionian Sea to take part in the NATO Operation 'Allied Force', the UK maritime element of which was designated Operation 'Magellan'. It was to defend the former Yugoslav state of Kosovo from ethnic cleansing by Serbia which had followed the breakdown of peace talks at Rambouillet in France. The first phase of the operation followed the now-familiar course of using cruise missiles to destroy enemy air defences and was interesting from an RN perspective in that it saw the first operational firing of a Tomahawk land attack missile (TLAM) by a British submarine.[12] The *Swiftsure*

class SSN *Splendid* fired a cruise missile as part of the opening NATO salvo, demonstrating that nuclear submarines now had a very effective strike capability over considerable ranges from a dived position that would be unknown to the enemy. For the opening stage of a conflict SSNs now offered a better strike capability than a carrier-borne aircraft with only one drawback. Unlike a carrier the TLAMs, once fired, cannot be replenished at sea, forcing the boat to return to a major base facility to be re-armed. *Invincible* stopped briefly off Cyprus to replenish and arrived in the Ionian Sea at the end of April in company with the RFA *Bayleaf*. She joined the USS *Theodore Roosevelt*'s battle group and her Sea Harriers were used exclusively on CAP over the enemy airfields at Pristina and Podgorica. Serbian fire control radars frequently locked-onto them but they were never engaged by surface-to-air missiles. By mid-May the NATO command decided that it had enough land-based aircraft to cope with the remainder of the campaign and *Invincible* was released to return to the UK. 800 NAS Sea Harrier F/A 2s had flown 300 hours on CAP in the area.

Operation 'Palliser', 2000

After some years of indecision, a new commando carrier was ordered in 1993, launched in 1995 and commissioned in September 1998 as *Ocean*. She had the outward appearance of a carrier with a 'through deck' and starboard-side island but her interior spaces were better laid out than the earlier light fleet carrier conversions. The deck was completely flat without an open forecastle but, for some unaccountable reason, the forward part of Fly 1 was made pointed like the 1920s *Hermes* and *Eagle*, significantly reducing the parking space available for aircraft, vehicles and pre-prepared underslung loads. The deck was marked with a runway centreline and Harriers could land-on easily and, theoretically, carry out a flat-deck short take-off but a Vulcan Phalanx gun situated at the point of the bow would represent a hazard for an aircraft that drifted right on take-off.[13] *Ocean* had no aircraft workshops like those in a carrier: instead she loaded a containerised amphibious support package which could be modified to suit the tailored air group (TAG) embarked for a specific operation. From the outset she was heavily committed to operations and her initial shake-down deployment to the Caribbean with Sea King HC 4s embarked was interrupted when she was diverted to give humanitarian aid to Honduras and the Mosquito Coast area of Central America after Hurricane Mitch caused devastation. Her helicopters carried food and medical supplies to communities up to 100nm inland and she provided up to 300 tons of fresh water per day.

In early 2000 she sailed with the Amphibious Ready Group (ARG) as part of the Aurora 2000 deployment with 846 (Sea King HC 4s) and 847 (Lynx AH 1s)

NAS embarked together with 42 RM Commando and part of 3 Brigade Headquarters. She carried out a series of work-up amphibious exercises including 'Rock Wader' in Gibraltar; 'Pine Wader' in Portugal and 'Ambrose Hill' at Camp de Canjeurs, a large artillery range in the South of France. Meanwhile *Illustrious*, which was also intended to join the Aurora deployment, was taking part in Exercise 'Linked Seas' in the Atlantic with RAF Harriers embarked in addition to her normal air group of Sea Harriers and Sea Kings. On 8 May 2000 she was diverted with her task group and ordered to proceed to Sierra Leone with all despatch as a key element of Operation 'Palliser' which was intended to evacuate British nationals, insert troops to restore calm and allow the UN peacekeeping forces in the country to resume their duties. At 02.00 on 5 May the amphibious ready group, including *Ocean*,[14] was ordered to prepare for Operation 'Palliser' and proceed as quickly as possible to Sierra Leone[15] where it was to join *Illustrious* and the frigate *Argyle*, the West African guard ship. Exercise 'Ambrose Hill' was terminated, the amphibious force re-embarked and the ARG sailed for Gibraltar where operational stores, more personnel and ammunition were loaded and then proceeded to West Africa.

By May 2000, Sierra Leone had been ravaged by nine years of civil war between rival factions that threatened to overthrow the elected Government of President Kabbah. A West African military peacekeeping force known as ECOMOG had been withdrawn and replaced by a small UN force known as UNAMSIL which had yet to make its presence felt and the Revolutionary United Front (RUF) tried to exploit the power vacuum. It attacked UN troops, killing seven and taking over 400 prisoners. British military observers escaped RUF encirclement around the town of Makeni and their leader, Major Phil Ashby, was taken out to *Ocean* as soon as she arrived to brief on the situation ashore. RUF fighters advanced on Freetown, the capital, with very little opposition and scenes of panic in the city raised fears for the safety of UK citizens. One British military observer, Major Andy Harrison, remained in the east of the country, surrounded by RUF fighters but still in radio contact with the outside world. The UK Government decided to fly in the 'Spearhead Unit', the 1st Battalion, Parachute Regiment Battle Group to conduct a national evacuation operation on 11 May. It was deployed around Lungi Airport and Freetown very quickly and restored calm to the region which allowed the build-up of UN troops to continue without interference. Foday Sankoh, the RUF leader, shot his way out of his house and fled into the bush. Troops loyal to President Kabbah's government numbered only about 2000; they had British rifles but lacked vehicles, uniforms and disciplined leadership. As might be imagined their discipline was low but their most useful asset was a single Mil-24 Hind helicopter gunship flown by a contract crew. It was effective against rebel targets but maintenance and the supply of ammunition were constant problems. The so-called Armed Forces Revolutionary Council (AFRC) comprised former soldiers loyal to Sergeant Johnny Koroma. In May 2000 they were nominally loyal to the elected Government but several factions, including the Occra Hill Faction, the West Side Boys and the Sierra Leone Border Guards followed their own lawless ideas and refused to fight the RUF. When 1 Para arrived, there was a very real threat that the RUF would overwhelm both the UN peacekeepers and the motley array of pro-government forces and seize both the capital and its airport.

Illustrious and the ARG took up a position off Sierra Leone on 14 May, carried out reconnaissance, for which the camera-equipped Sea Harriers were invaluable, and began to put vehicles and equipment ashore. On 17 May RUF fighters attacked a pathfinder picket position in the village of Lungi Lol where Captain Rich Cantrill RM of 42 Commando was carrying out a reconnaissance. The RUF leader was captured and a number of rebels killed in the ensuing fire-fight. By 25 May the whole amphibious force was ashore and the paratroops were brought out to *Ocean* to 'chill out'. They had arrived in theatre with nothing but what they stood up in and were delighted to have showers, good food and clean uniforms. The commando group's operations ashore were particularly notable for their sheer variety; apart from providing stability, they prepared for an evacuation, mended Government vehicles, trained recruits for the Sierra Leone Army, supported local police units and hunted for the remaining RUF rebels in the jungle to the north of the capital. Extensive river patrols were established to prevent the RUF from using boats to infiltrate behind the area now controlled by the British. Foot patrols established positive contact with the inhabitants of small villages and restored confidence. The Lynx helicopters of 847 NAS gave a capability to search the jungle for rebels at night giving the commandos 24-hour coverage of movement in the immediate area. Sea Harriers of 801 NAS from *Illustrious* were used to photograph villages and islands beyond the immediate area controlled by the Commando Group. They were also ready to use lethal force if necessary but the threat of it, together with artillery and helicopter gunships proved sufficient to deter further action by the RUF. The fact that they did not have to use force is a positive example of the deterrent effect of sea power. One other, unusual, aspect of Operation 'Palliser' was the establishment of an effective Sierra Leone Army training camp at Benguema and aid to the civil power as part of a 'hearts and minds' campaign to assist the local population. 42 RM Commando medical staff screened over 1000 potential army recruits and sixty RM personnel helped with their training. This task was handed over to a British Army team when the ARG withdrew in June. Members of the various ships' companies also helped by augmenting Royal Marines as guards around Freetown and by rebuilding and painting two school buildings. The latter task was

A posed PR photograph of Sea King HC 4s rapid-roping Royal Marines Commandos from the LPH *Ocean* onto a beach in Sierra Leone to demonstrate capability in 2000. (Crown Copyright)

particularly significant as the fighting had ended all other overseas development and, in May 2000, the sailors' efforts represented the only development of any sort in the country. *Ocean*'s engineers also carried out work on local electrical generating systems, so that the suburbs of Freetown were able to enjoy a supply of electricity after a considerable period without.

Operation 'Palliser' was rightly regarded by the new British Labour Government as an outstanding success and added impetus to its plan to build a new generation of aircraft carriers. The essential point to notice is that it worked well as a joint operation and that the various components formed an interlocking whole, not disparate and rival elements of single Service capability. This is what the RN had been saying since Admiral Lambe's proposal in the early 1960s. Airlift had moved the 'Spearhead Battalion' of 1 Para into Sierra Leone quickly but once there they had little but what they stood up in and had to rely on local resources of dubious value. British airlift capability was not sufficient to deliver vehicles, ammunition and logistic support on the scale required. It was a very necessary but

AIM-9 Sidewinder missiles being brought onto the flight deck to arm Sea Harrier F/A 2s in the range. (Author's collection)

complementary capability. The ARG with the carrier, commando carrier and RFAs brought with it all the facilities of a major base and was consequently able to do far more once it was deployed. The use of force where required, mobility provided by both helicopters and vehicles, support for the 'Spearhead Battalion' to keep it in action, riverine patrols with landing craft and helicopters and even aid to the civil power were all part of its repertoire operating for a lengthy period a long way from the nearest British base.

Operation 'Telic', 2003
The MOD had planned a major deployment to the Far East in 2003 to take part in Exercise 'Flying Fish 3', the next Five-Power Defence Agreement exercise in the region, but in the latter part of 2002, UN arms inspectors had continuously met obstruction whilst attempting to do their work in Iraq and armed action appeared to be inevitable. The programme for the deployment was, therefore, modified and a number of RN ships were deployed to the Gulf as part of the US-led Operation 'Iraqi Freedom'. The long, relatively slow build-up of Coalition forces included a number of land-based fixed-wing squadrons and their logistic support, so the UK Government decided that a carrier was not necessary. The UK contribution was unimaginatively designated Operation 'Telic' and included *Ark Royal* and *Ocean*.[16]

Ark Royal was re-roled from a fixed-wing carrier into her secondary LPH/ commando carrier role and sailed from Portsmouth in January 2003. She had a TAG comprising the twin-rotor Chinooks of 18 Squadron RAF and the Sea King ASaC 7s of 849A NAS embarked. *Ocean* and her accompanying RFAs embarked 845 (Sea King HC 4s) and 847 (Lynx AH 1s) NAS together with 3 Commando Brigade Headquarters, 40 and 42 RM Commandos together with 539 Assault Squadron RM, 29 Commando Regiment RA and 59 Independent Commando Squadron RE. The UK Task Group Commander, Rear Admiral David Snelson, was based ashore alongside the USN Fifth Fleet command in an integrated headquarters from where he was in constant communication with the UK PJHQ at Northwood in the UK. 3 Commando Brigade was commanded by Brigadier Jim Dutton RM and worked in close co-operation with the 3rd Marine expeditionary Force of the US Marine Corps. The primary objective of the RN Task Group was an amphibious assault on the strategically-significant Al Faw peninsula which covered the approached to the main waterways in the region to Umm Qasr and the port of Basra. It also contained the important oil installations at the Shatt al-Arab.

Hostilities opened with attacks by Tomahawk cruise missiles against Iraqi command and control facilities in which the RN SSNs *Splendid* and *Turbulent* took part. The commando assault began at 22.00 on 20 March 2003 with night landings by 40 RM Commando in Sea King and Chinook helicopters from *Ark Royal*. The second wave was delayed by the crash of a USMC CH-46 Sea Knight helicopter which killed the crew and the personnel from 3 Commando Brigade Reconnaissance Group that it was carrying. The assault eventually went ahead using RN Sea Kings and RAF Chinooks that had carried the first wave. The second wave was about six hours later than planned and conducted in deteriorating weather against heavy opposition but proved successful and achieved its objectives. Very accurate naval gunfire support for 3 Commando Brigade was provided the frigates *Richmond*, *Chatham* and HMAS *Anzac*. In the early hours of 22 March 2003 two Sea King ASaC 7 helicopters of 849A NAS collided at about 04.30. One had been returning to *Ark Royal* and the other was outbound at the start of its mission. Sadly all seven aircrew were killed, one of them a USN exchange officer. The Searchwater 2000 radar and its associated Cerberus system in the upgraded Sea King ASaC 7 had shown remarkable accuracy over both land and water and was even capable of tracking human beings and vehicles as they moved across the desert.[17] The combat phase ended shortly afterwards and a number of RN ships, including *Ark Royal*, were withdrawn. She arrived back in Portsmouth in May 2003 to be relieved as high-readiness fleet flagship by *Invincible*. *Ocean* arrived with the naval air commando squadrons soon afterwards. Far from being the period of unbroken peace that so many people had expected after the collapse of the Soviet

Ark Royal during the Second Gulf War in 2003; she is at anchor operating RAF Chinooks during the assault on the Al-Faw peninsula by the Royal Marines. There are three Chinooks and an RN Sea King ASaC 7 on deck with a fourth Chinook landing. (Author's collection)

Union, the decade after 1991 had been remarkable for the number of small conflicts in which the UK had been forced to take action. They were exactly the sort of scenarios that the Admiralty had predicted before its demise and the *Invincible* class ships had made a valuable contribution but, it has to be said, they were not as effective as the ships that the Admiralty had wanted to build. The key thing to understand, though, was that they existed and they were either close to the scene of action or could quickly be so when they were needed.

A Sea King HAS 6 of 814 NAS landing on *Invincible*. The aircraft nearest the camera is painted in 'Tiger squadron' markings based on the squadron's badge for its participation in a recent NATO 'Tiger Meet' of units with tiger-related badges. The next aircraft astern is also a HAS 6 and the three landing-on are all Sea King AEW 2s. (Author's collection)

20 New Defence Reviews, Carriers and Aircraft

The twenty-first century brought new challenges and disappointments for the RN carrier force but the first two decades were to be dominated by decisions taken at the end of the previous century and their half-hearted implementation. From the early 1980s the primary role envisaged for the surface fleet in the event of war with the Warsaw Pact was the operation of anti-submarine striking groups to prevent Soviet submarines breaking through the Greenland/Iceland/UK gaps into the North Atlantic. New passive towed-array sonars could detect submarines at ranges of up to 100nm and the Sea King lacked the radius of action to prosecute a contact at that sort of range from its parent ship. Even so, the Sea King HAS 6 had a formidable capability within its endurance limitations. New types of ship were considered, among them the frigate design that evolved into the Type 23 that is still in service in 2015. At first it was thought of as an austere towed-array 'tug' with little in the way of armament but a flight deck and hangar capable of taking a Sea King. Thankfully, more realistic ideas prevailed, because the ships would have operated a long way from any kind of support and had to be capable of defending themselves against a wide range of attackers. Recent experience in the South Atlantic taught that every available frigate had to have a general-purpose capability, including a medium-calibre gun, so that it could contribute to anything required of it from local constabulary actions to full-scale war. At the time it was thought that the *Invincible* class would provide command, air defence and area ASW support for the UK group and that other helicopters would prosecute long-range towed-array contacts. The way in which this was to be done struck me as complicated and so it proved to be.

A new class of 'one-stop' replenishment ships was specified capable of providing the anti-submarine task force with fuel, ammunition and stores. The MOD staff believed that building these ships with a flight deck aft of a standard 'box-shaped' hangar would allow them to embark four Sea Kings to provide a cheap moving base from which individual helicopters could be detached temporarily to towed-array frigates.[1] In fact, the aviation arrangements added to the ships' cost and together with varied replenishment arrangements required to transfer both solids and liquids at sea it made these ships so expensive that the RN could only afford to procure two for the RFA and they were very expensive to operate.[2] They also suffered from the fact that their stock of fuel, ammunition or spares was insufficient to support a large deployment or task force so they either had to operate together or with other single-role RFAs to make up the difference.

The 1998 Strategic Defence Review

The new Labour Government elected in 1997 spent fourteen months carrying out a Strategic Defence Review (SDR), which could actually claim to have based its re-assessment of the UK's security and defence needs on its proposed foreign policy. It was announced in the House of Commons on 8 July 1998 and noted that the collapse of the Warsaw Pact meant that there was no longer a direct military threat to the UK.[3] It also acknowledged, however, that the world was 'an increasingly unstable and unpredictable place where indirect threats to the UK still persist and can arise in many areas around the globe'. To combat this, the SDR called for a major shift from the existing force structure towards more mobile, joint expeditionary forces capable of 'the rapid deployment of sustainable military force often over long distances'. Given this realignment of emphasis, the RN was to 'change its bias from open-ocean warfare as formerly[4] envisaged in the North Atlantic, to force protection and near coast (littoral) operations'. The new force projection strategy was to be centred on two new aircraft carriers, notionally of about 40,000 tons with a complement of 'up to 50 aircraft' to replace the three light carriers of the *Invincible* class. Readers were reminded that the latter were originally designed for anti-submarine operations rather than force projection. The 'think-of-a-number' thought process that led to the notional tonnage for the new carriers was not made clear but it is interesting to note that 40,000 tons was the same figure that Lord Carrington had proposed in 1963 when alarmed by the growth of the CVA-01 design. The figure seemed to have a magic resonance with politicians. The cabinet was said to have been impressed by the recent RN carrier operations in the Adriatic in support of the British expeditionary element of the NATO-led force and George Robertson, the Defence Secretary, had argued strongly for an improved British carrier strike capability. Despite this enthusiasm, however, the research paper that backed up the SDR White Paper[5] was surprisingly timid on the subject and noted that the new carriers would be expensive. It also stated that New Labour's decision to procure a new, larger generation of aircraft carriers had a certain irony since it had been an earlier Labour Government which had decided to scrap plans for a new generation of large fixed-wing aircraft carriers in 1966.

'Jointery'

A key element of the SDR was the establishment of structures to support one, or potentially two, Joint Rapid Reaction Forces (JRRF) to implement the expeditionary strategy which bore a strong resemblance to the ideas taken forward after the 1957 review. This was part of a wider joint vision intended to maximise the cost and operational effectiveness of the armed forces through inter-Service co-operation or pooling in what was expected to be a three-dimensional battle space. Responsibility for command of these joint forces was to rest with a new Chief of Joint Operations at the PJHQ at Northwood. Initially he would have equal status with the single-Service commanders-in-chief but by 2012 he would subsume them and command all combat forces. The single-Service organisations became administrators, passing on worked-up and combat-ready formations to tri-Service command for operations. The First Sea Lord was to become a 'figurehead' responsible for standards and practices and no longer an operational commander. In addition to the PJHQ Northwood, a dedicated expeditionary JRRF HQ was established together with the nucleus of another. The joint approach was to bring the three single-Service logistical organisations under a new Chief of Defence Logistics charged with merging them into a single organisation after 1999. A fully unified explosives storage and distribution organisation came into effect in 2005 and a joint Defence Aviation Repair Agency followed it, the latter replacing the RN aircraft repair organisation and its RN air yards at Fleetlands and Perth.

Those who think logically might have supposed that a modest expansion of the Fleet Air Arm would have been the best way of meeting the requirement for a fixed-wing expeditionary force since they were already trained to operate at sea and were perfectly capable of operating from a land base. It was certainly the case that RAF Harrier detachments had shown themselves capable of embarking but their use failed to take heed of the lessons of the past. Since the RAF made up embarked detachments from different squadrons, their maintenance personnel had to be given naval training in fire-fighting, damage control and whole-ship responsibilities such as replenishment at sea and aircraft handling every time a detachment was formed. This would not have been the case with a naval air squadron.[6] Worse, every time a new RAF detachment embarked it was made up with pilots who had no previous deck landing experience. Their training to achieve day deck qualification could be achieved in a few days but full operational qualification for night and bad weather sorties came only with experience and took months. Then as soon as the pilots reached this standard they went back to their squadrons ashore and the next detachment would be made up with yet more novices. It is arguable that, culturally, RAF officers thought in terms of carriers as a means of travelling to an operational area and not as weapons systems in their own right with long-term needs for training and application. Because RAF embarkations were relatively rare, the ship had to take time to get used to their strengths and weaknesses and they seldom ran as smoothly as the embarkation of worked-up naval air squadrons. Notwithstanding all this, the RN Sea Harrier squadrons and the RAF Harrier squadrons were formed into a new Joint Force 2000, later re-named Joint Force Harrier (JFH) to 'harmonise operational practice and orchestrate joint RN/RAF Harrier forces able to operate from both land and sea'.[7] Unfortunately, despite its supposed joint status, it came under the administrative control of RAF Strike Command which showed little enthusiasm for embarked operations and took every opportunity to limit the aircraft's time spent at sea, culminating in the Command's recommendation to withdraw the Sea Harrier from service prematurely in 2006 because it believed the fleet had no need for fighters in the short term and the replacement JSF was supposed to be in service by 2012. From 2006 JFH was reduced in size to four squadrons, two of which were to be RN manned and two RAF; a fifth acted as a combined training unit. In the event only one RN squadron was ever formed, 800 NAS, and Strike Command used the shortage of RN personnel with certain key qualifications to delay the formation of the second, which was to have been 801 NAS. The bulk of the manpower for the second unit was available and used to increase the size of 800 NAS, the larger unit being known between 2006 and 2010 as the Naval Strike Wing. The RN requirement for embarked fixed-wing units on a permanent basis seems to have been given insufficient priority as the fundamental drawback with any combined force is that it can only be in one place at a time. Once JFH was committed to operations in Afghanistan, 800 NAS spent much of its time deployed ashore in support of the NATO-led expeditionary force, preparing to do so or recovering after having done so. Carrier deployments, such as those of *Illustrious*,[8] had frequently to embark USMC, Spanish and Italian Harriers as none were available from JFH. Joint air co-operation also formed the basis of a new Joint Helicopter Command which exercised operational control of the RN commando helicopter force, Army Air Corps attack helicopters and RAF battlefield support helicopters, all of which could be used to form a TAG for embarked operations. Again the drawback was that the Army and RAF helicopters were not designed for embarked operations and the cost of modification was seen as an 'overhead' rather than an 'enabler'. To be fair, once the Army realised the potential for carriers to take their aircraft to the scene of action, they took to the role with enthusiasm and carried out extensive training that led to an operational capability that was demonstrated off Libya in 2010. RAF Chinooks proved capable of operating at sea during the Second Gulf War in 2003 despite being too big to strike down into the *Invincible* class hangars. The aim of all this 'jointery' was to spread 'best practice' and make efficiency gains. Whilst this undoubtedly proved to be true in some cases, there were others in which the largest organisation took an attitude that things had always been done their way and the smaller organisations that had joined them would have to put up with it.

AgustaWestland Merlin

In 1977 the MOD issued a requirement for a new anti-submarine helicopter to replace the Sea King; it was envisaged, initially, that it would enter service from about 1985. Its concept of operation was that flights of four would embark in the 'one-stop' RFAs and deploy aircraft to towed-array frigates while they were deployed. Aircraft that required maintenance would return to the RFA and a replacement would be provided. The frigate would only have sufficient sailors to refuel and re-arm the aircraft, lash it to the deck or use powered handling equipment to move it in and out of the hangar. This method of operation produced so many 'what-ifs' when it was considered rationally[9] that it was soon dropped and more sensible schemes prevailed. As the Type 23 frigate grew in capability it was eventually accepted that they would embark aircraft as autonomous Flights with a full maintenance team in each ship, even though this would require extra manpower.[10] The aircraft to meet this requirement evolved slowly. Westland Helicopters put forward a proposal designated the WG-34 for a three-engined helicopter with greater range and endurance than the Sea King with an advanced carbon-fibre airframe. For some years this formed the basis of the RN's future plans but the Italian Navy also required a large helicopter to replace its Sea Kings and Westland and Agusta finalised an agreement to work together on a joint project that was accepted by the MOD. They formed a joint company known as European Helicopter Industries (EHI), and since the Sea King replacement was its first design it was designated the EHI-01. Unfortunately a press release was widely misread and the aircraft became known as the EH-101, a simple but fundamental mistake. Eventually Agusta and Westland took their collaboration a stage further and merged to form AgustaWestland in 2000 and the helicopter was re-branded as the AW-101. For the sake of commonality I will refer to the manufacturer as AgustaWestland from now on. In June 1981 the UK Government confirmed its participation in the project and in 1984 the British and Italian Governments agreed on joint production of the aircraft in two versions, anti-submarine and troop assault/cargo-carrying and the latter version was ordered for the RAF.[11] The first of nine prototypes flew in October 1987 but development was slow and the first operational aircraft to meet the full RN requirement did not fly until 1997. The name Merlin was selected for both the RN and RAF versions and the RN version was at first designated the HAS 1 but this was changed to HM 1 before it entered service, indicating a wider surface reconnaissance role. Merlins entered service with 700M NAS, the IFTU at RNAS Culdrose where all subsequent units have been shore-based, in 1998 and because of the aircraft's complex systems the unit took on a development role and, unusually, remained in commission for a number of years until it was disbanded in 2008. 824 NAS was formed in 2000 as a training and headquarters unit followed by two front line squadrons intended for service in carriers, 814 and 820 NAS. After 2010 these were assigned for embarkation in the Response Force Task Group LPH[12] or in RFAs as part of a tailored air group, TAG. A third front line unit, 829 NAS, formed in 2004 to provide detached flights in six Type 23 frigates.[13] The initial, and to date only, RN order for Merlins was for forty-four aircraft which were delivered between 1998 and 2002.

The Merlin HM 1 was a much larger helicopter and, therefore, more expensive both to buy and operate than the contemporary USN Sikorsky SH-60R Seahawk.[14] Its maximum take-off weight is 32000lbs and it can carry up to four Stingray lightweight torpedoes, depth charges and door-mounted machine-guns.[15] Unlike the SH-60R, however, it cannot carry air-to-surface missiles, limiting its usefulness in anti-surface operations. Its three Rolls-Royce RTM 322 engines each develop over 2000shp and it can remain airborne for six hours, nearly twice as long as a 'Romeo'. The type's Blue Kestrel radar is mounted in a large radome under the forward fuselage which allows 360-degree coverage, unlike the dorsal-mounted scanner in the Sea King. Merlin's principal anti-submarine sensor is the Thales Type 2089 folding lightweight acoustic system for helicopters (FLASH).[16] This dipping sonar has a range-scale from 1nm to 26nm and uses high-resolution doppler processing and shaped pulses to detect slow submarine targets. Like its two contemporary sea control helicopters, the Merlin can deploy both active and passive sono-buoys. It processes information from them through an AQS-903A acoustic processor and all information from them can be recorded for analysis after the sorties in the parent carrier. The original concept of operation was for the Merlin to be launched from a towed-array frigate to fly along the bearing of a submarine contact until it was over the approximate target position. Once there it would lay a pattern of sono-buoys to localise it, if necessary laying successive 'chevrons' of buoys to gain a pinpoint position, a process known as chevron-tracking. Once sure of the exact target location, the Merlin would attack it with a homing torpedo. If only passive buoys were used, the target would only be aware that it was being attacked when it heard the torpedo running, by which time it should be too late to evade it. Of interest, the Canadian Government also ordered the Merlin in 1987 as both a Sea King replacement and to replace Boeing Vertol CH-113 Labrador helicopters in the SAR role. The opposition Liberal Party bitterly opposed the deal which they said was

A Merlin HM 1 hovering over an RN *Swiftsure* class nuclear-powered submarine. (Author's collection)

unnecessary after the end of the Cold War and when they were elected into government in 1993 they cancelled it, incurring cancellation costs of $Canadian 470 million. In one of the most appalling sagas of inept procurement, subsequent Canadian Governments re-ordered Merlins as Labrador replacements but decided in 2000 to procure an undeveloped version of the Sikorsky H-92 passenger transport helicopter for anti-submarine warfare duties on RCN frigates and destroyers to be designated the CH-148 Cyclone. The contract called for twenty-eight helicopters to be in service from 2008 but in 2015 the RCN still lacks a single Cyclone that meets the specification.[17] Twenty-eight years after the decision to replace Sea Kings that entered service over fifty years ago, they are still in service. Perhaps one of the Canadian shortcomings was the lack of a partner; no other navy has shown interest in the H-92 and the Canadian Department of National Defence has had to bear the entire burden of project management and cost. In the UK, the RN has had to seek partners for every military aircraft project since the 1970s. In the case of the Westland Lynx, intended for operation from ships other than aircraft carriers, development was shared with France and, as we have seen, Merlin development was shared with Italy. Before that the RN had bought USN designs in the case of the Sea King and Phantom, albeit with expensive alterations in the case of the latter.

Early in its service life, work started on a capability upgrade and life-sustainment programme for the Merlin intended to maintain its operational viability until the type's projected out-of-service date in 2029.[18] Designated the Merlin HM 2, it was decided to upgrade thirty Mark 1s to Mark 2 standard in a £750 million programme that was completed in 2015. There are a number of major improvements over the earlier variant, among them a new flat-panel multi-function cockpit display based on five night-vision goggle compatible displays with touch-screen panel units, all capable of showing either flight information or tactical information and data. The biggest improvement, however, was an open architecture system giving a 'human machine interface' (HMI) which was said to be 'vastly superior' to that in the HM 1. The observer and systems operator in the rear cabin have new tactical consoles with 24in primary tactical display monitors situated in a more ergonomic and comfortable way. A new digital map system allows information from up to four map channels to be displayed on the tactical units[19] and an upgraded version of the Blue Kestrel radar incorporates a new synthetic aperture radar/inverse synthetic aperture radar facility together with an enhanced 'track-while-scan' performance. A new acoustics suite includes better sonics processing, new detection algorithms and a common acoustic processor for active and passive systems. With the shift to littoral and amphibious operations in the twenty-first century, ASW activity had tended to focus more on active sonar because the high level of background noise limits the effectiveness of passive systems; they remain important in open ocean warfare, however. The new acoustic systems are backed up by a solid-state mass storage and recording system. There are many more improvements but I will only mention two more, a new navigation suite including an attitude and heading reference system and an embedded GPS/inertial navigation system which gives an accurate aircraft position to within a few yards. Communications include second-generation, anti-jam, tactical UHF radio for NATO, SATURN, and HF systems and data-links capable of transmitting data to surface warships.

Replacing the Sea King ASaC 7

After the 2010 MOD decision that all marks of Sea King were to be withdrawn in March 2016, a series of studies investigated replacement options for the Sea King ASaC 7. The obvious choice was the USN E-2C Hawkeye, given that the new carriers would be big enough to operate them[20] but the MOD refused to learn from the lessons of history and, for some unaccountable reason, refused to make the airborne surveillance and control aircraft the driver for carrier design. STOVL options were considered including a derivative of the MV-22 Osprey tilt-rotor and a Merlin with the same Cerberus mission system as the Sea King ASaC 7.[21] The

MV-22 development would have to be funded by the UK Government as the USN and USMC have no requirement for such a variant and would not have been cheap. A Merlin conversion was an obvious way forward, especially since there were twelve HM 1 airframes in storage that had not been converted to HM 2 standard. Once more, however, the MOD elected to follow a lonely and unproven route that has not been used by any other Navy. Project 'Crowsnest' seeks to use the open architecture mission system of the Merlin HM 2 to allow the aircraft to be role-changed into the ASaC mission whilst embarked in a carrier when required. A competition is being run by Lockheed Martin UK, the project managers, to choose between two different systems, one of which is based on Cerberus. The idea is apparently that from a given number of Merlins embarked in a *Queen Elizabeth* class carrier, the command would decide how many would be configured in the ASW and ASaC roles at any one time. The advantage would be a minimal number of embarked multi-role helicopters in a given TAG but I find it hard to believe that effective skill levels can be maintained among the embarked squadron observers. ASW and ASaC specialist observers undergo very different operational training and, while there is some cross-over in surface surveillance technique, ASW observers are not trained as fighter controllers or in strike fighter tactics. ASaC observers are not trained in the application of sonics or anti-submarine tactics. In my opinion any attempt to produce a 'super observer' will prove as big a failure as the attempt to produce an all-embracing pilot/observer in the 1940s. The training will be very long and very expensive and once they are in a squadron it will be impossible to maintain the necessary high skill levels to be ready for combat at short notice. It is difficult enough to maintain skills for the separate disciplines in 2015 with the lack of realistic task force training at sea. MOD dithering meant that 'Crowsnest' Merlins will not be in service in March 2016 when all Sea King variants are withdrawn from service. To fill the gap and provide capability for *Queen Elizabeth* in her first years of service, the MOD decided in 2014 to run on seven Sea King ASaC 7s until 2018, by which time the Sea King airframe will have been in RN service for just short of fifty years. Few of my colleagues who worked on the 'urgent need' to replace the Sea King in the early 1980s because 'it was over ten years old' would have believed that to be possible.

The Search for a Sea Harrier Replacement

The Sea Harrier F/A 2 development can be considered a mid-life upgrade for the type, addressing the shortcomings identified in the Falklands and subsequent conflicts. Although the RN budget for the work was minimal, the resulting aircraft with its Blue Vixen radar and AMRAAM missiles was arguably the best fighter in Europe when it entered service although the airframe itself was becoming decidedly

A Sea King ASaC 7 on a surveillance sortie with its radome inflated and lowered into its operating position. (Crown Copyright)

dated. The extra 'black boxes' for the radar and weapons aiming system required an 18in avionic bay extension to be built into the fuselage aft of the wing[22] and the aircraft's basic weight was significantly increased[23] although the maximum all-up weight remained the same at 26,200lbs and a weapon load up to 5000lbs could still be carried. The contemporary US Marine Corps McDonnell-Douglas AV-8B, which was also produced for the RAF as the Harrier GR 5/7/9, had a slightly lower empty weight because of the extensive use of carbon fibre rather than aluminium in its construction and did not need it. The RN lacked the funds to develop the engine to produce greater thrust without a partner and neither the USMC nor the RAF was interested. Selection of the STOVL Sea Harrier had, metaphorically, 'painted the RN into a corner' where it had no choice but to land vertically, accepting the thrust available from the standard Pegasus engine. In the North Atlantic this might not have posed too great a problem but after the end of the Cold War the RN found itself having to operate in the Eastern Mediterranean, Arabian Sea, Persian Gulf and the Far East where high temperatures limited engine thrust. This minimised the weight at which the aircraft could hover, especially when it brought back unused weapons. It was often necessary for aircraft to land on with only a few seconds' fuel remaining. The alternative was to jettison unused weapons which could be very expensive, in some cases wasting some of the stock that had only been procured by the UK in limited numbers. This, together with the claim that the Harrier GR 7 was easier to upgrade, was the official reason given by the MOD for the Sea Harrier's early withdrawal from service in 2006. A number of Sea Harriers had less than 1000 hours' flying time and their disposal was, in my opinion, a tragic waste.

All military aircraft increase in weight throughout their service lives so it was obvious to the naval officers within the MOD staff that a replacement aircraft would be required and that a partner would be required to help fund its development. The RAF showed little interest since it was procuring different versions of the Panavia Tornado multi-role combat aircraft in the strike and fighter roles and had the Jaguar and Harrier for the close air support role. In the longer term, air staff officers stuck to their mantra that land-based aircraft could do anything and their attention was focused on the new design that was to become the collaborative Eurofighter Typhoon. In stark contrast, the French Navy and Air Force collaboratively produced carrier and land versions of the Dassault Rafale with common development and training regimes, the RAF had no interest any aircraft intended to operate from ships, even those intended for the joint expeditionary operations recently highlighted by the Government. The only possible partner for the RN requirement was the US Marine Corps which was seeking a replacement for the AV-8Bs which it operated as part of composite air groups with helicopters in their amphibious carriers. The MOD, therefore, held talks with the Pentagon in the late 1980s which agreed to investigate the joint development of an 'affordable', supersonic STOVL fighter to replace the Sea Harrier and AV-8B Harrier. The US designation AV-16 was tentatively allocated to one of the proposed designs. At about the same time the US Navy and Air Force were also considering a range of joint and single-Service fighter options that were variously intended to be 'affordable', 'stealthy' or simply better than the variety of types that they were intended to replace. With the end of the Cold War in 1991, US legislators sought a 'peace dividend' and decided to impose collaboration to achieve the perceived economy of a large production run of a single basic fighter design produced in different versions for the Air Force, Navy, Marine Corps and export customers.[24] By 1994 this had evolved into a project known as the Joint Strike Fighter (JSF), to be produced in three versions, each with the same sensors, weapons and an intended 80 per cent commonality in airframe design. The UK joined the project and designated its variant the UK Future Carrier-Borne Aircraft (FCBA), although most people referred to it as the JSF. The UK paid a share of the projected development cost and provided some naval and civilian staff for the Joint Project Office, the first time that 'foreign' officials had participated in a US Government procurement programme.

This made the UK a Level 1 Partner. Other Governments subsequently bought into the project at various levels but the UK remained the only Level 1 partner throughout the development life of the JSF. At the time it was assumed that the RN would capitalise on its recent STOVL experience and, although no final decision was taken, the STOVL variant was the one considered most likely and was the one that had significant British input. The other versions were a conventional version for the USAF to operate from land bases and a big-winged version for the USN with a tail-hook to operate from carriers. British involvement changed with the 1998 defence review, however, when the UK Government announced that the JSF would also be procured to replace the Harrier in RAF service[25] rather than the Typhoon. The FCBA was, therefore, re-designated the Joint Combat Aircraft (JCA), although most people still referred to it as the JSF. There seems to be no way of avoiding acronyms when it comes to this aircraft and its equipment. Three industrial groups were invited to put forward proposals and the first to be eliminated, surprisingly, was McDonnell/British Aerospace who designed and built the AV-8B Harrier. Their design was dismissed by the US Defence Advanced Research Projects Agency (DARPA) as being 'not sufficiently advanced in concept'.[26] A Boeing design was eliminated in 2001 and Lockheed-Martin was awarded a $19 billion contract for JSF design and development that was expected to take ten years to complete. The UK contributed $2 billion at first. The aircraft was now given the US designation F-35 and the name Lightning II. The airframe is built in three versions, each with distinct differences in the way it is to take-off and land. The F-35A is for the USAF and has a small wing and very high landing speed; the F-35B is a STOVL version with swivelling nozzles for the USMC, RN and RAF and the F-35C is the carrier variant for the USN with larger wings to lower the landing speed within acceptable limits for deck landing, a tail-hook and a nose-tow catapult launch system. Its maximum weight is 10,000lbs heavier than the other two, giving greater fuel and weapons carriage capability. It is fair to say that the 'A' and 'C' versions were heavily penalised to achieve commonality with the very specialised 'B' version. Designed on their own they would have been more robust, twin-engined aircraft built in both single and two-seat versions. By 2015 many US analysts believed that it would have been cheaper, quicker and more efficient to build two separate designs, conventional and STOVL using common avionic systems where possible and in my opinion they are probably right. One of the first major project delays that affected all three versions was the need to reduce airframe weight dramatically from that of the original design so that the aircraft could successfully land vertically from a hover onto an amphibious carrier with unused weapons, exposing an early critical weakness in the very area that had led the UK Government, supposedly, to be forced into removing the Sea Harrier from service early.

Lockheed Martin Lightning II

The aircraft that evolved from the JSF development and demonstration programme was given the name Lightning II[27] but, unusually for a British aircraft, it has not been given a British designation at the time of writing in 2015. For instance, the McDonnell Phantom had the USN designation F-4H,[28] but was designated the Phantom FG 1 in RN service. The Lightning is referred to, even by the MOD, using its American designation F-35. Its primary feature is stealth and the airframe is designed to offer minimal radar reflection against radars operating at certain frequencies. One of the original design concepts absorbed into the JSF was the common affordable lightweight fighter (CALF), but the Lightning proved to be far from lightweight and could certainly not be described as affordable. The STOVL version being procured for the British armed forces, the F-35B, has a maximum take-off weight of 60,000lbs.[29] If this is compared with the last conventional RN air group operated from *Ark Royal* IV it shows that the Lightning II will be the heaviest aircraft ever operated from a British carrier. Maximum weights of *Ark Royal*'s fixed-wing aircraft were:

Phantom FG 1	54,000lbs
Buccaneer S2	45,000lbs
Gannet AEW 3	26,000lbs

The aircraft itself is complicated with flight and engine controls, radar, communications, navigation, electronic warfare, sensor fusion and weapons control and many other systems driven by software. Software programmes are released in numbered Blocks after testing and, at the time of writing, the latest is Block 2B which is fitted in the early British development aircraft and with which the USMC plans to achieve initial operational capability. Block 3F, which is still under development, is the final Block for use in the operational evaluation phase of development and is to be used by USN and British aircraft from 2019 and by all Lightnings as they are upgraded after that. Block 3F gives greater combat capability than 2B, allowing the use of a wider range of weapons and the full transfer of imagery and data. The Northrop-Grumman AN/APG-81 active electronically-scanned array (AESA) radar has hundreds of transmit/receive modules built into the nose of the aircraft which have no mechanical motion. Beams are shaped by software to give thirty-two radar functions, twelve of which are air-to-air, twelve air-to-surface including ship tracking and sea-surface search, four are electronic warfare, two navigation and two weather warning. The AESA array itself is designed to last for the life of the airframe with an anticipated 10,000 flying hours between failures and the 'health' of the 'black boxes' that support it is checked by a built-in monitoring system that specifies which line-replaceable component to change if a fault develops. Track information from the radar is fed into an integrated core processor that fuses data with information from other sensors digitally to give the pilot what Lockheed-Martin describes as 'outstanding situational awareness'. The resulting target symbology is fed to the pilot through his helmet-mounted display and the panoramic cockpit display. There is no head-up display in the Lightning II. Another of the Lightning II's unique features is the AN/AAQ-37 distributed aperture system (DAS),[30] which comprises infrared sensors positioned around the aircraft to provide an uninterrupted spherical view which is fed into the integrated core processor and fused to give missile and aircraft detection, tracking and warnings, including ballistic missile launch from a considerable distance. It also gives the pilot 360-degree spherical vision by day or night through his helmet-mounted display, even through the floor of the aircraft under his feet. In whatever direction the pilot looks, he will see through the sensor that best supports his or her eye-line. The sensors are passive and do not reveal the aircraft's presence to an enemy but some of them are positioned close to airframe hot-spots, and have to be cooled by a cryogenic coolant system which adds complexity. Everything that moves on the aircraft is electrically actuated, generating a considerable amount of heat inside the airframe. Fuel is used as a 'heat sink' to cool it.

The Lockheed-Martin AN/AAQ-40 electro-optical targeting system (EOTS) feeds information to both the helmet-mounted display and the panoramic cockpit display via the integrated core processor. It has to fit into a cramped space between the radar and the cockpit in which it was not possible to contrive the straight optical path used in previous targeting systems. EOTS 'folds' the optical path via mirrors and prisms to create the most compact optical system ever devised. The primary lens is fitted inside a 'stealth window' assembly under the fuselage, aft of the radar and made up with seven sapphire facets. It complements the radar and DAS to provide designation for laser-guided weapons, a laser spot tracker for co-operative engagements using other aircraft's weapons, forward-looking infrared air-to-air and air-to-surface tracking over a wide area with digital zoom capability and the generation of geo-coordinates to allow the use of GPS-guided weapons. Previous tracking systems were fitted into air-cooled pods mounted under aircraft on external pylons but such an installation would have compromised the Lightning II's stealth characteristics. The fused data provided to the pilot is said to give a more accurate target location than in any previous fighter but AAQ-40 is another equipment that requires its own liquid coolant system using a specialised fluid. The BAE Systems AN/ASQ-239 'Barracuda' electronic warfare system inter-operates with the other sensors in the aircraft and, through networks, with other aircraft, ground stations and ships. Data is transferred via a multi-function advanced data link (MADL), which allows data transfer in real-time. Like EOTS, the ASQ-239 has to be mounted internally to avoid compromising the aircraft's low-observable stealth shape and it uses ten sensors located around the airframe and the radar receiver array itself to provide radar warning and to analyse and identify the emitter. The system provides electronic surveillance including the geo-location of radars, allowing the Lightning II to evade, jam or attack them either on its own or as part of a network-connected force. It can collect signals intelligence and the APG-81 radar can be used as a stand-off jammer although its use at high power would betray the presence of the aircraft. The USAF has formed a specialised unit at Eglin Air Force Base, Florida, the 513rd Electronic Warfare Squadron, which is manned by personnel from all three US forces that fly the Lightning II; it constantly updates the Barracuda system with the latest threats but I do not know if British Lightning II units will use the same system or if an alternative national system will be established in the UK.

The Lightning II's cockpit is remarkably clean and un-cluttered with very few switches. The panoramic cockpit display comprises touch-screen panels 20in wide by 8in high divided into four 'portals' in which the pilot can set any arrangement he or she prefers. Most to date have set tactical information on the left and a display of fused sensors on the right.[31] A strip across the top shows engine temperature and fuel gauges, a caution and warning panel, weapons status, undercarriage position and other administrative data. The aircraft is flown by a side-stick controller on the right of the cockpit with an arm rest just aft of it. The throttle on the left hand side has linear rather than rotary movement and both have 'hands on throttle and stick' controls so that the pilot does not have to release his hold on either in combat to make selections. There is a small battery-powered standby flight display on the central console which provides sufficient information, in the event of the single engine failing or being damaged in combat, to allow the pilot to fly the aircraft until the engine is re-lit or he is forced to eject. The F-35B variant being procured for the USMC, RN and RAF has 11 weapons stations numbered from 1 on the outboard port wing to 11 outer starboard wing, capable of carrying a combined total of 12,000lbs of weapons or fuel tanks.[32] Numbers 4, 5, 7 and 8 are internal and can be used in stealth mode but the others can only be used with external pylons fitted which negate the airframe's stealth characteristics. The internal weapons bays on the F-35B are smaller than those on the F-35A and F-35C. The inner wing pylons, stations 3 and 9 can each carry weapons of up to 5000lbs or 426 US-gallon drop tanks. The pylons immediately outboard of them, stations 2 and 10, can carry 1500lb weapons and the outermost stations, 1 and 11, are designed for air-to-air missiles only. Block 2B software will allow the carriage and operational use of AIM-120 AMRAAM air-to-air missiles, GBU-12 laser-guided bombs and GBU-32 joint direct attack munitions. Block 3F software will add the British advanced short-range air-to-air missile, ASRAAM, together with US weapons such as the AGM-154 joint stand-off weapon; GBU-39 small-diameter bomb and Paveway IV precision-guided munition. The UK Government is procuring a stock-pile of US weapons for use on British Lightning IIs and future software development may be funded to allow the carriage of other British weapons such as Meteor and Brimstone.

All three variants of the Lightning II are powered by Pratt & Whitney F-135 engines, the most powerful production engine ever fitted in a fighter. The F135-PW-600 version fitted in the F-35B is unique in that the spool to which the two low-power turbines are attached turns a drive-shaft, through a clutch and gearbox, that drives the horizontal Rolls-Royce lift fan, situated just aft of the cockpit. When it is clutched in for hovering flight, this delivers 18,000lbs of thrust, making the Lightning II arguably the world's most powerful turbo-prop aircraft, albeit with a vertical rather than a horizontal thrust line when the fan is engaged. Because the F-135 engine was specified to have 'tri-variant compatibility' and the STOVL F-35B powerplant needed a second low-power stage to turn the driveshaft, the versions fitted in the F-35A and F-35C also have a second low-pressure turbine although they do not have a driveshaft or lift fan and do not therefore strictly need it. The PW-600 also has other features designed by Rolls-Royce to give vertical thrust and allow the aircraft to hover in controlled flight. The swivelling tail nozzle deflects hot exhaust from the engine's high-pressure core downwards and the roll post puffer jets give roll control and some lift to 'balance' the hover using high-pressure air bled from the engine. Using the dry engine thrust through the swivelling tail pipe, the lift fan and the roll posts, a new F-135 engine in ideal conditions can generate 40,650lbs of downward thrust in hovering flight and this sets the limit at which the aircraft can land on a carrier. With full re-heat in conventional horizontal flight the F-135 can develop 41,000lbs of thrust giving a maximum speed of about Mach 1.6, significantly less than a Phantom FG 1 which was capable of speeds up to Mach 2.2 without external stores.

ALIS

The Lightning II airframes are only part of the system and they cannot be operated without the autonomic logistics information system (ALIS), which is used to manage flight operations, planned maintenance, aircraft diagnostics and repair, supply chain management, both pilot and technical training and qualification, all individual aircraft documentation and manuals. Early in the development phase a laptop computer, known as a portable maintenance aid (PMA), was plugged into the aircraft to install and retrieve information but after Block 2B software installation, communication between the PMA and the aircraft is by Wi-Fi data link. The PMA itself forms part of the ship or squadron operating kit which also includes standard operating unit servers, paperless manuals, maintenance, low-observability management and mission planning software. Data from the server is sent to a central server in each Lightning II user country, known as the central point of entry (CPE). The CPE for the US armed forces is at Eglin Air Force base in Florida; that for the UK is expected to be at the joint force base at Marham. The individual aircraft information held within each national CPE cannot be accessed by other nations but a core set of data will be passed the global sustainment system run by Lockheed-Martin at Fort Worth in Texas to provide maintenance data for the global Lightning II fleet. When the new carriers *Queen Elizabeth* and *Prince of Wales* come into service they will have ship operating kits that will exchange data with the UK CPE. Mission-planning software is accessed through laptop computers and ALIS downloads data into individual aircraft mission systems and passes the required weapon load and fuel state information to the maintenance team. ALIS calls up routine aircraft inspections and maintenance routines and is constantly updated, via the CPE, to ensure that all information is correct to the latest standards. If an aircraft develops a fault it sends a code to the PMA together with 'troubleshooting' information, a video clip of the appropriate repair procedure, the identity and location of the line-replaceable units or spare parts required to cure the problem and a list of technicians qualified to do the work. Information about every fault is passed to the global sustainment system at Fort

A British F-35B Lightning II, ZM 136, taking off from Eglin AFB with its undercarriage in the final stage of retracting. (Crown Copyright)

Worth to add to the total statistical knowledge of the aircraft's systems and their support requirements. The ship operating kits are meant to be mobile but there are doubts about their viability in USMC expeditionary operations and their development continues; it will probably do so for decades to come. ALIS can be used by aircraft operators for short periods without connection to the CPE but it will obviously not receive updated information. At the time of writing, this may limit operations at remote locations to a matter of twenty-eight days. Little has been said by the MOD about ALIS and its application in the RN.

The Lightning II has the most advanced systems ever installed in a fighter and its international development is, unsurprisingly, the most expensive weapons procurement programme in history. Hyperbole from the MOD press department focuses on the aircraft's undoubted virtues but I doubt that when the MOD began to discuss the need for an affordable Sea Harrier replacement it had any idea of the scale of the project it was becoming involved with. To be fair, I do not think that any of the US armed forces did either. Different US agencies give figures for the Lightning II that are calculated in different ways and are, therefore, impossible to compare. Lockheed-Martin quotes $98 million for a single F-35A airframe, to which the cost of the engine plus 'fixes' designed to cure problems found in the test programme have to be added, taking the total cost to a figure considerably in excess of $100 million. The F-35B is significantly more expensive than the 'A' both to procure and to operate. Whatever figure proves to be the correct one for British Lightning IIs, the cost of the individual airframes is only part of the picture. Before they can be flown or used operationally the cost of ALIS and all the infrastructure to support stealth, weapons and training has to be added. The Lightning II is already the most expensive system ever procured; calculations have shown that it will be the most expensive aircraft ever operated. In 2015 the UK had four development aircraft in the USA. Two of the British aircraft spent 2014 undergoing modifications to the latest production standard at the Fleet Repair Centre, East, at Marine Corps Air Station (MCAS) Cherry Point and these were used with a third to commission 17 Joint RAF/RN Squadron at Edwards Air Force Base in California where they form the UK element of the joint operational test team evaluating Block 2B and, eventually, Block 3F software. It is the first non-American F-35 unit to be formed. The unit is likely to remain permanently in the USA to act as a development 'conduit' between UK and US armed forces. British pilots and maintenance personnel undergo training with USMC training squadron VMFAT-501, the 'Warlords', at MCAS Beaufort in South Carolina where the fourth aircraft will be interchangeable on the flight line with American aircraft. RN and RAF pilots and maintenance technicians are trained alongside their marine counterparts as part of an Anglo/US partnership deal over carrier operations. The first operational British unit is to be 617 Joint RAF/RN Squadron which will have equal numbers of RN and RAF personnel. It is planned to commission the unit at MCAS Beaufort in 2016 and it will initially be equipped with the four production Lightning IIs ordered in 2014. The MOD has announced that further production batches are to be ordered on an annual basis after the 2015 Defence Review. It will take two years for 617 to work up to initial operational capability and in 2018 it is planned to move to Marham in the UK. A second British operational unit, 809 Joint RN/RAF Squadron, is due to form up at Beaufort after 617 but no date for its formation has been announced by the MOD.

The MOD plans to carry out three periods of fixed-wing first-of-class flying trials for *Queen Elizabeth* to test and accept her ability to operate embarked Lightning IIs on a regular basis. All of them will take place in US waters as the facilities do not exist in the UK to conduct the full range of assessments. The first is set to begin in 2019 with 17 Squadron embarked. The third will culminate with the carrier's operational readiness inspection (ORI), with 617 Squadron embarked at some stage in 2020. In 2014 Commodore Rick Thomson RN, the UK lead officer for Lightning II procurement who is based at the Joint Programme Office in Crystal City, Virginia, said that 617 Squadron will be operating a naval variant of the F-35 from a carrier and 'will be a naval air squadron in everything but title'.[33] In any other nation's defence forces it would be a naval air squadron, manned by people trained for the role from the outset and determined to achieve the best results and one has to wonder why the UK Government felt it had to be different. There is no evidence to support a claim that such a system is cheaper, more effective or better suited to unitary command and control and, on the contrary, there is a lot of evidence to show that it is not. A British training squadron, with an identity that has yet to be announced, is be formed at Marham in 2019 with production aircraft from a further UK order, yet to be announced, and instructors trained at MCAS Beaufort. Work started at Marham in 2015 to prepare it for Lightning II operations with the construction of specially-designed hover pads to withstand the powerful jet efflux when the aircraft lands vertically.[34] Before 2018 there are to be new runways and taxi-way surfaces and two new, specialised F-35B hangars; one for general maintenance, repair and the installation of upgrades and the other for stealth coating repair. The UK plans to be the first nation to set up its own maintenance and training centre, complete with its own low-observable verification facility, outside the USA and hopes to attract other user nations to make use of it and, therefore, help to fund it. Lockheed-Martin claims that all signals between the aircraft and the PMA, laptops, the ship operating kit, the CPE and the global sustainment system are completely secure but cyber-security has become a big issue in 2015 with specialised UK and US military units to fight cyber-warfare. It remains to be seen if a potential enemy can 'hack into' ALIS and, if it does, whether the aircraft will be operable without it.

The New Carriers

The decision, announced in July 1998, that the UK was to build two larger carriers to replace the three light carriers of the *Invincible* class was entirely the right way forward and should have been straightforward to implement. Given the wealth of RN experience, a tough chief executive who was expert in his field, the equivalent of Admiral Mackenzie who drove the Polaris project forward to meet time, cost and effectiveness targets, could have produced an effective ship at sea with a capable naval air group within a decade but it was not to be. Indecision, political influences and the lack of an expert leadership have all taken their toll. The resulting two ships of the *Queen Elizabeth* class will be later, more expensive and less capable than they should have been. Preliminary studies had fully understood the recent effectiveness of carriers in the South Atlantic War of 1982, the operations in the Adriatic during the 1990s and even some of the earlier operations described in this book. In 1998 the Defence Secretary George Robertson spoke of building two 'larger and more flexible aircraft carriers'. These ships were, he said, to enter service in 2012 and 2015. At last it seemed that politicians had understood that the structure of a modern warship was not a cost driver and that, therefore, its tonnage was not a critical element of the procurement cost. In fact structure amounted to only about 20 per cent of the cost of such a ship, the remaining 80 per cent comprising command, control, communications and technical systems that would allow it to operate with a minimal manpower requirement. This meant that increased steelwork to provide a larger hull volume would add only a small percentage increase in cost but deliver a far more flexible and versatile ship. The old shipbuilders' adage about hull volume that 'air is free and steel is cheap' is worth quoting again.

Unfortunately the good ideas seem not to have been carried forward into the design and development phase and it should be noted that by then the Admiralty's Ship Department with its talented and famous directors was just a memory and the design was the responsibility of the MOD Procurement Agency which placed contracts with industry. By 2000 the RN had been transformed into an administrative arm which provided forces for use in unified joint task forces and had lost the forceful characters who had done so much to take forward the design and development of aircraft carriers and their aircraft in the 1940s and 1950s. When it had been thought that the FCBA would begin its life operating from the *Invincible* class the MOD partially funded the development of the STOVL F-35B. As it became clear that the future carriers could be much larger ships with dedicated strike aircraft back on the agenda after three decades in which they could hardly even be mentioned, the STOVL option appeared much less clear cut. The carrier-borne F-35C version of the Lightning II being developed for the USN seemed, to many, a wiser choice but there were fears in the RAF that if this were bought for the RN, its own chances of procuring a long-range strike aircraft to replace the Panavia Tornado would be diminished.[35] A carrier of about the size of CVA-01 with two steam catapults and arrester wires could have operated a wide choice of very effective aircraft types available 'off-the-shelf' without the UK having to wait for development, or indeed to fund it. These included the Boeing F/A-18E/F Super Hornet strike fighter, the Dassault Rafale omni-role fighter, the E-2C airborne surveillance and control aircraft and even the EA-18G Growler electronic attack aircraft. Any of these could have been in service with naval air squadrons by 2010 and would have represented an affordable and viable capability for decades ahead, still leaving the opportunity to procure the F-35C after its development was complete and production cost reduced after 2020, if the type still appeared to be viable and cost-effective. All the aircraft I have named are expected to remain in service for another two decades at least.

By 2000, however, the MOD central staffs had moved even further away from the Admiralty's specialised directorates and now comprised joint teams focused on capability-led subjects such as long-range strike and expeditionary warfare, none of which fully described what an aircraft carrier could do. Instead of a single carrier-expert body, a number of specialised departments made their individual inputs. Few of them had any real knowledge of embarked aviation and the 'blind' therefore 'led the blind' though a series of arguments about what the new ships could or should look like with politics playing as big a part as operational capability. Instead of seeking advice from experts, if necessary from the USN, and proceeding immediately with a capable medium-sized conventional carrier, the MOD's procurement executive attempted, expensively, to evaluate alternatives, taking no notice of the development work that had taken place between 1943 and 1966. Unsurprisingly they arrived at many of the same conclusions but not the most obvious one that the new ships should be built with catapults and arrester wires.

Rather than take a decision, design contracts were given to two firms, BAE Systems and Thales UK. Each was instructed to produce two designs, one for a smaller STOVL carrier and one for a larger conventional carrier. It was anticipated that one of the four would be selected and built at about the time that the aircraft to be operated from it were selected but even this simple concept proved to be beyond the project's management. Obviously the larger ships were found to be more flexible and theoretically imposed fewer limitations on the type of aircraft that could be embarked in the ASaC, strike fighter and anti-submarine roles or even the degree of 'cross-over' capability to embark assault helicopters and Royal Marines

Queen Elizabeth being manoeuvred out of Number 1 Dock into the fitting-out basin at Rosyth in July 2014. Note the two islands, large flight deck and the 'ski-jump' on the port side forward; Flyco is in the after island. She represents a vast improvement over the tiny, narrow decks of the *Invincible* class. (Crown Copyright)

Commandos in a secondary LPH role. USN, USMC and French carrier-borne fighters could be recovered in coalition operations allowing greater inter-Allied co-operation. MOD(PE)'s eventual decision was, therefore, both complex and surprising and imposed limitations on the large hull that were unnecessary. It was certainly not going to be cheap either. The smaller STOVL designs clearly lacked flexibility and were rejected.[36] The Thales conventional design, which bore a clear resemblance to the aborted Admiralty design for the 1952 fleet carrier with its two islands reflecting the need for widely-spaced exhausts from the separate machinery spaces,[37] was selected as the basis for further development. However, it was to be developed and built by a consortium of both companies and re-designed to operate the STOVL Lightning II F-35B variant which remained the focus of UK strike fighter plans and a helicopter ASaC aircraft. To answer critics who pointed out that these ships were projected to have a life of up to fifty years but were locked into a configuration that only STOVL aircraft could use like the *Invincible* class before them, MOD(PE) contracted the consortium to design and build these ships to 'an innovative and adaptable design'. They were to be constructed with a 'ski-jump' and associated equipment to operate the F-35B but to an essentially conventional carrier design with an angled-deck sponson so that, after the F-35B, they could be modified in refit to operate aircraft requiring catapult launch and arrested recovery. In the 'small print' of the agreement, however, it was apparently specified that launch would be by the C-13 steam catapults and recovery by the Mark 7 Mod 3 arrester gear used in the USN *Nimitz* class and the French *Charles de Gaulle*. Subsequent design work concentrated on such a ship, identified as Design D, and was to have important ramifications.

The design demonstration phase was completed in 2007 and 'Main Gate' government approval to proceed with the build phase was given in July 2007. The final approval to begin construction was eventually given in May 2008, a few days short of a decade after the SDR had announced their procurement. By then the team responsible for the manufacture of the two carriers had evolved into the Aircraft Carrier Alliance comprising BAE Systems, Thales UK, BAE Systems (Marine and Insyte) and Babcock Marine together with the MOD, both as a partner and as the customer. Within the alliance, BAE Systems had responsibility for design integration, construction, commissioning and acceptance of the two ships. BAE Insyte was responsible for the design and installation of the command system which was the most complicated (and, therefore, the most expensive) ever built into a British warship and Thales UK was responsible for the Stage 1 design, power and propulsion systems and the aviation interface. When construction started the lead ship was to have been completed in 2014 but, having ordered the ships, the Government announced in December 2008 that the completion of the first ship was to be delayed until 2016 to reduce expenditure in the short term although cost in the longer term would be considerably increased. A similar delay would, necessarily be imposed on the second ship which could not be assembled in Number 1 Dock in Rosyth until the first ship was floated out of it. Metal for *Queen Elizabeth* was first cut on 7 July 2009 and that for *Prince of Wales* on 16 February 2011. Politicians soon made another dramatic intervention with the 2010 Strategic Defence and Security Review (SDSR), rushed though by a new Conservative/ Liberal Coalition Government in 2010. This sought, mainly, to reduce short-term expenditure and withdrew *Ark Royal*, by then the only operational carrier in the RN, from service with immediate effect.[38] Joint Force Harrier was 'axed' immediately at the same time and its aircraft, recently expensively modified with open-architecture systems to Harrier GR 9 standard, were sold to the USMC as a source of spare parts for their AV-8B force. Bizarrely, the same SDSR stressed the Government's continued belief in rapid-reaction expeditionary forces and the aircraft carriers needed to support them. The new carriers were not cancelled, therefore, but the gap in naval strike capability created by the review before the first ship could became operational in 2020[39] was said to be acceptable in the present world situation. Throughout the review process it was widely thought that substantial numbers of aged Tornado bombers would be withdrawn from service to save money and that the Harrier GR 9s of the joint force would be retained since they were the only British expeditionary strike aircraft capable of operation at sea as well as on land and offered the most flexible deployment capability as part of joint rapid-reaction expeditionary forces to meet unexpected, contingency operations. At the last moment, literally during the weekend before the review was to be completed, the Chief of the Air Staff, Air Chief Marshal Sir Stephen Dalton, is rumoured to have called on the Prime Minister, David Cameron and, perhaps because it was a joint force and not therefore central to RAF ethos, recommended the complete withdrawal of the Harrier force and retention of the Tornado. Whatever the reason, the Harrier squadrons were soon disbanded and many of their pilots made redundant.

Having destroyed the small RN strike force for the present, the SDSR still placed great emphasis on carrier strike after 2020 and stated that the best aircraft for operation from the *Queen Elizabeth* class would be the carrier version of the Lightning II, the F-35C. This was a decision that should have been taken at the outset and, taken now, it largely negated the significant sums of money spent by the UK on the F-35B, upon which the UK staff embedded in the Project Office had had some influence on the design and British industry was a considerable stakeholder.[40] Over a year into her build, it was already too late to alter the design of *Queen Elizabeth* and the changes to *Prince of Wales* would mean that she could not enter service until after 2020.[41] The UK had, by 2010, ordered three development F-35B aircraft and negotiations began to swop the last of these for an F-35C. Having worked with the 'B' for over a decade, the UK had, of course, made no input into the 'C' which was tailored to the USN *Nimitz* and CVN-21 designs.[42] It was decided that *Queen Elizabeth* would complete with a flat deck and no 'ski-jump' for a two-year first-of-class trials programme after which she would run for a short time as the world's largest and most expensive helicopter carrier until replaced by *Prince of Wales*, completed as a strike carrier to embark F-35Cs. The decision whether to convert *Queen Elizabeth* with catapults and arrester wires at her first refit was to be taken in the next SDSR planned for 2015. For over a year the Alliance worked closely with the USN on the adaptation of the design to incorporate catapults and arrester gear. The USN could not have been more helpful in many ways and an Anglo/US agreement on the development of mutual strike carrier operational techniques led to fifteen pilots flying F/A-18E fighters in USN squadrons and several hundred personnel going to sea in US carriers for training in their operation. It was decided not install C-13 steam catapults and Mark 7

Queen Elizabeth being fitted out in Rosyth in 2015. (Crown Copyright)

arrester gear but, instead, to install the new electromagnetic launch system (EMALS) and advanced arrester gear (AAG) designed for installation in the new USS *Gerald R Ford*, CVN-78, the first ship of the CVN-21 design, due for completion in 2015. The first set of equipment was earmarked for her but, generously, the USN made the second set available for *Prince of Wales*. By 2012, however, it had become painfully obvious that in this instance as well as many others the 2010 SDSR had been hastily put together without full analysis of the facts. The Alliance quoted a price of £2 billion, about half the original build cost, to install EMALS and AAG in *Prince of Wales* during her construction. If it was decided to fit them into *Queen Elizabeth* after her completion, a cost greater than her original build cost was quoted. Sources in the USN said that the actual cost of the equipment, sold on a government to government basis, was about £450 million although this was never confirmed in a contractual arrangement. The extra £1.5 billion was to cover the cost of installation plus the provision of extra generating capacity to supply the enormous peaks of electrical energy needed to 'fire' the catapults while the ship's electric motors maintained high speed. One cannot rule out the possibility of political influence by industry to protect its investment in the STOVL F-35 design but what was now certain was that the design was never really going to be adaptable after construction had started and the money spent on this aspect of the design was wasted. On 10 May 2012 the UK Defence Secretary announced that the Government had elected to return to the procurement of STOVL F-35Bs for operation from both ships which would, after all, be fitted with 'ski-jumps'. What interests me most in this inept saga is the apparent failure of the MOD to consider the installation of C-13 steam catapults and Mark 7 arrester gear as specified in the contract. The design potential must have been there and failure to fit it when requested could, perhaps, have represented a breach of contract by the Alliance upon which the MOD could have acted. The *Nimitz* class and *Charles de Gaulle* will be using this equipment for decades to come, why on earth did the MOD even consider EMALS and AAG when it had never been part of the specification or design process? Another facet of this convoluted design process that was not explained either was the apparent failure of the MOD to even consider the short take-off but arrested recovery (STOBAR) technique used by India, Russia and China. This involves powerful fighters, such as the MiG-29K and Shenyang J-15 with tail hooks, being launched using 'ski-jumps' but carrying out arrested landings using conventional arrester wires. The decision to operate conventional carrier aircraft was the right one but taken far too late to be capable of realistic implementation. Instead of producing carriers capable of operating a wide variety of aircraft that are available now or in the foreseeable future, the UK has produced expensive hybrids that are less capable of operating strike, ASaC, electronic attack or unmanned aircraft nationally or in close co-operation with Allies. The 2012 decision has effectively 'locked' these ships into a configuration which can only operate STOVL fighters and helicopters since the installation of catapults and arrester gear in some future refit is likely to be no less expensive than the figures quoted in 2012. The adaptable design would seem to be one more in a line of ill-advised and expensive errors of judgement by the project's management. However, I must emphasise that whatever criticism can be levelled at these ships compared with what they could, or should have been, they are nevertheless large aircraft carriers capable of operating a version of the world's most advanced fighter, the F-35B. They will still be capable of acting decisively in the national interest if they are manned and handled sensibly and are far better ships than the diminutive *Invincible* class that they replace.

Their Design

The *Queen Elizabeth* class carriers were built in blocks constructed by BAE Systems at Govan, Scotstoun and Portsmouth; Babcock at Rosyth and Appledore; Cammell laird at Birkenhead and A & P on the Tyne.[43] The sections were taken to Rosyth on lighters and assembled in Number 1 dock which had originally been built in 1916 and was just large enough after its entrance was widened from 124ft to 138ft and the sides re-profiled with the removal of steps to make the dock floor 30ft wider. The ships' two island structures contain the exhausts from widely separated machinery spaces and both ships have all-electric propulsion with power provided by two Rolls-Royce MT-30 gas turbine alternators, each developing 36 MW and four Wartsila auxiliary diesel generators, each developing 7 MW.[44] A number of emergency 2 MW diesel generators are fitted throughout the ship to provide power if the main machinery is damaged. Two shafts are each driven by 30 MW electric motors, giving the ship a design maximum speed of 26 knots, about a knot slower than the nuclear plant in *Charles de Gaulle* but considerably slower than the 30+ knots of a *Nimitz* class CVN. The motors are situated in the after part of lower block 04, fairly well aft to minimise the length of the shafts since, surprisingly, these ships are not fitted with azimuth thruster pods like other new electric warships in order to save cost. An economical cruising speed of 15 knots gives an endurance of 10,000nm and the design allows for the ships to operate at maximum intensity for seven days without needing to replenish at sea. All machinery is controlled by an integrated platform management system which, together with the operations room, navigation and flight planning areas, uses open architecture systems to allow continual upgrades to be applied. The completed ships are 932ft long with a waterline beam of 128ft and a width across the flight deck of 239ft. The planned ship's company is only 679, which compares very favourably with 4660 in the larger *Gerald R Ford*. An embarked air group will raise this figure by up to another 1000 with room for more in austere conditions. The flight deck and hangar are the largest ever built into a British carrier (which makes it even more frustrating that the types of fixed-wing aircraft that can be embarked is so limited). Like CVA-01, they are designed to operate a 'standard' air group of up to thirty-six strike fighters plus helicopters but in 2015 it appears that they will operate with a small air group of about six Lightning IIs and six Merlin HM 2/Crowsnest helicopters at any one time, a force that will be only just sufficient to maintain operational proficiency. One piece of good news was announced in 2014; this was the statement by the UK Prime Minister, David Cameron, that both ships will be taken into service by the RN. There had been some doubt after the SDSR in 2010 that one might be put into long-term reserve or even sold and only one operated. Operating both means that at least one will always be operational with the other replacing it when necessary, operating as an LPH or refitting as necessary.

Into the Future
It will be clear from my earlier comments that I think this project could have been managed more cheaply, expeditiously and effectively. Far more use could have been made of the wealth of UK carrier design experience and other very effective

options could have given the RN an effective strike fighter capability by 2012 without having to wait until 2020. Both the Boeing F/A-18E/F Super Hornet and Dassault Rafale M would have been effective and affordable and were available 'off the shelf' with the possibility of shared training and logistical support, retaining the possibility of procuring the F-35C after 2020 when its development was completed. Within a few months of the announcement of the SDSR in 2010, the Government elected to launch air strikes against dissident forces in Libya who opposed what was thought to be an emerging democratic regime. USMC Harriers from the LHD *Kearsarge* and French Rafales from *Charles de Gaulle* were able to react quickly from positions off the coast to engage targets of opportunity and fly multiple sorties in a single day. The RAF was forced to fly long-range sorties from the UK at first and later from bases in Italy, with air-to-air refuelled Typhoons that could not react quickly enough to attack time-sensitive targets. The Government must have wished that it could have reversed its hasty decision to scrap *Ark Royal*, which would have offered the ideal flexible capability with Joint Force Harriers embarked, but by then it was too late. At least the helicopter carrier *Ocean* with Army Air Corps Apache 'gunship' helicopters embarked was able to show glimpses of what a UK strike carrier could have achieved if one had been available. Whatever their convoluted procurement background, the *Queen Elizabeth* class will give the UK

Prince of Wales under construction in Number 1 Dock at Rosyth in 2015. This view of the incomplete ship shows the tiny gap between the sides of her hull and the dock walls to good effect. (Crown Copyright)

a flexible strike capability for as much as fifty years to come, well into the 2060s. Properly handled, they have the potential to become outstanding national assets. Once the design was settled, their actual construction in Rosyth has been a major engineering achievement, of which the nation should be justly proud.

A British F-35B Lightning II of the Joint Lightning Force at Eglin Air Force base in the USA where pilots and technicians were initially trained. Note the open weapons bay doors with attachment points for an AMRAAM missile on the inboard one. (Crown Copyright)

21 Reflections

Despite the massive run-down in the number of ships and the manpower crisis that followed the end of the Second World War, the RN carrier strike force maintained a viable capability that was emphatically demonstrated throughout three years of war in Korea. Carrier-borne aircraft were in action within days of the conflict's outbreak, immediately ready without having to wait for logistic support to be built up, aircrew to be trained in deck landing or technicians taught how to live in a ship and operate it. They could have been switched at short notice to operate in defence of Hong Kong, Okinawa or other Allied interests if required and their continued presence showed the US Navy that it did not have to fight alone. The conflict underlined the ability of the British and Commonwealth forces to work seamlessly together and as part of a coalition with the USA and other allies. Flexible methods of maintenance evolved from the need to keep aircraft serviceable for extended periods of embarked operation and a generation of pilots learnt realistic combat techniques and tactics. There were good reasons why the Admiralty took time to introduce jet fighters but piston-engined strike aircraft continued to be affordable and effective into the early 1950s. Contrary to the views expressed by many experts, nuclear weapons had not made navies obsolete and conventional forces, including carriers and their aircraft, clearly continued to have a most important part to play in the full spectrum of modern warfare. Conflict in Korea and a number of other theatres underlined the lessons, first learnt in the Second World War, that RN would have to fight air forces and armies in defence of the UK's national interest, often having to do so alone when no other British forces were available.

When jets were introduced, changes had to be made in the way carriers operated their aircraft and the RN led the world in designing and producing ships with innovative features such as the angled deck. However, the Government decision to miss out a generation of aircraft to save money prior to what were expected to be the years in which there would be the maximum danger of conflict in the late 1950s proved to be a dangerous failure that actually led to the retention of obsolescent airframe designs that had been bright ideas over a decade earlier but were no longer the best available. The inability of the Ministry of Supply and the run-down British aircraft industry give due importance to naval requirements or to progress designs quickly didn't help either and compared unfavourably with American aircraft projects such as the F-4H Phantom II. There was also a political tendency to assume that because both the RN and RAF both flew aircraft, they must have similar requirements. In fact they operate their aircraft in very different ways and there is much greater synergy between allied navies than there ever has been between air forces and navies. Naval air squadrons thrive on the mobility of the weapons system of which they form part, the carrier task force, meeting and overcoming a range of threats as wide as warfare itself. Air Force squadrons generally spend long periods operating from fixed bases from which they cannot, quickly, be moved and this may be ideal for static defence such as the air defence of UK bases or as a contribution to NATO forces in Germany. This is a good thing if long-term static defence is what the Government requires; it is not good if the Government wants rapid reaction forces capable of going into action immediately after they arrive at a crisis-point. Air Force squadrons also tend to be deeply specialised in specific roles, as we saw with the arguments over the Hawker P 1154, whereas naval aircraft and air crew have to be trained and capable of carrying out a variety of tasks. In my experience many RAF aircrew have enjoyed the experience of exchange appointments with naval air squadrons and have adopted a wider and more balanced outlook afterwards; the reverse is not always the case.

I hope that having nearly finished this book you will, by now, have a better understanding of the unique and vital role that aircraft carriers and naval aircraft have played in the UK's defence and of the shallowness of the arguments that have been levelled against them. They have frequently proved to be the only option open to a British Government that is desperately seeking ways to resolve a crisis of national defence but they have also played their part in humanitarian operations around the world and will, no doubt, continue to do so. They should be recognised as an important part of an inter-locking national system of defence and politicians should ask themselves why the Air Staff has consistently and deliberately objected to procuring aircraft that could be operated from a ship, as proposed by Field Marshal Festing in his study into tactical British air power. Spending the taxpayers' money to remove carrier operating equipment from the F-4 Phantom which could otherwise have been operated in a reinforcement role or as part of a joint force is but one of a number of cases in point. Reviews have invariably focused on specific aspects of defence and have often failed to comprehend the wide range of capabilities that aircraft carriers offer as 'floating bases' or 'sovereign territory' that is difficult for an enemy to attack or even locate. Perhaps their true capabilities are just too wide-ranging for inexpert politicians to comprehend. It is noticeable that RAF attempts to limit the existence of the RN carrier force only became really intense after the decision taken in 1963 to remove the nuclear deterrent from Bomber Command and replace it with the submarine-launched Polaris missile system. Much of the argument since then can be seen as the RAF struggling to preserve not only its independence as something other than a support arm to the other two Services, but its very survival. It is certainly no longer the independent force that it was originally created to be. Fortunately the Army Air Corps has learnt the lesson and is, in 2015, an enthusiastic supporter of joint carrier-based operations.

Aircraft carriers are widely seen as expensive platforms to build, although successive governments have made them much more so than they should have been. The series of studies after 1966 that looked at ways of creating a Navy without aircraft carriers found that attempting to do so was even more expensive and much less effective. It took time for some senior officers to realise that advances in technology had made every aspect of defence expensive, not just aircraft carriers. At least the initial cost of a carrier can be amortised over a fifty-year life span. Temporary bases built up to operate land-based aircraft like the Typhoon cannot and may even have to be abandoned after the operation for which they were built and equipped is over. Readers will, I hope, have deduced that I consider that the cancellation of CVA-01, the earlier *Queen Elizabeth*, in 1966 by a government that clearly had little idea of the damage it was doing to the Navy, the Nation and its shipbuilding industry was the most traumatic shock of this period, from which it took decades for the RN to recover, if indeed it can be said to have fully done so. In 1982 a later Government did everything that the 1966 Review had said would never happen again; it carried out an opposed, amphibious landing at a great distance from the UK without allies. Fortunately, there were still carrier-borne fighters to support the UK's liberation of the Falkland Islands and their dependencies, flown by well-trained pilots who believed wholeheartedly in what they were doing. After the 2010 Review there would not have been.

Looking back on the carrier replacement crisis of 1966, it is clear that there were three principal factors at work and these combined to make a lethal combination. First, the failure of successive Governments to order a new carrier for two decades after 1946 meant that that a growing number of replacements would eventually come to form an expensive 'bow wave' of new construction cost towards the end of the long-term planning period; exactly what was predicted for the late 1960s. If one carrier per decade had been built, expenditure would have been more even, with no 'bow wave'. As we now know, new construction would actually have been cheaper than the modernisations of *Victorious*, *Eagle* and *Ark Royal*. The second factor, not appreciated at the time, was that the naval staff actually precipitated the crisis to a certain extent by arguing retirement dates for its existing carriers that were up to a decade earlier than was strictly necessary. There was little of the original hull left in the modernised *Victorious* and she had been rebuilt from the hangar deck upwards with new boilers and re-fitted turbines. The US Navy would certainly have planned to run her on until 1980 at least and there is no reason why the RN should not have done so. *Vengeance*, the last of the 1942 light fleet carriers, was only withdrawn from service by the Brazilian Navy in 2001 when she was fifty-six years old, albeit extensively modernised. *Hermes*, the last of the 1943 light fleet carriers is to be withdrawn from service by the Indian Navy in 2016, fifty-seven years after her completion, so she could certainly have served effectively for a longer period in the RN. The failure of governments to order new ships was surprising in view of the many successful operations described earlier but can largely be ascribed to a lack of ministerial understanding of their true worth. The demand for the existing ships early replacement proved to be extremely unhelpful but was based on the contemporary belief that systems needed rapid replacement to reflect advances in technology and the perceived Soviet threat. The senior members of the naval staff had started their careers flying aircraft such as the Swordfish and Seafire and were already talking about the supersonic aircraft that would replace the Buccaneer. They could hardly have realised that airframe and warship technology was about to reach a plateau with systems remaining in service for decades in many instances. The big strides would be made in electronics but these did not, necessarily affect platforms themselves. The pernicious impact of air staff arguments against naval aviation during this period made the replacement situation worse and this is not a period of its history in which the RAF can take pride. The third factor was the poor state of the British economy in the mid-1960s and this was something over which the naval staff had no control. It is at least arguable, however, that big orders for technologically advanced warships on the Clyde would have given a major boost to the regional economy and could have encouraged export orders for a variety of ships. Unfortunately, we will never know.

One of the interesting trends that emerged during this period was the broadening capability of amphibious helicopter carriers to 'cross-over' between capabilities. The light fleet carrier conversions *Bulwark* and *Albion* had all their fixed-wing facilities removed and could only operate as helicopter carriers. Captain D B Law RN of *Bulwark* thought these large ships were under-utilised, however, and could do much more. He reported on trials carried out in his ship with P 1127 STOVL prototype aircraft during March 1966, only days after the cancellation of CVA-01, and recommended their use as close air support fighters to support the commandos once they were ashore. His work pre-dated the US Marine Corps decision to operate P 1127 derivatives from amphibious helicopter carriers by more than five years but, at the time, there was little appetite in the UK's MOD for carrier-borne fighters and the concept was not taken forward in Great Britain for some years. The idea of getting the most from these large hulls was gradually recognised, thankfully, and both *Albion* and *Bulwark* eventually embarked anti-submarine Sea Kings as well as assault Wessex helicopters. *Hermes* took the concept a stage further by embarking a Sea Harrier squadron as well as anti-submarine and assault helicopters. *Ocean* was, arguably, a retrograde step in that she could only operate assault helicopters and, for short periods, ASaC Sea Kings. She lacks the facilities to support anti-submarine operations. In the USN today, amphibious assault carriers are able to modify their air groups to embark either a mixed assault air group with MV-22 Osprey tilt-rotors, helicopters and some STOVL fighters or, alternatively, up to twenty-two F-35Bs, giving them a strike potential second only to a CVN or, if she is able to reach her full embarked potential, *Queen Elizabeth*. The *Queen Elizabeth* class has an impressive 'cross-over' capability and is capable of embarking STOVL strike fighters, ASaC, anti-submarine and assault helicopters in a tailored air group, if necessary all operating concurrently with appropriate command, control and communications facilities built into the ship's open architecture systems. If only they had been built with catapults and arrester wires they would have had capabilities that could fairly be described as outstanding with the ability to operate the widest range of British and Allied tactical aircraft and helicopters and to support them for prolonged periods anywhere on the oceans that cover 70 per cent of the earth's surface.

What would I have done? Argued immediately after SDR for a big-deck carrier of about 60,000 tons, a parallel deck, two C-13 steam catapults and Mark 7 arrester gear to be taken forward by a dynamic chief executive, an admiral with carrier experience and attitude, able to fight for what he wanted. The air group could have comprised F/A-18E/F Super Hornets, E-2C Hawkeyes and AgustaWestland Merlins in naval air squadrons with training and support for the first two types shared with the USN. I believe that apart from being more effective than the ships and aircraft we have procured, such a scheme would have avoided decades of unnecessary studies into concepts that were not taken forward and would have proved cheaper both to implement and to deploy. Versions of the F-35 would still have been options in the longer term after full development had reduced their unit cost considerably and improved reliability.

As I was finishing this chapter I noticed a newspaper headline that quoted several retired officers as saying that the F-35 version being procured for the RN should be known as the Sea Lightning, presumably to distinguish them from the RAF version. Possibly they have missed the point that there is actually no physical difference between them and UK F-35Bs are being procured from the outset as joint aircraft for a Joint Lightning II Force. They are not intended to form a naval air squadron and 17 (Reserve) Squadron, which has recently been formed at Edwards Air Force Base in California, has manpower which comprises 50 per cent RN and 50 per cent RAF. The first commanding officer is a Wing Commander RAF but he will in due course be replaced by a Commander RN or Lieutenant Colonel RM and the two Services will rotate command throughout the life of the unit. The same thing will apply to 617 Squadron which will be a joint-manned unit and so will 809 Squadron. It remains to be seen how effective these joint units will be, and Joint Force Harrier certainly gave no cause for complacency, but we are committed. Given the way the Lightning is procured and operated, I do not see the benefit of giving some aircraft within a joint unit a different name. 'Jointery' may not be the way forward I would have chosen but, in 2015, it is the one to which the RN and its Fleet Air Arm are committed and those involved are trying to make the best of it and, surely, a name change will not help them. The name Lightning II has been accepted internationally and may well achieve a considerable allied synergy as it becomes operational and for this reason, too, I do not really see a positive reason for the expense and complication of a name change. This leads me on to my last point. *Queen Elizabeth*, *Prince of Wales* and their embarked squadrons of Lightning II strike fighters and Merlin HM 2/Crowsnest helicopters represent a new and exciting era for British aircraft carrier aviation after 2020. It will be a joint future, however, that will not simply replicate the method of operation that worked so well in the past. RAF elements of joint units and both RAF and AAC helicopters will have as big a part to play as the RN elements of joint units and helicopter squadrons. I would hope that the Fleet Air Arm, at home in the sea environment, will act as the arbiter of 'best practice' and 'sea standards' and that their joint colleagues will appreciate that they will always have high standards to maintain if they are to live up to the outstanding achievements of the Royal Navy's aircraft carrier strike fleet after 1945. We shall see.

Notes

Chapter 1: Manpower, Fleets and Changes

1. Statement of the First Lord of the Admiralty, Explanatory, of the Navy Estimates 1947-48 (London: HMSO), Command 7054, p 5.
2. Ibid.
3. Bringing the combined total number of mines swept by British Empire minesweepers since September 1939 to 34,600.
4. Explanatory Statement 1947-48, p 6.
5. CB 03164 Progress in Naval Aviation Summary #1, year ending 1 December 1947, Directorate of Naval Air Warfare (London: Admiralty, April 1948), p 18.
6. Ibid, p 17.
7. Ibid, p 18.
8. Significantly, CB 03164 Progress in Naval Aviation from which part of the material for this chapter was derived has, inside its front cover, the statement that 'this book is intended for the use of the recipients but may in certain cases be communicated to persons in HM Service not below the rank of commissioned officer'. It could not, therefore, have been seen by rating pilots.
9. CB 03164(48) Progress in Naval Aviation Summary #2, year ending 1 December 1948, Directorate of Naval Air Warfare (London: Admiralty, May 1949), p 15.
10. A small number of air engineer officers qualified as pilots; after a front-line tour many of them became maintenance test pilots and even those who did not produced a wider knowledge of flying matters in the technical community and of maintenance among other pilots.
11. CB 03164 Progress in Naval Aviation Summary #1, p 4.
12. CB 03164(49) Progress in Naval Aviation Summary #3, year ending 31 December 1949, Directorate of Naval Air Warfare (London: Admiralty, April 1950), p 10.
13. Ibid, p 5.
14. CB 03164 *Progress in Naval Aviation #2*, p 5.
15. CB 03164(49) *Progress in Naval Aviation #3*, p 18.
16. David Hobbs, *British Aircraft Carriers* (Barnsley: Seaforth Publishing, 2013), contains details of all British carriers, their design, construction, modification and operational service.
17. David Hobbs, *Aircraft of the Royal Navy since 1945* (Liskeard: Maritime Books, 1982), p 95.
18. Ray Sturtivant, Mick Burrow and Lee Howard, *Fleet Air Arm Fixed-Wing Aircraft since 1946* (Tonbridge: Air Britain (Historians), 2004), p 301.
19. CB 3053(11) Naval Aircraft Progress & Operations Periodical Summary No. 11 - Period Ended 30 June 1945, p 17.
20. Tony Buttler, *STURGEON – Target-Tug Extraordinary* (Ringshall: Ad Hoc Publications, 2009).
21. Captain Eric Brown CBE DSC AFC RN, *FIREBRAND – From the Cockpit 8* (Ringshall: Ad Hoc Publications, 2008), p 25.
22. David Hobbs, *A Century of Carrier Aviation* (Barnsley: Seaforth Publishing, 2009), p 186.
23. Ray Sturtivant and Theo Ballance, *The Squadrons of the Fleet Air Arm* (Tonbridge: Air Britain (Historians), 1994), p 166.
24. Alan J Leahy, *SEA HORNET – From the Cockpit 5* (Ringshall: Ad Hoc Publications, 2007), pp 9 et seq.
25. Owen Thetford, *British Naval Aircraft Since 1912* (London: Putnam, 1962), p 91.
26. Hobbs, *Aircraft of the Royal Navy Since 1945*, p 14.
27. Sturtivant, Burrow and Howard, *Fleet Air Arm Fixed-Wing Aircraft since 1946*, pp 124 et seq.
28. The Sea Fury was the naval variant of the Hawker Fury intended for service with the RAF. To avoid confusion over mark numbers, therefore, the naval versions began with the Mark 10, followed by the Mark 11. RAF versions were to have been designated the F 1, FB2 etc but in the event all

were cancelled and only the naval variant built. Similar logic led to the RN Sea Hornet versions beginning with the F 20 and the Sea Vampire jet with the F 20.

29. Hobbs, *Aircraft of the Royal Navy Since 1945*, p 34.
30. Alan J Leahy, *SEA FURY – From the Cockpit 12* (Ringshall: Ad Hoc Publications, 2010), p 13.
31. Thetford, *British Naval Aircraft Since 1912*, pp 156 et seq.
32. J G S 'Joe' Norman, *FIREFLY – From the Cockpit 4* (Ringshall: Ad Hoc Publications, 2007), p 7.
33. Hobbs, *Aircraft of the Royal Navy Since 1945*, p 26.
34. The British system of allocating mark numbers changed from Roman numerals to Arabic in 1947. Confusingly, therefore, the last Merlin-engined Seafires were designated the Mark III and the Mark XV which replaced it was re-designated the Mark 15.
35. Captain Eric Brown CBE DSC AFC RN, *SEAFIRE – From the Cockpit 13* (Ringshall: Ad Hoc Publications, 2010), p 49.
36. Graeme Rowan-Thomson, *ATTACKER – From the Cockpit 9* (Ringshall: Ad Hoc Publications, 2008), p 12.
37. CB 03164 Progress in Naval Aviation Summary #1, p 21.
38. Ibid, p 21.
39. Ibid.
40. Ibid, p 23.
41. Ibid, p 10.
42. Geoff Wakeham, *Royal Naval Air Station CULDROSE 1947-1997* (RNAS Culdrose, 1997), p 10.
43. CB 03164(49) Progress in Naval Aviation #3, p 9.
44. Hall replaced A V Alexander who became Minister of Defence. Interestingly, unlike his predecessor, Hall was not made a Cabinet member although his own successor, Lord Pakenham, was.
45. Statement of the First Lord of the Admiralty, Explanatory, of the Navy Estimates 1947-48 (London: HMSO, 1947), p 2.
46. Statement of the First Lord of the Admiralty, Explanatory, of the Navy Estimates 1948-49 (London: HMSO, 1948), p 5.
47. Douglas Morris, *Cruisers of the Royal and Commonwealth Navies* (Liskeard: Maritime Books, 1987), p 199.
48. Eric Grove, *Vanguard to Trident* (London: The Bodley Head, 1987), pp 128 et seq.
49. Naval Historical Branch, *The Royal Navy – Incidents since 1945, Notes of HM Ships Involved* (London: Ministry of Defence, 1963).

Chapter 2 – The Korean War
1. David Hobbs, 'Inter-Allied Communication during the Korean War' in David Stevens (ed.), *Naval Networks: The Dominance of Communications in Maritime Operations* (Canberra: Sea Power Centre – Australia, 2012), pp 169 et seq.
2. The Soviet delegate, Mr Malik, was not present because he had boycotted the Council since January 1950. The Yugoslav delegate abstained from voting.
3. BR 1736 (34), Naval Staff History, British Commonwealth Naval Operations Korea 1950-53 (London: Admiralty, 1967), pp 1 et seq.
4. Hobbs, 'Inter-Allied Communication', p 170.
5. Now preserved by the Imperial War Museum on the Thames in London near Tower Bridge.
6. FO2FES, Report of Proceedings in Korea #1, preserved in the National Archives at Kew and quoted in the Naval Staff History. This was the first in a series of sixty-two detailed and informative accounts written by three successive Flag Officers.
7. Admiralty Signal 281702A June 1950.
8. Norman Polmar, *Aircraft Carriers* (London: Macdonald & Co, Publishers, 1969), pp 523 et seq.
9. Interrogation Friend or Foe; a system which allowed aircraft to transmit coded signals when detected by friendly radar, thus showing themselves to be friendly. Land-based RAF and USAF aircrews over the decades have shown themselves to be forgetful about turning it on, hence their interception by fighters when approaching fleets.
10. FO2 FES ROP #1.
11. I was once told by a former member of 800 NAS that the USAF B-29 squadrons had been briefed at Guam that the only aircraft in the war zone with 'in-line' piston engines were communist Yak-9 fighters but I have never found this confirmed in a written report. If true, the briefing authority clearly forgot, or never troubled to find out, about RN Seafires and Fireflies, not to mention USAF Mustangs.

12. John R P Lansdown, *With the Carriers in Korea 1950-53, the Fleet Air Arm Story* (Worcester: Square One Publications, 1992), p 36.
13. More detailed light fleet carrier histories can be found in my book *British Aircraft Carriers*, Chapter 20.
14. Awarded annually for the most outstanding feat of naval aviation, the Trophy was instituted by Admiral Sir Denis Boyd who had been the captain of HMS *Illustrious* during her aircrafts' attack on the Italian fleet in Taranto in 1940 and subsequently the second C-in-C of the BPF. Until his death in 1965, Admiral Boyd presented the Trophy, a silver model of a Swordfish aircraft, in person whenever possible.
15. Confusingly two ships named *Bataan* operated off Korea, the USN CVL and HMAS *Bataan*, an Australian destroyer.
16. The majority of which exploded when hit!
17. David Hobbs, 'HMAS *Sydney* III – A symbol of Australia's growing maritime capability' in David Stevens and John Reeve (eds), *The Navy and the Nation* (Crow's Nest NSW: Allen & Unwin, 2005), p 223.
18. David Hobbs, *Aircraft Carriers of the Royal and Commonwealth Navies* (London: Greenhill Books, 1996), p 101.
19. The Carrier Air Group system had ended in the RN during February 1952 and after that squadrons embarked in carriers as individual units under the line authority of the ship's Commander 'Air'.
20. Neil McCart, *HMS GLORY 1945-1961* (Liskeard: Maritime Books, 2002), p 84.
21. I served under Captain 'Pug' Mather in the Director General Aircraft (Naval) Department in 1979.
22. Hobbs, *British Aircraft Carriers*, p 233.
23. These lessons are taken from 'A Report of Operations in Korea' in *Flight Deck – The Quarterly Journal of Naval Aviation* published by the Naval Air Warfare Division of the Admiralty, Winter 1952 edition. It was written by Major B P W Clapin DFC RE who commanded Number 67 Carrier-Borne Ground Liaison Section in HMS *Glory*.
24. Lieutenant P Carmichael RN, 'Korean Diary', *Flight Deck* (Spring 1953), p 29.
25. David Hobbs, *Moving Bases – Royal Navy Maintenance Carriers and MONABS* (Liskeard: Maritime Books, 2007), p 58.
26. David Hobbs, *'C' Class Destroyers* (Liskeard: Maritime Books, 2012), p 117.
27. David Hobbs, 'Korean Warriors', *Aircraft* (October 2011), p 35.
28. The Army Air Corps was not formed until 1957.
29. Hobbs, *'C' Class Destroyers*, p 127.
30. David Hobbs, 'British Commonwealth Carrier Operations in the Korean War', *USAF Air and Space Power Journal* (Winter 2004), p 68.
31. Following the stipulations of the 'Morrow Board' in 1925 which stated only aviators could command aircraft carriers and naval air stations ashore. Furthermore, only admirals qualified as aviators could command carrier task forces. This rule encouraged a number of 'mature' naval officers including Reeves and Halsey to become aviators so that they could take command.
32. David Hobbs, 'British Commonwealth Carrier Operations in the Korean War' in Jacob Neufeld and George M Watson Jr (eds), *Coalition Air Warfare in the Korean War* (Andrews AFB, Maryland: USAF Historical Foundation, 2002), pp 154 et seq.
33. F W Cagle and F Manson, *The Sea War in Korea* (Annapolis: Naval Institute Press, 1957).
34. Naval Staff History, p 31.
35. FO2FE/2960/11 of 19 January 1951 quoted in the Naval Staff History, p 324.

Chapter 3 – Assistance for Commonwealth Navies

1. J D F Kealy and E C Russell, *A History of Canadian Naval Aviation* (Ottawa: Naval Historical Section, Canadian Forces Headquarters, 1965), p 35.
2. After the war she was returned to the USN in 'as lying' condition, sold to a Dutch shipyard in 1947 and rebuilt as a merchant ship. She was eventually broken up for scrap in Taiwan in 1977.
3. Kealy and Russell, *A History of Canadian Naval Aviation*, p 36.
4. Leo Pettipas, *The Supermarine Seafire in the Royal Canadian Navy* (Winnipeg Chapter of the Canadian Naval Air Group, 1987).
5. Ibid, p 33.
6. David Stevens and John Reeve (eds), *The Navy and the Nation* (Crow's Nest, NSW: Allen & Unwin, 2005), pp 211 et seq.
7. Letter from Admiral Sir Louis Hamilton to the First Sea Lord, Admiral Sir John Cunningham dated

18 March 1947 held in the Sea Power Centre – Australia, a copy of which is in the author's archive.

8. A Wright, 'Australian Aircraft Carrier Decisions', *Papers in Australian Maritime Affairs Number 4* (Canberra: Maritime Studies programme, 1998).
9. Stevens and Reeve (eds), *The Navy and the Nation*, p 212.
10. J Goldrick, T R Frame and P D Jones, *Reflections on the Royal Australian Navy* (Kenthurst: Kangaroo Press, 1991), pp 225 et seq.
11. Later Admiral Sir Victor Smith AC KBE CB DSC RAN.
12. Details of all the aircraft carriers operated by Canada and Australia are contained in my book *British Aircraft Carriers*.
13. Which, in the end, was not adopted but only after a considerable amount of development effort had been devoted to it.
14. Studied with the benefit of hindsight, the Australian carrier procurement has remarkable synergy with the views expressed by critics about the UK's *Queen Elizabeth* class carrier project in the twenty-first century.
15. Stevens and Reeve (eds), *The Navy and the Nation*, p 216.
16. Agenda Item 5/1947 for the Council of Defence meeting held on 3 July 1947 with comments by Admiral Sir Louis Hamilton to the RN First Sea Lord, Admiral Sir John Cunningham in the Archive of the Naval Historical Society of Australia with a copy in the author's archive.
17. Both squadrons had served in HMS *Ocean* prior to disbanding in July 1948 and their re-commissioning followed the normal RN sequence providing the squadrons for a newly-commissioned carrier. The original choice of numbers for the first RCN squadrons have followed the same pattern
18. 'A Survey of Naval Aviation in Australia', *Flight Deck* (Winter 1952), p 9.
19. Hobbs, *British Aircraft Carriers*, p 209.
20. Vince Fazio, *RAN Aircraft Carriers* (Sydney: The Naval Historical Society of Australia, 1997), p 39.
21. In order, the first two were HMS *Ark Royal* in February 1955 and the USS *Forrestal* in October 1955.
22. Colin Jones, *Wings and the Navy 1947-1953* (Kenthurst: Kangaroo Press, Kenthurst, 1997), pp 62 et seq.
23. Hobbs, *British Aircraft Carriers*, p 350.

Chapter 4 – Invention, Innovation, New Aircraft and Rebuilt Ships

1. *Flight Deck* (August 1944), p 1.
2. *Flight Deck* (Winter 1952), p 2.
3. Ibid, p 4.
4. Ibid, p 5.
5. Air-intercept radar fitted in the aircraft.
6. Two-seat, rather than single-seat, radar-equipped night fighters had been chosen after the trials carried out in *Ocean* during 1946.
7. The rocket-powered Saunders-Roe SR 177, described in a later chapter, was the manifestation of this consideration.
8. At high throttle settings the early jets accelerated reasonably quickly but at the lower throttle setting commonly used on finals it could take ten seconds or more for the engine to wind up sufficiently to make a safe climb-away. Worse, slamming the throttle forward could flood too much fuel into the burners and cause the engine to flame out. At high level it could be relit by the pilot pressing the igniter button on the throttle but at circuit height there was insufficient height to do so.
9. Hobbs, *A Century of Carrier Aviation*, pp 195 et seq.
10. US Naval Air Material Centre, 'Rubber Carrier Decks may be on the Way', Confidential report (November 1952), passim.
11. The engine had to be shut down so that the aircraft could be lifted safely by the crane and, without the engine running, hydraulic services had to be actuated by a hand pump.
12. US Naval Air Material Centre, 'Rubber Carrier Decks may be on the Way'.
13. Captain D R F Campbell DSC RN, 'The Angled Deck, A brief Review of its significance', *Flight Deck* (Summer 1953), pp 10 et seq.
14. One of the conditions of the wartime Lend-Lease Agreement was that the UK would keep the USA advised of all naval and military developments for two decades after the end of the Second World War. Angled decks, steam catapults, mirror landing aids, the rubber deck and gyro-gunsights for fighters were just a few of the 'reverse Lend-Lease' items from which the USN benefitted.

15. Hobbs, *A Century of Carrier Aviation*, p 204.
16. On high-performance aircraft these were often inside the wheel wells so that they did not obtrude into the airflow in normal flight to cause extra drag.
17. Hence the name slotted-cylinder catapult. The more common name, 'steam catapult', is not strictly accurate since, in theory, any convenient high-pressure gas such as slow-burning cordite or compressed air could be used. In 1951 steam was the most convenient gas in a steam-powered warship.
18. Hobbs, *Moving Bases*, pp 78–80.
19. Of interest, the RN gave its dead loads names such as 'Flossy' and 'Noah'; the USN gave its dead loads serial numbers such as 207698.
20. Hobbs, *A Century of Carrier Aviation*, pp 206 et seq.
21. This was *Indomitable*'s last period at sea. After the trial she paid off into unmaintained reserve.
22. CB 03164(52), Progress in Naval Aviation, Summary #6 (London: Admiralty, December 1952), p 13.
23. Which was to become the Scimitar F1. After protracted development caused by the outdated British procurement system and an inadequate number of prototypes, the type did not equip a front-line squadron until 1958.
24. Roger Lindsay, *de Havilland Venom* (Stockton-on-Tees: privately published, 1974), pp 10 et seq.
25. To meet the RN requirement, the DH110 eventually had to undergo a 90 per cent re-design and probably absorbed as much, if not more, effort than the DH116 would have done.
26. During the mid-1950s de Havilland worked on projects as diverse as jet engines, the Comet, Trident and DH125 commercial aircraft, the DH110, the 'Blue Streak' ICBM and the Firestreak air-to-air missile.
27. A similar helicopter, the Bristol Type 171, eventually did see service in the transport role with the RAF as the Belvedere but the Type 173 for the RN was cancelled in 1957.
28. Of interest, the USN was sufficiently impressed by the RN system to adopt it and USN surveillance aircraft, such as the E-2D Hawkeye in 2015, fly with specialist observers in the rear seats.
29. CB 03164(52), Progress in Naval Aviation, Summary #6, p 15.
30. The new Soviet *Sverdlov* class cruisers were the intended targets.
31. CB 03164, Progress of the Fleet Air Arm, Summary #8 (London: Admiralty, June 1956), p 15.
32. The RAF planned to fit Red Dean to the advanced, thin-wing, development of the Gloster Javelin but when this was cancelled in 1957, they too cancelled the missile.
33. CB 03164, Progress in Naval Aviation, Summary #6, p 18.
34. Range at this speed was about 2000 yards, although the exact distance depended on the state of the torpedo's battery when high speed was activated.
35. Hobbs, *British Aircraft Carriers*, pp 267 et seq.
36. Her modernisation is fully described in Hobbs, *British Aircraft Carriers*.

Chapter 5 – 'Cold War', NATO and the Middle East

1. Norman Friedman, *The Postwar Naval Revolution* (London: Conway Maritime Press, 1986), pp 9 et seq.
2. In late August 1945 the USA had only three atomic bombs left; of the first production batch one was expended in a test at Alamogordo and two dropped on Japan.
3. Eric J Grove, *Vanguard to Trident* (London: The Bodley Head, 1987), pp 38 et seq.
4. A V Alexander, Cabinet Defence Committee DO948)1, CAB131/6 in The National Archives, quoted in Grove, *Vanguard to Trident*, p 39.
5. Friedman, *The Postwar Naval Revolution*, p 14. UK GDP was about $35 billion compared with the US $258 billion. In real terms, the UK spent about $3.6 billion on defence in 1948 compared with about $9.75 billion by the USA.
6. Grove, *Vanguard to Trident*, pp 51 et seq.
7. Sturtivant, Burrow and Howard, *Fleet Air Arm Fixed-Wing Aircraft since 1946*, p 562.
8. Admiral Sir Rhoderick McGrigor, Field Marshall Sir William 'Bill' Slim and Marshal of the Royal Air Force Sir John Slessor.
9. Grove, *Vanguard to Trident*, p 83.
10. Friedman, *The Postwar Naval Revolution*, p 10. Friedman points out that the Polaris missile was developed on the basis of a prediction that a suitably-sized warhead could be produced by 1963.
11. Statement of the First Lord of the Admiralty Explanatory of the Navy Estimates 1954-55, Admiralty, London, February 1954, p 6.

12. Eventually sold to India and re-named *Vikrant*.
13. Used as a floating store, canteen and workshop near *Victorious* during her eight-year modernisation and eventually scrapped without ever having been completed. Her boilers and turbines were removed to replace the units damaged by fire in *Karel Doorman* in the early 1960s.
14. *Jane's Fighting Ships*, 1954-55 Edition (London: Sampson Low Marston & Co, 1954), p 305
15. The maximum effective range of the RN's 4.5in guns with a Mark 6 director against aircraft was 7000 yards. The maximum effective range of the Soviet 3.9in guns would have been similar. Using radar-ranging on the target, a toss-bombing attack aircraft such as the Buccaneer would release its bombs whilst pulling into a high-G climb that would difficult to track at about 9000 yards. The circular error of probability with this form of attack was about 50 yards so an attack along the line of ship with a group of bombs was likely to obtain a hit or hits without the aircraft entering the maximum effective range of the target's guns for more than a few seconds.
16. *Jane's Fighting Ships*, 1961-62 Edition (London: Samson Low, Marston & Co, 1961), p 411.
17. NATO intelligence officers found Russian names difficult to pronounce and so they allocated reporting names that were easier to say. The first letter gave a an indication of the type of aircraft. 'B' was allocated to bombers and 'F' to fighters. Different versions were given an identifying letter; for instance 'Badger A' was the medium bomber used by the Soviet Air Force and 'Badger B' the anti-shipping variant used by the shore-based Soviet Naval Air Arm.
18. William Green, *The World's Fighting Planes* (London: Macdonald, 1964), pp 62–5.
19. Ibid, pp 65–7.
20. *Flight Deck* (Winter 1952), pp 25 et seq.
21. An Admiral of the Fleet in the Royal Navy in addition to his Norwegian titles and honours.
22. *Flight Deck* (Spring 1953), pp 36–7.
23. Robert Jackson, *Suez 1956 – Operation Musketeer* (London: Ian Allen, 1980), p 9.
24. Grove, *Vanguard to Trident*, p 160.
25. Jackson, *Suez 1956*, p 9.
26. Royal Naval Historical Branch, The Royal Navy – Incidents Since 1945. Notes of HM Ships Involved (London: Admiralty, 1963), p 9.
27. Ray Sturtivant, *The Squadrons of the Fleet Air Arm* (Tonbridge: Air-Britain (Historians), 1984), p 329.
28. This short description of Naval Aviation's structure is based on a briefing written by the Admiralty for publication in *Flight & Aircraft Engineer*, the official organ of the Royal Aero Club, in a special edition on British Naval Aviation published on 20 April 1951.
29. The author served in DGA(N) between 1979 and 1982 as the aircraft carrier desk officer, Ships & Bases Section within DAE. It was fascinating to be there as the new *Invincible* class was brought into service, Sea Harriers introduced to operate from them and from *Hermes* after her modification with a 'ski-jump' to operate them.
30. Basic flying training for pilots at this time was carried out by the RAF in the UK and, for sixty student pilots a year, with the USN at NAS Pensacola. A number of observers were trained by the RCN in Canada.
31. This section was compiled from DAOT's Newsletter dated 5 November 1952 and distributed from the Admiralty, London on 21 November 1952, a copy of which is in the author's archive.

Chapter 6 – A Royal Occasion and the Radical Review
1. Donald Macintyre, *Wings of Neptune – The Story of Naval Aviation* (London: Peter Davies, 1963), p 5.
2. And those of the Army.
3. Trenchard was Keyes' wife's brother-in-law and it seemed to those in Government, therefore, that they would have to get on. Their discussions were chaired by Lord Haldane. Cecil Aspinall-Oglander, *Roger Keyes* (London: The Hogarth Press, 1951), pp 265–6.
4. Queen's Counsel – the highest rank of barrister in the British legal system.
5. His instructions were subsequently known as the 'Inskip Award'.
6. Hugh Popham, *Into Wind – History of British Naval Flying* (London: Hamish Hamilton, 1969), pp 116–17.
7. Although the official Admiralty Account of Naval Air Operations published by HMSO in 1943 was, surprisingly, entitled 'Fleet Air Arm'.
8. The RANVR and RNZNVR followed suit but the RCN had no Air Branch of its own and so members of the RCNVR serving in RN air squadrons had no 'A' in the curl of their sleeve lace.

9. Helicopters embarked in ships of the RCN and RNZN are operated by the RCAF and RNZAF respectively and the term Fleet Air Arm has become more historic than current in those countries.

10. HM Ships *Eagle, Indomitable, Implacable, Indefatigable, Illustrious, Theseus* and *Perseus*, HMCS *Magnificent* and HMAS *Sydney*.

11. Published under the authority of the Commander-in-Chief, Portsmouth by Gale & Polden Ltd, Portsmouth, 1953, price 2 shillings. Page 51.

12. A new Royal Yacht, *Britannia*, was under construction but was not completed until 1954.

13. 'Coronation Review Fly Past', *Flight Deck* (Winter 1953), pp 39 and 40.

14. Except for the Attacker squadrons from RNAS Ford which flew twelve.

15. '807 Squadron Flies Past', *Flight Deck* (Winter 1953), p 42.

16. Hobbs, *British Aircraft Carriers*, p 190.

17. Minute C.(54)329 dated 3 November 1954 from the Prime Minister, contained within CAB 129/71 in The National Archives at Kew.

18. Also contained within CAB 129/71.

19. Grove, *Vanguard to Trident*, pp 92 et seq.

20. He had married Winston Churchill's daughter Diana in 1935. The couple were subsequently divorced in 1960.

21. Grove, *Vanguard to Trident*, p 95.

22. Later Viscount Cilcennin.

23. ADM1/24695 'The Role of the Aircraft Carriers', quoted in Grove, *Vanguard to Trident*, p 102.

24. The only Chief of the Air Staff to have served in the RNAS. He joined the RNAS in 1916 and served in the first commission of the prototype aircraft carrier *Furious* during 1917. Serving under Squadron Commander Dunning at first, he was the third pilot to have deck landed an aircraft. After being commissioned into the RAF in 1918 he continued to fly on naval duties as a test pilot for a while and even in 1953 he may have retained a degree of loyalty for his former Service.

25. ADM205/94, 'Enclosure to First Sea Lord's No 2829' of 22 December 1953.

26. ADM205/102, Section 8A, 'Long Term Plan for the Navy' in The National Archives at Kew.

27. Flown by Gary Powers, the U-2 had been overflying the Soviet Union to photograph ICBM sites at what was considered to be a safe altitude on a flight from Peshawar to Bodo. A salvo of SA-2s was fired against it, one of which hit the U-2 and brought it down. Another hit a Soviet MiG-19 fighter which had been trying to intercept the U-2 but had omitted to change its IFF to the May setting.

28. Details of this aspect of the Review are contained in Section 8C of ADM205/102 at The National Archives at Kew.

29. Quoted in Grove, *Vanguard to Trident*, p 111.

30. C954/332, Defence Policy – The Fleet Air Arm', contained in CAB129/71, paragraph 1 at The National Archives, Kew.

31. It was felt that, with his forceful personality, he would be able to present a better case than the First Lord who was widely seen as a mild and gentle man despite his undoubted support for Admiralty policy.

32. Contained in ADM2015/99 at The National Archives at Kew.

Chapter 7 – The Suez Crisis

1. Grove, *Vanguard to Trident*, pp 178 et seq.

2. Jackson, *Suez 1956*, pp 7 et seq.

3. Geoffrey Carter, *Crises do Happen – The Royal Navy and Operation Musketeer, Suez 1956* (Liskeard: Maritime Books, 2006), pp 2 et seq.

4. Jackson, *Suez 1956*, p 10.

5. This approach had the obvious weakness that a far less robust approach had been taken when the Egyptian government arbitrarily closed the canal to Israeli shipping, despite Anglo-French ownership of the Company.

6. Department of Operational Research Report Number 34, 'Carrier Operations in Support of Operation Musketeer' (London: Admiralty, 1959).

7. Hobbs, *British Aircraft Carriers*, p 245.

8. Formerly HMS *Colossus* which had served in the BPF.

9. Formerly the USS *Langley*.

10. Brian Cull, with David Nicolle and Shlomo Aloni, *Wings Over Suez: The First Authoritative Account of Air Operations during the Sinai and Suez Wars of 1956* (London: Grub Street, 1996), pp 96 et seq.

11. Including Rav-Aluf Dayan and Mrs Golda Meir.
12. Details of the Sèvres Agreement are quoted in detail in Cull et al., *Wings Over Suez*, pp 102 and 103.
13. Reputedly, Anthony Eden destroyed his own copy, thus giving the impression that he was not proud of the role he had played in the slide towards hostilities.
14. I remember my father driving me to school at this time, past rows of sand-coloured vehicles parked at Plumer Barracks in Crownhill, just outside Plymouth, with 'H' painted prominently on their mudguards while we listened to a BBC radio news bulletin which stated that force would only be used as a last resort against Egypt.
15. The RAF airfields at Akrotiri, Nicosia and Tymbou. The build-up was complicated by the fact that Akrotiri was being modernised and expanded in 1956 and Tymbou, normally a relief landing ground, had to have its runway extended to operate the big transport aircraft based on it.
16. RAF airfields at Akrotiri, Nicosia and Tymbou in Cyprus; RNAS Hal Far and the RAF airfields at Luqa and Takali in Malta.
17. Group Captain L M Hodges DSO RAF.
18. Although many, apparently, thought it would be the former in defence of Jordan.
19. Cull et al., *Wings Over Suez*, pp 190 and 191.
20. A former Royal Naval Air station.
21. Carter, *Crises Do Happen*, pp 7 et seq.
22. The modification was adopted by all Sea Hawk squadrons and its inventor, Lieutenant Commander A B B Clark, CO of 899 NAS, was awarded £60 from the Herbert Lot Fund as a reward for his idea. The light was controlled by a switch in the cockpit and was known by various squadrons as either 'Nobby's Light' or the 'Mosquito Light'.
23. *Flight Deck* (Autumn 1956), p 63.
24. *Flight Deck* (Winter 1956), pp 3 et seq.
25. 1956 was not a good year for Lieutenant Middleton, who had three major incidents flying Sea Hawks. On 13 July he was forced to eject from WM 916 when the engine flamed out off Malta; on 5 September WM 966 caught fire while being launched by catapult from *Eagle*. He ditched ahead of the ship and was rescued by helicopter. On 29 October XE 441 had only reached 80 knots when the catapult failed after a series of jerks. He ditched off the bow and passed under the ship before being rescued by helicopter. His helmet was damaged when he hit the bottom of the ship but he was still judged fit to fly operationally during Operation 'Musketeer'.
26. Cull et al., *Wings Over Suez*, pp 273 and 274.
27. Considering that the bridge was built by British engineers and had clear tactical significance to the landings at Port Said, the failure by the targeting authority to describe its construction and optimum method of attack has no excuse.
28. *Flight Deck* (Autumn 1956), p 42.
29. *Flight Deck* (Winter 1956), p 9.
30. A local modification carried out on board.
31. Ray Sturtivant, *The Squadrons of the Fleet Air Arm* (Tonbridge: Air Britain (Historians), 1984).
32. *Flight Deck* (Winter 1956), p 13.
33. A normal peacetime average would be about 20 hours in a month.
34. Quoted in *Flight Deck* (Winter 1956), p 15.
35. Raymond Blackman, *The World's Warships* (London: Macdonald, 1960), p 24.
36. *Jane's Fighting Ships*, 1961-62 edition, p 319.
37. Norman Friedman, *US Aircraft Carriers – An Illustrated Design History* (Annapolis: Naval Institute Press, 1983), p 360.
38. *Flight Deck* (Autumn 1956), p 22.
39. *Flight Deck* (Winter 1956), p 16.
40. In this era both fixed- and rotary-wing aircraft used gravity refuelling like the petrol pumps at contemporary filling stations used by motorists. Faster pressure refuelling came in with the next generation of aircraft. Helicopters and Skyraiders had piston engines and used avgas. The jets and turbo-props all used avcat with its higher flashpoint and greater safety factor.
41. ADM1 – 27051, 'Operation Musketeer Carrier Operations', Appendix 5, The use of helicopters to lift 45 Commando Royal Marines in the National Archives, Kew.
42. ADM116 6136 section 4, 395 (a) in The National Archives, Kew.
43. *Flight Deck* (Winter 1956), p 39.
44. Carter, *Crises do Happen*, pp 67 et seq.

45. 1400 yards. One cable is 200 yards.
46. Formerly the RN 'River' class frigate *Nith*.
47. Local time was 'B', two hours ahead of 'Z'.
48. Department of Operational Research Report Number 34, 'Carrier Operations in Support of Operation Musketeer'.
49. *Flight Deck* (Spring 1957), pp 13 et seq.

Chapter 8 – New Equipment and Another Defence Review

1. Hobbs, *British Aircraft Carriers*, pp 268 et seq.
2. This description of CDS is taken from notes I made when serving in *Victorious* as a midshipman in 1966.
3. The suffix letter that followed the naval specification indicated whether it was for development or production aircraft. In this case N113D was for development aircraft and it was followed by N113P for production aircraft.
4. The AJ-65 evolved into the successful Avon series of engines.
5. Ray Williams, *Fly Navy – Aircraft of the Fleet Air Arm since 1945* (Shrewsbury: Airlife Publishing, 1989), pp 105 et seq.
6. Hobbs, *Aircraft of the Royal Navy Since 1945*, p 46.
7. Michael J Doust, *Scimitar – From The Cockpit #2* (Ringshall: Ad Hoc Publications, 2006), p 6.
8. 800, 800B, 803, 804, 807 and 736 NAS.
9. Society of British Aircraft Constructors. Later in the decade the word 'Aircraft' was replaced by 'Aerospace'.
10. With a top speed of 480 knots it was some 50 knots slower than the Vickers Valiant, a typical medium bomber of the period.
11. Purchased by de Havilland from Airspeed after 1945.
12. Tony Butler, *The de Havilland Sea Vixen* (Tonbridge: Air Britain (Historians), 2007), p 18.
13. Where aircraft were procured jointly by the RN and RAF at the time, RN variants were given higher mark numbers; for instance the Vampire FB 5 operated by the RAF and the Sea Vampire F 20 operated by the RN. When it became clear that the RAF had no interest in the Vixen, the first RN mark was re-designated as the FAW 1 rather than the FAW 20.
14. Hobbs, *Aircraft of the Royal Navy since 1945*, p 20.
15. One could, of course, argue that for exactly the same reason, if the aircraft was not going to operate in daylight, there was no reason not to fit a clear canopy for the observer like that in the Sea Venom but the aircraft's designers obviously did not think that way.
16. 890, 892, 893, 899 and 766 NAS.
17. AP101B-2803-15A. Pilot's Notes – Gannet AEW 3, May 1960 Edition, Amended to AL-14, Chapter 2, paragraph 3b.
18. The pylons could also be fitted with inert 1000lb bombs. During a deployment in the USN Atlantic Fleet Weapons Range during 1976 *Ark Royal* sought to get rid of a number of outdated inert bombs which proved more than the Buccaneers and Phantoms could use. My Flight, 849B, volunteered to help and we livened up AEW barrier patrols by attacking splash targets towed by an RFA tanker. Despite not having a sight (I used a chinagraph mark on the windscreen), I scored a direct hit on one target and completely destroyed it.
19. AP 4487D-PN. Gannet AS 4 Pilot's Notes, May 1957 Edition, p 115.
20. Thetford, *British Naval Aircraft since 1912*, p 101.
21. Details of all British aircraft carriers can be found in the author's *British Aircraft Carriers*.
22. Norman Friedman, *British Carrier Aviation* (London: Conway Maritime Press, 1988,) pp 197, 198, 230, 281, 326 and 345.
23. I was told by a test pilot that Short's considered fitting explosive bolts to the main oleos so that they could be blown off before a water landing but that the idea was not taken forward because the weight of the system with its safety interlocks would have been heavier than a hydraulic retraction mechanism. This may or may not be true but the story does illustrate the desperate need to put right the defects in the basic design.
24. Given the acceptance of a fixed undercarriage to save complexity and cost, one is forced to ask why the Seamew AS 1 had power-folding wings when wartime aircraft, on which the concept was based, did not.
25. Williams, *Fly Navy*, p 103.
26. Bill Gunston, *Early Supersonic Fighters of the West* (Shepperton: Ian Allen, 1976), pp 47 et seq.

27. The advantage of 'collision course' interception in which the fighter can engage a target from ahead, without having to turn in astern of it was obvious and the Firestreak Mark 4 missile was designed initially for the SR-177. It was later re-named 'Red Top' to differentiate it from the earlier missile and armed the Sea Vixen FAW 2.
28. Hobbs, *British Aircraft Carriers*, p 273.
29. 'Defence – An Outline of Future Policy' (London: HMSO, April 1957).
30. Gunston, *Early Supersonic Fighters*, p 45.
31. Ibid, p 46.
32. ADM1/27827 contained in The National Archives at Kew.
33. Richard Moore, *The Royal Navy and Nuclear Weapons* (London: Frank Cass Publishers, 2001), p 140.
34. William Green, *The World Guide to Combat Planes – Two* (London: Macdonald, 1966), p 13.
35. In flight the missile was designed to roll in order to minimise launch dispersion.
36. *Flight Deck* (Summer 1961), p vii.
37. AP(N) 144 – Naval Aircraft Handbook, 1958 Edition, p 237.
38. An American U-2 spy plane was shot down by a Soviet SA-2 missile at about this time showing that high-altitude operations offered little defence against anti-aircraft missiles.
39. The RAE feared that a conventional booster fitted to the tail would produce a cloud of ionised particles astern of the missile which would interfere with the radar beam. This largely theoretical fear proved to be unfounded.
40. CB03164. *Progress of the Fleet Air Arm Summary* #8 (London: Admiralty, June 1956), p 15.
41. *Flight Deck* (Autumn/Winter 1960), p xii.
42. *Flight Deck* (Winter 1958/59), p 14.
43. AP 4360D -PN. Pilot's Notes for the Sea Venom FAW 22, 1957 edition, p 8.
44. Fireflies were not the ideal missile target but there were plenty of them surplus to operational requirements now that the Gannet had entered service and the second cockpit gave ample space for equipment and controlling pilots in chase aircraft when necessary.
45. *Flight Deck* (Autumn/Winter 1960), p xii.
46. *Flight Deck* (Summer 1961), p vi. In my opinion it would have been a better choice for the Sea Vixen which could have carried eight.
47. Later versions of Sidewinder grew in sophistication with un-caged seeker heads which searched for a target all the time. Pilots could see where the 'eye' was pointing by the position of a moving cross fed into the head-up display. If the cross was over a target he could fire, even if the aircraft was not pointing at the enemy.
48. Sandys' background is interesting. As an MP, he served with the 51st Anti-Aircraft Brigade RA, a Territorial Army (TA) unit, early in the war and saw action in Norway. Later, in 1941 he was wounded in action and subsequently always walked with a limp. From then on he served as Finance Member of the Army Council and was given a minor ministerial post in the Coalition Government by his father-in-law Winston Churchill. In 1944 he was appointed Chairman of a War Cabinet Committee that examined the German use of V1 and V2 rocket weapons and considered defences against them. This left him with a life-long fascination for rocket and advanced technology weapons and a distrust of the RAF fighter community which he never lost. He lost his seat in the 1945 general election but regained it in 1950. He resigned his TA commission as a Lieutenant Colonel in 1946. Though disliked by many and trapped within his own appreciation of warfare, it has to be admitted that he was one of the most influential British Ministers of Defence.
49. Grove, *Vanguard to Trident*, pp 200 et seq.
50. 'Defence – Outline of Future Policy' (Command 124), April 1957.
51. Ibid, paragraph 24.
52. Possibly he saw such a project as another reason for cancelling the SR-177.
53. P Darby, *British Defence Policy East of Suez* (London: Oxford University Press, London, 1973), p 114.
54. Quoted in Grove, *Vanguard to Trident*, p 213.

Chapter 9 – Helicopters and Helicopter Carriers
1. Hobbs, *A Century of Carrier Aviation*, pp 241 et seq.
2. Thetford, *British Naval Aircraft since 1912*, p 328.
3. Sturtivant and Balance, *The Squadrons of the Fleet Air Arm*, p 26.
4. *Flight Deck* (Summer 1953), p 22.

5. The flight was of historical significance as the first time a formation of helicopters had crossed the English Channel.
6. Hobbs, *A Century of Carrier Aviation*, p 254.
7. Gordon Swanborough and Peter M Bowers, *United States Navy Aircraft since 1911* (London: Putnam, 1990), p 467.
8. *Flight Deck* (Autumn 1953), pp 20–3.
9. 5SL 2058 dated 27 August 1955 contained in ADM1/25901 – Naval Anti-Submarine Aircraft, at the National Archives, Kew.
10. Their original specification had stated that they should be expected to last for three years or the duration of the war, whichever was less. By 1955 they were ten years old and some had seen arduous service in the Korean War. In fact the last ship of the class, the Brazilian *Minas Gerais*, formerly HMS *Vengeance*, was not de-activated until October 2001.
11. Whirlwinds that ditched were seldom recoverable because they literally dissolved underwater in a matter of days. Popular Fleet Air Arm myth alleged that the few that were recovered quickly could be heard 'fizzing', despite being washed in fresh water.
12. The Skyraider also used avgas but by 1960 it had been replaced by the Gannet AEW 3.
13. Defined in D(57)27 as 'a balanced force of the largest number of vessels which we could expect to man with 88,000 UK adult males'. The actual manpower ceiling in 1957–8 was 121,500.
14. Figures contained in ADM1/27685 in the National Archives, Kew. They did not include ships in reserve or those engaged in fishery protection, trials or training.
15. Board Memorandum B.1325 contained in ADM1/27685 at the National Archives, Kew.
16. A Number of Gannet pilots were made redundant in the late 1950s.
17. Board Minutes, agenda item 5401 – The Helicopter Ship, contained in ADM1/27685 at the National Archives, Kew.
18. Contained within ADM1/27685 in the National Archives, Kew.
19. Able to carry a single Wessex helicopter with a flight deck and hangar aft.
20. Significantly he did not employ words such as 'essential' or 'vital'.
21. Details of which appear in ADM1/27685 in the National Archives, Kew.
22. These studies and figures are taken from a Ship Department, Product Group Constructive Paper dated 6 October 1960 contained in ADM1/27685 in the National Archives, Kew.
23. Recently modernised to act as carrier task force escorts.
24. Navy estimates show a reduction from a force of twenty-six cruisers in 1955 to nine in 1961, including ships in reserve and refit. In the same period the active destroyer/frigate force rose from fifty-two to fifty-four ships.
25. AOD/D.95/60 dated 10 October 1960 contained in ADM1/27685 at the National Archives, Kew.
26. M1.288/8/60 dated 14 December 1960 contained in ADM1/27685 at the National Archives, Kew.
27. DNAW D/151/60 dated 20 December 1960 contained in ADM1/27685 in the National Archives, Kew.
28. Note carriage, not operation.
29. TWP 4548/60 dated 20 December 1960 contained in ADM1/27685 in the National Archives, Kew.
30. M1/288/8/60 dated 20 January 1961 contained within ADM1/27685 at the National Archives, Kew.
31. Details taken from CB 01815B, Particulars of British Commonwealth War Vessels, April 1949 Edition.
32. Military Branch 1 AAP/MG/CCB.11 dated 8 March 1961 contained in ADM1/27685 in the National Archives, Kew.
33. The original Sikorsky design from which the Westland Wessex was derived.
34. COS (61) 480 and COS (62) 3rd Meeting.
35. COS (62) 1.
36. Board Minute 5627, a copy of which is contained in ADM1/29053 in the National Archives, Kew.
37. She could even have operated Gannets if given a more extensive refit with a steam catapult and upgraded arrester wires like her sister-ship *Melbourne* but this would have raised the cost of refit significantly.

Chapter 10 – A Range of Carrier Operations
1. Naval Staff History, 'Middle East Operations' (London: Ministry of Defence, 1968), p 2.
2. David Hobbs, 'A Maritime Approach to Joint and Coalition Warfare' in David Stevens and John Reeve (eds), *Sea Power Ashore and in the Air* (Ultimo, New South Wales: Halstead Press, 2007), p 199.

3. Flag Officer Second-in-Command, Mediterranean Fleet, Vice Admiral Sir Robin Durnford-Slater, Report of Proceedings, May 1958.
4. Naval Staff History, p 6.
5. Hobbs, *British Aircraft Carriers*, p 180.
6. FOAC Report of Proceedings, 14 to 24 July 1958 contained in MII/276/153/58 at the National Archives, Kew.
7. The contrast with the long-drawn-out British build-up before the Suez landings is striking.
8. Commander-in-Chief Mediterranean Report of Proceedings MII/282/5/59 in the National Archives, Kew.
9. Something the escort cruisers could not have done nearly as well. It is surprising how 'blind' their protagonist were to the events of 1956 and 1958. Those who looked back to the ability of cruisers to carry troops in the 1920s and 1930s failed to take into account that infantry battalions of that period were un-mechanised. Cruisers could not carry the vehicles and equipment needed by contemporary military formations, only specialised amphibious ships and carriers could do that.
10. Hobbs, *British Aircraft Carriers*, p 245.
11. FOAC ROP MII/276/153/58.
12. Popham, *Into Wind*, p 240.
13. *Flight Deck* (Winter 1958/59), p 9.
14. Hobbs, *British Aircraft Carriers*, p 248
15. Naval Staff History, 'Middle East Operations – Kuwait 1961' (London: Ministry of Defence, 1968), pp 41 et seq.
16. RTP(AP) Number 7 in the National Archives at Kew.
17. COS(59)268.
18. Hobbs, 'A Maritime Approach to Joint and Coalition Warfare', p 204.
19. *Flight Deck* (Autumn 1961), p 2.
20. J David Brown, Naval Historical Branch Study 1/97 (London: Ministry of Defence, 1997).
21. *Flight Deck* (Autumn 1961), pp 3 et seq.
22. It was part of her former outfit as a strike carrier and had been left in place as a useful task-force asset. Exactly how useful rapidly became apparent during the Kuwait Crisis and the second commando carrier, *Albion*, was fitted with a more capable Type 965 air-search radar during her conversion.
23. Former RN ships operated on behalf of the War Office by P & O Limited. They were given the names of birds preceded by 'Empire'.
24. A former 'River' class frigate modified with extra Naval and Army communications equipment for service with the Amphibious Warfare Squadron. Her sister-ship *Waveney* had also been modified for the role but had been discarded as an economy measure in 1958.
25. FOME 356/ME 386/70 dated 15 September 1961 in the National Archives, Kew.
26. David Hobbs, *The British Pacific Fleet* (Barnsley: Seaforth Publishing, 2011), Chapter 5, pp 108 et seq gives background on the wartime MONABS and their use.
27. *Flight Deck* (Autumn 1961), p xiii.
28. Hobbs, *British Aircraft Carriers*, p 278.
29. Joint Intelligence Committee JIC(61) 53/10 in the National Archives at Kew.
30. Hobbs, *British Aircraft Carriers*, p 241.
31. HMS *Victorious* 130/5 dated 30 July 1961 in the National Archives at Kew.
32. Naval Staff History, 'Middle East Operations', p 58.
33. Hobbs, *British Aircraft Carriers*, p 242.
34. D K Hankinson, 'HMS *Centaur* at Dar-es-Salaam', *US Naval Institute Proceedings* (November 1969).
35. Although their yellow cabin roofs, so painted to make them obvious to maritime patrol aircraft while they were in the hover with their sonar 'ball' in the water during anti-submarine operations, were less than ideal for assault operations.
36. The name 'Dar-es-Salaam' translates into English as 'Haven of Peace' in English.
37. In effect, a precursor of the 'shock and awe' tactics used by the Coalition allies in Iraq in 2003.

Chapter 11 – The Evolution of Strike Warfare

1. And, one must accept, against fixed targets when necessary.
2. I am grateful to my friend Norman Friedman for making this point, which stimulated my thought process, in an article published in *Headmark*, the Journal of the Australian Naval Institute (Autumn 2014).

3. The Technical Editor, 'Buccaneer – An Outstanding Strike Aeroplane', *Flight International* (4 April 1963).
4. John D Atinello of NACA, later NASA, in the USA first produced the concept of blowing supersonic, high-pressure air bled from the engines over a wing at low speed to improve its lift coefficient. The idea was taken forward in the UK and improved by Dr John Williams at the National Physical Laboratory and Lewis Boddington of the Admiralty.
5. Passive receivers will always detect a radar transmission before there is a sufficient strong return echo to betray the presence of the aircraft in which they are fitted.
6. Among other applications it was used in the de Havilland Trident airliner.
7. All Rolls-Royce jet engines have been named after British rivers.
8. Hobbs, *Aircraft of the Royal Navy since 1945*, p 6.
9. Williams, *Fly Navy*, p 131.
10. Correspondence between the Staff of the Commander Far East Fleet and the Admiralty, 1963, a copy of which is in the author's archive.
11. The author was serving in her at the time as a midshipman.
12. The only element of this joint programme to see operational service was the Type 192 which eventually entered service with the RAF as the Belvedere troop-carrying helicopter.
13. The basic Sikorsky S-58 was adopted by the French Navy for operation from *Jean d'Arc.*
14. Artists' impressions look rather like a 'chubby' American S-3 Viking with similar swept wings and underslung turbofan engine nacelles.
15. For comparison, CVA-01 at the same time was expected to cost £60 million to build.
16. Although a developed version of this radar was selected and flown in prototype form in the abortive Nimrod AEW 3 project.
17. Eric Morgan and John Stevens, *The Scimitar File* (Tunbridge Wells: Air Britain (Historians), 2000), p 210.
18. Loose Minute from First Lord to Minister of Defence, Copy to DCNS dated 12 May 1961. A copy is in the Naval Historical Branch Files and the author's archive.
19. Loose Minute dated 1 May 1961 from the files of the Admiralty Library; a copy is in the author's archive.
20. Loose Minute dated 1 June 1961 from the files of the Admiralty Library; a copy is in the author's archive.
21. COS (60) 168 in the National Archives, a copy of which is in the Admiralty Library.
22. Ministry of Defence Letter MM:67/61 dated 4 December 1961, a copy of which is in the Admiralty Library.
23. Ibid, p 2.
24. Loose Minute from Head of Military Branch 1 to First Lord dated 4 December 1961, copy to 1SL, other Board Members and relevant Staff Divisions, a copy of which is in the Admiralty Library.
25. Cabinet Defence Committee Meeting held on 6 December 1961, D(61) 17th Meeting, Minutes dated 7 December 1961, a copy of which is in the Admiralty Library.
26. Loose Minute from Head of Military Branch 1 to 1SL and Heads of Naval Staff Divisions dated 2 March 1962, a copy of which is in the Admiralty Library.
27. Only 5000lbs more than a Buccaneer S 1.
28. David Hobbs, Naval Historical Branch Study 62/4 Paper 62/4 (3) (97) (London: Ministry of Defence, October 1997), p 13.
29. Ibid.
30. When the RAF did eventually form Harrier squadrons for operation in Germany in 1969, each unit needed in excess of 200 off-road vehicles to support twelve Harriers. Their movements were plainly visible and thus would have been fairly easy to interdict.
31. Which had separate thrust and lift engines, the latter developed by Rolls-Royce.
32. Tactical Air Navigation equipment which showed the bearing and range to selected beacons provided that the aircraft was above the beacon's horizon. All RN fighters and AEW aircraft were fitted with TACAN and all carriers were fitted with beacons.
33. Drafted in a series of papers filed under NAD 202/62, a copy of which is in the Admiralty Library.
34. NHB Study 62/4 Paper 62/4 (3) (97) pp 15 et seq.
35. JP.53/63 (Final) dated 5 June 1963, a copy of which is in the Admiralty Library.
36. Hawker Design Office memorandum by Ralph Hooper, Project Office RSH/EJP dated 4 April 1962, a copy of which is in the author's archive.
37. Underlined in the original.

38. Actual figures, including prototypes, were 149 and eighty-one.
39. Taken from ADM 1/27966, 'Future Naval Aircraft' in the National Archives at Kew.
40. P 1154 – Meeting in the Ministry of Defence on 4 October 1963, No 7/63, dated 4 October 1963 and signed by Sir Solly Zuckerman CB.
41. 'Assessment of the P 1154 vis a vis Joint Staff requirement AW 406/OR 356 Annex A', distributed by Military Branch 1, Admiralty, undated.
42. A similar undercarriage was later fitted to the Sea Harrier and actually proved to be acceptable.
43. In a Loose Minute, NAD 202/62, dated 7 May 1963, a copy of which is in the Admiralty Library.
44. Politicians failed to understand the different Navy and Air Force aircraft designations and, although the F4H-2 and F-110A were essentially the same aircraft, there were heated arguments in Congress about which was the better aircraft. Thus the Phantom II was the catalyst for introduced a joint US system of aircraft designations that is still in use today.
45. The RAF version, based on NBMR 3, continued in development for another year before it, too, fell victim to the first round of defence cuts ordered by the new Labour government. Without partners a new airframe with a new engine designed to operate in a revolutionary new way was just too expensive compared with more conventional aircraft.
46. All export Phantoms were assembled in St Louis except for those intended for the Japanese Air Self Defence Force which were assembled in Japan by Mitsubishi, who built 138 Phantoms, including the very last of all versions to be delivered in May 1981.
47. Bill Gunston, *F-4 Phantom – Modern Combat Aircraft 1* (Shepperton: Ian Allan, 1977), pp 53 et seq.
48. Comments noted from conversations with former RN Phantom aircrew.
49. Sturtivant, *The Squadrons of the Fleet Air Arm* (Tonbridge: Air Britain (Historians), 1984), p 381.
50. The Anglo/French supersonic airliner Concorde was its last major politically-inspired project. Designed to demonstrate a capability that ministers assumed would be the next step in passenger-carrying aviation, it was not designed to any airline specification and, whilst technically brilliant, it was not what any airline wanted. Always in the shadow of the Boeing 747 'Jumbo-Jet', Concorde was a commercial disaster.
51. The substitution of a single-word name for something, for instance 'Whitehall' as a substitute for 'the British Government'. In this instance politicians misguidedly took 'RAF' to be a substitute for 'British Military Aviation'.

Chapter 12 – Brunei and the Indonesian Confrontation
1. Thus avoiding criticism that he favoured one or other of the former port divisions.
2. *Flight Deck* (Winter 1962/3), p 17.
3. Singapore left the Federation of Malaysia in 1965 and became an independent state within the Commonwealth.
4. John Roberts, *Safeguarding the Nation – The Story of the Modern Royal Navy* (Barnsley: Seaforth Publishing, 2009), p 48.
5. *Flight Deck* (Winter 1962/3), p 22.
6. Grove, *Vanguard to Trident*, pp 245 et seq.
7. *Jane's Fighting Ships*, 1964–5 Edition, p 126.
8. William Green and Dennis Punnet, *Macdonald World Air Power Guide* (London: Macdonald, 1963), p 13.
9. Roberts, *Safeguarding the Nation*, pp 49 et seq.
10. Ibid, p 50.
11. Denis Healey speech to the House of Commons given on 27 November 1967 and quoted in Hansard.
12. Sturtivant and Ballance, *The Squadrons of the Fleet Air Arm*, p 268.
13. *Flight Deck* (Winter 1963/4), p ii.
14. *Flight Deck* (Summer 1964), p 23.
15. Reputedly Mountbatten had used his influence to ensure that the RN got the very latest film titles to circulate to the fleet and film shows in ships and establishments were always a very special event. Sadly, the excitement this used to generate has now faded with contemporary easy access to a vast range of films as DVDs or on line that can be watched at any time individually or collectively.
16. *Flight Deck* #3 (1965), pp viii et seq.
17. *Flight Deck* #4 (1965), p 26.
18. It should not be thought, however, that high-intensity operations against sophisticated opposition

would be possible by units other than Royal Marines.

19. Hillers were light helicopters with a maximum weight of 2500lbs used for tactical reconnaissance in support of RM units ashore. Their function was eventually taken over by 3 Brigade Air squadron and then 847 NAS.
20. *Flight Deck* #4 (1965), p 41.
21. A local type of long-bladed knife.
22. *Flight Deck* #1 (1966), p 23.
23. Robert Jackson, *The Malayan Emergency & Indonesian Confrontation – The Commonwealth's Wars 1948-1966* (Barnsley: Pen & Sword Military, 2011), p 139.

Chapter 13 – The British Nuclear Deterrent and the End of the Admiralty Era

1. Although the choice of *Plym* was largely due to her availability as a suitable hull capable of steaming from the UK to Australia with the bomb components safely stowed on board. This first device was too big for a bomber to carry effectively.
2. A break with the RAF tradition of naming bombers and other large, heavy aircraft after cities – Lancaster, Halifax, Stirling, Canberra etc.
3. Green, *The World's Fighting Planes*, p 125.
4. John Baylis, *Ambiguity and Deterrence, British Nuclear Strategy 1945-64* (Oxford: Clarendon Press, 1995).
5. Which burned hydrogen peroxide and kerosene like the Armstrong Siddeley Spectre in the P-177 'rocket fighter'.
6. C Gibson and T Buttler, *British Secret Projects – Hypersonics, Ramjets and Missiles* (Leicester: Midland Publishing, 2007).
7. A former RNAS pilot who taken part in the early deck landing experiments.
8. H Wynne, *RAF Nuclear Deterrent Forces* (London: HMSO, 1994), p 275.
9. Group Captain Chris Finn and Paul Berg. 'Anglo-American Strategic Air Power Co-operation in the Cold War Era and Beyond', *The Royal Air Force Air Power Review*, Volume 7 Number 4 (Shrivenham Joint Doctrine & Concepts Centre, Winter 2004).
10. Ibid, p 49.
11. At RAF Feltwell, RAF Hemswell, RAF Driffield and RAF North Luffenham.
12. The Feltwell satellites were at Shepherds Grove, Tuddenham, Mepal and North Pickenham. The Hemswell satellites were at Ludford Magna, Bardney, Coleby Grange and Caistor. The Driffield satellites were at Full Sutton, Carnaby, Catfoss and Beighton. The North Luffenham satellites were at Polebrook, Folkingham, Harrington and Melton Mowbray. The sites were spread across a number of English counties from Suffolk, through Lincolnshire to Yorkshire to give some dispersion in case of a surprise attack but there were none in Scotland, Wales or Northern Ireland.
13. Kenneth Cross, 'Bomber Command's Thor Missile Force', *The RUSI Journal*, Volume 108, Issue 630 (May 1963), pp 131 et seq.
14. Thor's empty weight was only 6889lbs; the balance making up the total launch weight of 109,800lbs was all fuel and oxidant.
15. Another example of Anglo-American co-operation; the radar formed part of the US distant early warning line and was built with US funds but manned by the RAF.
16. Peter Morton, *Fire Across the Desert – Woomera and the Anglo-Australian Joint Project 1946-1980* (Canberra: Australian Government Publishing Service, 1989), pp 436 et seq.
17. Blue Streak fuel tanks were formed of stainless steel sheet, less than half a millimetre thick, seam-welded into a cylinder. When empty they were so fragile that they had to be pumped up hard with nitrogen to prevent them from collapsing under their own weight using the same principle as pneumatic vehicle tyres.
18. The term 'underground launchers' was used at the time; the word 'silo' was subsequently imported from the USA.
19. Complete blueprints for the K-11 silo design can be found in DEFE 7/1392 in the National Archives at Kew.
20. The heat shield was tested by a Black Knight rocket and found to work perfectly.
21. Quite why Sir Robert Menzies, the Prime Minister, allowed Australia to become so deeply involved is still uncertain. He certainly believed in a more unified Commonwealth defence posture than subsequently became the case and, no doubt, believed that his country would gain considerable technological expertise from the Blue Streak project.
22. Morton, *Fire Across the Desert*, p 444.

23. At least Blue Streak did have some use as the first stage of the European Launcher Development Organisation satellite launching system and Woomera was used for its testing.
24. The Victor had too little ground clearance to carry Skybolts on pylons under the wings.
25. Derek Wood, *Project Cancelled – A Searching Criticism of the Abandonment of Britain's Advanced Aircraft Projects* (London: Macdonald & Jane's, 1975), p 144.
26. Ibid, p 148.
27. Commander H B Grant AFRAeS, AMIMarE, RN, 'Polaris', *Flight Deck* (Spring 1961), p vii.
28. Captain J E Moore RN, *The Impact of Polaris – The origins of Britain's seaborne nuclear deterrent* (Huddersfield: Richard Netherwood Limited, 1999), pp 14 et seq.
29. Ibid, p 18.
30. Later to become the Chief Polaris Executive who drove the project forward on time and on cost.
31. V B Blackman, *Jane's Fighting Ships, 1972-73 Edition* (London: Jane's Yearbooks, 1972), p 341.
32. Captain Richard Sharpe RN, *Jane's Fighting Ships*, 1995-96 Edition (Coulsden: Jane's Information Group, 1995), p 759.
33. Ibid.
34. Ibid, p 758.
35. This brief history of the Naval Staff was informed by a monograph on the subject written by the Naval Historical Branch, NHB, in 1930 and by a study of the organisation in its later years I carried out while serving in NHB during 1997.
36. A shortcoming for which, as a former Sea Lord, he was himself partially responsible.
37. The creation of the unified Canadian Armed Forces in 1965 was rumoured by my contacts in the RCN to have been based on suggestions by Lord Mountbatten that were, thankfully, not taken up by the UK Government.
38. The title was passed to HRH Prince Philip, the Duke of Edinburgh in 2013.

Chapter 14 – The Cancellation of CVA-01

1. The initials stood for Tactical Strike and Reconnaissance, roles that were carried out by the obsolescent Canberra which had been in service since 1951. Although never referred to as such, the Canberra had effectively been the TSR 1.
2. Hobbs, *British Aircraft Carriers*, pp 289 et seq. The same volume contains the design, development and service histories of every British aircraft carrier.
3. Of interest, in 1959 the sixty silos needed to protect Blue Streak missiles were estimated to cost £150 million. This figure was just for the silos and did not include the cost of developing and manufacturing the missiles, their warheads and the extensive infrastructure needed for the support and maintenance of both. Although critics of aircraft carriers often describe them as 'big ticket' items, their cost was not remarkable when compared with other contemporary weapons systems.
4. The very term 'aircraft carrier' is not very precise and can be applied, with similar exactitude to the 1951 *Eagle* capable of operating a mixed air group of up to 100 aircraft and the 1943 MAC-Ship *Empire MacAndrew* capable of operating four Swordfish in a specialised convoy-protection role.
5. This section of the chapter has been based on Naval Historical Branch Study 1/97 (D/NHB/9/8/61) in which I was involved. Copies are held in the Naval Historical Branch and in the author's archive.
6. It should be noted that the Sea Harrier FRS 1, derived from the original P 1127, which did so well in the South Atlantic War of 1982 had the benefit of a further twenty years of development. It was fitted with radar and air-to-air guided missiles which had not even been considered for the potential armament of the original development aircraft.
7. This section of the chapter was derived from NHB Study Paper 62/7(94) dated January 1997 by J D Brown, Head of the Naval Historical Branch, with which I helped.
8. Sixteen were exported to the South African Air Force which operated them very successfully from shore bases.
9. The prototypes were 89ft long with a maximum take-off weight of 95,900lbs. At about 1000nm its radius of action was twice that of the Buccaneer so it can be presumed, as a 'rule of thumb' that it carried twice as much fuel.
10. Comprising the former Hawker, de Havilland and Blackburn companies.
11. The 'A' in CVA.
12. But it should be remembered that the Buccaneer's origin, stated in Requirement NA 39, had been to counter the threat of *Sverdlov* class cruisers acting in the commerce-raiding role, not as a deep-penetration land attack aircraft. Given the capability required for the primary purpose, however, it was always going to be very good at the second.

13. NHB Study 62/7(94) p 3.
14. It was known colloquially in the Admiralty as the 'Pike Ship'.
15. NHB Study 62/7(94), p 3.
16. Ibid, p 4.
17. Thus firmly rebutting CAS's view that the existence of the RN carrier strike fleet did not allow any reduction in the RAF front-line.
18. Although as the RN was subsequently to learn, growing international awareness of the RN nuclear capability might limit the number of potential diplomatic port visits.
19. Which would have pushed up the TSR 2 unit cost still further.
20. £0.62 million per Buccaneer S 1 in 1961.
21. NHB Study 62/7(94), p 5.
22. The original minutes are contained in D(62)6 dated 26 January 1962 in the National Archives at Kew.
23. Note that the McDonnell F-4H Phantom II entering service with the US Navy in 1961 came close to meeting this requirement but a STOVL equivalent was probably beyond the capability of British industry.
24. This sentence was, surprisingly, not well worded. What it was trying to say is that while the radius of action at only 400nm was a _disadvantage_, the P 1154's projected early entry into service was a distinct advantage. Like so many recommendations in this difficult time, recommendations were made before the facts were fully understood and the difficulty of developing such an aircraft was not, widely understood.
25. By when _Eagle_ would be thirty years old and _Hermes_ twenty. The USN kept carriers in service for far longer than this.
26. Hansard, 30 July 1963 Edition, p 237.
27. Loose Minute 133/64, 1SL to CDS dated 3 January 1964 taken from papers found in ADM 205 in the National Archives at Kew. A copy of this minute is in the author's archive.
28. Naval Historical Branch Study 1/97 dated 28 January 1997, p 13.
29. Ibid, p 15 et seq.
30. The somewhat pedestrian title that replaced that of First Lord after the expanded role of the MOD on 1 April 1964 removed the incumbent's Cabinet status.
31. Grove, _Vanguard to Trident_, p 277.
32. Statement on the Defence estimates 1966, Part I, Command 2901 (London: HMSO, February 1966), p 10.
33. Statement on the Defence estimates 1966, Part II, Command 2902 (London: HMSO, February 1966), p 27.
34. My own underlining.

Chapter 15 – Rundown of the Carrier Force

1. Papers contained within ADM1/24695, formerly CS 150/53 – Committee on the Defence Programme, at the National Archives, Kew.
2. 1SL Letter 133/63 dated 22 August 1963, contained within ADM/205 at the National Archives, Kew.
3. Ibid, pp 2 of 18 et seq.
4. Ibid, p 17 of 18.
5. Contained in ADM/205 at the National Archives, Kew.
6. Exactly the form of attack used by Argentine aircraft against a politically-weakened RN during the South Atlantic War of 1982.
7. Showing how quickly the FFWP got down to business.
8. DNAW FFWP/P(66)9; one of a number of documents retained by Section NA/W1 at the Ship Department at Foxhill, near Bath, that I examined in 1997. Copies are held in the Naval Historical Branch in Portsmouth and in the author's archive.
9. DNTWP 4197/66 dated 11 March 1966; another of the papers retained by Section NA/W1 at Foxhill which I examined in 1997. Copies are held in the Naval Historical Branch in Portsmouth and in the author's archive.
10. 50ft shorter than a 1942 light fleet carrier.
11. Large, mundane objects like pontoons and floats could be carried on the light fleet carrier conversions and lowered into the water by their cranes. None of this could be done by a commando cruiser.

12. Details of all the cruiser designs from this period are taken from the documents examined in NA/W1 Section of DG Ships at Foxhill, copies of which are now held in the Naval Historical Branch at Portsmouth.
13. 'Cost of Ships – presentation to Controller on 12 July 1968 – Introductory Remarks by AD/DC3'. One of the documents retained by Section NA/W1 at the Ship Department, Foxhill which I examined in 1997. Copies are retained in the Naval Historical Branch in Portsmouth and in the author's archive.
14. When I joined the Royal Navy in 1964 over half my Dartmouth intake was expected to be directly involved with naval aircraft and their operation. Apart from pilots. like myself, and observers there were direction officers, fighter controllers, air engineers and other specialisations centred on the Fleet Air Arm.
15. Richard Baker, *Dry Ginger – The Biography of Admiral of the Fleet Sir Michael le Fanu GCB DSC* (London: W H Allen Ltd, 1977), p 219.
16. Ibid.
17. Hobbs, *British Aircraft Carriers*, p 280.
18. For part of which time I lived on board before joining *Victorious.*
19. *Albion* operated 826 NAS, an anti-submarine unit, for the last few months of her operational career in 1972.
20. Laid down 1943, launched 1950, completed 1955.
21. With no new orders for anything else the RAF was relying on former naval aircraft to retain its capability within NATO.
22. The question of retaining the existing carriers and the arguments over whether it was worth doing so were contained in the papers retained by Section NA/W1 at the Ship Department, Foxhill which I examined in 1997. Copies have been retained in the Naval Historical Branch at Portsmouth and in the author's archive.
23. All were contained in the documents retained by Section NA/W1 at the Ship Department, Foxhill that I examined in 1997. Copies are now held in the Naval Historical Branch at Portsmouth and in the author's archive.
24. In the US designation system, the 'X' denoted the type's experimental status and the 'C' its intended role as a transport aircraft.
25. The same engine as the Hawker P 1127.
26. Shackletons were being replaced in the maritime reconnaissance role by the Nimrod MR 1.
27. This view was explained to me by RN observers who trained RAF aircrew at RNAS Lossiemouth in 1972.
28. The squadron in which I served at the time and for some years afterwards. Lossiemouth had a new wardroom and a number of other outstanding facilities. It was widely considered to be the best RN Air Station at the time and the announcement of its closure caused considerable sadness.
29. I recall one incident which shows how difficult relations between RAF group staffs and naval air squadrons could be. Shortly after disembarking from *Ark Royal* we were told emphatically by the group captain of RAF Lossiemouth that were now under the operational control of 11 Group, Strike Command. We learnt that a group of 11 Group staff officers were coming to Lossiemouth to discuss AEW operations so we procured 11 Group ties and, to show willing, wore them with our plain clothes when greeting the visitors in the Wardroom/Officers' Mess. The result was not quite what we expected; the senior staff officer pointed at our ties and said 'What are you wearing those for, you are nothing to do with 11 Group, take them off immediately.' As might be imagined the subsequent discussions were not cordial and the staff were reluctant to accept anything that did not fit their 'traditional picture'. Were we part of 11 Group while we were ashore or not? We never really found out and as far as we were concerned we remained part of the Fleet organisation that actually wanted us.
30. The author took part in 'Clockwork '71' with 846 NAS and 'Clockwork '72' with 845 NAS while serving as a commando helicopter pilot. 'Clockwork' training detachments have continued into 2015.
31. In which the author served on more than one occasion.
32. About £30,000 at the time.

Chapter 16 – Capability, the Beira Patrol, Aden and Belize
1. Statement on the Defence Estimates 1966, Part 1, The Defence Review, Command 2901 (London: HMSO, 1966), p 10, paragraph 4.

2. 'HMS VICTORIOUS 1966-1967', Commission Book published privately and printed by Gale & Polden, Portsmouth, 1967, p 34.

3. Author's recollection.

4. I was appointed to her to obtain my Bridge Watch-keeping and Ocean Navigation certificates before commencing flying training.

5. Neil McCart, HMS HERMES 1923 & 1959 (Cheltenham: Fan Publications, 2001), p 114.

6. Baker, Dry Ginger, p 220.

7. We were aware that something was afoot because two admirals were on board, Vice Admiral W D O 'Brien the Commander Far East Fleet and Rear Admiral A T F G Griffin FO2 Far East Fleet. A few hours after 803 NAS's embarkation Rear Admiral M H Fell, FOAC, embarked to carry out the ship's operational readiness inspection (ORI), so there were four admirals on board that night.

8. Sturtivant and Ballance, The Squadrons of the Fleet Air Arm, p 322.

9. Not least the USN who found that the extreme heat of the re-heated Spey exhaust in the British Phantoms actually melted Saratoga's jet blast deflectors, emphasising the importance of the water-cooled JBDs fitted during Ark Royal's refit! After the first few launches, RN Phantoms were launched in military power without re-heat.

10. Referred to simply as Rhodesia after the grant of independence to Northern Rhodesia in 1964.

11. Roberts, Safeguarding the Nation, pp 70 et seq.

12. Green and Punnet, Macdonald World Air Power Guide, p 19.

13. It was approximately 500nm from the coast the Kariba Dam and it could hardly be said that this was too far for realistic air cover to be provided because that was exactly the radius of action at which the RAF claimed that it could easily provide air cover for a task force in the Atlantic.

14. Neil McCart, HMS EAGLE 1942–1978 (Cheltenham: Fan Publications, 1996), p 100.

15. Roberts, Safeguarding the Nation, p 72.

16. Seen at first as a temporary undertaking, it was to continue until June 1975 although no carriers were used on it after 1966. It became a routine commitment for destroyers, frigates and RFAs on passage to and from the Far East Station.

17. 'HMS ARK ROYAL 1964-1966', Commission Book published privately and printed by Latimer Trend & Co, Plymouth, 1966, pp 108 and 109.

18. Ibid, p 5.

19. She had had a fire in 'B' boiler room in October 1965 and was still not in good mechanical condition.

20. Hobbs, British Aircraft Carriers, p 286.

21. Quoted in McCart, HMS EAGLE, p 104.

22. Conversation with Lieutenant Commander Martin Rotheram RN, who had formerly served in 849 'C', when we served together several years later in 849 'B' NAS.

23. Sturtivant, Burrow and Howard, Fleet Air Arm Fixed-Wing Aircraft since 1946, p 328.

24. Michael Apps, The Four Ark Royals (London: William Kimber, 1976), pp 220 and 221.

25. Tony Buttler, The de Havilland Sea Vixen (Tonbridge: Air Britain (Historians), 2007), p 190.

26. Neil McCart, Three Ark Royals 1938 – 1999 (Cheltenham: Fan Publications, 1999), p 122.

27. McCart, HMS HERMES 1923 & 1959, p 101.

28. Roberts, Safeguarding the Nation, pp 79 et seq.

29. Although there was one difficult point of detail caused by the different Service criteria for the award of medals. The RAF crews of 78 Squadron were awarded the General Service Medal (1962) for Operation 'Magister'. The RN and RM crews of 848 NAS, who had also flown from Khormaksar, were not and nor were the ship's companies of TF 318.

30. From Albion.

31. From Eagle's air group.

32. Rowland White, Phoenix Squadron (London: Bantam Press, an imprint of Transworld Publishers, 2009).

33. Of course, none of the islands proposed by the RAF for its 'Island Strategy' was even in the same ocean as British Honduras.

34. Flight Deck No 2 (1972), p 30.

35. Green and Punnett, Macdonald World Air Power Guide, p 12.

Chapter 17 – Small Carriers and Vertical Landing

1. Ministry of Defence MO.9/1/7/1 dated 28 June 1967; one of a number of documents held by Section NA/W1 of the Ship Department at Foxhill, Bath that I examined in 1997. Copies are now

held in the Naval Historical Branch in Portsmouth and in my archive.

2. Statement on the Defence Estimates 1966, Part 1, The Defence Review, Command 2901, HMSO, London, p 9, paragraph 2, lines 11 and 12.

3. In conversations with officers who had served in DNAW during the 1960s, I came across several who stated that Healey had felt that CVA-01 was, itself, viable but that during the 1970s the remaining elements of the strike fleet, and especially *Hermes*, were too small to be effective. If he really did think this he was wrong; *Hermes* was to be the most important element of the successful British operations in the South Atlantic during 1982.

4. It is worth noting that a cost-benefit analysis of the many roles that could be undertaken by CVA-01 had not been ordered by Healey. Also, his recent Defence Review had only considered carriers in the context of expeditionary operations in the Far East; it had not really considered mentioned their value in a NATO context.

5. All the details in the chapter were taken from documents held in Section NA/W1 of the Ship Department at Foxhill, Bath that I examined in 1997. Copies of all these documents are now held in the Naval Historical Branch in Portsmouth and in my archive.

6. Hobbs, *British Aircraft Carriers*, Chapter 31, pp 304 onwards describes many of these sketch designs and those of the previous commando-cruiser concepts.

7. Originally allocated to the ill-fated P 1154.

8. Originally allocated to the proposed RN version of the P 1154.

9. David K Brown, *A Century of Naval Construction* (London: Conway Maritime Press, 1983).

10. Designed originally for use as the forward lift in CVA-01.

11. Some press commentators referred to it as the 'see-through cruiser' because of its resemblance to a small carrier.

12. It was one of the documents held by Section NA/W1 of the Ship Department at Foxhill, Bath that I studied in 1997 and copies are now filed in the Naval Historical Branch at Portsmouth and in my archive.

13. By then, both yards actually formed part of the nationalised 'British Shipbuilders'.

14. Dare I say, not far short of the projected cost of CVA-01!

15. This is slack terminology, the same sentence and the remainder of the NSR states that the ship was to command a task/contingency force.

16. Each of the nine Sea Kings embarked could carry four on a single sortie.

17. *Illustrious*, the last of the class to be withdrawn, was in service for thirty-two years, the longest life of any British aircraft carrier to date.

18. Ship Department Remarks Sheet 1220/061/01/01 dated 15 December 1971 originated by M J Westlake. This was one of the papers retained by Section NA/W1 at Foxhill, Batch and copies are now held in the Naval Historical Branch at Portsmouth and in my archive.

19. In 1971 the planned completion dates were 1977, 1979 and 1981. The first two were three years later than that and the last one four.

20. Contained in D/DS4/81/6/9 dated 4 May 1972; one of the papers retained by Section NA/W1 of the Ship Department at Foxhill, Batch that I examined in 1997, copies of which are held in the Naval Historical Branch and my archive.

21. An aircraft carrier-style flight deck forward would have given a longer deck run and it is difficult to avoid the conclusion that the open forecastle, which was of little use to anyone including the cable party, was included in the design to make the ship look less like an aircraft carrier to those who were concerned about such things.

22. D R Taylor, 'The operation of Fixed-Wing V/STOL aircraft from confined spaces'. This was Lieutenant Commander Taylor's M Phil thesis written in 1973 and published by the University of Southampton in 1974.

23. The RN used the word 'ramp' to describe the curved structure at the rear of the flight deck. The term 'ski-jump' was, therefore, deliberately used from the outset to avoid confusion.

24. I performed the same function with *Illustrious* and then joined *Ark Royal* to stand by her during build.

25. Some of them stripped out of the old cruisers *Tiger* and *Blake*.

26. Author's opinion.

27. I was present on handover day when the Commodore Naval Ships' Acceptance (CNSA), said to Captain M H Livesay RN, *Invincible*'s first commanding officer 'Well captain, there is your ship, what is she?' The hesitant reply was that she was a cruiser. 'No she is not,' said the Commodore, 'there is an "R" pennant number, she is an aircraft carrier.'

28. Known as the Horizontal Approach Path Indicator/Close Approach Indicator.
29. Hobbs, *British Aircraft Carriers*, p 260.
30. Actual build costs in the post-Admiralty era are difficult to calculate because different contracts were placed with different firms for the hull, machinery, systems and weapons. A number of fixtures, still known as 'Admiralty supplied items' were provided from MOD stores.
31. It is ironic to think that the first British ship specifically designed to operate the Sea King, *Invincible*, was to be even smaller.
32. Patrick Allen, *Sea King* (Shrewsbury: Airlife Publications, Shrewsbury, 1993), p 3.
33 The anti-submarine version had a retractable undercarriage so that the sonar cable, when deployed, was not snagged by the wheels. This provision was unnecessary in versions not fitted with sonar.
34. Williams, *Fly Navy*, p 147.
35. HMS BULWARK 01/15 dated 29 March 1966, copies of which are held in the Naval Historical Branch in Portsmouth and in my archive.
36. HMS BULWARK 4/25/11 dated 28 June 1966, copies of which are in the Naval Historical Branch in Portsmouth and in my archive.
37. Originally intended to provide both a carrier-borne version for the French Navy and land-based versions for the RAF and French Air Force. The former was cancelled because of an inadequate single-engined recovery performance; a defect that could have been rectified by fitting export-standard engines that were developed for the aircraft sold to Oman.
38. Stewart Wilson, *Combat Aircraft Since 1945* (Shrewsbury: Airlife Publications, 2000), pp 23 and 124.
39. 'Fixed-Wing VTOL Aircraft and their Application in Small Ships', CAGH/865 dated 4 April 1966, copies of which are held in the Naval Historical Branch in Portsmouth and in my archive.
40. DGA(N) SB/VTO/66 'Take-Off Methods for P 127 Aircraft from Ships' dated 2 August 1966, copies of which are in the Naval Historical Branch at Portsmouth and in my archive.
41. NSR 6451 contained in ADDC3/1220/650/01, a copy of which is in the Naval Historical Branch in Portsmouth with Background Aircraft Carrier papers 12 and in my archive.
42. My underlining.
43. Essentially a small pilotless aircraft launched from a frigate that dropped a torpedo or NDB accurately over a submarine. The airframe crashed into the sea after weapon release and could not be recovered. It was an expensive system but gave more rapid reaction than a MATCH helicopter in any weather.

Chapter 18 – The South Atlantic War
1. Peter Hore (ed), *Dreadnought to Daring – 100 Years of Comment, Controversy and Debate in The Naval Review* (Barnsley: Seaforth Publishing, 2012), pp 358 et seq.
2. J David Brown, *The Royal Navy and the Falklands War* (London: Leo Cooper, 1987), pp 22 et seq.
3. Roberts, *Safeguarding the Nation*, p 55.
4. Ibid, p 121.
5. Ibid, p 126.
6. Ibid, pp 136 et seq.
7. Including but not exclusively *Canberra, Queen Elizabeth 2, Astronomer, Atlantic Conveyor, Contender Bezant, Baltic Ferry, Nordic Ferry, Europic Ferry* and many others.
8. Henry Leach, *Endure No Makeshifts – Some Naval Recollections* (Barnsley: Pen & Sword Select Books, 1993), pp 216 et seq.
9. Admiral Sandy Woodward, *One Hundred Days – The Memoirs of the Falklands Battle Group Commander* (London: Harper Collins Publishers, 1992), p xii.
10. *Bulwark* was alongside in Portsmouth in a sorry state awaiting disposal to a scrapyard. At one stage I was tasked to evaluate whether she could be brought forward to act as a maintenance and repair carrier, if necessary by being towed to the South Atlantic. The idea was not taken up because she was in extremely poor condition; SBS commandos had used her as a training facility and blown up a number of internal features. The main reason, however, was that she could only have been fitted out by stripping RNAY Fleetlands of its equipment and machinery and this would have halted all work on UK helicopters not involved in the conflict.
11. Including David Brown, *The Royal Navy and the Falklands War*, Admiral Sandy Woodward, *One Hundred Days*, Michael Clapp and Ewen Southby-Tailyour, *Amphibious Assault Falklands – The Battle of San Carlos Water* and Max Hastings and Simon Jenkins, *The Battle for the Falklands*.
12. Among them Commander 'Sharkey' Ward DSC AFC RN, *Sea Harrier Over the Falklands*

(London; Leo Cooper, 1992), Lieutenant Commander David Morgan DSC RN, *Hostile Skies – My Falklands Air War* (London: Weidenfeld & Nicolson, 2006) and Richard Hutchings, *Special Forces Pilot – A Flying Memoir of the Falklands War* (Barnsley: Pen & Sword Aviation, 2008).

13. Statement on the Defence Estimates 1966, Part 1, The Defence Review, Command 2901, HMSO, London February 1966, p 10.

14. Sold to India in 1986, she is still operational in 2016 as INS *Viraat* and still operates a mix of Sea Harriers and Sea Kings.

15. Supermarkets were used for the first time as a rapid source of victualling stores but vegetable varieties were limited by the short 'opportunity window'. Broccoli was about the largest by volume and I was told that *Hermes'* chefs even experimented with broccoli-flavoured ice cream at one stage until RAS provided greater variety.

16. The USN had designed a system of prefabricated structures, known as the 'Arapaho System' that could be assembled onto a container ship in a time of emergency to provide hangarage, fuel and a flight deck. When not in use the idea was that it could be stored in a naval base. We examined it and recommended against its adoption by the RN because it seemed a big capital investment that might see very little operational service. *Atlantic Conveyer* did actually have better facilities and having been converted in only six days showed that there was little need to procure Arapaho. It would have taken that long to install it on a suitable ship. Despite DGA(N)'s negative assessment the MOD did buy a single Arapaho outfit and fitted it onto what had become the RFA *Reliant*, formerly the STUFT container ship *Astronomer*. It was used to provide support for UN forces in the Lebanon in 1984 and then ASW protection for the Falkland Islands between 1984 and 1986 with 826 (Sea King HAS 5s) NAS embarked, spending 566 days at sea and steaming 100,000nm. Despite these impressive statistics, the aircraft support arrangements were, as we predicted, not a great success and she was withdrawn from service in 1986. There is little point in having a prefabricated structure that remains in constant use; if it is needed with that degree of permanence, a dedicated helicopter ship would have been preferable and, probably cheaper.

17. *Flight Deck*, Falklands Special Edition (1982), p 46.

18. Formerly the USS *Phoenix*, one of the few ships to survive the Japanese attack on Pearl Harbor unscathed. She was sunk by HM Submarine *Conqueror* using Mark 8 Mod IV torpedoes that were nearly as old as their target. This was the first torpedo attack ever carried out by a nuclear submarine and the first British torpedo attack for thirty-seven years. The boat's CO, Commander C Wreford-Brown RN, was awarded the DSO and *Conqueror* flew the traditional 'Jolly Roger' flag with appropriate markings when she returned to Faslane.

19. MOD intelligence had thought that she could not launch Super Etendards but after checking with the engineering firm of Brown Brothers I was able to confirm that her steam catapults had recently been refurbished to enable them to launch the new jet. The only limitation would have been the ship's relatively slow top speed which meant that she would have needed some natural wind to give enough wind over the deck to launch a fully-armed and fuelled Super Etendard.

20. Hore (ed), *Dreadnought to Daring*, p 371.

21. An export version intended for land-based use of the Seacat close-range anti-aircraft missile system used by the RN.

22. David Morgan subsequently transferred to the RN and eventually achieved the rank of Lieutenant Commander.

23. The term 'Alert 5' means that the aircraft was manned with mechanics and handlers close by, capable of starting, setting position information in the Navigation, Heading and Attitude Reference System (NAVHARS), while the ship turned, hard, into wind and being launched in five minutes or less.

24. San Carlos Water was chosen because it was surrounded by land on almost every side and it was felt that this would restrict the ability of enemy aircraft to manoeuvre into positions to attack the amphibious shipping at low level. Whilst this might have been true, it also limited the radar and visual warning time as attacking aircraft closed in over the 'clutter' on radar screens caused by the land.

25. Basic radar contacts with no form of enhancement such moving target indicator (MTI) or doppler effect.

26. The standard fuel load for a Sea Harrier in the CAP fighter role was 600 gallons.

27. Her Senior Naval Officer, Captain M Layard RN, survived.

28. T-Shirts were produced with the 'El Muerte Negro' legend which a number of Sea Harrier pilots wore proudly under their flying overalls for some years afterwards.

29. But, I have to point out, not from ships the size of CVA-01. Her longer hull would have been less susceptible to pitch motion and her arrester wires were near the centre of pitch; she would not been as limited as the smaller carriers in the sort of sea states found in the South Atlantic. Arguably this was just the sort of situation she was designed for in either the Northern or Southern Hemisphere.
30. David Hart-Dyke, 'HMS *Coventry* in the Falklands Conflict – A personal Story', *The Naval Review* 1, 9 (1983).
31. Hore (ed), *Dreadnought to Daring*, p 364.
32. Statement to the Author during a conversation with *Coventry*'s anti-air warfare officer in 1991 when we were subsequently serving together in the MOD.
33. Low-Altitude Surveillance Task.
34. One Gannet AEW 3 and one T 5 had been preserved for possible use by the RN Historic Flight and others were still considered to be recoverable at RN Air Stations and research establishments. I was one of a number of former Gannet pilots warned that we might be required at short notice to fly them. I understood, from conversations within DGA(N) that Gannet spares might have been loaded in *Atlantic Conveyor* against this eventuality but that may just be a rumour.
35. Another contemporary rumour was that her original arrester-wire machinery had not been removed, merely plated over and left. Even if this was true it would have needed extensive refurbishment which was not possible in the time available.
36. Designed for the RAF Hawker Siddeley Nimrod MR 1 maritime patrol aircraft.
37. RAF maintenance personnel worked on the radar in a dust-free, air-conditioned environment in a large workshop complex at RAF Kinloss. They were appalled when they saw the tiny space in which the radar was to be maintained on board *Illustrious*. Their feedback in the earlier arguments when the RAF said the RN did not need a large carrier would have been very useful.
38. One of my abiding memories was standing on *Illustrious*' floodlit deck at 02.00 in the middle of a dark wet night alongside the Walker Naval Yard in Newcastle to evaluate the flight deck lighting system and accept it for operational use. A shipyard worker came and told me that there was a phone call for me in his hut. The call turned out to be from the Fleet Staff at Northwood asking for approval to operate Wessex helicopters from a particular merchant ship that had been taken up from trade. Fortunately I carried sufficient briefing documents with me to 'multi-task' and, after a few minutes research, I was able to give him the answer he wanted and by 02.30 I was back with the deck lighting.
39. The first attack on a submarine by a British aircraft since 1945.
40. Hobbs, *British Aircraft Carriers*, p 324.
41. Lawrie Phillips, *The Royal Navy Day by Day* (Stroud: Spellmount, an imprint of the History Press, 2011), p 340.
42. *Antelope*, *Ardent*, *Coventry* and *Sheffield*.
43. I remember being driven through a city at rush hour in a police car with its blue lights flashing to get to a trial involving the new deck approach projector sight so that it could be ready to fit in *Illustrious* before she sailed. The police and everyone else concerned were desperately keen to 'do their bit' for the RN.
44. *Flight Deck*, Falklands Special Edition (1982), p 52.

Chapter 19 – A Decade of Operations
1. Hobbs, *British Aircraft Carriers*, p 320.
2. David Stevens, *The Royal Australian Navy* (Melbourne: Oxford University Press, 2001), p 227.
3. Ibid, p 228.
4. Roberts, *Safeguarding the Nation*, p 209 et seq.
5. My recollections from service in the MOD at the time.
6. Hobbs, *British Aircraft Carriers*, p 332.
7. Gary E Weir and Sandra J Doyle (eds), *You Cannot Surge Trust* (Washington DC: Naval Heritage & History, Department of the Navy, 2013), pp 46 et seq.
8. Nick Richardson, *No Escape Zone* (London: Little, Brown and Company, 2000), p 137.
9. Hobbs, *British Aircraft Carriers*, p 326.
10. Neil McCart, *Harrier Carriers Volume 1 HMS INVINCIBLE* (Cheltenham: Fan Publications, 2004), p 97.
11. Roberts, *Safeguarding the Nation*, p 246.
12. Ibid, p 259.
13. Hobbs, *British Aircraft Carriers*, p 338.

14. In addition to *Ocean*, the ARG comprised the frigate *Chatham* and the RFAs *Fort Austin*, *Fort George*, *Sir Bedivere* and *Sir Tristram*. In addition to 42 RM Commando, *Ocean* had embarked the Commando Logistics Regiment Royal Marines, 8 Alma Commando Battery of 29 Commando Regiment, Royal Artillery, and 59 (Independent) Commando Squadron, Royal Engineers.
15. MOD, *The ARG in Sierra Leone – Operation 'Palliser'* (London: HMSO, 2000).
16. Roberts, *Safeguarding the Nation*, p 276.
17. Ibid, p 277.

Chapter 20 – New Defence Reviews, Carriers and Aircraft
1. My recollections from the time spent serving in DGA(N), 1979–1982.
2. So much so that one of the two, RFA *Fort George*, was withdrawn from service in 2010 when only seventeen years old and scrapped as part of the 2010 Defence Review. The second ship, *Fort Victoria*, is still in service in 2015.
3. 'The Strategic Defence Review', Command 3999 (London: HMSO, 1998).
4. Ibid, p 36. SDR does not seem to have been edited as well as one might expect and the original document used the word 'formally' which makes little sense.
5. Strategic Defence Review White Paper, Research Paper 98/91 dated 15 October 1998, International Affairs and Defence Section, House of Commons Library, London, 1998, p 37.
6. Also, naval air squadrons are manned for mobility and have their own cooks, stewards and administrative personnel to augment the carrier, air station or FOB, wherever they are operating. RAF squadrons do not since they are mostly designed to operate from a permanent base. The shortfall had to be made up from men and women drafted from all over the RAF, not just those allocated to a joint force. Many were deeply unhappy with this, making the decision not to use naval units even more difficult to understand.
7. Research Paper 98/91, p 28.
8. Hobbs, *British Aircraft Carriers*, p 330.
9. What if the aircraft was to become badly unserviceable while it was forward-deployed on a frigate? If maintenance personnel were flown from the RFA to a frigate to fix an aircraft, what if another aircraft returned to the RFA for maintenance or repair while key personnel were deployed elsewhere? How would the aircrew in the RFA be kept up-to-date with the latest tactical picture as the frigates saw it?
10. The need to cut manpower to the minimum was probably the main driver for the earlier concept of detached flights.
11. The order was probably intended to provide continuing work for AgustaWestland's workforce at Yeovil but the RAF made no secret of the fact that it would have preferred an all-Chinook fleet.
12. The NATO designation LPH for Landing Platform – Helicopter replaced the earlier term commando carrier after the completion of *Ocean* which has a pennant number with 'L' flag superior.
13. The remainder operate Lynx helicopters to be replaced after 2015 by Wildcats.
14. The SH-60R maximum take-off weight is only 23,000lbs.
15. Conrad Waters (ed), *Seaforth World Naval Review 2011* (Barnsley: Seaforth Publishing, 2010), pp 178 et seq.
16. The SH-60R has the same dipping sonar, designated the AN/AQS-22 in USN service. The Eurocopter NH-90 in service with the French, Dutch, Italian and other Navies also has the same FLASH dipping sonar giving the three types a comparable active sonar capability.
17. Conrad Waters (ed), *Seaforth World Naval Review 2015* (Barnsley: Seaforth Publishing, 2014), p 166.
18. *Air International Magazine* Vol 85 No 5 (November 2013), pp 88 et seq.
19. Charts are important for ASW and surface surveillance operations for showing, among many other things, the known position of wrecks which might be detected by sonar and shipping routes through littoral areas.
20. The French Navy bought E-2Cs to operate from its nuclear-powered carrier *Charles de Gaulle* and uses USN training and support facilities to reduce cost.
21. The option chosen by the Italian Navy.
22. They had to be mounted aft to balance the heavier radar scanner in the nose, dividing the weight of the system equally on either side of the aircraft's centre of gravity when the nozzles are rotated down for a hover landing. The cabling between the two elements added more weight than an

installation in the nose of a conventional fighter would have done but that was one of the penalties of the STOVL configuration.

23. Empty weight of the Sea Harrier FRS 1 was 13,884lbs. That for the F/A 2 was 14,585lbs. Both had the same maximum all-up weight of 26,200lbs. Both used Pegasus vectored thrust turbofans with 21,500lbs maximum thrust.

24. David Hobbs, 'Lockheed-Martin F-35 Lightning II', *Warship World* Vol 14 No 2 (November/December 2014), p 16.

25. Prior to the review, the Harrier was not going to be replaced by a STOVL aircraft; the RAF expected the Eurofighter Typhoon to replace the Tornado, Jaguar and Harrier in every role from tactical strike to reconnaissance and close air support. There were also hopes that a 'future long-range offensive' aircraft would follow the Typhoon as a collaborative bomber project.

26. A description that must have come back to haunt them every time the JSF was delayed by a design or development shortcoming. At the time of writing in 2015 it was meant to have been in UK service by 2012 but is unlikely to be operational before 2020.

27. Lockheed's first fighter was the P-38 Lightning used by the US Army Air Force in the Second World War. The name also has an Allied connotation because the RAF had operated the English Electric Lightning fighter between 1960 and 1985.

28. F-4B, J etc after 1962.

29. Lockheed-Martin official website, 2015.

30. I am afraid that there really is no way to avoid acronyms with the Lightning II, there are just so many of them.

31. Information based on a conversation I had with Lockheed-Martin simulator exports at the Farnborough Air Show, Trade Day in 2012.

32. Lockheed-Martin official website, 2015.

33. Mark Ayton, *F-35 Lightning II – An Air Warfare Revolution* (Stamford: Key Publishing, 2014), p 138.

34. Yes, the F-35B, designed for the US Marine Corps to undertake remote-area landings away from normal bases, does need specially-designed pads to avoid destroying the ground underneath it if it lands vertically.

35. I actually heard an RAF staff officer in the MOD say that the RAF could not possibly buy the F-35C because it had been designed as a naval aircraft. The antipathy shown by the RAF to the Buccaneer was repeating itself.

36. Hobbs, *British Aircraft Carriers*, p 344.

37. Ibid, p 262.

38. Her ship's company, including the Captain, heard the news as they drove into Portsmouth Naval Base on the morning SDSR was announced. Having been one of the senior officers that stood by *Ark Royal* during the final stages of her build at Newcastle in 1985, I attended what had been planned as a birthday party at Portsmouth days after the ship's demise was announced. By then it had turned into a 'wake' and I well remember the sense of shock felt by all those present.

39. Completion in 2016 followed by four years of acceptance and first-of-class flying trials.

40. The lift fan and swivelling tail nozzle are designed and built by Rolls-Royce.

41. Twenty-two years after the SDR decision to build larger and more capable carriers!

42. Although, like all F-35 variants, the after fuselage is made by BAE Systems, the ejection seat by Martin Baker and many other components are made in Great Britain, adding up to about 15 per cent of the aircraft by value.

43. Hobbs, *British Aircraft Carriers*, p 347.

44. Presumably these were not enough to power EMALS and propulsion together and major upgrades would have had to be added.

Bibliography

Unpublished Primary Sources

ADM1/22418   Proposal to fit angled decks in future carriers.
ADM1/22667   The versatility of naval air power.
ADM1/22672   Support of land forces by a British carrier task force.
ADM1/23069   Hooked Swift fighter project.
ADM1/23245   1952 requirements for strike aircraft.
ADM1/23263   Report of the 1952 catapult committee on the BS-4.
ADM1/23452   Exercise 'Mainbrace' – report of observers on USS *Midway*.
ADM1/23788   Command facilities in aircraft carriers.
ADM1/23981   Motion of carriers at sea in relation to aircraft operation.
ADM1/24145   Specifications for new aircraft carrier designs.
ADM1/24508   New design for a fleet carrier.
ADM1/24518   Naval aircraft – future needs and tactical roles.
ADM1/24623   Deck landing – proposed investigation of problems.
ADM1/24695   Formerly Chiefs of Staff 150/53
              The role of aircraft carriers and the Radical Review.
ADM1/25057   HMS *Glory* – return from Korean operations to the UK.
ADM1/25058   Future of HMS *Indomitable*.
ADM1/25061   HMS *Glory* – proposal to re-commission.
ADM1/25062   HMS *Glory* – programme.
ADM1/25067   HMS *Glory* – proposed use in Training Squadron.
ADM1/25076   Naval aircraft requirements.
ADM1/25083   Super-priority production of the Supermarine N-113.
ADM1/25111   HMS *Ark Royal* – approval to fit angled deck.
ADM1/25149   Cheapest possible carrier capable of operating modern jets.
ADM1/25282   RAF Coastal Command – proposed transfer to RN.
ADM1/25288   Operation of aircraft carriers – aircraft complements.
ADM1/25318   NA-19 requirement for a single-seat strike aircraft.
ADM1/25405   Comparative merits of DH-110 and N-113 aircraft.
ADM1/25419   Draft sketches for 20,000-ton carriers.
ADM1/25794   All weather fighters – respective merits of DH-110 and N-113 designs.
ADM1/25795   Memorandum on Fleet Air Arm by serving officers.
ADM1/25891   Long term plans for the RN in 1954.
ADM1/25901   Naval anti-submarine aircraft – comparison of fixed and rotary wing
ADM1/25931   Amphibious warfare – 1955 helicopter requirements.
ADM1/25933   Trade protection carriers.
ADM1/25934   Surface strike potential of aircraft carriers.
ADM1/25935   Fighter development.
ADM1/25987   Cost of HMS *Centaur* 1950–9.

ADM1/26006   1955 study into high-altitude fighter requirements.
ADM1/26009   Integration of fighters and missiles.
ADM1/26139   Reserve ships – worth for retention.
ADM1/26357   1955 NATO Review – carrier-borne aircraft.
ADM1/26437   Helicopter platforms on RFA vessels.
ADM1/26450   HMS *Ocean* – mass helicopter trials.
ADM1/26468   Plans for air defence of the fleet in 1965–75.
ADM1/26655   Attacks by helicopters on long-range sonar contacts.
ADM1/26676   Naval aviation matters from 1956 Navy Estimate debate.
ADM1/26689   Staff targets for atomic weapons.
ADM1/26720   Aircraft Carrier squadron Memoranda.
ADM1/26842   Staff requirement for HMS *Hermes*.
ADM1/26966   HMS *Eagle* – voice-controlled catapult launch.
ADM1/27047   Air defence of a carrier force.
ADM1/27051   Operation 'Musketeer' – carrier operational analysis.
ADM1/27153   HMS *Bulwark* – requirement for conversion to a commando carrier.
ADM1/27359   Steam catapult development.
ADM1/27371   1957 Defence Review – long-term plans.
ADM1/27441   Naval staff requirement for the Bullpup missile.
ADM1/27685   Case for the Escort Cruiser Project.
ADM1/27811   Sidewinder missiles for Scimitar aircraft.
ADM1/27814   1960 views on naval air defence requirements.
ADM1/27845   The P-1127 aircraft.
ADM1/27871   Aircraft complements of carriers.
ADM1/27966   Future naval aircraft.
ADM1/28592   *Tiger* class cruiser conversions.
ADM1/28609   Formally M1/288//2/63
               Fleet air defence, V/STOL fighters and threats.
ADM1/28617   Planned RN amphibious capability 1966–72.
ADM1/28644   Planned aircraft carrier programme for 1963 to 1973.
ADM1/28853   Work study report on flight deck layout for CVA-01.
ADM1/28876   Staff requirement for CVA-01.
ADM1/29044   Name for CVA-01.
ADM1/29048   McDonnell Phantom – Admiralty fact finding mission to USA.
ADM1/29052   CVA-01 – development and design contracts.
ADM1/29053   Escort cruiser construction and conversion programmes.
ADM1/29054   Meeting between First Lord and Minister of Aviation to discuss areas of
               difficulty.
ADM1/29055   Replacement of the Sea Vixen by the F-4 Phantom.
ADM1/29065   Long-term carrier plan 64A.
ADM1/29132   Bid to Treasury for P-177 aircraft.
ADM1/29135   Continued development of P-177.
ADM1/29144   Wartime reinforcement of the Far East Fleet.
ADM1/29154   P-1154 – a Joint Strike Fighter to replace the Sea Vixen.
ADM1/29156   P-1154 costing.
ADM1/29323   Review of 1957 air defence working party report.
ADM 205/195   CVA-01 papers.
ADM 205/196   CVA-01 papers.
ADM 205/197   CVA-01 papers.
ADM 205/200   CVA-01 papers.
ADM 205/214   CVA-01 papers.

Documents studied while carrying research at Section NA/W1 at the Ship Department, Foxhill, Bath during 1997 and referred to in the text are identified as end-notes to the relevant chapters.

Secondary Sources produced by the Royal Navy and Royal Canadian Navy

BR 1736(54)   Naval Staff History – British Commonwealth Naval Operations Korea 1950–53.
                   (London: Ministry of Defence (Navy), Naval Historical Branch, 1967).
BR 1736(55)   Naval Staff History – Middle East Operations – Jordan/Lebanon 1958 and Kuwait 1961. (London: Ministry of Defence (Navy), Naval Historical Branch, 1968).
Flight Deck –   The Quarterly Journal of Naval Aviation published by the Naval Air Warfare Division of the Admiralty. Every edition between Winter 1952 and Number 1 in 2000.
CB 3053(11)   Naval Aircraft Progress & Operations, Periodical Summary No. 11 – Period Ended 30 June
1945.
CB 03164   Progress in Naval Aviation, Summary 1 for period ending 1 December 1947.
CB 03164(48)   Progress in Naval Aviation, Summary 2 for year ending 1 December 1948.
CB 03164(49)   Progress in Naval Aviation, Summary 3 for year ending 31 December 1949.
CB 03164(50)   Progress in Naval Aviation, Summary 4 for year ending 31 December 1950.
CB 03164(51)   Progress in Naval Aviation, Summary 5 for year ending 31 December 1951.
CB 03164(52)   Progress in Naval Aviation, Summary 6 for year ending 31 December 1952.
CB 03164(54)   Progress of the Fleet Air Arm, Summary 7 for year ending 31 December 1954.
CB 03164   Progress of the Fleet Air Arm, Summary 8. 1 January 1955 to 30 June 1956.
BR 642B   Summary of British Warships.
AP(N) 71   Manual of Naval Airmanship. Admiralty, London, 1949.
AP(N) 144   Naval Aircraft Handbook. Admiralty, London, 1958.
Kealy, J D F and Russell, E C, *A History of Canadian Naval Aviation* (Ottawa, Naval Historical Section, Canadian Forces Headquarters, Department of National Defence, 1965).

Published Secondary Sources

The following books from my own library were consulted during my research for this book.

Allen, Brian R, *On the Deck or in the Drink* (Barnsley: Pen & Sword Aviation, 2010).
Allward, Maurice, *Buccaneer* (Shepperton: Ian Allen, 1981).
Anon., 'HMS *Hermes*', a special edition of *The Vickers Magazine* (1960).
Anon., *Les Marines de Guerre du Dreadnought au Nucleaire* (Paris: Service Historique de la Marines, 1988).
Anon., *The ARG in Sierra Leone – Operation Palliser* (London; HMSO, 2000).
Allen, Patrick, *Sea King* (Shrewsbury: Airlife, 1993).
Apps, Michael, *Send her Victorious* (London: William Kimber, 1971).
_____,*The Four Ark Royals* (London: William Kimber, 1976).
Arnold, Lorna, *A Very Special Relationship – British Atomic Weapon Trials in Australia* (London: HMSO, 1987).
Askins, Simon, *Gannet – From the Cockpit 7* (Ringshall: Ad Hoc Publications, 2008).
Baker, Richard, *Dry Ginger. The Biography of Admiral of the Fleet Sir Michael Le Fanu GCB DSC* (Letchworth, The Garden City Press, 1977).
Benbow, Tim (ed), *British Naval Aviation – the First 100 Years* (Farnham: Ashgate, 2011).
Berg, Paul D (ed), *USAF Air and Space Power Journal* Vol XVII No 4 (Winter 2004).
Bishop, Patrick, *Scram* (London: Preface Publishing, 2012).

Black, Admiral Sir Jeremy, GBE KCB DSO, *There and Back* (London: Elliott & Thompson, 2005).

Blackman, Raymond, *The World's Warships* (London: Macdonald, 1960).

Blundell, W G D, *British Aircraft Carriers* (Hemel Hempstead: Model & Allied Publications, 1969).

Boswell, Richard, *Weapons Free – The Story of a Gulf War Helicopter Pilot* (Manchester: Crecy Publishing, 1998).

Brown, D K, *Rebuilding the Royal Navy: Warship Design since 1945* (London: Chatham Publishing, 2003).

Brown, Captain Eric, CBE DSC AFC RN, *Wings on my Sleeve* (London: Weidenfield & Nicolson, 2006).

————————————————————, *Firebrand – From the Cockpit 8* (Ringshall, Ad Hoc Publications, 2008).

————————————————————, *Seafire – From the Cockpit 13* (Ringshall: Ad Hoc Publications, 2010).

————————————————————, *Wings of the Navy -Testing British and US Carrier Aircraft* (Manchester: Hikoki Publications, 2013).

Brown, J David, *HMS Illustrious – Warship Profile 11* (Windsor: Profile Publications, 1971).

————————, *Carrier Air Groups – HMS Eagle* (Windsor: Hylton Lacy, 1972).

————————, *The Royal Navy and the Falklands War* (London: Leo Cooper, 1987).

————————, *The Seafire – the Spitfire that went to Sea* (London: Greenhill Books, 1989).

————————, *Aircraft Carriers* (London: MacDonald & Jane's, 1977).

Burns, Ken and Critchley, Mike, HMS *Bulwark 1948 – 1984* (Liskeard: Maritime Books, 1986).

Buttler, Tony, *The de Havilland Sea Vixen* (Stapleford: Air Britain (Historians), 2007).

————————, *Sturgeon – Target Tug Extraordinaire* (Ringshall: Ad Hoc Publications, 2009).

Carter, Geoffrey, *Crises do Happen – The Royal Navy and Operation Musketeer, Suez 1956* (Liskeard: Maritime Books, 2006).

Chant, Chris (ed), *Military Aircraft of the World* (Feltham: Hamlyn, 1981).

Chartres, John, *Westland Sea King* (Shepperton: Ian Allen, 1984).

Chatfield, Admiral of the Fleet Lord, PC GCB OM etc, *It Might Happen Again*, Volume II of his autobiography (London: William Heinemann, 1947).

Childs, Nick, *The Age of Invincible – The Ship that Defined the Modern Royal Navy* (Barnsley: Pen & Sword Maritime, 2009).

Clapp, Michael, and Southby-Tailyour, Ewen, *Amphibious Assault Falklands* (London: Orion Books, 1997).

Cooper, Geoffrey, *Farnborough and the Fleet Air Arm* (Hersham, Midland Publishing, 2008).

Crosley, Mike, *Up in Harm's Way – Flying with the Fleet Air Arm* (Shrewsbury: Airlife, 1995).

Cull, Brian, with Nicolle, David and Aloni, Shlomo, *Wings Over Suez* (London: Grub Street, 1996).

Davies, Brian, *Fly No More* (Shrewsbury: Airlife, 2001).

Davies, Giles (ed), *Murricane's Men* (Paisley: Giles Davies Ltd, 1997).

Doust, Michael J, *Phantom Leader* (Ringshall: Ad Hoc Publications, 2005).

————————, *Scimitar – From the Cockpit 2* (Ringshall: Ad Hoc Publications, 2006).

————————, *Buccaneer S1 – From the Cockpit 6* (Ringshall: Ad Hoc Publications, 2007).

————————, *Sea Hawk – From the Cockpit 3* (Ringshall: Ad Hoc Publications, 2007).

Dyndal, Gjert Lage, *Land-Based Air Power or Aircraft Carriers?* (Farnham: Ashgate Publishing, 2012).

Dyson, Tony, HMS *Hermes 1959 – 1984* (Liskeard, Maritime Books, 1984).

Ellis, Herbert, *Hippocrates RN – Memoirs of a Naval Flying Doctor* (London: Robert Hale, 1988).

Ellis, Paul, *Aircraft of the Royal Navy* (London: Jane's, 1982).

Fazio, Vince, *Australian Aircraft Carriers 1929–1982* (Garden Island, Sydney: The Naval Historical Society of Australia, 1997).

Fox, Robert, *Iraq Campaign 2003 – Royal Navy and Royal Marines* (London: Agenda Publishing, 2003).

Friedman, Norman, *Carrier Air Power* (Greenwich: Conway Maritime Press, 1981).

_____, *US Aircraft Carriers – An Illustrated Design History* (Annapolis: Naval Institute Press, United States, 1983).

_____, *The Postwar Naval Revolution* (Greenwich: Conway Maritime Press, 1986).

_____, *British Carrier Aviation* (London: Conway Maritime Press, 1988).

Gibson, Vice Admiral Sir Donald, KCB DSC, *Haul Taut and Belay – The Memoirs of a Flying Sailor* (Tunbridge Wells: Spellmount, 1992).

Gillet, Ross, *HMAS Melbourne* (Sydney: Nautical Press, 1980).

Glancey, Jonathan, *Harrier – The Biography* (London: Atlantic Books, 2013).

Goldrick, James, *No Easy Answers* (New Delhi: Lancer Publishers, 1997).

_____, with Frame, T R, and Jones, P D (eds), *Reflections on the RAN* (Kenthurst, NSW: Kangaroo Press, 1991).

Godden, John (ed), *Harrier – Ski-Jump to Victory* (Oxford: Brassey's, 1983).

Graham, Alastair, and Grove, Eric, *HMS Ark Royal – Zeal Does Not Rest 1981 – 2011* (Liskeard, Maritime Books, 2011).

Green, William, *The World's Fighting Planes* (London: Macdonald, 1964).

_____, *The World Guide to Combat Planes* ,Volumes 1 and 2 (London: Macdonald, 1966).

_____, and Punnett, Dennis, *Macdonald World Air Power Guide* (London: Macdonald, 1963).

Grey, Jeffrey, *Up Top – The Royal Australian Navy and Southeast Asian Conflicts 1955-1972* (St Leonards, NSW: Allen & Unwin, 1998).

Grove, Eric J, *Ark Royal – A Flagship for the 21st Century* (Privately published by the Ship's Company, 2001).

_____, *Vanguard to Trident – British Naval Policy since World War II* (London: The Bodley Head, 1987).

Gunston, Bill, *Attack Aircraft of the West* (Shepperton: Ian Allen, 1974).

_____, *Early Supersonic Fighters of the West* (Shepperton: Ian Allen, 1976).

_____, *F-4 Phantom* (Shepperton: Ian Allen, 1977).

_____, *Harrier* (Shepperton: Ian Allen, 1981).

_____, *Fighters of the Fifties* (Cambridge: Patrick Stephens, 1981).

_____, *The Development of Jet and Turbine Engines* (Sparkford: Patrick Stephens, 2006).

Hall, Timothy, HMAS *Melbourne* (Sydney: Allen & Unwin, 1982).

Harding, Richard, *The Royal Navy 1930-2000 – Innovation and Defence* (Abingdon: Frank Cass, 2005).

Harrison, W, *Fairey Firefly* (Shrewsbury: Airlife Publishing, 1992).

Hezlet, Vice Admiral Sir Arthur, KBE CB DSO DSC, *Aircraft and Sea Power* (London: Peter Davies, 1970).

_____, *The Electron and Sea Power* (London: Peter Davies, 1975).

Hibbert, Edgar, *HMS Unicorn – The Versatile Air Repair Ship* (Ilfracombe: Arthur Stockwell Limited, 2006).

Higgs, Geoffrey, *Frontline and Experimental Flying with the Fleet Air Arm* (Barnsley: Pen & Sword Aviation, 2010).

Hirst, Mike, *Airborne Early Warning* (London: Osprey Publishing, 1983).

HMS *Ark Royal* – 1956–7 Commission, published by the Ship's Company.

HMS *Ark Royal* – Third Commission 1959–61, published by the Ship's Company.

HMS *Ark Royal* – Fifth Commission 1964–6, published by the Ship's Company.

HMS *Ark Royal* – 1970–3 Commission, published by the Ship's Company.

HMS *Ark Royal* – 1974–6 Commission, published by the Ship's Company.

HMS *Bulwark* – 1969–71 Commission, published by the Ship's Company.

HMS *Bulwark* – 1974–6 Commission, published by the Ship's Company.

HMS *Centaur* – Fourth Commission 1963–5, published by the Ship's Company.

HMS *Eagle* – 1970–2 Commission, published by the Ship's Company.

HMS *Hermes* – Third Commission 1966–8, published by the Ship's Company.

HMS *Victorious* 1960–2 Commission, published by the Ship's Company.

HMS *Victorious* 1963–4 Commission, published by the Ship's Company.

HMS *Victorious* 1966–7 Commission, published by the Ship's Company.

Hobbs, David, *Aircraft of the Royal Navy Since* 1945 (Liskeard, Maritime Books, 1982).

_____, *Aircraft Carriers of the Royal and Commonwealth Navies* (London: Greenhill Books, 1996).

_____, *Moving Bases* (Liskeard: Maritime Books, 2007).

_____, *A Century of Carrier Aviation* (Barnsley: Seaforth Publishing, 2009).

_____, *The British Pacific Fleet – The Royal Navy's Most Powerful Strike Fleet* (Barnsley: Seaforth Publishing, 2011).

_____, *British Aircraft Carriers* (Barnsley: Seaforth Publishing, 2013).

Hore, Peter (ed), *Dreadnought to Daring– 100 Years of Comment, Controversy and Debate in The Naval Review* (Barnsley: Seaforth Publishing, 2012).

Howard, Lee, Burrow, Mick and Myall, Eric, *Fleet Air Arm Helicopters since 1943* (Stapleford: Air Britain (Historians), 2011).

Howard, David, *Sea and Sky – A Life from the Navy* (2011).

Humble, Richard, *Fraser of North Cape* (London: Routledge & Kegan Paul, 1983).

Hunter, Jamie, *Sea Harrier – The Last All-British Fighter* (Hinckley: Midland Publishing, 2005).

Hutchings, Richard, *Special Forces Pilot* (Barnsley: Pen & Sword Aviation, 2008).

Jackson, Robert, *Strike from the Sea – A History of British Naval Air Power* (London, Arthur Barker, 1970).

_____, *Suez 1956* (Shepperton: Ian Allen, 1980).

_____, *The Malayan Emergency & Indonesian Confrontation 1948–1966* (Barnsley: Pen & Sword Aviation, 2011).

John, Rebecca, *Caspar John* (London: Collins, 1987).

Johnstone-Bryden, Richard, HMS *Ark Royal IV – Britain's Greatest Warship* (Stroud: Sutton Publishing, 1999).

Jones, Barry, *British Experimental Turbojet Aircraft* (Marlborough: Crowood Press, 2003).

Jones, Colin, *Wings and the Navy* (Kenthurst, NSW: Kangaroo Press, 1997).

Kemp, P K, *Fleet Air Arm* (London: Herbert Jenkins, 1954).

Knowlson, Joyce, HMS *Ocean* 1945 – 1957 – *Peacetime Warrior* (Privately published, 1998).

Laming, Tim, *Buccaneer – The Story of the Last All-British Strike Aircraft* (Sparkford: Patrick Stephens, 1998).

Lansdown, John R P, *With the Carriers in Korea* (Worcester: Square One Publications, 1992).

Leach, Admiral of the Fleet Sir Henry, GCB, *Endure No Makeshifts – Some Naval Recollections* (Barnsley: Pen & Sword, 1993).

Lehan, Mike, *Flying Stations – A Story of Australian Naval Aviation* (St Leonards, NSW: Allen & Unwin, 1998.

Leahy, Alan J, *Sea Hornet – From the Cockpit 5* (Ringshall: Ad Hoc Publications, 2007).

_____, *Sea Fury – From the Cockpit 12* (Ringshall: Ad Hoc Publications, 2010).

Lindsay, Roger, *de Havilland Venom* (Privately published, 1974).

Lord, Dick, *From Tail-Hooker to Mud Mover* (Irene, South Africa: Corporal Publications, 2003).

Lygo, Admiral Sir Raymond, KCB, *Collision Course – Lygo Shoots Back* (Lewes: The Book Guild, 2002).

Lyon, David, HMS *Illustrious – technical history*, Warship Profile 10 (Windsor: Profile Publications, 1971).

MaCaffrie, Jack (ed), *Positioning Navies for the Future* (Broadway, NSW: Halstead Press, 2007).

Marriott, Leo, *Royal Navy Aircraft Carriers 1945-1990* (Shepperton: Ian Allen, 1985).

_____, *Jets at Sea – Naval Aviation in Transition 1945 – 1955* (Barnsley: Pen & Sword Aviation, 2008).

Mason, Francis K, *Harrier* (Cambridge: Patrick Stephens, 1981).
_____, *Hawker Aircraft since 1920* (London: Putnam, 1993).
_____, *The Hawker Sea Hawk* (Leatherhead: Profile Publications, n.d.).
_____, *The Hawker Sea Fury* (Leatherhead: Profile Publications, n.d.).
McCandless, Robert, *Barracuda – From the Cockpit 16* (Ringshall: Ad Hoc Publications, 2012.
McCart, Neil, HMS *Albion 1944–1973* (Cheltenham: Fan Publications, 1995).
_____, HMS *Eagle 1942–1978* (Cheltenham: Fan Publications, 1996).
_____, HMS *Centaur 1943–1972* (Cheltenham: Fan Publications, 1997).
_____, HMS *Victorious 1937–1969* (Cheltenham: Fan Publications, 1998).
_____, *Three Ark Royals 1938 – 1999* (Cheltenham: Fan Publications, 1999).
_____, *The Illustrious and Implacable Classes of Aircraft Carrier 1940–1969* (Cheltenham: Fan Publications, 2000).
_____, HMS *Hermes 1923 & 1959* (Cheltenham: Fan Publications, 2001).
_____, HMS *Glory 1945 1961* (Liskeard: Maritime Books, 2002).
_____, *The Colossus Class Aircraft Carriers 1944–1972* (Cheltenham: Fan Publications, 2002).
_____, *Harrier Carriers #1* – HMS *Invincible* (Cheltenham: Fan Publications, 2004).
Mills, Carl, *Banshees in the Royal Canadian Navy* (Willowdale, Ontario: Banshee Publications, 1991).
Moore, Captain J E, RN, *The Impact of Polaris – The Origins of Britain's Seaborne Nuclear Deterrent* (Huddersfield: Richard Netherwood Limited, 1999).
Moore, Richard, *The Royal Navy and Nuclear Weapons* (London: Frank Cass, 2001).
Morgan, Eric, and Stevens, John, *The Scimitar File* (Tonbridge: Air Britain (Historians), 2000).
Morgan, David, *Hostile Skies – My Falklands Air War* (London: Weidenfeld & Nicolson, 2006).
Morton, Peter, *Fire Across the Desert – Woomera and the Anglo-Australian Joint Project 1946-1980* (Canberra, ACT: AGPS Press, 1989).
Nash, Peter V, *The Development of Mobile Logistic Support in Anglo-American Naval Policy 1900–1953* (Gainsville: University Press of Florida, 2009).
Neufeld, Jacob, and Watson, George M (eds.), *Coalition Air Warfare in the Korean War 1950 to 1953* (Washington DC: US Air Force History & Museums Programme, 2005).
Newton, James, *Armed Action – My War in the Skies with 847 Naval Air Squadron* (London: Headline Review, 2007).
Norman, J G S ('Joe'), *Firefly – From the Cockpit 4* (Ringshall: Ad Hoc Publications, 2007).
Oldham, Charles, *100 Years of the Royal Australian Navy* (Bondi Junction, NSW, Faircount Media Group, 2011).
Orchard, Ade, *Joint Force Harrier* (London: Michael Joseph/Penguin, 2008).
Parry, Chris, *Down South – A Falklands War Diary* (London: Penguin Group, 2012).
Pettipas, Leo, *The Supermarine Seafire in the Royal Canadian Navy* (Winnipeg: Canadian Naval Air Group, 1987).
Phillips, Lawrie, *The Royal Navy Day by Day* (Stroud: Spellmount, 2011).
Polmar, Norman, *Aircraft Carriers* (London: Macdonald, 1969).
_____, *Aircraft Carriers Volume II 1946-2006* (Washington DC: Potomac Books, 2008).
Popham, Hugh, *Into Wind – A History of British Naval Flying* (London: Hamish Hamilton, 1969).
Reece, Colonel Michael, OBE, *Flying Royal Marines* (Eastney: The Royal Marines' Historical Society, 2012).
Richardson, Nick, *No Escape Zone* (London: Little, Brown & Company, 2000).
Roberts, John, *Safeguarding the Nation – The Story of the Modern Royal Navy* (Barnsley: Seaforth Publishing, 2009).
Rodger, N A M, *Naval Power in the Twentieth Century* (Basingstoke, Macmillan Press, 1996).
Ross, T, and Sandison, M, *A Historical Appreciation of the Contribution of Naval Air Power* (Canberra, ACT: Sea Power Centre – Australia, 2008).
Rowan-Thomson, Graeme, *Attacker – From the Cockpit 9* (Ringshall: Ad Hoc Publications, 2008).

Shaw, Anthony, *The Upside of Trouble* (Lewes: The Book Guild, 2005).

Smith, Admiral Sir Victor, AC KBE CB DSC RAN, *A Few Memories of Sir Victor Smith* (Campbell, ACT: Australian Naval Institute, 1992).

Snowie, J Allan. *The Bonnie – HMCS Bonaventure* (Erin, Ontario: Boston Mill Press, 1987).

Soward, Stuart E, *Hands to Flying Stations – A Recollective History of Canadian Naval Aviation, Volume 1 1945 to 1954* (Victoria, Neptune Developments, 1993).

Stevens, David, *The Royal Australian Navy* (Melbourne: Oxford University Press, 2001).

_____(ed), *Maritime Power in the 20th Century* (St Leonards, NSW: Allen & Unwin, 1998).

_____, *Naval Networks: The Dominance of Communications in Maritime Operations* (Canberra, ACT: Sea Power Centre – Australia, 2012).

_____, and Reeve, John (eds), *The Face of Naval Battle* (Crow's Nest, NSW: Allen & Unwin, 2003).

_____, *The Navy and the Nation* (Crow's Nest, NSW: Allen & Unwin, 2005).

_____, *Sea Power Ashore and in the Air* (Ultimo, NSW: Halstead Press, 2007).

Sturtivant, Ray, *British Naval Aviation – The Fleet Air Arm 1917–1990* (London: Arms & Armour Press, 1990.

_____, and Ballance, Theo, *The Squadrons of the Fleet Air Arm* (Tonbridge: Air Britain (Historians), 1994).

_____, Burrow, Mick and Howard, Lee, *Fleet Air Arm Fixed-Wing Aircraft since 1946* (Tonbridge: Air Britain (Historians), 2004).

Swanborough, Gordon, and Bowers, Peter M, *United States Navy Aircraft since 1911* (London: Putnam, 1990).

Taylor, H A, *Fairey Aircraft since 1915* (London: Putnam, 1974).

Taylor, John W R, *Fleet Air Arm* (Shepperton: Ian Allen, 1958, 1959 and 1963 editions).

Thetford, Owen, *British Naval Aircraft since 1912* (London: Putnam, 1962).

Till, Geoffrey, *Air Power and the Royal Navy 1914-1945 – a historical survey* (London: Macdonald & Jane's, 1979).

_____, *Seapower – A Guide for the Twenty-First Century* (London: Frank Cass, 2004).

Treacher, Admiral Sir John, KCB, *Life at Full Throttle* (Barnsley: Pen & Sword Maritime, 2004).

Vicary, Adrian, *Naval Wings* (Cambridge: Patrick Stephens, 1984).

Wakeham, Geoff, *RNAS Culdrose 1947–2007* (Stroud, Tempus Publishing, 2007).

Ward, 'Sharkey', *Sea Harrier over the Falklands* (London: Leo Cooper, 1992).

Warner, Oliver, *Admiral of the Fleet – The Life of Sir Charles Lambe* (London: Sidgwick & Jackson, 1969).

Watkins, David, *De Havilland Vampire* (Stroud: Sutton Publishing, 1996).

Weir, Gary E, and Doyle, Sandra J (eds), *You Cannot Surge Trust* (Washington DC: Naval History & Heritage Command, Department of the Navy, 2013).

Whitby, Michael, and Charlton, Peter (eds), *Certified Serviceable – Swordfish to Sea King* (Canada: CNATH Book Project, 1995).

White, Rowland, *Phoenix Squadron* (London: Bantam Press, 2009).

Williams, Ray, *Fly Navy – Aircraft of the Fleet Air Arm since* 1945 (Shrewsbury: Airlife Publishing, 1989).

Wilson, Stewart, *Sea Fury, Firefly & Sea Venom in Australian Service* (Weston Creek, ACT: Aerospace Publications, 1993).

_____, *Combat Aircraft since 1945* (Shrewsbury: Airlife, 2000).

Wood, Derek, *Project Cancelled* (London: Macdonald and Jane's, 1975).

Woodward, Admiral Sir Sandy, *One Hundred Days. The Memoirs of the Falklands Battle Group Commander* (London: Harper Press, 2012).

Wright, Anthony, *Australian Carrier Decisions – The Acquisition of HMA Ships Albatross, Sydney and Melbourne* (RAN Maritime Studies Programme, 1998).

Young, Kathryn, and Mitchell, Rhett (eds), *The Commonwealth Navies – 100 Years of Co-operation* (Canberra, ACT: Sea Power Centre – Australia, 2012).

Reference Works Published Annually
Jane's Fighting Ships (1950/51 to 2012/13 Editions).
Seaforth World Naval Review 2010 to 2016 Editions.
Conway/NIP Warship (Volume 1 to 2014 Edition).

Reference Journals Published Monthly or Quarterly
Air Enthusiast International Volume 1 Number 1 (June 1971) to Volume 88 Number 6 (June 2015).
Warship World Volume 1 Number 1 (November 1984) to Volume 14 Number 5 (May/June 2015).
The Navy Volume 63 Number 2 (April 2001) to Volume 77 Number 2 (April/June 2015).
Headmark, Journal of the Australian Naval Institute, Volume 26 Number 4 (Summer 2000) to Issue 153 (December 2014).
Proceedings, the Journal of the United States Naval Institute, Various Editions from 1964 to date.

Index